DISPERSING THE FOG

DISPERSING THE FOG

INSIDE THE SECRET WORLD OF OTTAWA AND THE RCMP

PAUL PALANGO

KEY PORTER BOOKS

Library and Archives Canada Cataloguing in Publication

Palango, Paul, 1950–
    Dispersing the fog: inside the secret world of Ottawa and the RCMP / Paul Palango.

ISBN 978-1-55470-042-4 (bound)

    1. Royal Canadian Mounted Police. 2. Justice, Administration of— Canada. I. Title.

HV8157.P345 2008   363.20971   C2008-902211-4

ONTARIO ARTS COUNCIL
CONSEIL DES ARTS DE L'ONTARIO

THE CANADA COUNCIL | LE CONSEIL DES ARTS
FOR THE ARTS | DU CANADA
SINCE 1957 | DEPUIS 1957

The author acknowledges the generous support of the Canada Council for the Arts.

The publisher gratefully acknowledges the support of the Canada Council for the Arts and the Ontario Arts Council for its publishing program. We acknowledge the support of the Government of Ontario through the Ontario Media Development Corporation's Ontario Book Initiative.

We acknowledge the financial support of the Government of Canada through the Book Publish-ing Industry Development Program (BPIDP) for our publishing activities.

Key Porter Books Limited
Six Adelaide Street East, Tenth Floor
Toronto, Ontario
Canada M5C 1H6

www.keyporter.com

Text design: Marijke Friesen
Electronic formatting: Alison Carr

Printed and bound in Canada

08 09 10 11 5 4 3 2

For Sharon
Her strength, intellect and beautiful spirit made this all possible.

CONTENTS

[preface]

THE IMPENETRABLE FOG

As I embarked on this project in early 2007—the completion of an unlikely trilogy of books about the Royal Canadian Mounted Police—my original mandate was to look at the recent state of the force. The RCMP was in great turmoil after a long series of missteps and scandals. For the first time in its history, an RCMP commissioner had been forced to leave office in disgrace. Pursuing the threads of this story, however, took me to places I had not originally contemplated exploring.

Canada is a democratic country, but in so many ways it doesn't feel like one. Its major public institutions—Parliament, government, and the police—are all housed in impressive buildings. But, like a Potemkin village, there is not much behind the walls.

It might sound old-fashioned to say so, but those institutions are the bedrock of any democratic nation—the upholders of the rule of law. The people who oversee, administer, and work in them are our guardians—the protectors of our country, its integrity, its wealth, and its freedoms. Without strong and properly motivated guardians, any country exposes itself to tyranny.

In this day and age, examining the health and integrity of a country like Canada through its political window is all but impossible. As Dr. Donald Savoie has pointed out in a series of books over the years, the most recent being *Court Government and the Collapse of Accountability in Canada and the United Kingdom*, the processes of government have become all but dysfunctional. Too much power has become concentrated at the top and there has been a noticeable decline in checks and balances within the system.

The police, on the other hand, are sworn servants of the law and their country. The vast majority of them are single-minded in their commitment and true to their oaths of office. Viewing Canada through their eyes and experiences, therefore, might well provide a unique and much clearer perspective of the state of the country.

After Parliament, an apolitical police force is the most important institution in a democratic country. The police must be disinterested. Their job is to enforce the laws and regulations passed by Parliament without fear, favour, or affection. If the police do not or are not allowed to operate independently under the law and treat every citizen equally, the integrity of the entire justice system is compromised.

The role of the media is to provide checks and balances against abuse by both government and the police. Unfortunately, the media coverage of the police has been all but reduced to ambulance chasing—"if it bleeds it leads." There are no reporters dedicated to covering the police as a fundamental institution in our democracy largely because police issues are deemed by the media elite to be little more than an entry-level job—writing not so much about the police but the exploits of criminals. "I am not a police reporter," is a phrase all-too-many editors have heard from journalists who view themselves more as celebrities who deal only with important matters like Question Period, foreign policy, and economics. But the mechanics of law and the justice system are at the root of our freedom. If no one is interested in who the police are, what they are doing, and how the laws of the land are being enforced, then all else is endangered. If Parliament, the police, and the media are not functioning in their proper, unencumbered roles, democracy becomes a flimsy concept.

Throughout the course of this book, every political interest in Canada—from the far right to the far left—will come under examination for what each has advocated, achieved, or ignored. Bureaucrats, police, business leaders, and the media also come under scrutiny.

I come to this work with a unique advantage. I am not beholden to the government or any political party, nor to any police service, club, brotherhood, secret society, or corporation, other than my publisher and editors at Key Porter Books.

My independence, therefore, allows me to tell this important, serious, and extremely controversial story to the best of my ability—as well, I hope, as it deserves to be told.

For the sake of clarity—because so many elements overlapped and were intertwined—I have chosen to tell the story thematically and as chronologically as possible. In a few places I have used examples from my personal experiences. To do otherwise would have been disingenuous and misleading.

I have striven to provide all points of view in the story, although there has been no official comment from government or the RCMP. There are a number of reasons for this, part circumstance, part design. The communications strategy of government and the RCMP is to control their respective messages. Prime Minister Stephen Harper does not grant open interviews.

In September 2007, Sergeant Natalie Deschênes, an RCMP media relations officer, informed me that I would have to submit my questions about the RCMP in advance. She told me I would have to give the force at least two weeks to consider them before it responded. Deschênes later reiterated that the force would only respond to written questions.

Due to the sensitivity of many of the issues I was exploring, I took the position that scripted, rehearsed answers would be a disservice to the reader. By May 2008, it was clear that all information emanating from the RCMP was being vetted by the government.

The RCMP may have lost its official voice but the voices of many Mounties can be heard in this story.

In an attempt to make the story coherent and self-contained I have also eschewed footnotes. I have attempted to give credit within the story to everyone on whose work and words I relied. When I sometimes found that I could not say something better than someone else, particularly in published chronologies of undisputed material, if possible I either gave the original author direct credit, or, if not, credit "in the neighbourhood." A good example of this is my treatment of Terence McKenna's work on the Khadr family in Chapter 5.

In many ways, *Dispersing the Fog* is three books. The first is about espionage and subterfuge and the sometimes elaborate gymnastics governments have used to deflect the public's attention away from the truth. The second is a virtual autopsy of the Royal Canadian Mounted Police. The final section is about the continuing crisis in Canada, the consequence of too much unchecked power being placed in the hands of too few people.

The title came to me as I drove down the road on which we live in Chester Basin, Nova Scotia. On a clear day driving south one can see many of the islands in Mahone Bay, right out to the open Atlantic Ocean on the horizon. On this particular autumn morning there was a thick sea fog and I could not see Oak Island or Marvin's Island, Shaw Island or, off in the distance, Big and Little Gooseberry islands. The thought crossed my mind that it would be wonderful to have the power to just make the fog disappear so that I could see what it had hidden.

Paul Palango
Chester Basin, Nova Scotia
July 31, 2008

PART I

THE MOUNTIES GET SPOOKED, AGAIN

Is all that we see or seem but a dream within a dream?
—*Edgar Allen Poe*

[1]

A TYPO: THE KEY TO A MONUMENTAL INTRIGUE

This all begins with a single typo, a simple misprint, which seemed to have slipped by everyone. It was the name of a company—CIM21000 Inc. That name had been reprinted so many times in newspapers, magazines, and on the Internet that it had become an accepted fact. The original source was an official document, the Report of the Commission of Inquiry into the Actions of Canadian Officials in Relation to Maher Arar. On the pages of that report were those same eight characters in black and white—CIM21000.

The Arar Commission, as it came to be known, was headed by Dennis O'Connor, the former associate chief justice of Ontario. How could an esteemed, experienced judge, dozens of lawyers, and countless proofreaders have made such an obvious clerical mistake in a matter so important? Was it merely the result of an oversight—one glitch in more than 12,000 pages of evidence, analysis, and the published findings?

The more I tried to investigate those eight characters, the more apparent it became likely that something was amiss. While it seemed inconceivable that it could have been done deliberately, the evidence suggested otherwise. It looked like some form of trickery. Did the perpetrators expect that everyone in the world would just gloss over the typo and forget about it?

In the context of that scenario there can only be one explanation for a deliberate typo—to hide something. But what? Was the typo a veritable microdot whose eight characters hid something fantastic, available only to those who could break the code?

By the time the first draft of this book was written, the riddle had not been solved but I had strong suspicions about what it might contain. So, as you shall learn, I built my case based on the evidence and circumstances and inferred from those facts. Yet the typo was always there, looming in the background. Then, in a propitious turn, I found my way inside it.

The name of one of the people concealed inside that typo was Parto Navidi. The first and last names were Iranian, but who was Parto Navidi? A worldwide search by private investigators, ex-RCMP, ex-FBI, ex-CIA, and ex-Mossad agents could not find this person. Trying to pin down the identity of Parto Navidi seemed about as fruitless as determining the identity of Keyser Soze, the dark spectre in the wonderful 1995 film *The Usual Suspects*. Like Keyser Soze, did Navidi actually exist?

Just before this book was to be edited, however, Navidi emerged and the secrets hidden deep inside the typo began to tumble out.

Unravelling that single typo confirmed the existence of a fantastic, orchestrated deception that had been consciously concealed from public view. But the typo was not the only mystery to be investigated. Another involved an extraordinary public statement with profound implications made in Ottawa in September 2000. Once mentioned, however, the entire matter dropped under the radar and disappeared into the political ether—soon to be forgotten by almost everyone.

Hunting down the story locked inside the typo and explaining what happened after that public statement had been made became the twin engines driving this story through the all-but-impenetrable political fog which has come to engulf us these past three decades.

[2]

JEAN CHRÉTIEN AND
GIULIANO ZACCARDELLI

In recent years, many Canadians have been forced to contemplate how the Royal Canadian Mounted Police has gone from being a revered icon and symbol of all that is good in Canada to a tattered, dishevelled caricature of itself. The warning signs have been there for decades, the mistakes and calamities all too apparent, but the root of the RCMP's countless problems could not be explained. It all seemed so complex and complicated, but there really was a simple, straightforward, and understandable explanation—the role of Quebec in promoting the failure of the Canadian federal government model. Canada is a country without checks and balances on power. The notion that public office is a public trust has long been lost as all Canada's institutions, including its police, have fallen susceptible to politicization.

Jean Chrétien was first elected prime minister of Canada in 1993 after his predecessor-once-removed, Brian Mulroney, had all but destroyed the Progressive Conservative Party. There had been a brief six-month interregnum during which Kim Campbell was elected leader by her party to replace the reviled Mulroney, which allowed her to become Canada's first female, though unelected, prime minister. The voters rejected her in favour of the Liberal, Chrétien, who proclaimed himself to be the one man who could keep Canada united in the face of the constant separatist threats from Québec. The Progressive Conservatives went from 169 seats to two.

It has long been the view of Quebec that Canadian federalism is a voluntary association and that the powers of the federal government should be limited to the collection and redistribution of taxes. Chrétien's approach to federalism didn't really matter to voters in his home province. Quebec found

9

another way to enforce its parochial vision. In 1993, the nascent Bloc Québécois, which ran candidates only in Québec, won 54 of the 295 seats in Parliament, while gaining only 10 percent of the national popular vote, a pattern that would hold through the next four general elections. By comparison, the New Democratic Party received 17 percent of the national vote, but only managed to win 19 seats. Chrétien would win three comfortable majority governments in 1993, 1997, and 2000, while receiving only between 38 and 42 percent of the popular vote. Chrétien's base of support was Ontario, Manitoba, and Atlantic Canada. Once in power, Chrétien proved himself to be anything but liberal, carrying on Mulroney's policies and ushering in the most right-wing government in Canadian history. He was also more of a Québec man than either that province's or other Canadian voters seemed to appreciate.

The Québec issue has shaped Canadian politics for four decades. The election of Chrétien continued a line of power in Canada that began in 1968 with the election of Pierre Elliott Trudeau. Trudeau, Mulroney, Chrétien and, eventually, Chrétien's finance minister and successor as prime minister, Paul Martin, all had two things in common. Each was from Québec and each had links to one man and his company—Paul Desmarais and Power Corporation. It has been said that Trudeau's campaign for prime minister was cooked up in Power Corporation's Montréal offices. After leaving politics, Trudeau went to work for Desmarais on Power Corp.'s international board of advisors. Mulroney considered Desmarais his business mentor and had worked for him as his labour negotiator in more than 30 subsidiaries of Power Corp. Afterward, Desmarais became Mulroney's key political supporter. A year after leaving office, Mulroney accompanied Desmarais to China to advise him on Power Corp.'s role in the massive Three Gorges Dam project and a $60 million real estate development near Shanghai.

Martin had worked as an executive for Desmarais at Canada Steamship Lines, and was eventually allowed to buy the company, making him a wealthy man. In his years out of politics before he became prime minister, Chrétien had been an executive at Consolidated Bathurst, a Power Corp. subsidiary, as well as doing other business with the Desmarais family. Chrétien's daughter, France, had also married Paul's son, André, who became president and chief executive officer of Power Corp. in 1996.

Over the years Paul Desmarais magically transformed a rundown bus company in northern Ontario into the appropriately-named Power Corporation. It became a formidable Québec-based conglomerate with enterprises in Canada, Europe, the Middle East, and Asia. Power Corporation's primary business was the development of infrastructure, utilities such as generating stations and water purification plants around the world, a noble enterprise. Power later diversified to control a number of leading Canadian financial institutions, many newspapers, and other media outlets.

Through an alliance with the secretive and aristocratic Baron Albert Frère of Belgium, Power Corp. all but controlled the infrastructure of Belgium, with major holdings in utilities, gas and oil, steel, transportation, banking and investment, and the media. Frère and Desmarais also had a major stake in the Iraqi oil business at the outset of the last Gulf War. In an almost cartoonish sense, Power Corp. has lived up to its name in more ways than anyone could ever have imagined.

Many consider the billionaire Desmarais to be not only the most powerful man in Québec, but in Canada as well. He is the equivalent of former Chase Manhattan chairman and chief executive officer David Rockefeller in the United States—a kingmaker who decides who will lead the country and what its policies should be.

Rockefeller and the Desmarais family have been close philosophical and business associates for decades. Paul and André Desmarais each served on the Rockefeller-inspired Trilateral Commission and on the international advisory committee of Rockefeller's Chase Manhattan Bank. Both families have long been among the world elite in promoting the concept of sustainable growth or sustainable development, which were coined in 1980 by the International Union for the Conservation of Nature and reiterated in 1987 by the Brundtland Commission, the United Nations World Commission on Environment and Development. Originally, these phrases described environmentally-friendly development. However, the phrase was co-opted by the industrial barons of the West, bent solely on securing and exploiting natural resources to ensure the growth of their enterprises. In that world of sustainable growth, Canada has the natural resources needed to fuel a large portion of the world's economy.

For four decades, the relatively small circle of Desmarais, his family, associates, and agents have had the vision, means, and motive to run Canada as they saw fit, as if the country were Potterville and Desmarais the real-life Mr. Potter from *It's A Wonderful Life*. In Canada's fractured electoral system, enough voters have gone along with them to make sure their influence continued unabated. The power of Power Corp. has been treated almost as an amusement in Canada, as if the Desmarais family are just good judges of political flesh and lucky to have backed winners so often. There has been little concern about the possibility that they were, in fact, making their own luck.

All these imperatives would soon collide with the rule of law in Canada.

✠   ✠   ✠

During the summer of 2000, Prime Minister Chrétien was looking for a new commissioner of the RCMP to replace Philip Murray, who was retiring after five years on the job. Chrétien had not been a fan of Murray or the RCMP. There had been plenty of bad blood. The RCMP had been poking around in some areas the prime minister considered touchy, and Chrétien had returned the favour by starving the force of money. And he had still not forgiven the RCMP for what had happened to him on November 5, 1995, when RCMP security guards were found to be asleep at the switch.

At 2:10 a.m. that morning, a 34-year-old paranoid schizophrenic named André Dallaire from Longueuil, Québec, had arrived at the fence surrounding the prime minister's residence, 24 Sussex Drive, in Ottawa. For 20 minutes he had thrown stones onto the grounds and had waved at security cameras that were supposedly being monitored by RCMP officers guarding the property. Dallaire then climbed the fence and made his way to the house, where he smashed a window to gain entry. Armed with a three-inch knife, he wandered around in the basement and on the ground floor for another half-hour before going upstairs. The prime minister's stunned wife, Aline, confronted him in the hallway and retreated to the bedroom. She locked the door. Either she or the prime minister (the story has never been made clear) then picked up an Inuit stone sculpture for protection and telephoned for help. It took the RCMP seven minutes to get to the scene.

In 2000, Chrétien wanted a commissioner who could protect him in more ways than Canadians might have expected. The various candidates for the job were invited to Chrétien's cottage in Québec to meet the boss. There would be no confirmation hearings or public examination of the candidates. Neither Parliament, the RCMP, nor the public would have input in the matter. Since 1984, after the last reform of the RCMP, the commissioner had been made a deputy solicitor general, appointed by and serving at the pleasure of the prime minister.

A leading contender for commissioner was a relatively young, politically astute, well-educated Mountie officer, Assistant Commissioner Tim Killam. Aline Chrétien, however, had taken a shine to Killam's boss, Deputy

Commissioner Giuliano Zaccardelli, the number-two man in the RCMP in charge of operations. He spoke French and Italian just like she did and he knew Québec almost as if he were a native son. Born in Italy, but raised in Montréal, Zaccardelli was easily more engaging than the average by-the-book senior Mountie. Zaccardelli was Aline Chrétien's man and her husband agreed. It was an easy sell. Appointing a one-time immigrant to such a powerful post brought with it the promise of continued support in the multicultural communities across the country which formed a large part of the Liberal party's political base. That the prime minister's wife seemed to have a say in the selection process of Canada's top police officer, and that no politician or editorialist thought much about it, shows the world just how quaint a dominion is Canada.

A few days later, on the evening of Tuesday, August 28, Chrétien and Mel Cappe, the Clerk of the Privy Council and head of the federal public service, placed a conference call to Zaccardelli's suburban Ottawa home. Chrétien asked Zaccardelli if he was prepared for a new challenge, to become the 20th commissioner of the RCMP.

Zaccardelli, an admittedly emotional man, felt his heart race as he accepted the offer. He noted the time: 9:05 p.m. He hung up the telephone and kissed and hugged his wife Bette. He would never forget the exact moment he got his dream job. Life would never be the same for them, but what they didn't know then is that it would become far more interesting than they could ever have imagined.

Chrétien announced Zaccardelli's appointment three days later, on August 31. It was greeted with enthusiasm by a majority of Mounties. With his 30 years of experience as a criminal investigator and manager, a degree in commerce, and years of on-the-job studying and tutoring, Zaccardelli was deemed the man who could turn the RCMP around. Zac, as he was known, was seen to be a good man with a great record and not inconsiderable charm, the kind of leader the force desperately needed.

As commissioner of the RCMP, Zaccardelli became the chief executive officer of one of the largest corporations in the country, directing and managing the activities of 26,000 employees—16,000 of whom were police officers—from coast to coast to coast and abroad. He had more power than just about anyone in the country. In some ways, he had more power than the prime minister. All the considerable powers of the RCMP Act were vested in his office. He could call for investigations, make and break careers, and do pretty well anything he liked, as long as he lived up to the oath he swore when he became a Mountie to abide by the force's rigid code of conduct as defined in the RCMP Act. The one thing he could not do was anything that might tarnish the image of the force.

If the RCMP has been good at anything in recent years, it was using the media to promote its image. When bad news hit the force, it always attempted, often successfully, to create good news to change the subject, such as announcing its winning awards for management excellence at the same time as it was being pilloried in Parliament and the press over its apparent incompetence. After a new commissioner assumed office, the marketing campaign to promote that person's profile usually began within hours. Zaccardelli officially became commissioner on Saturday, September 2, 2000.

Five days later, he held his first press conference in Ottawa. What he had to say was both striking and alarming. He told the astonished assembled media: "For the first time in this country, we are seeing signs of criminal organizations that are so sophisticated that they are focusing on destabilizing certain aspects of our society. There are criminal organizations that target the destabilization of our parliamentary system." It was a stunning and completely unexpected debut. He wasn't talking only about traditional organized crime.

When asked by reporters to explain what he meant, Zaccardelli said he could not go into detail. One reporter asked if he was just fear-mongering. Zaccardelli denied the suggestion. "It is not fear-mongering in the least. I can't give you, obviously, specific details, but we clearly have information that indicates that criminal organizations, sophisticated criminal organizations, as part of their strategy is not only to maximize their profits through illegal activities, but it is also, in doing that, in maximizing their profits, where they can attempt to try and corrupt and try to destabilize situations," he explained.

Many reporters that day, however, knew what he was referring to: Project Sidewinder, the joint RCMP–CSIS investigation that had begun eight years earlier following discoveries of irregularities at the Canadian consulate in Hong Kong. As investigators followed the trail, they became concerned about the apparent links between the Chinese government, Chinese criminal Triads, and leading Canadian business leaders and politicians. There were leads that investigators were eager to pursue back to Canada, but the controversial on-and-off investigation had been wound up without charges years earlier in puzzling circumstances. Yet it would not die.

For police and intelligence insiders, the inexplicable demise of Project Sidewinder was perceived to have been the latest and best example of politicians influencing police investigations. The leading Canadian businessman in China was Chrétien's son-in-law, André Desmarais, and the leading company operating there was Power Corp. Inside the RCMP, members had been grumbling that something needed to be done to save the force from political piranhas. To their delight, Zaccardelli seemed to be carving out an independent course for both himself and the force. His was the kind of leadership the RCMP craved, a commissioner who would finally stand up to the politicians and let the police do their job, without political interference. The rule of law would trump the rule of politics. It looked as if Canada was finally headed on the right track.

The day Zaccardelli spoke, Chrétien was in New York attending the two-day Millennium Summit of the United Nations, where he addressed a plenary session on the conflict in East Timor. "An incredibly diverse nation, we are deeply committed to freedom, tolerance, justice and equality. We know the sense of community that comes from sharing prosperity and opportunity," Chrétien told his fellow world leaders. "Alleviating world poverty is our common cause. We must share the benefits of globalization. We must give it a human purpose and a human face."

When he got back to Ottawa, Chrétien was first shocked and then furious about Zaccardelli's apparent ambush, a confidential source said. He could not fire Zaccardelli only a week into his job—even after a public performance like the one Zaccardelli had just given.

Though politicians, critics, and the Mounties themselves complained that the RCMP had become a politicized police force, no one has ever found the smoking gun. What happened that weekend in September 2000 might well be one. Confidential sources say Zaccardelli was summoned to an emergency tête-a-tête with Chrétien. He showed up in full dress uniform.

Chrétien let him cool his jets for two and a half hours in the foyer before having him ushered in. The Commissioner was looking like a loose canon, but Chrétien had to be extremely careful about what he said and how he said it. The Desmarais connection was as touchy a subject as there could be. Chrétien's predecessor, Brian Mulroney, was back working with the Desmarais family on Power Corp.'s international board of advisers. Chrétien did not even risk raising the family name. He also knew that he could not threaten Zaccardelli or order him to do anything untoward because the commissioner might just turn around and use that against him. Delicacy was the watchword.

Sources familiar with what had taken place that day said that Zaccardelli told the prime minister that he had only been doing his job the way the law demanded and the public expected. The Canadian Security Intelligence Act of 1984 lists specified "threats to the security of Canada," which includes "foreign-influenced activities within or relating to Canada that are detrimental to the interests of Canada and are clandestine or deceptive or involve a threat to any person." RCMP investigators had reasonable suspicions of a possible criminal conspiracy and were thus duty-bound to revive the Sidewinder file and pursue the case. Of course, Zaccardelli stated, a useful by-product was that such a public display of independence helped to raise the morale of the force. It showed the world that he was not in the government's pocket, like a few of his predecessors; that he was truly independent. Only in this way could his leadership be accepted by his fellow Mounties and ultimately be effective.

Chrétien was too cagey not to see where all this was headed. He told Zaccardelli that it would be wrongheaded for him to pursue the investigation because it had already been settled a year earlier. A source said the conversation went something like this:

"There was nothing to it," the prime minister told the new commissioner. "It's no good for the image of the country if the police are seen to always be chasing the prime minister or prominent business leaders, like they did with Mulroney."

Chrétien hammered out a deal with Zaccardelli. Chrétien implied he did not care what the RCMP did—or how it did it—as long as it respected *his* turf. "I don't want to know anything," he said, disingenuously. But he really did want to know and had ways to find out.

Business links to Chrétien in China were a matter of public record. He had worked closely with Hong Kong tycoon Li Ka-Shing in one of Li's companies. The Desmaraises were just about the only Canadian capitalists making a killing in China. It was clear to Chrétien that the end result of the Project Sidewinder investigation—should it continue—would lead inevitably to an investigation of him, his extended family, and their considerable corporate holdings. Power Corp. also had a large stake in China where it was heavily invested in a multitude of projects. For Chrétien, protecting his corporate interests and contacts was much more important than the public interest.

Chrétien decided that if Zaccardelli and the Mounties backed off, he would stay out of Zaccardelli's business and let him run the force as he saw fit. Zaccardelli's gambit had been as cleverly designed as an undercover police operation. He had lured the prime minister into a confrontation and then presented him with an offer he could not refuse. It had worked perfectly. Both men had received what they wanted. The Sidewinder file evaporated into the mists, and was never again pursued, to the surprise, if not shock, of the rest of the RCMP.

"Zac made this big announcement about organized crime and all these threats and we were all revved up to get going, and then nothing ever happened. It just dropped off the radar, never to be seen or heard again," said former RCMP Superintendent Garry Clement. Clement had been intimately involved in the Sidewinder investigation. "It was weird the way that whole thing happened."

Zaccardelli believed he now had a free hand to run the RCMP any way he pleased. In only his first week as commissioner, Zaccardelli had effectively created a sinecure for himself, unencumbered by oversight or political criticism. Feeling politically safe and protected, he soon began to reveal his true nature. And the dominoes that would lead to his downfall began to fall.

[3]

THE EMPEROR COMMISSIONER

That Giuliano Zaccardelli would land himself and the RCMP in a huge mess was not entirely his own doing. He had inherited more than a century of tradition and myths about the force which had been nurtured and enabled by successive governments largely uninterested in the efficacy and integrity of the force. Zaccardelli knew from the outset that the RCMP was a rent-a-wreck of a police force, but no one was going to admit that. Keeping a brave face and abiding by those traditions and practices, no matter what the consequences, had a single purpose—the protection of the force's good name and the maintenance of its myriad jurisdictions.

He knew that any attempt to transform the RCMP was not going to be easy. Canadians, raised on RCMP hagiography from writers like Pierre Berton, had come to see the force as heroic and necessary. Real and manufactured RCMP heroes abounded in Canadian history. Many in the country had an emotional attachment to the force, often expressed in that most visceral of terms, love.

Government reports, findings by the auditor general, and the RCMP's own internal investigations had determined that the force was suffering from serious fundamental cultural and structural problems. It was in desperate shape: underfinanced, understaffed, mismanaged, and up to its collective neck in controversies. As a guardian institution, it was a disaster.

Each of the two previous commissioners, Norman Inkster and Philip Murray, had been human resource officers in the force and each enjoyed a dubious legacy among the ranks for their less than astute leadership. From 1987 to 1994, Inkster had wanted a more businesslike RCMP, more focused on the bottom line. His crowning achievement had been selling the worldwide rights to the RCMP's logo and imagery to the Disney Corporation to generate a little cash. Over the next six years, Murray had taken Inkster's "innovations" even further, as he attempted to make the RCMP less top-down driven in its command structure, spreading responsibility and authority to lower levels—"empowering the officer on the street"—as Murray called it. Although the primary role of the RCMP should be federal policing, Murray had decentralized the command structure of the force, which only served the interests of its municipal and provincial contract responsibilities and even then, not all that well. Murray also firmly believed that any police officer could do anything. Specialization bred elitism, and his RCMP would be an army of handymen, anything but elitist.

Having been human resource administrators, Murray and Inkster believed in and were slaves to modern management theories about team-building and achieving consensus before moving forward, making as many employees as possible happy. Their efforts, however, had resulted in inertia, stagnation, and deceit, as the RCMP struggled to both meet its obligations and cover up its glaring weaknesses and amateurish mistakes. On the street, the RCMP had gained a well-deserved reputation for being a force that rarely got its man. Inside its own walls, discontent was evident everywhere. Hundreds of work-related grievances had built up in the system. Many were more than two years old. Harassment, especially sexual harassment, and womanizing were rampant. One high-ranking officer (not Zaccardelli) was thus described by his fellow Mounties: "He never passed a vagina that he hadn't met personally." Accountability at any level was seen as a vague and distant concept.

In Zaccardelli's view, the RCMP had gone soft. It had lost its focus, and no more so than at RCMP headquarters in Ottawa. Everyone was told that they had to play nice with each other, the clear intention being to create a civil and pleasant atmosphere. The older definition of the word nice, however, seemed more apt for describing the underlying attitude: mean and obsequious. Zaccardelli found himself surrounded by medal-hungry officers, too many of whom were more interested in endless promotion, pay increases, and pension packages than in doing the job that needed to be done.

Zaccardelli despised the all-in-the-same-boat approach of his predecessors. "Phil Murray wanted us to march hand-in-hand across Canada as if we are the Royal Canadian Mounted Boy Scouts," Zaccardelli told his underlings. "We're not Boy Scouts, damn it, we're the Royal Canadian Mounted Police. We are police and that's what we are going to be."

Saying it was one thing; doing it quite another. Zaccardelli set out on a nearly impossible mission to reconstruct the force from the destruction left by his predecessors. One of the biggest holes in the RCMP was the lack of a formal structure to gather criminal intelligence activity. Inkster and Murray did not believe in or support intelligence gathering and let that function wither. But solid intelligence makes police officers more efficient and effective. Without a centralized, coordinated intelligence wing, the RCMP was reduced to being a merely reactive police force, all but flying blind, gathering evidence day-by-day in a piecemeal fashion, with no meaningful strategy or vision.

Zaccardelli set out to swim against the tide: he would institute change his way. He needed a consensus, but he wasn't the kind of person who was willing to wait for everyone to get into the lifeboat before he paddled off. Someone had to be in charge and he was convinced he was that someone.

"Call me an autocrat, if you must, but if that's what it's going to take to fix the RCMP, then I will be an autocrat." It was one of his favourite sayings.

In his own eyes, Zaccardelli had begun his tenure as RCMP commissioner as the Great Hope, on a mission of restoration and revitalization. Once ensconced at the top, however, he revealed himself to be someone who even those closest to him never expected to meet—a bully who insulated himself with sycophants.

Zaccardelli's vision of how he would resuscitate the RCMP could best be described as anachronistic. In preparing the modern RCMP for the future, he was determined to connect its members with its past, as if the lessons learned in 1874 might provide guidance in the post-millennium years.

One of his priorities in taking command of the RCMP was to learn to ride a horse, a talent one might not think necessary in this day and age. He had taxpayers buy him a sharp new saddle and a pair of custom-made riding boots. The boots alone cost $1,064. In defending the purchase, he said he needed the boots for attending performances by the RCMP's entertainment division, the Musical Ride, with its dancing horses and regimental band. Zaccardelli wanted to take the salute from the 32 riders while seated on a horse, unlike his recent predecessors, who had always sat in the grandstand. He was the self-appointed guardian of the faith, as it were, the custodian of the RCMP's iconic image and valued traditions—the Horsemen. Those expensive, shiny boots would be a mere visual aid to help both the riders and the paying audience distinguish between the commissioner and the rest of the cavalry. The symbolism was all too rich for many of his underlings and for former Mounties.

For some in the RCMP, the new saddle and boots got Zaccardelli off on the wrong foot with his underlings. After all, most Mounties were adept at reading body language and nuance. To them it looked as if Zaccardelli wasn't just making a fashion statement, but was actually openly telling everyone what he really thought when he got up on his high horse with his new footwear. Many inside the RCMP were prepared to write off the riding boots. Dressing up and looking good was certainly part of his nature and nurture. To each his own.

Nevertheless, unease about Zaccardelli set in early in his tenure. The long-term goal of the RCMP was to become a diverse organization to better reflect multicultural, multilingual Canadian reality, but inside the RCMP, "being different" had not been the road to success. By nature, the RCMP had evolved as an organization with an outer persona of pomp and circumstance, scarlet red tunics, wide yellow stripes down each pant leg and, of course, those horses. After the tunics were stowed away in protective garment bags, the everyday Mountie tended to be dour, frugal, and austere, blessed with a get-by-with-what-you-got mentality.

The riding boots weren't the only accessory Zaccardelli coveted. He soon became fixated on the twin-engine 9-seater Piaggio P180 Avanti corporate turbojet to help him get to where his horse wouldn't take him. Today the RCMP has about 40 aircraft, with the backbone of the operation being the single-engine 9-seater Swiss-made Pilatus PC-12. The Pilatus is a dependable utility plane that can be reconfigured for a variety of uses. In any case, the RCMP air force is designated for operational, not administrative, use, which means that RCMP officers should fly commercial when they have to travel. The federal Treasury Board, which writes government cheques, wasn't convinced of the need for the Piaggio, but Zaccardelli would not budge. He knew that Chrétien would give him what he wanted. All he had to do was frame the argument in a politically acceptable fashion, which was what he did. He said the plane would be used to ferry RCMP emergency response teams to crisis situations.

At one point, Zaccardelli and his best friend in the RCMP, Superintendent Ben Soave, who had been the RCMP's liaison officer in Rome for many years, flew to Italy to inspect the plane. They cut a deal for the $10 million aircraft and its purchase was approved in 2002.

If the riding boots made Zaccardelli look good, the Italian-made jet was so downright sexy that it is the plane of choice for Maserati, the Ferrari racing team, and was used by one of the bad guys in the 2006 film *Miami Vice*.

Inside the RCMP, however, the whisperers questioned the propriety of Zaccardelli and Soave's trip and the reason for the purchase. Everyone knew that the Piaggio was too small for any emergency response team; another plane would have to follow it with equipment. But no one went public. In the crooked little world of the RCMP, reporting the truth could be construed as a violation of the internal code of conduct. Others wondered why the government was letting Zaccardelli get away with it.

With Chrétien in his hip pocket, Zaccardelli continued to spend. RCMP headquarters on Vanier Parkway, three kilometres east of the Parliament Buildings, had once been a monastery. Renovations had been made over the years but the building was tired and austere. In Zaccardelli's remaking of the RCMP in his own image, he spent $180,000 fixing up the executive offices there. He continued with "improvements" to his own office on the fifth floor. The commissioner's office is roomy but in no way fancy. The dominant art, if you can call it that, is a giant buffalo head mounted on a wall, making the place look more like a hunter's party room than the office of the highest police officer in the land. There are two entrances to the office, one from the foyer and the other a panic door with a separate, sheltered stairway designed for a sudden escape.

The big buffalo head on the wall got to stay because it would have been sacrilegious to tear it down, but Zaccardelli insisted something had to be done with the dowdy private washroom. He installed Italian marble and a gold sink, spending $42,000 on bathroom upgrades. The RCMP doled out another $30,000 for some fine Natuzzi leather furniture. And then there was the "improvement" to the main door, which we'll get to in due course.

Bit by bit the personality of the respected police officer that Zaccardelli had been began to melt away, replaced by one that better resembled another boss, George Steinbrenner—both the real Steinbrenner, the shipping magnate and tempestuous owner of the New York Yankees; and the pompous Steinbrenner of *Seinfeld*, the Larry David caricature of an authoritarian despot all too ready to bark out orders from behind his desk to the hapless George Costanzas who worked for him.

Like the general he seemed to think he was, Zaccardelli began readjusting his soldiers. This was one of his prerogatives as commissioner. In the old days there had been only three deputy commissioners, each of whom were quietly vetted by the Privy Council Office. The reason for this was that succession planning was always in the mind of both the force and the government. The next officers in line had to be judged capable of being commissioner before they were appointed as deputy. That all changed after Zaccardelli's predecessor, Philip Murray, decentralized the force in the mid-nineties in an attempt to make it appear more modern, more accountable, and more politically correct.

Until Murray's day, RCMP commanders had resisted the push to decentralize, recognizing that it would make the force even more unmanageable, weaker, and likely less accountable than it already was. But Murray, backed by the first Chrétien government, charged ahead, creating eight deputy commissioners across the country. Along the way, the vetting process disappeared, and promotions became dependent more upon the cut of one's jib, the turn of another's ankle, and other ephemeral criteria.

Soon, mimicking both the real and fictional George Steinbrenners, Zaccardelli began to surround himself with cronies. Steinbrenner favoured his family and in-laws; Zaccardelli chose associates and neighbours from the years he had spent in New Brunswick's "J" Division where he had been the assistant commissioner in charge of criminal operations during the nineties. Eighty percent of RCMP members are stationed in the four western provinces. New Brunswick is considered to be an outpost, not the place to develop leaders of the future. In New Brunswick, however, almost everyone had to be bilingual, which was an added bonus for anyone going to Ottawa, where 80 percent of the force's leaders had never served in the West.

There is an element of schizophrenia to the RCMP. To get to the top levels and to key positions in the RCMP bureaucracy, one had to speak French. Yet the RCMP's sensibilities have always been very British, even Scottish. Throughout its history it has been an organization governed and populated by Mc-Mounties, O-'Mounties, and Mountie-smiths, as it were. He surrounded himself with such people, as if to prove that 30 years of trying to diversify and reflect the evolving demographics of Canada had been a waste of time. Of the 43 top managers in the RCMP at one point, the only others with vowels at the end of their name were Assistant Commissioners Line Carbonneau, Brendan Dunne, Darrell LaFosse, and Kevin Mole. But there were eight Mcs and Macs—Macintyre, MacKillican, MacLaughlan, Mc-Callum, McCloskey, two McDonnells, and a McFadyen.

One by one, the Boys from New Brunswick rocketed to the top, and began calling themselves the "J" Division mafia. It was a terminology many other Mounties found offensive. Pierre Yves (P.Y.) Bourduas, a Zaccardelli acolyte, quickly became a deputy commissioner. Dan Killam joined his twin brother Tim, who was already an assistant commissioner. Another set of twins, Mike and Pat McDonnell, moved in as assistant commissioners. Gary Bass was made an assistant commissioner in British Columbia. This incestuousness did not go unnoticed.

"What are the odds that of all the police officers in the RCMP, two sets of twins are the best and brightest?" It was a question asked by many Mounties, who were more than a little nervous about the direction in which the force seemed to be headed.

Zaccardelli took his new charges under his wing and began to school them in what he considered a most important subject, the history of the RCMP. He devised his own cult-like program for his underlings. Officers were assigned required reading about RCMP history so they might better understand who they were and how they should view the world. In Zaccardelli's primer courses, however, there was one notable exception to the rule: himself. The RCMP was commanded to do as he and the RCMP's history had dictated, not as he did.

The terrorist attacks of September 11, 2001, and the ensuing invasions of Afghanistan and Iraq over the next two years forced the RCMP to shift its priorities away from domestic policing to national security. After years of having its budgets pared by the Chrétien government, Ottawa was now pouring money into the RCMP. In the huge adrenalin rush caused by the seemingly never-ending emergency situation, Zaccardelli got even more pumped up. The RCMP needed strong leadership in this time of crisis, and he was going to give it to them, or so he imagined. The problem he faced was that the RCMP he commanded was not quite the RCMP of its own marketing campaigns.

When Zaccardelli travelled, he demanded comforts befitting his self-perceived high status. His predecessor, Murray, had been keenly aware that rank-and-file Mounties respected a commissioner who was one of them—someone who shared their misery. Zaccardelli made it clear he was the chief executive officer: He deserved the best room in a hotel. He rarely left Ottawa without his golf clubs.

With the world in a state of turmoil a week after September 11, 2001, for example, Zaccardelli travelled to Toronto for a scheduled convention of the Canadian Association of Chiefs of Police. His flight landed at the executive terminal at Pearson International Airport. He was met there by a junior officer—Constable Pat Douek. That day other dignitaries in the Toronto area were also being escorted by the RCMP. When Douek arrived at the car pool, all the roomy, splashy vehicles had been checked out. Douek did the next best thing: he selected a silver-grey Ford Taurus, the newest car in the fleet. When Zaccardelli's aide-de-camp, Adjutant Officer Denis Constant, saw the Taurus, he was livid.

"The commissioner of the RCMP can't be seen in that," Constant told Douek. "Get a proper vehicle."

A search began for a Lincoln Town Car, which cost the force more than $1,000 in rental fees. But Zaccardelli made good use of the car. He demanded to be chauffeured everywhere, including the short, three-block walk from his hotel, the Fairmont Royal York, to the Toronto Convention Centre.

"Every morning he would come out of the hotel with his buddy, (then-Toronto police chief, now Ontario Provincial Police Commissioner) Julian Fantino, and get into the car, while Fantino walked," Douek recalled. "It was always rush hour, and Fantino always beat us to the convention centre."

That Zaccardelli felt compelled to travel in style that week in no way reflected the operational state of the RCMP. Across the country, politicians everywhere were complaining about the force being undermanned, under-financed, and spread as thinly and erratically as the hairs on a balding man's head. Even inside the force, the RCMP knew that it did not have the structure, experience, or specialists to deal with all its jurisdictions, never mind national security. In the media, American authorities were regularly warning that country's investors to be wary of investing in Canada because the laws were equivocal at best and the policing of the financial markets invisible. The biggest concern for Zaccardelli, however, was that his accord with Chrétien was being put to the test.

First, there was the so-called Shawinigate Scandal, a controversy which first raged from 1999 to 2001 after it was revealed that Chrétien had a conflict of interest surrounding his interest in a golf course in his riding and that he had lobbied the Federal Business Development Bank of Canada on behalf of an adjacent hotel. Chrétien had denied the allegations, claiming that he had sold his shares in the golf course in November 1993, and released to the public the bill of sale to confirm that sale to Toronto hotelier Jonas Prince. Opposition MPs argued that the prime minister effectively had a conflict of interest when he lobbied the Federal Business Development Bank to provide a $615,000 loan to the Auberge Grand-Mère, a hotel next to the golf course. The Opposition insisted that Chrétien was in conflict because the prime minister would have been more likely to collect his debt if Prince had been able to resell the shares, and Prince would have had trouble reselling them if the adjacent hotel was in financial difficulty.

On two other occasions, Chrétien tried to lobby François Beaudoin, the head of the Business Development Bank, for a $2-million loan for the same group of people, but Beaudoin refused to cooperate and eventually turned on Chrétien.

Although the RCMP announced in February 2001 that there was no basis for a criminal investigation of Chrétien, it did not waste any time going after Beaudoin, who was summarily sacked from his job. He sued and won his job back as well as being awarded $4.3 million in damages. Québec Judge André Denis issued a scathing 200-page judgment on the Beaudoin case, describing the actions of the RCMP and Chrétien's own goon squad as "an unspeakable injustice."

As Greg Weston of *The Ottawa Sun* later put it:

> One of the most shameful chapters in the Mounties' recent history was their unconscionable harassment of François Beaudoin, the former head of the federal Business Development Bank. Among other tactics later condemned by a Québec judge, the RCMP raided Beaudoin's home, cottage, and country club after he blew the whistle on Jean Chrétien for trying to lobby the federal bank boss to approve a loan for the "Shawinigate" inn. Was someone in the Chrétien government directing the RCMP in those police-state activities?

Chrétien defended himself by trying to argue that he was just a lowly member of Parliament working for his constituents. When the federal ethics commissioner, Howard Wilson, who reported to Chrétien, absolved him of wrongdoing, Chrétien crowed that he had been vindicated. The "vindication" didn't amount to much when it was learned that Chrétien had been more than a little deceptive in his claims. Chrétien acknowledged later that, beginning in 1996, his lawyer had acted to collect the debt owed on the sale by helping Mr. Prince resell the shares, which he had eventually done in 1999.

Meanwhile, the RCMP was bursting at the seams with potential disasters. One by one they began to explode in Zaccardelli's face. In early 2002, a seemingly obscure controversy in the handling of RCMP pension funds broke inside the force. The Ottawa police were called in as independent investigators to conduct a criminal investigation. However, charges were never laid, which sparked even more internal controversy. Zaccardelli said that he had everything under control, but there would be more to the story than that.

In late September 2002 came the case of 34-year-old Maher Arar. A Syrian-born Canadian who had graduated from McGill University and was working as a communications engineer, Arar had been arrested at New York's JFK Airport by U.S. authorities on his return from Tunisia via Zurich on his way back to Canada. Thirteen days later, on October 8, the U.S., under that government's "extraordinary rendition" policy, shipped Arar to Syria. The reality was that the U.S. was using third-party countries to interrogate and torture suspected terrorists. Word leaked that Arar had been "set up" by the Mounties, who were accused of both conducting a sloppy investigation and illegally passing erroneous information about Arar to the U.S. Federal Bureau of Investigation (FBI).

Once again confronting bad press, and public and Opposition demands for an investigation, the Mounties sprung into action. Only, instead of an internal review of its own failings, the force appeared to mount an attack on the press.

Armed with a search warrant, the RCMP raided the home of *Ottawa Citizen* reporter Juliet O'Neill and the *Citizen*'s newsroom on January 21, 2004. O'Neill was the reporter who had broken a story about Arar based on leaked government documents. The RCMP even convinced Ottawa Justice of the Peace Richard Sculthorpe to issue an order under the Security of Information Act to seal the file and keep the reasons for the warrants secret.

The Arar case continued to hold the headlines as Shawinigate faded from view. But another overlapping scandal began percolating to the surface. In 1995, Québec had held a referendum on sovereignty. The federalist opposition was led by a complacent and almost uninterested Chrétien. The federal side won by a hair. The "scare" caused Chrétien to orchestrate a secret sponsorship program to promote federal interests in the province. As much as $350 million in federal money was quietly redirected through Liberal-friendly Québec advertising agencies to so-called federal forces in the province, but in reality, most of the millions of dollars involved just disappeared.

In 2002, an internal government audit had detected evidence of the scheme, but, mysteriously, the RCMP had declined to investigate. In her 2004 report, Auditor General Sheila Fraser concluded that the Royal Canadian Mounted Police had been an active participant in the sponsorship scandal. The RCMP had accepted millions of dollars to display the "Canada" symbol wherever they could. Fraser said the RCMP illegally received $3 million in sponsorship money to help it celebrate its 125th anniversary in 1998, and that another $1.7 million received by the RCMP had been placed in an illegal, non-government bank account. The Mounties had used some of the cash to rent a train for a festive ride through Québec, complete with lavish dinners and expensive fine wines that had been stored in the evidence room at Montréal's "C" Division.

Even worse, public monies had been funnelled from the federal public works department through three Québec advertising firms and back to the RCMP. In return, the advertising firms received $1,324,380 in fees for "make-work" from the force. "We found no documented evidence of any additional visibility received in return for the sponsorship money," the report concluded.

Zaccardelli could blame that debacle on his predecessor Murray, but the meltdown continued and spilled into his watch. Auditor General Fraser also reported that $100,000 of the federal money directed through the RCMP had been donated by one of the advertising company executives to the separatist Parti Québecois, the enemies of federalism. When all this was later revealed, eight years after the fact, the PQ returned the contribution. No one in the RCMP was ever held accountable for what had taken place.

True to his tough-guy public persona, Chrétien never flinched, right to the end. Unbowed, he was finally hounded out of office and resigned in 2003 to be replaced as prime minister by Paul Martin.

Martin, lost in Chrétien's shadow for so many years, immediately tried to portray himself as being his own man, someone with clean hands, courage, and integrity, who was dedicated to serving the public interest. That he was eager and unafraid to dig through the detritus of his predecessor would prove to be a dangerous and somewhat naïve political course of action, and entirely unappreciated by many Canadians.

Among his first acts as prime minister was to set up a Commission of Inquiry into the Sponsorship Program and Advertising Activities, headed by retired Justice John Gomery. The judge got to the bottom of the mess and filed his report in 2005 (the report can be viewed online on a government website). Charges were laid, and a number of Québec business people who benefited from the government's largesse were fined and even sent to prison. Some cases continue to this day. But the Mounties escaped unscathed. No one lost his or her job over the scandal.

For his part, Chrétien, who had a deserved reputation as a bully, did not relish the thought of someone poking into his affairs. He tried—unsuccessfully—to have Gomery removed in 2004, citing bias, among other things. What galled Chrétien more than anything was an interview with the media in which Gomery referred to the former prime minister as being, among other things, "small-town cheap."

Both Auditor General Fraser and Gomery would exonerate Martin, pointing out that he had been kept in the dark by Chrétien, his loyalists, and their co-conspirators. Early in 2008, however, Chrétien, his ex-chief-of-staff Jean Pelletier, and former public works minister Alfonso Gagliano went to federal court to file an application for a judicial review. Their lawyers argued that Gomery was "seduced by the media and the limelight to such an extent that the judicial instinct for fairness, objectivity and restraint which [Chrétien] was entitled to expect of him gave way to a preoccupation on his part with focusing media [and public] attention upon himself, a course of conduct which preordained unfavourable findings." Although Gomery in his final report in 2005 did not link Chrétien and Pelletier to the kickback scheme, the two men argued that their reputations had been damaged by the report. They demanded that some of the unfavourable conclusions drawn by Gomery regarding the three men be quashed or annulled to restore their reputations. A few weeks after launching the suit, Chrétien was awarded the Order of Canada.

On June 26, 2008, Federal Court Justice Max Teitelbaum ruled that Gomery's inappropriate comments to the media throughout the hearings be-trayed bias against Chrétien and Pelletier. Teitelbaum struck down some of the contentious findings, stating: "The comments made by the commissioner, viewed cumulatively, not only indicate that he prejudged but also that the commissioner was not impartial toward the applicant [Mr. Chrétien]." Teit-elbaum also chastised Gomery's zeal to remain in the media spotlight which, he said, trivialized the proceedings and tainted the perception of fairness.

Chrétien and Pelletier claimed "total vindication." However, editorialists across the country were quick to point out that while Gomery may have been slapped on the wrist, the fact of the matter was that the Chrétien govern-ment had been entirely responsible for the scandal and that it was unseemly for the former prime minster to be gloating about such a small—even tech-nical—victory.

Meanwhile, back in 2004, Martin found himself being maligned both by his own party for airing its dirty linen and for singling out Québeckers for investigation and prosecution. The Opposition and other critics argued that, as finance minister during the sponsorship scandal expenditures, he had been asleep at the switch, as it were. He was portrayed as a "ditherer," when, in truth, he had acted with commendable directness.

The one issue where successive governments could rightfully be accused of dithering was the state of the RCMP. Hidden from the public was the fact that the RCMP had been reduced to a shambles and that it was a very dangerous place to be employed.

This all came into focus on March 3, 2005, when four young Mounties—Tony Gordon, Leo Johnston, Brock Myrol, and Peter Schiemann—were gunned down in an ambush at Mayerthorpe, Alberta, by a local madman, James Roszko. It was the largest single-day loss of life since the modern Royal Canadian Mounted Police was formed in 1920, equal to the fabled lost patrol of the North-West Mounted Police in which four Mounties in the Yukon froze to death in February 1911. Among other things, the Mayerthorpe massacre suggested incompetence within the ranks of the RCMP, but nothing was done.

In December 2005, in the midst of a federal general election, Zaccardelli did something extremely unusual. In November, before the election was called, Finance Minister Ralph Goodale had announced in Parliament that the government was going to change the tax treatment for so-called income trusts, a popular tax avoidance vehicle for corporations. Before the statement was made, unusual fluctuations in the stock market indicated that someone with inside knowledge was illegally trading securities to their advantage. The debacle helped cause the downfall of the Martin government and the calling of the election.

In response to a letter from New Democratic Party finance critic Judy Wasylycia-Leis, Zaccardelli confirmed that the RCMP had launched a criminal investigation into the release of information by the Department of Finance. In a subsequent press release on December 28, 2005, Zaccardelli personally inserted the name of Finance Minister Ralph Goodale as being a target of the RCMP investigation. The force said it was looking at Liberal insiders who might have benefited on the stock market from inside knowledge about the new tax treatment for previously tax-exempt income trusts.

An RCMP commissioner would normally acknowledge acceptance of such a letter without giving details—especially in the midst of an election. That is what happened in 1988, when the RCMP did not reveal an investigation into the activities of Mulroney government member Richard Grisé until after the election date. Grisé won the election, but was subsequently charged and convicted of fraud and forced to resign his seat in the House of Commons.

Zaccardelli's press release had an immediate impact on the January 2006 election. Paul Martin was leading in the polls but the Liberals plummeted

18 points almost overnight, losing the election to Conservative Stephen Harper. Just about everyone in Canada was wondering why Zaccardelli would openly interfere in an election. Zaccardelli said he had no choice but to release the information. "It was my duty," he said, but few believed him. Others wondered whether he was deliberately trying to help the Conservatives get elected.

The truth was more complicated. Zaccardelli had managed to have the RCMP avoid mounting an investigation into the sponsorship scandal while Chrétien was in office, but once out of office, events out of his control forced him to move forward. Mountie insiders believe the leak was instigated by Chrétien as a payback to his archenemy Martin for, among other things, muddying Chrétien's name in the sponsorship scandal inquiry and bringing down his Québec associates. Zaccardelli, forever the grateful loyalist, was merely Chrétien's tool.

Meanwhile, Auditor General Fraser was once again breathing down Zaccardelli's neck, reporting in late 2005 that the RCMP was failing to meet its duties across the country. The biggest gap was in federal policing where at least one quarter of vacant positions were not filled. The next year Fraser reported that the RCMP's National Police Service branch, its forensic and criminal labs where all the CSI (crime scene investigation) work was done, had a backlog of files extending more than 1 1/2 years. It was not as if the RCMP was doing the work for the entire country—Ontario, Québec, and the city of Vancouver had their own separate facilities. Added to these shortcomings were reports from the RCMP's public complaints commissioner and its ethics commissioner. Each slammed the force over its attitude toward civilian oversight and accountability. Again, the Liberal government did nothing.

On July 7, 2006, two more Mounties, Marc Bourdages and Robin Cameron, were shot near Spiritwood, Saskatchewan. They died within minutes of each other nine days later. Eighteen Mounties would die on the job during Zaccardelli's tenure—the most for any commissioner. No one in government seemed curious enough to wonder why all these things were happening.

And all this was only some of the national news. Elsewhere, a Mountie constable in northern British Columbia was accused of shooting a young man, Ian Bush, in the back of the head in a local lock-up. Staff Sergeant Ken Smith, a Mountie in New Brunswick, complained that the force had used illegal surveillance and other techniques on him to discredit him. Tori Cliffe, a female constable in Alberta, openly talked about how she and others had been sexually assaulted by a superior officer and how the force had tried to cover it by paying them off with substantial out-of-court settlements. A number of Mounties were so fed up with the system that they tried to run for Parliament in a desperate effort to get reforms.

There was not much good news, but Zaccardelli took it in stride. He would don his dress uniform, head up to Parliament Hill, and dazzle the politicians there with his charisma and bafflegab. He felt bulletproof.

Zaccardelli dismissed his critics, saying they were ill-informed about the state of the force. The RCMP had been named one of Canada's top one hundred employers in October 2006. That same year it was added by the Harvard School of Business to its Balanced Scorecard Hall of Fame—for its "excellent management practices." Inside the force, Mounties laughed at the plaudits, knowing full well that whoever was handing them out did not have a clue about how the RCMP really worked.

Zaccardelli continued to charge ahead. He believed that nothing would stick to him. The worse things seemed to get for the force on the outside the more confident he seemed to become.

The charm that worked on Parliament Hill, however, wasn't working inside the RCMP, where Zaccardelli had a magical touch for creating enemies. He made good use of the P-180 by flitting here and there around the globe, sometimes in the company of his friends, Soave and Fantino. But ordinary Mounties weren't so lucky getting lifts on the P-180.

One low-ranking Toronto-based RCMP officer who was urgently needed in Ottawa in 2006 was offered a ride on the P-180. Before the Mountie boarded he was told by Zaccardelli's aide that he should: "Sit at the rear of the plane, and don't address the Commissioner or make eye contact with him." The story quickly made the rounds inside the force.

His office renovations completed, Zaccardelli began to forge ahead on his next big projects. First would be the $29 million RCMP Heritage Centre in Regina, designed by internationally renowned architect Arthur Erickson. Next was a brand-new RCMP headquarters building in Ottawa, presumably with Zaccardelli's own name on it for posterity. He openly talked about becoming the longest serving commissioner in the history of the RCMP, that is, longer than the almost 23 years served by Aylesworth Bowen Perry. He had led the North-West Mounted Police from August 1, 1900 to March 23, 1923. For any ambitious up-and-comers, Zaccardelli's message was plain and simple: Forget about it. In the unlikely event he was hit by a car or his Piaggio P-180 Avanti missed a runway, the commissioner was grooming a successor—Deputy Commissioner P.Y. Bourduas.

Discontent about Zaccardelli was growing daily, not only in Ottawa but also across the country, over his imperial style and the RCMP's pedestrian policing practices. Zaccardelli was seen to be consumed with his image and legacy. Over the years he commissioned a number of official portraits of himself, including one by a female relative. Like so many of his underlings, he was a hound for public recognition. The problem was that every time he received a new medal for his uniform, Zaccardelli felt compelled to have the force pay for an updated portrait to capture it.

Zaccardelli had worked hard all his life. He and his wife Bette had never had children. He put in 18-hour days. He expected the same from his staff. He demanded respect and dished out contempt for anyone who didn't agree with him. He was used to being served and getting his own way. Near the end of his days as commissioner a deputy commissioner asked him, "Zac, I'm working hard, when am I going to get a promotion?"

"You are making $160,000 a year," Zaccardelli told the man. "You are expected to work hard for that money. That's why you get paid that much. So get back to work."

It was a loaded question because there is only one more promotion for a deputy commissioner, and Zac had no intention of resigning. All of which brings us to that other renovation he undertook in his office—the main door. Zaccardelli had an electric door opener installed that could be operated by a remote-control garage door opener.

"If it got to a point in a conversation when Zac didn't like something you were saying he would push the button and the door would open," said one Mountie who had experienced the treatment. "It was your cue to shut up right there and leave."

All Zaccardelli wanted to hear was the good news from his yes-men— which is what he got. By 2006, however, the world had changed. Zaccardelli was oblivious to the very real threat posed to the RCMP and himself from the swirl of controversies that would not die, and no one had the will or gumption to tell him to duck. But Zaccardelli wasn't the only one with a bullseye pinned to him; the entire force was being lined up for another political hit.

[4]

THE INVISIBLE HAND OF
STEPHEN HARPER

As Giuliano Zaccardelli and the RCMP began to implode, Stephen Harper was taking it all in. He had long ago come to his own conclusions about the RCMP, but had never been in a position to do anything about it, until now. In January 2006 he had been elected Canada's 22nd prime minister, promising to make the federal government an institution accountable to the people, and the state of the RCMP was clearly on his mind.

From his early days in politics in 1987 as chief policy officer for the Alberta-based Reform Party of Canada, Harper and his right-wing Albertan colleagues had been bent on changing the face of Canada. Their enemy was the eastern Canadian establishment, in particular the Québec political mafia which was seen to be led by the Desmarais family. Reformists believed the Québeckers had betrayed the entire country with their self-interested policies, like Trudeau's hated National Energy Program in 1980, which had applied double taxation to Alberta oil in the name of energy conservation.

For almost four decades beginning in April 1968, Québeckers Pierre Trudeau, Brian Mulroney, Jean Chrétien, and Paul Martin had held the post of prime minister. Non-Québeckers Joe Clark, John Turner, and Kim Campbell never got much of a chance to implement their ideas before being voted out of office.

In the view of the Albertans, Québeckers were reaping the economic advantages of Canada without being committed to the country as a whole. The Reformers were not entirely wrong about that. The Québeckers had insinuated themselves into the intersections of power in the federal government. The Québec political mafia—politicians from across party lines, wealthy old-family interests, latter-day tycoons, bureaucrats, and even criminals—worked as a cult-like unit.

The disproportionate representation of francophones in key positions in the federal government, its bureaucracy, and its agencies had clearly skewed public policy to a more Québec-friendly perspective than might be warranted by Québeckers' twenty percent representation in the general population. The Québeckers held their noses and paid lip service to federalism while deftly controlling and steering the country—always focused on their first priority of keeping key federal institutions weak.

Shortly after being elected prime minister, Jean Chrétien bragged about his own similar feelings in a December 1, 1994, interview with two reporters from the French newspaper Le Monde, which was subsequently reported in Canada by the Calgary Sun's Paul Jackson. "French Canadians are martyrs. They had been humiliated by the English. Obviously, I would have been happier if Canada had not been conquered in the past by the English. If this part of North America had remained French . . . but you can't rewrite history." But he had a plan to do just that: "For example, I have just appointed an Acadian to the office of Governor General. So the Governor General is a francophone. The same is true, among others, of the prime minister, the Speaker of the House of Commons, the Speaker of the Senate, the Chief Justice of the Supreme Court of Canada, the minister of Foreign Affairs, and the minister of Finance."

From Harper's perspective, Ottawa was littered with land mines and secret agents who had the tenure, experience, and ability to thwart anyone bent upon changing the status quo. As righteous as the reform-minded Harper might be, the public had him on a short leash.

The most serious problem Harper and his Reformists confronted was that no matter how much Albertans like him complained about the apparent rigging of the country, Albertans were not trusted by many in the rest of Canada. The perception was that Albertans were too American in their attitudes, too conservative, and out of touch with Canadian social sensibilities. Ideas from Alberta were often dismissed by the rest of Canadians as the arrogant, dangerous preachings of a bunch of rednecks who thought they were smart only because they had the good fortune to be sitting on vast reserves of valuable oil.

The very makeup of the Reform Party played into that skepticism. One of its gurus was Tom Flanagan, an American-born political science professor at the University of Calgary. Flanagan's social conservatism had become a lightning rod for controversy. He had argued, for instance, that Canada's Aboriginals were merely "first immigrants" and not entitled to land-claims settlements. Other Albertans—Rainer Knopff, Ted Morton, and Barry Cooper—openly railed against Québec, the Charter of Rights and Freedoms, feminism, abortion, and same-sex marriage. Cooper was also a frequent commentator on policing in Canada.

Western Canadian journalist Ted Byfield, the godfather of Alberta politics, had this to say about Harper and his followers to Marci MacDonald in a 2004 article, "The Men Behind Stephen Harper," in the *Walrus* magazine: "Those people who said they're dangerous—they're right! People with ideas are dangerous. If Harper gets elected, he'll make a helluva change in this country."

Since the recent oil boom had begun in the 1990s, Albertans had lorded their wealth over the rest of Canada and had often proclaimed that their province was as unique in the Canadian confederation as Québec. Though Alberta was an engine of the Canadian economy there was no more visible reminder of its continuing colonial status than the ubiquitous presence of the federal RCMP patrolling the streets and highways of the province. The very presence of the RCMP was a glaring manifestation of all that was wrong with the way Canada was being governed.

Albertans could talk all they wanted about being different and independent but the province did not even control its own police. It looked like a mere colony. The RCMP—a federal institution—was responsible for provincial policing and most of the municipal policing in Alberta. The RCMP reported to Ottawa, not Edmonton. That was a clear intrusion on provincial rights and Harper and his like-minded reformists believed that Alberta should have dominion over its own police in every way, much like the policing model in Ontario, Québec, or the United States. The FBI, for example, did not hire itself out to patrol the streets of North Dakota in marked vehicles. Harper was determined to clarify that important distinction because he did not want the federal government—the agent of Québec and Ontario—having influence where it should not.

As prime minister, Harper's moment may well have arrived but he knew that to realize his ultimate ambition and those of his home province he could not walk into Parliament humming Bruce Cockburn's "If I Had A Rocket Launcher." His chance of success would depend upon timing, luck, and a bundle of finesse. Harper recognized that no matter how logical and right he might be in taking on the Mounties, he could not do it directly. With rare exceptions in Canadian politics, obfuscation has always trumped clarity.

To tackle the Mounties, therefore, Harper had to hide in the political weeds as best he could. That was his style, anyway. "Stephen has an incredible strategic sense," Barry Cooper said in the *Walrus* article. "It's like playing chess: he can always see five or six moves ahead."

But with only 125 of the 308 seats in the House of Commons, Harper did not have any wiggle room. To survive, he had to depend on an unlikely ally—the Bloc Québecois. Harper's popular support since the January 23, 2006, election had continued to hover at about 36 per cent but his advantage was that no other parties were doing any better, in some cases even worse, than they had on election day.

The mystique of the Mounties has a powerful, if not irrational, pull on the majority of Canadians. On the political left and right, Canadians worry aloud about the dangers of the police having too much power and the country slipping into a police state. Yet Canada is the only democratic country in the world whose largest police force is treated as an icon. Not only that, it is blessed by the British Crown—a foreign icon.

Throughout its history, the RCMP has stumbled from one debacle to another. The willingness of Canadians to forgive the Mounties has been astonishing, as if the old saw, "If it ain't broke, don't fix it," had been transmuted into something more perverse: "If you don't admit it's broke, you don't have to fix it."

The RCMP myth is that it is a superior police force—the best in the world. In spite of all the RCMP's self-promotion about its accomplishments and its Hollywood image of always getting its man, the public record speaks otherwise.

Harper recognized that his biggest obstacle in promoting change was having to contend with the myths and confusion about the RCMP among the general population—particularly in his home province of Alberta.

+ + +

The Mounties and Alberta have been inextricably entwined since the force's inaugural mythical journey, the Great March West in 1873. The catalyst for the creation of the North-West Mounted Police was the Cypress Hills Massacre which occurred 65 kilometres south of Medicine Hat, June 1, 1873. There, ten Montana wolf hunters, who suspected local Aboriginal people of stealing their horses, murdered at least 20 Assiniboine men, women, and children and kidnapped and raped the Assiniboine women. News of the massacre did not reach Ottawa until August. Ten days after learning about it, Canada's first prime minister, Sir John A. Macdonald, ordered the creation of a new hybrid paramilitary force that would combine the best elements of the Royal Irish Constabulary and the mounted rifle units of the United States Cavalry. Enabling legislation to create the force—the North West Mounted Police Act—was passed August 30, 1873.

Three 50-man troops began the arduous trek across the country. The Horsemen, as they came to be called, followed the Dawson Trail, entering Manitoba at its southeast corner on their way to Fort Dufferin. The next year they were joined by another 125 members and the Mounties began their work in parts of Saskatchewan and Manitoba, enforcing federal laws, protecting Canada's sovereignty, and helping to create law and order in the wilderness. By the turn of the century, their jurisdiction had been expanded to include all of Alberta and Saskatchewan, the Yukon, and the Northwest Territories.

While the RCMP has long promoted itself as being invaluable to Canada, the country has not always thought of it that way. In 1896, Wilfrid Laurier—the Stephen Harper of his day—had campaigned on a provincial rights platform, part of which included the disbanding of the Mounties and turning policing over to the provinces. Laurier won the election, but after becoming prime minister reneged, and the force was spared.

In 1905, when Alberta and Saskatchewan entered Confederation as provinces, the Mounties were retained on contract by each province to provide provincial policing services. This arrangement only lasted until 1917, when then-Commissioner A. Bowen Perry unilaterally cancelled the Mountie contracts in a dispute over Alberta and Saskatchewan's plans to adopt Prohibition. Perry argued that Prohibition had not worked in the United States and that such laws were unenforceable. This led to Alberta and Saskatchewan each setting up its own provincial police forces. The Mounties, in any case, were all but bankrupt. The force had dwindled to just 300 men.

A new strategy was needed to pump life into the RCMP. That came with the demise of the Alberta Provincial Police in the early years of the Great Depression. The bankrupt province was forced to dismantle the provincial police force. The Mounties returned to contract policing in the province in 1932. The advantage to the province was that the federal government provided a hefty subsidy to any province which hired the Mounties. That same year the RCMP absorbed the men and vessels of the Preventive Service of the National Revenue department. It soon took over contract work in Nova

Scotia, New Brunswick, Prince Edward Island, Manitoba, and Saskatchewan, each of which folded its provincial police forces. Outside Ontario and Québec, the RCMP had a foothold in every province except British Columbia.

After the bloody Winnipeg General Strike in 1920, the Mounties absorbed the Dominion Police, based largely in Ontario. The Dominion Police enforced federal law in eastern Canada and had its own protective service, a counter-intelligence agency of the time. The protective service morphed into the RCMP's Security Service and continued its counter-intelligence work inside the RCMP. The RCMP Security Service had operated behind a wall of secrecy within the force. The police did not know what the Security Service was doing and vice versa. This is the usual arrangement, even today, in federal police services around the world.

Newfoundland entered Confederation in 1949, and the RCMP soon extended its reach, replacing the Newfoundland Rangers as the provincial police service. The Royal Newfoundland Constabulary continues to call itself the provincial police but only provides police services for the three largest urban centres on the island. With Newfoundland in the fold, there was now a political imperative to have the RCMP take over British Columbia as well.

The early days of the Cold War between the democratic west and the communist east were well underway in 1950. A Liberal, Louis St. Laurent, was the prime minister. In British Columbia the provincial government was a Liberal–Conservative coalition that had won an overwhelming majority in the previous election. The coalition was designed to block the Co-operative Commonwealth Federation—the forerunner of today's New Democratic Party—from gaining power. The B.C. premier was Liberal Byron Ingemar (Boss) Johnson and his attorney general was former defense lawyer Gordon Wismer—also a Liberal.

The 92-year-old British Columbia provincial police had built a solid reputation for its work. However, in a sudden policy change engineered by the Liberals in Ottawa and Victoria it was disbanded and replaced by the RCMP. The federal government convinced the British Columbia government to hand over provincial policing to the RCMP in return for a sweet subsidy. When handed the contract the RCMP did not have the manpower to police the province; it could only afford to pay 25 men. So 502 former BCPP officers simply switched uniforms and taught the Mounties how to police British Columbia. The Mounties could now claim to be Canada's national police but the entire affair helped cost the coalition its majority and left a sour taste for many British Columbians.

The issue of who controls the Mounties has long been a sore point between the provinces and the federal government. In 1959, a violent strike by loggers in Newfoundland led the RCMP superintendent in charge of that province to call for help from Ottawa. RCMP Commissioner Leonard Hanson Nicholson assembled 50 Mounties in Moncton and was about to send them to Newfoundland when Prime Minister John Diefenbaker stepped in and blocked the move. Diefenbaker did not want to be seen using the police to crush a labour dispute. Nicholson was furious about the political interference. Failing to persuade the government to change its mind, Nicholson resigned on March 31, 1959, on a point of principle, the first and only RCMP commissioner to leave office in that manner.

Over time, the RCMP continued to become even more hybridized. It assumed responsibility for all federal work, international policing, national crime laboratories, provincial and municipal policing, and just about everything that might loosely be construed as policing. Most Canadians, unaware of much of this history, can't describe what kind of police force the RCMP is. Some call it a national police force, and others think it is a federal police force: two different beasts. Still others believe it is the local provincial police. Few understand the multitude of jurisdictions policed by the RCMP. There is no other police force in the world like the Mounties, with good reason. On any given day, the organization and its members are asked to go in so many directions that in recent times, it has been rendered all but catatonic.

By the mid-sixties, this was all evident to the Mounties themselves. Theoretically, the primary role of the RCMP is to be a federal police agency. It was in that capacity that the RCMP had evolved to become, not a feared and respected investigative apparatus, but rather scarecrows in scarlet tunics sunning in a field of crime. History has shown that Mountie investigators were very good at building files—but not successful cases. The force earned a reputation for being shy about getting involved in controversy and finishing off a case, which will be explored in greater detail later.

RCMP Commissioner George Brinton McClellan began an overhaul of the force in the sixties. No longer would every new cadet have to literally earn his spurs. McClellan decided that in modern Canada, with growing organized crime, commercial fraud, and illegal drugs, learning to ride a horse was not the most important thing a Mountie needed to learn. In a controversial decision decried by RCMP traditionalists he cut equitation from the RCMP curriculum and began to focus on specialized training.

Specialists in commercial crime and other federal offences were trained and given free rein. The result was a number of high-profile successful investigations of malfeasance and fraud in the stock market. There were also controversial probes into such powerful politicians as Joey Smallwood, the founding premier of Newfoundland, and his unusual relationship with fraud artist John C. Doyle.

Throughout the sixties, separatist extremists in Québec, who today would be labelled terrorists and openly subjected to vilification, began to promote their cause through bombings, bank robberies, kidnapping, and murder. It was the role of the Security Service to investigate and neutralize them, although there were serious political concerns about having all that power resting within one organization.

In 1968, a Royal Commission chaired by Maxwell MacKenzie recommended that the Security Service be split off from the RCMP, but his recommendation was rejected by Prime Minister Pierre Trudeau. Trudeau believed that the timing was not right. In October 1970, British diplomat James Cross and Québec Labour Minister Pierre Laporte were kidnapped. Laporte was murdered. Trudeau invoked the War Measures Act and sent the army into Québec and Ottawa to quell the so-called "apprehended insurrection." The threat of continued violence ended and RCMP federal criminal investigators continued forward, seemingly undeterred.

The Québec crisis appeared to be over by the mid-seventies and the newly energized and confident RCMP federal police investigators ended up doing more work than they had originally intended in Québec. The trail of investigations started elsewhere often led the police to prominent Québec politicians, businessmen, and crooks. The most high-profile of these cases were the Dredging Scandal, the Hamilton Harbour Investigation, and the Skyshops Affair. The chain that linked each was a system whereby Québec-based individuals had found ways to defraud the federal treasury. As the Mounties began closing in on the province's elite, including then-Premier Robert Bourassa, a senator, and a leading business family, all hell broke loose. The Québec establishment pushed back to the point where Québec police tried to have RCMP Inspector Rod Stamler arrested for conducting the investigation.

The counterattack against the RCMP continued around allegations made by two former Mounties, Staff Sergeant Donald McCleery and Sergeant Gilles Brunet, the son of a former RCMP assistant commissioner. They alleged the Security Service had acted illegally in dealing with the Québec terrorists in the sixties. Mountie insiders were suspicious of the two because of their spotty history and erratic behaviour—rightly so, as it turned out.

At that time in the mid-seventies, however, Québec politicians at both the provincial and federal level were all too eager to seize on McCleery and Brunet's claims. The two whistleblowers said the force had committed break-ins and unlawful surveillance and had even burned a barn in Québec's eastern townships to prevent a planned meeting between the FLQ (Front de libération du Québec) and members of the American Black Panther movement. Five public inquiries were eventually held across the country touching on the activities of the RCMP. In each of them the lines between the Security Service and the criminal investigators became extremely blurred in the public mind. Just about everyone thought the RCMP were the bad guys when they were not. The most important of those inquiries—the McDonald Commission—made its report in 1981.

The McDonald Commission found that the RCMP as a police force had done nothing wrong and that, while the Security Service may have gone a little overboard, it had done so with the best of intentions. Nevertheless, the commission made a number of recommendations which included separating the Security Service from the RCMP.

Throughout all this controversy there was a further hidden complication. Since 1972, there had been an ongoing hunt for a Soviet spy inside the RCMP. A powerful Canadian bureaucrat had been photographed in a compromising situation. The Soviets had the pictures and were trying to leverage them. Since similar spy scandals in Great Britain had targeted homosexuals, the Canadian government and the RCMP sought out someone they thought was a likely suspect within their own ranks. The RCMP locked onto Leslie James Bennett, one of its intelligence officers. Bennett, a married man with a family, was pursued for more than a decade as a suspected Soviet mole. The force had even gone so far as to subject Bennett to "the fruit machine," which it believed could detect homosexual responses. As a result, Bennett's family was destroyed and he was forced to leave the country for Australia where he continued to be pursued and harassed until the late eighties when the real spy was uncovered after the fall of the Berlin Wall.

Then RCMP intelligence officer Peter Marwitz found something completely stunning in the secret Soviet records. The Soviet mole had been none other than RCMP Sergeant Gilles Brunet. The Soviet documents showed that Brunet had been paid at least $700,000 over the years to disrupt Canadian intelligence-gathering capabilities, a job at which he obviously excelled. It was a most uncomfortable disclosure for the RCMP. Being the son of a former assistant commissioner, Brunet had been above suspicion in spite of his shenanigans instigating the McDonald Commission.

The RCMP brass did everything it could to suppress and diminish the Brunet story. Marwitz's credibility was attacked. Bennett was eventually exonerated and paid a pittance for the damage done to him. But the larger questions still remained. Why did the Russians infiltrate the RCMP? What was their interest in destroying the RCMP Security Service? It was unlikely that Brunet was the only spy operating in Canada. Did he do it all on his own or were there more spies embedded in Canadian federal institutions, determined to keep them weak and ineffective? These were questions that would never be addressed by governments because any investigation would inevitably focus not only on the Russians and Americans, the likely suspects, but also on Québec.

The government adopted the McDonald Commission recommendations and severed the Security Service from the RCMP. It was transformed into a separate agency, the civilian Canadian Security Intelligence Service (CSIS). It was a bastard birth—a spy agency created by the sinister actions of a foreign spy agency.

The creation, shape, and mandate of CSIS were driven by Senator Michael Pitfield. A former "super bureaucrat" in the Trudeau governments, Pitfield went on to become a director of Power Corp. CSIS reported to the Security Intelligence Review Committee (SIRC), a panel comprised of privy councillors who would oversee its operations and performance.

In the context of this story, the Privy Council, its members, and bureaucrats play an important role. The Privy Council is the secretariat of the federal cabinet and the department of the prime minister. It is the bastion of the most powerful politicians and bureaucrats in Canada. The purpose of the Privy Council is to provide non-partisan advice to the prime minister, cabinet ministers, and the leaders of government in the House of Commons and the Senate.

The Prime Minister's Office—the PMO—is political, whereas the Privy Council Office—the PCO which operates the mechanics of government—is deemed to be non-political. Anyone who is going to be anyone in Ottawa must serve in the Privy Council Office. That is where Canadian bureaucrats destined to become leaders of government, as well as diplomats and ambassadors, receive their training. In recent years, the Privy Council Office has been accused on a number of occasions of stepping over the line into politics, operating more like the U.S. executive branch, which is political by design.

The Clerk of the Privy Council is the prime minister's deputy minister, secretary to the cabinet, and head of the civil service. He or she wields formidable influence. One of the Clerk of the Privy Council's key functions is chairing a deputy-minister-level group, the Interdepartmental Committee on Security and Intelligence. This committee discusses strategic policy and resourcing issues, considers sensitive national security matters, reviews proposals destined for Cabinet, and recommends the annual intelligence priorities for the meeting of ministers on security and intelligence.

One important function of the Privy Council is to disclose sensitive information to councillors under the Security of Information Act. In addition, it is required by law that members of the Security Intelligence Review Committee be Privy Councillors. Appointees to the Queen's Privy Council must recite the requisite oath:

> I, [name], do solemnly and sincerely swear (declare) that I shall be a true and faithful servant to Her Majesty Queen Elizabeth the Second, as a member of Her Majesty's Privy Council for Canada. I will in all things to be treated, debated and resolved in Privy Council, faithfully, honestly and truly declare my mind and my opinion. I shall keep secret all matters committed and revealed to me in this capacity, or that shall be secretly treated of in Council. Generally, in all things I shall do as a faithful and true servant ought to do for Her Majesty.

With CSIS reporting to the Security Intelligence Review Committee and its panel of privy councillors, the government guaranteed that anything CSIS touched would be kept secret—possibly forever.

While there was no investigation of or complaints made to the McDonald Commission about the RCMP as a police force, the commission recommended, among other things, that the policing operations also be made more politically accountable. To that end, in 1984 the RCMP commissioner was made a deputy minister, appointed by and serving at the pleasure of the prime minister. The word "accountability" seemed to assuage Canadians, although the government never clearly described what it meant by the term. It was as if a coup d'état had quietly taken place.

From the earliest days of this regime, the new "politically accountable"

RCMP operated like a blind dog on a short leash. After another Québecker—Brian Mulroney—formed a government in 1984, the politicization of the RCMP was effectively sealed.

The Mulroney government became the first Canadian government to have political control of the federal police, with the power to dictate what the force was supposed to do and how much of its energies were to be devoted to its chosen initiatives.

On March 16, 1985, Air India Flight 182, a flight from Vancouver and Toronto to London, England, exploded off the coast of Ireland, killing 329 people. It was Canada's largest mass murder.

That summer Norman Inkster was appointed the RCMP's deputy commissioner of operations. He would become the man ultimately in charge of the Air India investigation. Inkster, a career Mountie, was more experienced in human resources and administration than in police work. He was an odd fit for the job, to say the least. Under his leadership, the politically explosive Air India investigation zigged and zagged its way to nowhere. From the outset, CSIS was well aware of the threat and the perpetrators but, naively and stubbornly, would not share its information with the RCMP, a relationship that will be examined in greater detail later. The Mounties were highly offended by and dismissive of CSIS, whose agents they considered incompetent interlopers on their turf. It was the first major conflict between the RCMP and CSIS. There would be many more.

Thwarted by CSIS and its own investigative failings and shortcomings, the RCMP was able to supply only enough evidence for the Crown to convict one man, Inderjit Singh Reyat. He pleaded guilty in 2003 to manslaughter for manufacturing the bomb and received a five-year sentence. The Mounties's embarrassment would continue. It would take 21 years, until June 2006, for the Canadian government to hold a public inquiry. It was led by retired Supreme Court Justice John Major and finished in early 2008.

That many Mounties thought Norman Inkster was out of his depth as deputy commissioner did not matter to the Mulroney government. Inkster had a champion in Solicitor General James Kelleher. In 1987, Inkster was promoted to the rank of commissioner. His mandate was to operate the RCMP in a more businesslike fashion and to ensure that the force was more accountable. With his appointment, Inkster also became a deputy minister. To that end, one of Inkster's first moves was to move to an office next to Kelleher's in the solicitor general's department. Together, the two men began to reshape the force.

Kelleher soon appointed another of his deputies, Michael Shoemaker, as the first civilian deputy commissioner of the RCMP. It was another appointment unappreciated by insiders who feared the growing political influence on the force—Kelleher, Inkster, and Shoemaker were all directly beholden to Mulroney, which made just about every Mountie queasy.

At headquarters in Ottawa, a relatively low-ranking officer was assigned to be a liaison between underlings of the prime minister and solicitor general. As described in *Above the Law*, Mountie investigators began to find strange things happening. In one case, the police found a document in a government file. When they returned the next day with a search warrant, it was gone. In another case, the police found a copy of a search warrant in the desk drawer of the politician's Montréal office—one day after the warrant had been issued to the police.

In the mid-to-late eighties the Mounties found themselves back in La Belle Province—on treacherous ground. Just about everything the Mounties touched had tentacles leading back to Québec. Nothing good could come of it. The province had effectively held the country hostage for years, whining at the least perceived insult, attempting to extort power and federal money by threatening to separate.

After stories about possible corruption were published in newspapers such as *The Globe and Mail* and the *Montreal Gazette*, and by *the fifth estate*, the CBC TV investigative show, RCMP federal commercial crime investigators became involved in a series of scandals involving members and acquaintances of the Mulroney government. The federal police were once again thrust into an awkward world where the more they chased the suspects the closer they got to the pinnacle of Québec power—Mulroney and his cronies. The Mounties found themselves thwarted at almost every turn by their own force and by the government. The penultimate case was the Airbus investigation which involved suspected payoffs by German businessman Karlheinz Schreiber to Mulroney and some of his key associates as a consideration to persuade Air Canada to purchase Airbus passenger jets (which it did in 1988).

The on-again off-again investigation would result in a $50 million lawsuit against the RCMP, filed by Mulroney in 1995. He claimed that a letter to the Swiss government seeking its assistance in accessing bank records had defamed him—merely by naming him to foreign authorities as a target of police inquiries. Two years later, without warning, Mulroney's successor, Jean Chrétien, authorized a settlement. The government and the RCMP agreed to pay Mulroney $2.1 million for his legal fees and provide him with apologies from each institution. Chrétien said he had had "no choice" but to accept at face value the word of a former prime minister that he had done nothing wrong. Chrétien must have been the only person in Ottawa not to have heard the term "Lyin' Brian"—the nickname Mulroney earned among his own caucus and in the media during his first government. Chrétien later wrote in his memoirs, *My Years as Prime Minister*, that he was "relieved" Mulroney had taken the money.

The message to the Mounties was clear and decisive—don't mess with the country's elite. Mulroney crowed about being "vindicated." He now re-established his political presence after having all but single-handedly destroyed the Progressive Conservative Party by abandoning them to slaughter in the 1993 general election—held five months after he had left office.

In 2003, lawyer and author William Kaplan reported in *The Globe and Mail* that Mulroney had received $300,000 from German–Canadian businessman Karlheinz Schreiber shortly before leaving office. Mulroney said the money was for consulting work on a pasta business. Schreiber denied the existence of such a business proposal. Over the next few years, as he tried to cover up the payments, Mulroney changed the story many times, making it vaguer and vaguer.

Kaplan's story was ignored. Mulroney's political restoration was all but completed when Stephen Harper appointed him to an important post on his transition team in 2006. Mulroney would become one of Harper's closest confidants and most trusted advisers.

As we have already seen, the problems between the powerful of Québec and the RCMP had not ended with Mulroney's formal departure from politics in 1993—far from it. Before he left office, Mulroney made one other move that spoke to his hidden agenda.

Traditionally, the Privy Council has been composed of many current and former cabinet ministers, prime ministers, and some former provincial premiers. Under the guise of a national celebration—Canada's 125th birthday on July 1, 1992—Mulroney unilaterally appointed 18 people as privy councillors, unprecedented in Canadian political history. Among them were former politicians and ordinary citizens like hockey great Maurice Richard and war artist Alex Colville. Four of the appointees raised eyebrows and controversy: former Power Corp. boss Maurice F. Strong, current Power Corp. chairman Paul Desmarais, controversial media baron Conrad Black, and Montréal whiskey mogul Charles Bronfman.

In 1994, seemingly protected by his new Privy Council status, Bronfman paid back the country for the privilege and honour by secretly transferring $2 billion in assets out of the country without any tax consequences courtesy of his benevolent friends Mulroney and Chrétien.

The other major legacy of the Mulroney–Chrétien years that would have a profound effect on the RCMP was the way its budgets were controlled. Virtually every aspect of the RCMP's operations was approved by the Treasury Board. The result was that discretionary spending by the RCMP was reduced to almost zero. Its managers had no flexibility to react to situations and deal with them efficiently without wading through layers of bureaucracy, seeking to gain approval for unforeseen expenditures. The restrictions were so onerous that by 2007, the RCMP had to make 900 separate requests to obtain goods and services worth a total of $250 million. When Parliament approved money for the RCMP, the Treasury Board also had the power to order that the new money be fenced in for the sole purpose of a chosen project, such as tobacco enforcement or youth programs. By 2007, there would be 35 such government-imposed fences within the RCMP. In effect, the government was dictating what the police should be doing. This politicization did not go unnoticed.

In November 1999, retired Assistant Commissioner Robert H.D. Head published a paper called "The Politicization of the RCMP." He focused on the RCMP commissioner's dual role. "Too often, the thinking of the Commissioner (and the Force) can be diverted from law enforcement to social policy issues," Head wrote. "As a government bureaucrat it is too easy to lose sight of law enforcement and align one's thinking to support political initiatives. For example, the Commissioner's 1998 Directional Statement indicated a need 'for aligning our priorities with those of government.'"

Head continued:

Due to the Commissioner's position as a Deputy Minister in government, there have been instances of government interference into policing decisions. In the past, the RCMP were even providing the Ministry with details of crimes under investigation—some involving MP's and Senators. . . . It may be interesting to know that when Warrants to Search are issued in cases of suspected fraud/misappropriation of public funds, an entirely different set of rules apply to the offices of Parliamentarians. The Commissioner becomes involved with the Speaker of the House, before a warrant can be executed. This tells me that investigations alleging fraud against elected politicians are more liable to be sidetracked than those allegations against ordinary citizens!

The entire system of operating the Force as a business is contrary to ideals of law enforcement. In fact, the correspondence emanating from RCMP management makes little mention of law enforcement and considerable reference to programs such as crime prevention and client relationships. While that is all well and good, the average Canadian still holds the opinion that the police are in place to enforce the law—to catch crooks! The enforcement aspect seems to take a back seat.

There are complaints that bilingualism has resulted in most of the senior management positions being filled with officers who have little practical experience "on the street." Many members feel that in order to be a senior manager in the Force's Ottawa headquarters, preference is given to Québeckers who possess French as their first official language. Additionally, the bilingual bonus paid to members in the so-called "bilingual positions" is causing friction between members—members who are doing the same work and who rarely use the second language....

By being a Deputy Minister in government, the RCMP Commissioner is frequently seen as being in a conflict position. On one hand he/she has an obligation to Canadians to ensure that the law is enforced "without fear, favour or affection" but this is not possible if government (in which he/she holds a position of executive status) imposes restraint that causes investigations to be abandoned or ignored. In my opinion, the RCMP Commissioner should not be in a Ministerial organization but rather, that this position report to Parliament in the same manner as the Auditor General of Canada. It follows that candidates for this position ought to be publicly examined by a Parliamentary Committee before the appointment is ratified.

Because of the Deputy Minister position in government, the RCMP Commissioner has become much too political. He/she should not be publicly lobbying in support of any particular legislation, such as Bill C-68. Rather, the RCMP administration should simply appear before any Parliamentary Committee and provide the Committee with details of the cost and ramification of any particular legislation that is being proposed. No pro or con position should be taken by a police agency; they are in business to enforce the laws of Parliament.

Robert Head's assessment and recommendations, like all those before and after him, about reconstructing, rebuilding, and strengthening the federal police, would be shelved by Mulroney and Chrétien during, collectively, their two decades in power. As we have seen, and will see in the following pages, each man had the power, will, and influence to protect himself, his friends, and acquaintances from the prying eyes of the police, and neither was afraid to use that power.

All this could prove to be a hidden advantage later on for Harper, however. The more trouble Québec made for the Mounties, the better for Alberta.

☩ ☩ ☩

After seven balanced budgets, Paul Martin bequeathed to his successor Harper an operating surplus and a subtly reshaped bureaucracy through which Harper's government could better control spending.

The electorate expected Harper as prime minister to rise above mere provincialism but he was not the kind of person who would quickly forget who brought him to the big dance—the people of Alberta. Just as most Québec politicians were Québeckers first and Canadians second, Harper would always be an Albertan first.

From his earliest days in the Reform Party and, later, as leader of its offspring, the Canadian Alliance, Harper has been determined to have Alberta treated not, as it were, like a juvenile by Ottawa, but as a mature, adult province like Ontario and Québec. It had earned that right. To that end, in January 2001, while on a hiatus from formal politics and serving as president of the ultra-conservative National Citizens Coalition, Harper co-signed what has come to be known as the Alberta Firewall Letter. The open letter to then-Alberta Premier Ralph Klein was published in the *National Post*. It urged Klein to protect and expand the sovereignty of Alberta by standing up to Ottawa. Joining with Harper were the previously mentioned Tom Flanagan, political science professors Ted Morton and Rainer Knopff, Andrew Crooks of the Canadian Taxpayers Foundation, and Ken Boessenkool, once a policy adviser to former Alberta Treasurer Stockwell Day.

The letter, a manifesto for change, set out "the Alberta agenda." It called for reforms in the Canada Pension Plan, income tax collection, and health care. It promoted an elected Senate. High on its list of priorities was the state of policing in Alberta: "Start preparing to let the contract with the RCMP run out in 2012 and create an Alberta provincial police force. Alberta is a major province. Like the other major provinces of Ontario and Québec, we should have our own provincial police force. We have no doubt Alberta can run a more efficient and effective police force than Ottawa can—one that will not be misused as a laboratory for experiments in social engineering."

Now that he was prime minister, the timing was right for Harper to make his long-desired move—a first step in redefining both Alberta and the RCMP. The RCMP's provincial contract with Alberta was set to expire in 2012, which would give Harper almost five years to try to maneuver the country and his home province into accepting responsibility for its own policing—leading to the likely reconstitution of the Alberta Provincial Police.

Keith Brownsey, a professor at Calgary's Mount Royal College, told D'Arcy Henton of the *Calgary Sun* in 2006 that he believed Harper was determined to implement the ideas expressed in the firewall letter. "I don't think his views have changed on that one bit. If Stephen Harper is anything, he's an ideologue. He's held these views for most of his adult life. He won't change now."

As a graduate student at the University of Calgary, according to author William Johnson in his book *Stephen Harper and the Future of Canada*, Harper was intrigued by Adam Smith's theory of the "invisible hand" that guides the marketplace. From the moment he took power in February 2006, Harper, oblivious to most Canadians, had begun to use his own invisible hand to shape events. His ultimate goal was to release the federal government's grip on Alberta. Naturally, the RCMP, the dominant symbol of federal power, with its highest profile in the provinces outside Ontario and Québec, appeared to be high on his to-do list. Here and there, seemingly unconnected things were happening—but they weren't random at all.

To implement his ideas about policing, Harper began lining up his ducks one by one. James Kelleher and Norman Inkster—two of the RCMP's old nemeses—would have important roles to play. To make it all work, Harper and his Albertan elves still required some luck. If they could not get lucky, they would have to make their own luck.

It would not be an easy road. Mulroney and Chrétien had left a number of ticking time bombs. Harper would have to defuse them if he didn't want them to blow up in his face. Being a keen student of Canadian politics, Harper also knew that his would not be the only invisible hand at work.

[5]

MAHER ARAR TAKES THE STAGE

By the late summer of 2006, the RCMP was becoming overwhelmed by controversies from coast to coast, from lingering political debacles like Airbus and the sponsorship scandal to botched undercover operations and the shooting deaths of suspects in custody, among many other things. Almost every day, it seemed, some new horror would be revealed. Politicians, editorialists, and columnists were calling for one public inquiry after another into RCMP activities across the country. The most visceral ongoing case, however, was the case of Maher Arar, the Syrian-born Canadian communications engineer from Ottawa, who maintained the citizenship of both his native country and his adopted one. Arar is the best known of several Canadian Muslims who found themselves the victims of the U.S. government's secret rendition policy.

Rendition, the capturing of wanted felons in another state or country, had long been a policy of the United States government. Escaped slaves were subject to rendition and captured in faraway places to be returned to their owners. Although the concept of rendition was outlawed in the 1880s, it lived on. For instance, the U.S. Postal Inspection Service chased outlaws Butch Cassidy and Harry Alonzo Longabaugh (aka the Sundance Kid) all the way to Argentina and Bolivia where they were killed in a shootout in November 1908.

In another example, in 1989 the United States invaded Panama and captured its president, Manuel Noriega. Noriega was shipped to the United States, where he was tried and convicted of cocaine trafficking, racketeering, and money laundering. In 1993, the United States began to use a revised concept of rendition, working with unlikely allies like Albania, among others, to secretly kidnap Islamic terrorists who had been convicted of crimes in absentia and send them to foreign countries for imprisonment.

Michael Scheuer, a former senior analyst for the U.S. Central Intelligence Agency (CIA) and one of the architects of a 1995 agreement with Egypt to accept such prisoners, later described the rationale for rendition in an interview with the *New Yorker* magazine in February 2005: "It was begun in desperation. . . . We were turning into voyeurs. We knew where these people were, but we couldn't capture them because we had nowhere to take them," due to legal and diplomatic complications. A willing third-party country was needed, and Egypt was willing to participate, particularly because Islamic jihad was also the prime political enemy of the Egyptian government.

The rendition policy was designed to pinpoint legitimate targets and extract them from society. In February 2000, CIA Director George Tenet testified before Congress that: "Since July 1998, working with foreign governments worldwide, we have helped to render more than two dozen terrorists to justice. More than half were associates of Osama bin Laden's Al-Qaeda organization."

On September 14, 2001, President George Bush proclaimed a Declaration of National Emergency by Reason of Certain Terrorist Attacks, which gave him extraordinary powers to deal with the terrorist crisis.

Two days later, Vice President Dick Cheney went on *Meet the Press* and made this momentous statement: "This is a different kind of war. You're not going to see our victories. Our victories are going to occur in dark alleys as our intelligence forces and law enforcement forces go after this threat."

What and where was the dark side?

On September 22, 2001, an important date in the context of this story, the attitude of the U.S. government toward the practice of rendition changed. President George W. Bush and Vice President Dick Cheney had gotten over the shock of the September 11th attacks and along with the U.S. military and intelligence communities had begun to focus on how to meet the threat from Islamic fundamentalists. The wars to be launched in Afghanistan and Iraq were still only a gleam in their eye, but they approved a daring scheme that many would later call ill-conceived and even venal.

As the *New York Times* reported at the time, the government was going to become more aggressive, "forward-leaning. . . . We want to take risks." The government wanted to get ahead of its enemies, find out what they knew or were planning to do, and cut off any future attack before it could be mounted. The centrepiece of this bold plan was to expand the definition of rendition into what would unofficially become known as "extraordinary rendition." This involved a coordinated program run with the help of like-minded countries in capturing suspected terrorists almost anywhere in the world and transporting them, often by private airplane, to secret prisons in Eastern Europe, the Middle East, or the British base on the Indian Ocean island of Diego Garcia. The most notorious rendition site was at the U.S. naval base at Guantanamo Bay, Cuba, a facility which began to take prisoners in January 2002.

One year later, on September 26, 2002, Maher Arar was stopped by U.S. authorities at New York's John F. Kennedy International Airport, held in detention for 13 days, then sent to Syria where, it was soon being reported, he was tortured and imprisoned for a year. It was easily the most public case of "extraordinary rendition," to have taken place in North America.

Based on what they had heard in the news, the opinion of many Canadians and others regarding the Arar case was, and continues to be, one of astonishment. It appeared that the Royal Canadian Mounted Police had defied the laws of Canada and leaked erroneous information about Arar to the Americans and others, which had been used to justify his arrest, incarceration, and torture.

A majority of Canadians were incensed by what they believed was the callous behaviour of the RCMP and the damage done to the country's reputation, and to Arar and his family. As clear-cut as the story might have appeared, that Arar was undeniably an innocent victim of sloppy and, possibly venal Canadian police work, the story is somewhat murkier and more curious than what was revealed to the public.

Peter Worthington, a columnist for the right-wing *Toronto Sun*, summed up some of that confusion well in September 2006, when he wrote:

> What I don't get—and have never gotten from the start of this weird miscarriage of justice and accountability—is why the Syrians would imprison and torture Arar if the Americans (and RCMP) thought he was an Al-Qaeda or any other sort of terrorist?
>
> Since when have the Syrians—big supporters of Hezbollah and a sanctuary for anti-American fighters from Iraq—been torturing people suspected of seeking to undermine Americans?
>
> Heck, if he were what the RCMP thought he was, you'd think the Syrians would roll out the red carpet for him and honour him with a state dinner or something, not jail and torture him for a year.

Something seems out of kilter in this case.

Maybe there's a reasonable answer why Syrian intelligence elements would co-operate and torture someone like Arar on behalf of the Americans, or because the Americans didn't like or want him around?

Makes no sense.

Also, it makes little sense in Canada that there now seems a lynch-mob attitude towards the RCMP.

There are short versions of stories and long ones and sometimes neither gives a clear picture of what really took place. Telling a story chronologically is sometimes effective but the Arar story has so many overlapping threads, each with twists of its own, that a straightforward recounting would be mucky and almost impossible to read. Sometimes the best way to tell a story is to turn it over and examine it from different angles to find the key. Therefore, in an effort to better reveal its essence and implications, I will attempt to tell it from a number of points of view, breaking the story into five parts: 1) an overview of Islamic terrorism with the links that lead to Arar, essentially the known public story; 2) the genesis of the RCMP's involvement from the investigators' perspective, the problems, and the ensuing controversies; 3) the activities of the CIA and FBI in Canada; 4) the hidden heart of the matter, the key, as it were, which shows the reasons why the government had to invoke national security confidentiality in the matter, and 5) the machinations employed to cover up the real story and the creation of a necessary scapegoat.

In approaching the story this way, please bear with me through the sometimes non-chronological retelling and occasional repetition, but I can see no better way to cut through the thick fog of deception to best reveal how in this case the public was manipulated by governments in pursuit of the so-called greater good.

✠ ✠ ✠

First and foremost, this story is about the fundamentalist Sunni Islamic vision of a restored "world caliphate." This does not mean that these Muslims believe the entire world should be Muslim, because they would never accept infidels, that is, anyone who is not Muslim, into their mosques and allow them to pray to Allah. Rather, these extremists have what has been described as a fascist vision of the world: in their perfect world, everyone would have to submit to Islam and its laws. In their jihad, there are active soldiers fighting the infidels and hidden ones, sleepers, burrowed into an enemy society awaiting the call to action.

This radical view of Islam took root in 1928 with the creation of the Muslim Brotherhood by 22-year-old elementary school teacher Hasan al-Banna. At the time, Syria, which had once dominated the region, had been reduced to virtual colonial status, controlled by a series of other countries, including Jordan, Turkey, England, and France, for much of the previous 200 years. The Muslim Brotherhood included not only students of the Quran, but also students of the controversial nineteenth-century theory of eugenics, which advocated societies built on selective breeding and the creation of a perfect race.

Eugenic theory was much admired across the political spectrum around the world, even in western countries like the United Kingdom, the United States, and Canada. In 1893, for example, Professors B.G. Jefferis and J.L. Nichols published *Safe Counsel*, a 500-page guide with illustrations for healthier living based on the "science of eugenics." By 1928, their book was in its 39th edition, and was reprinted again as recently as 2005. In the West, eugenics received significant support among a minority but never gained a political foothold.

However, the theory of eugenics was seriously adopted by fascists in Germany, Italy, and Japan, among other countries, all intent on building a master race of their own. In Germany, for example, eugenics was fused with mystical, religious-like thinking which helped fuel the Holocaust. Although the fascists were eventually defeated in the Second World War, lost in the mists of time was the fact that Middle Eastern countries were also fascist strongholds during the war. For a time, Syria was ruled by the fascist Vichy government of France.

With the creation of the state of Israel in 1948, the Muslim Brotherhood immediately became focused on its destruction. During this period, Sayyid Qutb, an Egyptian-born intellectual, was studying in the United States. Qutb travelled throughout the U.S. from 1948 to 1951, and later wrote about how disgusted he was with its people, calling the men and women animal-like for mixing together, even in church, and dancing to black-inspired jazz music.

Qutb returned to Egypt where he became a member of the Guidance Council and head of the propaganda section for the Muslim Brotherhood. In 1953, he became editor-in-chief of the Brotherhood's newspaper, *al'Ikhwan al-Muslimin.* The next year, after an attempt on the life of Egyptian President Gamal Abdel Nasser by a member of the Muslim Brotherhood, Qutb was arrested and imprisoned for 10 years.

He wrote a number of books about Islam that would become the foundation of modern Islamic radicalism. Among the many ideas he propounded, a key one was that secular governments were illegitimate, *Jahiliyya*, or pagan, because they were manmade, and that the only legitimate government was one that served God—divine governance or *Hakimiyya*. To restore true Islam, Qutb called for martyrs willing to fight revolutionary warfare against infidels everywhere. In a perfect world, Qutb argued, every aspect of non-Muslim society would be eliminated, and there would eventually be a world caliphate. In the world caliphate, Muslims would control everything—government, business, and society—which meant that every non-Muslim would be forced to submit, like fundamentalist Muslim women, to the will of Muslim men. Qutb wrote that non-Muslims could look forward "to lives of poverty, difficulty, frustration, torment and sacrifice."

After his release from prison, Qutb was implicated in another plot to assassinate Nasser, and arrested, tried, and executed in August 1966, but his writings lived on. His philosophy became known as Qutbism.

When the Soviet Union invaded Afghanistan in 1979, the call went out around the world for all Muslims to come to Afghanistan and fight a holy war against the Soviet infidels. The Mujahedeen, as they were called, were supported by the United States with financing, technical help, and armaments. At the end of the bloody war in 1988, Osama bin Laden, Egyptian jihad leader Ayman al-Zawahiri, and others rose out of the Muslim Brotherhood to form Al-Qaeda. Bin Laden called himself a disciple of Qutb, and stated that he would use Al-Qaeda to implement Qutbism's vision and conquer infidels anywhere in the world. The primary targets were Israel and the United States.

Throughout the Soviet–Afghanistan war, significant amounts of money, as much as $1 million a week, were being raised in the United States and Canada by the Islamic sect Ismailiya. The money was being shipped weekly by armoured truck from Vancouver to Toronto and then on to Switzerland. In 1989, one such shipment, containing $1,080,000 in U.S. bills, was seized by customs officers at the U.S.–Canadian border in British Columbia. It was never claimed. In Canada, fundraising for the Islamic jihadists was being conducted all over the country and put to use by those back home.

In 1993, Al-Qaeda made its first strike in North America by setting off a massive truck bomb in the parking garage of the World Trade Center in

New York, but failed to knock down the twin towers, as planned. One of the plotters was Pakistani-born Ramzi Youzef, a well-educated communications engineer. Among other crimes, Youzef went on the next year to bomb Philippine Airlines Flight 434 flying from Manila to Cebu. The explosion killed a Japanese businessman, but the bomb was not powerful enough to bring down the plane. In January 1995, police in the Philippines started a fire in Youzef's apartment to give themselves a reason to enter it. Inside they found plans for what came to be known as the Operation Bojinka plot.

The centrepiece of Bojinka was the planned assassination of Pope John Paul during a visit to the Philippines, which was to take place 10 days later, on January 15, 1995. While police attention was focused on the visit, bombs hidden in toys were to be placed on 11 U.S.-operated commercial airplanes flying out of Bangkok to the United States on January 21 and 22, 1995. A third phase was to crash a plane into CIA headquarters at Fairfax, Virginia. The plot was foiled and Youzef was eventually captured in Pakistan after a confidant took a $2 million payoff from the CIA and turned him in.

These were clearly dangerous times. Although no terrorist attack had ever been made on Canada, international terrorists had long ago adopted Canada as a base of operations. Canada was conveniently located right next door to their Great Enemy, the United States. Unlike Mexico, which is also next door to the United States, Canada has a solid banking system, strict privacy laws, and the rule of law. Canada was a near-perfect soil in which to grow Muslim fanatics' hatred and dreams of world submission to their faith. In his 2002 book *Inside Al-Qaeda: Global Network of Terror*, author Rohan Gunaratna, a Sri Lankan-born expert on terrorism, wrote that terrorist groups base themselves in Canada so that they can develop "support networks" to generate propaganda, raise funds, recruit new members and procure materials for struggles elsewhere.

CSIS offered a similar assessment in one of its own reports to Parliament in 2002: "With the possible exception of the United States, there are more international terrorist organizations active in Canada than anywhere in the world." The common meeting places for Islamic terrorists were radical mosques, and the preferred way of raising money for their overseas efforts was through crime and phony Islamic charities.

Both the U.S. and Canadian governments were well aware that the battleground wasn't limited to the Third World. Sunni fundamentalist leaders spouting Qutbism were not shy about proclaiming their ultimate world caliphate vision. Their war campaign was based, not so much on overt acts of terrorism, but on subverting the political and economic system to meet their ultimate ends by promoting acceptance for their ideas, such as the use of Sharia law and banking systems in western society and public funding for Islamic schools. Despite threats of attacks with suitcase-sized nuclear weapons and chemical warfare in North America, many experts believe such a scenario is unlikely because it would destroy the land the terrorists want. They were playing the long game, infiltrating society, and gradually changing perceptions and rules in an attempt to win influence and power.

The Canadian connection to modern Islamic-based terrorism began with Algerian Ahmed Ressam, who had come to Canada in 1994. The PBS show *Frontline* detailed Ressam's so-called Millennium plot in an October 2001 broadcast "Trail of a Terrorist," produced by award-winning Canadian documentary filmmaker Terence McKenna. "Using a doctored French passport with his picture crudely glued in, the twenty-seven-year-old Ressam flew from France to Montréal. At the airport he was stopped by immigration officials who suspected that his passport was false. Ressam requested political asylum, claiming in a sworn statement that he had been tortured in Algeria and that he was falsely accused of arms trading and other terrorist activities. Apparently without checking with Algeria, France, or Interpol, Canadian immigration agents accepted his story and released him pending a hearing on his refugee status. Canada's Immigration Minister Elinor Caplan later said it was not a serious offence to present a false passport to gain entry to Canada, noting that many legitimate refugees resort to doing so."

In Montréal, Ressam made a living as a thief stealing from tourists but all the while he maintained his ties back home to the GIA, or Armed Islamic Group, a violent terrorist organization based in Algeria. The first major international incident involving the GIA was the hijacking of an Air France jet in Marseilles in 1994. A group of hijackers planned to crash the fully-loaded plane into the Eiffel Tower. From 1996, Ressam and other suspected terrorists linked to the radical Assuna Annabawiyah mosque in Montréal were being watched by CSIS. CSIS agents watched Ressam commit his thefts and robberies but did not report him to police because it was outside their mandate. Their sole role was to gather information concerning national security. In 1998, CSIS lost track of Ressam. Only after he was arrested did CSIS learn that he had gone to Afghanistan where he trained at a terrorist camp run by Osama bin Laden.

By April 1999, Ressam was being pursued by French authorities for his involvement with the GIA. *Frontline* later reported: "French investigating magistrate Judge Jean-Louis Bruguière sent a formal letter to Canadian justice authorities asking for search warrants to be executed in Montréal in his investigation of Algerian terrorists, including Ahmed Ressam, who was specifically named. It took Canada six months to process the request."

By the time the Canadians got around to thinking about rounding up Ressam he was already headed west. On December 14, 1999, travelling under an assumed identity, Ressam was arrested at the U.S. border at Port Angeles, Washington. He had arrived by car ferry from Victoria, B.C. An alert officer pulled Ressam aside. In a search of the vehicle he was driving, two passports in different names were found, along with 50 kilograms of explosives in a wheel well in the trunk of the car. Ressam was on his way to California where he planned to set off a bomb at Los Angeles International Airport on December 31, 1999, earning him the sobriquet of the Millennium Bomber.

In its extensive series in 2002, "The Terrorist Within," the *Seattle Times* reported what was going on in Montréal and what CSIS was doing or, as the case may be, not doing:

> While the physical setting of the Assuna mosque was unimpressive, it was a community magnet. On Fridays, it attracted about 1,500 worshippers, most of them Algerians. Even between prayers and services, the mosque was busy. Children played in its well-worn hallways. Young men congregated in its bookstore, which sold tapes imploring them to join the global jihad. In one such tape, Sheik Abu Abdul Aziz—a leader of jihad in Bosnia and Kashmir—gives his recruitment message: "Come to Afghanistan," he says in heavily accented, broken English. "Only pay the fare for tickets. I am not asking you to get rid of your vacation or retire from your job or get rid of your business. I suggest that you come with vacation for training, and next year, second vacation, you come for jihad. If you are real believers, Allah is expecting you to do an extra job."
>
> One thing Ressam noticed about Hannachi, the recruiter, and Fateh Kamel, another friend who had fought jihad, was their status among Montréal's Arabic extremists. In those circles, they were men of respect, addressed as "important brothers."
>
> Such status appealed to Ressam and his friends. Soon, in smoke-filled sessions at their apartment at 6301 Place de la Malicorne, they were planning their own jihad excursions.

What they didn't know was that Canadian intelligence agents were listening to their every word.

A few months earlier, the Canadian Security Intelligence Service (CSIS) had heard from Jean-Louis Bruguière, France's top terrorism sleuth, that he believed terrorists had formed a "cell" in Montréal. In particular, Bruguière told CSIS, watch for a man named Fateh Kamel.

At first, CSIS ignored the tip from Bruguière, who was seen by some in intelligence circles as an alarmist. But after Italian agents issued a similar warning, the Canadians began monitoring the Malicorne apartment and snapping photographs of Ressam, Kamel, and others.

CSIS agents quickly learned of Ressam's frauds and thefts. They also knew Ressam and others were wanted on immigration warrants. But they could barely bring themselves to call Ressam and the Malicorne denizens a "cell." That sort of hyperbole was for Bruguière, who referred to the address as the "appartement de conspiracie."

The Canadians instead gave the men at the apartment a derisive nickname, the "BOG"—short for "Bunch of Guys." To CSIS, they seemed more pathetic than dangerous—unemployed, no girlfriends, living on welfare and thievery, crammed into a flat reeking of cigarette smoke.

When they were overheard recruiting, plotting and spewing anti-Western vitriol, the agents found it nearly comical. An official would later refer to the sessions as "terrorist Tupperware parties."

Back at Canadian intelligence headquarters, CSIS Deputy Director for Operations Jim Corcoran would read summaries of the intercepted conversations.

"Some of these guys were killers," Corcoran said. The others "sat at their feet, enthralled. There were bragging rights. There was a certain cachet to it all."

Eventually, CSIS built a 400-page file on the men who came and went from the apartment. Some were identified as worth continuing to watch. The thief Ressam, though, was seen as the least likely to pose a serious threat.

The intelligence agency did little with the dossier, not even sharing it with Montréal police or immigration officials. Much like the CIA in the United States, CSIS was restricted to gathering foreign intelligence and protecting security. Its mission did not include chasing down ragtag thieves and immigration violators.

So the "bunch of guys" went undisturbed, even as they continued to plot their part of the holy war against the West.

CSIS may have been asleep at the switch but the CIA had not been. The CIA had been well briefed on the problem and high on its list was the Khadr family of Ottawa—the so-called "first family" of Islamic terrorism in Canada.

Ahmed Sa'id al-Khadr, the family's patriarch, had moved from Egypt to Canada in 1975. He was married to a Palestinian woman, Maha Elsamnah Khadr, and they lived in Toronto. He had studied computer engineering at the University of Ottawa and was involved in telecommunications research. During the Russian invasion of Afghanistan in the 1980s, Khadr, now a Canadian citizen, answered the Muslim call to fight a jihad against the Soviets. In Peshawar, Pakistan, he volunteered at an Ottawa-based registered charity, Human Concern International. The charity, established in 1981 with a goal to "alleviate human suffering," had been the beneficiary of $325,000 in Canadian government grants in the late eighties and nineties.

In the early 1990s, according to Terence McKenna who produced "Son of Al-Qaeda" for both the CBC's *the fifth estate* and PBS's *Frontline*, the Khadr family became extremely close to Osama bin Laden. In a family chronology published online by *Frontline*, much of which is included verbatim in the following paragraphs, McKenna showed just how close they were.

While in Afghanistan and Pakistan, Khadr met and became friends with Osama bin Laden, at which time Khadr was believed to have become one of the founders and leaders of Al-Qaeda.

Khadr's oldest sons, Abdullah and Abdurahman, attended the Al-Qaeda training camp at Khalden, Afghanistan, where both received weapons training. Abdurahman was repeatedly punished and expelled from the camps for rebellious behaviour.

In 1993, Khadr moved the rest of his family—his wife and their four other children—to Afghanistan.

Two years later, Pakistani authorities arrested Khadr, alleging he had financed the November 19, 1995, bombing attack on the Egyptian embassy, which had resulted in the deaths of 18 people. It was believed that Khadr had diverted funds directed to Human Concern International—without the charity's knowledge—to terrorist activities. Khadr went on a hunger strike, proclaimed his innocence, and quickly generated sympathy in Canada, although the charity immediately cut its ties to him.

Two months after the bombing, in January 1996, Khadr was set free after Prime Minister Chrétien, during a state trade visit to Pakistan, lobbied Prime Minister Benazir Bhutto about the case. Bhutto said there was no evidence linking Khadr to the Egyptian embassy attack.

Khadr returned to Canada where he and his wife soon set up a new Islamic charity, Health and Education Project International. However, when the Taliban took control of Afghanistan later that year, the Khadr family left Canada and moved to a large compound of houses near Jalalabad, Afghanistan. This city was home to Osama bin Laden and his family as well. Khadr was known to have used a number of aliases during this period, including Al-Kanadi, Arabic for "The Canadian."

On February 23, 1998, Osama bin Laden used a video broadcast to issue a fatwa in which he called for war against the West and Israel. Khadr was there by his side. Over the next three years, the world would be rocked by several Al-Qaeda attacks. At least 220 people were killed and more than 5,000 injured in simultaneous attacks on the U.S. embassies in Kenya and Tanzania on August 7, 1998.

According to McKenna's research, bin Laden attended the 2000 wedding of the Khadrs' daughter, Zaynab, and the next year the Khadrs attended the wedding of bin Laden's son, Muhammad.

Prior to the Al-Qaeda attacks on the battleship USS *Cole* in 2000 and the World Trade Center on September 11, 2001, the Khadr family were well-known in the intelligence community as Islamic terrorists. In October 2001, Ahmed Sa'id Khadr was one of nine men on a U.S. terror watch list, his photograph was distributed to U.S. troops in Afghanistan, and he was one of 39 people whose assets were frozen by the U.S. Treasury department.

Two months after the 2001 attacks on the United States, Abdurahman Khadr became separated from his family in Kabul, Afghanistan. He was eventually captured and handed over to U.S. authorities, one from the FBI and the other from the CIA. Abdurahman would later describe publicly how he helped the Americans by pointing out, over the next several months, Al-Qaeda hideouts and operation centres around Kabul. He talked about how he had lived for nine months in a CIA safe house and was paid a $5,000 bonus and $3,000 a month for his assistance. He even volunteered to go to Guantanamo Bay, where he served as a CIA informant. He didn't find out much and later became a CIA operative, first in Bosnia and later elsewhere.

The Khadr family credentials as committed terrorists were cemented on July 27, 2002, when 15-year-old Omar Khadr was captured in Khost,

Afghanistan by U.S. special forces. The U.S. first alleged that Omar was the sole survivor of a massive air attack on an Al-Qaeda compound. Although no one actually saw him, the U.S. military said Omar threw a grenade over a wall which killed a U.S. medic leading a commando squad into the ruins. In early 2008, the U.S. released information that indicated another man had been found with Omar, but that Omar had, nonetheless, been the grenade thrower. Omar was eventually shipped to Guantanamo Bay, where his protracted incarceration as a child soldier continues to be debated by Canadian politicians and civil rights lobby groups. His trial was scheduled to begin in October 2008.

On October 2, 2003, in the Pakistani province of Waziristan, family patriarch Ahmed Sa'id Khadr was killed after Pakistani forces laid siege to a suspected Al-Qaeda safe house. Wounded in the battle was Khadr's youngest son, 14-year-old Abdul Karim, who was paralyzed. He and his mother later returned to Canada seeking medical treatment.

So, knowing all this, let's go back to the time just before September 11, 2001. Intelligence agencies around the world and the police knew much about militant activities in Canada, the Khadrs, and their relationship to bin Laden. Among the lessons quickly learned was that terrorists and radical mosques went hand in glove. When they returned to Canada, the Khadrs settled in Ottawa, but preferred to pray a five-hour drive away, at the militant Sunni Salaheddin Islamic Centre, in the Toronto suburb of Scarborough. The imam there was the radical Egyptian-born Aly Hindy. His vehement anti-American rhetoric had not gone unnoticed. The elder Khadr was described by some who knew him as also being absolutely vitriolic in his hatred of the West. Khadr and his wife were proven to be accomplished liars, proclaiming their innocence and good intentions in the face of their obvious links to terrorism. But that came as no surprise to some of the more knowledgeable investigators schooled in Islamic thinking, particularly the concept of al-taqiyah or taqya, two of the many ways it is spelled.

Taqya is usually seen as a concept adopted by Shi'ite Muslims, who constitute a minority of Muslims, and are often governed by Sunni Muslims, their arch-enemies. Taqya is a principle endorsed in the Quran that encourages a Muslim to dissimulate or deceive to protect their faith, property, or life. It is a subject taught in fundamentalist schools and universities. Due to the Shi'ite reliance on taqya, many Sunnis do not trust Shi'ites. At the same time, the traditional Sunni belief is that taqya is a great sin because resorting to lies shows one's lack of faith in Allah. Sunnis believe that they must have faith in God at all times to protect them, which obviates the need for deception.

Nevertheless, Sunni intellectuals and religious leaders have also endorsed the use of taqya for Sunnis. In his book, *al-Durr al-Manthoor Fi al-Tafsir al-Ma'athoor*, author Jalal al-Din al-Suyuti quoted Ibn Abbas, one of the most renowned and trusted narrators of Sunni traditions. Ibn Abbas says: "al-taqiyya is the uttering of the tongue, while the heart is comfortable with faith." Sunni writer Abdul Hamid Siddiqi in *Sahih Muslim* elaborated on the many justifications a Sunni can use to invoke taqya, other than to hide one's real belief for the sake of safety. Taqya is obligatory for a Muslim, for example, to save a life, "when there is no possible benefit from the person's death." At other times, taqya could be used to "strengthen the truth." A Muslim cannot use taqya to spread falsehoods that might be damaging to other Muslims or the faith itself by bringing about "oppression." Finally, taqya is acceptable when a Muslim is in danger of being killed, jailed, or tortured.

Finally, there is this commentary by Sunni Najmuddin Tufi Hanbali, who wrote: "Know that the long arguments for and against taqiyah are useless. . . . but there is no doubt in its validity and legality. Of course, common people do not like its name (taqiyah) because it has been identified with the Shi'as. Otherwise, the whole world uses it naturally, though some call it 'tolerance,' others name it as 'diplomacy,' and some call it 'common sense.' And it is proved by proofs of Shari'ah (Islam)."

The investigation of the Khadrs led CSIS to focus on Abdullah Almalki, a Syrian-born electrical engineer from Ottawa. He had immigrated to Canada as a 16-year-old in 1987. He completed his high school education in Ottawa and became a Canadian citizen in 1991, but never gave up his Syrian citizenship. Of his connection to Khadr, this is what Almalki wrote in his own online biography:

> Abdullah sponsored an Afghani orphan through Human Concern International in the early 1990s and was anxious to learn more about the refugees in Pakistan. He took a break from school and traveled to Peshawar, Pakistan in the fall of 1992 for three months. From there he traveled to Islamabad and to refugee camps and to "Hope Village," a village built by HCI for Afghani orphans. Seeing the human impact of the war in Afghanistan was a life-changing

experience for Abdullah, and he committed to finding a way to apply his skills to improving these peoples' lives.

Abdullah returned to Canada in the late summer to marry Khuziamah, who he had met at Carleton University. The two married in October 1993, and travelled to Pakistan that fall. Abdullah continued working on the reconstruction project. At the time, Ahmad Said Khadr was the Regional Director for HCI. Abdullah did not agree with how Khadr was managing the organization, and he and his wife returned home to Canada in April 1994, earlier than they had planned. Their first of five children were born that July.

Back in Canada, Almalki and his wife started an electronic components export business, hoping to become a supplier to Micro Electronics International, Pakistan's largest privately-owned military and government manufacturer and supplier. Their company, Dawn Services, did well and the company soon branched out, developing a more diverse clientele. Almalki says he travelled extensively for his work, to the United States, Asia, the Middle East, and Europe. He finished his engineering degree at Carleton University in 1995 and then expanded the business to importing cellphone accessories. He was also a conservative, pious, religious man, who was considered an elder in his community, a person from whom others sought advice and direction.

Almalki was first questioned by CSIS in the early summer of 1998 by CSIS agent Theresa Sullivan. Almalki told Sullivan he had been a project director for Human Concern International. He also talked about knowing Ahmed Sa'id Khadr, and told Sullivan that he didn't like Khadr, and had not seen or talked to him since returning to Canada. A few months later, Agent Sullivan questioned Almalki again about Khadr and Khadr's relationship to bin Laden. Almalki said he didn't know anything about such a relationship. He was also asked if he had sold equipment to the Taliban. He said that he hadn't. The agent believed he was merely invoking taqya. The investigation continued.

In 1999, Almalki correctly concluded that he was under surveillance. Packages to his business had been opened and resealed. Whenever he crossed the border into the United States, he was routinely detained for secondary examination and questioned extensively about his business and contacts. In a curious twist, an Ottawa taxi driver, who was a Muslim acquaintance, approached Almalki and told him that CSIS had asked the taxi driver to enter Almalki's home and search for bomb-making materials. The taxi driver told Almalki that he had refused because he knew Almalki to be a good man, that is, a religious leader.

In February 2000, Almalki was questioned again in Ottawa by CSIS about a trip he had made to Hong Kong in the company of another Muslim businessman. This time, agent Violaine Pepin grilled Almalki about apparent discrepancies between what Almalki had told customs agents in Vancouver and what had actually happened. The focus of the questioning concerned Almalki's travelling companion, who also held a commercial pilot's license. Almalki denied that he had misled the customs agents in Vancouver.

In the months leading up to the September 11, 2001, attack, security agents on both sides of the U.S.–Canada border were being warned about an impending attack on the United States.

On August 16, 2001, just 26 days before the fatal day, Toronto-area truck driver Ahmad Abou El Maati arrived at the U.S. border at Buffalo, NY, carrying a cargo of old batteries destined to be recycled at a facility in Philadelphia. Border officials were already on the lookout for possible truck bombs, and El Maati and his vehicle were subjected to a thorough search. In a drawer in the driver's sleeping cabin, agents found papers and a map that detailed the location in Ottawa of a government virus laboratory, Atomic Energy Canada, the Parliament Buildings, and the U.S. embassy. El Maati was not driving his regular truck, which was being repaired in Montréal. The truck he was driving had previously been driven by an Ottawa-based employee, who made deliveries in the Ottawa region. El Maati said he had found the papers, map, and reading glasses when he got into the truck, and had put them in the drawer. They weren't his, he said. He had been to Ottawa, yes, but he hardly knew his way around the city, he said.

The Kuwaiti-born El Maati was 17 when he and his brother Amer had arrived in Canada with their parents in 1981. He held Canadian and Egyptian citizenship because his father was Egyptian. He came from a good family and was a devout Muslim, who had attended the *hajj* (obligatory Muslim pilgrimage to Mecca) twice. His parents, both Canadian citizens, were accomplished. His father, Badr El Maati, was an accountant, auditor, and business consultant, and his Syrian-born mother, Samira Al-Shallash, was a teacher.

The El Maati family had settled in Toronto where Ahmad completed high school. Over the years, he worked as a taxi driver in London, Ontario, and later took courses in electronics and computer technology, but never earned a degree. In 1991, he travelled to Afghanistan to join the American-backed Mujahedeen in the holy war against Soviet invaders. He couldn't fight because of a pre-existing knee injury but over the next six years he did odd jobs until the Mujahedeen were pushed out of Afghanistan by the victorious Taliban in September 1996. The next year El Maati spent six months travelling through Syria with his mother in an unsuccessful search for a wife.

When he returned to Canada, he went to Montréal where he worked for two months as a mechanic's assistant in a garage operated by Abdelrahman Elzahabi. Elzahabi, it turns out, was also a pilot who owned his own plane, a Cessna. In the spring of 1999, El Maati returned to Toronto and began to take flying lessons at Buttonville Airport, as part of a plan, he said, to start up an air taxi business. He said he quit after five lessons because he was terrified of flying. Instead, he earned a truck driver's license and eventually started driving big rigs for Highland Transport of Markham, Ontario, the job he was doing when he arrived at the Buffalo, NY, border crossing on August 16, 2001.

U.S. border officials questioned El Maati extensively about his past, took his fingerprints, photographed him, and took a retina scan. They photographed the map and papers and returned the originals, but El Maati wouldn't be forgotten.

As it turned out, the map was an out-of-date one published by the government for tourists. The virus lab and Atomic Energy Canada had both relocated several years earlier, but that wasn't enough to get El Maati off the hook. During his few months in Montréal, as we have seen, CSIS and the CIA were actively monitoring the Muslim community. When El Maati moved back to Toronto, he became one of the 2,000 weekly congregants at the Salaheddin Islamic Centre in Scarborough, where intelligence agents were camped out both inside and outside the mosque. But it wasn't so much Ahmad that the authorities were interested in, it was his brother, Amer, whom Ahmad didn't mention much, if at all.

Amer El Maati was known by a number of aliases, including Amro Badr Eldin Abou El-Maati and Amro Badr Abouelmaati. A Canadian citizen, he had held an expired Canadian passport in the second alias name. Both his family and the police had long lost track of him, but intelligence agents around the world suspected him of being a hardened high-ranking operative of Al-Qaeda.

After September 11, back in his jail cell in the United States, Millennium Bomber Ahmed Ressam began to have a change of heart. The stakes had certainly been raised, which made life with his captors and interrogators even more uncomfortable. Ressam began to open up to U.S. authorities about possible Al-Qaeda sleeper cells in Canada based on his contacts and experiences in Montréal and elsewhere.

As Ressam started to sing, the heat was being turned up by the intelligence agencies on the roster of suspects in Ottawa and Toronto. Abdullah Almalki was beginning to see government agents everywhere. He was suspicious of an unidentified man who had entered his house twice in the company of different real estate agents who pretended to be interested in buying the house the Almalkis were renting. Was it CSIS? The CIA? The police? Or did that really happen? No one knows.

On another occasion, Almalki said that after he left his house he sprinkled baby powder in the foyer in an attempt to detect intruders. When he returned home, he said he found footprints. Old credit card and bank statements began arriving in the mail as "per his request." He hadn't requested such records, he said, but obviously someone had. Almalki went to see Ottawa criminal lawyer Michael Edelson for advice.

Almalki did not know it but the investigation into his activities had now been turned over to a task force of police agencies—led by the RCMP.

On October 11, 2001, Maher Arar made his entrance into the police surveillance of Almalki. Arar telephoned Abdullah Almalki and invited him to lunch the next day. Police were watching as the two men met at Mango's Café, located in a small mall on Bank Street in the south end of Ottawa. Arar would later tell reporters that he had never been to the restaurant before and that Almalki was a mere acquaintance.

Almalki later said that the reason for the meeting was an attempt by Arar to find a good doctor for his wife, Monia Mazigh, who was pregnant with their second child. Since the Almalkis already had four children, Arar believed Almalki might be able to help him.

After some time in the restaurant, the two men went outside for a 12- to 15-minute walk in the rain, during which they seemed overly cautious about not being overheard. This seemed odd to the police because, as one Mountie later put it: "In my experience the only guys who go for a walk and talk, so they can't be heard, are Mafioso and bikers, and even they don't go out in the rain."

Later, Arar and Almalki drove to a mosque to pray. Next they went to Future Shop, a retail electronics store, where they looked at computer equipment and purchased a printer cartridge. They then returned to the mosque. They were together for about three hours.

Born in Syria in 1970, Arar had come to Canada at the age of 17 with his parents to avoid mandatory military service. He became a Canadian citizen in 1991, but retained his Syrian citizenship. One of the first things he did as a Canadian citizen was apply for a gun permit, but he never bought a gun. He earned a bachelor's degree in computer engineering at McGill University and a master's degree in telecommunications from the Institut National de la Recherche Scientifique (a division of the University of Québec) in Montréal. While studying at McGill, Arar met Monia Mazigh, who had emigrated to Canada from Tunisia in 1991 at the age of 21. They were married in 1994 and continued to live in Montréal.

According to his incomplete published biography, throughout the nineties Arar had bounced from job to job, working for CIM21000 Inc., Nex Link Communications, and Alcatel Communications. At face value, the seeming instability in his career did not mean much because that kind of work pattern was typical of those times for most workers. In December 1997, Arar moved with his family to Ottawa into a townhouse he rented from Minto Corporation.

Less than two years later, in 1999, he rented a second house in Framingham, Massachusetts, after he began working in the Boston area for The MathWorks Inc., a privately-held multinational corporation that specializes in technical computing software. Mazigh stayed behind in Ottawa, raising one child while working on her doctorate degree in finance at McGill, which she completed in 2001, the same year their second child was born. Arar's job required him to travel extensively around the United States and Canada, which he enjoyed. Sometime in early September 2001 (no firm date has ever been established), Arar quit The MathWorks and returned to Ottawa to start his own wireless technology consulting company, Simcomms Inc., which he ran out of his home. In his statements to the press and in his online biography, he said MathWorks had promised him some consulting work.

Almost three weeks after Arar was first identified by the police as being an acquaintance of Abdullah Almalki, the RCMP learned on October 30, 2001, that Almalki was listed on a December 27, 1997, lease agreement for Arar's townhouse as a witness to the contract and as Arar's emergency contact. The number given was traced back to Almalki's export business. Arar has always played down any personal connection with Almalki, stating that he only called on him to witness the signing of the contract and to be the emergency contact when his friend, one of Almalki's brothers, wasn't available. To this day, the police have not talked to Arar and have no idea about the depth and nature of the relationship between him and Abdullah Almalki.

The police investigation intensified, which its suspects seemed to react unfavourably to. On November 11, 2001, El Maati and his mother suddenly left Canada for Syria to attend his arranged marriage in Damascus. They had finally found a wife for Ahmad. At Toronto's Pearson International Airport, El Maati was questioned by the Ontario Provincial Police about the Ottawa map found in his truck. He gave the police his lawyer's name and flew on to Syria, only to be arrested and incarcerated in the Far Falestin or Palestine Branch prison.

El Maati later said that after being tortured for two days, he broke. *The Globe and Mail*'s Jeff Sallot later interviewed him:

> This went on for two days until Mr. El Maati says he broke. He says he agreed to concoct a story that the Syrians wanted to hear, a fanciful tale naming Canadians of Middle East origin he said had trained in Afghanistan. He also said that his brother Amer had wanted him to become a suicide bomber and drive a truck full of explosives into a target in Ottawa.
>
> "Yes," the Syrians said. "The American embassy."
>
> Mr. El Maati says he had to think quickly. If the American embassy was supposed to be the target he might get sent to the United States for trial. Hoping to go home to Canada, Mr. El Maati says he "confessed" that the target was the Parliament Buildings.
>
> Even better, the Syrians said. They asked him to write it down. He says when he balked at that the torture began again.
>
> Mr. El Maati says he couldn't take it any more. He agreed to sign a written statement they prepared for him and seal it with his thumb print. He says he was not allowed to see the final document.

El Maati said he was making it all up—invoking taqya—but police continue to insist that a subsequent investigation in Canada confirmed many of the elements of the story he had told in Syria. El Maati had told the Syrians that he knew Arar only by sight, having seen him once in Abdelrahman's Montréal garage, where he had worked, because Arar had contacted Almalki about how to obtain a Syrian passport for a trip to Damascus to meet his potential bride.

Canadian police found themselves targeting a small, seemingly disparate group, who appeared to know each other only casually. Perhaps it was just a coincidence that Khadr, Almalki, and Arar were all engineers and involved with computers and electronics. Perhaps it was a coincidence that so many of their apparent associates had suddenly taken up flying as a hobby. No one was admitting to being a friend of anyone else but the reality was that of the 1.5 billion Muslims in the world there were only two or three degrees of separation between any of them—Arar to El Maati and Almalki to the Khadrs to Osama bin Laden. Although it was only a case of guilt by association, the police were determined to learn more about the associations— but they never got much of a chance.

Two weeks after El Maati left Canada, the Almalkis decided to leave too. They said they were going to visit Khuziamah's ailing mother in Malaysia, but the manner in which they left raised the suspicions of police investigators. On November 27, 2001, Abdullah left Canada and flew alone to Amsterdam, leaving his wife and four children in Ottawa. The bag in which his computer was stashed didn't make the trip cleanly, arriving a week later with a notification that it had been seized and studied by the police. The next day the rest of the family met up with him in Amsterdam, and they all continued on to Kuala Lumpur. The family carried return air tickets and planned to come back to Canada four weeks later, on Christmas Day. Once in Malaysia, however, Almalki said in his online biography, Khuziamah was having difficulty with her pregnancy, which made an immediate return to Canada unsafe. The family decided to remain in Malaysia until the baby was born in February.

Back in Canada, spurred on by the capture of British shoe-bomber Richard Reid, who had unsuccessfully tried to bring down a commercial jet over the Atlantic Ocean on December 22, 2001, the RCMP–CSIS hunt for the Al-Qaeda sleeper cell switched gears. Triggered by Ressam's statements in prison, likely contributions from Abdurahman Khadr, who was helping authorities overseas, and their own information, a series of raids were launched on January 22, 2002. Armed with search warrants, the police targeted the homes and businesses of the El Maati and Almalki families and others in Ottawa, Toronto, and London, Ont. One of the Almalki brothers, Youssef, called his lawyer, who talked with the police. For reasons unknown, the police left the house without enforcing their warrant. During the searches, however, police found 26 hard drives, about 40 VHS tapes, 100 CDs and diskettes, around 20,000 pages of documents, and two boxes of shredded documents. Some of the computers, CDs, and diskettes had been hidden in walls and rafters. There was family information and photos on some of the documents, but to this day no one knows the entirety of what the police found.

Abdullah Almalki lingered for months in Malaysia after his child was born in February. In April, Almalki travelled to Singapore and Saudi Arabia for what he described only as "business reasons." While there, he checked with his extended family in Syria, and they told him that everything seemed fine there. On May 3, 2002, Almalki flew to Damascus and was immediately arrested and incarcerated in the Palestine Branch prison, where El Maati was being held. He said he was tortured too and then eventually shipped to Egypt where, he claimed, he was tortured in a more "sophisticated" fashion.

Meanwhile, Arar continued to travel between Canada and the United States. Police had asked customs officials in Canada and the United States to look out for him. He was stopped twice at Ottawa International airport for secondary examinations. Canadian officials seized his travel documents and recorded information about his trip on one occasion. On the second occasion, airport customs officer Rose Mutombo did the same. She also seized Arar's laptop and Palm Pilot, both of which had been purchased in the United States. He had not declared the items in Canada and owed duty. He paid the bill the next day and got back his equipment. Arar noted that someone had used the computers for 25 1/2 minutes, based on the rate of battery depletion.

J.P. Theriault, the regional intelligence officer for Canada Customs, had spent that time trying, unsuccessfully, to get into the computer engineer's computer. Canada Customs had high-tech equipment which could have opened the computer and read its contents as easily as opening a can of peaches. For whatever reason, however, Theriault did not use that equipment. Instead, he just downloaded names and phone numbers from the Palm Pilot.

It wasn't until 7:30 a.m. on the morning of January 22, 2002, the day of the aforementioned raids on El Maati and the Almalkis, that the RCMP would try to make contact with Arar. That day, Corporal Randy Buffam visited Arar's house. He was chosen for the assignment because he had taken an RCMP-authorized course on Islamic sensitivity training. Buffam was told by Arar's wife, Monia, that her husband was in Tunisia, having flown there via New York. The police did not know he had left the country. Mazigh also told Buffam that Arar had travelled to Tunisia to visit her ailing father, which struck the Mounties as being somewhat odd. The police thought it was a somewhat lavish gesture—it is a rare husband who would travel that far to visit his father-in-law.

The Tunisia trip was intriguing to the police in another way. The country was a hotbed of Al-Qaeda activity.

In any event, the police weren't there to search Arar's house but, they hoped, to enlist him as a witness. When Arar learned from his wife that a lone, male RCMP officer had visited his home and confronted his wife at such an early hour, he was furious. He called the police from Tunisia to protest the perceived breach of Muslim protocol—a woman should never see a man alone so early in the morning.

Two days later, Arar flew home. Amazingly, he was not searched by customs agents in the United States or Canada. When Cpl. Buffam called Arar the next day, on January 25, 2002, an angry Arar answered the phone. He calmed down enough to agree to meet the next day for an interview at RCMP "A" Division headquarters in Vanier, in the east end of Ottawa. But he did not show up.

Instead, Arar contacted lawyer Michael Edelson, who was already representing Abdullah Almalki and a number of Muslims in the community. Arar told Edelson, a top criminal lawyer in Ottawa, that he did not know Abdullah Almalki all that well, but was closer to Safa, one of his brothers.

Edelson later wrote in a letter to the police that Arar had told him he was dumbfounded by the police interest in him. He quoted Arar as declaring that he "admired Americans." Edelson said Arar told him he had nothing to hide and that he wanted to talk to police. Edelson drafted a letter (described later in the O'Connor Commission report, introduced below), setting out the conditions that the RCMP would have to meet for an interview with Arar:

Mr. Edelson would not consent to a videotaped, sworn statement because he wanted to avoid a situation where the interview would later be admissible as evidence in court—referred to colloquially in criminal practice as a "KGB" statement, after a Canadian case involving the admissibility of out-of-court statements; the statement could be audiotaped; a transcript could be prepared, if Mr. Arar was given an opportunity to review the transcript to correct anything erroneous or mistaken; the statement would not be "under caution," i.e. the typical police caution indicating that the interviewee waived the right to remain silent, then anything said could be taken down and used as evidence; Mr. Edelson would be present throughout the interview; if Mr. Edelson objected, certain questions would not be answered; Mr. Arar and his counsel would be free to leave at any time.

Edelson later said that in his experience the conditions were appropriate and not at all restrictive for the police. Whatever Arar said could be used only for "intelligence purposes." The police knew Edelson was being disingenuous. They were effectively being blocked from talking to Arar about anything substantive. The police never came back to interview Arar.

Three months later, in April, 2002, Arar and Mazigh drove to the United States. They crossed the border at the Thousand Islands Bridge. Once inside the country Arar had no problem renewing his U.S. work permit.

In June, Mazigh and her two children travelled to Tunisia, ostensibly to visit her ailing father. Arar followed her in July, after cleaning out his house and putting the contents in storage. Once in Tunisia, however, he began to look for work which suggested he had plans to stay there. The Canadian police, convinced Arar had left Canada for good, contacted the Tunisian intelligence service. They raised their concerns about Arar and his possible links to Al-Qaeda. Arar and his father-in-law were subsequently questioned by the Tunisian investigators, who made it clear that the Canadians wanted answers to some of their questions. Arar would later say that the information from Canadian authorities made the Tunisians nervous about him and that they did not feel comfortable about him being in their country.

In August, Arar said, his old employer The MathWorks told him it might have a job for him with a prospective client. A month later, Arar says he cashed in air miles points and took the only route he could find back to Canada, via Zurich and New York to Montréal.

As Don Butler later wrote in "The Arar Chronicles," a series published by the *Ottawa Citizen* in 2006, "He kissed his wife and children goodbye, slipped into a taxi and left for the airport for a flight to Montréal via Zurich and New York. It was Sept. 25, 2002. More than a year would pass before he would see or talk to them again."

Arar had been travelling in and out of the United States for almost a year since first being identified by police at Mango's Café. On September 26, 2002, however, Arar was taken into custody by U.S. agents at New York's John F. Kennedy International Airport. Arar was held in confinement for 13 days in New York and then secretly sent to Jordan and Syria where he was confined by Syrian authorities for 359 days.

In landing in Syria, Arar appeared to have unwittingly followed the footsteps of El Maati, Almalki, and two other less-celebrated Canadians, Syrian-born former Ottawa resident Arwad Muhammad 'Izzat Al-Boushi and Toronto-area geologist Muayyed Nureddin. Their cases were all similar. They had all left Canada sometime in 2002 or early 2003 and all ended up in the Palestine Branch prison. The image of an innocent Arar being tortured in a Syrian prison hellhole played out in the media for a year.

What also made the Arar case different from the others was politics. After his rendition to Syria, Monia returned to Canada. She began a high-profile and effective campaign to have the Canadian government intervene in the case and have him released.

It wasn't a one-woman show, however. Virtually every major human rights and Arab–Islamic lobby group on the continent put their collective voices behind her, including Amnesty International and the relatively unknown Canadian Council for American–Islamic Relations, or CAIR-CAN.

CAIR-CAN is described as a grassroots organization designed to promote understanding between members of the Islamic community and other North Americans. It had distributed a pocket guide for Canadian Muslims entitled "Know Your Rights," advising Muslims what to do if CSIS or the RCMP tried to interrogate them. In CAIR-CAN's view, Canadian Muslims were a "community under siege" since September 11, 2001, and it feared people were being targeted through so-called racial profiling for investigation.

But the U.S. version of the organization—the Council for American–Islamic Relations—had a controversial history in the United States regarding its status as a charity and its ultimate goals. It would be fair to say that in the United States, CAIR was seen to be a radical Islamic group with a somewhat shadowy history, including former high-ranking officials who had been convicted of having links to terrorist entities—including Al-Qaeda.

Some detractors saw similarities between CAIR and the infamous Italian-American Anti-Defamation League, which made headlines beginning in the seventies. That group was founded by longtime Mafia boss Joe Columbo Sr. after his son and namesake had been arrested in New York by the FBI. Proclaiming to be defending the good name of all Italians, Columbo Sr. headed anti-defamation marches on the FBI offices and even a rally, which was attended by at least 50,000 people. According to the website gangstersinc, the group won the support of respected politicians with its message that the government was tarring all Italians by using the words Mafia and La Cosa Nostra. The police soon dropped the terms in their public pronouncements. The words were deleted from the scripts of the *Godfather* movies and from television productions. Frank Sinatra and other top stars performed at a Madison Square Garden benefit and raised $500,000 for the anti-defamation league, monies that went straight into the Mob's pockets.

Before long the Italian-American Anti-Defamation League had grown to 150,000 members, with more than 50 chapters across the United States, raising millions for the Mob. In the media, Columbo was treated with respect, even being interviewed by top talk-show hosts like Dick Cavett. Columbo was named "Man of the Year" in March 1971, by what had now become the Italian–American Civil Rights League. "The league is under God's eyes and those who try to stop it will feel his sting," Columbo said in his acceptance speech.

The police knew it was a scam but all the uncritical political and media support made it all but impossible for them to do anything about it. Finally, the Mafia, tired of Columbo's attention-getting grandstanding and public persona, put out a contract on him. On June 29, 1971, Columbo was shot and killed by an assassin on his way to deliver a speech to the Italian–American Civil Rights League Rally in Columbus Circle.

Others such as Israel-born author and terrorism-financing expert Dr. Rachel Ehrenfeld, liken the tactics of the Council for American–Islamic Relations to those of the Church of Scientology, which has used monstrous lawsuits and outrageous claims in attempts to silence its critics. The highly litigious CAIR uses similar tactics, particularly against journalists and talk-show hosts. Some believe the organization uses such spectacular lawsuits to intimidate its critics and opponents in an attempt to silence them, all of which CAIR denies.

CAIR-CAN became the driving force behind the free-Arar campaign. With Mazigh as its public face pushing her cause into headlines around the world, Arar became a cause célèbre. He was portrayed as an innocent man who had been terribly wronged. Canada was being squeezed and looked bad, but no institution was being squeezed harder than the RCMP. The indelible impression created was that the RCMP had enthusiastically provided U.S. authorities with erroneous and overstated information about Arar and Mazigh, which fuelled the rendition action by the Americans. The RCMP was further accused of feeding information and questions to the Syrians, who in turn used it as part of their own interrogation of Arar, El Maati, and Almalki.

Efforts to free Arar seemed to be getting nowhere. In fact, to some it appeared the Canadian embassy in Syria was undermining and obstructing diplomatic initiatives, as if to ensure that Arar not get out of the Syrian prison too soon. Years later, a *Globe and Mail* editorial would highlight that intriguing point.

Frustrated by the apparent lack of action, Mazigh appeared before the House of Commons Foreign Affairs Committee on September 25, 2003. She implored members of Parliament to continue working on her husband's behalf. At the same hearing, RCMP Assistant Commissioner Richard Proulx refused to discuss the case with MPs. This made the RCMP look even worse in the eyes of the Canadian public and the world.

Ten days later, on October 5, 2003, however, Arar was set free by the Syrian government and handed over to Canadian diplomats in Damascus. Foreign Affairs Minister Bill Graham attributed his release to the success of "quiet Canadian diplomacy."

National and international anger about Arar's capture and incarceration had reached a fever pitch. Human rights groups were demanding to know who was responsible for railroading an innocent like Arar.

At the same time, covert attacks on Arar and his character began to spring from the shadows of government. The leaks were peculiar in the way the information was distributed, not to a single reporter, as is usually the case, but scattered almost randomly across a spectrum of media outlets.

Three days after Arar arrived back in Canada, on October 9, 2003, he had still not made a public appearance. That day, Graham Fraser reported in the *Toronto Star* Canadian authorities told their U.S. counterparts that Arar had been to Afghanistan a number of times.

The next day, Jeff Sallot reported in *The Globe and Mail* that unnamed Canadian sources said Arar had not been tortured in Syria but merely roughed up.

On October 23, CTV reporter Joy Malbon stated that unnamed government sources had told her that Arar had divulged information about Al-Qaeda, the Muslim Brotherhood, and radical cells operating in Canada.

The Muslim Brotherhood was of particular concern to the Syrians. The ruling party of President Bashar al-Assad is controlled by the Alawite sect, which represents merely 11 percent of the country's population. The vast majority of Syrians, 74 percent, are Sunni Muslims, the base of Muslim Brotherhood support.

On October 29, 2003, Curt Petrovich of the CBC reported on a private meeting between Arar and officials from the Department of Foreign Affairs in which Arar told Foreign Affairs Minister Bill Graham that he had been tortured while in Syria. Arar wanted to make that announcement himself, which he did at a press conference on November 4.

Arar was pressing for an inquiry, but government documents indicate that Graham was lobbying against one. Graham had even asked U.S. Secretary of State Colin Powell to intervene with his government to do whatever it could to help block such an inquiry. He said he was looking for "another way" to relieve the pressure.

On November 8, Juliet O'Neill of the *Ottawa Citizen* reported that the reason the government had opposed an inquiry into the Arar case was because "a group of Ottawa men with alleged ties to Al-Qaeda" was at the root of the controversy. In the article, O'Neill published previously secret details of the investigation into Arar in Canada. She included comments attributed to Arar from his interrogation in Syria.

The leaks about Arar were also spilling out in the United States. On November 19, the *Washington Post*, quoting anonymous U.S. officials, reported that then-Deputy Attorney General Larry D. Thompson had personally approved sending Arar to Syria after consulting with CIA officials, according to anonymous U.S. officials. Sending him to Canada would have been "prejudicial to the interests of the United States," a government spokesman said, adding that when Arar was apprehended in New York he had the names of "a large number of known Al-Qaeda operatives, affiliates or associates" in his wallet or pockets.

On December 30, 2003, Robert Fife of the *Ottawa Citizen* cited high-level sources in Canada and the United States who had access to extensive secret intelligence on Arar. Fife reported that Arar had travelled to Pakistan in the early 1990s and then entered Afghanistan to train at the Khalden camp. "This guy is no virgin," one source was quoted. "There is more there than meets the eye." Fife also reported that an Arar family spokesperson, Kerry Pither, had denounced the leaks as being "an anonymous smear campaign."

The Fife story was picked up and elaborated on by the CBS show *60 Minutes*. In that report, RCMP and U.S. officials were described as being in regular contact with each other after Arar was arrested in New York.

By now, the all-powerful Privy Council Office had long been trying to identify who was leaking information. Inside the bureaucracy, security officers were busy trying to root out and identify offenders, and a complaint was eventually filed with the RCMP. More than any other leak, Juliet O'Neill's had been almost entirely on point. Whoever her source—or sources—were, her information had come from deep inside the investigation tent.

On January 21, 2004, armed with a search warrant issued by Ottawa Justice of the Peace Richard Sculthorpe, RCMP officers raided O'Neill's home and office and seized contact lists, a Rolodex, and other materials. The search warrant, sealed for national security purposes, was issued under the new Security of Information Act, which had been rushed through Parliament after September 11, 2001. The RCMP was acting at the behest of the government but the raid proved damaging for the force. It created a firestorm of opposition among politicians and the public about the seemingly police-state tactic. (In November 2004, Ontario Superior Court Judge Lynn Ratushny ruled that the sealing of the search warrants was unacceptable, and violated guarantees of a free press, freedom of expression, and the public's right to an open court system. In October 2006, Ratushny struck down Section 4 of the Security of Information Act, ruling that it was "unconstitutionally vague" and broad, and an infringement of freedom of expression.)

The political pressure generated by the Arar case in 2004 was becoming explosive. Monia Mazigh was on the verge of announcing her intention to seek election to Parliament in the upcoming general election. She had been courted by both the Liberal and New Democratic Parties to stand as a candidate in the upcoming June 28, 2004 federal election. She chose the NDP after becoming close to Alexa McDonough, its Foreign Affairs Critic and former federal NDP leader. Mazigh was a hot commodity, so much so that the NDP was willing to overlook her stand against same-sex marriage, a position no other candidate could possibly hold and still win a nomination. Mazigh ran against Liberal David McGuinty, the brother of Ontario Premier Dalton McGuinty, and lost to him, finishing a decent third. Afterward, she went on to work as a policy researcher at NDP headquarters.

This process ensured that Mazigh and Arar were politically bulletproof. They were protected by political defenders cheering on their cause. They were in the NDP fold and the Liberals had also wooed Mazigh. Neither party was about to give Mazigh or her husband any grief, if it came to that.

Prime Minister Paul Martin, therefore, believed he had little choice but to accede to the calls for a public inquiry to investigate the Arar case. The press release describing the inquiry set out its extraordinarily narrow terms.

DEPUTY PRIME MINISTER ISSUES TERMS OF REFERENCE
FOR THE PUBLIC INQUIRY INTO THE MAHER ARAR MATTER
OTTAWA, February 5, 2004—The Honourable Anne McLellan,
Deputy Prime Minister and Minister of Public Safety and Emergency
Preparedness, today announced that the Government of Canada has
issued Terms of Reference for the Commission of Inquiry into the
Actions of Canadian Officials in Relation to Maher Arar.

On January 28, 2004, the Deputy Prime Minister announced that Mr. Justice Dennis R. O'Connor would undertake a public inquiry into the actions of Canadian officials dealing with the deportation and detention of Mr. Maher Arar and then, as a second task, make recommendations concerning an independent, arm's-length review mechanism for the RCMP's activities with respect to national security.

Mr. Justice O'Connor is to investigate and report on the actions of Canadian officials in relation to Maher Arar, including the following:

- the detention of Mr. Arar in the United States;
- the deportation of Mr. Arar to Syria via Jordan;
- the imprisonment and treatment of Mr. Arar in Syria;
- the return of Mr. Arar to Canada; and
- any other circumstance directly related to Mr. Arar that Justice O'Connor considers relevant to fulfilling this mandate.

Under the policy review of possible review mechanisms for RCMP national security activities, Mr. Justice O'Connor will examine domestic and international review models. He will make such recommendations as he considers advisable on the creation of a new mechanism and in doing this, he will consider how the recommended mechanism would interact with other Canadian review bodies.

The terms of reference, published later, strictly limited the scope of O'Connor's activities to a mere public review of the actions of Canadian officials in relation to Arar. The commission was authorized to make recommendations on the creation of an independent review mechanism of future RCMP activity with respect to national security. Most important, O'Connor was explicitly ordered not to ascribe blame or express any conclusion or recommendation regarding the civil or criminal liability of any person or organization.

In the 1,201 pages of the three-volume O'Connor report, as well as the 12,672 pages of public transcripts, the 36-page factual analysis, and the pages of edited in-camera testimony, one might think that everything there is to know about the story might be found there, but that is not the case. Public inquiries in Canada have usually been used as an excuse for a failed or derailed police investigation or as vehicles for governments with a hidden agenda either to cover up the real issue or to introduce new ideas which might otherwise be politically unpalatable. The O'Connor Commission would prove to be both such an excuse and such a vehicle.

Like so many Canadian public inquiries of the past, all those words—and all those gaps.

As journalist Peter Worthington suggested at the outset of this chapter, there was something about the official Arar story that just did not make sense.

[6]

THE MOUNTIES CHARGE INTO THE FOG

When Islamic fundamentalist terrorism exploded into the world view on September 11, 2001, RCMP Commissioner Giuliano Zaccardelli was beginning his second year on the job. His plan to reshape and reinvigorate the RCMP was still very much a work in progress. The force was short on everything it needed—money, staff, and specialized talent. It had virtually no capacity to gather useful criminal intelligence, and most of its investigators, new to their jobs, were in the perpetual training mode that is the everyday world of the RCMP.

This was especially the case with terrorism. After the McDonald Commission, the RCMP was prohibited from fishing around in national security investigations, which was the responsibility of CSIS. Inevitably, interest in national security issues eventually withered in the RCMP, even as the threat of terrorism grew dramatically throughout the 1990s.

One of the problems in Canada was the definition of terrorism itself. Until recently, terrorism had been considered to be a "political" act and the Canadian government was overly sensitive about appearing to repress the legitimate political aspirations of anyone. The fine line between radical politics and terrorism was best defined by a protocol that defined the difference. For example, at Toronto's Pearson International Airport, it was once posited that any terrorist activity at the airport would be handled by the Peel Regional Police force, the local police responsible for protection of the airport. However, if the act were deemed to be "political terrorism," then the RCMP would be responsible.

By 1994, western governments had begun to agree that terrorism of any kind was a criminal act, which should have focused the attention of all

Canadian police on what they should be doing, but it didn't. The police talked a lot about it among themselves, but did little. When it came to counter-intelligence, Canada relied only on CSIS and the Communications Security Establishment, which monitors the airwaves and cyberspace. There is no CIA or its British equivalents, the British Secret Intelligence Service or MI-6, to perform external intelligence. In theory and practice, Canada relied on its allies for their intelligence, a situation that has been profoundly criticized over the years by many knowledgeable observers, both in Canada and abroad.

Both the RCMP and CSIS fell under the umbrella of the department of the solicitor general, but the differences between the two services are profound. The RCMP is a servant and agent of the law. CSIS is another kind of animal. It reports to government. Its mandate is "to investigate, analyze, and advise government departments and agencies on activities which may reasonably be suspected of constituting threats to Canada's national security." CSIS investigates political violence and terrorism that advances a political cause in Canada or elsewhere. It investigates espionage, sabotage, and foreign-influenced activities, which might be considered detrimental to Canadian national interests, such as interference with ethnic communities in Canada. CSIS also conducts background and security checks for federal government departments and its agencies, including assessments of immigration, citizenship, and refugee applicants. CSIS also gathers foreign intelligence within the country at the request of the minister of Foreign Affairs or the minister of National Defence. The entire purpose of CSIS, therefore, is to collect information and direct it to the government through the Privy Council Office and other, sometimes informal, means. CSIS is overseen by the Security Intelligence Review Committee, whose role is to review the activities of CSIS to ensure that the extraordinary powers granted the Security Service are "used legally and appropriately, in order to protect Canadians' rights and freedoms." At any one time, there are five members on the SIRC committee, and all are privy councillors, sworn to keep all information secret.

By the late 1990s, the Chrétien government was treating CSIS in much the same way as it had the RCMP. The counter-intelligence organization was underfinanced and undermanned at a time when the threat to Canada and the rest of North America was growing. In 1993, CSIS had 2,465 employees, but by September 11, 2001, that number had decreased to 2,061, which included a large support staff. The total number of active agents was around 1,200 for all of Canada, about the same size as the Winnipeg Police Service.

In many other countries, policing and security are treated as an important function of government and overseen by senior and qualified ministers, but in the Chrétien government and Canadian provincial governments, the solicitor general or public safety department was usually handed to a junior minister, and was certainly not a funding priority. More important, as the Senate Special Committee on Security and Intelligence reported in January 1999, CSIS was more inclined to manage its meagre resources than to focus its full attention on potential threats. Like a team of five-year-old soccer players, everyone was rushing to the ball, wherever it might be. Although there were repeated calls for improvement, Chrétien had no inclination to change things.

Even if it did have the money and manpower, the problem for CSIS agents was that while they might think of themselves as spies, they are essentially civil servants on steroids. Their primary mission was to gather and analyze information relating to national security. The vast majority of CSIS agents were relatively inexperienced, with five or fewer years on the job. They did not have police experience and did not think like police, which CSIS deemed to be taboo. CSIS agents were trained to be blind to criminality, but they were good at taking notes the government could understand. The very nature of the job was to gather information from political and potentially subversive immigrant groups in an attempt to discern who might be a threat to Canada or another country. The role CSIS plays in Canada has always caused confusion in both CSIS and the government.

A further aggravation, as detailed in Richard Cleroux's 1990 book *Official Secrets*, was that CSIS was little more than a lapdog for the CIA and the U.S. National Security Agency. "When they said jump, CSIS asked, 'how high?'"

The bottom line was that in the RCMP's perspective, CSIS was deemed to be not only political, but stupidly so, not only the eyes and ears of the government, but an arm of both Canadian and U.S. government policy.

In its first test, the Air India investigation, CSIS officers were on the trail of the perpetrators in 1985, but believed that much of what they were doing was political in nature and not criminal. CSIS actually destroyed the mounds of evidence of criminality it had gathered for fear that it would fall into the wrong hands—the RCMP. CSIS took the position that because of Canadian disclosure laws—particularly the Stinchcombe decision—if CSIS were to share files with the RCMP, the RCMP might then be forced to reveal everything it knew as well as the identities of CSIS sources. It took more than two decades of government delay and obstruction before even that was revealed in 2007 at the Air India inquiry. Over that period, the RCMP took the rap for CSIS. In the ensuing years, the RCMP would be blamed many times for falling down on the job, when, in fact, it had been tripped over and over again by CSIS.

In effect, CSIS was little different from Canada's other spy agency, the Communications Security Establishment, which does little more than collect and analyze information. The two agencies were largely staffed with precisely the same kind of people: bright university graduates with multiple diplomas who spent more time analyzing information than collecting it. CSIS and the CSE operated under a legal regime less strict than the RCMP's and did not have to meet the same high standards of evidence as the police to be granted wiretaps and search warrants by a judge.

Then came September 11, 2001. Absolute panic set in. CSE, CSIS, and the RCMP were completely unprepared for the reality of the international terrorists who had infiltrated North America. CSIS suddenly woke up and realized that the "bunch of guys" it had lazily been following around Montréal and Toronto—specifically Ahmad Abou El Maati and Abdullah Almalki—might actually be part of a master terrorist plot.

By its own admission, CSIS was woefully understaffed; it did not have the manpower to keep up with all its investigations. Intense pressure was coming from the United States over a possible next wave of attacks. In the ensuing weeks and months, the U.S. government made 1,500 requests for assistance from Canadian authorities to help follow leads generated by U.S. investigators, which led them to Canada. On September 22, 2001, the day the U.S. government decided to boldly expand the concept of rendition, and after the FBI began pressing Canadians to get to work on the terrorist file, two urgent meetings were held at CSIS offices in Toronto.

The first was an all-agency meeting that included the RCMP, CSIS, and the FBI, as well as other law enforcement agencies. As Justice Dennis O'Connor would later report, at that meeting "the FBI asked the Canadian agencies to investigate certain individuals who allegedly had ties to persons whom the Americans suspected to be terrorists. The agencies were to provide further information about these individuals and, if possible, detain them for interviews. The RCMP did not act on the FBI's request, as it was not yet prepared to detain and interview the individuals named."

At the second meeting that day in the CSIS offices, Jack Hooper, director general of the CSIS Toronto office, chaired a meeting including CSIS, the

RCMP, the Ontario Provincial Police, the Toronto Police Service, and the Peel Regional Police, where he briefed them on the investigation of certain individuals identified as potential threats to Canadian security. CSIS wanted the police to gather information for CSIS, but the police argued that the investigation looked more like a criminal one and should be treated that way.

In response, on September 25, 2001, Zaccardelli authorized Project Shock. This involved the reassignment of 2,000-plus RCMP members and support staff to respond to immediate priorities, including the protection of VIPs and important buildings, airport security, and following up investigative leads. One initiative of Project Shock was the refocusing of the RCMP's Integrated Proceeds of Crime units across the country. The IPOC units were set up to gather incriminating financial information on suspected criminals which could be used to seize a suspect's assets as part of a prosecution. The RCMP also announced that it was establishing a new entity, the Financial Intelligence Task Force, "to co-ordinate research on the financial transactions of suspected terrorist organizations." This later came to be known as the Financial Transactions and Reports Analysis Centre of Canada, Fintrac for short. Its priorities, in order of importance, were prevention, intelligence, and prosecution. The overriding problem for the police was that they were being asked to venture into an area of investigation—the financing and abetting of terrorism—that successive governments had long ignored out of fear of enraging vocal ethnic and religious groups. The government was now telling the police to form a posse and charge ahead and that the law would catch up with them before they lynched the bad guys.

A day after the Toronto meetings, on September 26, 2001, Hooper accepted that the RCMP-led task force could not just gather information for CSIS but should conduct criminal investigations of its own. He turned over to the police a few of those cases, the likely suspects, as it were. In an unprecedented letter to the RCMP that day, Hooper described "an imminent threat to public safety and the security of Canada." What was so unusual was that CSIS was prepared to allow the RCMP to use information gathered by CSIS in any criminal prosecution. A protocol was set up so that liaison officers in both forces could transfer information back and forth.

This led to the formation of the RCMP-coordinated Project O Canada, based at the force's "O" Division headquarters in Toronto, which included the Ontario Provincial Police and Toronto Police Service, and others. The primary target was Abdullah Almalki who was, at the very least, suspected of working as a financier or facilitator for Al-Qaeda. The police were told, among other things, that Almalki was supplying computer equipment, components, and sub-components to Al-Qaeda through a maze of intermediaries. Equipment sold by Almalki had been found on the battlefields of Afghanistan. Then there was the rest of Almalki's family, including his three brothers, Nazih, Safa, and Youssef. Also targeted was the family of truck driver Ahmad El Maati, along with some others who had frequented the Salaheddin Islamic Centre in Scarborough led by the radical fundamentalist Imam Aly Hindy.

Within a week, the Project O Canada team was calling for help to monitor Almalki in Ottawa. To do that investigation, "A" Division set up Project A-O Canada. Both Project O Canada and A-O Canada had the same mandate as Project Shock: prevention, intelligence, and prosecution.

The investigations were growing and their focus showed just how unprepared Canada had been for the terrorist attacks. The RCMP had been allowed to coast along, as had CSIS, in typical Canadian fashion, hoping that nothing would happen. No expertise was being developed. Only a handful of RCMP officers had taken a national security investigations course.

"A" Division was also a most unlikely place from which to run a major criminal investigation because its main functions were policing federal properties in the national capital region and providing security and protection for VIPs.

Nevertheless, from the top down, the RCMP was on high alert. This was sexy stuff, likely the most important case in any of their lifetimes. A team was put together in Ottawa. Chief Superintendent Antoine Couture, the director of criminal operations (CROPs) at "A" Division, chose inspectors Michel Cabana and Garry Clement to assemble and direct a team. Cabana had experience in major case management and Clement was an expert on financial and undercover investigations.

Ottawa Police Staff Sergeant Patrick Callaghan, who had worked for nine years on investigations for the RCMP, and OPP Staff Sergeant Kevin Corcoran were chosen as assistant managers. It was known at the time that Corcoran wasn't familiar with RCMP procedures but it was believed that there would be enough supervision provided to guide him along the way.

RCMP Sergeant Randal Walsh was responsible for preparing affidavits for search warrants. Cpl. Robert Leman was the exhibit custodian. Constable Michel Lang from "A" Division's Customs and Excise unit had experience with Canadian and U.S. Customs lookout systems. Corporal Randy Buffam, a senior member of the RCMP's National Security Intelligence Service, was the only officer with previous experience with Sunni Islamic extremists. Back at RCMP headquarters, Deputy Commissioner Garry Loeppky, the operations chief, was keeping an eye on what was going on, with Zaccardelli peeking over his shoulder.

There was one other element to the investigation which would prove fateful. The U.S. government made it clear that it expected Canada to shed its "bunch of guys" mentality and deal immediately and conclusively with the looming terrorist threat. Due to this overriding sense of urgency, the Canadian government made it clear to the police that "the rule book" was effectively being suspended. The government expected all agencies to fully cooperate "in an integrated fashion" with each other and with American agencies. Project A-O Canada was considered an international investigation with "caveats down:" information would be freely shared with CSIS and U.S. authorities, who could use the information as they saw fit. To that end, liaison officers from the FBI would have access to the investigation.

Over the first few weeks, the FBI agents visited the RCMP's "A" Division in Ottawa and were escorted into the building where they were handed all the information the Canadians were gathering. As everyone got to know each other better, the formal relationship soon became more informal. The thinking at the time was that while the RCMP would have liked to have made its own case, it would be even better if the Americans could do its dirty work, shifting the burden of the cost of prosecution and the expected messy politics south. It would not have been the first time that Canada had taken that approach—nor the last.

On Parliament Hill, the government was on a war footing. Suspected terrorists were on their very doorstep. A new anti-terrorist act was being hurried together in order to give police more powers. CSIS was flowing information that it was gathering back to the government and Ottawa was in a tizzy. Everyone knew the history, too—that when the RCMP and CSIS worked together, bad news was not far away.

The Security Intelligence Review Committee would play a large role, but it couldn't be seen to be ordering the police around. Someone from SIRC would cover the CSIS end of things. The government, therefore, had to organize itself at the highest levels in such a way that it could monitor and direct the ongoing security operations at two levels. Each key department, the Privy Council Office, CSIS, the Solicitor General, the RCMP, the Ministry of Defence, and the Department of Transport, has its own war room for emergency situations like this. Each had its own responsibilities, but everything had to be coordinated, and the secrets kept in check. On paper, at least, the solicitor general's office, which was responsible for the police and CSIS, would take the lead. However, someone had to be in control of the trickier issues and the murkiness without leaving an obvious direct trail back for the curious to follow should anything go wrong.

There was no question that the quarterback of the entire operation was Ward Elcock, the CSIS director, guiding from above. Elcock, a lawyer, was part of the incestuous fraternity that ran the country. He was the nephew of Senator Michael Pitfield, the Power Corp. director who had overseen the creation of CSIS. Elcock's route to the top through the civil service was typical for such an insider. He had served as security and intelligence deputy clerk of the Privy Council Office for five years, assistant secretary to the cabinet, and as counsel for legislation and House planning for six years. He took over CSIS in 1994 for the first of two five-year terms.

Among the key players on Elcock's team were two other lawyers in the Department of Transport, which was responsible for airports and aircraft, among other things. They had similar credentials and were trusted behind-the-scenes movers and shakers, people experienced with shaping the government's policy initiatives and responses, while protecting the politicians—often from themselves.

Margaret Bloodworth was the associate deputy minister, and soon-to-be deputy minister of Transport. Bloodworth, the chief gatekeeper, had impressive credentials in security and was a dedicated protector of the government's interests. Like Elcock, she had begun her civil service career in 1989 in the Privy Council Office as assistant secretary to the cabinet. In 1994, Bloodworth was promoted to deputy clerk and counsel responsible for Security and Intelligence. With her, "Yes, Minister, but you should be aware of . . ." approach, Bloodworth was seen by many in Ottawa to be the Canadian embodiment of the manipulative, all-knowing bureaucrat.

William Elliott, the assistant deputy minister of Transport, was responsible for safety and security. Elliott had entered the civil service in 1988 as a political appointment, legal advisor, and special assistant to then-Progressive Conservative Deputy Prime Minister Don Mazankowski. Elliott quickly rose to become chief of staff, but by then the Conservatives under Brian Mulroney had become deeply unpopular. Before the Tories were massacred at the polls in 1993, Elliott moved into the Department of Justice. He worked there until 1998, when he became deputy commissioner of the Canadian Coast Guard, a post he held until he moved to Transport.

Elcock would lurk in the shadows of the espionage world but Blood-worth and Elliott would have a big say in current events, and later would become even more important when everything got a little too hot for the government.

+ + +

For a terrorist, sleeper agents or cells are beautiful weapons. They are individuals or groups of people who wiggle their way into an organization or society and then pretend they are part of the scenery. They tend to be reliable workers and appear to be the best of citizens, while flying below the radar of authorities. Their goal is to be innocuous and law-abiding until their masters hit the on switch. Detecting and investigating a sleeper cell, therefore, is extraordinarily difficult.

In the days and weeks after September 11, police and the media were uncovering the trail left by the terrorists who struck the United States. On September 27, the day after the creation of Project O Canada, the U.S. government released the names and photographs of the 19 men who had hijacked the four planes on September 11. Many of them had come from good families and were well-educated. Most of them had avoided contact with the authorities and in the years leading up to the attacks, many had travelled extensively through North America, the Middle East, Europe, and Asia, particularly Malaysia. The common link seemed to be a sleeper cell in Hamburg, Germany, but already intelligence agents were hearing about other sleeper cells around the world.

After CSIS put the RCMP on the trail of Ahmad El Maati, and Abdullah Almalki and his brothers, the police were desperately trying to find clues and follow them. This wasn't going to be like following Mafioso or outlaw bikers, where most of the players were already known. The police had only an inkling of who they were looking for: seemingly ordinary men who were probably well-educated, religious people, without criminal records, and with the means and wherewithal to travel just about anywhere at any time. They all knew that this was going to take a lot of time, but they had no idea how much time they had before the expected next attack.

On October 12, two significant events occurred. The first involved a move by the governments of the United States, Canada, and the United Kingdom to freeze the accounts of suspected Al-Qaeda financiers around the world. Those targeted were more than two dozen wealthy Saudi Arabian businessmen, including members of the bin Laden family, known in Al-Qaeda circles as "the Golden Chain." These people were suspected of raising money, usually through fronts operating as charities around the world, which was then directed to the jihadists.

Of interest to this story are two people in the Golden Chain. One was a Saudi Arabian investor, Yassin al-Qadi (Kadi), who operated the Blessed Relief Foundation and who owned properties in Vancouver. He was alleged by the U.S. government to have directed as much as $3 billion to the Al-Qaeda cause over the years. Al-Qadi also owned a number of businesses, not the least being Ptech Inc., a high-flying, fast-growing computer software company in the Boston suburb of Quincy. Ptech had numerous contracts with U.S. government agencies, including the Army, the FBI, and the White House. Ptech specialized in enterprise architecture, which encompasses the design and layout for the computer networks and computer systems that are going to be used by an organization.

The second person of interest was Ibrahim Afandi, owner of the Gang Ranch, near the interior British Columbia community of Clinton, south of Prince George. The ranch is the second largest in North America, and Afandi has lived there from time to time. Afandi was a director of the International Islamic Relief Organization, which was also cited as being an Al-Qaeda front. Each man denied he was involved in Al-Qaeda fundraising and al-Qadi was cleared of such charges in Switzerland but, as you shall eventually see, each may well have played an important role in this story.

The second event was the meeting between Abdullah Almalki and Maher Arar at Mango's Café. Arar later described the Mango Café meeting in an interview with CBC: "I used to see his brother at work, and sometimes at the mosque on Friday prayers, and so most of the time we talked business. And I told him I needed a printer cartridge for my printer, and he said, 'My brother knows a salesman at Future Shop,' and so I remember I called his brother and I said, you know, 'Can we see each other? I want to go to Future Shop.' And he said, 'No problem.' And when we went there, we didn't find the salesman, so what we did, we went to a nearby fast-food restaurant, and then we had lunch, and then we headed back to the Future Shop. I bought the cartridge and I went back home."

Arar made no mention of what Almalki had said the meeting was about, that is, to find a doctor for Monia, who was in her second trimester.

From the outset, Arar was not a suspect, and not actively pursued, which is clear from the approach the police took. They learned about his education and all the jobs he had held. It took the police 18 days after the Mango's Café meeting to track down Arar's landlord for an interview. On October 30, an RCMP officer went to Minto Corporation and asked for a copy of Arar's lease. He didn't have a search warrant, but the Minto manager gave it to him anyway. On the 1997 lease, Almalki was listed as a witness and as the emergency contact for Arar. That same day, Cpl. Buffam sent a note to U.S. Customs about Arar, and was surprised to learn that "he was already known to them." Constable Lang also sent a note to U.S. Customs about Arar, Mazigh, and others, to have their names entered as "lookouts" in the U.S. Treasury Enforcement Communications System, which is used by U.S. federal authorities to monitor cross-border traffic. Lang's note described the named persons as a "group of Islamic Extremist individuals suspected of being linked to the Al-Qa'ida terrorist movement." Based on what little the Mounties knew, it was a poor choice of words.

The fact that U.S. authorities already seemed to know about Arar fuelled suspicions in Canada, but not enough to make the Mounties increase their concerns about Arar. Over the next few weeks, the Mounties kept digging. They learned that Arar had applied for a gun permit in 1992, but had never bought a gun. They found nothing exceptional in Arar's financial records or those of his wife. The Mounties assigned an officer to dig into Arar's work history. A big question in the minds of the police was why Arar had left his last job with The MathWorks Inc. in Boston around the time of the September 11 attacks, the point of origin of two of the hijackings. Arar was likely returning home to be closer to his growing family, but in his own description later, he only said that he left The MathWorks in 2001 to set up his own consulting business at home, but has never explained exactly when. The exact date and the circumstances of his departure from Boston were the kinds of things that naturally piqued the curiosity of the police.

The Mounties also sought Arar and Mazigh's travel records, and requested that they and their vehicles be placed on a border watch on both sides of the border. Curiously, Arar was still not believed to be a priority risk, so little so that over the next ten months he would travel back and forth across the U.S. border on at least three separate occasions. On one visit his work visa was even renewed. Twice Arar re-entered Canada without having been pulled over at Customs for a secondary search, which customs officials later attributed to "human error."

Ahmad El Maati, meanwhile, left Canada on November 11 for his arranged marriage in Syria. Abdullah Almalki and his family slipped out of the country two weeks later to visit his ailing wife's ailing mother in Malaysia. The police had no way of knowing whether their stories were true or not. No one was talking. The police suspected they were just trying to get away from the heat of the obvious investigation.

In Ottawa, the Mounties were determined to enlist Arar as a possible witness, but were reluctant to approach him through his lawyer, Michael Edelson. Edelson argued that he was on a list of three lawyers recommended to the Muslim community in Ottawa and had been chosen by chance. This might have blurred the issue for some, but not for the police. Then there was the letter from Edelson to the RCMP described in the previous chapter. Edelson described the letter as containing a normal, unremarkable set of conditions: no videotaping; nothing Arar said could be used against him or anyone else, Arar could edit the transcript of an audio tape; Edelson could refuse any question; and Arar could leave at any time.

The police, naturally, took a different view. The fact that Arar had chosen the same lawyer as Abdullah Almalki and others in the community was viewed by the police as suspicious. If Arar was innocent, why did he need a lawyer? The RCMP wasn't creating the cat and mouse game atmosphere, Arar was. While Arar said he wanted to talk and wanted to help, the restrictions on the interview, including the fact that nothing Arar said could ever be used in any court case, anywhere, effectively rendered any interview useless. In fact, an interview conducted under such circumstances would only serve to reveal what the police knew or were thinking of doing, which the Mounties were not eager to reveal.

The RCMP, incorrectly, twice informed U.S. authorities that Arar had refused to be interviewed when, in fact, he had agreed to be interviewed but with extremely strict restrictions.

Throughout spring 2002, Arar quietly went about his business but he was no longer travelling as he had always done. He completed an article, "A Modified Constant Modulus Algorithm Enters the Scene," for a technical magazine called *Wireless Systems Design*. It was about wireless modems handling signal distortion and would be published in April 2003.

In June of that same year, recall that Mazigh flew to Tunisia. Over the next few weeks, police were alerted to what seemed to be odd behaviour in Arar. Arar cleaned out his house, put his family's belongings in storage, and in July flew to Tunisia, but took a convoluted route through Montréal, New York, and Zurich. To the police it appeared that he wouldn't be coming back, and they wondered if he had taken off, just as Ahmed El Maati and Abdullah Almalki had earlier.

In later explanations of why the family went to Tunisia, Arar offered different reasons on different occasions. At one point he said that they went to visit Mazigh's ailing father, while Mazigh's mother stayed in Ottawa. To the police, it looked like a lot of old people in faraway places were starting to get sick. Later, Arar described the visit as a family vacation. He also said he was looking for work in Tunisia, which apparently he couldn't find. Then, Arar says, The MathWorks called him in August with the news that it might have work for him with a prospective client.

More than three months later—when he passed through New York—he was detained by U.S. authorities and renditioned to Syria. American authorities kept the RCMP in the dark about their intentions with Arar until he had been shipped out of the United States. The RCMP and, apparently, the Canadian government had no idea in those first few days about what had happened to him.

☩ ☩ ☩

When Prime Minister Paul Martin created the O'Connor Commission to look into the politically charged Arar case, the RCMP, from Commissioner Zaccardelli down to the members of Project A-O Canada, believed it had little to fear because its members had done nothing seriously wrong. They might have made a few mistakes here and there, which they had, but nothing crucial.

"We did the best we could in the time that we had," said former RCMP Superintendent Garry Clement, who had run the early stages of the investigation, in an interview. "We had good investigators and we did a clean investigation. If I had to do it all over again, there wasn't much that I would change."

Zaccardelli, too, wasn't all that concerned about the RCMP's culpability. On February 13, 2004, he broadcast a message to all RCMP members, trying to steady the ship.

I am writing you today on the issue of increased attention that our organization has received lately in both the media and in the public domain. Much of this attention has been critical of our actions on a number of fronts. The public enquiries announced to review the role of Canadian officials in the detention and deportation of Mr. Maher Arar and the Government of Canada's sponsorship program, as well as the execution of search warrants on the media have, and continue to be, trying issues for the RCMP.

Many of you have either told me personally, or have spoken to your colleagues about the effect that these reports are having on morale. These are difficult files in a demanding environment, but I have confidence and great pride in the capacity of the men and women of the RCMP to meet these challenges with the professionalism and integrity that we bring to all our activities.

I want to assure you we are making every effort to dispel misconceptions about the RCMP and its actions. Our involvement in these issues will carry on for some time, and we can expect more scrutiny and criticism of our actions during the months to come. In the end, our story will be told.

I want to remind you that we have been through trying times in the past, and throughout those difficult periods, our values have sustained us. We, employees of the RCMP, have always lived up to them: integrity, honesty, professionalism, compassion, respect and accountability. Remember them, and continue to use them well as we serve Canadians and their communities.

Remember, too, that because our organization values its integrity, the RCMP has always been, and will always continue to be, accountable for its actions. I have committed that the RCMP will cooperate fully with both inquiries.

In the meantime, I encourage you to stay the course and remain focused on your work. Our duty is to uphold the law and keep citizens and their communities safe and secure. Canadians are counting on us to do just that.

If there was one thing that the RCMP could hope for, it was that the O'Connor Commission would pay some heed to Bill C-36, Canada's Anti-Terrorism Act, which had become law on December 24, 2001. The new law made it easier for Canadian authorities to use electronic surveillance against a charity or religious group suspected of financing terrorists or to uncover a potential sleeper cell. "This includes eliminating the need to demonstrate that electronic surveillance is a last resort in the investigation of terrorists," the law read. The Criminal Code was amended to create a "preventive arrest" power to impose conditions of release, where appropriate, on suspected terrorists. "This will prevent terrorist activity and protect the lives of Canadians." There were many provisions in the new law, which directly addressed perceived civil liberties infractions faced by the police in dealing with the El Maati, Almalki, and Arar cases. Most important, the law compelled individuals with suspected terrorist links to testify under oath or face jail. They could no longer hide behind a lawyer. The problem with the new law was that it wasn't retroactive to the previous 11 weeks.

The RCMP went on to conduct its own self-examination. On September 25, 2004, the results of the internal RCMP investigation by RCMP Chief Superintendent Brian Garvie were published. The heavily censored public version found that the RCMP had given American authorities information that should have been covered by caveats, that is, information that couldn't be used by the Americans without Canadian approval. The Mounties, of course, had been led to believe from the outset of the investigations that "caveats were down," meaning that information would be freely exchanged. It seems that no one had contemplated what would have happened to "an innocent" who happened to be caught up in the investigation. Garvie also found that Richard Roy, the RCMP liaison officer with the Department of Foreign Affairs, might have known of the plan to remove Arar to Syria but did not contact his supervisors. And Garvie noted that Deputy RCMP Commissioner Garry Loeppky tried to convince the government of the day not to say that the RCMP "had no evidence Arar was involved in terrorist activities." The RCMP still considered Arar "a person of interest." In other words, there was something fishy about him, but they could just not put their finger on it.

The Garvie report didn't go far enough for Arar, who publicly stated after reading it that he wanted to dig deeper into what the RCMP had done.

Whatever hopes the RCMP had for redemption in the O'Connor Commission died at the opening gavel. The O'Connor Commission was not interested in Arar's past, his actions, or anything the RCMP knew. The commission was not empowered to prove whether Arar had been to Pakistan or Afghanistan. The overriding presumption of the commission was that the RCMP had wrongfully sent erroneous information about Arar to U.S. authorities, who used that information to arrest him and have him sent to Syria where he was tortured. Justice O'Connor's job was simply to "prove" that Arar was tortured and to recommend remuneration for him and ways to fix the RCMP's approach to national security investigations.

Arar's lead lawyer, Marlys Edwardh, demanded that everything the government knew, even matters subject to national security confidentiality, be disclosed in the public hearings. To clear Arar's name, his lawyers' plan was to find out the entire workings of Canada's approach to counter-terrorism investigations. They were rebuffed on that one. But Justice O'Connor threw them a big bone—he decided that Arar would not have to testify until the end of the proceedings, until Arar had been made aware of all the facts. In many respects, the public policy train pulled out of the station and headed down the tracks with Arar as its engineer, his lawyers the conductors, and everyone else—the politicians, the media, and the public— along for the smooth, predictable ride to the inevitable collision with the Royal Canadian Mounted Police.

In place of Arar having to testify for himself, a neutral fact-finder, Pro-fessor Stephen J. Toope, was asked to determine whether Arar had been tor-tured. Toope's mandate was precise: "To investigate and report to the Commission on Mr. Maher Arar's treatment during his detention in Jordan and Syria and its effects upon him and his family."

Toope had glowing credentials. From 1994 to 1999, he had been the youngest dean of Law in the history of the McGill University Law School. He had also served as president of the Pierre Elliott Trudeau Foundation, which had an initial endowment of $125 million. Toope began his investigation with a review of public written materials, nine in all, including earlier testimony before the O'Connor Commission and articles about Syrian prisons and tor-ture. Seven of the reviewed articles related to human rights around the world, and had been published by the Canadian and U.S. governments, the United Nations, Amnesty International, and the Syrian Human Rights Committee.

Toope conducted ten interviews, none of them under oath, unusual for a public inquiry of such importance and magnitude. He talked to Arar, Ahmad El Maati, Abdullah Almalki, and one other man, Muayyed Nureddin, about their experiences in Far Falestin prison. Nureddin, a Canadian citi-zen, was a computer programmer analyst, who had been a principal of the Salaheddin Islamic School in Scarborough from 2001 to June 2003. CSIS approached him first in 1999 seeking information about his contacts. In 2003, he travelled with his brother to Germany and from there, they drove to Syria. Over the next few months Nureddin made a number of trips in and out of Syria before being arrested by Syrian police, placed in their prison, and tortured, based on information from the United States and Canada. El Maati, Almalki, and Nureddin had all since been released from Syria and had returned to Canada. Also interviewed was Monia Mazigh. Each told Toope their personal stories as part of a conversation. Toope did not ask any tough questions.

Dr. Doug Gruner, a family physician in Ottawa who worked in hospital emergency rooms in Smiths Falls and Alexandria, Ontario, was described by Toope as having "experience with post-traumatic stress." Gruner, who had been in practice "roughly a decade," had worked in Malawi and Tanzania and was with the International Red Cross in East Timor in 2000. Gruner had been recommended to Arar and one of the other "victims" by Amnesty International. "Gruner told me that the symptoms displayed by Mr. Arar, physically and psychologically, were completely consistent with the story Mr. Arar told of his confinement and torture," Toope wrote. Again, there was no cross-examination.

Dr. Marta Young, a clinical psychologist and tenured professor at the University of Ottawa, was also recommended to Arar by Amnesty International. Young told Toope she saw Arar for "approximately 12 visits" and found that Arar was "a straight, honest person.... He is not making things up." Toope added: "The story is simply too congruent with her own experience and with the literature on torture victims for that to be at all likely."

Toope did not refer to any comments made by the other three "experts" listed in his report. One was Kerry Pither, who had worked on the Arar case and served as the family's spokesperson. Pither had also acted as a spokesperson for the East Timor Action Network. For Toope's purposes, she was a spokesperson for The Committee of Organizations with Standing at the Arar Commission.

Another person Toope interviewed was Alex Neve, secretary general of Amnesty International in Canada. The final person interviewed was Riad Salojee, executive director of the Canadian Council on American–Islamic Relations.

What did those three people have to contribute? No one knows, but Toope wrote:

"In finding facts concerning Mr. Arar's experiences in Syria, I must conclude as to the credibility of his testimony, which was not taken under oath," Toope reported to the Commission. "Given the very nature of detention and interrogation, much of the detail concerning what happened to Mr. Arar in Syria cannot be verified by eyewitness observers. None of the jailers or interrogators was available for me to interview. To assess credibility, I have obviously had to judge the person sitting before me and telling me his story. I have listened to Mr. Arar attentively and watched him closely. I have tried to compare his demeanour and his reactions to the scores of other torture victims and detainees I have interviewed on human rights monitoring missions in numerous countries, and in testimony before me at the United Nations Working Group on Enforced or Involuntary Disappearances where torture victims have also appeared. I have also undertaken a careful comparison of public sources about detention conditions and interrogation practices in Syria and the testimony before me.

"Finally, I have cross-referenced the detailed descriptions provided to me by the four men I interviewed who discussed their detention and treatment in Far Falestin. In undertaking that cross-referencing, I have also implicitly had to assess the credibility of the descriptions offered by Messrs. Almalki, El Maati and Nureddin. To do this, I have repeated the same practices used to judge the reliability of Mr. Arar.

"I must emphasise that in assessing credibility, I am limiting myself to the parameters of my mandate: I am judging only whether or not the stories told to me concerning the conditions of detention in Syria and the practices of Syrian security services are believable and likely to be true. Within these parameters, I am confident in concluding that the descriptions offered by Messrs. Almalki, El Maati, and Nureddin were convincing."

Convincing? Toope painted a picture of Arar as a successful communications engineer who had been reduced to a broken and broke man, with family problems, who was ostracized by the local Muslim community, which was likely true. Arar himself said some people were suspicious of him, while others resented the fact that he allowed his wife to use her maiden name, which was a sign that Arar was not a good Sunni.

That the four men had in some way been tortured seemed not to be in doubt, but Toope could not say conclusively for how long and how badly.

All Arar's witnesses were linked to human rights movements and none were compelled to testify under oath. Nevertheless, the Toope report was entered into evidence and adopted. Toope went on to become the president and vice-chancellor of the University of British Columbia.

The impression left by the Toope report was that Arar had been tortured for a year to beat information out of him which could be used by the Canadians. While the Canadians did pass on questions to the oddly helpful Syrians, Arar himself would say that the Syrians were concerned about the fact that he had avoided military service and that his mother's cousin was a member of the outlawed Muslim Brotherhood.

On his website, Arar described six days of torture. Speaking in the third person, he grouped the events into two five-day periods.

October 11 to 16

Early the next morning Arar is taken upstairs for intense interrogation. He is beaten on his palms, wrists, lower back and hips with a shredded black electrical cable which is about two inches in diameter. He is threatened with the metal chair, electric shocks, and with the tire, into which prisoners are stuffed, immobilized and beaten.

The next day Arar is interrogated and beaten on and off for eighteen hours. Arar begs them to stop. He is asked if he received military training in Afghanistan, and he falsely confesses and says yes. This is the first time Arar is ever questioned about Afghanistan. They ask at which camp, and provide him with a list, and he picks one of the camps listed.

Arar urinated on himself twice during the interrogation.

Throughout this period of intense interrogation Arar was not taken back to his cell, but to a waiting room where he could hear other prisoners being tortured and screaming. One time, he heard them repeatedly slam a man's head on a desk really hard.

October 17 to 22, 2002

During the second week of the interrogation, Arar is forced into a car tire so he is immobilized. This was used to scare him, but he is not beaten while in the tire, as with other prisoners.

The intensity of the beating and interrogation subsides after October 17. Interrogators start using a new tactic, taking Arar into a room blindfolded so he can hear people talking about him, saying, "He knows lots of people who are terrorists," "We will get their numbers," "He is a liar," "He has been out of the country." They occasionally slap him on the face.

During his 359 days in Syria, it may well have been that while Arar was to some degree "tortured," it could also be argued that he likely got off lightly, considering how the Syrian justice system works. No one knows what really happened, but some people familiar with the Syrian prison system said they were anything but convinced by Arar's story. One of them is George Samuel, the *nom de plume* of a former Syrian soldier now living in Canada, who is a successful businessman. Samuel asked for anonymity out of fear of possible reprisals against himself and his extended family in Syria.

Samuel said in an interview that he has studied the Arar story and had been in the audience in Ottawa when Arar gave a speech after he had returned to Canada. He said that there are many things about the Arar story and the way he tells it that he found bothersome.

"In Syria, the Arar family name is well-known. It is linked to two places in Syria, Hamah and Aleppo," Samuel said. "The family's name is strongly associated with the Muslim Brotherhood."

That is not meant to suggest in any way that Arar was a member of the Muslim Brotherhood, but in the larger context of what occurred, it might prove to be an important clue to the true story.

When he was in Syria, George Samuel said he knew people who had been tortured in the Palestine Branch prison and was familiar with the techniques used.

"First, it is impossible to find someone in that prison," Samuel said. "Once you enter, your name is changed and the guards don't know your real name so that you can't be easily found. The first day they tell you this: 'You will tell us everything you know in the next 24 hours.' It is brutal. If a man survives, even after only one day he cannot be recognized by his family. It is that bad. Arar said that he was slapped on the wrists with a belt or something, and across the face a couple of times for a few days. That's not Syrian torture. I do not believe he was tortured. It is very strange to me what happened to him."

Samuel found it suspicious that the Syrians did not take issue with Arar for avoiding mandatory military service. "If that were the case, the punishment is to be sent to a city called Palmyra, where one is required to do hard labour. I'm sorry, it doesn't add up to me."

Another torture expert skeptical of Arar's testimony was Brian McAdam, a longtime Canadian immigration and control officer, who has spent more than three decades in the public service dealing with refugees and torture victims. "Every torture victim I had ever met did the same thing," McAdam said. "He or she would willingly take off their clothes and show me what had happened to them. Even if there are no visible signs, there is technology which can show underlying damage, which could substantiate a story. Arar said he was beaten and tortured, if only on the arms, but he would not even roll up his shirt sleeves for an examination. We just had to take his word for it. His behaviour was contrary to what I would expect in the circumstances."

No one knew what the Syrians really asked Arar or what he had told them. No one knew why the Syrians seemed to have treated Arar with relative deference. Arar's version of events was accepted at face value.

Throughout all his trials and tribulations, little of consequence was revealed about Arar's past or his family's history in Syria. His life remains a mystery.

In interviews, Arar never got into details. The *Toronto Star*'s Michelle Shephard published a story on May 1, 2004, describing Arar as "an intensely private man. Arar says that going public with his story has been incredibly difficult. . . . In his Ottawa living room, Arar looks wistfully at photos of his old Damascus neighbourhood shown to him by a reporter, and talks of a land he fears he may never set eyes on again."

In his bestselling 2006 book *Ghost Plane*, British author Stephen Grey described Arar, at one stage of his life, as being: "soccer obsessed, playing striker in a semiprofessional team." Grey described Arar as being a person with few hobbies or a large circle of friends, bent upon starting his own business and making a lot of money. If anything, Grey reported, Arar came off as a nerd who described himself as "a bit of a computer freak. . . . I suppose my idea of a good read was some business or electronics magazine." Of the article Arar published in 2003 in *Wireless Systems Design*, Grey wrote: "It is full of complicated jargon, meaningless to all but experts like him. It ended with this: 'Simulation results using 16QAM modulation prove that in the presence of light-to-moderate channel distortions, the new algorithm— known as baptized AMA—converges faster than CMA'. . . . You get the picture. It was technology, not radical jihad, that filled Maher's head."

When Arar spoke to reporters, he was never challenged. The published stories ooze with sympathy for him—an idyllic moment as a child in Damascus, the lost glory of his soccer-playing days, or an example of his intellect. There is never any detail about his life. His own online biography begins with his arrival at Kennedy Airport, his rendition, and his great fight against the RCMP and governments for the wrongs committed against him and his family.

After the issue of Arar's torture was settled by the O'Connor Commission, the next big matter to be resolved was whether the RCMP deliberately committed wrongdoings and had him sent to Syria.

During the commission hearings, much was made of the fact that Cpl. Buffam showed up at Monia Mazigh's door at 7:30 a.m., and that the RCMP was not being sensitive to Islamic traditions. This was not so. Buffam was trained in Islamic formalities and Mazigh never complained about his behaviour at the time. She was, in fact, cordial to the Mountie. On a couple of occasions, the RCMP, based on the available evidence at the time, overstated their case, calling Arar and the others "extremists," linking them conclusively to Al-Qaeda and so on. The overriding impression left in the media by the commission hearings was that the RCMP was not competent in investigating terrorism, that investigators were not properly supervised, and that the constitutional rights of innocent Canadians had been willfully and tragically violated. The RCMP has considerable faults and weaknesses, as you shall eventually learn, but the Arar investigation should not be considered one of them.

As one ploughs through the analysis and recommendations in Justice O'Connor's report, however, this is what leaps out:

"I am satisfied that, based on the information available to them, the Project members had reasonable grounds to conduct surveillance of this meeting [Mango's Café]. This was a routine and proper investigative step and was not the result of racial profiling," O'Connor wrote on page 18, adding:

"I conclude that there was nothing improper in Project A-O Canada obtaining these documents [Minto rental agreement] without a warrant."

On the next page: "I am satisfied that Project A-O Canada had sufficient reason at the time to request a lookout for Mr. Arar."

On page 22, O'Connor said he strongly endorsed the importance of information sharing with all the agencies involved, including U.S. authorities, adding, on page 27: "I conclude that Project A-O Canada did not act improperly in sending the questions [to U.S. authorities]." Further, he said:

"I am satisfied that it was appropriate for the RCMP to respond to the questions [that had been faxed by a U.S. agency]."

A major issue raised by Arar's legal team was that the RCMP knew or ought to have known that Arar would be sent to Syria. O'Connor wrote:

"I accept Corporal Flewelling's evidence that it did not occur to him that the American authorities were considering Syria as an option. He believed that Arar would be returned to Zurich or be sent to Canada. I am satisfied that the RCMP was not informed of the possibility of Syria as a destination until at least October 7. . . . I have thoroughly reviewed all the evidence relating to events both before and during Mr. Arar's detention in New York and there is no evidence that any Canadian authorities—the RCMP, CSIS, or others—were complicit in those decisions."

Arar's supporters argued that the RCMP should have notified the Department of Foreign Affairs and International Relations before passing information about Arar to U.S. authorities. O'Connor found that there was no such requirement.

Arar's supporters said the RCMP was biased and sloppy. O'Connor concluded otherwise: "The investigation was comprehensive and thorough, and involved co-operation with American agencies. . . . the remainder of the team [Project A-O Canada], which grew to include about twenty members, also had an impressive range of experience and skills. . . . I do not attribute bad faith to members of Project A-O Canada. They were dedicated officers who did their jobs in what they considered was an appropriate manner."

O'Connor reiterated this conclusion on page 78:

"There is nothing in the evidence to suggest that the decision was motivated by the fact that Messrs. Almalki and Arar were Muslims or of Arab origin, or that the surveillance was the result of racial profiling."

On the next page, O'Connor returned to the rental agreement:

"The fact that evidence might eventually be found to be inadmissible does not necessarily mean that the police officers acted improperly in obtaining it."

On page 81, O'Connor noted that:

"The RCMP did not request a search of Mr. Arar's person. The lookout that was issued indicated only an examination of his travel and business-related or commercial documents," adding: "Nonetheless, I am satisfied that Project A-O Canada had sufficient reason at the time to request the lookout for Mr. Arar."

Over and over again, O'Connor stated that in the substantive issues being discussed, the RCMP did not consciously do anything wrong. When it came to information sharing, he wrote on page 104:

"All in all, the RCMP has very sensible policies that require a thorough vetting of information before it is provided to other agencies. These policies do not in any way diminish the importance of information sharing. Rather, they help ensure that information is shared for appropriate uses only, that recipients are not misled about the reliability or accuracy of information, and that personal information is properly protected."

Returning to the question of Arar not being a suspect, but only a person of interest, O'Connor wrote on page 113:

"Even though Mr. Arar was only a person of interest in the investigation, I am of the view that it was appropriate for Project A-O Canada to share information about him with the U.S. agencies. The agencies were cooperating in the investigation, and information sharing was vital. Project A-O Canada was properly interested in Mr. Arar, and it was important that it investigate his connections to Almalki and others. There is nothing wrong with sharing information about a person of interest."

One of the most contentious issues in the Arar case was that all the information gathering in Canada about him, El Maati, Almalki, and others was shared with CSIS and U.S. agencies. O'Connor found this reasonable under the circumstances: "In light of the resources required to analyze this material, Project A-O Canada decided to share the seized information with CSIS and the American agencies, as a way of enlisting their help. I believe this was a reasonable decision. It was imperative that the information be analyzed and, given the continuing concern about terrorist attacks, that this be done as quickly as possible, but the RCMP lacked sufficient resources to undertake this enormous task."

O'Connor stated conclusively on page 156:

"There is no evidence to suggest that any members of the RCMP participated or acquiesced in the American decision to remove Mr. Arar to Syria."

In fact, if any organization knew what was really going on, it was CSIS. On October 10, 2002, Jack Hooper, at the time deputy director in charge of CSIS operations and second-in-command at the spy agency, had issued a memorandum with his thoughts on Arar's situation as he was being whisked off to Jordan and then Syria. "I think the U.S. would like to get Arar to Jordan where they can have their way with him," Hooper wrote.

We could go on, but the point seems obvious. O'Connor was convinced that the RCMP did not deliberately or knowingly have any involvement in the U.S. decision to ship Arar to Syria. O'Connor was not even sure if the Americans had used the information the Canadians sent to them, or had relied upon their own information before taking their actions against Arar. One might think that would be the end of it, but not so. Once again, the RCMP seemed to have dodged a bullet. It hadn't.

[7]

THE CROWNING OF AN
INFLUENTIAL MAN

On September 18, 2006, after 127 days of public and closed-door hearings, Justice Dennis O'Connor tabled his report, stating: "I am able to say categorically that there is no evidence to indicate that Mr. Arar has committed an offence or that his activities constitute a threat to the security of Canada."

Interestingly, in reaching his conclusions, O'Connor had never been briefed on a key piece of the puzzle: the entire RCMP slideshow which depicted all the links the police found between the various suspects and Arar. Instead, O'Connor had reviewed an edited version of the RCMP evidence, which contained about ten percent or less of the information. That the O'Connor Commission was not interested in all the information gathered by the RCMP was seen by some Mounties as a portent of what he would eventually "categorically" conclude.

Now all O'Connor's earlier compliments for the RCMP were transformed into brickbats. The government had indicated to the RCMP that, due to the dangerous circumstances that existed during the fall of 2001, the force should charge ahead and the law would catch up with them. The Anti-Terrorism Law, which came into effect on December 24, 2001, would have covered many of the situations in which the Mounties found themselves trapped, but O'Connor would have none of that. He found that the RCMP fuelled American suspicions about Arar by passing on details of their investigation to the Americans. He said that the RCMP wrongly described Arar in various communications as "a suspect," "principal subject," or "important figure." He said Arar was tainted in the Americans' eyes because the

RCMP told them that Abdullah Almalki was Arar's emergency contact on the Minto lease, that Arar had applied for a gun permit in 1992, and that he might have been the president of The MathWorks, which he was not.

During the January 22, 2002 raids on the Almalki brothers' houses, Youssef Almalki told the police that he was "not sure" if his brother had a business arrangement with Arar. The RCMP told the Americans that Arar did have a business relationship with Abdullah Almalki but that they did not know the details.

A RCMP situation report of the Mango Café meeting stated that Arar had travelled from Québec for the meeting, which was not true, although Gatineau, Québec is part of the local bus route in Ottawa and its environs.

And then there was that single failed attempt by the RCMP to interview Arar and the way it was construed to the Americans: that Arar refused to be interviewed, when, in fact, he had—but with restrictions.

O'Connor had harsh words for the RCMP: "The Commissioner also found that both before and after Mr. Arar's detention in the U.S. the RCMP provided American authorities with information about Arar which was inaccurate, portrayed him in an unfair fashion and overstated his importance to the investigation. Some of this inaccurate information had the potential to create serious consequences for Mr. Arar in light of American attitudes and practices at the time."

One important thing that O'Connor mused about was an everyday Canadian reality—the RCMP investigating itself. After Arar was released, the RCMP was asked to write a timeline about the investigation, which it did. The timeline, however, omitted potentially damaging disclosures about what it had actually done in giving information to U.S. authorities, like handing over its entire computerized SuperText file. O'Connor said: "Since the RCMP had in effect been asked to report on itself, there was a heightened obligation for it to be complete and forthcoming."

No sooner had O'Connor spoken than the government announced, on December 12, 2006, the formation of an internal inquiry, this one led by former Supreme Court Justice Frank Iacobucci, whose job would be to hold hearings into the cases of Ahmad El Maati, Abdullah Almalki, and Muayyed Nureddin. Following in Arar's footsteps, they were suing the government. Unlike the O'Connor Commission, this hearing would be held entirely in camera for national security reasons. There would be no witnesses or cross-examination, just a review of the documentary evidence. Neither El Maati,

Almalki, and Nureddin, nor their lawyers were allowed to attend the hearings. They weren't being treated like Arar had been treated, and with good reason, which we will soon get to.

As had been the case in the McDonald Commission in 1981, the Mounties had been vilified after becoming entangled in a nest of spies. No one was willing to stand up and defend them, except for one of the original RCMP investigators, Garry Clement. In the initial stages of the investigation, then-Inspector Clement had been charged with picking the personnel for the operation and running the investigation. He was subsequently promoted to superintendent, and assigned elsewhere, much to his chagrin, but that was the RCMP way of doing things. Shortly afterward, Clement left the RCMP to become the police chief in Cobourg, Ontario, a small city on Lake Ontario, about an hour's drive east of Toronto.

Clement could not take the bashing handed out by the O'Connor Commission. He thought it was not only unfair but distorted. He was so angry that no one was defending the RCMP that he went to the media with his observations. "It was not a fishing expedition," Clement told the *Toronto Star*. "What has to be underscored is that the investigation was not directed at Mr. Arar. He became a person of interest through his own actions."

In what he later described as a town hall-like speech, Clement continued with his assessment: "I want the public to know that at no time did the investigators mislead our American counterparts causing them to take action they would not have done on their own volition. I can state with confidence that we ensured all of our documents leading to search warrants etc. were legally scrutinized and met a very high standard. In any investigation involving thousands of pieces of paper, armchair quarterbacks can always find human error."

On September 20, 2006, two days after O'Connor's report came down, the House of Commons issued a unanimous apology to Arar.

On January 26, 2007, Prime Minister Harper issued a formal apology to Arar and his family. Eleven days later he announced a settlement of $10.5 million with an additional $2 million for his team of lawyers, led by Marlys Edwardh and Lorne Waldman. The inquiry cost Canadian taxpayers another $16 million. Arar and his family received $10.5 million tax-free for their pain and suffering, and none had to testify under oath. Harper also sent letters to the United States and Syrian governments to protest Arar's treatment. It was a touching ending to a story that outraged many Canadians, a humble immigrant who stood up to the greatest power in the world, and beat them. "I have cleared my name," Arar said.

The Arar settlement struck a few people as unusual. One of them was Thomas Rose, a senior producer at the CBC, who also taught law at Sir Wilfrid Laurier University and the University of Western Ontario. "There is something terribly wrong with simply giving Maher Arar $11.5 million [the original estimate for legal fees was $1 million]," Rose wrote in a published opinion piece. "It's not that he doesn't deserve compensation for the suffering and misery he and his family have had to endure. It's not even the amount Prime Minister Stephen Harper and his actuaries came up with. It's the way the payment is being made.

Few doubt anymore that Maher Arar was the victim of indifferent, overzealous and unethical actions of government officials and intelligence agents in at least three states: Canada, the United States and Syria. In this respect, the prime minister's apology is long overdue," Rose continued. "But a payment is being made for a grievous wrongdoing without Canadians ever having received answers to some fundamental questions that go to the heart of what our democracy is all about. Why did Canadian officials, for example, actively work to destroy the reputation of a man Justice Dennis O'Connor has determined committed no offence?"

Rose's intuition told him something was not right, but he could not put his finger on it. "When the prime minister announced the compensation package to Arar this past week, he was very careful with what he said about the deal. In a letter to Arar, Harper apologizes to him, his wife and his family. But what is he apologizing for? As the letter states, the prime minister is apologizing on behalf of all Canadians for any role Canadian officials may have played in his terrible ordeal.... Canadians deserve more. To quote Baron Gordon Hewart, Lord Chief Justice of England, 'It is not merely of some importance but is of fundamental importance, that justice should not only be done, but should manifestly and undoubtedly be seen to be done.'

The Arar settlement of $10.5 million in compensation, as well as legal fees, seems out of proportion with Canadian practices. In July 2008, for instance, Stephen Truscott was awarded $6.5 million in compensation when his conviction for murder was overturned. At the age of 14, Truscott was convicted and sentenced to death for the 1959 murder of Lynn Harper near

Clinton, Ontario. He spent four months on death row before the age of 16 and was eventually paroled in 1969 at age 24. He was forced to live under an assumed name his entire life until the Ontario Court of Appeal threw out his conviction in August 2007. His settlement, minus legal fees, works out to a little more than $100,000 a year for each spent in prison for a crime he did not commit. In the so-called "tainted blood" scandal, thousands of Canadians were infected with life-threatening hepatitis C through the negligence of the Canadian Red Cross. The average victim received about $109,000 in compensation.

Around the world, meanwhile, the O'Connor Commission was lauded for its transparency, and labelled as a shining example of how other countries should deal with similar situations. "Of all the countries to have launched investigations into rendition scandals, only Canada has made a real effort to put right the wrong done to the victim—and in a way that does not endanger its legitimate national-security interests," wrote Swiss parliamentarian Dick Marty in *The Globe and Mail*. Marty went on to quote Arar himself about why accountability is so important: "Accountability is not about seeking revenge; it is about making our institutions better and a model for the rest of the world. Accountability goes to the heart of our democracy. It is a fundamental pillar that distinguishes our society from police states."

Arar and Mazigh became instant celebrities, rocketing from obscurity to the centre of polite society at warp speed. *Time* magazine named Arar one of the 100 most influential people in the world. Cartoonists used him as a symbol of morality. *The Toronto Star* called Monia Mazigh "the Laura Secord of our time," likening her to the Canadian heroine who, during the War of 1812, made a heroic journey to warn British troops of an impending American attack near Niagara Falls. Arar was named *The Globe and Mail*'s Nation Builder of the Year in 2006. In 2007, Arar returned the favour and nominated Justice Dennis O'Connor for the same award, but he did not win. Arar had instantly becoming Canada's unofficial Ambassador for Moderate Islam.

On February 14, 2007, Senator Marcel Prud'homme announced an "important event" that day, a reception in the Senate, "where all Canadian communities will express their friendship to the couple." Later that day, Prud'homme said, he, along with Members of Parliament Meili Faille, Omar Alghabr, Bill Casey, Stéphane Dion, Jack Layton, and Gilles Duceppe, would present the couple with the Charter of Human Rights to mark the establishment of the Arar–Mazigh Scholarship in Human Rights, a bursary for human rights studies at the University of Ottawa, which had been announced that day. Nipissing University later bestowed honorary doctorates on both Arar and Mazigh.

Arar was even invited to speak and participate at the Global Investigative Journalism Conference, held for the first time in Canada from May 24 to 27, 2007. There, he entertained journalists and documentary filmmakers from Canada and about 30 other countries. The conference, hosted by the Canadian Association of Journalists, was billed as an opportunity for journalists to, among other things, "dig deeper on current issues such as terrorism, government corruption and corporate crime." Arar escaped the gathering unscathed as the attendees fawned over him and never asked him a tough question. For them the story was complete. There was nothing more to say.

Some bloggers, however, like Flaggman's Canada, had read between the lines of official reports and media coverage and were expressing their skepticism by raising questions on the Internet. "Is Maher Arar a liar? *The Globe & Mail* and O'Connor Commission all but says it," Flaggman wrote in the autumn of 2007.

The U.S. government, however, would not budge on its assessment of Arar. He was still barred from that country, and the U.S. has repeatedly made it clear that it has no intention of apologizing to him.

The last chance for a relatively transparent airing of what had happened to Maher Arar ended with a terse release from the O'Connor Commission on September 6, 2007. It read:

> The Commission of Inquiry into the Actions of Canadian Officials in Relation to Maher Arar, headed by Mr. Justice Dennis O'Connor, will not be calling Mr. Arar as a witness. The Inquiry has now been notified by Counsel for Mr. Arar that he is not asking the Inquiry to reconvene a public hearing as there is no need for him to testify. Mr. Arar advised the Commissioner that he made his decision in light of the Inquiry's very full review and report on the conduct of Canadian Officials.
>
> In his ruling of May 9, 2005, Commissioner O'Connor decided that the decision whether to call Mr. Arar as a witness should be deferred until there had been made available to him the maximum amount of information relating to the matters about which he could testify. Delaying the decision did not adversely affect the progress of the Inquiry as the mandate was to investigate and report on the actions of Canadian Officials that related to Mr. Arar.

In the view of the Commissioner, Mr. Arar's evidence was not necessary in light of his mandate. However, Mr. Arar was given the right to apply to the Commissioner to testify after full disclosure was complete.

With the release of further information authorized by the Federal Court of Canada, Mr. Arar and the public do have the maximum amount of information which will be disclosed.

Therefore, the Commission is of the view that its mandate is now fulfilled and has so advised the Government of Canada.

The Arar case was closed even though the subject of the inquiry and investigations never answered a single question under oath. Canadian journalists and commentators, meanwhile, were surprisingly silent on this matter.

The reference in the press release to a federal court decision was to the one announced six weeks earlier, on July 26, 2007. The O'Connor Commission had put up a fight over the government's refusal to disclose all it knew about the Arar case, citing national security issues. Federal Court Justice Simon Noël ruled that the government only had to release a little of the information the commission was seeking, while the rest would remain secret, due to national security concerns.

Commission counsel Paul Cavalluzzo said: "The Commission is content with Justice Noël's decision because the more important information in dispute will now be disclosed. We will not initiate an appeal to the Federal Court of Appeal." Cavalluzzo added that the judgment was "the culmination of a long process in which the government has released a great deal of information which it initially resisted and which the Commission felt should be disclosed to the public." Cavalluzzo concluded: "in the Commission's view, the public interest would be adequately served if Justice Noël's decision is accepted by all parties."

Throughout the entire process, Arar, his family, his myriad supporters, the Government of Canada, and the O'Connor Commission had argued that they were all working together in an attempt to shed light on the matters at hand. The only truly transparent thing in the entire O'Connor Commission was its evisceration of the RCMP. Important questions about what really happened in Syria and what the Americans knew were allowed to linger. At the end of the day, all that collective energy to get to the bottom of the story didn't really accomplish that, which provided a huge disservice to Arar himself. Arar was found to be innocent, but the lasting impression is that he might only have been found innocent because the police did not have the time or ability to collect enough evidence against him.

Yes, the RCMP made some mistakes, but one can only wonder if the errors, such as they were, might have been avoided if Arar had openly talked to the police. In that respect, it could be reasonably argued that he appeared to be deceptive and was the author of his own misfortune. Or was he a man who might have protested a bit too much?

✛ ✛ ✛

Maher Arar had carefully marketed his image almost from the moment the police showed up at his door in January 2002. Back then, instead of answering questions from the police, which Canadians do every day, he invoked his constitutional and Charter rights and called a top criminal lawyer for advice. He never once answered a question under oath. Why?

Considering the way in which he had been vindicated and handsomely remunerated by the Government of Canada, one might surmise that Arar would think that it was his moral and ethical duty to testify for the benefit of his fellow Canadians. You would almost think he would feel compelled to roll up his sleeves and tell his entire story, and clear up the incongruities left hanging over his head. What was there to lose? In such an extraordinary situation, one might have thought that Canadians would welcome his candour. If Arar did have something to hide, he could even have testified under the provisions of the Canada Evidence Act, so that nothing he said could be used against him in a court of law.

Arar's personal website begins with his arrest in New York and his rendition to Syria, but nothing before that and not much afterward, either. His story does not begin in New York but years before it. But what is that story?

In an article, "Outsourcing Torture," in the *New Yorker* magazine in February 2005, the Arar story was recounted by writer Jane Mayer, but the story, as always, began at JFK airport and—as always—begins with his detention at JFK airport. All we learn about Arar is what Arar says happened to him in Syria. "Not even animals could withstand it," Arar said. "You just give up . . . you become like an animal." Mayer wrote: "When Arar described his experience in a phone interview recently, he invoked an Arabic expression. The pain was so unbearable, he said, that 'you forget the milk that you have been fed from the breast of your mother.'" As heart-wrenching as it might all sound to some, the Arar story began, at the very least, a year earlier, and even farther back in time. If he had nothing to hide, why does he appear to be hiding something? His recent life was no mystery, but there are so many questions left unanswered, and enough missing in his story, that it makes some skeptical about what really happened.

Every one of the over 33 million Canadians alive today contributed 38 cents to Arar's settlement. For my 38 cents, it would be fair to say that I would have liked to have had answers to so many things Arar did or didn't do.

What was his family's history in Syria? Had he ever been to Pakistan or Afghanistan? He says not, but not under oath. This information, which the police believed to be true, seemed important in the circumstances, and spurred on their investigation.

When Arar lived in Montréal, did he attend the militant Assuna Annabawiyah mosque? Did he know Ahmed Ressam, the Millennium Bomber, who was in Montréal at the same time? Why did he apply for a gun permit, but never buy a gun?

The O'Connor Commission stated that Arar worked at four companies after leaving university: CIM21000 Inc., Nex Link, Alcatel, and The Math-Works. Those facts are repeated over and over again in the media, but never probed. When and where did he work at these companies? What did he do at each? Why did he leave?

I would have liked to have known more about his time spent at The MathWorks in Boston. What does The MathWorks do? How much was he paid? Did the company subsidize his second house there? Why did Arar leave The MathWorks in Boston when he did in early September 2001, to start up a consulting business from his Ottawa home? Presumably it was to be closer to his growing family, but I'd like to know more.

If Arar was so successful at his work, what happened to his business after the police began to look at him as a person of interest?

Arar's wife, Monia Mazigh, has a doctorate degree in finance. She is obviously an intelligent woman. She was in her second trimester with her second child when Arar went looking for a referral to a doctor from Abdullah Almalki at Mango's Café. Wouldn't Mazigh have already had a doctor? If he was only looking for a doctor's name, why did he go for a walk in the rain with someone he claimed was merely an acquaintance? Arar said that they talked about business, but what business? Almalki's "business" was the target of the investigation. If Almalki was a religious elder in the Ottawa community, was Arar confiding in him or vice versa? What did they talk about for three hours?

Arar went to Tunisia in January 2002. Why? To visit his in-laws alone? Who does that? An ailing father-in-law was the same reason Almalki used to go to Malaysia, months earlier. Why did Arar pack up his belongings in Ottawa and head back to Tunisia in July 2002, a month after his wife and children had gone there? Why did his mother-in-law stay in Ottawa? Why did Arar say he was looking for work in Tunisia? Why Tunisia? Why did his wife and family stay in Tunisia for four months, from June to late September 2002. When Arar headed back to Canada on September 25, 2002, why did he leave his family behind? He said he returned to North America because The MathWorks said it might have work for him from a prospective client. It seemed like a long way to go for a rather flimsy offer.

What about all that money for Arar? Why did the government feel so compelled to rush to pay Arar $12.5 million. His story was vague and incomplete. What makes him more special than any other victim in Canada? The settlement was entirely out of proportion to typical Canadian legal settlements.

There are hundreds of questions like that for which we deserve answers, but Arar has refused to submit himself to interviews. Instead, he tells the same story over and over again. In March 2008, Toope even joined Arar and Mazigh at the University of Victoria in a panel discussion on civil liberties and national security. They said they were using the Arar case to provide lessons for the future, but what really happened in the past? When pressed by a journalist, Arar's first response is to introduce his lawyers or his public relations agent. He says he has been besieged by interview requests or is too busy to answer questions. Yet in the seventeen months since he received his government settlement, I could find not one published interview with him.

Likewise, Ahmad El Maati's and Abdullah Almalki's personalized web stories, while touching, portray some events in a disingenuous manner, while skipping others, which only makes skeptical observers wonder what they were really doing.

Then there is the Peter Worthington question: why would Syria torture these men? It is an important clue to solving the ultimate mystery. On the face of it, if the Syrians had their own motives, they might have agreed to help the Canadians, who seemed to be addressing similar problems, all of which, in the context of the times, served to make Syria look less threatening to the West. But Syria has shown little interest in playing kissy-face with the West.

For two and a half years, Justice O'Connor struggled to find, or, it can be argued, to miss, the whole story. In his final report, O'Connor couldn't help but wonder out loud to himself on a number of occasions that he wished he had access to Syrian and American files. That would have been helpful, he kept saying, but the Syrians and Americans wouldn't cooperate. As you shall see, the Canadian government had its own reasons for keeping it that way, even if it meant, once again, conspiring to trash the RCMP.

[8]

MY ATTEMPTS TO INTERVIEW MAHER ARAR

Maher Arar is a very difficult person to talk to openly. In my attempts to reach him I approached him through his website, where he entertained requests for interviews. All such requests were directed to his volunteer public relations contact, Richard Swain. The following is a log of our communications, which has been edited to eliminate personal telephone numbers and repetition.

Monday November 12, 2007

Mr. Arar:

Good morning, sir.

My name is Paul Palango. I am a freelance journalist, based in Nova Scotia, and the author of two books about the RCMP: *Above The Law* (1994) and *The Last Guardians* (1998). I am currently researching and writing a new book to be published in 2008 by Key Porter Books of Toronto.

Your story is one of the many that form the entire story about the RCMP over the past decade.

I have read all the open-source materials available about your case and have conducted a number of interviews, but still have many outstanding questions, which only you and your wife, Monia Mazigh, can answer. I believe these questions need to be answered before I can be fully confident that I have everything correct.

To that end I would like to interview you and your wife, preferably on separate occasions and with all due considerations. I would prefer to do this in the next few weeks and am prepared to come to Ottawa.

Can you please get back to me at your earliest convenience?

Thank you

Paul Palango
902-. . .-. . . .

(Automated reply)
Thank you for your interest in interviewing Mr. Arar.

Your request has been received.

November 20, 2007

Richard: I sent a request to you on Monday, November 12 requesting an interview with both Mr. Arar and his wife, Monia Mazigh, for a book I am currently writing. I did not receive a reply, could you please get in touch with me as soon as possible. . . .

The original request follows . . .:

Thank you

Paul Palango
902-. . .-. . . .

(Automated reply)
Thank you for your interest in interviewing Mr. Arar.

Your request has been received.

Thursday November 29, 2007

Richard: I've waited several weeks for a reply to my request for interviews. This promises to be an important and controversial book which will focus, in part, on the Arar story. To be fair and balanced to all sides in my reporting of these issues, it is absolutely essential that I be able to conduct these interviews as soon as possible. My deadline is creeping up.

Thank you

Paul Palango
902-. . .-. . . .

Monday, Dec 3, 2007
Paul . . .

I'll be speaking with Maher about this today, and I'll let you know if he is available.

Cheers,
Richard

Thursday December 6, 2007

Paul . . .

I regret to report that Maher and Monia are not able to make themselves available to you for interviews. Although they find the work that you have done around these issues very interesting, when it comes to discussions about reform in our National Security apparatus, Maher feels that O'Connor's reports and recommendations speak very clearly. While there is always room for more discussion about these issues, Maher and Monia aren't able to satisfy even a small portion of the number of requests for personal interviews that they receive.

However, if you are interested, and think that it would be useful, I could certainly put you in contact with members of his past and current legal and support team, who may be better able to speak to you about this. Alex Neve of Amnesty Canada might be particularly helpful.

Best regards,
Richard

Thursday December 6, 2007

Richard:

I am dismayed by the refusal of Maher Arar and Monia Mazigh to be interviewed by me. While I respect the fact that they may well be besieged by requests from others, I cannot emphasize enough how important this story will be.

I have no interest in talking to their lawyers. In light of the public exoneration Mr. Arar received, I fail to understand why he and his wife find it necessary to have a lawyer vet a journalist's questions. I need to talk to them and will only talk to them.

My book will detail many serious matters which were addressed and not addressed by the O'Connor Commission and others. These matters are clearly in the public interest and require clarification or rebuttal by Arar and Mazigh.

I have conducted extensive research and already have interviewed a number of credible people who have provided information or opinion about the matters in question, some of which is divergent with what is publicly known about the case.

My deadline for completing this book is imminent. While I plan to provide their side of the story as gleaned from the public record and open sources, I am compelled to give Arar and Mazigh an opportunity to answer my own questions and comment on my findings.

Will you please forward this message to them or provide me with a telephone number so that I might better make my case directly to them. On the other hand, you can have them call me. You have my contact numbers.

Thank you

Paul Palango

Monday December 10, 2007

Paul . . .

I am sorry if I made it sound as if Maher and Monia refused to be interviewed by you. The fact is, Maher and Monia are unable to accommodate the number of interview requests that they currently have.

In my previous email, I offered to put you in contact with some of the many people who supported Maher and Monia through their ordeal. While some of these people happen to be lawyers, I did not mean to suggest that you speak to them on a legal basis, but instead as people who were intimately and openly involved in the process of bringing Maher home, and helped him through the public inquiry.

I'd like to make the same offer again, except to say that in particular, Kerry Pither (a well-known human rights activist), and Alex Neve of Amnesty Canada are extremely knowledgeable. And, if you have specific questions or areas of interest, there are many other supporters who could provide accurate and perhaps invaluable information.

I hope that this is helpful . . .

Best regards,

Richard

Friday December 14, 2007

Richard: Kerry Pither and Alex Neve might be wonderful and well-intentioned people, but they cannot answer the many questions for which I need answers. For me to interview them about Maher Arar and Monia Mazigh would be like them interviewing my auto mechanic about me. He knows my vehicles, that I pay my bills, and a little bit about my life, but he has no clue about my history, the way I think and what I really do.

For example: Can either of them answer any of these questions?

1) When Mr. Arar lived in Montréal, where did he live? Who were his friends and interests? Which Mosque did he attend?

2) His work history. What was CIM21000 Inc? Where was it located? Who owned it? What did he do there? Why did he leave? What are the precise dates of his employment there and what were his duties at Alcatel, Nex Link and MathWorks?

3) He seemed cash-strapped, living in a rental house in Ottawa? How did he afford a second house in the Boston area?

4) How did he find out about the MathWorks job? Did he have to pass a security clearance? What did he do at MathWorks? Where did he travel? Exactly when did he leave and why?

5) Can he provide as references the names of people with whom he worked at any of his places of employment?

6) In Ottawa, after Monia Mazigh went to Tunisia in June 2002, why did he clear out his house? What did he do with the contents?

7) It has been reported that he was seeking work in Tunisia, why?

8) What ever happened to the MathWorks job offer for a prospective client? Does he still do work for The MathWorks?

9) Did he ever have contact of any kind with the Boston office of the FBI?

10) Further questions which likely will arise from the answers to those questions?

Thank you

Paul Palango

December 21, 2007

Richard: It has been a week since I sent this to you. I want to make sure that you got it.
Paul Palango

Tuesday January 8, 2008

Richard: I still have not received a reply to my questions or my follow-up query to you. Can you provide me with a direct number so that I might personally make my case?
Thank you.

Paul Palango

[9]

ARAR RECONSIDERED

The concept of invoking national security confidentiality dates back to 1890s France when the French government declared that it could not discuss its actions in the prosecution of alleged German spy Captain Alfred Dreyfuss for *raisons d'état*. Dreyfuss, a Jew living in anti-Semitic times, was wrongly convicted and sentenced to prison.

As more and more people became aware of the injustice dealt to Dreyfuss, the French government was caught in a quandary. If it tried to exonerate Dreyfuss, it would be forced to admit to a cover-up designed to protect the French army, the true identity of the traitor, and the complicity of the government itself. As the government dug in and denied the truth, in spite of the evidence exculpating Dreyfuss, things only got worse.

In 1898, French writer Emile Zola sent a letter, headlined "J'Accuse," to a Paris newspaper about the perceived ongoing injustice. The letter has been called by some the single best piece of journalism ever written. Its publication led to the downfall of the government, the eventual discovery of the real traitor, and the cover-up employed by the government to conceal the truth. The Dreyfuss case defined the conflict between valid national security issues and the right of people living in a democracy to know what their government is doing. It also defined the difference between a government doing something moral and right as opposed to a government using political expediency as its guiding principle.

Was the O'Connor Commission an elegant and beautifully executed ruse designed to obscure something very important? Much was done behind closed doors in the name of national security confidentiality. The Rules and Procedures of the Commission set out what O'Connor could and could not do: "Insofar as he needs to hear evidence, the Commissioner is committed to a process of public hearings to the greatest extent possible. However, the Terms of Reference direct the Commissioner to take all steps necessary to prevent disclosure of information that, if it were disclosed to the public would, in the opinion of the Commissioner, be injurious to international relations, national defence or national security. The procedure which will govern hearings where such issues may arise is addressed in the section on National Security Confidentiality."

Although O'Connor's mandate theoretically allowed him to review everything he wanted to see, he did not look at all the RCMP evidence and he had no access to Syrian or American files. This would prove crucially important to a Canadian government that had something more substantial to hide than a bungled police investigation. Otherwise, why all the fuss, fanfare, and bullying in the pursuit of so-called clarity?

Concealing the development of an atomic bomb in the middle of a world war that can't be won is clearly a state secret worth keeping. The Canadian government does not have such a monumental secret. Historically, its biggest secrets have tended to be about petty intrigues and questionable behaviour by the government, as happened when the Diefenbaker government inexplicably scrapped the Avro Arrow advanced fighter jet program in 1958. During the FLQ crisis in Québec, Prime Minister Pierre Trudeau invoked the War Measures Act in an attempt to steamroll over Québec terrorist groups. Other than that, nothing much truly dangerous has ever happened in Canada, but national security is often invoked, and when it is, it usually has to do with espionage. In the Arar matter, the deepest secret was something very embarrassing to Ottawa, something the electorate could sink its teeth into.

When Ottawa called on the RCMP to investigate reporter Juliet O'Neill for her inside stories about the Maher Arar situation, she was not the only journalist with access to inside information who shared it with the public. Months after O'Neill's house and office had been raided by the police during the O'Connor Commission hearings, *Toronto Star* columnist James Travers wrote a column based on inside government information, but that was rare. Nobody went after Travers, but no one followed in his footsteps either.

By attacking O'Neill so forcefully and egregiously, however, the government got across the message that it wanted to make—that anyone who dared leak information or publish that information would become the subject of an attack under the Official Secrets Act. No one would be spared. Today, several years later, that message is still effective. Among the ranks of the police and bureaucrats who had some knowledge of what really happened, almost everyone who knows something is afraid to talk openly.

In Calgary, during the summer of 2007, I collared a couple of senior RCMP members who were familiar with what had happened. "The Arar case doesn't make sense to me," I said to one of them. "There's something missing. What really happened?"

"You're on the right track," the Mountie replied. "Just keep asking that question."

"What should I ask?"

"National Security," he said with a blank look on his face. "I can't say anything."

The other Mountie just nodded his head in agreement, and added: "National Security."

It was the same in Ottawa and elsewhere. When I confronted Giuliano Zaccardelli one day with the question, he just gritted his teeth, let out a weak smile, and said: "I can't talk about that."

But a French-Canadian RCMP member made a gesture and perfectly described the RCMP's view of the Arar case. He said with a knowing smile: "*C'est une grande fiction.*"

But what was that fiction?

In the world of policing, many of those who leave the service continue their association through private-sector contracts, veteran's associations, and longtime friendships. Many of these people, especially those who held senior ranks, are often called upon for advice. The Arar case was widely discussed inside and outside the RCMP by people in this milieu. Just about everywhere one goes in this world there are leads and solid information. But, again, no one wants to go on the record.

From a government's perspective, the umbrella of national security confidentiality creates a near perfect world. Even if a story does come out, it can only be done with unnamed sources, which diminishes its credibility. Most media are reluctant to publish stories with unnamed sources, and even if one is published, the government could easily deny it, arguing that if such a story were true, then the sources should be courageous enough to lend their name to it. So, what really happened? On the surface, it appears that at the very worst the government was investigating a group of low level Al-Qaeda sympathizers dabbling in used radios. What was there to hide?

What was the big secret?

✝ ✝ ✝

On or about September 22, 2001, the U.S. government completed the formulation of its new and aggressive plan to ferret out, secretly capture, and imprison potential Islamic terrorists around the world. It was what they had been doing over the previous eight years, since the World Trade Center bombing in 1993, but now they were going to kick into another gear. The U.S. and its disparate allies were prepared to take risks and do the unthinkable—extraordinary rendition.

That same day, as you may recall from an earlier chapter, CSIS called two meetings in Toronto with the RCMP and other police services, and asked the police to hit the streets and launch a criminal investigation because CSIS had determined that there was an "an imminent threat against the country." Being the only federal police service in Canada with jurisdiction, the RCMP became the lead investigative agency. It was a treacherous assignment for any police force, but even more so for the ill-equipped, under-prepared Mounties, and the boy-scout demeanour of so many of its members.

"The biggest problem for the RCMP is that in their training and approach to an investigation, they have a simple mindset and only see things in black and white. For them, it's either a crime or it's not a crime. They can't see shades of grey where, unfortunately, most criminality takes place," says former Toronto Police Chief William McCormack. Now retired, McCormack continues to be a respected member of the police fraternity and maintains contact with the highest levels of the police, military, and intelligence community. McCormack's view echoes that of many police experts in Canada, including current and former members of the RCMP itself.

The original agreement for Projects Shock, O Canada, and A-O Canada was that CSIS and the RCMP would share information with both themselves, the FBI, and the CIA. The RCMP charged onto the streets of Ottawa and Toronto, without CSIS giving them a clue about what had really been going on there.

CSIS had come running to the RCMP for help: according to highly placed sources in the intelligence community CSIS had recognized that it had a problem with one of its operatives in the Muslim community. It was assumed the operative had been turned by CSIS—that he was only pretending to work for a foreign agency while actually working for Canadian intelligence. However, it had come to light the agent was "playing more for the other side than for us." In the aftermath of September 11, there was a heightened sense of urgency, even panic, in CSIS and up to the highest levels of government. At the same time, CSIS never revealed any of this to the RCMP. The RCMP had no clue about the double agent's existence.

"I don't believe it was Arar," said a confidential source with access to the highest levels of the intelligence community. "But it does appear to have been someone in the Ottawa circle who likely got picked up in the RCMP radar."

Once the RCMP got involved, CSIS continued with its overlapping investigation, and strange things were happening. As had been the case all the way back to the Air India investigation, beginning in 1985 and ever since, the RCMP found that CSIS agents were still slipping out of the shadows and tripping them up.

Abdullah Almalki was the prime target, but by the time the RCMP started to look at him Almalki was so spooked by the obvious surveillance that he had gone to a lawyer. Remember how he complained that a cab driver had told him that he had been approached by a person identifying himself as a CSIS agent, who asked him to enter Almalki's house for the agency, which the man said he refused to do? Who was that CSIS agent? Or was it someone else? Did that really happen? Almalki also claimed that he had found that parcels to his business had been searched, old credit card statements were arriving in his mail, and there were unknown footprints in the baby powder in his foyer.

The Mounties forged ahead using their standard investigative techniques and tried to cultivate their own sources. Investigators identified a possible source they thought might have been able to assist them, circled him, and closed in, only to learn, after jumping through all the hoops, that CSIS had forgotten to mention the person to the RCMP. A CSIS agent told the RCMP: "We already knew about him. He's one of our sources."

It wasn't an isolated incident. Time and time again, CSIS agents were running in front of the Mounties, peering over their shoulders, or trying to steer the police away from their hidden assets in the community. The RCMP found that CSIS agents often beat them to an interview of a witness or suspect, effectively warning the subjects that the police were coming next. As for information sharing, the RCMP handed everything it had over to CSIS, but CSIS often held back what it knew, which was obvious to the Mounties, and their frustration grew.

CSIS's behaviour made for such a difficult relationship that at one point serious consideration was given inside Project A-O Canada to have CSIS agents charged with obstructing justice. Cooler heads prevailed because it was decided that the ensuing controversy would only cause more problems for the RCMP. Ottawa would stand behind CSIS in any situation.

A further problem inside the RCMP was the fear that CSIS had infiltrated the force and was monitoring the RCMP efforts from inside. There were suspicions about who the CSIS mole might be, but they were never pursued. Placing counter-intelligence moles inside police forces is a tactic used by the CIA, even inside the United States, though it is prohibited by law there. These agents, with non-official covert status, or NOC, are considered to be one of the most effective CIA tactics for gaining information and exerting influence, even inside the United States, where the CIA is prohibited by law from spying on U.S. citizens. The CIA will never acknowledge the existence or identity of a NOC, even if one is exposed. The NOC will also never admit who he or she really is.

These agents exist in a schizophrenic world, pretending to serve one master but in reality serving another. NOCs are commonly planted inside high-tech organizations, a one-person sleeper cell, as it were, often with the cooperation of the head of the organization. As the *Washington Post* reported in 2005, the CIA even has its own company, In-Q-Tel, which invests in high-tech companies as a way of buying intelligence and developing technology tailored to specific CIA needs.

Former Toronto Police Chief McCormack related a story from his personal experiences about a friend he had made years ago in the New York City Police Department. The man was a lieutenant in the NYPD, but told McCormack after his retirement that he had really been a CIA agent all along. McCormack says: "That's how intelligence agencies operate. The very nature of police work, responding to emergencies and developing intelligence about possible criminal behaviour, brings the police into contact with a wide assortment of individuals within a community. The police have the manpower that the intelligence community doesn't have."

As difficult as the relationship between the RCMP and CSIS might have been, there were two other factors that compounded the problem even more in Ottawa. Those were the active presence of both the FBI and the CIA.

It is normal for the FBI and CIA to have agents in Canada attached to the American embassy, just as the RCMP and CSIS have liaison officers in other countries. But the Canadian approach to such work is much different than that of the Americans, who feel it is their right to enforce their laws anywhere in the world. Canadian police do not work in foreign countries without local permission and escorts. Even in an emergency, Canadian police do not cross the border without giving notice to the Americans.

In Ottawa, there were usually four FBI agents working out of the U.S. embassy, three who coordinate joint criminal investigations between Canadian and U.S. police, and one who acts as a liaison to CSIS on intelligence issues. As you might expect, no one knows how many CIA agents work out of any U.S. embassy in the world.

After Millennium Bomber Ahmed Ressam was captured in late 1999 and his links to the Assuna Annabawiyah mosque in Montréal were established, both the CIA and the FBI had little confidence in CSIS being able to manage the terrorism file, even though the CIA and FBI were having their own problems and failures, such as missing the September 11 plotters.

The CIA had long been mining the Muslim communities in Montréal, Toronto, Ottawa, and Vancouver, while cultivating potential informants. CSIS knew this and so did the Canadian government, which had a history of turning a blind eye to CIA activity in Canada. As the CBC reported, previously classified U.S. documents revealed that during the late 1960s and 1970s, the CIA spied on Canadians critical of the Vietnam War in an operation code-named "MH Chaos." The U.S. spy agency targeted university professors, students, and other Canadians who the agency believed were espousing left-wing ideas. The CIA developed a network of informants on Canadian campuses in the late 1960s and had reports sent down from Ottawa to the CIA's headquarters at Langley, Virginia.

"Everyone knows how the Americans are, they just bully their way in," one high-ranking official told me in August 2006. "What were we going to do, tell them to leave?"

From Ottawa's perspective, CSIS needed all the help it could get, and if no one knew about the FBI and CIA, so much the better. As we already know, in the weeks and months after September 11, 2001, the U.S. government placed more than 1,500 requests for assistance from the Canadian government, most of those aimed at the RCMP. Some of those requests were coming from intelligence the U.S. was gathering abroad from captured informants; some from Ressam, who was singing to the authorities; and more from Abdurahman Khadr, who had been captured in November 2001 in Afghanistan. Khadr, who knew the Toronto-Ottawa Muslim communities intimately, was actively helping the U.S. authorities. Finally, there was the information coming from the CIA undercover agents on the ground in Canada.

During the fall of 2001, as the Mounties in Project A-O Canada tried to corral the El-Maati-Almalki suspects and attempt to gather evidence, they couldn't help but notice all the outside activity. After Arar was identified as a person of interest by the RCMP and his name discussed with U.S. authorities, a peculiar thing happened. The FBI office in Boston told the Mounties that they were already aware of Arar and were going to attempt a sting operation targeting him. No one in the RCMP seemed to know if that operation ever got off the ground, but the information planted a seed in the heads of the RCMP investigators, that they were onto something substantial.

It was getting confusing for everyone, an investigative nightmare filled with suspects, persons of interest, CIA spies, counter-spies, a couple of CSIS double agents and, as the Mounties would eventually figure out, a contingent of FBI agents who had sneaked into the country.

During the early weeks and months of Project A-O Canada, the Mounties realized that at least 12 FBI agents were working the streets in Ottawa, with as many as a dozen others, by conservative estimates, in Toronto, Montréal, and Vancouver. The Mounties wondered if it had something to do with the FBI's "sting" on Arar.

Meanwhile, in southern Ontario, FBI agents were crossing the border at Buffalo on day trips, "going to the casino," and then stalking suspects around Toronto and Hamilton. The Hamilton area was becoming a concern because of the high number of suspected Muslim Brotherhood members who had congregated in the engineering department at McMaster University, where there is a nuclear reactor. A large proportion of the staff and student body were identified as being potential radicals, with access to the reactor, which was raising obvious concerns in the United States, whose border was just a short drive away from the campus. The RCMP were never informed about the "official" presence of the U.S. agents, and it is not known whether they were officially approved by the Canadian government or not. The FBI agents weren't being escorted by Canadian police, as would be the custom.

"Everyone knows that's what they were doing," William McCormack said. "They shouldn't be here doing what they're doing, but the federal government has shown no interest in trying to stop them."

The problem for all the U.S. agents, however, was that they could not conduct an investigation openly, so that's where the Mounties came in. The Canadian government implicitly told the RCMP to fully cooperate with the U.S. agencies, which the Mounties did, to a fault. According to a confidential source close to Project A-O Canada, when FBI agents visited the RCMP operations office at "A" Division in Ottawa, they would sometimes come armed with their own questions and insights about the suspects in the investigation. "They knew what they were looking for, and it was clear that they were doing their own investigative work," the source said.

But that was not the only way the FBI and CIA were getting information. The Canadian legal system has evolved in such a way that makes it all but impossible for the police to conduct an investigation without revealing everything they knew or tried to do to the suspects. In 2002, Canadian courts ruled that the RCMP had to turn over all documents in a case, including the operation plans of any police force involved in an investigation. This decision made it all but impossible for foreign police services like the FBI, who are reluctant to let criminals know how it thinks and operates, to participate in any joint investigation with Canadian police.

"Everyone knows that Canada is a sieve for information," said a leading U.S. authority, who asked for confidentiality. "The Canadian legal system is set up to give criminals up-to-date access to police techniques." His words echo those of many others on both sides of the border.

To get around this, the FBI, the CIA, and presumably other foreign police and intelligence services have been exploiting a loophole in the Canadian system. Informed sources say it is not uncommon for foreign intelligence agencies to retain Canadian lawyers, who in turn hire accounting firms and private investigators—who can then hide behind the lawyers—while conducting an investigation. The private investigators, most of them ex-Mounties, operate without the encumbrance of search warrants and other legal niceties. They gather evidence against Canadians in Canada while circumventing the laws of the country. All of this is being done with the complicity of governments, which have collectively turned a blind eye to the practice.

The bottom line is that everyone from the top of the government down seemed to know what was really going on and what the true intent of Project A-O Canada was, that is, to investigate possible terrorist activity in Canada, assist the Americans at all times, and, if possible, help the Americans prosecute suspects, even Canadian citizens, in the United States.

In the post-September 11 climate, the Canadian approach to Islamic terrorism was typically pragmatic and political. The U.S. government would take the expense of prosecution and the political heat. The Canadian government, always sensitive to immigrant communities, would be left in a win–win position. It didn't have to undertake a messy prosecution and alienate potential voters and it would score points with the Americans for being cooperative.

From the Canadian point of view, therefore, there were at least three motives for the government to do what it eventually did. First, it helped to cover up the weaknesses and failings of CSIS. Second, it obscured the fact that the blundering and inaction of the Chrétien government over the years left it in no position to negotiate with the Americans after September 11. Canada was then forced to cede its sovereignty and willingly allow U.S. agents to operate openly in Canada. The third reason was to hide the identity of secret agents and double agents, as well as their investigative techniques, such as they were.

No one knows what information the Americans collected in Canada on Arar, or anyone else for that matter. What is known is that in spite of his eventual exoneration in Canada, Arar continued to be persona non grata in the United States and subject to an inexplicable, mysterious, and onerous "no-fly" order. What did the Americans know or think they knew?

In August 2007, the Canadian media became excited about a revelation from previously redacted materials before the O'Connor Commission which indicated the CIA had been involved in Arar's rendition to Syria. "CIA at the Heart of the Arar Affair," *The Globe and Mail* reported. Columnist John Ibbitson wrote: "The federal government fought like blazes to keep the fact that the CIA sent Maher Arar to Syria from you—they fought so hard that it took a court order for you to hear it—because Ottawa doesn't want to lose face with the Americans, or the Syrians, for that matter."

After everything blew up in their faces, meanwhile, some Mounties and others familiar with the situation took a step back to review what had happened.

"The whole thing was a CIA operation, not just the rendition. That comes from the highest levels," one highly placed source with access to the investigation told me in August 2007.

Further interviews confirmed that many in the highest levels of policing and government knew this but, once again, no one would risk the wrath of the government and speak on the record.

It seems evident now that Arar's trip to Syria might have been only a small part of a larger picture. The entire investigation was run by the CIA, in concert with the FBI and CSIS, who together used the unwitting Mounties as their investigative proxies. The hidden agenda was that in the process of that investigation a CIA operative or two would be brought into the mix.

In a very short time in October 2001, the RCMP had been thrown into a confusing and widespread investigation, and then served a lob—an agent. That the police became interested in the agent was not an accident, but part of the grand plan concocted by the CIA and approved by the Canadian government. At the time of its conception in the aftermath of September 11, there existed a worldwide fear of Islamic terrorists. Nobody knew what was coming next. Extraordinary rendition seemed like a good idea at the time, something that would be frowned upon but deemed necessary under the circumstances. But, like many of the ideas that trickled out of Dick Cheney's brain, it was half-baked. It would be fair to assume that those who conceived of and approved the plan did not anticipate the level of outrage and political controversy that it would generate in Canada and elsewhere. They had to ad lib or, as is common in U.S. football, call an audible here and there, to change the play as the game went on.

It is highly unlikely, therefore, that the subsequent O'Connor Commission inquiry was part of the overall scheme, but became necessary after the unanticipated public uproar in Canada. Instead of letting the courts and judicial process decide the matter as they should, the government's own statements and actions helped whip the public into a frenzy over the apparent mistreatment of Arar. This foment was then used to justify the manipulation of institutions and the public inquiry process to give the people what they thought they wanted, and to conceal the harsher reality.

The original police investigation centred on Ahmad El Maati, the Toronto truck driver and brother of terrorist Amer El Maati; Abdullah Almalki, who had gone to Pakistan with known Al-Qaeda member Ahmed Sa'id al-Khadr; and Almalki's three brothers. In light of their individual histories, the searches on their homes and the unknown contents seized, and their behaviour afterward, it seems likely that, at worst, El Maati and the Almalki brothers and others like them were low-level Al-Qaeda sympathizers. None of them appeared to be friendly secret agents. But anything was possible. No one else identified in the Muslim community appeared to have the right history to be a candidate for the job.

In their brief investigation, it does not seem that the RCMP had the time or manpower to focus on anyone else. They didn't have time to develop solid sources who might have been so utterly compromised as to cause such a furor. As we have seen, CSIS had sources, but it was CSIS and the U.S. agencies that laid the groundwork for the RCMP and set them off on the trail of El Maati, the Almalkis, and Arar. If anyone else had been working for the CIA, there would have been no need for all the smoke and mirrors that were employed in the Arar case. There seems to have been no investigative trail to anyone else.

Arar has insisted that he did nothing wrong, and he has the backing of the O'Connor Commission findings and his financial settlement to prove it. Yet his silence has left much room for alternative scenarios and hypotheses about what really might have happened.

The problem facing U.S. intelligence agencies in the late 1990s was that they were not very good at infiltrating the Islamic terrorist movement. The Americans needed help, and fast. Canada had become a staging ground for terrorists, but the Americans could not rely on the Canadians to serve their interests. The Americans knew from experience that neither CSIS nor the RCMP had the interest, ability, or experience to carry out a proactive investigation. In short, if there was one thing the Americans could expect from their Canadian counterparts, it would be that something was bound to go wrong, unless they took matters into their own hands. There was also a history of compliance between the government of Canada and the CIA.

✛ ✛ ✛

There are so many obvious, unanswered questions in the Arar story, but perhaps the missing information was not, by any means, an accident. What if the Maher Arar saga was an example of tricky playwrights and daring actors mounting a grand theatre production on a world stage, a show designed for a very select audience? Sound impossible? It would not have been the first time Canada had become involved in such an elaborate enterprise.

In 1980, Canadian Ambassador Kenneth Taylor became a hero for his efforts to help six stranded American diplomats escape capture in Tehran after Iranian students shouting "death to America" stormed the U.S. embassy and took it over. The official story told how Taylor and Canadian Immigration officer John Sheardown had given shelter to the Americans in their homes for months and how then-Prime Minister Joe Clark and the apparatus of Canadian government engineered a remarkable feat in dangerous circumstances. Parliament even held its first private session to discuss the matter and approve the rescue mission of the Americans. Canadian passports and identity papers were issued to the Americans and they were whisked out of Iran just ahead of the hordes seeking to lop off their heads.

Taylor was immediately celebrated. He was appointed consul general to New York City, made an officer of the Order of Canada, and was even awarded the United States Congressional Gold Medal. He became an instant celebrity, making the round of television talk shows, the subject of numerous newspaper and magazine profiles, and a popular speaker on the lecture circuit.

It was a fabulous story, but it was not quite true, and the Canadian government was not as courageous and innovative as it seemed to have been. It took almost three decades for the real story to emerge. Canada, as it turned out, had played a small but important role in the grand story. The reality was that the CIA had manipulated all the events from behind the curtain.

In April 2007, *LA Weekly* magazine editor Joshuah Bearman, writing in *Wired* magazine, described the lengths to which the CIA would go in terms of imagination and execution to make a sensitive project successful. Back in 1979, the Americans knew that their six missing U.S. diplomats and spies were hiding out in the homes of the two Canadians. Getting them out would not be simple. The Iranians had control of the U.S. embassy and access to its personnel files. They knew how many Americans had been in the country and how many had left. They also knew how many Canadians were there as well. The diplomats could not sneak to the airport or out of the country. They would have been stopped, questioned, and searched.

The Canadian government was also getting nervous. At a NATO meeting in December 1980, an antsy Flora MacDonald, Canada's minister of External Affairs, confronted U.S. secretary of state Cyrus Vance and suggested the six Americans make for the Turkish border—on bicycles if necessary.

By January 1980, nine weeks into the crisis, the CIA realized that it had to create a scenario to account for the six extra bodies. It fell to CIA agent Tony Mendez to orchestrate a plan. Mendez was in charge of logistical operations in support of the *tens of thousands* of false identities the CIA was running. He had spent 14 years in the CIA's Office of Technical Service and was a former head of the CIA's Disguise Section, among other postings. Those departments had done everything from wiring cats with microphones for eavesdropping to transforming a black CIA officer and an Asian diplomat into Caucasian businessmen—using masks that made them ringers for Victor Mature and Rex Harrison—so they could arrange a meeting in the capital of Laos, a country under strict martial law.

The Tehran operation was particularly difficult. The only three CIA agents in the country were in hiding. For a week, the Americans and Canadians could not figure out a workable scenario to fool the Iranians. A novel approach was needed.

Mendez, who had contacts in Hollywood, invented a character, Kevin Costa Harkins, an Irish film producer leading his pre-production crew through Iran to do some location scouting for a big-budget Hollywood epic. The Iranians needed the money and a big budget film could be an enticing proposition to them. Following is an edited excerpt from Bearman's story about what the American and Canadian governments cooked up together.

In just four days, Mendez, (John) Chambers, and (Bob) Sidell created a fake Hollywood production company. They designed business cards and concocted identities for the six members of the location-scouting party, including all their former credits. The production company's offices would be set up in a suite at Sunset Gower Studios on what was formerly the Columbia lot, in a space vacated by Michael Douglas after he finished *The China Syndrome*.

All they needed now was a film—and Chambers had the perfect script. Months before, he had received a call from a would-be producer named Barry Geller. Geller had purchased the rights to Roger Zelazny's science fiction novel, *Lord of Light*, written his own treatment, raised a few million dollars in starting capital from wealthy investors, and hired Jack Kirby, the famous comic book artist who cocreated *X-Men*, to do concept drawings. Along the way, Geller imagined a Colorado theme park based on Kirby's set designs that would be called Science Fiction Land; it would include a 300-foot-tall Ferris wheel, voice-operated mag-lev cars, a "planetary control room" staffed by robots, and a heated dome almost twice as tall as the Empire State Building. Geller had announced his grand plan in November at a press conference attended by Jack Kirby, former football star and prospective cast member Rosey Grier, and several people dressed like visitors from the future. Shortly thereafter, Geller's second-in-command was arrested for embezzling production funds, and the *Lord of Light* film project evaporated.

Since Chambers had been hired by Geller to do makeup for the film, he still had the script and drawings at his house. The story, a tale of Hindu-inspired mystical science fiction, took place on a colonized planet. Iran's landscape could provide many of the rugged settings required by the script. A famous underground bazaar in Tehran even matched one of the necessary locations. "This is perfect," Mendez said. He removed the cover and gave the script a new name, *Argo*—like the vessel used by Jason on his daring voyage across the world to retrieve the Golden Fleece.

The new production company outfitted its office with phone lines, typewriters, film posters, and canisters, and a sign on the door: Studio Six Productions, named for the six Americans awaiting rescue. Sidell read the script and sketched out a schedule for a month's worth of shooting. Mendez and Chambers designed a full-page ad for the film and bought space in *Variety* and *The Hollywood Reporter*. The night before Mendez returned to Washington, Studio Six threw a small party at the Brown Derby, where they toasted their "production" and Mendez grabbed some matchbooks as additional props to boost his Hollywood bona fides. Shortly thereafter, the *Argo* ads appeared, announcing that principal photography would commence in March. The film's title was rendered in distressed lettering against a black background. Next to it was a bullet hole. Below it was the tagline "A Cosmic Conflagration."

The ruse worked. The film crew contacted the hidden Americans and gave them their new "Canadian" identities. The Iranians bought into it. The Canadians got the credit and no one breathed a word about what had taken place.

Now, when it came to infiltrating the ranks of potential Islamic terrorists in Canada and elsewhere in the aftermath of September 11, 2001, the Americans knew that if they were going to achieve any success, they would have to take matters into their own hands, which is precisely what they did. As later events would show, the CIA and the FBI were working together around the world to penetrate Al-Qaeda.

✠ ✠ ✠

I tried to follow up on the Arar story during the summer and fall of 2007, but information was difficult to find. Before long, those who would cooperate stopped doing so.

"The hammer came down," one of my sources told me. "They're on to you. The word is out that no one is to discuss Arar with you."

Other sources later confirmed the same thing: that the government, the RCMP, and the intelligence community was watching and would take action, if necessary, if official information was deemed to have been leaked. Most of my sources soon dried up, but not all.

One way to dispel such conjecture would have been for Arar to sit down and answer any questions asked, but he has adamantly refused to do that, which in the context of events seems absolutely incongruous. It would be fair to say that Arar has a moral obligation as a citizen of Canada to tell his whole story.

Why the secrecy?

The facts of the Arar case raise serious questions and concerns about the government's role in the story. Not the least of these was the Canadian government's interest in gaining even more political control over the RCMP.

[10]

BEHIND THE TYPO: CIM 2000 INC.

Maher Arar graduated from university in 1992, and was living in Montréal, where the CIA was known to be active and had a history of trolling Canadian university campuses for recruits during this period. This has been well documented in news accounts and other books.

It is not known what Arar did in 1993 or when his official work history began. The O'Connor Commission listed his employment history in chronological order—CIM21000 Inc., Nex Link Communications, Alcatel Communication, and The MathWorks—but gave no specifics. The latter three companies are well known multinational entities and easy to locate, but not CIM21000 Inc. There is no record of it anywhere in the world.

Private investigator Kevin Bousquet of Corpa Investigation Inc. of Burlington, Ontario, conducted an extensive search of government databases and old microfiche records in Canada. He confirmed my own findings. There was no record of anyone in Canada ever registering the name or style of CIM21000 Inc.

Bousquet said the closest match he could find was on a Québec government database. It was a company named CIM 2000 Inc. and had registered its incorporation on April 14, 1997. Its place of business was Suite 406 at 3750 Crémazie Boulevard, Montréal—a mundane, six-storey building on the service road below the elevated TransCanada highway passing through the east end of the city.

The timing and location was right but there was no other available information about the company or what it did. Only two pages of corporate records, the bare minimum, had been filed with the Québec government.

The documents indicated that the company was set up and controlled by

Parto Navidi of 13309 Chelsea Street, Pierrefonds, Québec, which is in the northwest corner of the island of Montréal.

If Navidi had actually lived there, it was long ago, as a tenant. Navidi was not listed as the previous owner and no one living there now remembered the name. There was no telephone listing for any Navidi in Québec. There were two telephone listings for P. Navidi at the same address in the Toronto suburb of North York. A woman who answered one of the phones at the house said she knew of no such person at that address. She added that she did not know anyone named Navidi who had lived in Pierrefonds. It looked like the investigation was at a dead end.

CIM 2000 Inc. had twice been found in default of its business filings and its charter was revoked on May 5, 2000—just as the Bloc Québecois moved its party headquarters into Suite 307, a large office space directly below. The Bloc moved out of the Crémazie building in 2005 and no one in the party's office could remember the situation back in 2000.

An Internet search found many Navidis. The late Dr. Aziz Navidi, a lawyer, was revered for his defence of the human rights of the much persecuted members of the Baha'i faith in Iran. Pirouz Navidi was a leader of a banned Marxist–Leninist political party known today as the Union of People's Fedaian of Iran. It was once an anti-Soviet group, which had participated in overthrowing the Shah of Iran. However, after defeating the Soviets in Afghanistan its members became the victims of oppression in Iran. In recent years, the party had split and dropped the word "guerrilla" from its original name. The larger group took on a more Russia-friendly approach. The Fedaian is vehemently anti-American and in recent years has forged alliances with various like-minded groups in Kurdistan, Iraq, and the surrounding region. The Fedaian and its leaders consider themselves part of the Iranian government in exile. But all that had proved to be a dead end as well.

In the United States, some of the Navidis had a common interest—mathematics and computers.

The most intriguing discovery, however, was an Iranian-born Washington D.C.-area computer consultant who had emigrated to the United States in 1977, at the age of 18. He had graduated from Catholic University with a degree in chemical engineering. On his website, Al Navidi, as he is now known, boasted about his marathon running, triathlon participation, and his travels around the world. Oddly, he also listed his high-level CIA-FBI security clearances. One of his computer programs, he said, "interfaces with the FBI, INS, and CIA systems."

One of Navidi's associates was a prominent Iranian–American named Emmanuel Soheyli of Huntington Beach, California. They were partners in a Maryland company, Visual Development International LLC, which specialized in computer software design and development. Soheyli even had his own website dedicated to all things Persian—music, information, and a link to the Al Jazeera news channel, among other things.

Could CIM 2000 Inc. actually be the CIM21000 Inc. referred to in the O'Connor Commission? Was the name change just a typo, a mere printing error—the only one I could find in more than 12,000 pages of material? Was the name deliberately obscured?

If the O'Connor Commission was worried about any connection to CIM 2000 Inc., why did it just not mention the company instead of creating a deliberate typo? What did the government know about CIM21000? What did the company do? How long did Arar work there? What were his duties? Why did he leave? Who else worked there? What did they remember of him?

As it turned out, CIM 2000 Inc. provided a clue to what Arar might really have been doing and why the government had bent over backwards for him.

The Parto Navidi mystery seemed unsolvable, but then, after the first draft of this book was written, Navidi popped out of the shadows.

As an investigative tool, the Internet can be a wonderful surveillance mechanism. Every so often I would use different search strategies to find a mention of CIM 2000 Inc. and Parto Navidi. On March 6, 2008, one of my volunteer researchers, Brent Belesky, telephoned me to give me an update. During our conversation, he asked me if I had ever found "that guy Navidi." As we talked, I twiddled away on the computer and googled "Iranian baby names." Parto was not a man but a woman! Having a Muslim woman as the head of a company was certainly not Sharia. These were thoroughly modern Muslims indeed.

One more google of Parto Navidi proved invaluable. As luck would have it she had recently placed her Ottawa-area townhouse up for sale and had posted the listing on an Ottawa real estate website—along with her business telephone number. She ran a laser hair-removal service.

I called Navidi, hoping to catch her out of the blue. I explained who I was and what I was doing and that it had something to do with Maher Arar.

When I mentioned Arar's name, Navidi said: "Oh, Maher," her voice trailing off. I could almost hear her eyes roll.

"I'm calling you because your name is listed on a company in Montréal that has been out of business since 2000. I would like to know what that business was doing."

"The company was set up by my husband and Maher. He was his partner," Navidi said. "They put my name on it. I didn't know they had used my name. I didn't know anything about the company or what it was doing. I didn't even know where it was."

She would not tell me who her husband was. "We have been divorced for five years. I have not talked to him since."

"What is his name?"

"I'm not going to tell you," she said. "I'm making it difficult for you, but if you look for Maher his name will be there right beside him. That is where you will always find him."

I soon learned that Parto Navidi's ex-husband was Mourad Mazigh, the brother of Monia Mazigh and therefore the brother-in-law of Maher Arar. Like his sister Monia, Mourad was well-educated, having studied advanced mathematics at the École Polytechnique in Montréal.

Returning to the O'Connor Commission report I was now able to find a single, veiled reference to Parto Navidi buried in the "Report of the Events Relating to Maher Arar—Factual Background Volume II." On page 506, there was this entry: "On February 4, 2004, Project A-O Canada attempted, unsuccessfully, to interview Mourad Mazigh's ex-wife, who was listed as an administrator of CIM2000."

CIM2000? Another typo?

This was one day before the O'Connor Commission was established on February 5. Arar was back in Canada by then and the RCMP was continuing its investigation of Arar, picking up the loose ends they missed in 2001 and 2002.

Like so many other journalists, my research had focused on what the RCMP had discovered before Arar had gone to Syria and what had happened there and afterwards—and not on what the police had dug up after he had returned to Canada. I had allowed myself to be subconsciously directed by the mandate of the O'Connor Commission and had stayed inside the boundaries that had been set out.

On the next page of the Factual Background, Volume II, there was this important entry I had originally overlooked: "August 2004: In August, Project A-O Canada produced several pages of documents, both personal and commercial, indicating contact between the following individuals and companies:

Abdullah Almalki, Youssef Almalki, Safa Almalki, Nazih Almalki, Maher Arar, Mourad Mazigh, and CIM2000. The documentation ranged in date from 1996 to 2002, often related to computer equipment."

That was it. There was no mention of what else the company was doing or with whom.

Once again, CIM 2000 Inc. was described inaccurately, but only just. I was not able to obtain the original RCMP documents but it is unlikely that the Mounties had wrongly described CIM 2000 Inc. The very fact that the police had uncovered the company and submitted their findings to the commission meant that the commission was compelled, in its final report, at the very least to acknowledge its presence, even if it meant creating typos here and there to cover the trail.

When told about the typo, a confidential source who had worked at the top levels of the federal bureaucracy had this to say: "Inserting typos is an old trick governments use to throw people off the path of something it doesn't want known."

The circumstances surrounding the creation and operations of CIM 2000 Inc. would pique the interest of any police investigator. It was set up in the name of a nominee who had a different name than the actual operators. The nominee, for one, said she did not know her name had been used. The company did not keep up its regulatory filings and eventually vanished into thin air.

If CIM 2000 Inc. was a legitimate company, then why all the silence about it from Arar and Mourad Mazigh? There is nothing illegal in Canadian or U.S. law about selling used radio equipment and telecommunications equipment to other countries.

This led me to invest in one more title search. Who owned the property at 13309 Chelsea in Pierrefonds, which was listed in the government file as Navidi's residence in 1997?

The Chelsea Street house had been sold for $120,000 on September 9, 1988, by its builder, Maison Tops Inc., to Pietro Rigolli. He and his wife, Mihan Haghighi Talab, resold the house in 2003 to a Sikh–Canadian couple for $180,000. The Rigolli name did not mean much to me until I googled him. Pietro Giovanni Rigolli was no ordinary landlord.

Rigolli held dual Italian and British citizenships. Born in 1953, he had moved to Canada in 1989, where he set up his base of operations in Montréal. Rigolli used at least five aliases. Sometimes he called himself Peter Rigolli. One of his favourite alternate identities was Ian Falcon. His wife, Mihan

Talab, was Iranian and sometimes he passed himself off as an Arab, using the name Farid H. Talab. At other times, he was a Latino known as Rafael Heredia, or an Italian, G. Tedaldi. He had a previous conviction for forgery in Great Britain.

Rigolli's business, Air Rig Inc., was operated out of his family home on Northview Street, a cul-de-sac which runs into the large park and lake at the heart of Dollard des Ormeaux, a northwest Montréal suburb.

Air Rig purported to be a legitimate dealer of aircraft parts and components. One of its favourite suppliers was Pratt & Whitney, the Connecticut-based designer and manufacturer of aircraft engines and components. Rigolli began to do business in 1991 with Pratt & Whitney, purchasing materials from it in Connecticut and California. Rigolli told the company and the U.S. government, which approved such restricted exports, that he was shipping the parts—valued in the millions of dollars—to customers in Switzerland or Singapore. In fact, the parts were going to the Islamic Republic of Iran whose commercial and military fleets were each suffering from severe shortages caused by an ongoing U.S. embargo.

Iran had enjoyed a tricky relationship with the United States. After the storming of the Iranian embassy in November 1979, and the ensuing Canadian caper to spirit out U.S. diplomats, President Reagan had overseen a covert program to ship tanks and missiles to Iran, although he had told the American public he would never do such a thing. The profits generated from the secret sales were used to buy weapons for U.S.-backed Contra rebels in Nicaragua. The infamous Iran–Contra affair, as it came to be known, blackened the reputation of the Reagan administration, leading to convictions against a number of high-ranking officials, all of whom were eventually pardoned by President George H.W. Bush or had their convictions vacated, as was the case with Oliver North.

In May 1995, a full U.S. trade embargo was placed on trade with Iran, based on the U.S. government's contention that Iran supported international terrorism, but Rigolli, nevertheless, continued buying from Pratt & Whitney.

By 1999, Rigolli had conducted $20 million in illegal business with Iran over an eight-year period, but then his world came crashing down. An informant, whom the prosecution refused to identify, had tipped off the U.S. Customs Service about Rigolli's activities. On March 3 of 1999 Rigolli made the two-hour drive from his home to the U.S. border at Burlington, Vermont. Customs officers were waiting in an Emery Worldwide warehouse for Rigolli to arrive and clear for export two shipments of Pratt & Whitney components worth $65,000. Rigolli told the customs officers that the materials would be transhipped through Canada to Singapore, but somewhere along the line he had been introduced to an undercover agent who could prove otherwise.

The trap was sprung. Rigolli was arrested and shipped to New Haven, Connecticut, for trial on charges filed in both Connecticut and California. He tried to make bail. His wife even tried to pledge $1 million in real estate assets owned by her family in California, but the courts were not about to let him go free.

Rigolli languished in jail for a year and went through a number of lawyers before negotiating a guilty plea over the illegal sale of $7 million worth of Pratt & Whitney components—$2.8 million of which had been transacted in 1998 and 1999. Rigolli was convicted of conspiracy to defraud the United States, exporting war materials, and violating presidential authorities. Federal Court Judge Janet C. Hall sentenced Rigolli to 56 months in prison and levied fines in excess of $100,000 against him. Rigolli was shipped off to the medium security Otisville penitentiary, northwest of New York City, near the Pennsylvania–New Jersey border. He was also deemed a "denied person" on a published list of the U.S. Bureau of Industry and Security, a division of the Department of Commerce. The "denied persons list" cited 118 Northview, Dollard des Ormeaux as being Rigolli's home address.

The story received scant press coverage and was not even reported in most major newspapers.

Rigolli thought he had a foolproof system, which also involved dummy companies set up by his brother in England and other cutouts. The scheme, however, had been sabotaged. A newspaper reporter speculated that Pratt & Whitney had ratted him out but the company would not comment. In the end, Rigolli had no idea who had betrayed him and how it had been done.

The Rigolli-owned house linked to Maher Arar's then-sister-in-law Parto Navidi is two kilometres west of Dollard des Ormeaux in the adjacent community of Pierrefonds. Was it the same Pietro Rigolli? The answer could be found in the government's property rolls.

According to Québec records, Mihan Haghighi Talab purchased 118 Northview on April 20, 1998 from 2832-8559 Québec Inc. She took out a $400,000 mortgage with the CIBC bank, which was guaranteed by Farid Haghighi Talab, one of the known aliases of Pietro Rigolli as cited in his case files. After Rigolli was arrested in March 1999, Mihan sold the property in October of that year for $565,000. Rigolli and Talab's names were listed on each property.

The information contained in all the criminal court documents pointed to an even deeper story. The prosecution only presented a bare-bones outline of its case because Rigolli had pleaded guilty. What the U.S. government did reveal in its prosecution was that the RCMP had searched Rigolli's house on Northview in Dollard des Ormeaux, and little more.

After Rigolli had been placed in custody in New Haven, on April 15, 1999, Mary Troland, deputy director of the U.S. Department of Justice, sent a nine-page request from "The Central Authority of the United States" to the "The Central Authority of Canada." In that document, Troland sought the Canadian government's assistance in obtaining a search warrant for 118 Northview. The Canadians did not immediately spring into action. The RCMP decided to mount its own case.

Five months later, on September 16, 1999, having built its evidence, Montréal-based RCMP member Rénald Gauvin applied for and was granted search warrants for both the RCMP in its own capacity and in the assistance of the Americans.

The RCMP searched, not only the house, but also a building at Montréal's Pierre Elliott Trudeau International Airport in Dorval. The RCMP laid two charges against Rigolli over the illegal importation and exportation of the airplane parts. Those charges were dropped the next year after he pleaded guilty and was imprisoned in the United States.

Normally, there would continue to be a complete paper trail in the court records. Ronald Thibault of Mo-Ro Inc. in Montréal was hired to conduct such a search. He found that the two files had been placed in archives. It took a week to retrieve them. When he was allowed to look at them in the courthouse, Thibault found the letter from the U.S. Department of Justice in one jacket with an outline of the case. There were also two pages listing 1,500 exhibits seized from the Rigolli house and, presumably, the airport, but without much detail. Most of what was seized had been documents. The evidence was thus tersely described: "documents found in the second drawer of the filing cabinet" or "files found in the second drawer . . ." or "1,051 rivets."

What should have been in the files were the affidavits to support the search warrants, and the search warrants themselves, providing details of what the police knew. Instead, Thibault noticed, scribbled in French on the back of each file, this notation: "June 8, 2000. Request to withdraw authorized." A further note in a space left for bailiff's comments are the words "*mandate entrouvable.*" Translation: the search warrants and any other accompanying documents had been lost.

In light of the lengthy investigation and arrest of Rigolli and the RCMP involvement in the investigation with their search of his house and home business at 118 Northview in Dollard des Ormeaux, it seems impossible that the RCMP, CSIS, FBI, and CIA could have missed the connection to the second house at 13309 Chelsea in Pierrefonds or a previous house Rigolli had owned in the area. They were all listed in public records. There were also property tax, income tax, and utility company records, among others. In any police investigation—especially one involving national security—it would have been routine for the police to conduct searches of public databases for any links to a suspect or suspects.

Whatever the case, the links between Pietro Rigolli, Parto Navidi, Mourad Mazigh, Maher Arar, and CIM 2000 Inc. were incontrovertible. This raises an entire new set of questions.

No one knows where Arar and his wife lived while in Montréal. Did they live at 13309 Chelsea with their in-laws, Mazigh and Navidi?

I travelled to Ottawa to meet Parto Navidi. She operates a laser hair-removal studio above a strip mall in Bell's Corners, on the western outskirts of the city. Her new husband and her son from her previous marriage were sitting on a couch in the foyer watching television. She introduced me to her young son as "this is the man asking questions about Uncle Maher." The office door opened and two clients shrouded in traditional Gulf-style black abayas drifted to a back room and waited for service.

"I knew they were setting up a company," Navidi said, "but I did not know what they were doing with it."

When I asked her about 13309 Chelsea in Pierrefonds and Pietro Rigolli, Navidi vaguely recalled Rigolli and his wife, Mihan. "We found the house through an Iranian real estate agent. Mihan was an Iranian like me. We were not related. She was an interesting woman who was involved in all kinds of things like charities and causes."

Asked if her husband and Arar had had any interactions with Rigolli, Navidi said: "They did not do business with him. He was only the landlord."

"Did you know that he had been arrested in the United States?" I asked.

"We found out about that only after he stopped coming around," she said, "and then we moved out soon after that."

I pressed but she became fidgety. She said she did not know Rigolli and his wife but then she admitted that he had often come to their house. When I tried to ask her who had lived in the house in Pierrefonds or any more details about CIM 2000 Inc., she ushered me out the door. She said she was busy. I asked if I could call her and she said, "No problem." After numerous attempts, however, she refused to talk to me: "I don't know why you want to ask me questions. I have nothing to say. You had better stop calling me." She hung up the phone.

✛ ✛ ✛

No one knows specifically what Arar was doing in the years leading up to Rigolli's arrest. All we have been told is that Arar had been in Ottawa from 1997 to 1999, and that sometime in 1999 he went to work near Boston at The MathWorks. The RCMP's submission to the O'Connor Commission about CIM 2000 Inc. stated unequivocally that documents showed that Arar and his brother-in-law were operating CIM 2000 Inc. as a business from 1996 to 2002, and that some of that ongoing business was with the Almalkis.

Recall that CSIS agent Theresa Sullivan first interviewed Abdullah Almalki during the summer of 1998 about his activities. Since Almalki was being monitored by CSIS, it would be fair to presume that his activities included doing business with Arar and Mazigh during the previous two years. The CSIS surveillance of Almalki continued. In 1999, CSIS agent Violaine Pepin interviewed Almalki about a trip he had made to Hong Kong with a Muslim businessman who happened to hold a commercial pilot's license. Almalki, his three brothers, and their father were being watched closely. It seems inconceivable that the business dealings with Arar and Mourad Mazigh could have been missed during this period.

In the same vein, the RCMP federal officers in Montréal, through their involvement in the Rigolli investigation in 1999, must have known about CIM 2000 Inc., Arar, and Mazigh. It is also inconceivable that there would have been no contact by the RCMP or CSIS with them during that period or that no files were opened on them. The seriousness of the case mounted by the Americans had caused the RCMP to launch its own investigation—complete with property searches.

But the RCMP federal investigators at Ottawa's "A" Division who became entangled with Arar in 2001 and 2002 were not told about Arar's past. The search warrants in the Rigolli case, which may or may not have mentioned CIM 2000 Inc., Arar, or Mazigh, had disappeared in June 2000. The Mounties had no background on them when they were sent out urgently on Almalki's trail.

When informed about the existence of CIM 2000 Inc., Navidi's comments, and the links to Pietro Rigolli, former RCMP Superintendent Garry Clement—who had overseen the original Arar investigation—was flabbergasted.

"Somebody at the top of the RCMP had to know all this, but we were never told. If we had known about that company back then, it would have changed the whole course of the investigation. We would have had a clear link between Arar and the others, particularly Almalki, and would have not been left stumbling around.

"It was a big mistake by us," Clement said, "because as soon as you see a company where the principals are hiding behind a nominee, there can only be two reasons for doing that—tax evasion or criminal activity. This puts a whole new light on things and raises serious questions about Arar's version of events and what he was really doing."

The RCMP investigators tried to provide a hint of impropriety at CIM 2000 Inc. to the O'Connor Commission, but the commission downplayed the evidence as not being part of its mandate. But the Mounties had put the commission on a hook by revealing the documents. O'Connor was forced to acknowledge Arar's relationship to CIM 2000 Inc. in some form, even it that meant fudging the name in a clear attempt to cover the trail back to it.

After my first interview with Parto Navidi on March 6, I wondered if there was a trail that linked Arar and Parto Navidi with Arsalan (Al) Navidi in the Washington area.

On March 15, I went back to track down Al Navidi using the Internet. I found that I was blocked out from any searches related to him. When I tried to search his biography, companies, and virtually every reference to him, all of which had been there ten days earlier, time after time my search engine locked up. I called Brent Beleskey, who was more sophisticated in searching. He found that the memories on various Internet servers had been erased. "There's nothing but black," he said. "That's strange." Maybe I was on to something and maybe not, but I let that sleeping dog lie.

Knowing all this, let us return to the known, yet vague, official chronology of Arar's activities and follow his barely visible trail and try to put his story into an understandable context.

[11]

ARAR'S TRAVELS

In December 1997, Arar and his family moved from Montréal to Ottawa where he hooked up with Abdullah Almalki, who signed his lease as a witness and contact person.

Sometime in 1999, Arar moved to his fourth job in two years with The MathWorks in Boston. He was living in a rented townhouse in Ottawa. Monia was pregnant and studying for her doctorate in finance at McGill University. She stayed behind. Arar had the financial wherewithal to rent a second house in Boston. Arar's work with The MathWorks allowed him to travel extensively around the United States. He has never elaborated on his work there, his travels, or his sources of financing.

The MathWorks employs about 1,800 people and develops powerful computer programs used by governments and industries around the world, including Agriculture Canada. During its early investigation, the RCMP believed the business of The MathWorks was developing computer learning programs for schools and other programs for industry and government. The MathWorks' most important business, however, was with the U.S. government, in defence and security. As The MathWorks says in its own literature: "Every major aerospace and defense organization in the world uses Math-Works products and services to develop air, naval, land, and space systems. Engineers and scientists rely on MathWorks tools for Model-Based Design and technical computing in programs such as the Airbus A380, F-35 Joint Strike Fighter, Mars Exploration Rover, as well as unmanned aerial vehicles and advanced wireless systems." The MathWorks, as it turns out, is a CIA contractor. Its Matlab and Simulink products are high-speed graphic and sorting programs, which have proved invaluable to the intelligence community.

In the mid-to-late nineties, Boston had become a gathering point for many radical Islamic proponents, including one large group of taxi drivers linked to Al-Qaeda and another formed by expatriate Somalis. Each was being investigated by the Boston office of the FBI.

The biggest concern in Boston, however, was with Ptech Inc., and its fundamentalist Islamic connections. In 1998, Yassin al-Qadi had made a $14 million investment in Ptech, making him the major shareholder in the company. Over the next year, he directly put in at least another $4 million, says Dr. Rachel Ehrenfeld in an interview for this book. Ehrenfeld, who is a leading authority on all facets of illegal money transfers, including money laundering, organized crime, drug trafficking, political corruption, and terrorism, has been used by the Canadian government as a consultant on such matters.

Ehrenfeld found that $5 million of al-Qadi's Ptech purchase monies came from the Isle of Man, $9 million indirectly through BMI, a former New Jersey-based Islamic investment firm with connections to other Ptech management members and investors in the company, and $2 million from Switzerland. Ptech had contracts with the U.S. Army, the Air Force, Naval Air Command, Congress, the Department of Energy, the Department of Justice, Customs, the FAA, the IRS, NATO, the FBI, the Secret Service, and the White House. "Al-Qadi's purchase of Ptech, with all the sensitive work it was doing for the government, set off alarm bells in Washington. There was very much concern," Dr. Ehrenfeld said. "He who controlled the architecture of the computer systems had the ability to control and destroy them, as well."

Devlin Buckley, a contributing writer to *Online Journal*, picked up the story in an article published in March 2006:

> Adding further concerns, al-Qadi was only one of many Ptech investors and managers with alleged connections to terrorist financing. Former Ptech board member Soliman Biheiri, who was recently convicted of lying to investigators regarding his affiliations with known terrorists, was in charge of the above-mentioned New Jersey investment bank, BMI, which according to court documents was used as a financial conduit for Al-Qaeda and Hamas supporters. The FBI discovered the true principals behind BMI were actually Yassin al-Qadi and Hamas leader Musa abu Marzook.
>
> Investigators also accuse Ptech's Biheiri of using BMI to funnel $3.7 million from an Islamic charity, entitled the SAAR Foundation, to Islamist terrorists. The president and CEO of the SAAR

Foundation was Yakub Mirza, who was also on Ptech's board of directors, and who is said to have contacts high within the FBI.

Furthermore, Ptech's vice president and chief scientist, Hussein Ibrahim, was the founder and president of the aforementioned BMI. In fact, Ptech, al-Qadi, Biheiri, Ibrahim, BMI, Mirza, and SAAR, all maintained financial connections with one another, as well as with other organizations and fronts allegedly connected to money laundering and terrorist financing, such as the Muslim Brotherhood, al-Taqwa, the Safa Foundation, the International Islamic Relief Organization (IIRO), and others. Ptech's chief architect, Suheil Laher, headed yet another Islamic charity entitled Care International, which the FBI and IRS claim was "engaged in the solicitation and expenditure of funds to support the mujahideen and promote jihad."

Top Ptech investor and manager, Muhamed Mubayyid, served as Care's treasurer, and has since been indicted for lying on tax returns and concealing the charity's true activities. Mubayyid also donated money to the Alkifah Refugees Center, which maintained the same corporate office as Care, and from where the 1993 World Trade Center bombing was launched.

Also part of this financial nexus was Ptech founder Abdurahman Muhammad Alamoudi, who, according to the US Treasury Department, "had a close relationship with al Qaida and had raised money for al Qaida in the United States." He has since been sentenced to a maximum of twenty three years in prison for illegal dealings with Libya, including his admitted involvement in a plot to assassinate Saudi Crown Prince Abdullah.

Alamoudi also founded a US Army chaplain program for which he served as a consultant for over a decade. A former Justice Department official has described the program as a "spy service for Al-Qaeda."

With all those suspicions, the FBI was getting nowhere. The formal investigation was dropped in 1999, or so it seemed, stunning the investigator in charge, Robert Wright. He believed that the Saudis had used their considerable political influence to get the FBI off their backs. Buckley quoted Wright as saying the FBI "intentionally and repeatedly thwarted and obstructed" his attempts to arrest terrorists, seize assets, and expand his investigation into the financial network, of which al-Qadi allegedly was a part.

Virtually nothing is know of Arar or his activities during the entire time he was in Boston. Two years later, however, Arar had returned to Ottawa, the home of the Khadr family, who were well-known Al-Qaeda members. He set up a business, Simcomms Inc., in his home, with a promise of "consulting work" from his former employer, The MathWorks. What was that work? Neither he nor The MathWorks will say, but presumably he had done a good job in Boston and was still held in high regard by his employers. At least, that is the impression the public has been left with.

In Ottawa, Arar wrote and published an article in *Wireless Systems Design* magazine about wireless modems and a way to overcome distortion. As was pointed out earlier, *Ghost Plane* author Stephen Grey concluded that, based on that article, Arar was a harmless computer nerd. The article contains details about a "new algorithm," improvements to a technology that at the time was not commercially viable in some applications.

Shortly after arriving back in Ottawa, Arar met with Almalki at Mango's Café. The two men apparently didn't communicate with each other again. The police, naturally, became curious about Arar, and began to investigate him as a person of interest.

In January 2002, Arar flew from Ottawa via New York to Tunisia, where his father-in-law lived. The Americans said they were watching him, but did nothing, and allowed him to transit.

Two days after his wife received a visit from the RCMP, on January 22, 2002, Arar returned to Canada, via New York, again, to meet with the police, who wanted to interview him.

Recall that FBI agents in the Boston office told the RCMP that they were planning a sting on Arar, but nothing seemed to come of it? At the same time, the RCMP became aware that there were at least 12 FBI agents working in Ottawa, but the agents there didn't seem to gather much evidence about anything. The likely reason for that was because their job might not have been to gather evidence, but to monitor, guide, and protect their valuable secret agent, whoever it might have been.

In the interim, Arar and Monia, who were supposedly being watched carefully by the U.S. authorities, made another trip to the United States by car and, while there, Arar renewed his work visa. Anyone who has crossed the U.S.–Canada border since 2001 knows how difficult it can be getting into the United States. Arar not only had no difficulty, no flag was raised about him.

In June and July 2002, Arar's family and then Arar himself headed, via New York, back to Tunisia again, either, as he would put it in various statements, to visit Mazigh's ailing father or for a family vacation—in one of the most dangerous countries in the world. Why did they travel separately? Why did the Americans let him pass through?

Canadian police, meanwhile, learned he had packed up his household and was not likely coming back to Canada. He was even said to be looking for work in Tunisia. Why did he pack up his house? Did he think he was not coming back?

That August, Arar said his former employer The MathWorks had offered him a "possible" consulting job with a "prospective" client. We have never learned what the job might have been.

Arar lingered in Tunisia for another month until September 25, before heading, not to Boston for the "possible" job, but back to Ottawa where he had emptied his house months earlier. Why? The route took him through Zurich and New York. Why? He left his family behind in Tunisia. Why?

The RCMP never considered him a suspect, merely a person of interest. The police had never questioned him. Arar must not have expected that if he travelled across the Canadian border he would likely be challenged. These were dangerous times. Muslim men like him were suspect, even if they had nothing to hide. Many didn't travel because of that fear. Why did Arar not fly directly to Canada?

The Americans detained Arar on September 26, but did not secretly ship him off to a foreign country, as had been the case with many other extraordinary rendition victims around the world. American law prohibited both sending a refused passenger at its borders back to a third-party country or to a country where he would be tortured. Instead, the Americans made a bit of a show of it, allowing Arar a phone call to his mother-in-law in Ottawa, which put Canadian authorities on his trail. Why, with this one man and only this man, were the Americans prepared to flout their own conventions and laws and so obviously incite anger in a neighbouring country which is also its closest business partner and political ally?

From secret documents disclosed years later by *The Globe and Mail*, a mysterious high-level meeting took place in Washington on October 4, 2002, after which an order was signed by then Acting Attorney General Larry Thompson to have Arar sent to Syria. The rationale for the action was that the porous Canadian border would not keep him "from returning to the United States nefarious purposes."

After 13 days in detention in New York, the Americans then sent Arar, not so quietly, to Syria via Maine, France, and Jordan. The itinerary was easy to trace. Soon, everyone in Canada knew where he was, how he had arrived in Syria, and how he was being tortured.

The way the rendition was carried out was entirely extraordinary: the Americans deliberately brought an avalanche of unflattering attention to themselves. Under the rendition program, the U.S. had scooped up suspected terrorists around the world and shipped them to secret prisons. Some of those people seemed clearly linked to terrorism, but there's something about the way the extraordinary rendition program was carried out by the United States that doesn't pass the sniff test.

Michael Scheuer, the CIA agent who was the architect of rendition and ran the program from 1995 to 1999, confirmed, without going into detail, that there were differences in approach. Speaking at a conference in April 2008 at Duke University in North Carolina, the retired intelligence officer said: "The bar was lowered after 9/11."

One of the attendees at the conference was former Liberal cabinet minister Ron Atkey, who had worked inside the Arar Commission trying to dig out secrets about the case hidden by the government. *The Globe and Mail* described the following telling exchange between Atkey and Scheuer:

> Questioned about the Arar affair, Mr. Scheuer asserted that that rendition was not technically a CIA job, but rather an FBI initiative, by agents working in cahoots with unspecified agencies north of the border.
>
> That prompted a response from Canadian lawyer Ron Atkey, who was in attendance to give a speech about the years he spent inside the Arar Commission battling government secrecy to reveal what Canada knew about the CIA rendition program.
>
> Mr. Atkey pointed out Canadian agencies were found to have had no foreknowledge of the U.S. decision to put Mr. Arar on a Gulfstream jet and fly him to the Middle East, after his 2002 arrest in a New York airport.
>
> "The biggest piece of baloney," Mr. Scheuer said. "They [the Canadians] were totally surprised like Captain Renault in *Casablanca*," he quipped.
>
> The allusion referred to a scene in the 1942 film, where a duplicitous French gendarme shuts down an illegal casino operation in Morocco—saying "I'm shocked, shocked to find out that gambling is going on in here!" even as he is handed a big win from the roulette wheel.

The difference in the approach to rendition after September 11, 2001, was embodied in the statements by Bush, Cheney, and others within the next 10 days, that the U.S. government was "prepared to take risks ... to get out ahead of this thing."

In *Ghost Plane*, Stephen Grey estimated that several hundred people had become caught up in this system. There were obviously several categories of renditioned suspects. The first included those taken before September 22, 2001, when the new policies were implemented. Next are the known terrorists or combatants, whose crimes and deeds could be documented, such as Khalid Sheikh Mohammed, the confessed architect of the September 11 attacks, and Ibn al-Sheikh al-Libi, a senior Al-Qaeda figure. If they are excluded from the list, then the number of truly extraordinary renditions is sharply reduced.

In a story published in the *Washington Post* in December 2005, anonymous CIA sources are quoted as saying that there were 39 extraordinary renditions carried out, but not all of them had been hard-core Al-Qaeda members. In fact, Arar was not the only innocent person renditioned. There had been "ten or fewer of such erroneous renditions," the *Post* reported. Was this the risk the Americans were taking? Were some of these innocents merely actors in a play within a play?

The ten or so innocents all had similar stories. A few were sent to Guantanamo Bay, where the real bad guys landed, but most went to prisons where contingents of Al-Qaeda and Muslim Brotherhood convicts were being held captive. Most of the innocents said they were tortured, usually within earshot of other prisoners, but none all that badly. Most described their torture as being "psychological." All were released relatively unharmed, except, perhaps, for a marked loss in body weight. Arar's case wasn't that unusual, but even the definition of "innocents" seems somewhat blurry.

Khalid El-Masri, a Kuwaiti-born citizen with German nationality, ended up in an Afghanistan jail that housed prisoners from Pakistan, Tanzania, Yemen, and Saudi Arabia. A car salesman struggling to make a livelihood, he had the same name as a wanted Al-Qaeda member. As Stephen Grey described it, he was released after five months, flown to Tirana, Albania, and then driven for six or seven hours down bumpy back roads before being let out near where the borders of Albania, Macedonia, and Serbia converge. He was handed his belongings and money, which had been seized from him, and ordered to walk away. "At the end of the path he found three uniformed men. They appeared to be expecting him, and had a plastic bag with a packed lunch waiting for him," Grey wrote. The men asked to see his passport, told him he was in the country illegally, and then drove him to the airport, where he purchased his own ticket and flew back to Germany.

In April 2002, Martin Mubanga of London, England, was captured in Zambia, shipped to Guantanamo Bay, and detained there for two years before being released. He returned to London and became a human rights activist as well as a budding rap singer, a cause célèbre and a hero to many.

Australian citizen Mamdouh Habib was taken off a bus in Islamabad, Pakistan, in November 2001, and shipped to Egypt, where, he said, he was tortured for six months, before confessing to being a planner of the September 11 attacks. He said he told his interrogators that he had trained pilots and had even wanted to commandeer one of the planes himself. Habib was then sent to Guantanamo Bay. He was released in January 2005. Habib sued the Australian government, creating a public uproar, but the Australian government hid behind its Official Secrets Act and would not address the Habib case. He subsequently ran for election to the Australian Parliament as an independent, but won only 5 per cent of the vote.

Although there was a public outcry in many countries about the rendition practice, it is important to note that the Australian and several European governments and intelligence agencies refused to cooperate with investigations undertaken in their countries. That is probably because all the countries involved—the United States, Canada, Australia, Great Britain, Germany, France, Italy, Egypt, Syria, Jordan, Afghanistan, Pakistan, Uzbekistan, Zambia, and others—were acting together in a common cause.

They all knew that the extraordinary renditions had two purposes: the first, to move bona fide Al-Qaeda members to secure fortresses like Guantanamo Bay or the British base at Diego Garcia (an atoll in the middle of the Indian Ocean); the second, to provide a cover for secret agents who would be placed in prisons housing suspected terrorists and later replanted into their communities. There is no other explanation for how the U.S. managed to make such horrendous errors in ten of 39 cases, more than one in four. With all the planning and execution required and with everything that was at stake, such a high ratio of failure seems decidedly improbable.

Hassan Mustafa Osama Nasr, also known as Abu Omar, was taken in 2003 by the CIA in Italy and deported to Egypt. He wasn't released until 2007, after which he returned to Italy, where authorities had already filed charges against 26 Americans who were suspects in the affair. All 26 had registered under their own names at Rome hotels and were easily traced.

Likewise in Canada: everyone seemed to know there were FBI and CIA agents roaming freely, but no one raised an eyebrow.

In Arar's case, why would he have been sent to Syria? The common link between Syria and the United States was their mutual fear of the Muslim Brotherhood. Syria knew about the group, and the United States wanted to know more. This unlikely alliance was just another example of the adage, "The enemy of your enemy is your friend."

For Arar, being imprisoned in Syria would carry serious consequences. The Arar name was well known and carried considerable cachet in Muslim Brotherhood circles in Syria. His mother's cousin was a member of the Brotherhood. The region's popular revolutionary poet, Mustafa Salih Mustafa Yousof al-Tull Wahbi, was born in north Jordan but went to school across the border in Aleppo, Syria. He made a name for himelf in the 1920s for his strident anti-government stance. His *nom de plume* was Arar.

If Syria suspected that Arar had been a member of the Muslim Brotherhood, then that country's interrogators would certainly have done more to him than they actually did. No one but Maher Arar and the Syrians know where he was in the Palestine Branch prison, and the Syrians are not talking. The public impression was that Arar was kept in solitary confinement in a grave-like or coffin-like cell one metre wide, two metres long, and two and a half metres high, presumably out of contact with other prisoners. But that part was not entirely true.

There were 20 cells on that dark, dank range of the Palestine Branch. There was access to two disgusting Turkish toilets. When he was there, Toronto truck driver Ahmed El Maati had been held in cell number 5, and, he said later, he was able to have conversations with a young woman being held on the other side of the wall. El Maati had been sent to Egypt by the time Abdullah Almalki, the original target of the Canadian investigation, arrived. He was placed in cell number 3. Stephen Grey reported that when Arar showed up a few months later, he was next door to Almalki in cell number 2. There were prisoners from other countries in adjacent cells on the range, like Syrian-born Mohammed Haydar Zammer, a German locksmith, in number 13. Born in Aleppo, Zammer was a suspected Al-Qaeda recruiter who had been taken while in Morocco. According to Stephen Grey's research, the inmates on the cellblock were able to pass notes to each other and communicate in whispers.

What has also been lost in the hysteria is that Arar did not spend the entire time in the Palestine Branch. On August 20, 2003, he was sent to

Sednaya prison, north of Damascus, where Muslim Brotherhood members constitute a large proportion of the population. Seventeen days later, Almalki was transferred to Sednaya as well.

On Arar's website, he described, curiously in the third person, the move to Sednaya and what took place there:

> Arar is not tortured when he arrives at Sednaya prison. He is placed in a collective cell and is able to talk with other prisoners and move around. Arar says this was like heaven compared to where he was at the Palestine Branch. Then, Arar wrote the following, which he says happened on September 19 or 20, 2003: Arar is teaching English to some other prisoners in his cell when he hears others saying that another Canadian has arrived. He looks up and sees a thin man with a shaved head looking very weak. After some time he realizes this is Abdullah Almalki. Almalki tells Arar he has also been at the Palestine Branch, and that he was in a cell like Arar's for even longer. He tells Arar he has been severely tortured—with the tire and the cable. He says he was also hung upside down. Almalki also says he was tortured at Sednaya prison just weeks before.

Almalki had only arrived at Sednaya on September 6, two weeks earlier, which makes his torture there seem plausible. However, for whatever reason, Arar seems to indicate that he did not know that Almalki was being held next door to him on the same range at the Palestine Branch for at least eight months. Eight months? He had told the O'Connor Commission expert fact finder Stephen Toope that he and Almalki had talked "extensively."

In fact, in his public account, Arar leaves the impression that he talked to no one in the Palestine Branch. He made not a single reference to any conversations he might have had. That's his well-defended, uncorroborated story.

It is also important to note the Syrian response to all of this. Syria said Arar was not tortured and that he had no links to Al-Qaeda, which would be absolutely true within the context of the above scenario. Syria would say no more than that, perhaps because what they did say was slyly true.

The U.S. posture toward the entire affair is revealing. When the gun-shy RCMP pointed out to U.S. authorities that some of its information about Arar had been overstated or might be misleading, why did the Americans ignore that and press on? Why would the U.S. not come clean with what it said it knew about Arar? Why has it resisted cooperation? Why has it blocked every attempt by Canada, which wasn't trying very hard at all, to determine the facts of the matter? Why has it continued to badmouth Arar?

All of which brings us back to the unexplored issues surrounding CIM 2000 Inc. Mourad Mazigh, Arar's partner and brother-in-law, said he planned to testify before the O'Connor Commission. But in August 2004, after the RCMP found the business documents of CIM 2000 Inc. and were closing in on the company and, likely, the links between Mazigh, Arar, and arms dealer Pietro Rigolli, Mourad had a change of heart. Instead of taking the stand on his brother-in-law's behalf, Mourad opted to return to Tunisia.

Upon his arrival, Tunisian intelligence officers, at the behest of Canadian authorities, questioned him and his father about what they were doing. This led to a backlash of organized outrage in Canada, led by Arar and Monia. There was no basis for Mourad to be questioned, they protested, and insisted the police were on another illegal fishing expedition.

Arar and Monia held a dramatic, headline-grabbing press conference in September 2004 to denounce the so-called intimidation of Mourad and the Mazighs' father. "It's outrageous that they would have my father-in-law visited just because they are desperate to find evidence that isn't there," Arar said. He and Mazigh said their relatives were extremely frightened by the perceived "intimidation."

Arar's lawyers sent furious, outraged letters to Minister of Public Safety and Emergency Preparedness Anne McLellan, demanding to know "if Canadian officials shared any information which led to these interrogations and said that such contacts only intimidate a witness who has yet to give testimony." McLellan denied that there was intimidation and refused to say what the police were doing in the ongoing investigation. For his part, Mourad eschewed the opportunity to testify and stayed in Tunisia, and the CIM 2000 Inc. story all but disappeared.

By April 2005, Arar had accused the Canadian government officials of being complicit with his torture after released documents revealed that the police expressed an interest in information revealed to the Syrians during his interrogation. For the next two years, Arar complained about being virtually disabled from his experience in Syria and being unable to work. He was said to be suffering from post-traumatic stress syndrome and was unable to find a job in Ottawa. But then another interesting twist occurred in his life.

In the early summer of 2006, Arar headed west to Kamloops, B.C., where he bought a house with a two-car garage. On the surface it looked as if he were getting away from all the intrigue and pressure, but the B.C. interior was one of the unlikeliest places in the world for a devout Sunni Muslim like him. Before he arrived in the Kamloops area, about a dozen Sunni Muslims lived there and there was not even a mosque. The rationale for the move was that Monia had been offered her first teaching job, as a research and teaching professor of economics at what is likely one of the most obscure post-secondary institutions in Canada, Thompson Rivers University.

TRU, as it is known, opened in 2005. It is an amalgamation of the former University College of the Cariboo and B.C. Open University. The first chancellor of the university was former downhill skier and ski-resort operator Nancy Greene Raine. Among the many dignitaries who attended the university's opening was then-Conservative Leader Stephen Harper.

It looked as if Arar and Mazigh were ready to settle down out of the limelight, but landing out of the blue in Kamloops made them big news. *The Globe and Mail* sent veteran Ottawa reporter Jeff Sallot to cover the story. Sallot, an American, had a long career which had begun in Ohio where he shared a Pulitzer Prize for his coverage of the Kent State massacre on May 4, 1970. At the *Globe* he had spent most of his time in Ottawa covering police and security matters, although he did have a stint in Moscow as a foreign correspondent. Sallot's uncritical stories about Arar helped to drive home to the public how decent a man was Arar, and how dastardly he had been treated.

Arar told the *Kamloops Daily News* that since he could not find a job in Ottawa, he planned to complete his PhD while his wife taught. "It's such a beautiful, small community," he is quoted as saying of Kamloops. "The stress level is a lot less than big cities, less traffic, and we like the clean air." Reporter James Gordon then paraphrased Arar: "He added he never wanted to be a public figure, but he embraced it when circumstances made him one."

Everyone knew Arar and Mazigh were in town.

On June 23, 2006, just before Arar flew out to Kamloops to house hunt, Swiss investigative Judge Marie-Antonella Bino made a request to Canadian authorities for information about Ibrahim Afandi. Afandi ran the Gang Ranch in Clinton, British Columbia, and was the other Canadian connection in the so-called Golden Chain investigation of Al-Qaeda financiers.

In Canadian terms, Clinton is just around the corner from Kamloops. Each community is linked geographically through the Thompson River valley. To fly out of Clinton, the nearest airport is Kamloops, 120 kilometres away, about a 1 1/2-hour drive. With Arar and Mazigh in town, the number of practising Muslims had swelled to around 15. It was an active religious community, nonetheless, with an Internet presence. At the very least, did Arar and Afandi pray together?

The next coincidence?

The leading federal government politician in that region was none other than Public Safety Minister Stockwell Day, the cabinet minister in charge of the Arar file, CSIS, and the RCMP. Day was the member for Okanagan-Coquihalla, a riding that includes part of the Kamloops area. While Day usually is identified as being a political force in neighbouring Alberta, where he was a leading provincial politician, he had moved to British Columbia in 2000. Did Day have any influence on Mazigh's appointment at the university?

After Arar's arrival in the community was announced in the media, did Afandi try to contact him and commiserate with him? Did they ever meet? It's impossible to know because no one will say.

Arar and Mazigh, flush with their millions, suddenly had a change of heart. In the late summer of 2007, they announced that they had decided to give up their idyllic life in the mountains and return to Ottawa. Before they left, they donated $20,000 for a scholarship at Thompson Rivers University for a student pursuing studies in social justice. It was their "thank you" gift to Kamloops. The university was somewhat stunned by what had happened, said a campus source, who asked for anonymity. "We thought she was doing a good job and was happy here, and then they suddenly left, citing family reasons. It's not easy to find economics professors who want to come here. We still haven't been able to replace her."

A few weeks after Arar left Kamloops, the Canadian government finally "perfected" its file on Afandi, which was subsequently sent off to Judge Bino in Switzerland in October 2007.

Again, it could all be mere coincidence and conjecture. Maybe Arar did just sit around the house, babysit the kids, and bone up on computer engineering, while Mazigh conducted research or lectured the scholars at Thompson Rivers U. Again, like so much in the Arar saga, no one knows for sure. Arar, as we have seen, will not talk.

Finally, there is another possible clue pointing to what Arar may have been doing, that the O'Connor Commission had overlooked, which was revealed only after Arar had been paid off by the Canadian government.

Lost in all the confusion and histrionics of the time was a revealing story published on March 17, 2007, in *The Globe and Mail*, a story that didn't seem to go anywhere or appear to have much importance. In this story, reporter Colin Freeze attempted to explain the roots of the American government's intransigence in clearing Arar's name. His story centred on the relationship between Abdullah Almalki, the prime target in the Arar investigation, and two Lebanese-born brothers, Abdelrahman Elzahabi and Mohammed Kamal Elzahabi.

If the name Abdelrahman Elzahabi rings a bell, he was the fellow mentioned earlier who ran an automobile repair shop in Montréal in the late nineties. He had a pilot's license and his own Cessna aircraft which, he said, he had been forced to sell. The Montréal garage is where Almalki, Maher Arar, and truck driver Ahmed El Maati all admitted they had seen each other, but were mere acquaintances.

In the mid-nineties, before he opened his Montréal business, Abdelrahman Elzahabi operated Drive Axle Rebuilders (DAR), an automobile repair business in New York City.

The central player in *The Globe and Mail* story was truck driver Mohammed Kamal Elzahabi. Elzahabi had been held in a maximum security U.S. prison in Minnesota since his arrest in 2004 for lying to federal authorities. He was a suspected Al-Qaeda sleeper agent. Elzahabi had been a trained sniper fighting for the Mujahedeen in Afghanistan.

Elzahabi's arrest warrant contained information gained from the January 22, 2002, raid by the RCMP on Abdullah Almalki's house in Ottawa. In the nineties, Almalki, as we already know, was selling Canadian electronic equipment to Pakistan. He was also doing business with Arar and his brother-in-law Mourad Mazigh through CIM 2000 Inc., which was not mentioned in the Elzahabi arrest warrant.

In 1996, Almalki had sent a fax message to the Elzahabi brothers, who were running DAR in New York City, seeking their assistance. Almalki asked the brothers if they would help him buy cheap electronic equipment in the United States, consolidate the packages in New York, and ship them to Pakistan, which they did.

"The [Canadian] documents detail purchases and shipments of radios and other electronics worth hundreds of thousands of dollars, all shipped to DAR in New York," *The Globe and Mail* quoted from an FBI affidavit. The story continued: "Among the items shipped to Elzahabi's New York business were large quantities of portable field radios or 'walkie talkies,'" reads the affidavit. "Field radios of the same make and models as was shipped to DAR in New York have been recovered in Afghanistan by U.S. military forces during military actions following the attacks of September 11, 2001."

The export of the field radios was not a crime, but the FBI said that Elzahabi lied to them when he told an agent that he did not know much about the business. A 1996 fax from Almalki addressed to "Mr. Elzahabi" proved otherwise. "Mohammed Kamal Elzahabi did knowingly and willfully make a false material statement," the indictment says.

The *Globe* quoted court documents, portions of which had been made public, in which Elzahabi told the FBI about how he had become radicalized when he attended an Islamic conference in the United States in the eighties. Soon after, he joined a missionary group and found his way to Afghanistan, where he took the name Abu Kamal al-Lubnani. He became a sniper instructor, giving other Arabs small-arms training at the Khalden camp, a base for would-be Mujahedeen fighters that years later would be taken over by Al-Qaeda.

In the early nineties, Elzahabi "met men who would go on to become notorious terrorists, even the eventual mastermind of the 9/11 attacks, Khalid Shaikh Mohammed." As close as he appeared to be to Al-Qaeda, Elzahabi never admitted to being a member.

During the Afghan civil war, Elzahabi was shot in the gut and forced to return to the United States for treatment. He worked for a while with his brother at DAR before moving to Boston where he became one of the group of taxi drivers being watched by the FBI. "Three other former mujahedeen worked at the same company. One ended up jailed for an Al-Qaeda bomb plot in Jordan. Another was killed trying to lead a Sunni insurrection in Lebanon. The other is jailed in Syria," the *Globe* reported.

The FBI said that it started investigating Elzahabi in 1999, the same year Maher Arar moved to Boston to work with The Mathworks. The FBI could not find any evidence Elzahabi was a terrorist. Then it lost track of him. "Elzahabi went to fight the Russians in Chechnya—before an FBI public-record search found him driving 18-wheelers out of Minnesota."

Elzahabi's lawyer, Paul Engh, said he was flummoxed by why his client was being held for so long in a maximum security over such relatively minor charges. Engh could not understand why the government had bugged and videotaped his client's cell. "The presumption of innocence means nothing in this case," Engh told the *Globe*. His client's prison time was already "well past" any sentence he would get if convicted of lying about walkie-talkies.

Maher Arar's name came into the case because Elzahabi said the FBI questioned Elzahabi about him after he was arrested. In a court motion brought in 2006, Engh asked Judge John Tunheim to compel Maher Arar, who was barred from entering the United States, to give a statement about what he knew about the matter. Tunheim turned down the request, saying that whatever Arar had to say was not relevant.

Freeze then tried to contact Arar, whose name had by now been cleared officially in Canada and who was presumably resting on his settlement. Freeze wanted to ask Arar about the FBI's position. Arar would only speak through his lawyer, Lorne Waldman.

Freeze wrote: "'We have no idea why the FBI says this—Maher has never heard of a DAR in New York,' Mr. Waldman said in an e-mail to the *Globe*. Asked whether he knew Mohammed Kamal Elzahabi, the lawyer said only: 'Maher says he had his car fixed at [Abdelrahman's] garage a few times when he lived in Montréal.' Later, Mr. Waldman said his client doesn't recall ever meeting the other brother, Mohammed."

Freeze could not explain why the U.S. government was being so harsh toward Arar and so adamant about his involvement. "*The Globe and Mail* has spent months investigating Project A-O Canada and its tangled aftermath—the complex web of personal and police interactions that have remained an unsettling mystery."

In October 2007, I spoke with Freeze about the story, which had been completely ignored and had had no impact on the Arar matter. I asked him about Arar's demeanour. "I had to deal with his lawyer," Freeze said. "It would be fair to say that because of the story my presence is not welcomed by Team Arar."

Ottawa information research specialist Ken Rubin, a perennial thorn in the side of government, was hired by Team Arar to ferret out information about their case. Something about their approach, which he could not describe, made him leery and he withdrew his services. "Maher and Monia are nice people, but in my mind there was something fishy going on. I couldn't put my finger on it," Rubin said in an interview in March 2008. "There was this whole Team Arar thing. Arar's lawyers were acting kind of weird in my opinion, and the government lawyers were, too. It's like they all had a big secret, which they only knew, and they were playing some kind of game together. The only journalist the Arar team liked was Jeff Sallot because he wasn't threatening to them. I just didn't want to be part of it, so I pulled away."

Arar said he had known Abdelrahman Elzahabi in Montréal because he had brought his car there a few times to be fixed. The Elzahabi brothers had been doing business with Abdullah Almalki since at least 1996. Arar said he barely knew Abdelrahman Elazhabi and did not know Mohammed Elzahabi at all. In the past, Arar had denied being close to Almalki as well, although the documents submitted to the O'Connor Commission in August 2004 indicate otherwise. He and his brother-in-law, Mourad Mazigh, had conducted business with Almalki from 1996 to 2002. The "business" in which all of them—the Almalki brothers, the Elzahabi brothers, Mazigh, and Arar—were involved was buying field radios and other electronic equipment and shipping it to Pakistan or Afghanistan. Yet, when confronted with the evidence of both their mutual association and business ties, each either denied the existence of such relationships or, as in the case of Mazigh and Arar, refused to answer questions. Why was the Elzahabi case not explored by the O'Connor Commission? Or was it just one coincidence too many?

Arar had a knack of showing up in one hot spot before moving on to another. Wherever Arar seemed to go, the Boston FBI office seemed to be following not far behind—in Montréal, Ottawa, Boston, New York City, and who knows where else? Just as Arar had just set up residence to work with The MathWorks in Boston, the FBI began its investigation of Elzahabi in Boston. When Arar moved to Ottawa, the FBI were on the streets there. It was Boston-based FBI agents who told the RCMP they were planning to do a sting on Arar, knowledge of which helped spur the RCMP investigation, but it never seemed to happen. Finally, as Michael Scheuer put it, the FBI orchestrated Arar's rendition. Was that the sting? Perhaps all these examples are just one coincidence after another of Maher Arar landing in a place, taking the stage, and having the police soon pounce.

The Elzahabi matter, flimsy as it might seem to be on the surface, continued to muddy Arar's name in the United States. Over and over again, Arar has kept repeating his mantra about how he wants to clear his name. In Canada, he was called upon as a critic of government and police, an instant expert as it were, on how those institutions can better serve the public.

On October 18, 2007, Arar testified before a U.S. Congress subcommittee, via satellite link-up at the University of Ottawa. At issue were classified documents in which the imprisoned Mohammed Alzahabi told U.S. authorities that he had seen Arar in Afghanistan in the early nineties. Arar said he falsely confessed under torture in Syria to having been in Afghanistan, and denied that what Alzahabi said was true.

Arar told the subcommittee, according to *The Globe and Mail,* that he had been given "no explanation whatsoever" as to why his attempts to clear his name in the United States have stalled.

A week later, on October 25, 2007, U.S. Secretary of State Condoleeza Rice testified about the Arar case before the House of Representatives foreign relations committee. "We do not think this case was handled as it should have been," Rice said. "Our communication with the Canadian government about this was by no means perfect. In fact, it was quite imperfect." Nevertheless, Rice said, Arar would continue to be barred from the United States. "We and the Canadians do not have exactly the same understanding of what is possible in the future for Mr. Arar in terms of travel and the like," she said.

"You're aware of the fact that he was tortured?" Bill Delahunt, a Massachusetts Democrat and chairman of the Foreign Affairs Subcommittee, asked Rice, referring to the O'Connor report.

"I am aware of claims that were made," Rice responded.

Editorialists and civil libertarian groups in the United States and Canada were outraged by the position Rice had taken.

"What you're seeing is an American government in retreat," Arar lawyer Julian Falconer told CBC News. "It's extremely significant that for the first time what you're seeing is, slowly but surely, the U.S. Government is conceding that mistakes were made."

Had mistakes been made?

Prime Minister Stephen Harper said he was "encouraged" by Rice's comments. "We have raised this issue on many occasions with the Americans, and we hope that the U.S. government will act to fully address this matter," he told the House of Commons. By early 2008, Public Safety Minister Stockwell Day stated that he had made four more inquiries about Arar to the U.S. government.

As for Arar and his alleged ties to Afghanistan, the Canadian government and the O'Connor Commission showed no interest in the matter, leaving it to dangle—tantalizingly—in the wind. Paul Cavalluzzo, the O'Connor Commission counsel, reiterated that point to reporter Colin Freeze: "What the report says is that one's presence in Afghanistan is a very complicated and nuanced question. If the person is a mujahedeen fighting the Soviets . . . we looked at him as freedom fighters and nationalists. However, if they were in Afghanistan after 1996, when Al-Qaeda moved to Afghanistan, and attended an Al-Qaeda training camp, that's a different story. As far as Arar is concerned, there was the allegation and it wasn't proven either way."

The focus of the Canadian inquiry, Cavalluzzo said, was on the conduct of Canadian officials. "Whether Arar was in Afghanistan in 1993 wasn't related to that," Cavalluzzo told Freeze.

On the other hand, if everything were as above board as it seemed, a logical person would think that the very public stalemate between the United States government and Maher Arar could be resolved if one side or the other opened up with what it really knew. The Americans are not going to do it, so why not Arar?

To date, Arar has declined to testify under oath and has never been cross-examined by anyone. He wouldn't even take off his shirt to show his scars.

In September 2007 Penguin Canada announced that it had purchased the rights to a book by Arar spokesperson Kerry Pither. It would be "the inside story" of Arar, Ahmad El Maati, Abdullah Almalki and Muayyed Nureddin as told through their eyes. Three months later, in December 2007, McClelland & Stewart announced that it had struck a deal with Monia Mazigh to write her memoirs (first in French) to be published in 2009. The world wanted to know what her husband had to say, the real story, but she said he was not quite ready to tell it, if he ever would be.

✚ ✚ ✚

Compare the manner in which the government handled the Arar case with how it handled similar complaints made by Ahmad El Maati, Abdullah Almalki, and Muayyed Nureddin. Arar got the one-sided "open" public forum, while the inquiry into the cases of the other three, headed by former Supreme Court Justice Frank Iacobucci, was held entirely in secret. Not only were the three complainants not allowed in, but their lawyers were left to patrol the corridors, due to national security concerns. The original plan was that no witnesses would be called and the inquiry would merely be a review of the documentary evidence. But in early 2008, Iacobucci did call a number of witnesses, including RCMP investigators, to testify in secret. Why all the secrecy? Could it have been something to do with Maher Arar that El Maati, Almalki, and Nureddin should never know?

As this book was being completed, insiders suggested Iacobucci was planning to release an interim report during the summer and his final report in September 2008. In July, Iacobucci put out another "final, final" call for submissions. The deadline was October 20. "The whole thing is going to be another whitewash," a confidential source said. "I was told that it all came down to politics, the facts be damned."

[12]

THE CANADIAN CANDIDATE
AND THE SCAPEGOAT

When Stephen Harper became prime minister in February 2006, he arrived in Ottawa with a promise to reform government and make it more transparent. Among the first briefings he received was the Arar file. The O'Connor Commission was in its final stages. In the midst of the Arar controversy, significant changes in the bureaucracy had taken place, which had propelled Margaret Bloodworth and William Elliott out of the shadows and into key positions of control.

In May 2002, Bloodworth, who had been the deputy minister of Transport, was named deputy minister of Defence. Shortly afterward, Elliott, who had been her assistant deputy minister of Transport, in charge of safety and security, got another job. He was named assistant secretary to the cabinet, in charge of security and intelligence. In that role he supported the national security adviser to the prime minister, and was secretary of the Cabinet Committee on Security, Public Health, and Emergencies.

After Arar came home in October 2003, Bloodworth was promoted yet again, this time as the first deputy minister of the newly created Public Safety and Emergency Preparedness Canada. She was now the top civil servant in charge of, among other responsibilities, the RCMP and CSIS. Elliott was then named national security adviser to the prime minister in April 2005.

Bloodworth and Elliott emerged as the twin gatekeepers of the Arar story. What precisely they told Harper is not known, but it is evident that Harper was presented with a dilemma. He could blow the whistle on what really happened under the previous Liberal governments of Paul Martin and Jean Chrétien, but that was now politically impossible. The inflamed Canadian public and those around the world who were paying attention to what was going on at the O'Connor Commission would cry about a cover-up. If Harper revealed what the CIA and FBI had been doing in Canada, it would only serve to alienate the American government and its people. On the other hand, he could hold his nose and go along with the game, sacrificing the reputation of the RCMP for the greater good, as it were.

This brings us to the extraordinary $12.5 million awarded to Arar, his family, and his legal team. Arar had originally sued the government and the RCMP for $37 million in compensation for his damages. In terms of Canadian civil litigation, it was an extraordinarily high claim, but so was $12.5 million. However, when the O'Connor Commission recommended a settlement for Arar, there wasn't much debate inside government—as had been the case in the Mulroney matter—about how much should be paid. The government just cut a cheque and that was it. "It was a very un-Canadian thing to do," said a confidential source. "The question you have to ask yourself is this: did Canada really pay the money, or did the Americans?" Afterward, a number of others, including prominent civil litigation lawyers, made similar comments to me.

It is an intriguing possibility that the American government secretly slipped the money to the Canadians. As was pointed out earlier, the settlement was entirely out of proportion to previous Canadian legal settlements, but it does fall within the range of what American settlements look like. The $12.5 million sounds like a lot of money, but in 2007, the *Washington Post* reported, the U.S. budget for intelligence gathering was more than $50 billion. The Arar settlement would have been 1/5000th of the U.S. intelligence budget. To put that number in further context, a second $12.5 million could provide salaries, benefits, offices, and equipment to 60 people making $100,000 a year each. Each Canadian paying Arar 38 cents would be equivalent to each American paying him about four cents. It was chicken feed.

In either the O'Connor Commission's version of the story or in the context of the above scenario, the financial settlement to Arar was a magic, political bullet. It made Canada and Canadians feel good about themselves at the expense of the RCMP, which needed fixing anyway. It vindicated Arar and made him look like an ordinary, innocent good guy, a victim-hero. It also sent a signal to moderate Muslims that Canada was a fair country and that the rule of law prevailed for one of them. It polished Arar's credibility in both the secular and Muslim communities. He had seized, or had handed to him, depending on one's perspective, the moral high ground. The settlement also fully mitigated and effectively defeated any claim for damages that

Arar might have had under a 2004 lawsuit launched on his behalf by an advocacy group, the U.S. Center for Constitutional Rights.

That lawsuit named the U.S. government, Attorney General John Ashcroft, FBI Director William Mueller, Homeland Security Secretary Tom Ridge, and 10 "John Does." The U.S. government fought back, citing the State Secrets Privilege Act, which effectively prevented Arar's lawyers from seeing any of the government's evidence. The case was eventually thrown out in February 2006 by Judge David Trager of the U.S. District Court for the Eastern District of New York. Judge Trager cited national security and foreign policy concerns and found that Canadian officials were complicit in the U.S. rendition scheme for Arar.

"One need not have much imagination to contemplate the negative effect on our relations with Canada if discovery were to proceed in this case and were it to turn out that certain high Canadian officials had, despite public denials, acquiesced in Arar's removal to Syria," Judge Trager wrote.

Judge Trager gave Arar a chance to "better allege" his physical abuse and damages. The decision was appealed, but then became stalled in the courts due to "national security concerns." At one of those appeal hearings in 2007, Dennis Barghaan, the attorney representing Ashcroft, alleged in court that Mr. Arar had "unequivocal membership in Al-Qaeda."

But where was the proof?

On June 30, 2008, the U.S. Second Circuit Court of Appeals affirmed the lower court decision, ruling that Arar had failed to establish that the federal court had jurisdiction to hear his complaint.

"Arar has not adequately established federal subject matter jurisdiction over this request for a judgment declaring the defendant acted illegally by removing him to Syria so that Syrian authorities could interrogate him under torture," the ruling stated.

Judge Jose Cabranes, writing for the majority, said Arar had no federal standing in the case. He said the case could not be heard in federal court because Arar was an inadmissible alien and, as such, never entered U.S. jurisidiction.

A few weeks earlier, Richard Skinner, U.S. Homeland Security's inspector general, told a congressional committee that an investigation of U.S. officials involved in Arar's detention at a New York airport and subsequent deportation to a Syrian prison has cleared them of any wrongdoing. Skinner added, however, that the government was reopening the case after new, previously classified, information cast doubt upon the conclusions reached in the original finding.

In response to this news, on June 17, 2008, Arar published a brief article in *The Globe and Mail* under the headline: "With persistence, the truth will come out."

Mister Skinner's report clearly establishes that what happened to me was a rendition in disguise. Mister Skinner found that on Sunday, Oct. 6, 2002, the government prepared the "operations order" to remove me and sent flight clearances to Rome and Amman, so the United States could fly me on a private jet. These actions were taken before my six-hour interview with INS concerning my fears of being tortured in Syria, before the INS concluded it was likely I would be tortured there and before the INS received supposed ambiguous "assurances" that I would be protected.

In other words, my fate had already been decided—the "immigration process" meant to safeguard me from torture was a sham.

So far, these high-level officials have evaded accountability and public scrutiny of their own wrongdoing by keeping me on their watch list, thereby attempting to keep the focus on me. The U.S. government claims to rely on classified information to keep me on the watch list—information that New York congressman Jerrold Nadler has seen and called "nonsense," and the Canadian Public Safety minister Stockwell Day has seen and confirmed that it does not justify keeping me on a watch list.

The Canadian government has already apologized and launched a full public inquiry. It is only my hope that the U.S. government follows Ottawa's example and rights the wrongs by at least conducting an independent investigation examining the actions of all officials who shipped me off to Syria like a parcel without regard for my basic human rights, international law or the U.S. Constitution.

I would like to commend the efforts of the U.S. House of Representatives' foreign affairs and judiciary subcommittees trying to get tot the bottom of what happened to me. I appreciate their courage in standing up for justice and reminding Mr. Bush's administration that America is a country of the rule of a law. It is my hope that through their persistence and good work, the full truth will eventually come out.

As for Ahmad El Maati, Abdullah Almalki, Muayyed Nureddin, and the other Canadian Muslims who ended up in the Palestine Branch, their situations are much different. Each returned to Syria on his own and each of their backgrounds was markedly different from Arar's, which was why they were not treated the same. Their collective usefulness, if any, was for them to become supporting players in the Arar passion play. And at the end of any passion play, as you well know, someone has to die.

✛ ✛ ✛

At this point it might be useful to have a brief primer on the subtle distinctions and realities of Canadian federal politics, which is dominated by the Conservative and Liberal Parties. The New Democrats usually have been the third party at the federal level, but have occasionally held power in a few provinces. Nevertheless, the New Democrats often hold the balance of power in a minority government and are able to exert an influence disproportionate to their numbers. The other political factor in Ottawa is Québec which, in recent years, has sent the Bloc Québecois to represent its provincial interests.

In theory, parties work together in minority governments to build consensus, giving the appearance that the smaller parties have a say in how the country is run. But the reality is that since the Mulroney era in the late eighties, power has become consolidated—dangerously so, critics say—in the office of the prime minister. The prime minister, with the assistance of the Privy Council Office, usually gets what he wants.

On September 28, 2006, nine days after the O'Connor Commission's report had been made public, but months before Arar would receive his settlement package, RCMP Commissioner Zaccardelli was called to Parliament Hill to testify before the Standing Committee on Public Safety and National Security. Like all parliamentary committees, it is made up of members from all parties. Zaccardelli showed up in full-dress uniform, as usual, hoping to project his status and power.

Maher Arar was not there, and although the proceedings were televised, he did not have a television in his house in Kamloops, B.C., where he was still living. The committee provided a telephone link so that Arar could hear what Zaccardelli had to say.

In Zaccardelli's opening statement, he quoted historian Arnold Toynbee, who "wrote that the evolution of an individual, organization or society is determined by the ability to respond successfully to challenges, both human and environmental.

"Mr. Arar," Zaccardelli went on to say, "I wish to take this opportunity to publicly express to you, to your wife, and to your children how truly sorry I am for whatever part of the actions of the RCMP may have contributed to the terrible injustices that you experienced and the pain that you and your family endured.

"I know that an apology can never give back to Mr. Arar what was taken from him, but what we can do is move forward with changes and reform. That means in very concrete terms identifying and acknowledging errors that were made, implementing whatever change is required to address them, and by recommitting ourselves to the very heart of our purpose: to do our best to serve and protect all Canadians and our country."

Zaccardelli told the committee that it was not his plan to go into the details of the case, which had been "exhaustively addressed by Justice O'Connor." He had prepared himself for this moment and had no fear of taking questions. As it would turn out, his answer to the first question asked was all it took to put a fatal hole in Zaccardelli's career.

"My question then, to you, Commissioner, is this," Irwin Cotler, the Liberal from Mount Royal began. "What did you know and when did you know it? In particular, were you aware of the conveyance of false and misleading information by RCMP officials to a U.S. authority that likely contributed to his removal, for example, that Maher Arar and his wife were Islamic extremists, who were associated with the Al-Qaeda terrorist movement, a characterization that, as the commission put it, would have disastrous consequences if so made as it was?"

"Mr. Chairman," Zaccardelli said, with a nod and a slight smile, "with respect to what I knew about the mislabelling or false information concerning Mr. Arar, I was aware a serious investigation was going on for some time. I was aware that there was a person in the file by the name of Mr. Arar who was a person of interest. I personally became involved in the file after Mr. Arar was detained in Syria. After he was in Syria, the matter was brought to my attention. I informed myself of that. I asked for the file and for specific documents relating to what happened."

Zaccardelli carefully chose his words, as he continued: "In the process of getting that information, I found out that investigators were speaking with American officials while he was in detention. As part of that discussion or that correspondence with RCMP officials, I learned that in this process they tried to correct what was labelled as false or incorrect information with regard to Mr. Arar. That was the first time it came to my attention that there was a possibility or that we had mislabelled or mischaracterized Mr. Arar in our dealings with him in the investigation. That was my first point of knowledge about the matter, and I inquired further how this had happened. Does that answer the question? I'm willing to take further questions. I think the point was when did I know, and I think I've explained that."

The next questioner, Serge Ménard, the Bloc Québecois Member for Marc-Aurèle-Fortin, asked Zaccardelli about the typical flow of information from the RCMP to government in such a matter. He was particularly concerned about what Solicitor General Wayne Easter, who was the minister of the day, knew and when he knew it. "When the Minister enquired about this matter, why didn't you let him know that you were convinced that mistakes had been made and that Mr. Arar was not a terrorist, that there was no reason to send him to a country where he might probably be tortured?"

Zaccardelli said he had only learned about the information after Arar was in Syria, which prompted Ménard to ask: "Didn't you realize, at any time, that the minister believed that Mr. Arar was a terrorist when you knew that he was not?"

"Mr. Chairman," Zaccardelli replied, "usually, the Minister is not aware of a criminal investigation conducted by the RCMP. I cannot make any comments concerning the exact information in the hands of the minister. Normally, where there's a national security investigation, which was the case, the minister is not informed of what the RCMP is doing."

Ménard kept banging away until Zaccardelli seemed to relent: "When we learned what had occurred, we had discussions with the minister to inform him of the situation."

Liberal Mark Holland, the member for Ajax-Pickering, wondered aloud about the relationship and direction Zaccardelli might have received from the government. Zaccardelli said he had not received any direction. Zaccardelli was wary of Holland because he knew about the political gamesmanship that had taken place earlier. Normally, the Liberal on the Committee would have been Toronto-area Liberal Maurizio Bevilacqua, a fellow Italian–Canadian, whom Zaccardelli considered a friend. But Bevilacqua had stepped aside (or had been asked to step aside) and had relinquished his time on the committee to the pugnacious Holland.

"Did you at any time tender your resignation, in light of the report's findings?" Holland asked.

178 DISPERSING THE FOG

"You know," Zaccardelli replied, "there are two kinds of people in the world. There are those who are confronted by difficulties and they throw up their hands and walk away from a challenge. Then there are those who roll up their sleeves and decide they are going to fix what went wrong. I'm a person who fits in the latter category."

Holland persisted: "Just to repeat the question, Mr. Chairman, in light of the report's findings, did you tender your resignation, and did you, in fact, prepare a letter of resignation?"

"Mr. Chairman, I have just stated that I roll up my sleeves and do my work," Zaccardelli said, deflecting the question. "I'm the Commissioner of the RCMP and I intend to continue to be the Commissioner of the RCMP."

"Are you continuing not to answer the question?" Holland asked.

"Mr. Chairman," Zaccardelli pleaded.

"It's just yes or no," Holland said. "Did you offer your resignation at any point in time over the past nine days?"

"I did not," Zaccardelli finally said. He added, "But, as I said, Mr. Chairman, I accept my responsibilities; I accept Justice O'Connor's report, and I am working diligently to lead this great organization to be better than it is by learning from our mistakes, for the benefit of all Canadians."

Zaccardelli strode out of the room with a smile on his face, convinced he had done a good job in the morning session. Arar said that he was somewhat appeased by the apology, but that he was continuing with his lawsuit. A spokesman for him demanded that the individual police officers who had caused Arar to be harmed should be identified and punished.

In a press conference, Zaccardelli defended the RCMP members who he said had made "honest mistakes." He did not plan on reprimanding anyone. He said he had no intention of resigning, and Public Safety Minister Stockwell Day confirmed that the government had no intention of asking Zaccardelli for his resignation.

As careful as he thought he had been, Zaccardelli did not appreciate that he had made a huge blunder on the first question asked of him by Irwin Cotler in the committee room. He had said he knew about the Arar investigation, but had only become personally involved after Arar had been sent to Syria. He said it was at that time that he became aware of RCMP mistakes on the file. The answer seemed genuine and forthright. But back in 2001, the investigation into Abdullah Almalki had been the hottest thing in Ottawa. Deputy Commissioner Garry Loeppky, Zaccardelli's "right-hand man" in charge of criminal operations, was personally running the case. Yet Zaccardelli said he knew nothing. The story did not wash.

In his answer in the committee room, Zaccardelli had also linked the Chrétien government to the scandal by stating that in October 2002, after learning about the erroneous information transmitted to the Americans, he had informed Minister Wayne Easter about what had taken place.

By baldly stating this in public, he drew a direct connection between the RCMP and the government, in which he also served as a deputy minister, appointed by and serving at the pleasure of the prime minister. Any focused line of questioning that chased the Arar information up the food chain of government past Zaccardelli would put those hiding the big secret in the line of fire. Zaccardelli would soon have a private face to face with National Security Adviser William Elliott and others about his testimony, while the rest of Ottawa was abuzz about the scandalous possibilities.

The Standing Committee on Public Safety and National Security did not sit every day, but its members were now eager to pursue the line of questioning that Zaccardelli had opened up for them. In the grand scheme of things, Zaccardelli was now a sitting duck.

Over the next nine weeks, a delicate dance began in Ottawa, which had all the makings of a cover-up. Zaccardelli refused attempts by reporters eager to have him elaborate on his comments, which led to speculation that he was being muzzled by the government. The *Toronto Star*'s bureau chief, Susan Delacourt, received a call from a woman who was an "unofficial speech writer" for the RCMP commissioner and a close friend. The woman told the *Star* that Zaccardelli was, in fact, being told to keep quiet. The *Star* ran with the story, only to have Zaccardelli turn around and deny it, forcing the paper to retract. "We were set up," Delacourt said, and the *Star* began digging for dirt on Zaccardelli. It was war between the newspaper and the RCMP commissioner, who would not be trusted by the paper again.

Almost a month after Zaccardelli testified before the Standing Committee on Public Safety and National Security, former Solicitor General Wayne Easter was called to testify. On October 24, 2006, Easter denied just about everything Zaccardelli had told the committee on September 28.

"I was not informed," Easter said, reiterating, "I will state once again, I was not informed." Easter said that he didn't even learn about the RCMP mistakes until after he had read the O'Connor Commission report. "There is no situation where the RCMP came to me, and basically said: 'We screwed up. We provided improper information.'"

As *The Globe and Mail* reported, "Easter told the committee that he had spent hours going through his papers, ministerial briefing notes, and other official documents for his committee appearance. He also said that he had spoken with aides from that period. Easter said there was nothing he could find to suggest that Commissioner Zaccardelli or anyone else from the RCMP told him that they had given the Americans faulty intelligence."

Zaccardelli was left twisting in the wind. He and Easter were telling polar opposite versions of the same story. The government continued to express its support for Zaccardelli, but something obviously had to be done to rectify matters. On Parliament Hill, there were repeated calls for the government to fire Zaccardelli, but Prime Minister Harper stood firmly behind him, as did Public Safety Minister Stockwell Day, at least in public.

The standing committee, meanwhile, was into the chase. It called Margaret Bloodworth and William Elliott as witnesses. They declined to attend, however, each stating that they were "too busy." The rumour in the corridors of Parliament was that the government had ordered the two not to testify, which would make sense since they were the gatekeepers of the real story.

On November 2, Zaccardelli sent a note to the Standing Committee, advising them that he would like to come back to testify about "a contradiction" in his previous testimony. Meanwhile, the RCMP hired an Ottawa consulting firm, McLoughlin Media, which specializes in the training of executives and politicians for media interviews, presentations, and crises. "We just wanted to ensure that he was prepared fully for his appearance," said RCMP Assistant Commissioner Bernie Corrigan, adding that the force didn't have media consultants on its payroll. The RCMP paid McLoughlin $400 an hour to coach Zaccardelli, which cost the RCMP almost $25,000 in all.

The day before he was to return to face the committee, Zaccardelli gave a speech at the Chateau Laurier Hotel to the Canadian Club in Ottawa. In the speech he said he had first learned that the Mounties had passed on erroneous information about Arar only after he had read the O'Connor Commission report. "Senior officials, including myself, were not informed until the commission of inquiry had completed its work," Zaccardelli said. "There is discrepancy between what I said to the committee and what I am saying now." Zaccardelli said he would elaborate on his comments when he appeared before the committee. "If there is some misunderstanding ... I look forward to answering and clarifying that point."

The admission was called "jaw-dropping" by MP Mark Holland, who told the CBC: "I cannot imagine any scenario, I cannot imagine any circumstance in which he can explain the incredible number of contradictions that have been made."

As billed, Zaccardelli, again decked out in full regalia, showed up at the Standing Committee the next morning, where he faced the toughest assignment of his life. Committee chairman Garry Breitkreuz, the Conservative Member for Yorkton-Melville, was courteous in his introduction: "Mr. Zaccardelli, welcome to the committee. We appreciate your coming before us today."

Zaccardelli swore an oath to God to tell the truth, and it was all downhill from there, as he tried to explain how he had recently come to realize that he remembered that he forgot when he testified almost ten weeks earlier. "I believe that some aspects of my prior testimony could have been more precise or more clearly stated," he said. "A number of misconceptions have resulted, and, as I indicated in my letter to the committee, I have been anxiously awaiting the opportunity to set the record straight, both for the committee and the Canadian public."

The RCMP commissioner went on to outline the Arar case, once again attempting to show how he hadn't actually informed Solicitor General Wayne Easter in October 2002 about what the RCMP had done. Zaccardelli concluded his opening statement by saying: "I want to be very clear about the significance of what I have said here today. For a government official, nothing is more fundamental than ensuring that the information they provide to ministers is accurate and complete. To improperly withhold information or to misrepresent facts is a cardinal sin. If I had been guilty of such actions, no one would have to ask for my resignation, Mr. Chairman. The facts of the matter are, however, that due to circumstances I have described, we were unaware of some important information until the completion of Justice O'Connor's inquiry this year. My colleagues and I deeply regret that mistakes were made, but it is important to recognize that at all times we acted in good faith . . . I would like to thank you for giving me this opportunity to speak with you today. As I stated on September 28, it is such steps that assure all Canadians of the existence of transparent, accountable, and responsible leadership within the Canadian democratic system that is the very bedrock of a safe and civil society."

MP Mark Holland immediately went on the attack by referring to Zaccardelli's September 28 statement that he knew about the RCMP's mistakes while Arar was still being held in New York City. "That was my first point of knowledge about the matter," Zaccardelli said.

"This wasn't one reference," Holland charged. "We count eight separate references saying precisely the same thing, stating that your first point of knowledge of this matter was much, much earlier than you are saying today. Because you are now saying today that you were in the dark and you didn't know anything until Justice O'Connor's report came forward, I'm wondering on which day you perjured yourself before this committee, today or September 28?"

For a man who surrounded himself with yes-men, who demanded absolute respect from his underlings, who was now at the apex of his life as commissioner of the RCMP, the question was like a knife to his heart. Being labelled a perjurer by a parliamentarian was the last thing he had expected to happen to him. He calmed himself and tried to give a plausible answer.

"Mr. Holland," Zaccardelli replied, "I first had an opportunity to read Justice O'Connor's report when I returned from overseas. As soon as I received the 1,200 page report, I immersed myself in that report, and I tried to come before the committee as quickly as I could. We had contact with the committee. I tried to get as many of the facts as I possibly could.

"I have to honestly tell you that in preparation for coming here on September 28, I thought I was preparing myself to deal mainly with the recommendations on the way forward," Zaccardelli said, mildly expressing his dismay. The past was the past, he tried to persuade them, it was time to be positive and move on, words which likely came straight out of his own consultant's mouth.

"When I came here and testified, I gave the best answers with the best knowledge I had at the time. Subsequent to my testimony, in reviewing my testimony and in hearing comments, I realized that some of my testimony and comments were not as precise as they possibly could have been. That is why I did everything I could to try to get back before the committee to correct the record. The information I gave on the 28th was the best information I had. The first time I became aware of this matter was in 2002, after Mr. Arar was in Syria and it became very public. It was then that I started to inform myself. That's the first time I started."

Holland continued to press Zaccardelli. He wanted to know if anyone in government had helped him with his speech the day before and with his testimony before the committee.

"I made it very clear on September 28 and I've made it clear today that there was never any political direction or influence on my decision when to speak, how to speak, or what to say relative to this matter. Any suggestion along that line is totally inaccurate," Zaccardelli replied.

Holland then turned his attention to the media consultants hired to train Zaccardelli, something Zaccardelli thought was a secret. Holland had to virtually beat the answer out of the RCMP commissioner, who tried to deflect his questions twice, before he admitted, "Yes,"—the RCMP had paid for help. Zaccardelli now found himself being the one victimized by leaks from within his own organization.

Then came this question, which would serve as a portent of what was going to happen next to the RCMP. It was asked by Laurie Hawn, the Conservative Member for Edmonton Centre, who is a former lieutenant-colonel in the Canadian Air Force. "I have a very brief question. I know what the answer is going to be, but I want to get it on the record anyway. [Former Public Safety Minister Anne] McLellan said that perhaps it goes to something more important in terms of the culture of that organization. Is there a problem with the culture of the RCMP, for which I have the utmost respect?"

"I don't believe there is any problem at all with the culture," Zaccardelli replied, then listed everything the RCMP had done to fix itself since the O'Connor report was issued almost three months earlier.

"I agree with your assessment of your members," Hawn added.

Zaccardelli had no sooner left the House of Commons than calls for his resignation reached a crescendo, but he said he would not cave in. Only one other RCMP commissioner had ever resigned in the middle of a political fight, Len Nicholson in 1959, over John Diefenbaker's interference in RCMP operations. But Zaccardelli, as we have seen, was not cut from the same cloth as Nicholson, who believed in abstract notions like points of principle and the integrity of the RCMP. Zaccardelli's RCMP and the government were so intertwined that principle and integrity had long been washed away. "I've done nothing wrong. I told the truth. There is no way that I am going to resign," Zaccardelli said.

Zaccardelli felt safe for two reasons. Even with his angel Chrétien long gone, the RCMP commissioner expected the Liberals to put up a fight to defend him, even if the government turned on him. But the Harper Conservatives seemed to be ready to protect him. Public Safety Minister Day told the Standing Committee the next day that he "never once felt that the commissioner lied to me or deliberately in any way tried to lead me astray. There could be other reasons for the contradictions."

Zaccardelli failed to realize that as much as the public perception had been that the RCMP commissioner had helped to get Stephen Harper elected, with the income trust investigation leak in December 2005, the commissioner's actions, no matter what the motivation, would make any politician question his discretion and trustworthiness. Another well-timed leak could sink Harper someday in the future. In his flawed testimony, Zaccardelli had given Harper the perfect excuse to pull the floor out from under him.

Late on the afternoon of the next day, Zaccardelli was forced to swing in the wind.

December 6, 2006
Dear Prime Minister:

It is with regret and sadness that I am, with this letter, tendering my resignation as Commissioner of the Royal Canadian Mounted Police.

Let me assure you, Prime Minister, that I have at all times tried to do what is in the best interest of the Canadian public, the RCMP, and the institutions of Government. Clearly, the RCMP and I depend upon the confidence of Canadians and their elected representatives. Without this we cannot succeed.

However, the events subsequent to the release of Justice Dennis R. O'Connor's report on the Arar situation have taken on a life of their own. I must take responsibility for having added to the confusion in my first appearance before the Parliamentary Committee. My recent attempt to set the record straight and correct misperceptions I helped create has stirred new controversy.

I have always tried to be transparent and accurate in my dealings with the Government. This is precisely why I felt it important to appear again before Committee, notwithstanding the risks. The continuing controversy, however, makes it increasingly difficult for me and for the institution to fulfill its responsibilities to the Canadian people.

I am proud to have served my country as a member of the RCMP for 36 years, six as Commissioner. The RCMP is a great Canadian institution deserving of our collective respect and support.

I plan to make a brief public statement setting out my decision no later than tomorrow.

Thank you.
G. Zaccardelli

Harper immediately accepted the resignation which would be effective nine days later.

Dear Commissioner:

I hereby acknowledge receipt of your letter and accept your resignation effective December 15, 2006.

The Royal Canadian Mounted Police is one of the most respected and important institutions in Canada. I appreciate your dedication to the RCMP and I commend you for your desire to do what is in the best interests of this great institution.

I recognize that you have dedicated your life to law enforcement by serving in many capacities throughout the country, culminating in six years as Commissioner. On behalf of all Canadians, I wish to thank you for your long service to this country.

Yours sincerely,

Rt. Hon. Stephen Harper

In the House of Commons, Harper announced the resignation and fore-shadowed what the government was planning to do. The prime minister said that "a process for replacing the commissioner will be established. In the interim, an acting commissioner will be named shortly.... The RCMP is one of the most respected and important institutions in Canada. It is important that the men and women of the RCMP know that they continue to have the full confidence of the Government of Canada as they work tirelessly to keep Canadians safe and secure."

Zaccardelli had been made the official scapegoat in the Arar affair. He would not be overseeing the opening a few months later of the RCMP Heritage Centre in Regina, the cost of which had grown from $29 million to $40 million. The extra money was to be spent on a section depicting the history of the Mounties in modern culture and presumably would be filled with movie posters and photographs from the Hollywood films of the 1930s to early 1950s. Not much positive has happened since.

Zaccardelli's goal of becoming the longest-serving RCMP commissioner had crashed on the shoals of a mysterious case that had begun more than six years earlier. His name would not be attached to the new RCMP headquarters in Ottawa. He was gone for good and he could not believe what had happened to him. He resented having been forced to use the word "resign." He told his friends and acquaintances: "I did not retire. I didn't take a package. I didn't ask for one. I was disgusted by what had happened."

What really riled him was that the Liberals had abandoned him. He had always assumed that the deal he had brokered with Jean Chrétien, back in his first week in office in September 2000, would be honoured. He had been loyal. He had protected the Liberals. He expected that the Liberals would always hold power or enough power to guarantee his planned sinecure. But it didn't work out that way and he was angry. "All those politicians, they act like they are your friends. They want you standing beside them in uniform because it makes them look good, but then when it best serves them, they just turn on you. They can't be trusted. They are not your friends. They can never be your friends." Zaccardelli still had friends and sympathizers who believed that he had been treated poorly and effectively sacrificed by the government, but that would soon change as well.

In the days after Zaccardelli was forced out of his post, it was clear to all that there were serious problems within the RCMP that would require more than a band-aid to repair. The Arar powder keg wasn't the only area of concern. While the government had to keep a lid on that, it could not be seen to be heavy-handed in picking Zaccardelli's successor. People were already suspicious about Harper's extremist tendencies and intentions, so he was forced to undertake a delicate dance to get to where he believed the government needed to be.

RCMP insiders were demanding that only an RCMP member could serve as commissioner, but that was not going to be such an easy thing to do. It would be politically and operationally unwise to choose someone from the upper echelons in Ottawa, the Carpet Cops, as they were derisively referred to by the rank-and-file. Most of them had been tainted by their proximity to or association with Zaccardelli. The government needed someone safe in the short term, someone who had the respect of the force, who could buy time so that the government could do the things it needed to do to make their first choice for commissioner more politically palatable.

The day after Zaccardelli officially left the RCMP, on December 16, 2006, Beverley Busson was sworn in as 21st commissioner of the force, the first woman to hold the post. Busson would serve only as interim commissioner until the next full commissioner was appointed. It was made clear to everyone that Busson's tenure would be short.

Armed with a teaching degree, Busson was one of the first women to be accepted for training in the force in 1974. Like most Maritimers who joined the Mounties, she served her entire career in western Canada working in contract policing, where she met and married her husband Bob Busson, another Mountie.

Busson earned a law degree in 1990 at the University of British Columbia, and two years later was promoted to the rank of inspector. After a brief stint in Ottawa, she headed back out west to North Battleford, Saskatchewan, rising quickly to become assistant commissioner and commanding officer in that province. In 1999, Busson left the RCMP to head the Organized Crime Agency of British Columbia. She rejoined the RCMP in 2000 as the commanding officer of British Columbia and in 2001, she became deputy commissioner for the Pacific Region (British Columbia and Yukon), while retaining her role as the commanding officer of British Columbia.

Busson was much respected within RCMP circles but as her résumé indicates she was a typical Mountie. The vast majority of her experience was in municipal and provincial policing, mostly in Saskatchewan, which is light years away from the problems facing the federal police in Ottawa and elsewhere.

Back on Parliament Hill, with Busson temporarily in charge, Zaccardelli out of the picture, and the settlement to Arar imminent, the Standing Committee on Public Safety and National Security finally got around to examining two people they had hoped to speak to much earlier, Margaret Bloodworth (now national security adviser to the prime minister and associate secretary to the cabinet) and William Elliott (now associate deputy minister in the Department of Public Safety and Emergency Preparedness). On Tuesday, January 30, 2007, Bloodworth and Elliott turned up at the committee room to field what were mostly softball questions. Bloodworth said that she had met with Zaccardelli many times before his first testimony to the committee, but had not discussed with him what he would say. Elliott said the same.

After September 28, 2006, they both had meetings with Zaccardelli. Bloodworth said she did not discuss his testimony with him.

Elliott said: "Between the two appearances, I met with him on a number of occasions. On one occasion, shortly after his testimony, in the margins of a meeting on another subject, he mentioned that he was anxious to come back before the committee. I met with him just days before his testimony on December 5. We didn't talk about the appearance." Elliott added, a few minutes later: "I take his December 5 testimony as a more accurate reflection of his recollection of events."

Committee members Joe Comartin, Rick Norlock, Omar Alghabra, and Maria Mourani wanted to know about national security issues in the

Arar affair. For instance, who decides what constitutes a national security issue?

"There's a great deal of information that was not made public that Mr. Justice O'Connor agreed should not be made public because of potential damage to national security," Bloodworth said.

Holland, as usual, pressed a stern and steely Bloodworth about what she knew and when she knew it with regard to the Zaccardelli affair. Bloodworth, who is known for choosing her words carefully, said she had been out of the country at the time and had only read news reports. "I knew questions were raised in the media about it being unclear shortly after; I don't know what day, but shortly after."

Before long, the subject turned to how to improve the RCMP and CSIS. In response to a question from MP Blaine Calkins, Bloodworth said that Canadians are much better than other countries in some national security activities, while not as good in others.

"I think CSIS is an excellent organization," Bloodworth said. "I've had foreign counterparts tell me that they have a great deal of respect for what they do. I think CSIS would say they have a very young workforce. They've recruited a lot of new agents in the last five years, and experience will help in getting them even better."

CSIS is an excellent organization?

Bloodworth had to know about concerns raised in an internal CSIS study, a draft of which was dated January 2007, obtained through access to information a year later by Jim Bronskill of the Canadian Press. The consultant's report showed that CSIS was "lagging behind" other countries when it came to keeping the public informed about its activities.

Somewhat tellingly, CSIS had not issued an annual report since 2004–5, the height of the Arar years, something that is customary for police and intelligence agencies in democratic countries. The reports CSIS had issued were found by the consultants to be "dull, timid and full of recycled information.... A review of recent years' public reports indicates a fair amount of repetition from year to year, with few insights, facts or figures about actual CSIS operations.... Some respondents suggested that if CSIS does not move to increase its openness about its operations, its reputation and credibility may suffer."

Perhaps CSIS could not reveal what it had been doing because to do so would have been political dynamite.

Bloodworth and Elliott tapdanced through the session. MP Omar Alghabra expressed his personal frustration with their responses by telling the two witnesses: "You know, we're getting the sense that we're not getting a lot of clear answers."

The next week, Arar received his settlement from the government and moved back to Ottawa with his family to continue his work as the country's unofficial Ambassador of Moderate Islam.

Alghabra had been on the right track in his skepticism about Bloodworth and Elliott's testimony. If one believed what they had to say, the Privy Council Office was not abnormally involved in the investigations. Alghabra sensed that they knew more, much more, than they were admitting, but the evidence suggesting what their actual roles were would not be revealed until much later.

Between 2002 and 2007, while the Arar case had been playing out, Canadian authorities undertook two investigations which would provide some useful insight into what Alghabra was trying to find out from Bloodworth and Elliott.

Mohammad Momin Khawaja was arrested on March 29, 2004, and accused under the new Anti-Terrorist Act of participating in the activities of a terrorist group and facilitating a terrorist activity. The RCMP raided Khawaja's house in Orleans, a suburb of Ottawa, and his workplace. He was a computer software developer working on contract for the federal government in the Ministry of Foreign Affairs. The raid was part of an investigation involving Canada and Britain in which nine men of Pakistani heritage were arrested for plotting terrorist attacks in London. Khawaja was the only person arrested in Canada. Although he had travelled several times to London, he denied having a hand in any plotting. He was only going there "to find a wife," an alibi that might sound familiar to you by now.

News of the arrest of Khawaja attracted the attention of another man, Mubin Shaikh. He telephoned CSIS, told them he knew Khawaja, and volunteered to be a spy for the agency. He got the job. Two years later, on June 2, 2006, an RCMP-led police task force, with the help of CSIS, arrested 17 young Muslim men in the Toronto area. An 18th suspect was arrested two months later. Four of the suspects were juveniles. The RCMP alleged that the motley group had set up a makeshift training camp in Washago, in Ontario's Muskoka Lakes cottage country, north of Toronto. There the men were supposedly practising guerrilla warfare to conduct their jihad but did not have tents or clothing for the winter conditions. Bearded, wearing khakis, and dining at the local Tim Hortons donut shop was enough to arouse the curiosity of some of the locals in the small, peaceful community. When they started firing off guns at their "training camp," the police were alerted to their presence.

Two of the suspects were associated with McMaster University in Hamilton, whose nuclear reactor and concentration of Islamic professors and students had long been a source of concern to American authorities. The arrests made world headlines, replete with allegations that the group had planned to bomb the Ontario legislature, take over CBC headquarters in Toronto, and kidnap and behead politicians. The timing of the arrests was suspiciously propitious for the government, which was preparing to step up its anti-terrorism efforts with new powers.

Before long, however, things turned even weirder. Mubin Shaikh, the volunteer CSIS agent, went on television and told Linden MacIntyre on the CBC's *the fifth estate* about what he did and why he did it. Eventually, Shaikh began telling the media that the case against the suspects was weak. One sign of that weakness was the collapse in September 2007 of a preliminary trial into the matter after four months of testimony. As Shaikh was in the middle of his testimony, federal Crown attorneys stopped the proceeding and asked a judge to dismiss all the charges against the defendants. Fourteen of them were immediately recharged and the Crown indicated that it would waive a preliminary hearing and proceed by preferred direct indictment to trial. The Crown refused to say why it had taken such an action. A court-imposed ban prevented publication of any evidence already heard. Once underway, the trial was expected to last five to seven years.

"It's a stain on the administration of justice to deprive these accused persons of their constitutional right to have an effective trial," defence lawyer Paul Slansky told reporters outside the Brampton, Ontario, courtroom.

"We can't discount the political implications of this prosecution—showing the world that we're tough on terrorists," said Raymond Motee, who represented defendant Ibrahim Aboud.

By April 2008, charges against three more of the alleged co-conspirators had been dropped. Among those cleared to date are the McMaster University students and Qayyum Abdul Jamal—the oldest accused and purported spiritual leader of the group. His wife, Nova Scotia-born Cheryfa MacAulay Jamal, told the *Toronto Star* she wanted to sue the government for what it had done. "I want millions, seriously," Ms. Jamal said. "I know it sounds greedy, but I don't care. I want millions for what the kids have suffered and how much we've aged in this process."

The high-profile case was evaporating before the government's eyes. But judging by its behaviour behind the scenes, the government knew how flimsy the case was against the 18. A revealing story by *The Globe and Mail* in September 2007 described how the Privy Council Office had been involved in micromanaging the case. Reporter Omar El Akkad reported that bureaucrats were beginning to chafe under the pressure from above. After the arrests, the PCO wanted to know "what kind of outreach activities the RCMP and CSIS were doing with Muslim groups."

In the 1,700 pages of documents El Akkad received through an access to information request, a picture was painted of a politicized, overly controlling, and domineering Privy Council Office bent on sanitizing the government's image. "Just so we're all clear . . . in particular on issues of this nature with many depts involved, ALL electronic media interviews must be co-ordinated + OK'd by pco," one memo read. The PCO even went as far as to approve or reject talking points for an interview by Public Safety Minister Stockwell Day with international media. The *Globe* story showed that the Privy Council was not quite as detached from politics as the government's flow charts otherwise suggested, but rather an extension of Stephen Harper's invisible hand.

Inside the RCMP, the damage done by Arar was significant but not fatal. While the O'Connor Commission concluded the RCMP had made some mistakes, its findings, in many respects, were ambiguous. The members of the force had not acted out of malice, it said, but were merely under-supervised. There wasn't enough meat in the O'Connor report for the government to justify doing anything drastic to the RCMP command structure.

Nevertheless, dissension was brewing in RCMP ranks. Some Mounties were angry about the O'Connor report and the atmosphere was poisonous. The danger for the government was that disgruntled Mounties would start leaking embarrassing stories, things that would normally be kept secret.

Running on a parallel track to the Arar case was an obscure controversy within the walls of the RCMP. It had been allowed to simmer on the government's back burner for so long one might have thought that by 2007 it would have been forgotten. The government was now prepared to serve it to the public, fully heated, and deflect attention away from the Arar debacle.

The ensuing controversy would become the catalyst for the government to take its next steps in a plan to impose even more political control on the unruly, dysfunctional RCMP, and place a secure, hopefully leak-proof seal on what the American spooks had been up to and were continuing to do in Canada.

PART 2

STRANGERS IN A STRANGE LAND

*"There are no conflicts which cannot be resolved unless
the true promoters of them remain hidden."*
—L. Ron Hubbard

[13]

A CONVENIENT DIVERSION

S ituated an hour's drive north of the U.S. border at Ogdensburg, New York, Ottawa had long been a kind of grubby burg blessed with natural attributes. Across the Ottawa River lies the province of Québec. The Rideau River snakes through the city, as does the Rideau Canal, on which citizens like to skate to work during the bitterly cold winters. The dominant pieces of architecture in the city are the magnificent Parliament Buildings, the seat of government, nestled along the Ottawa River.

Government is the big business in Ottawa, although efforts over the past two decades have done much to diversify the economy and encourage the development of high-tech industries. Throughout the region, glass towers have risen in tribute to the dynamism of these enterprises, but Ottawa will always be a government town with a bureaucrat's mentality. The people who live in Ottawa, by and large, are conditioned by its rules, the demand for orderliness, consensus, and secrecy, which is offset by the well-paying jobs and lucrative government pensions. It is the kind of city where on a cold winter's day, a pedestrian risks the wrath of others if he should decide to cross a street on a red light, even if there are no cars around. I will never forget being told by someone that I had "no respect for authority" because I had done just that.

The people of Ottawa are good savers, according to the banking industry, and usually lead the country in the size of their portfolios. Tastes in the city run, as one prominent interior decorator once put it, "from off-white to mushroom." As Bob McKay, an old deskman at *The Globe and Mail*, once put it: "When two Ottawa guys go out for a night on the town, they are sure to paint the town grey." When it comes to spending money, Ottawa retailers know that it is hard to separate the locals from their cash. "Is it on sale?" or "Will I get a discount if I buy two?" are among the most frequently heard phrases in the city. In short, Ottawa is a place where people usually don't take risks.

In Ottawa, the flamboyant, sure-footed, authoritarian Giuliano Zaccardelli was the perfect person to wear the black hat in the grand, tawdry story that was being constructed for Canada and the rest of the world. Before Zaccardelli was made to fall on his sword in December 2006, there existed any number of reasons over the years for members of the RCMP to stage an open revolt against their leadership. Zaccardelli was deemed by many to be arrogant, out of control, and too political. Finance Minister Paul Martin's budget cuts of the mid-to-late 1990s had led to chronic understaffing. At RCMP headquarters, the Carpet Cops led a cushy life. Throughout the rest of the country, organized crime and financial fraud were rampant. The working conditions for members of the force had deteriorated to the point where it was becoming dangerous to be a Mountie. More and more members were off work on stress leave or giving up the job altogether. The political influence exercised by the government on the force was seen by many to be both alarming and demoralizing. RCMP leadership since the eighties had only exacerbated the situation, but few spoke up, even after retiring or resigning, and the few who did were readily dismissed as misfits, cranks, or troublemakers.

The RCMP rolled on, but within the force the grumbling was growing into a firestorm over something the Mounties in Ottawa truly valued and about which they could find the energy and courage to get truly exercised—the administration of their pension and insurance funds.

The seeds of the controversy had been planted in policies the government had been trying to perfect for four decades, that is, that the government and its agencies should operate like a business. As I reported in my first two books, in 1960 Progressive Conservative Prime Minister John Diefenbaker set up the Royal Commission into the Reorganization of Government. The three-man commission was headed by J. Grant Glassco, a prominent business mogul of the day, who had a history of giving the government the advice it wanted to hear. The key Glassco recommendation was that the post of the Comptroller General be eliminated, which it was, in 1965. The Comptroller General's office oversaw all spending by the government and its agencies. In Glassco's and Diefenbaker's view, the government and its members should be the ones held accountable for spending, not some stuffy, tightwad Ottawa bureaucrat. In theory, any poor decisions by government would be captured by the auditor general, at which time the government could be held accountable, presuming the same people would be holding the same offices three years later or more. In fact, dodging accountability was only a cabinet shuffle away, a practice perfected by successive Canadian governments. Running the government as a business is a politically appealing notion, a vote-getter in fact, but it has proven to be lousy in practice. Canada's accumulated deficit went from zero in 1965 to $610 billion in 1997. The size of government has grown at an almost exponential rate since 1965, and spending has never gone down on an adjusted per capita basis. Some business!

With no one overseeing the issuing of government cheques, fraud became rampant as people, almost always those politically connected from Québec, found ways to slip themselves into the purchasing process where they could siphon off substantial bogus fees. As obvious as it was that this was happening over the years—with the Airbus scandal, the sponsorship scandal, and so many others—neither the Mulroney or Chrétien governments had the appetite to do anything about it.

Inside the RCMP, there has long been resistance to the business mantra because the good dedicated cops there over the years know that the philosophy of business runs almost contrary to that of a guardian agency. Businesses make decisions based upon bottom lines, while guardian institutions are empowered to protect the public interest, as efficiently as possible, but at any cost, if necessary.

The Mulroney government addressed this intransigence by injecting civilians into the upper management of the RCMP, a move further resisted by many Mounties. The prime reason was that the civilians were not peace officers and were not subject to the provisions of the RCMP Act, which governs police officers. The civilians were still civil servants and subject to the Public Service Staff Relations Act, which made them beholden to the Privy Council Office. As we learned in Chapter 2, then-Solicitor General James Kelleher and Commissioner Inkster appointed Deputy Solicitor General Michael Shoemaker to become the first civilian deputy commissioner of the RCMP, creating a schism inside the force. The RCMP was force-fed the business mantra from that point forward, but it never really took hold.

By the time Zaccardelli became commissioner in 2000, he found that under the "progressive" leadership of previous Commissioners Philip Murray and Norman Inkster, every facet of the RCMP's operations and administration had fallen into disarray. Nurtured on the business philosophy himself, Zaccardelli was convinced that the RCMP needed outside help to manage its $3 billion budget. He hired three civilians for key positions: Paul Gauvin, as Deputy Commissioner of Corporate Management and Comptrollership; Jim Ewanovich, as Chief Human Resources Officer; and Dominic Crupi, as director of National Compensation Policy. All came with impeccable civil service credentials and were qualified for their jobs. The previous year Ewanovich had been named civil servant of the year. The hirings were not welcomed by many members inside the force.

Over the previous 50 years, Winnipeg-based Great West Life Insurance Company had handled the RCMP's $30 million insurance account, but changes were afoot. It cost the RCMP about $2 million a year to administer various insurance plans, but the force was looking to save money. There was also the RCMP's $12.3 billion pension plan to administer, which was costing the force "between $6 million and $14 million a year" to do itself, a direct quote from a report by the auditor general. Ewanovich and Crupi quietly approached Québec-based Morneau Sobeco to make a business case for outsourcing the administration of both the pension and insurance plans. Morneau Sobeco said it could do the whole job for only $2.8 million a year for the next two years, a great saving, if true.

Armed with the Morneau Sobeco proposal, Ewanovich and Crupi were demanding more from Great West Life, including high-tech services, all at a lower cost. As Great West Life tried to meet those demands, Crupi, the spearhead, would change them again, making negotiations difficult. To the managers of the insurance company it looked as if their company was being made to jump through hoop after hoop to the point of exhaustion. To a seasoned fraud investigator, making things unnecessarily complicated looked like the opening moves in a scam.

Feeling squeezed, but with nobody to complain to about the situation, in December 2001 Great West Life told the RCMP that it could not meet all the force's expectations. The insurance company was then told that it would be required to hire the RCMP's hand-picked subcontractor to do the job, Morneau Sobeco. Two months later, in February 2002, Morneau Sobeco got the job, without tender. The arrangement was a strange one from the start, including the fact that all of this was concealed from the eyes of Zaccardelli. RCMP monies flowed through Great West Life to Morneau Sobeco, with Great West collecting a 15 percent fee for doing virtually nothing. Meanwhile, Morneau Sobeco was charging full freight for its end of the deal. The RCMP was being double-billed.

The transition was anything but smooth. In 2001, Assistant Commissioner Bruce Rogerson complained about managers taking "freebies" from contractors, but his complaints were ignored, and he found his career effectively derailed. RCMP members began to complain about the service Morneau Sobeco was providing. Many were wondering how the company got the job. Along the way, Zaccardelli kept impatiently hammering away at his underlings about efficiency and doing a better job. The expected savings in the Morneau contract turned out to be just a dream. The $2.8 million lowball estimate grew quickly to $5.9 million in the first year and to $8.1 million in the second, almost three times the original estimate. By 2003, Zaccardelli, already caught up in the evolving Maher Arar scandal and a thousand other things, was becoming alarmed about what was going on inside his own force. The RCMP was supposed to be saving money, but now it was paying as much or more than it did when it handled everything itself. Concerned that the Human Resources Branch wasn't being efficient enough, he ordered an A-base review of the unit, an exercise to review, re-justify, and/or reallocate the core of ongoing funding of the organization. Little could he have known how much further misery he was about to cause for himself and the RCMP.

Denise Revine, a human resources director who had spent 36 years working as a civil servant for the RCMP, was placed in charge of the A-base review of the pension and insurance plans. As she poked her way through the files, she soon came across an account coded N2020, which piqued her curiosity. The account appeared to be a slush fund being operated by a small unit in the National Policy Compensation Centre. Laptops, computers, language classes, an online system for vacation leave, golf green fees in New Brunswick, gifts, travel, and contracts—as many as 31 of them—had been given to friends and family. The unit, which oversaw the RCMP's pension and insurance plans, was headed by Crupi, who reported to Ewanovich.

Revine followed her nose and soon uncovered a treasure trove of other disturbing behaviour. As part of its goal to become more businesslike, the RCMP was determined to have private companies and contractors take over more of the work that it had been doing internally. Revine discovered that some of these new contracts had let in apparent non-arm's-length deals, without being tendered, and had been awarded to relatives and friends of Ewanovich and Crupi. Ewanovich's daughter, Alexa, a student at Queen's University in Kingston, Ontario, was hired for summer work, as were Crupi's stepdaughter and niece. Although it is frowned upon, nepotism is not, in and of itself, anathema within the ranks of the RCMP. Ewanovich and Crupi, however, were perceived to have gone too far. Revine discovered evidence that some students were paid salaries more than double the rate allowed under the federal government summer student employment program.

In the single most egregious case, a consultant hired to do the compensation centre's staffing was paid $443,000 out of the pension plan coffers for 18 months' work, at a time when the RCMP had its own internal staffing officers. There was evidence of contract splitting in which untendered, single contracts were broken up into bite-sized pieces which would fly under the $25,000 approval process ceiling, only to be reassembled on the other side by the contractor. The trail led to what appeared to be a nepotistic network inside the compensation centre which was operating far outside the rules, some with ties to the governing Liberal party.

The conduit was Consulting and Audit Canada, a federal agency whose mandate was to arrange outside consulting work for the government. Frank Brazeau, a project manager at CAC, had previously worked with Crupi in the Public Works department. Revine found a link to two small companies, Abotech and Casey Computers, who were hired as subcontractors to work with other subcontractors.

Abotech was a computer consulting firm operated by David Smith, who was a low-level Liberal party backroom boy from nearby Pontiac County, Québec, not to be confused with a more powerful Liberal party backroom boy, Senator David Smith of Toronto. The Québec Smith operated the business from his home. He also happened to be Brazeau's cousin.

As Revine was conducting her probe, with the support and backing of Prime Minister Paul Martin, Smith won the Liberal nomination in the riding of Pontiac-Gatineau-Labelle. He won the 2004 general election, a campaign in which his brother-in-law, Frank Brazeau, was a key worker. To avoid conflict of interest rules, before taking his seat in Parliament Smith sold his company to his wife and two young children. His wife continued to work the contracts.

Abotech's "work," as it turned out, was to act at least 30 times as a middleman between Consulting and Audit Canada, which itself was a middleman, in the hiring of other subcontractors. Two of those contracts were with the RCMP, while others were spread around six other agencies. Abotech collected fees for doing nothing.

Casey Computers, a small Ottawa computer consulting company, obtained six contracts valued at more than $3.2 million as part of the RCMP's plan to outsource some of its administration. One of the contracts was not tendered and the cost of the service to the RCMP was astronomically higher than the force would have paid its own staff. At one point, as CTV News would later report, company owner Kim Casey added her husband to the contract at a cost of $675 per day—a move that drove up the contract's cost to the RCMP by 25 percent. Even as the controversy grew, Casey Computers kept getting contracts, one, in 2005, worth $500,000.

In all, 31 questionable sole-source contracts for so-called RCMP work were doled out by CAC, for which the RCMP was charged $667,000 for administration and overhead by the government's own agency. Revine also found that $3.1 million had been charged to the pension plan to pay for RCMP human resource projects that should have been paid for by RCMP appropriations funding. This had the effect of relieving budget pressure on managers responsible for these projects, which was not proper.

In its original plan to modernize its insurance plan by turning administration over to a private sector company, the RCMP had estimated that it would cost $3.6 million. Revine believed that the RCMP had spent more than $25 million on an ill-conceived plan, and was planning to spend another $30 million. It was running like a business, all right. All her sleuthing, however, placed Revine in a quandary. There was no question that something strange was going on, but who was she going to tell, the RCMP? The leads all pointed to the bosses above her.

Revine didn't realize it at the time, but someone else, coming from an entirely different direction, had also picked up the scent. Staff Sgt. Ron Lewis was the staff service representative for headquarters, a shop steward as it were, for the RCMP's company-run union. Lewis had been fielding complaints made by other RCMP members about harassment, nepotism, and abuse of authority by Ewanovich and his subordinates. Stewart collected the complaints and forwarded them to Zaccardelli in the hope of sparking investigation.

On May 28, 2003, Lewis met with Zaccardelli and coaxed him into calling for a criminal investigation by RCMP "A" Division into the allegations that civilian members of the force were dipping into the pension fund illegally. As is so often the case in Canada, the RCMP was being asked to investigate itself.

In June 2003, Revine, having documented her findings, visited her boss, Chief Superintendent Fraser Macaulay. In January 2002, Macaulay, who had swiftly risen through the ranks, had been named Director General of

Organizational Renewal and Efficiency, in the human resources branch. "The perception is that this is a cash cow and there doesn't seem to be an end in sight," Revine wrote in her report to Macaulay. To Revine's astonishment, Macaulay was not surprised. Soon after taking over the job 17 months earlier, Macaulay became aware of possible improprieties in the pension plan administration and other human resource issues involving Ewanovich and Crupi. He had talked about it with others, but chose to sit on his hands and do nothing. He feared that if he went to his higher-ups about what he suspected, he might be the one punished in the shoot-the-messenger world of the RCMP.

Armed with Revine's documented findings, Macaulay summoned up the courage to confront the issue head-on and called a meeting with Zaccardelli. As the *Ottawa Citizen*'s Kathryn May reported: "Macaulay laid out for Zaccardelli the alleged misappropriation of funds, the threats, excessive spending, staffing and contract violations and management's abuse of power to override the rules. Several weeks later, he followed up with a formal report, written by Revine, to flesh out the details for both Zaccardelli and the force's head of internal audit."

Zaccardelli was upset, mostly at Macaulay for not saying anything about what he had known for 17 months. Macaulay's fear that he would be "punished" proved correct, but Zaccardelli didn't see it that way. "Fraser was a good man, but he made a poor decision, a serious error in judgment," Zaccardelli said. "He has to spend some time in the penalty box." Deputy Commissioner George called Macaulay in and reassigned him to the Department of Defence as a liaison officer, a lateral transfer, but a cushy two-year job nonetheless.

Macaulay, Revine, and Lewis believed things were going smoothly until they learned later that the criminal investigation had been stopped after two days by Zaccardelli. Instead, the commissioner had ordered Gauvin to conduct only an internal audit of the 2003 fiscal year to determine if a police investigation was warranted. The auditors were instructed to investigate three matters: the use of pension funds for purposes other than the administration of pension and insurance plans; the retention of consultants at excessive remuneration and hiring children of consultants; and family members of the unit being hired and their salaries paid out of the pension plan. He referred the rest of the allegations to Assistant Commissioner John Spice, the RCMP's ethics officer.

Macaulay then learned that Assistant Commissioner Vern White had filed a formal complaint against him for raising suspicions of misconduct by Dominic Crupi, sending what appeared to be a strong message to the rest of the force.

Meanwhile, Zaccardelli extended Ewanovich's contract for another year, and both he and Crupi received a yearly performance bonus. In Zaccardelli's view, there had clearly been administrative foul-ups in the pension plan which cost the force about $3.5 million, but RCMP members' pensions and insurance were never compromised—because they are guaranteed by the government.

The new audit conducted by Brian Aiken, the Director General of Internal Audit, took four months to complete. Aiken found Ewanovich's dismissive attitude to be a large part of the problem, and recommended that Zaccardelli take action, which he did. Shortly afterward, Ewanovich left the RCMP, to be replaced by Assistant Commissioner Barb George.

George, a Newfoundlander, was married to an ex-CSIS agent who now worked for the RCMP as a polygraph expert. She had been promoted through the ranks and was championed by Zaccardelli. Like many of those who had risen to the top under Zaccardelli, insiders at headquarters were wary about her talents and abilities. "She was just another one of Zac's good corporals," was the opinion many had of her, a common RCMP description of someone who has been over-promoted.

On November 23, 2003, George relieved Crupi of his duties, although a combination of various leave entitlements left him on the payroll of the RCMP until he resigned in June 2005. A further review of the pension and insurance administration plan was undertaken and new controls were implemented.

Zaccardelli figured it was all over in 2003, and the RCMP was ready to move forward, but he had no idea about how incensed RCMP members could get when they believe that someone was allowed to fool around with their pension monies and get away with it. In their view, Ewanovich and Crupi got off lightly, with golden handshakes, much better than a regular RCMP member would have been treated in similar circumstances.

Staff Sgt. Lewis, who was on the verge of retirement himself, was like a dog on a bone. He soon enlisted Assistant Commissioner George in his attempts to have the criminal investigation reopened. George was prepared to leave the force if Zaccardelli wouldn't do that. George asked Lewis to prepare a formal complaint, in which Lewis alluded to the Mission Visions and Values (MVV) statement of the RCMP.

In his original e-mail to George, Lewis wrote:

> As an organization, we are expected to fully investigate wrong-doings by our employees. However, there are two overriding factors which highlight the necessity to do so with due diligence and clarity.
>
> Firstly, the RCMP is the authority which is expected to carry out this role for other federal government departments and throughout the rest of Canadian society. If we loose [sic] our credibility we loose [sic] our moral authority. Secondly, the MVV of the RCMP is the primary guiding principle for how its employees conduct business. That guiding principle has been seriously damaged. Many employees, and especially the senior managers, are dumbfounded how this behaviour has been allowed to happen with open knowledge at all levels of the RCMP.
>
> We now have a credibility gap which needs to be bridged. Without a full and transparent investigation with appropriate corrective action, these behaviours will be seen as condoned and even rewarded. The probability of employees and managers stepping forward to expose wrongdoings in the workplace is very low if they expect to be punished or ignored. **We have a serious crisis to resolve.**
>
> [Emphasis part of original e-mail.]

Six weeks later, with Lewis's complaint in hand, and with evidence collected by Denise Revine, George brought the information to her fellow assistant commissioner David Gork. He recommended an investigation and met with two senior "A" Division officers, one of whom worried about the propriety of the RCMP investigating itself. Several weeks after that, Deputy Commissioner Garry Loeppky recommended that the Ottawa Police Service be asked to lead the investigation. It was dubbed "Project Probity," a reference to a speech Zaccardelli had made in a 2003 speech in Hong Kong. The definition of probity in a police force, he had said then, was honesty and integrity.

The new investigation was all but run by the RCMP. It provided the offices, equipment, supplies, and most of the staff. The case even had the same file number as the previous, two-day-old investigation killed by Zaccardelli. Inspector Gork was the command officer. RCMP Staff Sergeants Mike Frizzell and Steve Walker were assigned to assist the Ottawa police investigation, which was led by Inspector Paul Roy. While Roy was focused on the past, Frizzell was concerned about what was still going on, particularly on the insurance side. He believed there was evidence of continuing illegal money transfers from the RCMP's insurance plan and he was determined to investigate that. Roy became irritated by Frizzell's activities, which were seen to be interfering with the Ottawa police investigation. His own RCMP superiors thought Frizzell was being overly aggressive and even harassing in his approach, although there was no evidence to prove those contentions. In fact, the evidence suggests that Frizzell was anything but harassing. Nevertheless, he was ordered by his superiors to cease and desist the investigation, and two RCMP superintendents confronted him and served him with a notice ordering him to leave the office. He was told to report back to "A" Division for his regular duties. George would later say that Frizzell was moved for "health" reasons, which Frizzell knew was bogus. His health was fine. "I was just sick and tired about what was going on," he said afterward.

All this internal turmoil eventually came to the attention of *National Post* reporter Andrew McIntosh. On April 7, 2004, McIntosh published a story about how Ewanovich and Crupi had lost their jobs after an internal audit determined that $4 million in expenses had been wrongly charged to the pension fund. The story, coming as it did in the early days of the new police investigation, became a one-day wonder.

Neither the RCMP nor Ottawa Police Chief Vince Bevan had any idea how complex the case would prove to be. Not enough resources were devoted to it, which caused the Ottawa police to take a year to complete its work on Project Probity. In so doing, it confirmed the findings of the internal audit and identified a number of additional instances of wrongdoing. The police couldn't just go to a justice of the peace and lay a charge, as they might in a minor case. In major cases like this, all police charges or information had to be approved by the Attorney General's office.

In mid-2005, a provincial Crown attorney concluded there was no reasonable prospect of conviction in the matter. That was the end of it, or so it seemed. Only after the Crown attorney made his finding did Zaccardelli call for an internal probe under the RCMP Act into the activities of three RCMP members, but the one-year statute of limitations had already run out, and the investigation ended before it had even begun.

Mounties of all ranks were furious. The behind-the-scenes shenanigans with Great West Life and the pension administration smelled of something bigger than "maladministration." With clear links to the Liberal Party through the presence of recently elected David Smith, whose wife now ran Abotech, it looked like something with which the RCMP had grown quite familiar over the decades: an old-fashioned Ottawa cover-up. If a police investigation can't be stopped from the inside, the other way to do it is through the prosecutor's office.

One by one, the principals who had pushed for an investigation found themselves sidelined. Macaulay went first, followed by Frizzell, each transferred elsewhere within the force. Denise Revine's job was, without warning, declared "redundant." Revine's responsibilities were cut back in a brutal and humiliating fashion to the point where after three months of "abuse" from her superiors, she was compelled to take paid stress leave for a year.

Inside headquarters, Assistant Commissioner Gork was openly critical of the investigation at a high-level meeting on June 27, 2005. He believed criminal charges should have been laid and that the RCMP had a duty to do more. He also recommended that the individuals who had discovered the problems and who had been punished for their courage should be rewarded for their efforts. When Zaccardelli learned about Gork's comments he went ballistic. Shortly afterward, Gork sent an e-mail to one of his colleagues:

> I told Barb George a year and a half ago that this would cost me my job. Now they are not going to fire me, but if they could they would. What they wanted was for me to say, everything is fine, and everything is looked after. It isn't. They did not want to hear that so it is now in their court to deal with. I even got a call from Barb late one evening to talk about how pissed the Commish was. I told her to give him a message for me. At first she balked, but then she said she would . . .
>
> 1) I am sorry he did not like it
> 2) If I were to do it again, I would do it exactly the same way
> 3) I will never be back to the HQ building again, and I will mail in my [retirement papers] to coincide with the spring of 2008.

Gork soon found himself shuffled off to Europe to be a liaison officer with Interpol. It might have looked like a cushy gig to some, but Gork knew he was being sent to one of the RCMP's plusher penalty boxes. Rank-and-file RCMP officers were up in arms. Members of the RCMP's staff relations representative committee drafted a memo describing the handling of the investigation as "truly unacceptable. . . . 'Accountability,' as specific and tough as that word sounds, has become a vague, loose term in our organization," the memo read. "We will not accept this behaviour from employee/members of the RCMP at any category or years of service, just as we would not expect members in the field to drop the ball on alleged wrongdoings."

Auditor General Sheila Fraser reviewed the case and found that the RCMP had quietly but quickly repaid $3.4 million to the pension plan. She also found that the RCMP had spent $1.3 million from the pension and insurance accounts on work of little value and "excessive payments" to families and friends.

As far as Zaccardelli was concerned, in the context of the RCMP's $3 billion-plus annual budget, the entire affair was small potatoes. He told his underlings that he couldn't really understand what all the fuss was about. "We made some mistakes, and we dealt with it."

Zaccardelli also knew what was going on elsewhere in Ottawa, specifically at the Department of Defence, where a massive fraud case against the government was about to be revealed.

In 2003, around the time Denise Revine had stumbled into the pension scandal, the RCMP had been called by the Department of National Defence to conduct a criminal investigation. The chief procurer for the DND, Paul Champagne, had been caught—along with two Ottawa businessmen—of running a billing scheme through which the government had been defrauded of at least $159 million over a period of years. The scam involved computer giant Hewlett-Packard, which provided servicing to the Defence Department. Hewlett-Packard says it was told to pay subcontractors certain fees for DND work that couldn't be disclosed. Until he was caught, Champagne lived an eponymous life with a mansion and a vacation property in the Turks and Caicos Islands. Champagne eventually pleaded guilty and was sent to prison, while Hewlett-Packard repaid $145 million to the government of Canada.

"That's a scandal," Zaccardelli said to his colleagues as the RCMP's pension scandal refused to go away. "Why isn't everyone looking at what happened over there at DND and what they did wrong? Why is no one asking questions of them? We didn't lose a dime. Our members didn't lose a dime in their pensions. I don't get it. We paid back the money [with taxpayers' dollars]. I don't get it."

The difference was that in the government's eyes the country's armed forces were not a threat to government and there was no political upside to taking them on, but the RCMP had long had a largely politically-promoted image of being incompetent and dangerous. They were easy targets.

One person who did get it, ironically enough, was Paul Martin. He had been the beneficiary, as it were, of almost two decades of Mulroney and

Chrétien government sleaziness. The Québec leaders had all but joked about the seemingly unending assaults on the public treasury by them and their friends. Scandal after financial scandal rocked the country during their leaderships, and all of them had one thing in common: it was so easy to dupe the treasury out of taxpayers' money.

Martin kept his own counsel but was quietly outraged by all the double-dealing. He was determined to put a stop to it all. One of Martin's overlooked accomplishments as prime minister was a little-noticed change in the way government would operate in the future. In his first budget, in March 2004, Martin promised to restore the powers of the Comptroller General. He intended to place a deadbolt on the backdoor of the government treasury, which had so long been left unguarded against political and bureaucratic kleptomaniacs. As you learned earlier in this chapter, the powers of that post had been eliminated in 1965 in an effort to make the government more "businesslike." In June 2004, accountant Charles-Antoine St-Jean was appointed Comptroller General of Canada. Few noted the significance, but is it any wonder why Chrétien and Mulroney continued to speak so ill of Martin? Stephen Harper, on the other hand, seemed poised to reap the many benefits of Martin's parliamentary courage and meaningful acts.

Jump forward to early 2007 as the Arar affair is finally winding down, the long-simmering pension scandal had finally reached full boil, and when what is left of Zaccardelli's credibility is about to be reduced to nothing.

✝ ✝ ✝

For four years, the RCMP pension scandal had bubbled beneath the surface of politics. Zaccardelli, quite mistakenly, believed he had dealt effectively with the matter. His own members thought otherwise. The media was onto the story, so the House of Commons Standing Committee on Public Accounts agreed to delve into the scandal and listen to what whistleblowers Macaulay, Lewis, and Revine, among others, had to say.

At first, the Harper government put up resistance, arguing that they were all disgruntled employees and not to be trusted. But being in a minority position in Parliament, the government could make the arguments, giving itself the benefit of plausible deniability, knowing full well that the opposition parties would win any vote to hear the evidence they wanted to hear, which was what happened. By forcing the discussion into the open in the Public Accounts Committee, the government would not be seen to be going after the

Mounties. In fact, with the encouragement of opposition members, the Mounties would be seen to be throwing mud at themselves in public, which would prove useful in the larger game being played.

On February 21, 2007, two weeks after Maher Arar received his $12.5 million settlement, the Public Accounts Committee began hearings on the RCMP pension matter.

Assistant Auditor General Hugh McRoberts opened the testimony with his department's summary review. "We concluded that the RCMP had responded adequately to the findings and recommendations of its internal audit and of the OPS investigation by addressing issues directly connected to the abuse. In particular, the RCMP reimbursed or credited about $3.4 million that had been improperly charged to the pension plan. It also took steps to prevent further inappropriate charges to the pension plan, and it strengthened staffing and contract controls. However, we found that the internal audit and criminal investigation raised additional issues that remain unresolved."

Recently appointed Interim Commissioner Bev Busson reviewed the history of the controversy from the force's perspective. "I would like to emphasize that the RCMP Pension Plan is not, and was never, at risk."

Ottawa Police Chief Vince Bevan testified that "the Provincial Crown Attorney concluded that issues uncovered, while serious, were administrative in nature rather than criminal and that there was no reasonable prospect of conviction on criminal charges."

That is where the civility ended. Like all House of Commons committees, Public Accounts comprised usually anonymous backbenchers who otherwise attract little attention in Parliament. Committee work, especially in a high-profile matter, is the one place they might earn camera time on the nightly news. The chairman of the committee was Liberal Shawn Murphy from Prince Edward Island. There were representatives from every party: Borys Wrzesnewskyj and Judy Sgro, both Liberals from Toronto; Paule Brunelle, the Bloc Québecois member for Trois Rivières; and Conservatives John Williams from Edmonton, Brian Fitzpatrick from Prince George, and David Sweet from Hamilton. New Democrat David Christopherson from Hamilton Centre had a slightly higher media profile, having once served as solicitor general when the New Democratic Party led by Bob Rae ran the government of Ontario in the early nineties.

Wrzesnewskyj, the Liberal member for the Toronto riding of Etobicoke Centre, opened the charge, quoting from Auditor General Sheila Fraser's 2005 report: "Millions of dollars of rank and file RCMP officers' pension and life insurance funds were misused due to management overriding controls. Much of these funds have still not been repaid. This appears to be a tale with no best-case scenario and the worst case of fraud, obstruction of investigations of whistleblowers, investigators punished and constructively dismissed, a criminal investigation suspended, evidence buried, and of wrongdoers rewarded with fraudulent leave payments."

Wrzesnewskyj turned to Deputy Commissioner Barb George, head of human resources, and asked her if she or Zaccardelli had anything to do with having Staff Sergeant Frizzell removed from the investigation.

"I can state with absolute finality that it was neither . . . Commissioner Zaccardelli nor myself that had anything to do, whatsoever, with the, as you say, removal of Sgt. Frizzell."

"Can you tell me who it was?" asked Wrzesnewskyj.

"No, I'm not aware of who it was," George replied. "The best that I can state is that I understood that when Sgt. Frizzell left, is that he returned to his home division, which is 'A' Division. Again, I'm careful with regards to the privacy concerns here, but I understood it was for health reasons."

Wrzesnewskyj then went after the RCMP's civilian Deputy Commissioner, Paul Gauvin, who was in charge of corporate management and comptrollership. Gauvin admitted he had been ordered to take a one-day ethics course after he was found to have failed to properly supervise underlings Ewanovich and Crupi.

"Mr. Gauvin, you assisted Mr. Ewanovich, appointed by Mr. Zaccardelli, Mr. Crupi and six others who were party to a golf game at St. Andrew's Golf Course in New Brunswick on August 26, 2001," Wrzesnewskyj stated. "I have here an e-mail from an official hired by Mr. Crupi with instructions on how to bury the cost into pension fund expenses. This e-mail clearly shows the intent and the mechanism on how to commit fraud against RCMP pension funds. It reads in part: 'I need to make adjustments on the rate for the RCMP Pension Advisory Board. The purpose of this is to hide the golf rates and to expense the golf.' How often did senior RCMP officials use the RCMP pension and insurance funds to cover inappropriate living, hotel, recreational and personal expenses?"

"I can't answer how often," Gauvin replied, "but I can say that this was done by individuals without any knowledge that we had."

One by one the members of the committee went over the evidence, but before long Wrzesnewskyj got another turn to ask questions and he lunged for Deputy Commissioner George's jugular over what he believed was the biggest issue: the removal of Sgt. Frizzell from the investigation and the appearance of a cover-up. He wanted to know who had ordered Frizzell off the investigation.

"I can speculate if you wish me to speculate," George said. "I wasn't involved in this criminal investigation."

"Ms. George, I am stunned," Wrzesnewskyj said. "Here you have criminal investigation following up on a criminal investigation that was shut down by the commissioner two days into it, an internal audit that recommends a criminal investigation, you have a criminal investigation, you're in charge of human resources, one of your officers, the lead investigator on an investigation going on for 15 months is physically removed by two officers from his office, and nobody seems to know who gave that order?"

"Mr. Chair, if I could speak, please," George interrupted, obviously disconcerted. "I was never and I am not in charge of the sergeant that we are speaking to right now."

And so it went. The meeting was soon adjourned but the smell of blood was in the air. The plan was to call more RCMP witnesses to the next session, which would be held five weeks later. In the interim, everyone inside the RCMP prepared for the worst. They would not be disappointed.

[14]

THE LOST GUARDIANS

The Harper government desperately needed help to pull off its planned drastic maneuver to gain control of the RCMP. It got all the help it needed from a decidedly unexpected quarter—inside the RCMP's own tent.

"Ladies and gentlemen," retired Staff Sgt. Ron Lewis began his testimony on March 28, 2007. "I appreciate the opportunity to appear before you today to clarify the issues of concern in relation to the RCMP pension and insurance plans. In particular, I would like to thank the MP for Etobicoke Centre, Borys Wrzesnewskyj, who has taken the time to read between the lines of the [auditor general's] report and uncover the real story. His persistence and dedication for justice has been extremely helpful to allow this story to be told, and a great service to the citizens of Canada."

Lewis, gruff and determined, was a man on a mission to settle old scores. The otherwise politically obscure Wrzesnewskyj was prepared to give him every opportunity to do so.

"I first became aware of the serious wrongdoings concerning the outsource of the RCMP pension and insurance plan in early 2003, and other related wrongdoings by senior executive-level employees of the RCMP as far back as 2001, which are kind of related to the whole story we're about to hear, today," Lewis continued. "While trying to expose these wrongdoings, which were both criminal and code-of-conduct violations, I had face-to-face meetings and produced written complaints up to and including Commissioner Zaccardelli. To my disappointment, I was met with inaction, delays, roadblocks, obstruction and lies. The person who orchestrated most of this cover-up was Commissioner Zaccardelli."

Lewis's testimony was riveting, unlike anything ever said in public about an Ottawa mandarin, never mind a commissioner of the RCMP. The committee members were clearly salivating at the possibilities.

"In retrospect," Lewis continued, "I failed in my attempt to rectify the wrongdoings, in my belief that the internal processes under the RCMP Act and related policies would do the job. I now know this to be untrue, after six years of trying. I've exhausted every process available, and now you, the lawmakers, are my last resort."

The former staff sergeant had only spoken for a minute or so, and the headlines were already being written, but he wasn't finished yet.

"A culture was created by several senior executives where it became very dangerous for employees to report wrongdoings," Lewis said. "The risk to their careers and financial well-being was high. On the other hand, wrongdoers were protected by these senior executives, and supported by Commissioner Zaccardelli. This culture exists today, since some of these senior executives are still in place. But, I wish to emphasize, the RCMP is not rotten to the core. The rot exists only within a small group of senior executives. Some are gone. Some have left recently. Some still remain. The good employees are still suffering emotionally, financially and career-wise, while the wrongdoers are back in the job reaping benefits."

Lewis concluded by making three recommendations to the committee: that an independent, external body be appointed to handle all allegations of criminal activity or violations of the RCMP Act; that all funds missing from the pension fund (about $200,000) be returned immediately; and that Deputy Commissioner Paul Gauvin not be involved in the process because he had "a conflict of interest, since he was accountable for the violations in the first place."

Next to testify before the committee, in full uniform, was Chief Superintendent Fraser Macaulay who, you will recall, was "sent to the penalty box," the RCMP liaison in the Defence Department, by Zaccardelli four years before. Macaulay's latest responsibilities were community, contract, and Aboriginal policing. He brought with him Denise Revine, the demoted auditor who had originally uncovered the mess. She sat beside him.

Macaulay reiterated some of Lewis's points, but added: "I would like to clearly state that we are here today, almost four years after reporting on these matters to Commissioner Zaccardelli, because we believe that he abdicated his responsibility by not immediately addressing the fraud and abuse reported to him, and that there were inappropriate actions taken to suppress the facts and mislead employees. For the record, we are here because it is the right thing to do."

Macaulay told the committee that the evidence presented by him to Zaccardelli on June 17, 2003, "was credible, undeniable and convincing. The commissioner was aware of misappropriations of funds; the threats, the excessive spending, the serious staffing and contracting violations and the gross abuses of power and authority.

"The truth of the matter," Macaulay continued, "is that the investigation was shut down prematurely, preventing the investigators from being able to link the numerous gains, promotions, performance pay, hiring of relatives, kickbacks and prospects of future consulting work to the abusers of the pension fund. Even under these circumstances, 21 individuals were highlighted as having committed possible code of conduct offences. Yet not one of them was held accountable for their actions. In fact, a number of employees were promoted immediately following the conclusion of the investigation."

Macaulay was followed by RCMP Staff Sgt. Steve Walker, who had been one of the RCMP's lead investigators in the investigation conducted by the Ottawa Police Service. Walker compared the core values of the RCMP—honesty, integrity, respect, compassion, professionalism, and accountability—to what had taken place. "The mechanisms for insuring the adherence to core values are accountability and supervision," Walker said. "The lack of proper accountability and supervision has been stated as an important contributing factor to corrupt behaviour. Proper supervision and accountability allows managers to identify warning signs and, by ensuring the rules are adhered to, they can remove the opportunities for corrupt behaviour. Corruption has a tremendous impact on public trust, faith and internal morale."

Walker would have headline-making quotes of his own.

"I have never heard of, or witnessed such wholesale violations of all our core values as I have seen and observed in the course of the pension investigation. . . . I believe we were intended to give this a quick once-over and to minimize the allegations. . . . This investigation and the outcomes are nothing short of sickening to any loyal and dedicated employee of the RCMP. . . . Millions of dollars of pension fund and insurance monies have been subject to misuse, misappropriation, and spent in violation of rules surrounding fenced funding and Treasury Board directives."

Walker outlined in detail the costly and probably inappropriate renovations to Zaccardelli's office which, among other things Zaccardelli had done, had been the subject of an earlier investigation. That investigation had led to criticism of the then-commissioner, but nothing more. Walker also pointed out that the RCMP had become caught up in the Gomery inquiry into Jean Chrétien's illegal federal sponsorship program in Québec and how it had flowed millions of dollars through illegal RCMP accounts to help Chrétien battle Québec nationalists.

"How many times is an organization allowed to make the same mistakes, before someone is held responsible at the highest levels and positive change can be seen to be done by employers and the taxpayer?" Walker asked in concluding his opening statement.

The final two witnesses, RCMP Staff Sgt. Mike Frizzell and now-Assistant Commissioner David Gork, added nothing new but they did lend their full and unequivocal support to the damning testimony of the previous witnesses.

As political theatre it was unprecedented. RCMP members, some in uniform, active and retired, speaking out against their leaders. The members of the Public Accounts Committee had received such a plethora of openings to explore it was almost impossible to know where to begin.

Wrzesnewskyj was the first to draw more blood. His target was Deputy Commissioner George, who had testified at the first hearing, five weeks earlier, that she had no idea who had Frizzell removed from the investigation. "I can speculate if you wish . . . I wasn't involved," she had said then.

Wrzesnewskyj tabled copies of two e-mail messages. The first, from RCMP Chief Superintendent Doug Lang, read: "I have an electronic copy of the written order we served on Frizzell at the request of Assistant Commissioner Gork and Deputy Commissioner George." The second, from RCMP Assistant Commissioner Bruce Rogerson, read: "Barb George called Assistant Commissioner Darrel Lafosse, then me, and then Dave Gork surrounding Mike Frizzell's harassing behaviour and he needed to be dealt with swiftly."

"Mr. Chairman," Wrzesnewskyj said, "I'm very concerned that Deputy Commissioner Barb George has perjured herself before the committee and will need to reappear to clarify the situation."

Wrzesnewskyj turned his attention to Macaulay. "What did Deputy Commissioner George say to you about your being seconded to the Department of National Defence?"

"Barb made it very clear to me at that time that I was alone," said Macaulay. "She advised me I was on an island by myself and that nobody was going to tell the truth. We had a lengthy conversation on the issues again and she explained to me how naïve I had to be to think anyone was going to stand beside me in this type of situation and to tell the truth."

Macaulay's bombshell was an even bigger bombshell than the other bombshells from the opening statements.

New Democrat David Christopherson·could hardly believe it. "Either this Chief Superintendent deserves to be medaled for courage or his career is effectively over. But that is one hell of a statement to make here in front of a parliamentary committee, that a deputy commissioner, as alleged by a chief superintendent, made the comments we've just heard. . . . This is far from over."

Conservative John Williams jumped in to ask if any of the witnesses had filed a complaint with Assistant Commissioner John Spice, the RCMP's ethics commissioner.

Macaulay said he and Revine had gone to Spice, but that the ethics commissioner told them even he was having difficulty getting answers. "He was struggling and kept telling us . . . that this wasn't going to work. He wasn't getting anywhere with the commissioner."

Conservative Brian Fitzpatrick, vice-chair of the committee, took up the charge at the end of the session. "I am a lawyer and I think a lot of the stuff I've heard—if it was somebody else, they would be in criminal court and they would have been dancing a tune. Some of them may have been packing their toothbrushes for the crowbar hotel visit."

Not to be outdone, Shawn Murphy, the committee chairman, said: "It seems to me that we're dealing with a cover-up. And a lot of times it's like Watergate, the cover-up is worse than the crime. It's getting such that I'm scared the next person to walk through that door is going to be the ghost of Richard Nixon."

☩ ☩ ☩

At his suburban home, east of Ottawa, Giuliano Zaccardelli was still numb from the humiliation of having been publicly forced out of the commissioner's office. He knew that it was inevitable he would be called before the Public Accounts Committee, so he kept in touch with brass, including Interim Commissioner Busson.

It took Zaccardelli a while to get his head around what exactly had just happened in the Public Accounts Committee. The RCMP had provided him with unedited copies of the testimony—the blues, as they are known—to help him prepare for his testimony. He had finished scanning the first volume from February 21, and had made some comments in the margins about the testimony. On Good Friday, April 5, 2007, he sat down with the two volumes of testimony, including the session from March 28. Using a yellow highlighter stick, he underlined key statements, while using various colours of ink to make notes in the margins. "Check further," he wrote about an Ottawa police finding about abuses in the pension fund. "Find out exactly what the funds had been used for." "Get more info on this." "Did I appoint Jim [Ewanovich]?" "Get more info from Paul [Gauvin]." "Get more info on why Bus Case was inadequate. Some say it was deliberately low?? Why??" "Why the business case low balled?" "Get all the facts contracts etc." "Follow up." "Clarify this." "Wasn't wasted. Was used for other HR issues. Clarify and get right."

When Bev Busson testified that "those funds were administratively ledgered improperly rather than stolen," Zaccardelli noted: "very important distinction . . . Get Paul to explain the confusion with T.B. [Treasury Board] rules at the beginning."

It is not clear if Zaccardelli was still trying to direct the RCMP's response to the crisis or just making notes for himself. In either case, his comments, while potentially self-serving, tend to reveal a man who saw himself as a chief executive officer of a 26,000-person company, but didn't know the nitty-gritty details of his organization. "Who made the decision to remove Frizzell?? Inspector Roy?" Zaccardelli wondered to himself.

With regard to the nepotism issue in the pension department, Zaccardelli scribbled: "We only found out about nepotism after the audit was complete."

Zaccardelli saw nothing wrong with the compensation packages awarded to Ewanovich and Crupi. "Find out exactly what Jim and Cruppi [sic] got re: their dismissal. Bottom line: they are entitled to be treated according to the rules." "They were removed from their jobs by me—same day I received Audit report. Get info on bonus from Barb." Later, on the same issue, he wrote: "Get Barb to get info on this. I believe I said no to performance pay—check."

He was adamant that Ewanovich and Crupi were just sloppy managers, not thieves, as suggested by committee member Brian Fitzpatrick: "Clear this up. There is no evidence that they personally took money for themselves." "Clear this up," he wrote again and again.

Clearly, Zaccardelli was upset by the allegations being made by his own members about corruption and cover-ups. In the margins of one sheet of blues, he wrote: "Important: [Ottawa Police Chief] Vince [Bevan] says no cover-up. They had benefit of independent crown and forensic audit."

Borys Wrzesnewskyj had stated that there was "more than enough evidence" of corrupt behaviour, but Zaccardelli wrote in the margins: "There was not—Important." "Important" and "Very Important" were words he would use many times for both himself and whoever his audience might be.

As for Staff Sgt. Ron Lewis's allegations, Zaccardelli was convinced that Lewis had tried to go too far and had overstated his actions, especially the fact that he had called for a criminal investigation.

"Lewis had no authority to call for a criminal investigation. His job was to report, then I decided what course of action was required. I decided the Audit as the best approach. Lewis was shopping his complaint around. This was inappropriate. Once he gave me the info I decided what should be done. Check with 'A' Div what complaint he had made. Had he made a previous request for a criminal investigation?" In another comment on Lewis's testimony, given later, Zaccardelli wrote: "Not so" and "This is slander."

Regarding Chief Superintendent Macaulay, Zaccardelli wrote: "Clear that he doesn't agree with the way I managed the allegations i.e. audit vs criminal investigation." "Note for Monday." "Macaulay never asked to see me. He was brought to me by Barb."

In his testimony before the committee, Macaulay stated at one point: "I originally went to Mr. Spice and advised him of the findings that Ms. Revine was starting to uncover." Zaccardelli underlined the testimony and wrote: "Very Important Re Fraser's duty to report. If she was starting to uncover— When did he learn of it? When did she start A-Base?" Later in Macaulay's testimony, Zaccardelli wrote: "Again why didn't he come forward?" "Wrong." "Never said anything to me." "Challenge this."

The issue of John Spice, the ethics officer, being ignored by Zaccardelli also rankled the former commissioner. "Be ready to address this. John never mentioned these issues to me. We only talked about Lewis/Jim [Ewanovich] personality conflicts."

His own testimony was only a few days away and Zaccardelli had concerns about the politicians on the committee, and what they were looking for. Comments made by David Christopherson caused Zaccardelli to note: "These are only allegations" and "Very Biased."

Of Shawn Murphy's allusion to Watergate and the ghost of Richard Nixon, Zaccardelli noted: "Bias on part of chair." And, a few paragraphs later: "So biased." "Important. Bring this out at hearing." "Wrong."

Wrzesnewskyj at one point had asked Inspector Gork: "What sort of relationship did Deputy Commissioner Barb George have with Commissioner Zaccardelli?"

"You'd have to ask her that," Gork had replied.

Zaccardelli seemed perturbed by the suggestiveness of the question: "Be ready to deal with this question."

The questions about George stung him partly because she was one of his top protégées, and in recent days she too had been made to walk the plank. Wrzesnewskyj's lethal accusation of her being a perjurer had pierced her otherwise respectable reputation. She had not even been given a chance to "clarify" her comments in public before Bev Busson called George into her office the day after the committee hearings. Busson subsequently announced that George was stepping down as deputy commissioner of human resources and from her senior executive and management duties. Busson's story was that George was merely going on paid leave to pursue educational opportunities, but that didn't wash with anyone either inside or outside the RCMP. The media were soon alerted to the real story, that George had been suspended with pay and that an internal investigation would be called to determine whether she had deliberately obstructed the Commons committee.

Having seen his own career already destroyed in another parliamentary committee appearance four months earlier, Zaccardelli had prepared himself as well as he thought he could. This time around he didn't have professional consultants to help him out. He had nothing to fight for now but his own pride and respect for the institution he loved. On April 16, 2007, he headed back to Parliament Hill and into the lions' den.

The atmosphere that afternoon inside the Committee room was electric with anticipation. Everyone there—the politicians, the reporters, and the witnesses—knew there was going to be a slaughter. Unlike U.S. committee hearings where a witness can bring a lawyer, the Canadian system is almost deliberately unruly and, arguably, unfair. The key witnesses were Zaccardelli, Jim Ewanovich, and Dominic Crupi. But two of their accusers, retired Staff Sgt. Ron Lewis and RCMP Chief Superintendent Fraser Macaulay, in uniform, were also witnesses. It was certain to be a free-for-all.

Zaccardelli made an opening statement constructed largely on the notes and comments he had made in his review of the previous evidence. He tried to control his anger with the process, but it wasn't easy.

"Now, I want to make one thing clear," he said as he was coming to the end of his summation, "I have never been under the apprehension that all parties are necessarily happy with the steps that were taken and the management approach to this issue that I was pursuing as commissioner. As you can imagine, there were very few of the thousands of decisions I undertook during my tenure as commissioner that were unanimously supported. That is one of the burdens and challenges of leadership, of course. However, there is a significant difference between disagreeing with the steps taken by management and making allegations that management is covering up or acting corruptly as Lewis, Macaulay, and others who disagreed have done.

"Mr. Chairman, I do not plan today, or in the future, to grant any quarter to remarks made at this committee or elsewhere inferring corruption at the RCMP or associated with me," Zaccardelli continued. "Such allegations are so completely baseless that I can only surmise that frustration and anger have badly clouded the thinking of the individuals who have made such unfounded and unsubstantiated statements. . . ."

Zaccardelli, obviously upset, had one final comment for the committee: "I am deeply concerned with the inferences and accusations that have been levied against me in this committee and in the public sphere as a result. I have not had before today any opportunity to provide information or respond to questions and yet, Mr. Chairman, it appears that many conclusions have been arrived at regardless. I am confident that this cannot have been the intention of the committee and I look forward to clearing up the misconceptions which have been allowed to flourish."

Ewanovich defended himself by stating that much of what had happened on his watch had been approved by one level or another of the RCMP bureaucracy. "I have been through four auditor general reviews, an RCMP internal audit, an internal investigation, and a year-long investigation by the Ottawa Police Service, which was conducted by thorough and professional investigators, as well as an independent forensic auditor. It was found that all monies were accounted for and that issues, while serious, were administrative in nature rather than criminal. I have not read in any of these reports that I was corrupt or responsible for fraudulent practices."

Ewanovich concluded by taking a shot at Zaccardelli: "When I read the draft audit report in October 2003, I was shocked at the seriousness of the findings, [and] although not directly responsible, disgusted with the commissioner. And, in spite of all our other successes, it happened on my watch. I took accountability, stepped down and resigned."

When Crupi's turn came, he took aim at Macaulay. "When I was appointed as director I had the responsibility for budgets. Financial coding inputs, spending authorities and administration for the group fell under the purview of Chief Superintendent Fraser Macaulay. I no longer had individuals under my control who could do that. During this time we were not permitted to direct access of financial records or reports, not until a pension accounting unit was created and given full access in 2003 to the financial system did this change. At no time was I ever told or asked by Macaulay or any of his staff to explain an action or a process or advised that we were doing anything wrong. Nor was I provided with any information or training in any of these areas. I fully cooperated with the police investigations."

Witness Staff Sgt. Lewis, in response to a question, was the first to go on the attack, calling Zaccardelli a liar for saying that he would investigate Ewanovich in 2003, and later stating he had no memory of such a commitment. "Mr. Zaccardelli pounded on his desk and said: 'Why are these officers coming to me?' And I said: 'The reason for that is because you treat them poorly when they come forward. As a result, I will not give you documents until you appoint an officer [to investigate].' They will all come forward at once, not individually because as they come forward, they get punished. And Fraser Macaulay is a good example."

Lewis told the committee that Zaccardelli told him to go directly to Assistant Commissioner Ghyslaine Clément, the commander of "A" Division, and have her open an investigation, which Zaccardelli stopped two days later, instead ordering an internal audit.

Zaccardelli was quietly incensed. Lewis had admitted that when he had first come to the commissioner demanding an investigation, there was nothing on paper. And he had no authority to launch his own investigation. The story was getting confusing, so Zaccardelli tried to clear things up.

"It doesn't make sense because that's not what I did," Zaccardelli said, responding to a question from Bloc Québécois Member Jean-Yves LaForest. "Mr. Lewis came to me. I met with him twice to discuss some concerns that he had. During the first discussion that I had with him, I was having difficulty understanding what he was talking about. I actually went to the NEC, which is the National Executive Committee of the divisional representative system. I said: 'I'm trying to understand what Mr. Lewis is trying to complain about.' They said to me: 'We have trouble understanding what he's trying to complain about on this also.'"

Zaccardelli tried to show that Lewis was not being entirely candid, but LaForest interrupted him, arguing that Zaccardelli wasn't answering his question.

"Mr. Chairman, I'm entitled to answer the question," Zaccardelli snapped, and he was allowed to continue.

"I went to my desk. I wrote down and summarized what I believed were Mr. Lewis's allegations and concerns. I showed it to him and I asked him: 'Do you agree with this?' He said: 'Yes, I agree, those are my concerns.' I then called my chief of audit and directed him to start the investigation immediately. I never ever instructed or told Mr. Lewis to go to 'A' Division to ask for a criminal investigation. That would be ridiculous because I'd already decided as the senior manager of the force who has received a complaint on a course of action. My course of action was the audit. There were never any instructions to go anywhere and to start a criminal investigation."

Lewis then referred to his own evidence, two memos to Clement in which he had written: "The Commissioner instructed me to contact you to investigate this matter." As for Zaccardelli's story, Lewis said: "He never said: 'I never told you to do that.'"

New Democrat David Christopherson soon homed in on "the issue of the alleged cover-up," a reference to the way Macaulay, Revine, Frizzell, and Gork had been treated after they spoke up about the problems in the pension administration office. "Are they coincidences? Is that merely a coincidence because it doesn't look good. I'd like to hear your thoughts on that."

Zaccardelli began to recount, case by case, what had happened to each person. He said he had had nothing to do with Revine. "I wouldn't know Frizzell if he walked in the room." Zaccardelli pointed out that RCMP Inspector Gork had already testified that it was Ottawa Police Inspector Roy who had asked that Frizzell be removed from the joint investigation.

Zaccardelli recounted how Barb George had raised Macaulay's concerns with him, and that he had invited George to bring Macaulay to his office for a discussion.

"These are my exact words," Zaccardelli told the committee as he recounted the meeting with Macaulay and the discussion about the problems Macaulay had found. He said that Macaulay told him he had known for more than a year and a half about what was going on, but had been afraid to say anything because it would affect his career.

"I was clearly very disappointed and hurt by the statement," Zaccardelli said of Macaulay. "I had Barb George in my office. I said to Barb George:

'Barb, Fraser has made a serious error in judgment in this case. He's a good young officer. I've known him since he was a very young member. I believe in him. I want him to recover from this and I want him to move ahead. I need you to get him out of this environment he's in, and I want you to find a good job for him. This is a man I want to save because I believe in him.'"

Zaccardelli went on to say that before Macaulay took up his next assignment, he had called him into his office and told him: "Fraser, I know you're not happy with this, but I believe in you. You're a good member. I want you to recover from this mistake. You go down to DND, show them what you're made of, and you'll come back and you'll have a very good job."

Zaccardelli thought he was doing well, until he said one more thing: "Now, I know, this notion has been thrown around about a punishment transfer. There are no punishment transfers in the RCMP."

Some members of the committee and the assembled journalists howled derisively at the comment.

"Well, I'm glad to see we have a lively audience," Zaccardelli said, inwardly astonished that the so-called dispassionate journalists had so openly declared their biases. It was a stunning moment for him, one that he would refer to over and over again in the months to come.

"I've never, ever transferred anyone or directed anyone to ever be transferred for a punishment purpose. When Fraser Macaulay—"

He was cut off by Christopherson who wanted to ask another question.

"No, but let me finish," Zaccardelli protested. "Let me finish my answer."

"No," Christopherson said. "Chair, I'm asking for my rights."

"No," Shawn Murphy told Zaccardelli, "I think you've gone on long enough."

The committee turned to Macaulay, who was sitting nearby, for his version of the story.

"The bottom line was it was a very clear message to the employees that you don't put your hand up," Macaulay testified. "If I was so afraid for my career—I'm back in the organization—why would I be here today? Why would I have done what I've done for the past 3 1/2 years? Why would I have continued hand in glove with Denise Revine, a commitment that I made to her when she found this out about my organization? I've heard many times. I've heard many times from Mr. Zaccardelli. He let us down. He came in here and he talks the values and he means them, most of the time. This is a leader who got to the top of this organization. He's made a mistake and now we're back into the same stuff. Now, we've got the notes; we've got the paper; we know what's going on here. I was removed because I came forward. That is all."

Conservative Brian Fitzpatrick accused Zaccardelli of having a "buck-passing" management style and that he only acted as he did because he had found himself trapped in a corner.

"I never passed the buck," Zaccardelli said, bristling. "I never abdicated and that is totally unfair what you've just said, and I totally disagree with that."

The committee members kept hammering away at the former commissioner. "What were you fearful of?" Wrzesnewskyj asked.

When Zaccardelli tried to answer, Wrzesnewskyj cut him off. "Mr. Chairman, may I have the decency to answer—"

"Mr. Zaccardelli," Wrzesnewskyj continued with a fistful of mud, "did a former chief financial officer of the RCMP advise you that Deputy Commissioner Paul Gauvin has a book with a record of all the requests you made to him which were improper and illegal and that if he goes down, he will take you with him?"

"I have no recollection of that," Zaccardelli said. When he tried to elaborate, Wrzesnewskyj cut him off again.

Conservative John Williams weighed in next. "It's the cover-up we're talking about."

"If this is a cover-up," Zaccardelli replied, "I think it's a pretty poor cover-up. We have a public audit by the RCMP that is shared by Treasury Board and the auditor general. We have a very public investigation that is going on by the Ottawa City Police. We have the Crown that says there's no reason to charge. I am communicating with my members giving them an update on what's going on. I am meeting with the NEC, the National Executive Committee of the reps. This is in the public domain. If this is a cover-up, Mr. Williams, I leave it to you."

The committee pecked away at Zaccardelli all afternoon. It all came down to whether or not there was a first investigation initiated by Lewis.

He said there had been, and Zaccardelli said there had never been a first investigation, but an audit. "That is the problem I've had for six years with this man. I keep telling him things, he keeps twisting and he keeps telling lies. I'm sick of it. And he's doing it here under oath," Lewis said, firing another sure-to-be quoted rocket at Zaccardelli.

"Please," Shawn Murphy reprimanded Lewis, "in your testimony, I'd ask you to refrain from making personal insinuations like you just did. We don't allow that in Parliament."

But the final nail was hammered into Zaccardelli by David Christopherson, who said that with Lewis and Zaccardelli embracing conflicting versions of the same story, one of the men was not telling the truth. "They're saying opposite things," Christopherson said. "So either an order was given that a criminal investigation start or it was not."

Zaccardelli, whatever his faults, didn't stand a chance. Nothing about the committee process was fair. Little light was allowed to shine on the so-called scandal, and what light there was didn't get reported. That night and the next day, newscasts and newspapers alike focused on the often outrageous comments by Macaulay and Lewis and certain committee members, doing everything they possibly could to tell a one-sided story, which every one of them did. Both the public and members of the RCMP were left with the impression that horrible things had happened under Zaccardelli's watch, but few, if any, knew with any degree of certainty what those horrors might be. They just knew that it was bad.

Christopherson was quick to take credit for all that had happened. In a subsequent committee meeting, he proudly stated: "The opposition all voted, in a formal vote against the government, to have Frizzell, Macaulay, Revine, and Lewis come to speak. Remember that when it happened, at that time, they were troublemakers. They were disgruntled employees. It's in Hansard. I won't name names, but government members said they weren't going to let them come here and be given a platform to launch against senior officers just because they were disgruntled employees. We brought them here and started to hear from them. It's when this started to unravel. It wasn't that long ago that the names—and I'm going to say them again—Frizzell, Macaulay, Revine, and Lewis, who are now going to be legendary heroes in the RCMP, were troublemakers."

The Public Accounts Committee voted that the whistleblowers should receive honours for their courage. Later, Interim Commissioner Busson hosted a private dinner at an Ottawa restaurant and awarded Revine, Macaulay, Lewis, Frizzell, and Walker the Commissioner's Commendation for outstanding service, the RCMP's most coveted award.

For the government, all this would prove to be an invaluable distraction from the troublesome subject of one Maher Arar.

✢ ✢ ✢

Giuliano Zaccardelli had twice been destroyed. Before he testified at the Public Accounts Committee hearings, Zaccardelli still enjoyed the support of many RCMP members who believed he had been railroaded in the Arar affair. Afterward, he had virtually no support inside the RCMP. And the knifing would continue.

Over the next weeks and months, more of the force's dirty linen would be aired in public. Four female Mounties came forward to talk about how they had been quietly paid off after their complaints about sexual harassment and assaults by a RCMP officer in western Canada had been ignored. Much of the mud thrown involved events that had preceded Zaccardelli's tenure as commissioner, but it hardly seemed to matter.

An allegation was made that the high-flying Zaccardelli had once charged $80 to his expense account for a single shot of cognac. It was a wonderful symbol of excess, even though those who knew Zaccardelli well were aware that he was proud of the fact that he had never had a drink of hard liquor in his life. "I had my first glass of wine when I was thirty-two," he said.

Forced out of office, Zaccardelli found it hard to let go. One day, while travelling with his wife Bette in western Canada, he came upon a Mountie patrolling the streets of Banff, Alberta. The Mountie wasn't wearing his hat.

"Where's your kit?" Zaccardelli asked the astonished Mountie. "Go get it, right now."

The Mountie returned to his detachment to relate the story about the former commissioner, to the guffaws of all who were there. Although RCMP rules state that in public all Mounties must be fully dressed, in Banff, with its wild bar scene, the Mounties are constantly battling drunks. The force had lost so many hats that the members just kept them stowed. That story made the rounds, adding to the considerable folklore about the former commissioner.

Zaccardelli wanted to write a book about his life in the RCMP and what had happened to him to set the record straight. But not one publisher in Canada was interested in his story. He had been "proven" a liar in public, he had been humiliated, and he was considered a disgrace by his former colleagues. His story was deemed not worth telling. His policing career was over—or was it?

In the aftermath of the Public Accounts Committee hearings, the government moved forward with the next steps in its plan. Resisting calls for a public inquiry which, he said, would take too much time, Public Safety Minister

Stockwell Day did something entirely unexpected and not a little bit curious. He appointed David Brown, Q.C., a Toronto lawyer who was once chairman of the Ontario Securities Commission, to conduct a quick and dirty one-man, independent inquiry into the RCMP. Brown was given just two months to conduct his special investigation and report his findings because, Day said, the RCMP's problems were obvious and urgent action needed to be taken. In fact, the RCMP's failings and dysfunction had been evident for decades.

In any event, it seemed like the perfect time for the government to call a time out, reassess the viability of the RCMP in its current structure, thoroughly think through all the ramifications involved with any change, and then move forward in a decisive fashion. Why the rush? As a consumer, when a salesperson is pushing you to sign a deal, your intuition should tell you that there might be something amiss. Rushing is what fraud artists do to dupe unwitting victims. As we already know, there were other things going on, and the expedited process was deemed the only way to escape the larger issues. The Mounties and the rest of Canada had no appreciation of how dangerous the issues were the government was juggling. Time and discretion were of the essence in its move to get more control of the RCMP.

[15]

THE ARAR GATEKEEPERS
TAKE OVER THE RCMP

It would be fair to say that, based on his past performance at the Ontario Securities Commission, few people in Canada expected much from special investigator David Brown. Appointed by Stephen Harper's political soulmates, the notoriously right-wing Ontario government of Mike Harris in 1998, Brown spent the next seven years at the helm of the OSC, Canada's largest market regulatory body. Under his leadership, the OSC became world-renowned for its tortoise-like pace in recognizing cases and investigating them, and its Bambi-like timidity in mounting prosecutions.

It was a period during which large-scale accounting fraud became a plague on the market, the high-tech bubble burst, and flagrant insider trading was depleting trust in the financial markets. Spectacular implosions of seemingly viable companies were happening on a regular basis: Bre-X, Livent, Philip Services Corp., and then Nortel and others. Conrad Black was treating his public companies like a personal piggybank. Shareholders and market watchers were complaining that the stock and mutual fund markets were little more than a casino, and that the OSC was only concerned about the interests of sellers—particularly the rich and powerful establishment. Otherwise, it was buyer beware.

During Brown's seven-year tenure, the OSC opened 1,700 files on suspect companies, but managed to gain convictions in only eight cases. It collected a paltry $15.5 million in fines against companies and individuals, a little more than $2 million per operating year. The OSC often left the dirty work to its U.S. counterpart, the Securities and Exchange Commission.

Stephen Jarislowsky, a prominent Montréal money manager and outspoken critic of the OSC, was one of many who had little faith in Brown's performance. He told *The Globe and Mail* in 2004 that under Brown's leadership, the OSC has been "a little bit too easygoing" on those who break the rules. "I'm a bit disappointed no one is in jail over Bre-X," he said, referring to the gold-mining scam that led to billions of dollars in losses for investors.

When the Ontario government indicated in late 2004 that it intended to separate the OSC's investigative function from its regulatory duties, Brown abruptly announced his resignation and walked away from his $606,000-a-year job.

He returned to his private law practice with the Toronto firm, Davies, Ward, Phillips and Vineberg LLC, and soon began receiving public honours and plaudits for his performance at the OSC. He was said to have transformed the OSC into a self-funded Crown corporation, a business model that helped him improve staff morale, while doubling the organization's budget and his own salary.

In the spring of 2007, the 67-year-old Brown had less than nine weeks to study the massive RCMP file, get to the bottom of its problems, and write a comprehensive report. It would be the seventh investigation of the matter, but there didn't appear to be enough time for Brown to even collect his thoughts. Not a single person inside the RCMP or in the rest of Canada held out much hope that anything meaningful would come out of his so-called "investigation."

Everyone was in for a huge surprise.

On June 15, 2007, Brown took a seat before the cameras in Ottawa and made a public statement about his 66-page report, entitled "A Matter of Trust." The report had been submitted much earlier to Stockwell Day, the Minister of Public Safety, and Vic Toews, the president of the Treasury Board. The government had had enough time to pull together a background paper on the report, as well as a question and answer format "for the sole purpose of providing media with a quick reference guide and is not intended to comprehensively cover all the details and subtleties of the report's findings."

Brown began his presentation with the familiar tribute to the RCMP.

"The RCMP is revered by Canadians and respected around the world. However, today a cloud hangs over the senior management of the RCMP as an institution as a result of the Arar inquiry, the sponsorship scandal, and the Air India tragedy, in addition to the pension and insurance plan improprieties I have discussed here. These events cannot be allowed to compromise the pride which the members of the force have in belonging to the RCMP or the confidence and trust which Canadians place in the RCMP. . . . It is not overstating the importance of these issues for me to also address my comments to all Canadians whose pride in the RCMP is fundamental to being Canadian."

It appeared Brown might be quoting directly from the RCMP media guide. That there are Canadians who believe that pride in the RCMP is fundamental to being Canadian is probably true, but in a 2007 public opinion poll of Canadians, the RCMP didn't even rank in the top 10. In the rapidly changing demographics of Canada, most Canadians have little or no idea about either the RCMP's history or the scope of its current policing practices.

Brown took pains to detail the work he had done. He had hired two dozen consultants, forensic accountants from KPMG, and some lawyers from his own Toronto law firm. Brown said he was determined to resolve "the confusing and conflicting information" that had arisen since 2003 from two internal investigations, parliamentary hearings, a criminal investigation, and an Auditor General's report. To that end, Brown and his team conducted structured interviews with 25 people, including the original whistleblowers and Zaccardelli. They examined 400,000 electronic documents and e-mails, "which revealed 3,500 e-mails of significance. . . . More than 35,000 pages of documents were reviewed. . . . before Brown began to write his findings."

Brown was actually building up to something quite spectacular. "What happened in the administration of the RCMP pension and insurance plans constituted a breach of fundamental trust between management of the RCMP and its current and retired members," Brown said, visibly warming to the task. "In preparing this report, I found myself forced beyond these events to comment on a broader breach of trust between RCMP management and its members. After sifting through the various versions of events, the picture of the RCMP and its culture that has emerged is one of mistrust and cynicism. Giuliano Zaccardelli was commissioner of the RCMP from 2000 to 2006. He is a central figure, not only in events described in this report, but, more generally, in the cultural issues facing the RCMP.

"Throughout this piece," he continued, "Commissioner Zaccardelli and other members of senior management failed to understand the significant issues at hand. As a result, they did not respond in a manner that was transparent, timely, effective or thorough. More than that, they did not understand the impact that their lack of responsiveness was having on the organization. In an already fractured culture, senior management was projecting the attitude of disinterest and callousness in respect of an issue of legitimate concern to every single member—past and present—of the force: their pensions. In the process, the commissioner lost his troops.

"Even today," Brown said, "neither Commissioner Zaccardelli nor Chief Financial Officer Paul Gauvin, Deputy Commissioner, has accepted responsibility for what happened or the impact on the organization. This has created the conviction on the part of many that the force's values—honesty, integrity, commitment, respect, accountability and professionalism—are routinely disregarded by management."

Brown found that "the current paramilitary, chain-of-command management structure at the RCMP works for a small police force but not a $3 billion enterprise." He slammed Zaccardelli for his passionate, dismissive, and autocratic leadership style. He said the whistleblowers had been treated unfairly by RCMP management and Zaccardelli, and should be commended for their efforts.

The investigation by the Ottawa Police Service was not independent, Brown said, and he recommended that the Ontario Provincial Police be asked to conduct a review to determine whether a new investigation was required. But, Brown added, he did not think a full-blown public inquiry was necessary.

Brown said there was no evidence of a cover-up but the implication was that it certainly looked like a cover-up. If the Canadian public had not yet come to realize that Zaccardelli, already twice excoriated in public, was the root of all the evil that had come to bedevil the RCMP, Brown took this opportunity to drive a stake into his heart. "He allowed a culture to exist—and grow—that displeasing the commissioner was career-limiting. . . . The comments received and uncovered about Commissioner Zaccardelli paint a picture of a man who enjoyed the status and privileges of his office and who used those things to keep people at a distance. . . . The force of Commissioner Zaccardelli's personality has been an important influence on the cultural problems of the RCMP today. The fact of a single individual—even the Commissioner—having unchallenged authority is rooted in the governance structure of the RCMP. I believe it is essential that both the governance structure and the culture at the RCMP should be reviewed by a task force of qualified individuals."

In his comments to reporters later, Brown gilded some of the phrases he had used in his report. "A fractured culture" became "a horribly broken culture." His suggestion for a review by a task force became "an urgent review."

The government's message had been shaped and clearly hammered home. That night's newscasts and the next day's papers were filled with the dramatic findings and focused on those phrases, which never appeared in the report or its summaries, a common tactic of those determined to "control the message." "RCMP 'horribly broken,' investigator finds," reported *The Globe and Mail*. "RCMP 'horribly broken': report," shouted the *National Post*. "Mounties left 'horribly broken,'" screamed the *Ottawa Sun*. The phrase was blasted across the airwaves and was picked up internationally. "Report critical of 'broken' Mounties," read the headline of the *New York Times*.

Public Safety Minister Day welcomed Brown's report, stating: "We think there's enough here to move ahead, and in a reasonable period of time see a fresh governance structure in place, that gives a breath of fresh air to an incredible organization." The government, he added, would name a new full-time commissioner of the RCMP in the coming days or weeks.

Brown's instant investigation and conclusions seemed to be not a little contrived. It was in no way a review of the force, but it perfectly suited the Harper government's agenda. As New Democrat David Christopherson put it: "You're going to tell me that one person, a super-investigator, was able to come bouncing out of a phone booth and go in there and by themselves, get to the bottom of this in a few weeks? It's ridiculous."

The RCMP had been thoroughly humbled and humiliated. Its tarnished image was now indelibly cemented in the consciousness of the nation and the rest of the world.

✛　✛　✛

Dr. Linda Duxbury is a professor in the Sprott School of Business at Ottawa's Carleton University. She is considered one of Canada's leading workplace health researchers. She has written hundreds of papers, journals, and books, is a much sought-after guest on radio and television, and much in demand as a speaker at corporate events.

In August 2007, she lectured at the annual meeting of the Canadian Association of Chiefs of Police in Calgary. The professor held the attention of everyone in the audience for three hours one morning, describing for the police leaders not only the problems they face today, but the ones looming on the horizon, such as the dearth of people willing to become managers.

"People do not leave an organization, they leave bad management," she said, using her own research to back up her observations. "Employees must be able to speak truth to power. A one size fits all approach will not work anymore."

Throughout her presentation, Duxbury directly commented on the state of the RCMP, a force she knows all too well, to the pleasure of the majority of the audience and the chagrin of the Mounties there, who were in the minority.

In fall 2000, Duxbury and her colleague, Dr. Chris Higgins, of the Richard Ivey School of Business at the University of Western Ontario, had undertaken a national study in which 100 Canadian organizations with 500 or more employees participated. The RCMP was one of eight federal departments or agencies who participated in the research, known as the Duxbury and Higgins 2001 "Balancing Work, Family and Lifestyle National Study." Slightly more than 3000 regular members of the RCMP, 577 civilian members, and 476 public servants who worked for the RCMP responded to the survey. What Duxbury and Higgins found inside the RCMP and reported to the force in 2002 caused RCMP managers to cringe. If Duxbury and Higgins were right, there was something drastically wrong inside the RCMP. Despite the force's perpetual self-promotion campaign, rank-and-file Mounties confessed to the researchers that, by and large, it wasn't as wonderful as its marketing suggested. The comprehensive range of complaints, from overwork and stress, to management indifference and a dysfunctional promotion system, landed with a thud on then-Commissioner Zaccardelli's desk. If he could find any solace in the damning report, it was that he had only been in the job for a few weeks and could not be responsible for those failings.

Zaccardelli knew that he had inherited all kinds of problems and employee discontent would be just another big one with which he would have to deal, a legacy of his predecessors. His major concern was the damage caused by Murray's decision to decentralize and empower his underlings. By the time Zaccardelli took over, managers were flying off in every direction, largely unaccountable, and the commissioner's role had been reduced to an all but ceremonial one. Zaccardelli thought that this would prove to be disastrous in the long run, and by the force of his own strong will attempted to impose structure, controls, and accountability on the force. This, of course, was bound to engender resentment in the ranks. And it did. But Zaccardelli believed he was on the right track and could weather any storm.

In 2003, the RCMP hired Duxbury and Higgins to come back and conduct more research. Completed the next year and titled "People Management at the RCMP: Key Findings from the 2001 National Work–Life Study," Zaccardelli was confident the report would confirm that he had made significant improvements within the force. That's the way it looked from his aerie at headquarters in Ottawa anyway. Duxbury and Higgins told Zaccardelli that he was right about his perspective of the force. Only one-quarter of those involved in the first survey volunteered to do the second one, which meant the researchers did not have a proper sample size for some groups.

The two professors and their team of researchers found that in the two years between the surveys, the higher one rose in the RCMP the better things seemed to be. At the top, life for the Carpet Cops was almost rosy. However, in the ranks there was all but a mutiny brewing. It didn't look good at all for the RCMP, then or in the future.

The 2004 study reported that women were still having a tough time in the force. Many felt harassed. Somewhat ironically, at the same time a higher percentage of women were reported to be happy with their jobs. Men felt overworked and stressed to the limit. Workloads were deemed "unsustainable over time." A high percentage of Mounties—33 percent—had no plans to stay in the force until retirement. Thirty-nine percent of them were planning to look for a job elsewhere. Relatively few wanted to become managers and there existed a high level of cynicism about the promotion process. An even higher percentage—50 percent—wouldn't recommend that their children join the RCMP. They said management was seen to be brutal, distant, and too political.

The researchers found that to be a Mountie meant not having much of a family life. The RCMP insisted that work always came first. Overtime could not be refused. Compared with other professions in Canada, divorce rates among employees at the RCMP were at the highest levels. "The data suggest that many employees at the RCMP do not cope well with the stressors they face," the report concluded. "To meet demands at work they work harder, cut back on sleep, prioritize and plan and schedule their work and let things slide at home. Most do not delegate or ask for help from others. A significant number practice unhealthy strategies such as displacement or avoidance. There has been little change over time in how employees cope with stress. That being said, the increased tendency to use alcohol to cope with stress is cause for concern."

In the two years since the first study, Duxbury and Higgins found that morale in the RCMP had worsened. Almost half of the employees at the lower ranks—49 percent of constables and corporals—said they were demoralized because of short-staffing, overwork, and inertia in the force. A majority of Mounties were willing and prepared for drastic changes to be made in the administration and operations of the force, but the brass didn't see that need. "One in five members of this group would not take a job at the

RCMP if they had to do it again and a similar number would not recommend the job to others," Duxbury and Higgins wrote.

They added: "The data indicated that the people at the top of the RCMP (commissioned officers from inspector to commissioner, the managers of the force) have a very different view of the world than the people that they manage. Consider the following: First, the survey data indicated that those in the Inspector and above grade had a highly supportive manager, are highly committed and loyal to their job and very engaged in and satisfied with their jobs. The data would suggest that this group loves their jobs and the RCMP. The situation has improved over time for this group—likely due to an influx of better managers into the area. It may be that 9/11 has made their jobs more relevant and interesting. In all cases, the attitudes and experiences of those at the top of the RCMP are more positive than those expressed by those in middle management and front line jobs at the RCMP."

Duxbury and Higgins found that one of the most aggravating things about the RCMP for individual Mounties was its arcane and bewildering promotion systems. They determined that 43 percent of women compared with 25 percent of men liked the promotion system because it allowed them to *not* seek advancement in their careers. These people wanted to nest right where they were and collect their benefits and full pension at the end of their careers. "These data are consistent with the low number of women in the upper ranks of the RCMP. If this issue is not addressed the RCMP is likely to have problems with succession planning as both men and women refuse to consider promotions to the upper echelon of the RCMP," the researchers wrote.

Duxbury and Higgins found that one in four RCMP employees had given the overall work a negative rating because of frustrations with the promotion process. They provided two tables, one seeking positive responses, the other negative, which served to reveal the level of discontent inside the RCMP.

Table 1: Perception of Change Within the RCMP: Percent Agreeing

Management of Change: Percent who Agree	2003
I am willing to contribute to the change process.	89.6
I see change as a positive thing.	68.5
RCMP has a clear focus and sense of direction.	36.8
The leadership team at the RCMP are knowledgeable about strategic issues.	31.3
RCMP is progressive.	30.7
RCMP is innovative.	25.8
Changes at the RCMP are made in a way that is consistent with the mission of the organization.	23.9
Creativity and innovation rewarded in the RCMP.	20.9
RCMP celebrates its successes with respect to change.	20.9
Change driven by facts and information.	19.1
Leadership team open to different ideas and opinions.	17.9
Employees are kept well informed about what is happening.	16.9
RCMP consistently follows through with plans and decisions.	16.6
Employees receive adequate training to keep up with the changes.	15.3
Employees actively involved in planning and implementing change.	14.9

Change at the RCMP is carefully considered and well planned.	14.8
Rationale for change effectively communicated.	14.1
Impact of change is monitored and evaluated.	11.1
Leadership team keeps employees motivated about change.	9.2
Adequate resources are provided to accommodate new processes.	6.2
Problems arising from the change are identified and resolved.	4.3

Table 2: Perception of Change Within the RCMP: Percent Disagreeing

Management of Change: Percent who Disagree	2003
Adequate resources are provided to accommodate new processes.	79.9
Problems arising from the change are identified and resolved.	71.2
Rationale for change effectively communicated.	71.2
Change at the RCMP is carefully considered and well planned.	67.3
Leadership team keeps employees motivated about change.	66.9
Impact of change in monitored and evaluated.	65.4
Employees receive adequate training to keep up with the changes.	65.3

Employees actively involved in planning and implementing change.	65.2
Leadership team open to different ideas and opinions.	63.6
Employees are kept well informed about what is happening.	60.7
RCMP consistently follows through with plans and decisions.	60.7
Changes at the RCMP are made in a way that is consistent with the mission of the organization.	55.8
Creativity and innovation rewarded in the RCMP.	52.1
Change driven by facts and information.	49.4
RCMP is innovative.	48.6
RCMP has a clear focus and sense of direction.	47.2
RCMP is progressive.	42.3
RCMP celebrates its successes with respect to change.	39.9
The leadership team at the RCMP are knowledgeable about strategic issues.	36.2
I am willing to contribute to the change process.	2.8
I see change as a positive thing.	7.4

Among their recommendations, Duxbury and Higgins suggested the RCMP rebuild trust with the rank and file: "The findings from this study suggest that the RCMP needs to consider cultural change if they wish to successfully address many of the issues uncovered in this study. Specifically they need to deal with the following dimensions of their culture: the focus on hours (if you do not work long hours you will not get ahead; it is unacceptable to say no to more work), the idea that one has to pick between work or family (family leave and family responsibilities limit career advancement), a focus on policy rather than practice (employees do not feel comfortable using supportive policies that are currently in place) and the idea that it is who you know and how you play the game that will get you ahead within the RCMP. The importance of addressing the issue of organizational culture cannot be overemphasized. A policy approach on its own will not fix the issues uncovered in this study. To successfully implement many of the recommendations given in this report the RCMP will need to change reward structures, accountability frameworks and measurement systems."

Zaccardelli and his subordinates were shocked by the report's findings. They understood there were serious problems inside the RCMP, but the recommendations in the Duxbury and Higgins report were more explosive than they could possibly have imagined. To implement the changes would mean changing the entire nature and structure of the RCMP. Its business model could not absorb giving staff more time off, paying overtime in cash to better reflect the true costs of overtime, or giving RCMP members more time for family and recreation.

As the RCMP brass reviewed the report, they found a number of outs. The sample was relatively small and, by the authors' own admission, the findings possibly skewed in some areas because of that. The RCMP reviewers also thought that Duxbury and Higgins had approached the force in an almost ingenuous fashion, in a way that fit their standard model for examining a corporation, as if the RCMP were a boxed-cereal manufacturer. The commissioner couldn't just wave a magic wand and make things better.

The RCMP was capable, to some degree, of setting regular hours for its staff, but a police service by its very definition is not a normal workplace. Criminals don't work from 9 to 5 and crimes often can't be investigated in one shift or by multiple investigators clocking in and out as their creature comforts dictate. Overtime is a necessary part of the job. Even by ordinary police service standards, the RCMP was an extraordinarily complex and abnormal entity, something the researchers glossed over.

"She's just a university professor," Zaccardelli scoffed, dismissing the report's lead author. "What do they know about the RCMP?" Instead of implementing any changes, Zaccardelli and the Chrétien government buried the report, and the commissioner continued down his established path of strong-arming the RCMP into shape.

The report didn't die, however. Three years later, when Special Investigator David Brown came looking for evidence, he was handed the research. He interviewed Duxbury, who briefed him on the phrase that became the headline: "a horribly broken culture." "Rebuilding trust" became the foundation and theme of Brown's own report "A Matter of Trust." It was supported by a couple of interviews with the pension scandal whistleblowers, whose echoes one can hear throughout Brown's report.

After the Brown report was tabled, Duxbury was called to the Public Accounts Committee to talk about her work. She told the assembled politicians that the RCMP had simply not adapted to the 21st century and was locked in an outdated paramilitary model, which was true. It was "not change ready" and "institutionally sick." Duxbury testified: "Cultural change is the most difficult kind of change and the majority of cultural changes fail. Even if all the stars are aligned, it's five to ten years for cultural change to occur and not all the stars are aligned here, so I caution the committee, give the RCMP a chance here. We can't expect miracles overnight.... Cultural problems arise when organizations that have been hugely successful in the past don't see how the environment has changed around them and they keep their culture and don't adapt," she said.

The politicians on the Public Accounts Committee accepted her testimony as if it were received wisdom, even though the previous Chrétien and Martin governments had known about her first report since 2000.

The way those previous governments handled the Duxbury reports put the notion of ministerial responsibility to shame. In 1984, recall, the government of the day made the commissioner of the RCMP a deputy minister in the Department of the Solicitor General in an effort to make the force more politically accountable. This suggested that the government, through the commissioner of the RCMP, would then have knowledge of reports like the ones conducted by Duxbury and Higgins, and would take appropriate action. That Chrétien did nothing shows how he had kept his part of the accord he made with Zaccardelli in September 2000—to keep his nose out of the docile, error-prone, and politically controlled RCMP.

In the intervening years, as the RCMP continued to self-destruct, absolutely nothing substantive was done to address its myriad internal problems. Successive governments continued to praise and put their faith in the RCMP. When the RCMP received third-party awards during this period for its organizational and business prowess—such as being named one of Canada's top employers or by receiving a citation from the Harvard School of Business—Zaccardelli cited these accolades as evidence that he was on the right path. Those who had bestowed the awards on the RCMP had obviously bought into the RCMP's own marketing and had conducted no independent research, showing just how hollow such recognition can be. For its part, the government doled out medals and honours like clockwork to the highest-ranking members of the force.

The entire David Brown maneuver also served Prime Minister Harper well. In the aftermath of the Arar matter, he needed to change the subject, but at the same time he had been presented with a momentous opportunity. Doing nothing, like his predecessors, was not an option, but what would he do? In the short term, he was compelled to ensure that the RCMP kept a lid on the Arar case and what had taken place. At the same time, events had conspired in such a way as to allow him to make fundamental changes to the structure and direction of the RCMP. These imperatives were not mutually exclusive. To take on the RCMP, however, he would need to inflict more damage on the reputation of the force. The weapon was already sitting there in the filing cabinet: the documents that should have been revealed by the Chrétien government. It was a no-brainer. Now there were no issues of ministerial accountability, because his was a different government. The time had come to reveal Duxbury's and Higgins' reports and clobber Zaccardelli and the RCMP with them.

✠ ✠ ✠

After the Brown report had been made public, the necessary next stage was implemented: the appointment of a new commissioner.

In December 2006, the government had hired headhunters Ray & Berndtson to search for a permanent commissioner to replace the recently appointed Busson. The candidates would be vetted by a committee appointed by the government. Mountie insiders found the makeup of the committee worrisome. It looked like a platoon of experienced political firefighters being sent out to douse a potentially dangerous blaze.

Heading up the committee was National Security Advisor Margaret Bloodworth. It included two former solicitor generals, Liberal Jean-Jacques Blais and Conservative James Kelleher, and Kelleher's protégé, former RCMP Commissioner Norman Inkster. Suzanne Hurtubise, Deputy Minister of

Public Safety, was the final appointee. The committee's job was to narrow the field of eight or so candidates to two or three. From that pool, Prime Minister Harper would make his choice.

The presence of the powerful mandarin Bloodworth on the committee sent chills up the spines of Mountie brass, who were both suspicious and fearful of her. Many believed she wanted the job for herself. It wouldn't have been the first time that had happened. Which brings us to Kelleher and Inkster.

In 1987, Inkster, then head of RCMP Human Resources, sat on the search and selection committee for a new commissioner to replace Robert Simmonds. A politically adept technocrat, Inkster managed to have the committee overlook every other candidate but him. Beginning in 1987, Kelleher and Inkster were the two people responsible for setting the RCMP on the course it took to the disaster it had become.

Blais was more than a token Liberal. A former solicitor general and former president of the Privy Council, he currently sat on the Security Intelligence Review Committee, which oversaw CSIS. Hurtubise, a career bureaucrat, was seen to be one of Bloodworth's allies.

There are many capable people in Canada. Why those five?

Rumours abounded about who might be chosen for the job. The general consensus was that none of the senior Carpet Cops in Ottawa had a chance, since they had all been associated with or groomed personally by the so-called madman Zaccardelli, and all were tainted by the fact that they had done nothing to stop him. No one fell into this category more than Zaccardelli's hand-picked man, Deputy Commissioner Pierre-Yves Bourduas. Inside the walls of the RCMP, he was seen to be more dismissive and demagogical than Zaccardelli. For many, this was summed up best by his nickname, achieved by reversing the first two initials of his name, "YP," French slang for "so what?"

Another insider considered was Assistant Commissioner Raf Souccar, who would have been politically attractive as an opportunity to showcase diversity in the RCMP, but whose experience was considered to be limited. He was also too close to Zaccardelli and, like him, had autocratic tendencies.

Top Mounties from across the country were being touted, people like Assistant Commissioner Peter German, who was in British Columbia. Tall, bright, and charismatic, German was a published author, but his recent career running the elite Integrated Market Enforcement Team had been a disappointment. The IMET squad was batting zero in convictions. German also had another problem. In the past, he had been one of the original investigators in the Airbus scandal, in which Prime Minister Harper's close adviser, former Prime Minister Brian Mulroney, had become snagged.

Deputy Commissioner William M. Sweeney was based in Edmonton where he was running the RCMP contract operations in "K" Division on the prairies. One of the many boys from New Brunswick, Sweeney had a brief tenure in Ottawa in the early 1990s, but had spent most of his career in the West. While he was liked and respected within the force, he didn't speak French, which was seen to limit his career. If he had a strong card, it was the fact that he was known to be close to influential Conservative party members from Alberta, who were promoting him within their government.

The search committee looked at a number of outsiders, including at least one retired former RCMP officer in western Canada, who didn't want the job. High-profile Ontario Provincial Police Commissioner Juliano Fantino was considered briefly, but he had too many strikes against him. He was cut from the same managerial cloth as was Zaccardelli, had spent too much time with Zaccardelli on the Avanti P-180, and he didn't speak French.

Jacques Duchesneau, a former Montréal police chief who went on to become president of the Canadian Air Transport Security Authority, was also given a look, but quickly rejected. The RCMP wasn't much of a force in Québec, compounded by a quiet war inside the RCMP over French language issues, and a perception of Québec influence at headquarters. A Québecker at the top was bound to ignite a mutiny.

Under the circumstances, the government made the only decision with which it felt comfortable. In early July, information was leaked to the media that Margaret Bloodworth's right-hand man, William Elliott, would be named the 22nd commissioner of the RCMP. The 53-year-old Elliott, the first civilian to be appointed to the post, was officially sworn in on July 16, 2007.

A tintinnabulation of alarm should have gone off. The Arar "cover-up" had now come full circle. The gatekeepers of the real story now were perfectly ensconced within an impenetrable protective shield: Bloodworth was the national security adviser and Elliott the new head of the RCMP. Those inside the RCMP got the message. The lid was secure. Stephen Harper had installed someone he could manage, secure in the knowledge that careerist RCMP leaders would never rebel.

"William has incredible and extensive experience that suits him well for the position that he is about to take on," Public Safety Minister Stockwell

Day told reporters in the foyer of the House of Commons. "He has political experience right here in this building."

Elliott's appointment received mixed reviews. Some thought the choice inspired, others worried about the growing politicization of the force. Zaccardelli was one of the first to call Elliott. He told him: "If a civilian was going to be Commissioner, you were the best choice."

Oft-quoted retired RCMP Staff Sgt. Ron Lewis told the *Ottawa Citizen*'s Kathryn May: "If the government wants to fully control the RCMP, then putting a bureaucrat in there is one step closer to shortening the arm's length." Lewis made it clear that Elliott should not attempt to wear a Mountie uniform: "He can't wear a uniform. Would you choose a person to be a captain of a hockey team who doesn't know how to skate? That's what they've done to the RCMP."

Even Colleen Myrol, the mother of murdered Mountie Brock Myrol (one of four killed on March 3, 2005, in Mayerthorpe, Alberta), jumped into the fray. She told *The Globe and Mail*'s Jane Taber: "As parents of a Mountie, we know that Brock would be truly dismayed and shocked that it is okay to take a bullet for Canada, die for your country as a Mountie, but a Mountie isn't good enough to be Commissioner."

Prominent human rights lawyer Clayton Ruby, the partner of Maher Arar's lawyer Marlys Edwardh, praised the appointment. Speaking to Richard Brennan of the *Toronto Star*, he said: "Every government of every stripe has been terrified to do this . . . this is courageous for Harper."

Day attempted to calm the waters within the RCMP with a strange e-mail he sent to "all members of the World's Finest." "Bill Elliott," the message read, "is the first one to admit he has not been a cop. It's true that he doesn't know what it's like to step out of that patrol car at midnight into a dark alley. And he doesn't know the feeling of being undercover and having a hardened criminal stare him in the face and say: 'If you're a cop, I'll kill you.' Nor does he know the gut-wrenching feeling of hearing the chilling call coming over the police-band car radio: 'Officer down!'"

Day continued: "He knows what it is like to deal with the impact on the transportation system in the aftermath of the 9/11 terrorist attacks on the U.S. He knows what it is like as deputy commissioner of the Canadian Coast Guard to see life-and-death rescue operations unfolding, and wishing the men and women risking their lives for others had better equipment."

Elliott took over in a low-key fashion. Some Mounties liked the new boss. Others were dismayed about how little he knew about policing. As a sop to the RCMP, Elliott's appointment was followed by the announcement that Deputy Commissioner Sweeney would be moving from Alberta to Ottawa. But only for eight months, it turned out. The grand plan was that during his short stay in Ottawa, Sweeney would become the number two man at headquarters as special adviser to the commissioner. His role would be to lead the RCMP's work with the five-person Task Force on the Governance and Cultural Change in the RCMP, which had been recommended by David Brown in his pension scandal report, and had been empanelled the same week Elliott had been formally appointed. The task force was asked to report back by the end of the year, five months hence. Elliott made it clear that in his first six months on the job he would be little more than a caretaker. Any *substantive* changes would have to wait until the task force report was completed.

Within the RCMP and the wider policing community, the promise of a task force that would set a new course for the RCMP had been in the wind for so long that many had begun to speculate that the report had already been written, and that the government was now looking for names to attach to it. When the panel was announced, their suspicions seemed to be all but confirmed.

As task force leader, Public Safety Minister Day selected former OSC chairman David Brown. Norman Inkster, the ubiquitous and politically malleable former RCMP commissioner was, once again, called on to set direction for the force. Also named were a trio of rather obscure individuals: Linda Black, the head of Alberta's Law Enforcement Review Board; former Navy admiral Larry Murphy, the federal government's deputy minister of Fisheries; and Richard Drouin, a former Hydro-Québec chairman, who now headed the North American Power Grid Regulator.

The five-person task force had just five months to examine the RCMP from top to bottom and then arrive at cogent recommendations that the government promised would be implemented by January 2008. We already know how quickly and decisively the newly energized Brown could work. But if he was intent upon doing a proper job, there was so much more to look at, more than what we've already seen. Would the task force bother to venture into the depths of the RCMP or had the government already made up the collective mind of the task force before it had even been sent on its momentous journey? Did the government already know what it was going to do?

It sounded like a Herculean task. But in his first few meetings with both RCMP members and officers from other Canadian police forces, Brown seemed to suggest his mandate was less sweeping and not as Herculean as promised. His mandate, he contended, was not to recommend drastic change but more a tweak here and a tweak there. Apparently, there was not going to be a "top-to-bottom" examination of the RCMP.

A complete examination of the RCMP sounded like an onerous task but if anyone had been paying attention to what had been going on inside the RCMP over the past three decades, the multitude of problems would have been easy to describe and the solutions readily apparent. The truth was that all the political choreography and drama over the previous years about Maher Arar and the pension scandal could have been avoided if the Chrétien government had lived up to its responsibilities and taken steps to confront and address the obvious. But, as we know, there was no intention of doing that.

By early 2008, William Elliott had made no major personnel moves. All the Zaccardelli loyalists were still in place. Even Deputy Commissioner Barb George, who had been suspended during the pension scandal hearings after being accused of being a perjurer, had been recently reinstated. The RCMP said in a statement welcoming her back to the force that her "suspension was neither disciplinary nor punitive in nature, but rather was a purely administrative measure. Furthermore, the RCMP wishes to clarify that the internal investigation into D/Commr. George's conduct did not involve any allegation that she had misappropriated public funds for personal gain, nor that she was personally involved in the mismanagement of the RCMP pension or insurance plans. The internal investigation concerned questions with respect to communication between D/Commr. George and other members of the Force. These questions have now been resolved to the satisfaction of the RCMP."

However, the RCMP's exoneration of George was shortlived. In February 2008, the Commons Public Accounts Committee recommended that George be found in contempt of Parliament for misleading politicians with her claims that she was not involved in the removal of Staff Sgt. Mike Frizzell from the pension fund investigation. Contempt of Parliament was a rare procedure and had been used only twice since 1991. When Parliament reconvened in April, in a controversial finding editorialists across the country likened to a kangaroo court, George was found to be in contempt. Even so, she continued to deny that she had done anything wrong.

One action Elliott did take seemed perplexing. He rehired Professors Linda Duxbury and Chris Higgins to do a third study of the force. Was he hoping that his mere presence at the top would heal what ailed the Mounties? Or was he just trying to confirm the previous two studies so that the government could move ahead with a clear mandate to provoke real change? There would be consequences to all this dithering, however, which would prove to be even more painful for both the RCMP and the Canadian public.

[16]

SHADES OF TRUTH

To fully appreciate the monumental problems facing the RCMP, one must first understand how the force thinks. From its inception, the RCMP has encouraged and enforced a mindset that makes everything that happens to it—from its countless mistakes to its susceptibility to being politically controlled—possible, even inevitable.

"The RCMP is a cult," said former RCMP Inspector Bill Majcher, who left the RCMP in 2007. "I didn't used to think that way, but now that I'm out and have had time to clear my head a little, it's pretty clear to me. When I took my commission and became an inspector, I just joined a cult."

The notion that the RCMP is a cult has even been picked up by credible journalists, including *Toronto Star* columnist James Travers, who wrote in 2007: "For far too long, no one was willing to peer too closely at the postcard force. Insiders happily drank the cult Kool-Aid, parliamentarians were afraid to impose discipline or oversight on an institution held in higher esteem than politicians and Canadians were understandably reluctant to tear down one of their few remaining 'icons.'"

A police force acting like a cult is not a new idea. Police live in a world of "them against us" where it is easy to become isolated from the rest of society. They eat, drink and, all too often, sleep with each other. Cops marry cops. Cop families beget more cops. Anyone who has read a Joseph Wambaugh novel knows about the thin blue line and "choir practice" and the unhealthy bond police officers often have with each other. Because of that, police forces are havens for secret societies like the Masonic Order—the mafia of the mediocre, as it has been dubbed. One can't get ahead, even today, in the Calgary Police Force without being a Mason, police insiders say. The Masons are also prominent in the RCMP, a fact in and of itself that should be disturbing. In England, for example, Masonic influences led to criminal activity in the 1970s and the breaking up of Scotland Yard's famed Flying Squad.

There is a profound difference between other police forces and the RCMP, which begins at the moment a Mountie cadet is sworn in as a peace officer. When he teaches comparative policing models, former municipal police officer Mark Lalonde focuses on the subtle but important difference between the Mountie oath and the one sworn by other police officers in Canada. "As an occasional college criminology instructor, one exercise I do with my students is to have them compare the RCMP oath of office with the oath of office used by various municipal and provincial police," said Lalonde, who has taught for 12 years at the British Columbia Institute of Justice and who is currently involved in training police overseas as part of a United Nations initiative. "It's an interesting exercise."

The oath of office for a municipal police officer in British Columbia is similar to those taken by other municipal and provincial police in Canada: "I, ... [name], do [swear/solemnly affirm] that: I will be faithful and bear true allegiance to Her Majesty Queen Elizabeth the Second, Queen of Canada, Her Heirs and Successors; I will, to the best of my power, cause the peace to be kept and prevent all offences against the persons and properties of Her Majesty's subjects; I will faithfully, honestly and impartially perform my duties as .... [office]."

The RCMP oath is: "I, ..., solemnly swear that I will faithfully, diligently and impartially execute and perform the duties required of me as a member of the Royal Canadian Mounted Police, and will well and truly obey and perform all lawful orders and instructions which I receive as such, without fear, favour or affection of or towards any person or party. So help me God."

Lalonde says: "The municipal police officer pledges allegiance to the Queen, Canada, to keep the peace, prevent crime and serve communities. The RCMP oath of office is essentially an oath of allegiance to the RCMP."

The difference in language might seem minor, but the implications for those who swear the RCMP oath are not. Each individual in the force is described as being a member, as if the organization is a club. Individual RCMP members are committed under the RCMP Act to uphold the honour of the RCMP first. Its roll of honour is not its great police officers and their accomplishments, but all its dead saints—the Cypress Hills Massacre, the Lost Patrol, and now Mayerthorpe. It is a police force whose collective self-image is defined by fictional police officers, contrived gentlemanly rubes from another era, like the determined Sergeant William Preston of the North-West Mounted Police and his lead sled dog, Yukon King, the heroes of a late-1930s radio series, or by U.S. singer Nelson Eddy's series of musical Mountie movies, beginning with *Rose Marie* in 1936. Over the past half century, the Mounties have done nothing to capture the imagination of the entertainment world, other than the relatively successful Canadian-made television series, *Due South*, in the late 1990s. As played by Paul Gross, hero Benton Fraser was a throwback to the Sgt. Preston days, an implacable Mountie from the Northwest Territories doing a fish-out-of-water turn in urban Chicago for four seasons. Even satirized Mounties, like comedian Dave Broadfoot's hilarious and feckless Sgt. Renfrew and the dozy Dudley Do-Right of the *Rocky and Bullwinkle* cartoon show, carry similar pedigrees.

Today's RCMP indoctrination process is straight out of the late nineteenth century, as if the world had stopped then. The RCMP's archaic Code of Conduct and rituals feed into the social needs and hunger for conformation of its cadets. Their guiding light is the premise that the RCMP are agents of the law and are bound to act ethically at all times, a symbol of all that is right and good in Canada, in spite of considerable evidence to the contrary. Once inside the confines of the force, these new recruits find themselves being instantly respected as part of the glorious continuum of the RCMP's grand history and traditions. They are new links in the golden chain, a perception that is fostered by the force's endless self-promotion.

Much of the RCMP's marketing, however, is undertaken with strategic intent to achieve two primary goals: to reinforce loyalty while at the same time blurring the public's view of the RCMP's myriad shortcomings, failings, and embarrassments.

Its cultish tactics go well beyond what Professor Duxbury merely hinted at in her 2004 study of the force, the basis for investigator David Brown's "horribly broken culture" assessment of the RCMP. The force is rife with accounts of the extent that its leaders will go to save the perceived "good" guys and banish the "bad" ones.

Those perceived to be good and onside are usually protected through a transfer, promotion, or sudden retirement. Charges of sexual harassment, assault, deceit, and others, are routinely buried and made to disappear, including those against some of the highest-ranking members of the force. Some Mounties can do no wrong.

One of the most visible examples of such protection in recent years was the sordid case of former RCMP Staff Sgt. Cliff McCann. He had been linked in the early 1990s to a sexual abuse case involving prominent New Brunswick men at a provincial institution, the Kingsclear Youth Training Centre. The controversy rocked New Brunswick and became national news. Kingsclear was closed, but neither the RCMP nor the New Brunswick government seemed interested in pursuing McCann, in spite of what appeared to be his clear connections to the case.

In October 2007, after spending three years investigating the matter, the independent Commission for Public Complaints Against the RCMP made its report public. The commission concluded that the RCMP had made mistakes in its investigation that created a perception of a cover-up and that RCMP investigators had given McCann preferential treatment. There had been inadequate note-taking, a lack of resources, and a lack of due diligence by senior officers to ensure the investigation was a priority, the report found. But it couldn't find evidence of a cover-up. The RCMP was seen to get off the hook on a technicality, created by its own seemingly deliberate ineptitude. McCann has denied the allegations and was never prosecuted, but is being sued by four former Kingsclear residents.

Meanwhile, others have been railroaded out of the force with blistering campaigns, trumped-up charges, and willful deceit by the RCMP brass, often because someone higher up was suspicious of them or because they might have suggested that there was a better way of doing things.

One of the most flagrant cases was that of Staff Sgt. Ken Smith. In 2001, Smith was promoted to staff sergeant and made the head of the RCMP drug squad in Saint John, to the chagrin of one of his superiors. That superior, Superintendent Louis Lefebvre, was upset that one of his friends, who had been acting head of the drug squad, didn't get the promotion.

An Orwellian campaign against Smith was then mounted by his superiors. He was followed by RCMP surveillance teams for six weeks, who documented his every move and those of his family. His wife was a decorated Mountie as well. A tracking device was attached to his vehicle illegally, without a warrant. In 2002, he was suddenly removed from his job by Lefebvre, for no apparent reason. Smith was then escorted to the Saint John office and taken inside to collect his belongings. His firearm was taken from him. The locks on the door had been changed.

Smith soon found himself facing trumped-up charges of, among other things, using a police car inappropriately and taking annual leave without documenting it. He was accused of swearing at a waiter in a restaurant while working a drug investigation undercover at a Holiday Inn. Contrived criminal charges were laid against him. All were subsequently thrown out.

Smith conducted his own investigation and then found information which showed Lefebvre had planned the attack on him even before showing up for work on his first day as the drug squad leader. Other senior members of the RCMP were implicated as well.

When it finally exploded into public view, it was the kind of case one might expect a democratic government to go wild over. If the RCMP had been prepared to use illegal surveillance to wrongfully entrap one of its own, one had to wonder what it might do to the general public. The New Brunswick solicitor general was powerless to do anything because the RCMP reported to Ottawa. The problem for Smith in Ottawa was that the men running RCMP operations in New Brunswick had close ties with the man who used to run those very same operations in the 1990s, Commissioner Giuliano Zaccardelli. The commissioner was not about to do anything, and he didn't. If Smith thought the federal government might intervene, he did not know about the accord between Zaccardelli and Jean Chrétien.

Smith filed an internal complaint with the company union, the Div Reps, but that went nowhere. He tried to have an investigation started by a municipal police force, but no one wanted to take on the Mounties. Like most controversies involving the RCMP, the force just ragged the puck, hoping against hope that it would go away. But Smith persisted in his legal counterattack. It is continuing at the time of writing.

In Nova Scotia, Constable David Moore was assigned to the Halifax Region detachment of Tantallon. Moore had enjoyed a successful business career before becoming a Mountie later in life. He owned apartment buildings and an historic restaurant on Cleveland Beach on the waters of St. Margaret's Bay. The restaurant was in the jurisdiction of his RCMP detachment.

Moore began to have problems with local hooligans living near his restaurant but his own superiors were deaf to his complaints. One day, he called for help after some of the young men began to act up. No one responded. Fed up, he went into the restaurant, got his badge, and arrested the individuals. At that point, his colleagues came but didn't bother to talk to three long-haired witnesses who were enjoying the beach. Moore was the one who came under fire. The force laid a number of charges against him. When the time came to go to court, the three formerly-long-haired witnesses, now looking quite respectable, showed up to testify for Moore. They were interns at the Capital Health Centre in Halifax. The charges were dismissed, and

Moore sued the force, one of his many actions against his superiors, whose actions were never questioned by the force.

Moore's restaurant was finally torched in 2004 and burned to the ground. He kept fighting the RCMP, however, and was declared surplus to establishment. He was seconded to work for the Nova Scotia government enforcing gambling laws.

"I won't give in to them," Moore said. "It has cost me hundreds of thousands of dollars to fight them, but I believe in the RCMP. I just want to make it right."

When one talks to other knowledgeable, concerned members of the RCMP about what is really wrong with the RCMP, former Inspector Bill Majcher's name is at the top of the long list of extraordinarily intelligent and talented people who have been unfairly victimized and blackballed by the force.

Majcher is one of the most celebrated police officers in the history of the Mounties, renowned for both his daring and his success. A specialist in undercover work who joined the force in 1985, one of Majcher's first assignments was to spend time in jail posing as a prisoner next to Air India suspect Ripudaman Singh Malik. Later he worked in the RCMP's proceeds of crime section where he traced criminal financial dealings around the world. For example, Majcher worked on the war crimes trial of former Yugoslavian President Slobodan Milosevic, tracking the illegally gotten gains he had tried to hide around the world.

One case, more than any other, gnawed at him. Although he is prohibited from talking about the specifics of the case, at the time it was the longest undercover operation in RCMP history. Conducted on both sides of the U.S.–Canadian border, the investigation involved the price fixing of a group of commodities by a powerful, politically-connected family in western Canada. Majcher believed he had gathered enough evidence to show that Canadian consumers had been ripped off for hundreds of millions of dollars over the years, but the case was derailed before it went to court. He said considerable political influence was brought to bear on both the RCMP and the prosecutors.

In the early 1990s and again, later in that decade, the baby-faced Majcher was the key player in joint investigations, including the Bermuda Short sting, between the RCMP and the FBI. In each, Majcher posed as a Vancouver businessman—"West Coast Billy"—operating out of Miami who said he could provide money-laundering services for drug traffickers. Ensconced on a yacht in Miami, he was so successful that the ultra-dangerous Cali cartel from Columbia wanted to make him their North American business agent. In another case, he snagged two prominent Canadian lawyers in his web. In 2004 and 2005 respectively, Martin Chambers of Vancouver and Simon Rosenfeld of Toronto were convicted and imprisoned for money laundering.

Another important person West Coast Billy lured onto his boat in Miami was a high-ranking general in the Chinese army. The general had been taking advantage of Canada's immigrant investment program and ploughing money into the Potash Corporation of Saskatchewan. The general proposed a scheme whereby he would allow shipments of goods to enter China without duty in return for a hefty payoff. That is when politics intruded on two fronts.

At the time Canada was already in a dispute with China over Lai Changxing, China's most-wanted man. Lai had run a multi-billion-dollar smuggling racket in Fujian which involved dozens of government officials, police, and military. He had fled to Vancouver in 1999 where he sought refugee status, and soon became involved in organized crime in the Lower Mainland. However, since he faced the death penalty in China, Canada has refused to send him back there, a case that is still being argued in Canadian courts. Back in 2002, the Lai case was the largest thorn in Sino–Canadian relations, and Majcher was told that Prime Minister Chrétien did not want to complicate matters any more than they already were by throwing a captured Chinese general into the mix.

But the RCMP was desperate in 2002 to deflect the public's attention away from the Maher Arar saga. Through the Bermuda Short sting, Majcher had infiltrated the Hell's Angels in Niagara Falls. "The RCMP was desperate for a good news story so the brass decided to shut down the Bermuda Short operation even though it was gathering steam," said Majcher. "By doing that they were going to expose me and my 13 years as an undercover operative were over. That is the way the force operates. The image of the RCMP always comes first. They are always looking for ways to change the subject, sometimes no matter what the cost to operations or the public interest."

Four tonnes of cocaine had been seized in the Hell's Angels operation and Majcher was outed by the force as its daring secret agent, exposing him to the wrath of the bikers and, eventually, his own commanders.

He was a golden boy within the RCMP but he made it clear to all that his successes were due to the fact that he didn't listen to his superiors, many of whom he did not trust or respect. "I was in life and death situations. I often didn't have time to clear things with my superiors. I didn't have time to do the politically correct thing or take the uncontroversial road. I had to do what it took to get me through alive."

When he was promoted to inspector in 2003, and became white-shirted RCMP management, Majcher was one of those designated to set up and run the new Integrated Market Enforcement Teams, a plan by Zaccardelli to fix something that was terribly wrong with the force, its inability to catch white-collar criminals. While the IMET teams looked great in theory, Majcher found that the RCMP had neither the will, talent, nor the mindset to do the job. The more he pushed for action to be taken, the more resistance he received from his superiors.

It seemed to him that the upper echelons of the RCMP were a fiefdom, a collegial world of buddies, relatives, and sycophants, unwelcome to outsiders. "The way in which the RCMP is organized allows too many people to rise to the top who do not have the intelligence, talent or skill sets to do their job properly," Majcher said in an interview. "This problem is compounded by the fact that with its cult mentality, the RCMP resists any criticisms. It does not respect the public, bureaucrats or politicians. If one of the RCMP brass gets involved in a controversy, there is no will within the force to assess that person's culpability. The saying is: 'Respect the rank, not the story.'"

Anyone who was not part of this group was considered a threat. That included anyone trying to rein in the force, like former RCMP Public Complaints Commissioner Shirley Heafey. For eight years, after assuming the post in 1985, Heafey was subjected to stalling, lies, and obfuscation by the force. Its favourite weapon against her was character assassination—she was labelled a left-wing loon who didn't understand the everyday world of the RCMP. As complaints mounted against the RCMP, Heafey became frustrated by the unwillingness of members of the force to hand over documents. "We keep asking and asking, and we'll get a little bit here [and] a little bit there, but there's never an explanation given," she told CBC news in 2005. "There are complainants that don't get answers. I can't answer their complaints, because I can't get the information from them, from the RCMP."

One notorious case was that of University of British Columbia professor Dr. Sunera Thobani. Thobani was the centre of media attention after she spoke out against the United States shortly after the 9/11 attacks on New York and Washington. Thobani filed a complaint that the RCMP had deliberately leaked erroneous information to the media, suggesting that Thobani was under criminal investigation. Heafey said it took her three years to get documents naming the sergeant who had admitted leaking the information.

"When we finally got the information that was being withheld, it actually confirmed everything that [Thobani] complained of," she said. The RCMP officer was never disciplined.

Majcher said such behaviour had become typical within the force. "The RCMP senior management actually believes that it is above the scrutiny of judges, politicians, civil libertarians and professors. They see Stockwell Day as weak and easily manipulated. They will never tell the truth to a minister or his representative, but will give shades of the truth, always manipulating. I became disturbed by the lack of impartiality. For some people it is rather intoxicating that people fear you rather than respect you but in today's climate, people fearing the police is not a good value proposition. Many politicians have told me that they were afraid of the RCMP. In a democracy that's not right. When police take actions for political reasons or for the purpose of appeasing politicians and government, we're not that far away from an oligarchy. The current structure appears to be an oligarchy."

Just as galling to Majcher was the systemic aversion within the RCMP about doing anything that might be considered controversial. The public expects that a police service will put the interests of the public first, but in the RCMP, Majcher learned otherwise. "With the growing sophistication of crime and the reality of international terrorism, the RCMP needs imaginative, conceptual and relational thinkers at the top, but that's not who gets to the top. Those who get promoted are unimaginative, not deep, and rather superficial. They are politicians with badges, high school kids with guns. Much of the decision making, such as it is, is visceral and emotional. There is no pursuit of excellence and when someone tries to excel, the group think is: 'He might get ahead of me, I might have to put him down.' When a decision has to be made, the thought process goes like this: 'What's good for my career? What's good for the RCMP? What's good for the public?'"

A prime example, he said, of how prevalent and ridiculous this thinking has become occurred in early 2007, as late spring flooding from the Fraser River threatened the Lower Mainland of British Columbia. "A memo went out in E Division which sought suggestions from members about how the RCMP could boost its public image while dealing with the flood," said Majcher. "Their first concern wasn't the public, it was the bloody image of the RCMP and the possible opportunities for self-promotion. That memo was soon destroyed."

Majcher said the out-of-control careerism within the RCMP was distressing. Over the years, many of those who have risen to the top have had relatively shallow experience in criminal investigation. Majcher explained it this way: "There's a saying in the RCMP, 'Big files make big problems, small files make small problems, and no files make no problems.' The less you do, the better you do. If you run into problems in the RCMP and you are not part of the in group, no matter how right you might have been or how small the problem, it is deemed to be a blemish on your career. You're done. That's why a lot of the leaders in the force come from the training academy and United Nations postings and the Musical Ride—those are deemed to be the most important and safest career paths."

Majcher was frustrated with what he saw happening: "We've lost a sense of balance. There is no purity of purpose. The RCMP has lost sight of what its objective is. You don't work for the commissioner or the government, you work for the public."

So Majcher decided do something proactive about the situation. He offered himself as a Conservative candidate in Richmond, B.C. in the 2004 federal election. If he had won, he would have had to turn in his badge and take an unpaid leave from the force, which are the rules in such a situation. Another serving Mountie, Constable Pete Merrifield, had been allowed by the force to run as a Conservative in the 2004 election in the Toronto suburb of Richmond Hill, where he finished a distant second to the Liberal candidate.

The Mountie brass became apoplectic about Merrifield and Majcher. In a force considered by many of its members to be overly politicized, actual participation in politics is considered to be taboo, even though it is a member's right to run for office.

The most celebrated case until then was that of Staff Sgt. Gaétan Delisle, who joined the force in 1969. In 1995, Delisle, a federal officer based in Montréal, was elected mayor of his small community, St-Blaise-sur-Richelieu, an area in which he had no policing conflict. RCMP brass went ballistic. Delisle was put on administrative leave for 18 months without pay, an unprecedented occurrence. Delisle fought the force and eventually won his back pay, but had to resign as mayor. The RCMP's ongoing battles with Delisle which continue to this day turned him into a pariah at the highest levels of the force, and a folk hero among much of the rank and file.

Merrifield's was a particularly vexing case for the Mounties. He had joined the force at 30, spent five years dodging bullets in rural Saskatchewan, and had then gone into federal policing. He spent time in the air-carrier protection program as an undercover air marshal and was then moved into counter-terrorism. This led him into situations where he had to protect politicians, like then-Prime Minister Paul Martin. "My personal politics had nothing to do with my job," Merrifield said in an interview. "I got into politics because I wanted to promote ethics and integrity in government. I guarded Paul Martin at least six times. I would have taken a bullet for that man. That was my job."

His superiors did not see it that way. In 2005, Merrifield put his name up for nomination in another riding in the next federal election. He did not have a campaign, he said, he just wanted to give speeches. He followed the same procedures as he had the year before, but this time the RCMP started harassing him, investigating his expenditures and, in spite of his glowing performance reviews, sent him to become the second person in an about-to-be disbanded customs and excise unit tucked away in a far-off corner of the detachment in Newmarket, Ontario. He was declared "surplus to establishment." The 41-year-old Merrifield continues to work with the RCMP in the customs and excise section in Newmarket. He has an ongoing lawsuit against the force, and expects to be a constable for a long while.

On June 27, 2008, Ontario Supreme Count Judge Ellen J. Macdonald, in siding with Merrifield in a pre-trial motion, ruled that his case should not be subject to the internal RCMP grievance process, as the force had tried to argue. "Understandably," Judge Macdonald wrote, "he has no expectation that he will be treated fairly in the grievance process. From his perspective, all of the evidence is to the contrary. Based on what he has pleaded, I can understand his skepticism."

The RCMP used all its artillery to attack Majcher, a senior officer and a member of the inner sanctum of the force, much like a cult would in dealing with a wayward acolyte. A Liberal candidate in the same election warned Majcher in advance that the force was going to attempt to destroy his reputation and credibility in his next annual work review.

In that review, shortly afterward, Majcher's superiors cited him for possible wrongdoing and policy violations in undercover investigations that had taken place 10, 12, and 15 years earlier. One of Majcher's Hell's Angels sources told him that the word on the street was that false complaints had been filed by either the Angels or organized crime figures against Majcher, knowing full well that he was now vulnerable. It is a tactic often used by criminals to get a particularly effective cop off their backs. The criminals knew how the RCMP would handle such a situation and the force never missed a step.

Majcher recognized what was going on—he had become fair game—and even offered to take a polygraph test to prove that he wasn't lying, but the RCMP wasn't interested in hearing his side of the story. It was a classic witch hunt and the RCMP had a long history of sacrificing its best and brightest in order to maintain the status quo. Majcher was harassed, smeared, and suspended and his political dream and policing career both went up in smoke.

He finally retired in 2007, after being offered a generous settlement in return for a strict non-disclosure agreement. That procedure, buying and dealing its way out of trouble and covering its tracks was, he knew, the RCMP way when serious issues arose from time to time inside the force. The day he left, he offered to take a polygraph just to clear the air and prove he had done nothing wrong. "It was without prejudice. It couldn't be used against me or them. It was just for the sake of clarity," Majcher recalled, "but they would have none of that. They weren't interested in clarity. Unless I was prepared to kiss the ass of the demigod in Ottawa [the commissioner] or his sycophants, I was not going to get ahead. I wanted to make a difference, but they didn't want to give me the chance. I would upset the status quo, and that made me too dangerous."

Majcher's view of the RCMP is that it has become an extremely wasteful and inefficient institution. "It's like a business that's doing $1 million a year when it should be doing $5 million."

Who is to blame? The downhill slide had begun in the early 1990s when then-Commissioner Norman Inkster brought in Dr. Anna Gray as a human relations consultant. "Since I left the force, I got to know Norm, and he's a good guy," Majcher said of Inkster. "But, I'm afraid to say that he was the one who started it all."

Under Inkster, Gray advocated a change in the RCMP promotion system which discounted experience on the job and focused instead on a 40-page written examination, the purpose of which was to identify, not the best police officers, but rather the best managers. Preparing for the exam, with its emphasis on social skills over knowledge of police administration and operations, took up a good portion of time for ambitious Mounties. "It's a horrible process," said Majcher. "Anyone off the street had a better chance of passing that test than most experienced police officers." Soon, the upper management of the RCMP was filled with gentle, forward-looking officers. "Promotion became the be-all and end-all," Majcher said. Getting angry, either out of frustration or incompetence, or just because an individual cared about what they should be doing, quickly earned any number of officers a ticket out of the inner circle. "The RCMP didn't call what it did punishment, because it was always couched in phrases like 'broadening one's career with new challenges or opportunities' or 'surplus to establishment.'"

The new cadre of managers at the top was inculcated in the myths, mystique, and hoary traditions of the force, but had little operational experience, which in any police force is important. Since the Carpet Cops didn't have an instinctive feel for a situation, they were less capable of understanding both what is needed in the field and why certain actions had to be taken, which is exactly what began to happen to the RCMP. From the time Inkster took the reins of the RCMP to today, the force has lurched from one disaster to another, never seeming to learn from its mistakes. "The RCMP is like the *Titanic*, but the difference is that the *Titanic* only hit one iceberg. After the RCMP hits an iceberg, it turns around and rams another one, and then another one," Majcher said. "It's not an accident that the RCMP runs into so many problems. There is no operational ability, no operational perspective at the top. There's no leadership. The force is living on a reputation built a century ago, it has done nothing in recent times to warrant that reputation."

After it headed in this direction, the RCMP realized it needed more than fond memories of the Musical Ride to get the job done. It was desperate to find an operating code, a bible as it were, something in which every member could put his or her faith. Just like the rest of the world, the philosophy of business became the RCMP's new religion.

A not-so-subtle shift in thinking was introduced, and the force began to promote itself as a business, adopting the language and attitudes of business. This was politically appealing because it all sounded so professional. The force even licensed its image to Disney Corp. But business and guardian institutions have different mandates and objectives and should also have different thought processes. While it seems obvious that the bottom line cannot be the only measure of success in a guardian institution, that's what it became in the RCMP.

Comporting itself as if it were actually a business, RCMP members from every rank were soon inundated with exposure to business gurus and crash courses in business philosophy. "Before long," Majcher said, "Mounties everywhere were talking about paradigm shifts and this theory or that one. There was a lot of experimentation going on as the force tried out different management principles and models. The problem was that an expert might take five or six years of schooling to understand these concepts, but the Mounties were taking three-day courses and then coming back with a whole new lexicon. They were parrots who didn't understand the fundamentals of the situation, but it was the parrots who kept getting promoted."

Of all the business gurus brought in to tutor the Mounties, none had a more lasting impact than Harvard-trained Stephen R. Covey. In 1998, at the beginning of the Covey influence, RCMP Staff Sgt. Jack Briscoe was quoted in *The Last Guardians* as saying: "We felt we needed him, because we are in transition and needed help. We are moving from crime-control policing to a collaborative, responsive, and client-centred model of service, which we call community-based policing. What we hope to achieve is quality service delivery through the application of the principles of community-based policing. What makes Covey an attractive process is that his principles are common sense to you and me. You just put them into the process, build trust and concepts such as improved interpersonal relationships, managerial alignment and stewardship. Those exposed to the training unanimously say everyone should experience Covey."

That was the plan 10 years ago, and look what has happened since. "The RCMP have been suckers for every business philosophy which had already been discredited at least 10 years earlier in the real world," said Majcher. "But it won't admit it. It can't admit it because, if it did, it would expose the hollow core at the centre of the force. They say they value honesty and integrity, but it's all talk. They don't really believe it."

The RCMP introduced businesslike slogans to help motivate and guide its staff, like Balanced Scorecards and Core Values, and has continually touted its success, even though the auditor general was less than enthusiastic about what the RCMP was doing. In her 2005 report, this is what she had to say:

> The RCMP tracks its priorities and activities but does not measure performance. To implement its priorities, the RCMP uses a management tool referred as the balanced scorecard. This management tool allows the RCMP to track its progress in carrying out activities and processes. While these activities may be sound management practices, they are not consistently aligned with its clients' priorities. The balanced scorecard tracks activities necessary to produce the outputs that may contribute to outcomes, but it does not provide information on actual outcomes—for example, "Safe homes, safe communities."
> The RCMP annually establishes initiatives at the federal and divisional levels. Responsibility for each initiative is assigned to an individual, and a series of actions are defined. During the year, the RCMP

monitors its progress by noting which actions have been completed. However, this does not give an overall picture of performance.

The RCMP all but ignored the auditor general and continued to pat itself on its back for a job well done. What did she know?

When it came to core values, Majcher remembered them by rearranging their order into the following acronym: HICRAP—honesty, integrity, compassion, respect, accountability, and professionalism.

As the RCMP embraced the appearance and trappings of business, business jargon and bafflegab became the standard operating language of the force. Other agencies or individuals became their partners or their clients, concepts which are normally anathema to most police. "The emperor had no clothes," Majcher said, "but no one wanted to tell him that because if you did, the force would rise up to protect itself. The RCMP talks about core values and integrity, but when the rubber hits the road, it hides behind its iconic status and traditions. That's anything but integrity, but the leaders are blind to the obvious."

At every level of the force, businesslike thinking is promoted like a mantra to the point of being ridiculous, and it still isn't all that well understood. Horst Baender, a former Saskatchewan civil servant who now makes a living in Moose Jaw as a photographer, related the story of an ongoing argument he had with his brother, Rolf, a now-retired RCMP staff sergeant. Rolf had run a number of six-member Mountie detachments in Alberta locales like Brooks and Manning. Horst was talking to Rolf about the difficulties of running his new business, when the Mountie said: "I'm an entrepreneur, too. I run a detachment. I have employees and vehicles and a budget, and I have to manage my money wisely." Horst told his brother that running a six-man police detachment was not entrepreneurship, but public service, and never the twain shall meet. The brothers no longer talk to each other.

The RCMP has convinced governments and itself that it knows what it is talking about when it talks about its "business," its "partners," and its "clients." But not everyone does. An infamous story which made the rounds within the RCMP illustrated the confusion, even for Mounties. A young RCMP member was seen to be treating a suspect with the utmost courtesy, above and beyond what might have been expected.

"Why are you doing that?" the constable was asked by another Mountie.

"He's our client, and that's how we're supposed to do it," the young Mountie replied.

"He's not our client," the first Mountie said. "The client is the victim."

The point of all this is that the RCMP has been allowed to evolve into a monster that even a conflicted, hardnosed manager like Giuliano Zaccardelli had no chance of defeating because even he had been touched by that system. As much as he recognized the problems, Zaccardelli was doomed from the start. Even though he was a product of the culture, his personality was the antithesis of those entrenched below him. Blind loyalty only went so far. In effect, he was a nearsighted leader who found himself beaten to death by single-minded, vicious butterflies.

✙ ✙ ✙

"The RCMP is a cult," said Dorothy Ahlgren Franklin, a civil servant since 1975. Franklin spent four years, from 1996 to 2000, as the director of law enforcement in the solicitor general's office and the next four years, until 2004, working inside the RCMP as the civilian officer in charge of its National Youth Strategy.

Franklin, who has never met Bill Majcher, painted a similar picture of the state of the force. In her view, the RCMP is composed of otherwise good and decent people who have all but surrendered their values, personalities, and ideals to the needs of the RCMP. She says the RCMP is systemically oblivious to the public interest, deceptive, and self-serving, like isolated inhabitants of an island fortress.

Franklin believes the problems within the force go back as far as the first days of training at Depot, the RCMP training facility in Regina, Saskatchewan. New cadets are not allowed to walk or use the sidewalks, so they run everywhere on the interior roads at Depot. Walking on a sidewalk is one of the many privileges to be earned. The air is filled with the sound of marching feet, drill sergeants shouting, and troops singing. As modern as the RCMP likes to pretend it has become, it can't shake its paramilitary traditions. At Depot, cadets live in barracks and are graded for their bed-making abilities. Each spends endless hours marching around a drill hall, forming fighting formations that were obsolete when the force was founded in 1874. It's all about camaraderie, working and fighting together as a unit.

"New members are indoctrinated very successfully at the outset of their careers from their first few minutes in training," Franklin says. "They are introduced to the RCMP history and traditions and the RCMP way of doing things. There is nothing empirical about the training, it's all about emotion.

A cadet dedicates his or her entire life to the RCMP, and the RCMP always plays on that emotion. That alone is cult-like."

During the four years she worked inside the RCMP, Franklin found the attitude of many of the members disturbing. "I've never been in an organization where career progression is such an obsession. I've never seen an organization where the 'groupthink' is so strong. Even people who had made their mark elsewhere succumb to it. Once they are inside the RCMP, they seem to lose the ability to think critically."

In her view, the so-called Coveyites dominate the organization and not in a good way. She saw them to be the arch-defenders of the status quo, never wanting to make waves, even when a tsunami might be required. "The entire corporate body has been indoctrinated by Covey. Everyone is over-influenced by the notion of team-building. There is no objectivity. Everything to these people is either black or white, and they refuse to budge."

She described the organization as one so driven by consensus that, as the old saying goes, every time it sets out to construct the perfect racehorse, it ends up with a camel. As a policy expert, Franklin found that once the RCMP locks onto a course of action, no matter how unsuitable or unsound it might be, it will stay the course to the point of its own embarrassment or disaster, whichever comes first. "The only thing that really matters is the image of the force."

One example Franklin uses is a program called D.A.R.E. (Drug Abuse Resistance Education), which was a product developed by a U.S. company to address the U.S. government's War on Drugs and then-First Lady Hillary Clinton's campaign to save children from drugs. Under the terms of the license purchased by the RCMP, only a uniformed officer can talk about D.A.R.E. and only in a school setting. All officers who "teach" D.A.R.E. are trained and monitored by the U.S. company, not by the RCMP.

In its own press releases, the RCMP describes D.A.R.E. as "a comprehensive prevention education program designed to equip school children with skills to recognize and resist social pressures to experiment with tobacco, alcohol, other drugs and violence. This unique program utilizes uniformed law enforcement officers to teach a formal curriculum to students in a classroom setting. D.A.R.E. gives special attention to fifth and sixth grade students to prepare them for entry into intermediate & high school, where they are most likely to encounter pressure to use drugs. . . ."

The RCMP uses D.A.R.E. as an example of its proactive, community-minded policing across the country. Hundreds and hundreds of Mounties across Canada are trained in D.A.R.E. Parents and children alike love the idea of the program, and every year schoolchildren who complete the D.A.R.E. program receive recognition at awards ceremonies. The RCMP looks touchy-feely and politicians love it.

"There is not one piece of empirical evidence that D.A.R.E. works," said Franklin, who had nothing to do with the administration of the program, but who has studied its efficacy. "Yes, everyone loves it, but it's just feel-good entertainment. If you look at the drug and alcohol use statistics for the same students in subsequent years, it doesn't make one bit of difference whether a child has been exposed to D.A.R.E. or not. It's a wonderful bit of marketing for the RCMP, but a complete waste of time and energy. The resources could be put to better use elsewhere."

Inside the RCMP though, Franklin couldn't make herself heard. Nobody wanted to look at the evidence she had to support her argument because to do so would mean admitting an error after so many medals and honours had been handed out to the RCMP officers who had been pushing D.A.R.E. all these years.

The primary reason why the RCMP continues to invest in, promote, and protect the D.A.R.E. program is that in most communities across the country, D.A.R.E. is the only positive contact the RCMP has with youth.

"The RCMP is constantly moving people around from detachment to detachment," Franklin said. "The individual members are usually policing communities they know little about. They don't know the people and the people don't know them. They are distant."

Her observation was supported by Sandy MacDonald, a teacher of "at risk" students at Tantramar Regional High School in Sackville, N.B. MacDonald comes from a family familiar with the law. His father is a judge and his brother a prosecutor. "In my job I know what's going on in the community. I'm someone the kids can talk to," he said. "They tell me about the things they are into and the crimes they are committing."

MacDonald says his own students tell him that the RCMP doesn't have a clue about how to deal with youth crime. "The Mounties are invisible. When you do see them, they're doing nothing to prevent crime. They don't know the kids. They don't know the families in the community. They don't know the history. They are always moving in and out of the detachment. They're little more than strangers in a strange land. They seem to think that their uniform earns them respect. It doesn't. Kids laugh at them. They seem to think that they can have a single contact with a child, scare them with their authority and move on. It doesn't work. All the Mounties do is react and arrest someone after the fact, when so much more could be done."

But getting the RCMP to admit to any of its shortcomings is all but impossible. When cornered, the force will invoke shades of truth to defend itself. Following are two examples, one from my own personal experience.

⊹ ⊹ ⊹

On February 1, 2006, *Maclean's* magazine published a story by Charlie Gillis headlined: "The Mounties give up: The RCMP is walking away from serious investigations, and failing to snag fraudsters, drug traffickers and white collar criminals." The content of the story should be obvious.

Five days later, the RCMP launched a counterattack against Gillis and *Maclean's*. Commissioner Zaccardelli sent off a long letter blasting the reporter. The force put out a press release, which it distributed widely through its detachments, other police agencies, and government agencies, and published on its website. It was an interesting document at the time because in spite of the obvious evidence, the RCMP refused to acknowledge any of its problems. With its all-out attack on a perceived enemy, the manipulation of facts and images, it showed just how entrenched the bunker mentality of the force was. No matter how well supported the arguments made by Gillis were to show that the RCMP was not doing its job, the RCMP continued to insist that it was on the right track in both its form and function. It was not prepared to accept any criticism of its philosophy, structure, or performance.

"In his arguments, the author, Charlie Gillis, demonstrates an incomplete understanding of the resource allocation, managerial approach and organizational philosophy of the RCMP. Mr. Gillis acts on the assumption that the RCMP's contract and federal policing efforts are separate and mutually exclusive. As such, he fails to grasp how law enforcement in the 21st century is understood and practiced both in Canada and around the world," the RCMP said.

The RCMP went on to describe how well it dealt with issues, without any specifics. "While the *Maclean's* article pointed out that real financial and human resources challenges exist within the RCMP, it fails to mention the ways in which the RCMP is actively addressing them," it wrote. It defended its policing model as being one of the best in the world and referred to how it meets its commitments, protects Canada, and always perseveres. One could almost feel the force's bruised ego and anger at being challenged about its perceived accomplishments.

The statement concluded with this almost snide final paragraph: "On the one hand, the title of the *Maclean's* article, 'The Mounties Give Up,' devalues the dedication and professionalism of all RCMP members and employees. On the other hand, the title could be interpreted to mean that we have indeed given up—we have given up the isolationist mentality that discourages communication among law enforcement organizations and across jurisdictions; we have given up any reluctance to work with our municipal, provincial or federal government partners to determine appropriate resource and officer deployment; and we have given up on any resistance to the notion that the best way forward is through dialogue and the free flow of ideas, even when they are triggered by negative or biased input. Indeed, all Canadians and all of our partners can rest assured that, in its 132-year history, the RCMP has never turned away from the people it serves, has never given up on its responsibilities, and will never give up on its commitment to safe homes and safe communities."

Gillis was taken aback by the attack. His piece was impeccable: well-researched and documented. "I couldn't believe what they did," Gillis said in an interview. "It was a coordinated attack to get me but they didn't really have anything to say. It was all a bunch of vague platitudes. *Maclean's* had never seen anything like it before."

Later that year, in December 2006, days before Zaccardelli would formally leave his job as commissioner of the RCMP, I wrote a freelance article, which was published in both the *Ottawa Citizen* and the *Winnipeg Free Press*. In that piece, "A Prescription for Fixing the RCMP," I set out a number of propositions. Three of the main ideas were that the RCMP had grown into an enormous and ungovernable entity. The RCMP was unique, I said: "There is no police force like it in the world, and for good reason." I wrote that many other police forces found it difficult to work with the RCMP, which was seen to be incompetent and overly secretive. Third, I recommended that the only way to fix the RCMP would be for it to give up its contract policing duties outside Ontario and Québec and to become entirely focused on its primary responsibility, federal policing, like the FBI and its counterparts in other countries.

A few days later, RCMP Assistant Commissioner Bernie Corrigan, head of the force's public affairs and communications services, sent a letter to both papers defending the RCMP, which was subsequently published in each paper. As it did after the Gillis story in *Maclean's*, the RCMP sent a copy of the letter, framed as a press release, to other media outlets across the country, all police departments and government agencies, and published it on its website. "The following piece has been written by the RCMP in response to the article by Paul Palango entitled 'How to Fix the RCMP' published in the *Ottawa Citizen* on December 13, 2006 and entitled 'Fixing the RCMP—The Mounties are long overdue for a major overhaul' in the *Winnipeg Free Press* on December 14, 2006. Both newspapers have published our response (on December 19, 2006, in the *Ottawa Citizen* and on December 21, 2006, in the *Winnipeg Free Press*)."

Following is an excerpt of the key comments Corrigan made on behalf of the RCMP:

> In his article "How to Fix the RCMP" (*Ottawa Citizen*—Dec. 13, 2006), Paul Palango expresses his personal views and opinions. We respect his right to do so. However, we also trust Mr. Palango and the *Ottawa Citizen* understand that the RCMP has the right to restore some needed balance and factual accuracy to his article.
>
> Mr. Palango suggests that other Canadian police forces find it difficult to work with the RCMP. But our 2006 survey of policing partners proves otherwise. It found that 82 per cent agree with the statement "Our organization highly values the RCMP's contribution to our partnership/collaboration." This is up from 77 per cent in 2003....
>
> Mr. Palango also falsely claims that the RCMP is an international anomaly because—in his own words—no democratic or totalitarian country would envision having one "monolithic beast" control its law enforcement structure. In fact, a number of countries including Sweden and New Zealand have one police service across their respective countries.
>
> He suggests we have contract policing because the 1929 depression forced the hand of provincial governments. But the fact is the first provincial contracts were signed in 1905.
>
> Contract policing supports the RCMP's federal mandate since uniformed officers can support federal investigators while performing general policing or traffic duties. As a result, some of our most significant drug seizures have been made during what Mr. Palango calls "handing out speeding tickets." In fact, RCMP members working on the frontline have had key roles in the arrests of wanted criminals and illegal aliens, along with the discovery of missing and abducted persons.

Mr. Palango goes on to recommend that the Government of Canada hand back provincial policing responsibilities to the provinces. But the model of policing we have in Canada has been built by the Government of Canada and the provinces and territories, working together, and the RCMP. It simply reflects the way in which our society has chosen to conduct policing activities. If this changes, the RCMP would adjust to the new environment.

And contract policing is a good deal for Canadians. A 2004 Deloitte economic study found at that time that the Government of Canada was receiving about $460 million dollars in benefit in return for its investment in contract policing. Twenty-two separate benefits were quantified.

In short, we strongly believe that the contributions of the 60,000 members of the law enforcement community working in a collaborative and integrated fashion helps make Canada one of the safest places in the world to live. They are owed, at the very least, an accurate accounting of the facts.

The RCMP had used all its power, authority, and credibility to mount a one-sided argument against me that looked pretty damning, at least on the surface. When the RCMP article ran, the *Winnipeg Free Press* allowed me to rebut some of what was said, but the *Ottawa Citizen* did not. The *Citizen*'s attitude was: "You had your turn, now they get theirs," as if this would be a fair fight in the minds of the public.

In the RCMP article, Corrigan had relied on a single answer to one question in an RCMP-commissioned survey to state that 82 percent of the RCMP's policing partners were satisfied with the RCMP. That number alone should have been a headline in any newspaper.

There are only 223 separate police services in Canada. By its own admission, the RCMP was saying that at least 40 police services had experienced difficulties with the RCMP. In Canada, the vast majority of small police services operating outside of Ontario and Québec are wholly dependent upon the provincial and federal services of the RCMP. The tiny Bridgewater, N.S. police force would not dare complain about the RCMP, nor would the Central Saanich Police on Vancouver Island, nor the Medicine Hat Police Service in Alberta. Which 40 police services had problems with the RCMP? Research indicates that it was the biggest ones, those that count most: Calgary, Vancouver, Toronto, the Ontario Provincial Police, the Montréal

Urban Community Police, and the Sûreté du Québec. As a number of senior police administrators told me confidentially afterward, the RCMP's so-called defence was anything but. Former Mountie Bill Majcher summed it up with these words: "In my travels I deal regularly with police services everywhere. I don't know of a police force that doesn't have serious issues with the RCMP."

Corrigan also argued that the Mounties were not unique in the world, and that Sweden and New Zealand had single police forces.

The fact is that Sweden, with a population of nine million people, does have a 25,000 member National Police force. What Corrigan and the RCMP conveniently left out was that Sweden also has a separate National Economic Crimes Bureau, effectively a federal police force whose jurisdiction is the investigation of financial crimes, fraud, and protection of the public treasury, something Canada doesn't have. Canada has depended on the RCMP to do that work, and has suffered from its lack of commitment and utter incompetence. Sweden also has distinct layers of accountability for all its police services, and the National Police do not investigate themselves, as is the case in Canada. Meanwhile, New Zealand is two islands with a population the size of Metro Toronto in the middle of nowhere. Of course it has only one police force.

Another point Corrigan made was that contract policing hadn't begun out of desperation in the Great Depression, but actually in 1905.

In fact, the RCMP did provide contract policing to the provinces of Alberta and Saskatchewan when they joined Canada in 1905. However, in 1917 Commissioner Aylesworth Perry had unilaterally withdrawn RCMP contract services over a dispute about Prohibition being enacted in the two provinces. Alberta and Saskatchewan then set up their own provincial police services, which were then taken over, like all the others, during the Depression. Shades of truth, indeed.

A few weeks after Corrigan's letter was published, the RCMP issued another press release. It was the announcement of a search for a suitable candidate for to replace Zaccardelli as commissioner. In the first paragraph, the release stated: "The RCMP is a unique police force in the world...." What happened to Sweden and New Zealand?

[17]

THE SECRET ARMIES OF THE RCMP

I f one were to accept at face value what the RCMP has to say about it, the concept of contract policing in Canada provides the most efficient and effective policing service in Canada.

If one were to accept the arguments of the critics of contract policing, they would say that it was conceived as an anti-union police force, scabs as it were, who have distorted the delivery, quality, and effectiveness of policing anywhere they might be hired.

RCMP supporters say that contract policing is the most efficient in the world—one police service doing everything—providing the best possible value for taxpayers and communities.

Detractors say the RCMP is an ungovernable monolith whose broad reach through contract policing is a threat to good governance and the rule of law. In other words, it does not serve the public interest very well.

Across the country, people have complained that it is not a friendly police force. Wendy Berry, a diminutive dental hygienist, moved with her family from Ontario to Chester, Nova Scotia, in 2002. A law-abiding citizen with two grown children, she was struck by the difference in attitude between the RCMP and typical Ontario municipal police services or even the Ontario Provincial Police.

"The Mounties are like dictators," Berry said. "In my contacts with them, I have found them to be arrogant and cold and defensive. They talk down their nose at you and treat everyone as if they are school children. I was really shocked because until I had come face to face with them, I had had a positive impression about the Mounties. I don't anymore."

Outside the provinces of Ontario and Québec, which operate and fully pay for their own provincial and municipal police services, the other provinces, three territories, and First Nations reserves get a deal on policing from the federal government. Until 1981, municipalities with fewer than 15,000 residents received a 44 percent federal government subsidy for hiring the RCMP, while municipalities larger than 15,000 residents received a 30 percent subsidy from Ottawa. After 1981, the federal government reduced that larger subsidy to 30 percent and the smaller to 10 percent. The rationale for the subsidy seems to be solely based on tradition. When the contract-policing system was inaugurated during the Great Depression, it was expected that a Mountie would spend a percentage of his time (there were no women until 1974) doing federal work, such as border patrols and enforcing federal government law.

Back then, the provinces were large open spaces with a thinly scattered population. Since then, the world has changed. The population has become more urbanized, but the policing concept has not. In labour-union terms, other police see the Mounties as scabs, stealing their jobs and tolerating unsafe working conditions.

One of the many myths of the RCMP is that it is an affordable police force. Its own internal estimates, however, which have been confirmed by outside agencies, agree that a uniformed RCMP patrol officer costs approximately $156,000 per year to put on the street. By comparison, a typical municipal officer costs about $105,000 or even less in smaller, out of the way locales.

Communities that hire the RCMP under contract believe that they are getting a better deal than they might otherwise receive by having their own police services.

The RCMP has been very good at selling its services. The appeal of the federal subsidy, even if it is only 10 percent, seems too good to turn down for many communities. However, after the RCMP wins a contract with a sizzling offer, communities get less steak than they bargained for. Because its per-officer cost is so high, the force meets budget obligations by downsizing the number of officers it deploys to the client. A community, expecting a full complement of officers, suddenly finds a reduced police presence. While the RCMP might appear to be an economical alternative to a municipal or provincial service, it runs like a business and bills its customers for anything it does outside of what might be stipulated in a contract, such as the use of tactical squads.

In its 2006 report on policing, Statistics Canada confirmed both the high cost of RCMP policing and the problem of hidden RCMP charges. In a foot-note, Statscan published a disclaimer about its own analysis stating that it could not determine the true cost of RCMP policing in any contract com-munity because of unknown "additional policing costs" for special services, which the RCMP would not disclose. In British Columbia, for example, there exists a program in which the RCMP charges a community "insurance" against murder. The fees are determined by a community's past criminal his-tory. In 2006, White Rock paid $79,000 to the RCMP for such protection. After a murder occurred in its jurisdiction and was investigated by the RCMP's integrated homicide unit, it was not billed any more. Communities that don't pay the insurance are liable to receive a huge bill from the force for investigating complex crimes.

In the boonies and around some large urban centres in Canada, the RCMP is the only police—the Everypolice. The force operates at the federal, provincial, and municipal levels. Often, a single uniformed officer can be responsible for all three functions. As well, a Mountie in a small town or city might be expected in the course of his or her duties to do public relations in schools, patrol local and provincial highways, provide security, investiga-tive petty and major crime, as well as organized crime, defend the country's border, and gather criminal intelligence, among other things. In this perfect world, the RCMP is both check and balance—the judge, jury, and execu-tioner too. The reason for this is a long-misunderstood anomaly about the nature of RCMP contracting.

Though provinces and municipalities pay for its services, RCMP mem-bers are not subject to provincial police acts or other provincial legislation, unlike municipal police officers in the same area. A premier or mayor may think he or she is the boss, but the RCMP everywhere reports to the com-missioner and its every action and deed is controlled by Ottawa.

If something goes wrong, the Mounties investigate the Mounties. Few politicians have seen anything wrong with this. The overriding principles are that the Mounties have the institutional integrity to do the right thing when called upon. Most importantly to politicians, there has been an irresistible allure to the RCMP. It had all the appearance of being a modern up-to-date organization regularly spouting new ideas and innovative programs on com-mand, with the promise that it could do the work required better and cheaper than anyone else. If only that were so.

With its 26,000 or so employees, the RCMP looks like a huge policing operation, but only 16,000 or so are sworn police officers. By comparison, at any time New York City has between 38,000 and 40,000 police officers on the street. Chicago has almost 14,000. The RCMP's own statistics from late 2007 shows that 47 percent—almost half—of its 16,000 sworn officers are rented out to the ten contract policing divisions across Canada. The RCMP, however, was playing with the numbers and minimizing the amount of manpower devoted to that "business line."

According to Statistics Canada's authoritative report, *Police Resources in Canada*, published November 15, 2006, there were 6,111 Mounties deployed in provincial contract work across the country and 4,268 officers employed in municipal policing. That's 10,379 of 16,000, which is approaching 65, not 47 percent. By any measure, contract policing is the huge tail that wags the scrawny dog that is the RCMP. But how big is that tail? Depends on who you believe: the Mounties or Statistics Canada. The question is: Why would the RCMP understate its own staffing levels?

Politics was the reason for this ongoing shell game by the RCMP, concerned that its activities and very presence in contract policing have become a matter of public debate and discourse. During the multiple Ottawa-centred debacles over the previous years—the Québec sponsorship scandal, the Arar debacle, and the RCMP pension kerfuffle—the spotlight had been shone on the RCMP's deployment of its staff and its accountability.

Questions began to be raised by the auditor general and in the media about the efficacy of contract policing at the expense of federal policing, which should be the force's first priority. Even inside the RCMP, particularly in British Columbia, Mounties were openly talking about the failure of contract policing and the deterioration of service. In November 2007, the Commission for Complaints Against the RCMP reported that in Nunavut, in Canada's far north, complaints had risen tenfold over the previous four years. Most were about the use of excessive force. The complaints from the North echoed what others across the country were saying about the RCMP.

To any objective observer, the broad-based political support the Mounties have enjoyed doesn't seem to be justified by a review of its overall performance.

In November 2006, when Giuliano Zaccardelli was on his last legs and about to walk the plank, Nova Scotia cabinet minister Bill Dooks approached me at a social function in Halifax.

"Hey, we've all got to get behind Zac, he needs our help, right now."

"Why do you we have to help him?"

"Because he's the commissioner and we need to protect him," Dooks said. "We love our Mounties, don't you?"

Across the country, one hears the same kind of blind devotion being expressed by people at all levels of government, but no place is more devoted to the cult of the Mounties than British Columbia. With a constant, almost predictable beat of questionable conduct, the RCMP had likely generated more bad press and infamy for British Columbia over the previous two decades than in the rest of the country combined. Unsolved murders, soaring crime, rampant financial crime, dubious political investigations; the list could go on and on, but the governors of the province seem hypnotized by the red serge. When it comes to the Horsemen, the same words flow out of the mouths of so many B.C. politicians like an eerie, zombie-like mantra.

"We love our Mounties," Premier Gordon Campbell told the *Maclean's* magazine editorial board during an off-the-record meeting in October 2007, after being asked if his government had any concerns about the RCMP.

"We love our Mounties," Solicitor General John Les was quoted as saying so many times in the Legislature and in public one might have thought it was part of his bedside prayers.

"We just love our Mounties," Coquitlam Mayor Maxine Wilson told a radio call-in show earlier in the year, where she was the guest of another guest, Assistant Commissioner Alistair D. Macintyre. Wilson was one of the local politicians the Mounties regularly called upon to defend them in public.

If one were to look at the past and present performance of the RCMP in British Columbia, political support for the force seems inexplicable. What is there to love?

While the politicians implicitly supported the Mounties, there was a growing anti-RCMP movement in British Columbia. It began in 1991 with the publication of a nostalgic yet critical book by Kamloops historian and author Lynne Stonier-Newman, *Policing a Pioneer Province, The B.C. Provincial Police, 1858–1950*.

"At one minute after midnight on August 15, 1950, the British Columbia Police ceased to exist. Ninety-two years had passed since James Douglas, Matthew Begbie and Chartres Brew had participated in its origin. There was no formal goodbye, no fanfare, no ceremony," Stonier-Newman wrote. It was her opinion that "it is entirely possible that the BCPP got torpedoed for political reasons," which it did. The B.C. government of the day had been made an offer they couldn't refuse, but no one could imagine that the RCMP would ever grow, like a cancer, from 500 officers to 6,000 and control the province like an occupying army.

Wallace T. (Wally) Oppal, then a justice of the Supreme Court of British Columbia, made public a report in 1994 which he had written after two years of exhaustive research. In an overview of the report, "Closing the Gap—Policing in British Columbia," Oppal observed that the RCMP had taken the position that the province had no jurisdiction to deal with complaints about its members.

"In discussing the future policing needs of this province, it is imperative to ask ourselves whether it is appropriate to have a provincial and municipal police force which has its headquarters in Ottawa," Oppal wrote. In referring to the fact that the RCMP Act places RCMP officers under the direction of the federal solicitor general, Oppal said: "Clearly, the Attorney General, the chief law officer of the province, now has less control over the RCMP than that which was agreed upon in 1950."

Oppal called for change, stating that the closed ranks and mindset of a quasi-military police force were anathema in modern British Columbia. "The RCMP must make fundamental changes and be more responsive to the needs of British Columbia communities," Oppal wrote. "The force simply must become more accountable to local needs and allow more participation by local government. British Columbians are entitled to an open and uniform system of policing. I am confident that the force is capable of accommodating the needs of this province. However, in the event that the RCMP is not prepared to undergo the necessary change that is suggested in this report, it will be imperative for the province to consider establishing its own provincial force."

Perhaps Oppal's informed opinion about the RCMP is one of the reasons why—following Oppal's retirement from the bench and switch to politics—Premier Gordon Campbell appointed him attorney general in his cabinet and not solicitor general in charge of policing.

RCMP Public Complaints Commissioner Shirley Heafey studied the force from the inside for eight years and concluded bluntly: "The RCMP should not be involved in contract policing."

Another log on the growing fire was Auditor General Sheila Fraser's 2005 report. Fraser concluded that the RCMP had too great a focus on contract policing, which contributed to relative underfunding of federal policing. "Since 2000, the RCMP has for the most part met its contractual obligations to provide the required number of peace officers to its clients, but has done so to the detriment of staffing its federal policing activities."

Fraser said "for the most part" but the gaps in RCMP contract service were significant to anyone who had to deal with the force. Her argument was picked up a few months later and carried down the field by one of Stephen Harper's closest allies, Dr. Barry Cooper, a professor of political science at the University of Calgary. The author of 20 books on public policy, Cooper wrote a scathing report that was published by the conservative think tank The Fraser Institute: "Bureaucrats in Uniform: The Politicization and Decline of the Royal Canadian Mounted Police."

Cooper argued that the RCMP was at a tipping point and that instead of making tough choices in difficult times, it was taking the easy road and easy money provided by the provinces.

"Contracting provinces have increased their demands for RCMP services every year since 1999 and they have provided budgetary resources to cover those increased requirements but the federal share of the increased costs was not covered by the federal government. The RCMP managed the shortfall by cutting back on federal policing. They could do so because the RCMP budget appropriation is a 'single pot of funds,' not divided between federal and contract policing."

In commenting on his report later, Cooper elaborated on his findings: "To fix what once was a decent and useful police force, a royal commission would be a good place to start. So would provincial police forces in Alberta and B.C. But most of all it would take some political will in Parliament and in the government to face up to the reality that the Mounties ain't what they used to be."

Two other heavyweights, former judge Wallace (Wally) Craig and former Vancouver police chief Bob Stewart, also expressed their views on the subject.

"The senseless dismantling of our provincial constabulary was an abject surrender of the provincial government's constitutional obligation under Section 92 of the British North America Act to be directly involved with policing in every nook and cranny of the province," Craig wrote in the *North Shore News* in 2005. "Since 1950, our attorneys general (or solicitors general) have had to endure the embarrassing fact that their actual authority over policing under the magisterial Police Act is confined to municipal police departments in Abbotsford, Central Saanich, Delta, Nelson, New Westminster, Port Moody, Saanich, Vancouver, Victoria and West Vancouver. Beyond reach of our law ministers is 'E' Division, a burgeoning paramilitary force . . ."

All this seemed to fall on deaf ears in the provincial and municipal governments. In late 2007, the Union of British Columbia Municipalities issued a memorandum regarding the upcoming renegotiation of the RCMP contracts in the province, which expire in 2012.

Craig fired back in another *North Shore News* piece: "It's time to bring back provincial police."

He wrote, in part:

When our provincial politicians rejected civilian provincial police under direct control, and embraced what would soon become and remain to this day a federal paramilitary police force, they knew full well that the force was completely unaccountable under our Police Act. Today's provincial politicians are tarred, too, with the same brush.

If our provincial government continues this aberrant and tunnel vision approach to the administration of justice and hangs onto "E" division for 20 more years beyond 2012—when RCMP contracts are up for renewal—then the misadventure of 1950 will be revisited and worsened.

Beware of things happening in the shadows of government, out of sight and untouched by the light of public scrutiny and debate. Take-charge bureaucrats, once civil servants, are already stirring the pot of renewal under the auspicious cover of the Union of British Columbia Municipalities.

Either the UBCM is filling a vacuum of inactivity on the part of the Solicitor General or acting on his instructions as it fusses along in a self-fulfilling process intended to bring about renewal of contracts with the RCMP.

I say this because a memorandum dated Oct. 9, boldly titled RCMP Contract Mandate, produced by a grandiosely styled UBCM Secretariat is a blueprint for the status quo. It includes the suggestion that the federal government and our provincial government "are in the early stages of the contract renewal process" and certain guiding principles have been adopted; the most telling of which is that "Continuation of the RCMP is beneficial to all."

I have questions for the secretariat.

1. Who is the exponent of the notion that "Continuation of the RCMP is beneficial to all"?

2. How can renewal of the contract be ". . . beneficial to all" when "E" division is already sapping away too many new recruits,

thus having a deleterious effect on the national strength and federal duties of the RCMP; a force so troubled in the senior ranks that it is being administered by a civilian commissioner?

3. Have you considered that it may be best for the RCMP to be told by its masters in Ottawa to prepare for the end of contracting out approximately one quarter of RCMP national strength?

We British Columbians must be loud, clear and relentless in demanding our constitutional right under the division of powers in the British North America Act, specifically the provincial right to administer justice: to begin again with our own civilian British Columbia Constabulary.

Craig called upon Premier Gordon Campbell to put Attorney General Oppal in charge of the police file. "Let him do the job of charting a course to civilian policing. To deny him the opportunity to take charge of policing matters in this time of urgency will be a sign of disrespect that may force the attorney general to consider whether he has any place in your government."

Bob Stewart had served as the chief of police for Vancouver from 1981 to 1991, longer than anyone else in the now-121-year-old force. After his police career ended, Stewart founded the Justice Institute of British Columbia, a training centre for those interested in careers in police and security. From his perspective, the time was well past due for the RCMP to leave British Columbia.

In early 2007, Stewart published a discussion paper, "The Buck Stops Nowhere," which was widely distributed. In that piece, Stewart's observations provide a useful context for what is happening across the country in RCMP contract jurisdictions. He wrote, in part:

In British Columbia at the outset of 2007, there are 126 RCMP detachments, 11 municipal police forces and other specialty services such as transit and railway police.

Over 70 percent of all B.C. police employment (officers and civilians) is within the mandate of the RCMP and, despite contracts with government to serve the province and municipalities, the force answers only to Ottawa.

For some inexplicable reason, suburban mayors think of their RCMP detachment commander as their "police chief," a local guy. They seem to think someone who reports to Ottawa is less of a threat than a district commander who would report to metro police headquarters which would most likely be centrally located somewhere within the region most convenient to the largest number of people.

They can move extra personnel from one area to another to ensure the maintenance of service levels. None of our municipal forces can do that. The RCMP has this ability among its large urban detachments, although it is common knowledge that municipalities contract for a set number of RCMP officers, but that this number is just about never realized. There is a lag time in filling vacancies and the number of officers taking in-service training at any given time (often education unrelated to municipal assignments), those who are ill and on vacation, significantly reduces the local force.

Unlike local police, the RCMP heritage is one of wilderness and colonial administration, evolved along military lines with strict chains of command. The culture is not local. The mandate is not local. The management is not local. RCMP regional and municipal officers argue that contracts make them locally accountable, but that is ingenuous at best. They "consult" locally. They "report" nationally. Their careers depend upon pleasing national headquarters.

Those who doubt any of the foregoing ought to read the RCMP Act. It can be noted in current debates that lines of authority between the Prime Minister and Solicitor-General over the RCMP remain unclear. There is no doubt at all about the status of a local Mayor and Council or even provincial governments. Zero authority. They have a civil contract only, not unlike the deal you might have with a home repair service.

The RCMP has its own Commission for Public Complaints, federally appointed. While the B.C. Legislature believes it is of paramount importance to have an independent Complaints Commission for municipal police, it apparently sees nothing odd about having complaints against 70 percent of the policing in the province handled by an agency appointed by Ottawa, not even resident in British Columbia.

"The RCMP is not suited to being a municipal police force. It doesn't have the proper instincts," Stewart said in an interview. "It doesn't do a very good job at all and, in fact, compounds the problems facing other police forces."

Stewart's observations were echoed by serving RCMP members like B.C.-based Constable Rob Creasser, a vocal critic and perennial black sheep of the force. On a province-wide radio talk show broadcast in December 2007, he called in to say this: "In my experience in the RCMP, the force should not be doing provincial or municipal policing. There should be a single metropolitan police force in Vancouver and a separate B.C. provincial police service."

This chorus of calls for the restoration of the provincial police forces in British Columbia was being echoed elsewhere, particularly in Alberta. Either or both provinces seemed like logical starting points for deconstructing and reconstructing the RCMP. Logical as it all might be, such ideas landed like a burning paper bag filled with dog feces inside RCMP headquarters. The RCMP brass recognized that the "starting point," the elimination of contract policing in British Columbia, would mark the end of the modern RCMP. If a single province stopped contracting with the RCMP, the "business case" for contract policing would evaporate. The entire contract regime would collapse, and the massive bureaucracy of Carpet Cops would no longer be needed.

To observers like Judge Craig and former Vancouver Police Chief Stewart, among others, the political support for the RCMP, in spite of its many shortcomings, high costs, and calamities, seemed inexplicable. Across the country, there were numerous complaints about the force being deceptive, self-serving, and incompetent, but no matter what the RCMP did there was no political will to take on the force in a substantive fashion. It was effectively unaccountable, yet the contracting provinces seemed reluctant or unwilling to do anything about it. How did the RCMP get away with it? Then I found the RCMP's magic wand.

✝   ✝   ✝

In the spring of 2007, another RCMP controversy was brewing in Moncton, N.B. over the cost of policing in Codiac Region, which was formed in the mid-1990s by the amalgamation of the communities of Moncton, Riverview, and Dieppe. At the time of the proposed union, Moncton city council, by far the largest of the three, voted unanimously against having the RCMP take over municipal policing. The provincial government ignored the votes and imposed the RCMP services, partly because French-speaking Dieppe wanted a guarantee that it would receive bilingual services. Now, ten years later, the entire region had found itself in a quandary.

The Moncton region (population 112,000) is the largest municipality policed by the RCMP east of Vancouver and its suburbs. Unlike the ten percent subsidy municipalities receive in the Lower Mainland of British Columbia, Moncton foots the entire RCMP bill and receives no federal assistance. Once again, you would think there would be an outcry about the double standard. Moncton politicians soon learned that even paying full freight for the Mounties doesn't guarantee full service. RCMP staffing was well below the previous municipal levels and costs were continuing to skyrocket. When Moncton moved to limit the pay of RCMP officers, it found that it had no control over it. Remuneration was an area controlled by the federal pay commission in Ottawa. All Mounties, no matter where they lived or the cost of living in that area, were to be paid on the same scale. Meanwhile, the rural villages of Hillsborough and Chipman, N.B. were so upset about the lack of RCMP service that they had each decided to hire private security guards, and deduct the cost from the RCMP bill they were paying.

In February 2007, I was called by CBC Radio, in a province-wide drive-home show broadcast, to comment on the situation. In that interview, I pointed out that the same argument had recently taken place in Lunenburg, Nova Scotia, where the town council found the RCMP wanting. I even related two personal stories from Chester, N.S., which is policed by the same RCMP detachment as Lunenburg. In the first, I described running into a woman on the street one day. The woman had learned about my interest in the RCMP and approached me. She told me about a meeting that had recently taken place at the town hall where the new RCMP sergeant in charge of the Chester sub-detachment laid out the force's community-policing "vision." The woman said: "He told us that the RCMP couldn't do everything, and that we had to be our own police. That's what community policing is. I'm a 70-year-old woman, what kind of policing can I possibly do? They are paid to protect us, and that's what they're supposed to be doing. It's ridiculous. I'm so mad."

She wasn't the only one. At around the same time, during a shopping trip at the local building supply, I had overheard three men talking about the RCMP. I worked my way into the conversation and met the man working behind the counter. His name was Ross Woronka. He had retired to Chester after a long career at the Calgary police department as a detective and senior officer. Woronka said that he had tried to get involved in the community and lend his expertise with regard to policing and security, but that he finally threw in the towel and gave up.

"The RCMP doesn't have a clue about how to do municipal policing," Woronka said. "They are completely out of their element. They don't have the manpower, the intelligence, or the commitment. They are distant and arrogant. They don't eat at the local restaurants. They don't know anyone in the town. I've never felt so unsafe as being in a RCMP policed community."

During the radio interview, I discussed in detail the many problems inherent in RCMP contract policing, about the indifferent staffing across the country and the lack of accountability. A few days later, I was contacted by two New Brunswick municipal police officers, Constable Mike Donovan of the Rothesay Regional Police and Constable Dean Secord of the Saint John Police Force. Secord was the president of the New Brunswick Police Association, a lobby group hoping some day to be a union. He represented non-RCMP officers in the nine municipal and regional forces in the province.

Secord, Donovan, and I soon met and they told me about the policing situation in the province. It was their view that the Mounties had all but abrogated their responsibilities and were not serving the public that well. Yet, the monolithic, voracious RCMP was threatening to gobble up another small municipal force in Grand Falls and make it a contract operation. The provincial government didn't look like it was going to do anything about it. Secord and Donovan had convincing statistics and events to back up their case, and a host of anecdotal stories.

"The RCMP comes in and offers a community the full-meal deal, municipal, provincial, and federal policing, all on one plate. It looks so tempting that politicians can't refuse it," Donovan said. "But once you pay for the meal, you get only the big, doughy bun and nothing else. The RCMP are spread so thinly that they are constantly robbing Peter to pay Paul. Even though they might have a contract with one community, they'll leave that place unmanned and cover it from another community, maybe 40 miles away. We've tried to document this, but it is virtually impossible to find out how many Mounties are on the job and what each one of them is doing. When you ask, they play 'Hide the Mountie' with you."

The two police officers said their association needed someone to do further research and write a position paper for them. I undertook the assignment because I thought it might open up some new ideas about the RCMP. In the process, I gained more insights and knowledge than I could have imagined.

New Brunswick is a small province with a population of 730,000. Most of its residents live on the perimeter of the province. Whereas there are nine municipal police forces, the rest of the province is served by the RCMP through three different forms of agreements: eleven municipalities with direct contracts, 58 with Provincial Police Services Agreements between the municipalities and the province, and 19 under the terms of an Extended Agreement between the municipalities and the province. The RCMP also provides First Nations policing to four of the five Aboriginal communities in the province, the fifth being St. Mary's in contract with Fredericton Regional Police.

These memoranda of understanding appear to be a sound business practice, setting out in advance what each party is expected to do under the terms of a contract. They are not dissimilar to joint-venture agreements between corporations undertaking a project together. Corporations normally set up protocols in such agreements in which each side agrees that it will share information with the other side and that no public statements about a project or its partners will be made by any co-signer without the consent of the others. Therein lay the insidiousness of the RCMP memoranda of understanding.

When the RCMP enters into an agreement, a stated or implied provision is that all concerns, criticisms, or comments will be worked out between the partners. Each side is bound not to make a comment about the other, and all public comments relating to the RCMP and its partners will be negotiated. Any violation would be considered a legal breach of the understanding.

The RCMP has working agreements with every police service in the country—a sword that it dangles over the head of its partners. No matter how poorly it might have performed, the language in the contracts binds its myriad partners across the country from saying anything about the RCMP without the consent of the RCMP, which is never given. The net effect is that the RCMP has the means to stifle any public discourse among policing agencies about its miserable performance, a virtually impregnable security blanket. Fear of retribution from the RCMP is one of the prime reasons why, in the midst of any controversy, other police leaders have little substantive, if anything at all, to say when called upon by the media for their insights into a debacle.

New Brunswick Constables Secord and Donovan had compelling evidence that the municipal forces were better trained and provided a higher level of service and a higher crime clearance rate than the RCMP. They were prepared to say what their own police chiefs knew, but couldn't publicly discuss.

Twenty years ago, it could reasonably have been argued that the RCMP provided the best-trained police officers in Canada. That is no longer the case. In the mid-1990s, New Brunswick implemented its Policing Standards program, which dictated that every serving officer require maximum training and retraining at prescribed intervals. In the RCMP, however, the reverse happened. Since the mid-1990s, the RCMP had reduced not only the length of training for recruits, but had also continually lowered its standards across the board. Governments demanded that the force better reflect the diversity of society, so big white guys were out, and 48-year-old cadets and slim, diminutive cadets of either sex became common. These new recruits could not meet the physical standards of the big guys and were not as capable at either defending themselves or safely restraining suspects.

A further effect of the downsizing of individual police officers was that new weapons had to be employed. A small police officer couldn't use his or her gun in every potentially dangerous situation. No matter how much self-defence training an officer took, the simple fact is that, as in boxing, heavyweights destroy middleweights, welterweights destroy flyweights, and someone who is mentally unstable or high on drugs can whip them all. Enter the taser, the controversial electronic stun gun, better than pepper spray and not as deadly as a bullet, though sometimes so.

Police used to be able to defend themselves and deal with unruly customers with open-hand techniques that were actually invented in Canada during the Second World War. During the war, the Canadian army quickly learned that Japanese soldiers were better trained in hand-to-hand combat. Japanese children are taught from childhood how to defend themselves with judo and karate. Knowledge of martial arts is part of their culture. Canadians grow up with a hockey stick in their hands and rudimentary skills in boxing and wrestling.

An innovative Canadian, Bill Underwood, recognized that Eastern martial arts were not the answer for western soldiers. It would take too long to teach and had limitations in close quarters. He broke down the basics of the Eastern approach, eliminated the long sweeps and circular swirls, and invented a self-defence system called Combato as a reply to karate and judo. Combato taught individuals how to position themselves by gaining proper angles, anatomical pressure points, and methods to use a person's nervous system against them. Combato was adopted by the Devil's Brigade, the first Canadian special forces service, and then by the RCMP.

Over the next 20 years Combato was adopted by army and police services around the world. It began to fall out of favour, however, in Canada and the United States. The so-called "sleeper hold" was banned after suspects died in police custody in a number of jurisdictions and the squeamish public and governments called for kinder, gentler policing, without understanding the ramifications that lay therein. The police might get smaller, kinder, and gentler, but the suspects and even ordinary citizens who came into contact with the police did not. The police and the public once enjoyed a kind of social contract. The police were respected and those who came into contact with them—even some hardened criminals—honoured that contract. Everyone had a role to play, and both sides, with some exceptions, stuck to their role. In recent decades, that informal agreement has broken down and incivility toward authorities has escalated to the point where even teenage girls now try to duke it out with uniformed officers. To deal with this, the police have found themselves in a constant search for new and more effective ways to deal with unruly people. As a group, many forces have become slaves to the latest fashions, none more so than the RCMP.

"They went from Bruce Lee movies to mixed martial arts, but it didn't work," said Robbie Cressman, a disciple of Underwood who trains police and military in Canada around the world in the latest version of Combato. "It takes five to six years to master Eastern martial arts, not just an hour a day for a few weeks. Even then, the Eastern arts are not designed for police work. The police are often operating in crowded corridors and halls with all kinds of physical restrictions. They are usually wearing full gear and need one hand free for their trigger finger should they need it. They can't get in a boxing match with a suspect. They can't use Tae Kwon Do or Karate or kickboxing. They can't kick to defend themselves or attack. All those things put them at a professional disadvantage."

According to Cressman, the reduction in useful self-defence training has filled the streets with police officers who are not confident about their abilities, and their fear makes them dangerous to themselves and anyone else. "My wife was a police officer. Every female officer she knew couldn't meet the training standards the first time, they had to go back for remedial work. The British are well-trained and disciplined, the exact opposite of the Americans, who instead rely on push-button warfare. The Americans have lazy skill sets, a coffee in one hand and a taser in the other. It takes away from their competency. Unfortunately, that is what has happened to the RCMP. Too many of them are out there and are not confident. They are bound to make mistakes, and when they do, the public gets into an uproar and governments then pass even more procedures and restrictions on police use of force. Then comes additional litigation and the fear of being sued. It becomes a vicious cycle because no one is prepared to address the underlying issues."

When he took over as police chief of Cobourg, Ontario, former super-intendent Garry Clement voluntarily took an Ontario Police training course with the relatively small Durham Regional Police. He was astounded by what he learned. "That was the best police training I could ever imagine," said Clement. "It was so far ahead of what the RCMP has been doing that I could see why [the Mounties] have had so many problems. They're not trained to a modern standard."

The gap between municipal police and the RCMP was cited by the fed-eral auditor general, who reported in 2005 that RCMP staffing levels are down significantly and that the force has long been shortchanging its clients in contract policing. The auditor general found gaps in training that could compromise the health and safety of police officers and the public, and gaps in completing training for newly graduated cadets. An RCMP survey sup-ported those findings. It found, among other things, that 16 percent of newly-graduated cadets did not receive the full six-month mandatory field coaching, and that overall the number of peace officers who met all six mandatory training requirements had dropped from 57 percent in 2003 to 6.2 percent in 2004. As the RCMP reported: "We have found that gaps in training may be preventing the RCMP of meeting its clients' expectations of fully trained peace officers."

In New Brunswick, the implementation of policing standards forced the municipal departments to become much stronger, more professional, better trained, and superior to the RCMP. All municipal police officers are now required to take prescribed courses over the first five years of their careers and continuous training afterward, but the Act did not apply to the RCMP, which is bound by federal regulations.

The RCMP claimed that its members also met the requirements of New Brunswick Policing Standards, but that was not entirely true. There was a sig-nificant and important difference. Every New Brunswick municipal police officer was required to have certain training. The RCMP countered that only some of its officers needed to be or are trained in the required prescribed areas. The net result was that all municipal officers are fully trained to provincial standards, but not all RCMP members are so well-equipped.

In practice, this is what that meant. The RCMP had a single emergency response team for the entire province, whose members are spread out across New Brunswick. That is the RCMP approach. Their ERT response time was severely affected by this reality, if it responded at all. Municipal forces had several ERT teams across the province, and their response time was significantly quicker. The RCMP had roughly twice as many officers in New Brunswick than municipal forces, yet the municipalities had more trained police dogs, more trained collision reconstruction experts, and more identification officers.

The issue came to a head in Grand Falls in the spring of 2008. In February, the local council had voted by a 4–3 margin to hire the RCMP as the municipal police force based on the promise by the Mounties to build a regional headquarters in the community. The Mounties would not put the promise in writing. The New Brunswick police association fought back and hired public relations consultants. Polling in the community determined that a vast majority of the citizens did not want the Mounties. The decision to implement the change was put off until after the May 12 municipal election. At the ballot box every councillor who backed the Mounties was voted out of office and the RCMP was forced to cancel its contract expansion plans.

The more I looked at the RCMP in New Brunswick, the clearer the picture became about how gerrymandered the force had been allowed to become. Its entire structure was illogical. Then I took a closer look at federal policing in the province. A light went on. Here is an excerpt from Dean Secord's discussion paper, "Our Province, Our Police."

The distortion of the delivery of policing is largely based on both the primary focus of the RCMP as a federal police force. There are 131 RCMP members fully dedicated to federal policing in the province of New Brunswick, an expense which is fully financed by the federal government. The 502 provincial RCMP officers in New Brunswick, theoretically devote 30 percent of their time to federal law enforcement. In effect, by combining the time spent by these two groups of Mounties conducting federal law enforcement, there were approximately 308 man years of RCMP members in federal policing in the province this year. The question is: does New Brunswick need 308 police officers doing federal law enforcement or does it need a better balance between municipal and provincial police functions and federal functions?

For example, Ontario with a population of 12.6 million people is home to 1,224 RCMP federal officers, many of them in Ottawa, effectively 1 per 10,000 residents. Québec's population is 7.6-million and there are 926 federal RCMP in the province, slightly, effectively 1 per every 8,200 residents. New Brunswick with a population of

730,000, with 131 fully dedicated RCMP federal officers, has one per 5,500 residents, not including the 30 percent of work to federal policing done by the 502 provincial officers in the province. If one takes the effective federal manpower in New Brunswick to be 308 man years, then the number of federal officers to residents is actually one for every 2,300 residents. The policing that a community receives from the RCMP is not the same policing most local governments and taxpayers think they are paying for.

Secord and Donovan told me that one way to understand how the RCMP rigs its own federal enforcement statistics is to look at the different ways suspects are treated during a routine traffic stop.

Donovan said: "When a municipal police officer makes a routine drug bust as part of their duties and seizes a small quantity of drugs, say, in Saint John, a charge may be laid for simple possession. Those cases are dealt with efficiently in provincial court, often with a summary conviction. When the Mounties make the same stop, just outside Saint John, it's a federal case. It's ridiculous."

The Mounties, it turns out, even if performing the same function as a municipal officer in the same geographic area, are required to treat all drug seizures as federal crimes. The RCMP claims that this is part of the force's federal mandate, as covered by the federal subsidy and/or its "fenced in" financing for special projects. Any offender charged by the RCMP in New Brunswick, or in any jurisdiction where it operates in a contract capacity, enters a different and more expensive stream of justice and could face stiffer penalties. In New Brunswick, such cases are not even dealt with at the local level. In that province, the procedure for the RCMP is to forward any drug-related information to Halifax headquarters where it must be approved by a prosecutor attached to the Health Canada-financed drug enforcement unit. If a charge is approved, the federal government then hires a private sector lawyer who acts as a special prosecutor for the case.

"What we have are two levels of justice for the same offence, which is patently unfair," said Donovan. "It's also inefficient and in no way cost-effective."

Unfair as it might well be, that system is used by the RCMP across the country and it helps the force pad its federal crime enforcement statistics. It could reasonably be argued, therefore, that there was no real efficiency or cost saving in RCMP contract policing, with or without a federal subsidy. In the alternative, since municipal police are doing much of the same work as the RCMP in its federal capacity, it would be much fairer to the taxpayer if the federal government subsidized municipal policing at the same level as the RCMP or dropped the subsidy altogether.

Since governments and the RCMP seem so consumed by the phrase "the bottom line," the true bottom line is that it costs more for a community to hire the RCMP—significantly more. The RCMP service is at best no better, no more effective, or cheaper than the same services provided by a traditional municipal police force, and likely less so in all categories. It was apparent that taxpayers would save money and receive better policing services if there were a better balance between federal, provincial, and regional municipal forces in New Brunswick.

I had found enough in New Brunswick to make me wonder how it was that the provincial government was not more concerned about the obvious shortcomings and failings of the RCMP.

"I can't understand why the government doesn't do anything about this," I said to Secord and Donovan one day.

"Because the RCMP controls how the government thinks," Secord said.

"How could that be?" I wondered.

✠   ✠   ✠

In its contract role, the RCMP is governed by the federal RCMP Act and not by provincial police acts. It is not subject to the authority of a provincial solicitor general. In New Brunswick, the previously described cases of former RCMP staff sergeants Cliff McCann and Ken Smith seemed to beg for provincial intervention. McCann had been a suspect in the investigation of sexual abuse at the now-defunct Kingsclear institution, while Smith had been victimized by illegal surveillance and other questionable tactics by his own force. Each case seemed to clearly fall under the jurisdiction of the province and its laws. Both the Smith and McCann cases suggested that there was something seriously wrong in New Brunswick, but what? Why was the provincial government reluctant to take on the Mounties in the face of such blatant wrongdoing?

Positioned as they are in Canada in the small cities, towns, and villages of the country, the typical Mountie begins rubbing shoulders with politicians at the lowest levels of the pecking order, town councillors, police services board members, and the like. Their proximity to the police and their power, in my experience, often rubbed off on the small-town politicians. So many become all but puffed up with an "I've got a secret" sort of countenance. Over time, small-town politicians move up the political food chain, while individual Mounties rise through their own organization. A reeve in some provincial backwater might eventually become solicitor general. The Mountie might become assistant commissioner, which made me wonder about the situation back in British Columbia. By late 2007, all hell seemed to be breaking loose there, but the government was adamant about doing nothing, and the RCMP was confident that nothing would be done.

Then-B.C. Solicitor General John Les hailed from Chilliwack, B.C., where he was municipal councillor for three years and mayor for 12 years from 1987 to 1999. Before he became involved in municipal government, Mr. Les was active in business and property development, as well as community activities, such as restorative justice, the Community Police Access Centre non-profit society, and the Fraser Valley Regional Library.

Who was the top cop in Chilliwack at the time? Assistant Commissioner Alistair Macintyre. He was now in charge of RCMP operations in that province. Across the country, there were similar relationships, but all that was so hit and miss. There had to be more.

Secord and Donovan pointed out to me that the bureaucrats who control the policing bureaucracy in New Brunswick are all ex-Mounties. In the opinion of Secord and Donovan, the only voice being heard in government was that of the Mounties, while the police association or anyone advocating their position was usually given short shrift. The bureaucrats often called meetings about policing and invited only Mounties to attend. On the other hand, if the municipal police sought a hearing, the bureaucrats almost always asked that the Mounties be there too.

The old saying in policing is that there is no such thing as an ex-Mountie. The Mountie oath has a powerful hold on its members even after their formal careers are over. The Mountie network is vast and complex. There are veterans' associations and clubs where the current and the former mingle regularly. There are Mountie chat groups and online newsletters and any number of social events. Mounties often only truly trust other Mounties.

In the course of their careers, members of the RCMP move frequently and can be posted anywhere in Canada or even abroad, as liaison officers or on peace-keeping missions in some foreign trouble spot. The federal government calls on Mounties to train police officers in other countries. The RCMP is also big on awards and medals and certificates. In the homes of many Mounties, it is not unusual to find all four walls of a dedicated room entirely covered with framed citations and award certificates. A typical Mountie résumé can go on and on and on. When an ex-Mountie applies for a position in government, the list of experiences and honours is irresistible, even if in so many cases it is a mile wide and an inch thin. On the other hand, a municipal police officer might have a short résumé but be long on what counts most. More often than not, however, the Mountie who looks more worldly and experienced on paper typically wins out.

Ottawa researcher Ken Rubin was hired to file access-to-information requests with the RCMP and the government to find out if there was a formal list of ex-Mounties, and where they might be working. Rubin reported that no such list was compiled because he was told that such a list would violate federal privacy laws.

A province-by-province search revealed that the people in charge of each government's police policy directorate, the people who gave the politicians advice and whispered into their ears, were ex-Mounties in every RCMP contract province except one, Alberta.

In British Columbia the axis of Solicitor General Les and Assistant Commissioner Macintyre was completed by the fact that the assistant deputy minister of Police Services was ex-RCMP member Kevin Begg. His office was stuffed with ex-Mounties.

Throughout the federal and provincial governments, ex-Mounties, each of whom had retired with sizeable pensions, were being hired back by governments, where they hold virtually every key position in every department dealing with law enforcement or public safety issues. As provincial bureaucrats, these ex-Mounties only oversee the operations of the municipal police forces in their respective provinces. The record is quite clear across the country that the municipal forces are held to a higher standard than the RCMP. The ex-Mountie bureaucrats are always vigilant about any perceived transgression, to the point of harassment. Whether a force deserves it or not, in the contract provinces the municipal police must walk on eggshells, with the constant threat hanging over their heads of the RCMP taking over their jurisdictions.

It made so much sense. The RCMP had its own invisible hand working behind the scenes, a fifth column defending its interests, not only in governments and its bureaucracies, but also in banks, other businesses, and private investigation firms. As private investigators, these ex-Mounties were not only working for Canadian businesses and wealthy individuals, but also for foreign businesses, police, and intelligence services.

The ex-Mounties are not only the eyes and ears of the force, but its hidden voice, passing on information, gathering intelligence, whispering in other ears, advocating RCMP policies, and watching the force's back. This unofficial arm of the force is a virtual secret agency, guiding situations and keeping the RCMP brass in the loop.

[18]

THE FOUR HORSEMEN OF
THE APOCALYPSE

Vancouver is world-renowned for its Downtown Eastside, an open market for drugs, sex, and crime. It was the hunting ground for Canada's best-known serial killer, Robert (Willy) Pickton. Throughout the 1980s and 1990s, he lured prostitutes to his pig farm in suburban Port Coquitlam, taking the women from the Vancouver police jurisdiction and into RCMP territory. At Piggy's Palace, as he called his "entertainment centre," Pickton drugged and slaughtered at least 49 women, although some believe the number might be much higher. Pickton was only caught after an RCMP officer arrested him on a gun charge, and the real investigation began.

Throughout the killing spree and after Pickton's 2002 arrest, the Vancouver Police Department was accused by community activists of being lax about the growing number of missing women and not responding quickly enough to the obvious presence of a serial killer. But it wasn't all the city police department's fault. In a normal, tiered policing milieu where there are clearly defined jurisdictions, municipal, provincial or state, and federal, police forces can look over each other's shoulder and bring a needed fresh view to any situation. But that's not the case in the Lower Mainland. The RCMP provides all those bodies under a unified command with a single perspective. If women were disappearing off the streets of Toronto or Montréal at the rate they were in Vancouver, the Ontario or Québec provincial police would have come in much earlier and widened the scope of the investigation.

In the Pickton case, the women were taken from Vancouver and murdered deep inside the RCMP's jurisdiction. Despite all the activity, the Mounties did not have the wherewithal to detect the crime pattern, develop informants, or solve a horrendous ongoing crime happening in its own backyard. In its capacity as a provincial force, it was invisible because the crime was all handled at the municipal level.

"Vancouver could only do so much," said former Vancouver Police Chief Bob Stewart in an interview. "Its jurisdiction is hemmed in by the RCMP. The media, with the assistance of the RCMP, sat back and criticized the city police. If the RCMP had been doing its job properly, that man would have been caught a lot sooner."

However, solving crimes has not been the RCMP's forte over the past few decades. Stumbling from one debacle to another has. During this period, at every level of the force and in every type of investigation, it has become apparent that there is a tried and true recipe for disaster in the RCMP— relative inexperience in a job function, under-supervision, under-financing, and an absence of accountability. When push comes to shove, as we've already seen and will continue to see, the RCMP's first instinct is to turn on the fog machine and cover up.

The brutality of the force was etched in the public's mind during the 1997 Asia Pacific Economic Conference in Vancouver. The lasting image is of Staff Sgt. Hugh Stewart using a Costco-size container of pepper spray to indiscriminately disperse protesters near a fence. Fifty-two formal complaints were filed over RCMP actions, including pepper spraying, strip searches, and violations of civil rights.

A public inquiry headed by former judge Ted Hughes spent $10 million and took three years to examine what had taken place. In his 453-page report, Hughes was critical of both the federal government and the RCMP brass in British Columbia. Hughes found that police actions "did not meet an acceptable and expected standard of competence and professionalism and proficiency." He found the RCMP had not properly prepared for or planned what it was going to do.

Hughes concluded that many of the protesters' complaints were well-founded. But he stopped short of blaming the officers on the ground. It was the poor planning of their supervisors, he concluded, which had led to an inevitable imbroglio.

The report was not binding on the RCMP and the force continued policing Lotusland without significant changes to its practices. Over the next few years, in British Columbia, as elsewhere across Canada, several RCMP officers were charged with assault and even sexual assaults. With rare exceptions, the accused Mounties were allowed to continue working, even after being convicted of their crimes. One Mountie convicted of assaulting a citizen was given a short conditional sentence. Days after he left court, he was promoted. The RCMP knew how to protect its own favoured members, but the public didn't always get the same degree of understanding.

The most dangerous place in the country for anyone to be a prisoner of the RCMP was in British Columbia. An internal government report, obtained by the *Vancouver Sun* through the Access to Information Act, showed that there had been 80 RCMP in-custody deaths from 2002 through 2006, including police shootings. The number accounted for 56 percent of all in-custody deaths at the hands of Mounties across the country, even though only one-third of all Mounties were serving in British Columbia.

Just before Christmas 2004, two RCMP officers in Vanderhoof, in northern B.C., confronted Kevin St. Arnaud, a suspect in a drugstore robbery. He was shot three times by Constable Ryan Sheremetta, who said St. Arnaud had threatened him—"You're going to have to shoot me"—and fired a shot at him. Sheremetta said his gun went off after he slipped and fell backwards onto the snow. He said it was self-defence, but his partner, 24-year-veteran Colleen Erickson, told a very different version of the story. She said St. Arnaud had given up and that Sheremetta was in a police firing stance when he shot the suspect. She said she didn't hear Arnaud threaten Sheremetta, as Sheremetta had claimed.

Cameron Ward, a veteran defence lawyer, told CBC Radio that witnesses at the scene heard someone shouting: "Get back here, you son of a bitch!" That suggested, he said, that St. Arnaud may have been moving toward Sheremetta because he had been ordered to do so. The greatest concern, however, was that the RCMP was allowed to investigate itself. "The investigators devoted all their time and effort to trying to justify the shooting and to defend their colleague," he said.

The forensic evidence supported both the witnesses and Constable Erickson's version of the story, but the RCMP stood behind Sheremetta. In its cultish way, both St. Arnaud and Constable Erickson were viewed as threats to the RCMP's image and prestige.

Less than a year later, on October 29, 2005, a Saturday night, 22-year-old Ian Bush, a popular sawmill worker, was at a hockey game at the local rink in the northern B.C. community of Houston. His friend Jeremy Stapleton was there when Bush was arrested for having an open beer in his hand. Stapleton later said that Bush didn't give RCMP Constable Paul Koester, who had been on the job for five months, his real name. Instead, he gave the name of a friend. The RCMP officer didn't find it funny, and carted him away in his cruiser. The last time anyone saw Bush, "he was laughing, joking, in a good mood."

An RCMP news release later said that Bush became violent at the police station lock-up, and that in a fight for Koester's gun, he was shot and killed. There were no witnesses. The smear campaign had begun.

Koester claimed self-defence. Forensic evidence showed that Bush had been shot in the back of the head. The RCMP vehemently denied any wrong-doing by Koester, who stuck to his story in spite of damning evidence presented at a coroner's hearing which ended in July 2007. Koester testified that Bush had pinned him face-down and was strangling him. Nevertheless, Koester said, he had still managed to pistol-whip Bush from that face-down position and shoot him in the back of the head.

Edmonton Police Services officer and forensic investigator Joe Slemko, however, testified that the blood splatter evidence placed Bush under Koester, and not on top of him, as the Mountie had testified. Slemko's evidence was dismissed by Coroner Shane DeMeyer. He ordered the jury not to apportion blame and to only make recommendations which, if implemented, might help to avoid a similar situation in the future.

Bush's family and supporters were outraged by what had taken place. In their view, there had been no accountability. The RCMP had been allowed to investigate itself. The provincial and federal governments stood by and watched. "He didn't have disrespect for police officers, not ever ... He just wouldn't go fighting with a police officer," Bush's sister Renée said in an interview with CBC News.

"We don't feel like it's going to be the truth because it's the RCMP investigating the RCMP. Maybe we would have more confidence if it was someone else investigating," said Bush's sister Andrea Patrick.

On November 29, 2007, the Commission for Public Complaints Against the RCMP exonerated Koester. Commission Chairman Paul Kennedy said that Koester had acted in self-defence and that the police investigation into the shooting was conducted fairly and without conflict of interest. "I concluded that Constable Koester had a reasonable apprehension of death and believed that he could not otherwise preserve himself from death other than to use lethal force," Kennedy wrote. "Accordingly, Constable Koester acted in self-defence. In addition, given Constable Koester had tried lesser forms of intervention that were not successful, Constable Koester was authorized under the RCMP's use of force policy to use lethal force."

As for the police investigation, Kennedy wrote: "I concluded that the

North District major crime unit conducted a highly professional investigation into Mr. Bush's death and exemplified the best practices for major crime investigations . . . in a timely manner and free from any manner of conflict of interest, bias or partiality."

The finding was not surprising coming from Kennedy, who, after taking over from the more controversial Shirley Heafey, had assiduously tried to cozy up to the Mounties and show them that he was a reasonable guy. In a speech to the National Press Club six months earlier in Ottawa, Kennedy talked about the RCMP and its glowing reputation, despite all the controversies. For him, there was no broken culture and all the reported problems were being blown out of proportion.

In that May 9 speech, Kennedy said, in part: "There is a tendency to string together a number of disparate events that occur throughout Canada, emerging from any one of the three different roles played by the RCMP, as evidence of a systemic problem within the Force. The RCMP has become a rolling stone that gathers moss. This conflation of disparate issues can contribute to the creation of a 'crisis.'"

It is inevitable that such a police service will be the subject of public complaints as to how it discharges its duties. Since 1988 there has been on average 2,000 annual complaints. They range in nature from complaints of rudeness, police shootings that result in serious injury or death, to appropriate response to large public protests such as those that took place at APEC in Vancouver and the Summit of the Americas in Québec City. The vast majority of these complaints can be adequately addressed under the current legislation. However, it is clear that individual cases can highlight glaring defects in the review mechanism which undermine its credibility, foster tension between the RCMP and the commission, and have helped spawn a growth in the "Public Inquiry" business.

Some of the accountability difficulties have, in my opinion, been overly simplified as personality conflicts between members of the commission and leadership of the RCMP. Such conflicts, if they exist, mask what is essentially a flawed statutory mandate; one that has been overtaken by time and evolving police practices.

In that speech, Kennedy seemed to be all but campaigning for the still-open commissioner's job that would go to William Elliott a few months later. He appeared to be oblivious to all that was going on around him, which strongly suggested that the RCMP was out of its depth in even the shallowest of waters.

The RCMP was caught up in so many scandals the public found it all but numbing. A number of the scandals involved questionable agents hired by the RCMP to infiltrate organized crime circles. Time after time, it seemed, the force was willing to pay out hundreds of thousands of dollars to con men who would take the money, change their identities, and go on to act with impunity, knowing that they were now untouchables. The most flagrant example was a Vancouver man who committed a murder while in the witness protection program, and who received more protection from the Mounties than anyone could have dreamed possible. Citing privacy issues, the RCMP did everything it could to protect the true identity of the man and his deeds, the revelation of which would show just how hollow the force had become.

Lawyers for *The Globe and Mail* and the *Ottawa Citizen* were tipped to the story and spent six months in court in an attempt to break the seal imposed on the case. Each paper published a remarkable front-page story on March 22, 2007. The usually staid *Globe* published a preamble in bold-face, italic, over-sized type, beneath the headline: "The secret agent who conned the Mounties: Richard Young's 'cruel charade.'" The preamble alone revealed just how scared the RCMP was to have the truth told:

> Editor's Note: The article that follows is incomplete. That is not normally something we do. Usually we make our work as complete as possible. In this case, we are hobbled by legal restrictions.
>
> The story is about a man who became an RCMP informant and was eventually enrolled in the Witness Protection program in spite of ample warning that he was an unreliable liar.
>
> This individual went on to commit a heinous crime. We can neither describe the details of the murder nor the current identity of the killer.
>
> *The Globe and Mail* publishes this story today in conjunction with *The Ottawa Citizen*, a highly unusual act in itself, and one which speaks to the importance the editors of the two newspapers place on this matter. Greg McArthur and Gary Dimmock researched and wrote this story at *The Citizen*. Greg is now a reporter with *The Globe and Mail*. For legal reasons it was modified jointly with *The Citizen* after he left.
>
> Both Greg McArthur and *The Citizen* have been waging a legal battle to publish it for the past six months. A court ruling yesterday allowed us to tell this part of the story.

But this is more than just the story of an individual gone bad. It is an issue of public policy. But the blanket legal requirement of the Witness Protection Act against ever disclosing the identity of a person accepted into the program—no matter how awful his subsequent actions—inhibits our efforts to not just tell this story, but to examine the RCMP's role in this affair.

Edward Greenspon, Editor-in-chief

Both stories chronicled the activities of "Richard Young"—Agent E8060. He was described as a jobless, pathological liar who had been accepted into the witness protection program even though an RCMP polygraph specialist raised concerns about the veracity of the informant's stories before he became a paid agent. A British Columbia judge later ruled that in fact the informant's so-called evidence was nothing more than a charade.

"Richard Young" was one of a number of foul balls used by the RCMP in Vancouver to investigate organized crime, a calling that neither Young nor the RCMP proved capable of undertaking. The full story about Young's true identity and his criminal shenanigans at taxpayer's expense under the watchful eye of the RCMP was eventually revealed. The real story was the inability of the hapless RCMP on the West Coast to do the job it was paid to do—protect the public by deterring, investigating, and solving crimes.

Surrey, once a largely rural farming area which stretches from just south of Vancouver to the Washington border, has been the fastest growing community in Canada for more than a decade. Pastoral though it might be in some places, it is today a sprawling community and the home of a wide variety of criminal elements including biker and ethnic-based criminal gangs. The community has been both the prime training centre for new Mounties and the biggest profit centre for the RCMP, the economic and policing implications of which don't seem to have dawned on the local guardians. Every six months, the RCMP spits out fresh new Mounties and sends the largest contingent of most graduating classes to Surrey. Until 2004, these rookies were paid the minimum wage of $32,000 a year. In 2007, the rate had risen to $44,513. The community, however, is billed for the full freight of an experienced three-year officer, whose pay is around $80,000 a year. In Surrey, young officers with little or no experience cut their teeth in policing, but never really get to know the community. A Mountie in Surrey with five years' experience is considered to be an elder statesman of the local force, but still wet behind the ears by the standards of any other major metropolitan police service. A new Mountie rarely lasts long enough in Surrey to get to the maximum pay level before he or she is shipped out to fill some other hole in the force. Some find it so difficult to exist in Surrey on RCMP wages that they are forced to take second jobs, like night security work at Wal-mart. Some left the RCMP for that reason.

That Surrey was the RCMP's kindergarten was formalized in a September 2007 memorandum of understanding brokered by the force's human resources officer. In it the federal divisions in Ontario, Ottawa, and Québec signed an agreement with "E" Division in British Columbia to put newly inducted members onto the streets of Surrey to whip them into shape for complex federal policing responsibilities back in central Canada. To quickly develop junior G-men and women, the RCMP paid for the entire exercise out of its federal budget, a sort of payback to Surrey.

In most communities they serve, the Mounties are strangers in a strange land. They gather so little criminal intelligence that there is virtually nothing the force can do to protect citizens. Their very presence makes life dangerous for everyone, including themselves.

On the Friday afternoon of October 19, 2007, six men were executed in a Surrey apartment. Four were young men connected to the drug trade, but two were innocent bystanders. Edward Schellenberg, 55, was a gas appliance repairman doing work in the building, while Chris Mohan, 22, lived next door to the murder scene and apparently walked out of his apartment and into the hands of the killers. Crimes like that can happen anywhere, but in the Lower Mainland gang-related murder was well on its way to soaring out of control.

In the days after the six murders, a wide variety of concerned people in the Lower Mainland began to come out in public to complain about the Mounties and the organization of the force in British Columbia. One of those was the new West Vancouver Police Chief, Kash Heed, a former Vancouver police officer, who had been appointed two months earlier. Heed added his voice to the growing debate in an opinion piece published in *The Vancouver Sun*. Heed called for a regional police force in Vancouver, a direct attack on the RCMP kingdom. The morning the article was published, an irate Solicitor General John Les phoned West Vancouver Mayor Pamela Goldsmith-Jones and told her to order her police chief to zip up his lips. A few days later, Les relented and said that the discussion of a regional force in Vancouver was "a valid discussion," although he made it clear he stood four-square behind the RCMP. In the background, however, the details of one of the most explosive stories in RCMP history were being hidden by both the Mounties and the Solicitor General's office. It had begun five days earlier in the neighbouring community of Richmond.

✟ ✟ ✟

In the early morning hours of Sunday October 14, 2007, Polish native Robert Dziekanski was wandering around Vancouver International Airport, located in the suburb of Richmond. The 40-year-old Dziekanski had come from the impoverished town of Pieszyce to Canada seeking landed immigrant status. A part-time construction worker, he had had minor run-ins with the law in his small, poor town. He had just quit smoking, didn't speak any English, and had never been outside Poland in his life. He was on his way to live with his mother, Zofia, who worked as a cleaning lady in Kamloops. She had remarried eight years earlier and had moved to Canada. His dream, he told his friends back home, was to kiss a grizzly bear.

Dziekanski had arrived in Vancouver around 3:30 p.m. the previous day after a 17-hour flight from Frankfurt, Germany. He had cleared the first stage of customs at 4 p.m., but then seemed to get lost. His mother was in another part of the airport looking for him. She had her son paged over the airport intercom, but the speakers couldn't be heard in the baggage area. After many hours of waiting, she figured that he had missed his plane, so she took the long drive back to Kamloops.

At 10:30 p.m. Dziekanski finally showed up at a baggage carousel, needing help to find his luggage. Officials located the luggage for him and then led him to an office where his immigration papers would be processed. At 12:30 a.m., his paperwork completed, he left the immigration area and wandered around the airport, eventually arriving in a secure area in the baggage concourse.

To those around him, the tall, burly, imposing man seemed dazed and confused, possibly suffering from a psychiatric disorder. Over the next hour or so, he was periodically observed by airport security staff and Canada Border Service Agency officers, but no one did anything to help him. RCMP officers, who are assigned to protect the airport as part of their municipal responsibilities, were nowhere to be seen. In the understaffed Lower Mainland, it was approaching 2 a.m., near the end of shift for most Mounties on patrol in Richmond. At that time on Sunday morning, there was only a skeleton crew on duty.

The RCMP story was that Dziekanski, big and swarthy, had become violent and that *three* RCMP officers had tried to subdue him. The RCMP said that because of the crowd in the room, the officers could not use pepper spray on Dziekanski, so were forced to employ a taser, an electronic stun gun, on him. Dziekanski, however, died on the spot.

RCMP spokesman Sgt. Pierre Lemaitre, of the Richmond city detachment, told CBC Television that despite police efforts to calm him, "the officers were met aggressively and confrontationally by Mr. Dziekanski . . . The officers were using gestures saying, 'you know, relax, relax, put your hands on the desk there where the computer was taken.'" Lemaitre said Dziekanski wouldn't cooperate "and was still throwing things around."

Sgt Lemaitre later told the *Vancouver Sun*: "The officers tried to speak to him, tried to calm him down, but he continued to throw things around and yell and scream." In another commentary on CTV News, Lemaitre said: "He was pounding on the windows behind us, he was throwing chairs."

Lemaitre said that the first taser shot "didn't seem to have any kind of effect on him . . . even after the handcuffs, he continued to fight."

The RCMP went into its familiar dance. The RCMP described what had taken place as "an isolated incident," "an occupational hazard," and "an unforeseen tragedy." This was followed, as has often been the case in similar situations, by government officials spouting their uncritical support for the force: "We have 100 percent confidence in the RCMP;" "All the evidence isn't in yet;" "We'll have to wait for the inquiry before we can pass judgment;" all of which happened in the days after Dziekanski was killed.

Despite the RCMP's story, many people were appalled by what the RCMP had done. Police instructor Mark Lalonde put it this way: "The morning after the death of Mr. Dziekanski at the hands of the RCMP, I was deeply disappointed by the comments of the RCMP spokesperson. There was no expression of regret, condolences to the next of kin, or call for an outside independent review. Rather, it was corporate spin control and justification for the actions of the police. . . . truth management. It's not about the quality of public service, but rather brand protection. I expect this from the private sector, not from a public service."

As is the case in most deaths at the hands of police, a coroner's inquest was called. The Mounties involved went back to work. The RCMP continued to suggest Dziekanski was the author of his own misfortune, while the media whipped itself into a frenzy over the use of the taser. The Mounties, meanwhile, sent investigators to Poland to dig up dirt on Dziekanski.

Paul Pritchard, a young Victoria, B.C. schoolteacher present in the baggage concourse at the time, had filmed the last minutes of Dziekanski's life. The RCMP members had seen him shooting what had happened and seized his camera. They promised to return it to him in two days. When he did not get the camera back, Pritchard hounded the Mounties for it. Pritchard was subsequently told that the images on his camera were prime evidence and that he would not likely get it back for two and a half years. Under Canadian law, without a warrant, the police have no right to take away the camera of a witness. Pritchard decided to fight the Mounties. He threatened court action. Finally, after 30 days, the RCMP returned the camera to him, stating that the evidence was not as conclusive as the force first thought it might be.

Pritchard reviewed the tape himself. He loaded the two-minute-and-ten-second video onto YouTube and distributed it to the media. Within hours, it was being widely viewed—to the horror of both Canadians and the international community.

On Pritchard's video, Dziekanski seems to be in obvious mental distress. He appears terrified. He is sweating. His shirt is wet. He appears to be attempting to barricade himself inside a secure area of the airport's arrivals terminal. Dziekanski lines up desk chairs, a small wooden table, and a clipboard along the doors separating the secure zone from the public waiting area. The doors wave open and shut as he builds a barricade. He steps outside the doors wielding a chair in front of him. His voice is audible. He is muttering something in Polish, which some in the crowd think is Russian.

"There's nothing wrong, it's OK," one civilian says.

A dark-haired woman, later identified as Sima Ashrafinia, approaches Dziekanski and reaches out to him, trying to calm him down. Members of her own family were deaf, so Ashrafinia uses hand gestures in an attempt to communicate with Dziekanski. When he throws a small chair against the thick glass that separates them, she does not flinch. It was clearly not aimed at her. She calls for help, but Dziekanski never threatens her. He continues to move about, ignoring her. "He's so scared," a woman can be heard saying on Pritchard's video. "Just leave him."

According to the tape, *four*—not three—RCMP officers arrive on the scene. All four are powerfully built men, each wearing body armour. They each climb over a railing and walk toward Dziekanski, who is behind the glass doors. He strenuously gestures at his luggage as they appear to be talking to him. He throws up his hands in the air and walks forward toward a glass wall. The officers follow him, indicating that he should put his hands on the counter of an information desk. Dziekanski is standing with his back to the counter as the officers fan around him.

There is the crack of the taser. Fifty thousand volts of electricity from an officer's gun shoot into Dziekanski. He winces and starts screaming. It appears he has a stapler in his hand. His arms flail. He grabs his chest and lunges to his right through a doorway, howling. He is zapped again and lands on his chest. "Hit him again! Hit him again!" a voice can be heard yelling. The Mounties said they fired the taser twice at Dziekanski. Sima Ashrafinia remembered four zaps. As Dziekanski writhes on the ground, the Mounties move in to pin him and handcuff him. In doing so, one of the Mounties places his knee into the back of Dziekanski's neck, applying his full weight. Another does the same to his lower back. Dziekanski twitches for a few seconds and then is still.

It had taken no more than 25 seconds from the time Dziekanski had been confronted by the RCMP members to the moment he passed out and, to all appearances, died. It took eight minutes for rescue workers to get to the scene, eight minutes during which the Mounties and airport staff stood around doing nothing. No one tried to resuscitate Dziekanski, although the Mounties later said the officers were monitoring his vital signs. Firefighters were the first to respond to the RCMP members' call for emergency help. When they tried to treat Dziekanski, the Mounties refused to remove their handcuffs from him. When emergency medical attendants arrived moments later, the Mounties removed the handcuffs, but Dziekanski was dead.

"There was nothing that man was doing that was threatening," police self-defence trainer Robbie Cressman said in an interview. "In a situation like that, the first thing an officer should do is assess a person's body movements. His body posture was that of confusion. He was venting and in obvious distress. He wasn't aggressive. One properly trained officer could have handled that situation, but the four of them did nothing. They didn't move him from side to side to get an angle on him. They didn't even try to take him down. It was an excellent example of improper training and the application of that poor training."

In fact, before firing at Dziekanski with the taser the four RCMP members had done nothing right. They had not correctly followed a single procedure in the National Use-of-Force Framework protocol, which was part of their training. They had made no attempt to assess Dziekanski's state of mind, talk him down, get an interpreter, or, if necessary, subdue him with hands-on physical force. They violated every protocol for confronting a person and bringing the person under control. Whatever had happened before the police arrived should have been considered by them to be in the past. At the time the police confronted him, Dziekanski, by any definition, was passive and not threatening. Reports indicated that the airport wanted the area cleared because a Singapore Airlines jumbo jet had just arrived and the passengers would be coming to that baggage area in three or four minutes. The passengers couldn't be diverted to another area?

The RCMP announced that a criminal investigation into the matter would be conducted by the Lower Mainland Integrated Homicide Unit— you got it, the RCMP—along with members from four of its captive municipal forces in the metropolis. The RCMP was investigating itself again. The federal government, provincial government, and the RCMP each announced that the investigation would be thorough and "independent," whatever that meant. The province of British Columbia, meanwhile, did nothing. Solicitor General John Les said he saw no need to do anything further. Everything was under control.

It was at this point that I was called to comment on the affair on radio and television. I conducted 15 interviews across the country on November 15 and 16, as well as participating in a lively 40-minute radio phone-in show on Vancouver's CKNW. The anger toward the RCMP was palpable and overwhelming, greater than anything reflected in the coverage of the local and national newspapers. People wanted the RCMP out of British Columbia. In all my appearances, I stated that the RCMP or any municipal force that works with the RCMP could not be trusted to do an indifferent investigation. I pointed out that, given the circumstances, particularly the appearance of a cover-up that was broken by Pritchard's videotape, Solicitor General Les was, I put it quite harshly, "nothing but a stooge for the RCMP." I suggested that the only police forces capable of standing up to the Mounties were the Toronto or Montréal city police, or either the Ontario Provincial Police or the Sûreté du Québec. Something more had to be done.

The next day, Saturday November 17, Deputy Commissioner Gary Bass announced that he had asked the Ontario Provincial Police to authorize an external and independent review of the investigation. It looked like a small victory for those who wanted the RCMP to be held accountable. Commissioner William Elliott also issued a statement in which he said that the four officers involved in Dziekanski's death had, finally, "been reassigned." To what or where, no one knew. "I recognize . . . that the RCMP cannot provide effective policing services without the support of the communities we serve, and I am concerned that growing misperceptions are eroding the public's confidence in the RCMP," Mr. Elliott wrote in a statement. "I would like to make clear that this incident is being treated very seriously by the RCMP, up to and including by me as commissioner."

The thin veneer of respect for the force shattered that weekend. Until then, the general assumption was that the RCMP's mistakes were only those of its leaders and that the Mountie on patrol was by and large a good, well-intentioned individual. That was no longer the case. Mounties on patrol found themselves being openly taunted and yelled at by bystanders. People began throwing eggs at RCMP vehicles. All the controversies had combined to take on a new dimension of mistrust of the force.

After the weekend, the B.C. government had no choice but to do something. Premier Gordon Campbell apologized to Dziekanski's mother in the Legislature for what had happened to her son. "I'm glad to apologize for what took place," Campbell said that Monday. "That was something that was devastating to her in more ways than I can even begin to imagine. I'm sure the RCMP would be glad to apologize. So I'm glad to apologize on behalf of people in British Columbia for what took place." Solicitor General Les followed with a similar apology, after, sources said, being taken out to the political woodshed that weekend.

Attorney General Wally Oppal announced a provincial inquiry into taser use headed by Tom Braidwood, a retired B.C. Court of Appeal judge. Oppal said the government was forced to launch its inquiry because all the agencies involved—the RCMP, the Canada Border Services Agency, and airport security—were being less than forthcoming. "I think it's safe to say that we were waiting for some kind of appropriate answer from the authorities and nothing was forthcoming at all," Oppal said. "We thought someone might step up and offer an explanation about what happened. You think of the repercussions here and the public deserves answers. It's all the parties who were involved. . . . There was a huge vacuum of information there."

Former judge Wally Craig later pointed out in the *North Shore News* that it was a useless gesture: "The truth of the matter: The inquiry commissioner will have no authority to deal with the RCMP and this avoidable and regrettable death."

By Tuesday, the usually truculent Solicitor General Les was now openly talking about the possibility of a single metropolitan police force for the Vancouver area, barely two weeks after he had publicly berated West Vancouver Police Chief Kash Heed for saying the same thing. "I'm interested in new ideas when it comes to policing," Les said, grudgingly.

The furor over the Dziekanski incident was so great that the RCMP, for the first time in its history, was all but forced to shut down its propaganda machine, which had always been so effective. Nobody believed the RCMP's explanations. As *The Globe and Mail* put it in an editorial: "Only the RCMP know the truth. Don't expect a straight answer."

But they still weren't beyond trying to pull strings behind the scenes. On November 19, I received a call from the CBC national radio show *The Current*, asking me to appear the next morning with host Anna Maria Tremonte. The producer asked me who the show could get to defend the RCMP's position. I told her that I didn't think there was anyone who could or would defend it. The problem she faced was that CBC policy required all stories to appear to be balanced.

"The biggest problem with so-called balanced reporting is that it is an artificial construct," I said. "It is one of the reasons why the RCMP has survived doing what it has been doing for so long. It and its partners in propaganda regularly distort or outright lie when defending the force and its actions. They have been allowed to do this in the name of fairness, but what they are actually doing is creating doubt in the mind of the public where there should be no doubt."

Ten hours later—late into the evening before the morning broadcast— senior producer Susan Campbell called me. She told me that the CBC had tried to get more than 20 current and former senior RCMP officers to go onto the show, but all had refused. Ontario Provincial Police Commissioner Julian Fantino, who was flogging his own book, had already proven in previous media appearances that he did not want to wade into the discussion. He was more interested in selling his book.

In a most telling revelation, Campbell told me that she had spoken to Ottawa Police Chief Vince Bevan, and had asked him to speak for the RCMP. "He told us that he would only do it if the RCMP was represented on the show and had invited him as a guest," Campbell said.

The Ottawa Police Service has numerous memoranda of understanding with the RCMP and must work with the force every day in the nation's capital. There was no way Bevan would dare violate any agreement the Ottawa force had with the RCMP and risk the wrath of the RCMP and its proxies. "It's pretty well a breakaway on an open net," I told Campbell.

"I can't believe it's come down to that," she said. But it had. I went on the show alone, and spoke for ten minutes. I was followed by outspoken RCMP Constable Pete Merrifield, the former Conservative candidate in Richmond Hill, who had been reassigned to the bowels of the RCMP in Newmarket, Ontario. Merrifield effectively described "the total lack of accountability in the force," as his bosses across the country took it on the chin, word after word after powerful word. A similar scenario would play out over the next few weeks, as the RCMP hunkered down. When it did speak, as Deputy Commissioner William Sweeney did on CTV's *The Verdict*, it was in a non-combative setting, where Sweeney, in full-dress regalia, downplayed all the negative talk and urged Canadians to support the RCMP in its time of need and recognize all the good it does.

Two days later, an RCMP corporal was trotted out before the cameras in one last valiant attempt to explain what had happened to Dziekanski. The corporal gamely attempted to explain how the four RCMP members had been monitoring Dziekanski's vital signs while waiting for emergency medical teams. But playing in the background of Pritchard's eyewitness video, one can clearly see one Mountie wrapping up his taser and another kneeling off to the side doing nothing. The pathetic response was a Marx Brothers moment, evoking Chico Marx's response in the 1933 movie *Duck Soup* after he had been caught in an obvious lie: "Well, who you gonna believe, me or your own eyes?"

There would be yet another major RCMP controversy in British Columbia, as if the world needed more proof of its duplicity and incompetence. Commissioner Elliott's description of "growing misperceptions . . . eroding the public's confidence," was made within days of a disturbing story making headlines in British Columbia. It involved the RCMP's greatest ever debacle, one which had been playing out for more than two decades, since the failed Air India bombing investigation begun in 1985.

Tara Singh Hayer, editor of the *Indo-Canadian Times*, was an internationally known, moderate voice in the volatile Sikh community in British Columbia. He had fearlessly campaigned to expose the criminality and dangers to be found within the extremist Sikh movement. In 1985, shortly after the Air India bombing, Hayer had been present at a meeting in London in the offices of the Punjabi-language newspaper *Desh Pardesh*, where he overheard a conversation between editor Tarsem Singh Purewal and one of the suspected bombers, Ajaib Singh Bagri. What he heard implicated a number of people, including Talwinder Singh Parmar, the accused mastermind of the plot. Three months later, Purewal was murdered near his offices, leaving Hayer as the only witness to what had been said.

In Surrey, B.C., in 1988, Hayer was shot and paralyzed. The Sikh youth arrested in the shooting was tried and convicted of attempted murder. But it was common knowledge that he had not acted on his own. Someone had hired him to shoot Hayer. From his wheelchair, Hayer continued on with his crusading journalism. Threats against him mounted, particularly after October 15, 1995, when he gave the RCMP a statement about the suspicious meeting in London ten years earlier.

The climate had become so dangerous in the Lower Mainland that the RCMP told Hayer and *Vancouver Sun* reporter Kim Bolan, who had been reporting extensively on the issue, that they had each been targeted for assassination. Shots were fired at Bolan's house and she was forced to move. The RCMP promised Hayer round-the-clock protection and even installed surveillance cameras around his Surrey residence which were connected to the nearest police station, but the family didn't think the police took the threats all that seriously. In fact, RCMP Sgt. Laurie MacDonnell had once suggested to Hayer that the best way to end the threats against him might be for him to tone down his stories and not be so critical of the people he attacked in his newspaper. Hayer refused to take the Mountie's advice.

"How can I ask someone else to stand up if I am not willing myself to stand up?" he told his son David Hayer, now a Liberal member of the British Columbia legislature. On November 18, 1998, Hayer was maneuvering his wheelchair out of his vehicle in the driveway of his home when someone shot him, execution-style. He died instantly.

Immediately, the RCMP went into its patented truth-management mode. A favourite tactic is to hide behind the cloak of an official inquiry or investigation, criminal or otherwise, so as not to disclose pertinent information—especially information that might prove to be embarrassing to the force. In 2000, the RCMP charged Bagri with Hayer's murder. Like so many botched RCMP cases, however, after the credibility of a key witness was called seriously into question, the case collapsed. For nine long years, Hayer's grief-stricken family wondered how the prosecution could have failed, especially when the crime had supposedly been caught on camera.

The answer came to light in the days after Paul Pritchard's damning video evidence of the Dziekanski incident was made public. The venue was the continuing Air India inquiry headed by former Supreme Court Justice John Major. Internal RCMP documents obtained by the inquiry showed that the force had long known that the surveillance cameras installed outside Hayer's home by the RCMP were not working, and that—unbelievably— the force had done nothing to fix them.

"It's only when I read these documents that I found out, actually, nothing worked," David Hayer told Jim Brown of the Canadian Press. "Nobody came back to us and explained *this is what had happened.*"

Hayer recalled how the RCMP had repeatedly reassured his mother about the protective measures they were providing. "They used to tell my mum, you know, nothing can happen in here, we're watching everybody, we're watching all the cars that come around the house."

"We placed our trust in the police," said Isabelle Martinez Hayer, David's wife. "They always told us that they'll take care of us, they'll take care of dad. And now to discover this is pretty tough ... It really makes you wonder."

To Commissioner Elliott, however, the content of all the criticisms about the RCMP was just so many "misperceptions."

But were they?

The tangled relationship between the RCMP and its political masters exploded into view in the spring of 2008, when B.C. Solicitor General John Les was forced to suddenly resign after it was revealed the RCMP had been investigating a shady land deal in Chilliwack in which Les seemed to have gained an illegal benefit. The investigation had been going on for at least nine months and a special prosecutor had been appointed to investigate, but the Mounties had conveniently kept a lid on it until a CBC reporter revealed what had been going on.

In spite of the fallout from the Dziekanski tragedy, the RCMP seemed to learn nothing from the experience. Its taste for tasers continued unabated. In May 2008, three officers in Kamloops were called to the Royal Inland hospital to deal with 82-year-old Frank Lasser who used an oxygen tank to survive after heart surgery. Bedridden and suffering from pneumonia, the obviously delirious Lasser was wielding a three-inch pocket knife. Rather than overpower him, the Mounties zapped him three times with a taser. "I was laying on the bed by then and the corporal came in, or the sergeant, I forget which it was, and said to the guys, 'OK, get him because we got more important work to do on the street tonight,'" Lasser told CBC news. "And then, bang, bang, bang, three times with the taser, and I tell you, I never want that again."

The Lasser story triggered another which served to confirm the extent of the problems within the RCMP. It began with a statement by psychologist

Mike Webster to the media in which he said: "I'm embarrassed to be associated with organizations that taser sick old men in hospital beds and confused immigrants who are arriving in the country."

Webster had worked with the RCMP for more than three decades and was considered to be one of the leading police psychologists in the world. It was not the first time he had spoken critically of the force. He had been frequently quoted by the media after Dziekanski's death, which he had called, among other things, "disgraceful." What happened to him after he made those comments supported what so many others have said about the force and its cult-like demand for absolute loyalty.

As Gary Mason of *The Globe and Mail* reported: Even as the words spilled from his mouth, Mr. Webster knew they had the potential to cause him more trouble with the RCMP. Mason wrote:

> In early December, Mr. Webster says he received a call from Richard Bent, chief superintendent of the RCMP E Division in Vancouver. The senior Mountie asked Mr. Webster, who lives on Denman Island, B.C., if the two could have a meeting. Mr. Webster knew something was amiss.
>
> He wanted to know immediately what it was about.
>
> "That's when he said it was about the nature of my comments to the media about the Dziekanski incident," Mr. Webster revealed in an interview Wednesday. "He said: 'You've upset some of the members here and they're saying things.' I said, 'Like what?' And he said: 'Well, they're saying that maybe you shouldn't be getting any more work with the RCMP.'"
>
> Mike Webster nearly dropped the phone.
>
> "There was only one way to interpret that comment," Mr. Webster said. "It was a clear threat."
>
> Mr. Webster said he told Chief Supt. Bent that he didn't respond well to threats. And that they wouldn't change his mind in any event. After stewing about the incident over Christmas, Mr. Webster articulated his anger in a letter to Chief Supt. Bent, which he copied to Gary Bass, the RCMP's top man in B.C. In it, he reiterated how offended he was by Chief Supt. Bent's comments, which he considered a blatant form of intimidation.
>
> He said he heard nothing back. But he did begin hearing from his friends inside the force. He said one relayed to him that Mr.

Webster's outspokenness cost the psychologist a small fee-for-service job. One of Mr. Webster's friends was told: "Don't be hiring Mike Webster. He's in shit with us for being disloyal." Another told him to expect a call from a top RCMP official in Ottawa who was going to fly out to talk to him.

Sure enough, the call came. Two weeks later, Mr. Webster said he was having lunch with an RCMP inspector from headquarters who scolded him for his Dziekanski comments. He suggested the psychologist was being disloyal to an organization that had been good to him over the years. He said Mr. Webster should have waited until the RCMP had concluded its investigation into the incident before giving any kind of opinion on it.

"I told him I didn't need anything more than the 25 seconds of video that we've all seen over and over again to offer my analysis," Mr. Webster said. "I really gave him a blast. It was just more of the same. The expectation is that if you work for the Mounties you align your values with the corporate culture and if you don't that's being disloyal and is unhealthy. . . ."

To Mr. Webster, his run-in with the Mounties reflects a more serious and systemic problem inside the organization, one recognized in the report into the RCMP pension-fund scandal. That report suggested the force was a troubled organization that did not abide dissent of any kind. And those who did offer opposing views were often shunted off to dead-end jobs and forced to wave promotions goodbye.

"As a psychologist, I know it's not healthy for people to live in such an oppressive climate," Mr. Webster said. "Being a member of the RCMP today is like being part of Putin's Russia; they don't tolerate any opinion that doesn't reflect the party line."

In June 2008, eight months after Dziekanski's death, the integrated homicide unit recommended that no charges by laid against the individual Mounties. Walter Kosteckyi, a Vancouver lawyer who represents the Dziekanski family, told the *Vancouver Sun* he could not understand why it took the police so long to finish the investigation. "The issue seems to be how could they recommend charges if that's how the officers had been trained? Of course, that raises serious concerns and questions about that training."

A few weeks later, the CBC's Kurt Petrovich used access to information legislation to uncover RCMP e-mails about the Dziekanski affair that cast doubt on the force's sincerity in getting to the bottom of the scandal. The RCMP e-mail exchange showed the forced moved quickly to create a public relations strategy. All answers were to be vetted in Ottawa—"including ones described by RCMP commissioner William Elliott as 'tough or dirty questions' from the media."

Petrovich wrote:

A day after the release of eyewitness video of the events leading up to Dziekanski's death, the RCMP commissioner called the four officers involved in the incident and expressed his support, according to the partially redacted e-mails.

"I have just now placed calls to all four members. I spoke to three or four," Elliott wrote in an e-mail dated Nov. 15, to Gary Bass, the RCMP deputy commissioner for the Pacific region.

"I know this is tough on you and all our folks in E Division. Please be assured of my ongoing support," Elliott wrote.

Bass responds the next day, writing that the commissioner's calls "were a big hit" at the Richmond detachment where the four officers work.

In another e-mail from Bass, dated Nov. 24, he describes bumping into B.C. premier Gordon Campbell at the airport, saying the premier also expressed support for the offices and the continued use of Tasers. Campbell said Wednesday that he offered support out of compassion for the officers, not as a signal he was siding with them.

The e-mails also suggest that a number of senior RCMP officers were worried about being portrayed negatively in the media, but felt the four officers at the airport had acted properly.

But the e-mail exchange between the RCMP in British Columbia and the force's headquarters in Ottawa has prompted questions from the B.C. Civil Liberties Association and Walter Kosteckyj, a lawyer representing Dziekanski's mother. They say the e-mails call into question the RCMP's public vows for transparency and accountability in the case.

✠   ✠   ✠

The deceptiveness about staffing levels and the way the RCMP spends money didn't go unnoticed in some places around the country.

For years, communities across Canada have justifiably complained that the RCMP had become a virtually invisible police force in its contract duties. When it enters into a contract, the RCMP promises 24-hour service with the best-trained police officers in the country at a price that no other police service can match. The reality is somewhat different—more like a 9 to 5 police service.

In 1996, the government of Nova Scotia ordered that several smaller communities be amalgamated into larger regions. The deployment of police became an issue since the RCMP already held contracts in some of the affected areas.

The cities of Halifax, Dartmouth, and Bedford were joined into a single political unit—the Halifax Regional Municipality—merging their police services. Halifax Region is a huge political unit, a nearly-two-hour drive from its northern boundary to its southern one. The outlying areas were policed by three RCMP detachments, Tantallon, Sackville, and Cole Harbour. Together, they employed about 200 Mounties. In the first years of the awkward relationship between the Halifax Regional Police and the RCMP, the Halifax force found that it was being called upon to do a lot of the Mounties' work. There were never enough Mounties available to do the job.

Halifax took a novel approach to the situation. The local government decided that the regional police and the Mounties should use the same record-keeping system. The Mounties at first demurred and fought the incentive. The secretive RCMP never wants anyone to know what they are really doing and had always demanded control of everything about themselves or the lead role in any joint investigation. Halifax told the RCMP that there would be no negotiations—it was their way or the highway. The Mounties caved in and adopted the Halifax Regional Police record-keeping system.

Before long, Halifax police chief Frank A. Beazley noticed something curious.

"We began to look at RCMP staffing in the area and what individual officers were doing," Beazley said in an interview. "Beside some officers' names we'd find a zero for time, zero files, zero investigations, even though they were listed as being on the roster. We asked the Mounties what was going on, but they wouldn't tell us. We sent 1,500 e-mails to the RCMP about this, but never got one reply. Eventually, we learned that one of the officers who was on our roster, was also on the roster of a force in B.C. Another was on a federal police roster, and so on."

In Alberta in 2005, complaints about invisible Mounties came to the attention of Brian Skeet, a former Calgary police officer, who that year had become assistant deputy minister in the Ministry of Public Safety. He was in charge of police services. As Skeet and his staff reviewed the RCMP records, they found themselves trying to master a maze of incomprehensible data.

"It was very confusing trying to figure out who was on the roster and what each Mountie was doing," Skeet said in an interview. "We couldn't determine for certain what they were spending their money on or how much they were spending. It was very confusing."

"Deliberately confusing?" I asked.

Skeet just raised his eyebrows, smiled, and made a facial gesture, but he wasn't prepared to put his thoughts on record, at least not at that time.

[19]

ALL THE DEAD YOUNG SAINTS

"A career nowhere near ordinary."

In 2007, the RCMP spent $800,000 on an unprecedented "award-winning" recruiting drive across the country, using a five-word slogan that seemed clever to them but suggested more than anyone might have intended. "Nowhere" is the location of many RCMP detachments. "A career nowhere" is what had happened to so many Mounties, as researchers Linda Duxbury and Chris Higgins learned in their previously-reported study of the force. In their reports on the force, they discovered that a disproportionate number of Mounties wanted out of the "horribly broken culture" that characterized the RCMP.

By October 2007, the RCMP had already admitted that it was going to fall 300 recruits short of its target of 2,000 for that year. Over the next four years, the force projected that 600 members per year were expected to retire, with others leaving for personal reasons or other jobs, often with other police forces. There was no way the RCMP could train enough new members to fill its ranks. The force had no long-term succession planning in place. It just lived day to day.

The RCMP wasn't the only police service with a recruitment problem. Geoff Gruson of the Police Sector Council said that policing is virtually off the radar for most young people these days. Fewer than 5 percent of students would even consider it as a job, certainly not as their first choice. Most recruits are anxious for jobs in urban areas with big city departments that offer interesting work and a clear career path, unlike the RCMP, despite its protestations to the contrary.

Of the many problems facing the RCMP in making itself an attractive employer, the two most important are its structure and federal government hiring mandates. To be a Mountie means that one must, in most cases, leave home and create a life elsewhere, in fact, in *many* elsewheres over a lifetime, a police vagabond.

Federal government policies on hiring have also served to cripple the force in many ways, some of which are not apparent to either the politicians or the public. In Ottawa, it is a given that Mounties be bilingual—in English and French. But in 2001 only 60 percent of Canadians reported that English was their mother tongue, and 22.9 percent that French was their mother tongue. Both are in decline, with increasing immigration from non-English and non-French-speaking countries. Chinese dialects were the third most-spoken language in Canada in 2001. Eighteen percent of the population, almost the same number as French speakers, reported that they had grown up speaking neither English nor French. By 2006, Statistics Canada found that number had risen to 20 percent. Further findings showed that the number of those who spoke French at home was in decline and that popular French immersion programs were not working all that well. "The ability of young Anglophones to maintain their knowledge of French as a second language appears to decline with time," concluded the report. Yet within the RCMP, the view was that in spite of the obvious demographic trends, the ability to speak French was more important a career-path skill than expertise in investigating crime. Officers are regularly pulled from their assignments to take French-language training.

Bilingualism is a fact of life on Parliament Hill, parts of Québec and New Brunswick, and in isolated pockets around the country. In 2006, for example, a New Brunswick woman created a brief political tempest when she filed a complaint to the federal government after a Mountie had stopped her vehicle for a traffic violation near Moncton. The Mountie couldn't speak French. RCMP policy required that a French-speaking officer be called to the scene. The woman complained that all Mounties patrolling the Trans-Canada highway be able to speak French, no matter that the Trans-Canada runs through Québec, where English-only speakers are often confronted on the highway by Sûreté officers who can't say more than "Hello" in English. Who's going to make them speak English? That's a Canadian reality. In fact, on the West Coast, Mounties say the ability to speak Mandarin or Punjabi would be more useful than English or French.

The politically motivated policy of bilingualism is an entry-level deterrent for any ambitious potential Mountie who doesn't speak French. This resulted in a skewing in the promotional system to those who speak French. This can be verified by the Mounties' own data which showed that a member in "C" Division in Montréal and to a lesser extent in "J" Division in bilingual New Brunswick earned promotions at a rate almost twice as fast as Mounties working anywhere else in the country. The upper level of the force, therefore, has become over-represented by a relatively small demographic pool, mainly individuals from Québec.

Then there are the dual issues of equality and diversity. As the RCMP states in its own literature:

"Employment equity is of crucial importance in ensuring that the Royal Canadian Mounted Police has a diverse, innovative and responsible work force fully capable of achieving its mission. The RCMP remains committed to the principle that it should reflect the diverse population of Canada to ensure effective police/community relations and the effective delivery of police services. The RCMP has committed to ensure that all employment policies, practices and standards are fully inclusive and provide all Canadians with equal and fair opportunities within the spirit of employment equity policies and legislation."

Until 1974, the RCMP was a male-only club, mostly the big white guys from small towns mainly in the Maritimes and western Canada. True to its paramilitary origins, the RCMP controlled everything about a member's life to the point where a Mountie had to receive permission from the force to marry. When women were allowed into the RCMP, it came at a price. Most of the women, naturally, couldn't meet the physical requirements facing the men, so the standards were relaxed somewhat. Those women who did make it onto the force often found themselves in a hostile environment, replete with psychological and sexual harassment. As fast as they became Mounties, they left. The RCMP churned through women for the next 35 years but has had difficulty pushing them to the top. The reason for this is because, as Linda Duxbury and Chris Higgins found in their 2004 study, women who join the RCMP aren't all that interested in promotion. They would rather nest in a place, collect the benefits, and retire with a lucrative full pension.

Too many of these female Mounties, lured by the status and security of the position, had gone into policing for wrong reasons. The RCMP soon found that one of the first things many of the young new female officers did was to get pregnant and begin raising a family. The force had no plan for covering the missing members who were off on generous federal government extended leaves. Many female members thought that they'd spend a few years on the job and then graduate to school safety officer or something just as sublime. Back on the job, the women found that the endemic short-staffing meant that they would have to undertake the kind of dirty police work they didn't relish or had not even contemplated doing, even though they were earning equal pay for work of equal value. Being a young mother and grappling with rowdies outside town bars five nights a week was not their intended career path. All this has been further aggravated by the fact that a high proportion of female officers were among the first to book off on stress leave, and to stay off the job for prolonged periods.

It is a serious problem across the board in all policing agencies and correctional institutions, a story that has gone unreported because it is deemed to be so politically incorrect and controversial to state such facts, in spite of the abundant evidence. In prisons, the big guys—white, black, and any other colour for that matter—do most, if not all, the dangerous work. They know that in life-and-death situations, few women have the physical strength to defend either themselves or their partners or the mental toughness to fire a weapon when required to do so.

Although many Mounties complain privately or off the record about this, only a few will speak openly. One of them is undercover specialist, former RCMP Inspector Bill Majcher, whom we met previously. "In my experience," Majcher said, "about one or two of any ten female police officers has the mental and physical ability to do the entire job. When it comes to heavy lifting, the men have to do it all. In most places, the women arrange their lives so that they don't have to go out after dark. It's rare to find a woman doing a dangerous assignment at 3 a.m. That's not fair to anyone."

It is less than fair and not good public policy. Since physically capable men are the ones who get thrown into the most dangerous situations, they are more likely to end up in controversy. In the RCMP, controversy is the kiss of death to a career. The men are in a no-win situation and morale plummets along with effectiveness. Many women, meanwhile, fly under the radar, having never been exposed to the heat. With their clean records and unblemished careers, like so many other male Mounties in non-contact postings they earn quicker promotions, much of it based on fantasy.

All this was compounded by the disastrous recruitment policies of the 1990s. The perfect Mountie on recruiting posters was anything but a big white guy—a female, a visible minority or even someone in their forties or fifties. The stated rationale for the older recruits was that the force wanted to attract mature people with life experience. What that really meant was that the RCMP was hoping to find Mounties who didn't need much supervision, a way of saving money. As then-Commissioner Philip Murray put it at the time: "We want to empower the Mountie on the street."

A further difficulty in achieving this goal was that people who reflected diversity were being asked to take positions across the country in communities where they were sometimes the only member of their ethnic group. A black man or woman from northwest Africa didn't stand a chance in northwest Alberta, or many other locales for that matter. For those interested in a career in policing, therefore, the Mountie uniform might be iconic, but the Mountie way of life a personal disaster. The choice was easy. For those people, municipal forces were a much more attractive alternative.

In 2007, the RCMP's recruitment campaign didn't delve into such subtleties and verities. It didn't talk about the high divorce rate, the alcoholism, and the constant debilitating stress, but rather it took a leaf, as usual, from the Johnny Mercer songbook, "Accentuate the Positive," and it only sang about its perceived glories and the privilege of wearing the scarlet red tunic. The most important thing that the RCMP didn't tell its potential recruits was something about which its own members were well aware after the 1990s: the RCMP had become the most dangerous law enforcement agency in North America for a working police officer.

✝ ✝ ✝

Of all the Mounties to whom a new cadet might be introduced, the last would be Staff Sgt. Gaétan Delisle, the one-time mayor of St-Blaise-sur-Richelieu, introduced earlier. I first met Delisle at Magnan's, a popular restaurant and tavern in Pointe St. Charles, overlooking the shipping canal which cuts through Montréal. I didn't know what to expect. In any military or paramilitary force, it has often been said that the staff sergeants command the most respect. After 38 years in the RCMP, his red hair turning grey, Delisle still physically fits his title. He is the kind of imposing, chiselled bull who might cause an unsuspecting criminal caught in a dark alley to wet his pants. In his almost four decades inside the RCMP, Delisle has taken no bull from anyone, not even the commissioner of the day.

Delisle is the godfather of the union movement within the force. He was at the first meeting in 1974, when disgruntled RCMP members gathered to complain about their horrible working conditions. In response, the RCMP set up the Staff Relations Representative (SRR) Program, copied from a similar program in the United Kingdom. The difference, however, was that unlike the British model, the RCMP version wasn't independent and wasn't allowed to negotiate with the government. The SSR's motto is "Members First," but Delisle and thousands of other Mounties believe that its true motto is: "RCMP First, Members Last." By 2007, the backlog of unresolved grievances was almost two years long.

Within the SSR system, each division has a representative, a DivRep, as that person is called. For the past 31 years in Québec, the elected DivRep for "C" Division has been Delisle, precisely the antithesis of who the RCMP had envisioned as shop steward in the company union. His constant hammering away at the system has earned him four SSR suspensions, and each time he has fought his way back, stronger than ever. As he describes his trials and tribulations, he pounds the table with his massive fist and often uses the mild French epithet, "*tabernac*," to help express his dissatisfaction. What drives Delisle is not better pay, because the Mounties are now well paid, but the treatment and safety of officers.

"It is a joke," Delisle said of the SSR system. "We get young members who transfer to Québec and they learn for the first time that they are entitled to family leave. In the contract provinces, the RCMP takes advantage of the young. The system is corrupt. All the supervisors are getting bonuses for meeting their budgets. The young members can only earn their scheduled salary increases, at six months, twelve months, and twenty-four months, if there is a recommendation from the supervisor. Is a young Mountie going to say no to a supervisor and insist on backup before taking an assignment or is he just going to go ahead and take a risk to please his supervisor? You know the answer to that one. The supervisors have a conflict. When the capacity to manage a budget is directly linked to promotion, which one does a supervisor give up? The RCMP tries to run detachments as if each were a Wal-mart store, and that's wrong.

"The RCMP does what it wants and its employees have no protections. They must just follow orders, even if those orders are questionable. There is no major police force in North America that operates like the RCMP. In other places the union and management work together as a check and balance. In the RCMP, members have no say in what they do or about their personal health and safety. They can't refuse work without losing their jobs. If members had a say, someone they could talk to without being punished, a lot of the crazy things that have happened would not have taken place. The

RCMP is a dangerous place to work, and I have spent my life trying to improve things for the members."

Dangerous it is.

With 16,000 or so sworn officers, the RCMP is by any standard a large police service. In its contract capacity as a provincial or municipal police service, its jurisdictions are largely rural, even territorial. It provides only federal policing for the almost 20 million Canadians who live in Ontario and Québec. It doesn't service any of the larger cities in western Canada—Winnipeg, Brandon, Regina, Saskatoon, Edmonton, Calgary, Vancouver, or Victoria. With the exceptions of the large suburbs of Vancouver and the Codiac Region in New Brunswick, the land of the Mounties is the vast expanses of Canada, with a force of about 10,000 members in contract policing. Canada is a country that prides itself on strict gun control and one of the lowest murder rates in the industrialized world. With a total population of more than 33 million, Canada recorded only 605 murders in 2006.

A comparable-sized service with similar conditions can be found in the Australian state of New South Wales. Australia, with a population of almost 21 million and strict gun controls, has about the same per capita murder rate as Canada. The jurisdiction of the New South Wales Police Force is the entire state of seven million people, including Sydney, where four million people live. In 2007, the NSW Police Force employed 14,454 sworn officers, and was continuing to grow. Like the RCMP, the NSW does international policing and peacekeeping work for the United Nations.

But since Canada is situated next to the United States, a bastion of weapons of every sort as well as having a violent, murderous culture, the best comparison might be with U.S. police services. With a population nearly 10 times larger than Canada, the United States had almost 30 times more murders in 2006, a total of 17,034. Most Canadians believe that U.S. cities like New York, Philadelphia, Washington, and Chicago are dangerous places, which they are. Charlotte-Mecklenburg, N.C. is about a quarter the size of Toronto, but has about the same number of murders annually. The murder rate in some of those cities is almost equal to all of Canada. For example, New York City, with eight million residents, had about 500 murders in 2007, down from 596 murders in 2006. Los Angeles had almost 500, while Chicago, Detroit, and Philadelphia each had more than 400.

One would assume that being a police officer in Canada would be about as safe as in New South Wales and inherently less dangerous than in the United States. In general, that is true. Over the past decade, every year, between

145 and 170 U.S. police officers die on the job. In Canada, every year a handful of officers might die in the line of duty, as is the case in New South Wales, Australia.

Since September 2000, for example, seven NSW officers were killed in the line of duty, one by gunshot and the others in motor vehicle accidents or chases. Four others died from illness on the job or work-related illnesses, which I will ignore for the purposes of this analysis.

In Toronto, Canada's largest city, only one officer, Constable Laura Ellis, has died on duty since September 2000. She was killed in 2002 when her patrol car was involved in a collision with another vehicle while responding to a call. The Ontario Provincial Police has lost six members through various automobile accidents. Montréal police have had two of its officers killed since 2000, one in a motorcycle accident and the other, Constable Benoit L'Ecuyer, shot after a police pursuit.

All those numbers are reversed, however, when it comes to the performance of the RCMP. Since September 2000, when Giuliano Zaccardelli became commissioner, the RCMP has had 20 members killed while doing their job, 18 under Zaccardelli and two more in the first few months of William Elliott's tenure. If we were to expand the criteria to include the two months before Zaccardelli took over, there have been 23 RCMP deaths since July 2000.

By comparison, the New York City police department maintains a staff of officers that fluctuates between 38,000 and 41,000 depending on budgeting. There are also an additional 13,000 special purpose police on the streets of New York, involved in schools, transit, and housing. Since September 2000, the New York City police department has had 34 officers killed in the course of carrying out their duties. Twenty-three of those died in the World Trade Center attack, while only 11 NYPD officers have died on the streets since that time, including two auxiliary police forces. The Chicago Police Department employs more than 13,000 officers and is almost as large as the RCMP. Since September 2000, it has had eight officers killed in the line of duty, including three in automobile crashes, one who was hit by a train, and one in a training accident. In Philadelphia, where there are almost 7,000 officers, five have been killed during that period, one of whom was struck by a vehicle. In Charlotte-Mecklenburg, three died. The only U.S. police service with a death rate comparable to the RCMP is the California Highway Patrol, a force with about 7,000 uniformed members. The CHP also had 20 members killed during the same period, 16 of them in traffic or vehicular pursuit situations.

In virtually every case with a Mountie fatality, it comes down to a combination of the same four equations: poor training, relative inexperience on the job, inadequate resources, and under-supervision. The warning signs have been there for years.

In my second book, *The Last Guardians*, published in 1998, I went out on a night patrol with Constable Ken Aspen out of Winnipegosis, Manitoba. The closest Mountie on duty that night was 150 kilometres or so away. When Aspen stopped a car in the middle of nowhere, filled with a group of men, Aspen told me how to use the shotgun if the situation went south. He said his best weapon was his mouth. That night it worked.

In another vignette, I related the story about a police chase and head-on crash well after midnight on a dark road in the Vancouver suburb of Burnaby. There were not enough police officers available to properly cordon off the area, so I ended up having to stop a speeding car hurtling toward the crash site. It was clear to me that RCMP officers were being asked to do more than they possibly could safely accomplish, but the message was ignored, with dire consequences.

"The past seven years have been a disaster," said Staff Sgt. Delisle, "but the brass don't care. They say they care, but then they do nothing. They hold a regimental funeral, lots of tears are shed, much alcohol is drunk, and then they move on to the next one. Nobody wants to do the right thing."

✝ ✝ ✝

The first Mountie to die on Giuliano Zaccardelli's watch was Constable Jurgen Seewald. A 26-year veteran of the RCMP, he was a decorated peacekeeper for his work in Bosnia. In the early-morning hours of March 5, 2001, Seewald responded alone to a domestic dispute in Cape Dorset, Nunavut Territory, in Canada's sparsely populated far North. The female complainant had told the RCMP dispatcher that her common-law husband, Salomonie Jaw, was threatening violence and had a gun. Seewald was killed by a shotgun blast inside the residence. Seewald became the first Mountie to be killed in Canada's North in 25 years, since the 1979 drownings of two other Cape Dorset Mounties during a walrus hunt. He was not going to be the last.

Constable Peter Magdic had been a Mountie for 11 months when he rolled his Chevrolet Tahoe police vehicle off a road south of Portage la Prairie, Manitoba on November 18, 2001. He was returning from a routine call on Long Plain First Nation.

The next month, on December 21, 2001, and only a few miles away, Constable Dennis Strongquill, 52, an Aboriginal and father of six, was on his way back to his detachment after buying a coffee. He stopped a suspicious car near Dauphin which had been stolen by three gun-toting youths who were on a crime spree. He ordered the youths to follow him back to the detachment. When he got out of his car, coffee in hand, he was gunned down. One of the suspects was shot by police later that day after a standoff in Saskatchewan.

In March 2002, Constable Christine Diotte was killed after being struck by a vehicle that had lost control on icy roads. She had been investigating another accident.

Two weeks later, Constable Wael Audi attempted a U-turn to chase another car and was broadsided by a bus in Squamish, B.C. In September of that year, Constable Jimmy Ng, 31, was killed by a hit-and-run driver in Richmond, B.C. Three months later, Superintendent Dennis Massey of Calgary died after a tanker-truck driver lost control of his vehicle and his trailer broke loose and slammed into Massey's vehicle, a truly tragic, and unavoidable, accident. On June 10, 2003, the string of traffic deaths ended with the death of Constable Ghislain Maurice whose unmarked vehicle collided with a dump truck near Sherwood Park, Alberta, east of Edmonton.

Eight months later, in Sherwood Park, on February 8, 2004, Constable James Galloway, 55, a dog handler with 35 years service in the force, was called to the scene of a standoff involving Martin Ostopovich, a man with known psychiatric problems. He was armed with a high-powered rifle.

The standoff became a prolonged one because the RCMP did not have a dedicated emergency response team in the area. As is the custom, members of the ERT teams were spread out around the province. It wouldn't be the first or the last time RCMP officers across the country would have to fend for themselves because their superiors, mindful of their budgets, didn't want to use the ERT teams for the precise purpose for which they were intended. One of the ERT members who was at the Ostopovich property was Constable Stephen Vigor, who took command of the situation.

When Ostopovich tried to leave the scene in his own vehicle, Constable Galloway rammed it with his cruiser. Ostopovich shot Galloway, killing him. The other officers then shot and killed Ostopovich.

Judge Peter Ayotte led an inquiry into the shooting. Ayotte recommended that the RCMP increase its resources for emergency response teams. The RCMP paid only lip service to the notion. It was a lapse that would come to haunt the force and the country a year later.

One more Mountie would die on the job in 2004. At 2 a.m. on November 13, 2004, in Vernon, B.C., RCMP officers became involved in the chase of a stolen truck, a chase that was eventually called off. But it wasn't over. Auxiliary Constable Glen Evely, 39, was one of the late-bloomer RCMP members, who had joined the force two years earlier. He was riding in a police vehicle that was rammed at an intersection by the fleeing truck and killed instantly. Throughout all these events, the RCMP wrote off everything as being coincidence, the regrettable but expected tragedy that often comes with doing a dangerous job like police enforcement. All those who died were described by the force as heroes, brave people who just happened to be in the wrong place at the wrong time. The RCMP's bad run of luck, ten dead Mounties in three years, was about to get even worse. As it did, it became even more difficult for the RCMP to tell the truth about anything it was doing.

Mayerthorpe, Alberta, is a small farming community northwest of Edmonton, on the edge of the Alberta foothills. It is known as the starting point for the Cowboy Trail, a 700-kilometre drive south to the Montana border. The area has become popular for filmmakers hoping to capture an authentic western feel. Clint Eastwood's Oscar-winning movie, *Unforgiven*, was filmed along the Cowboy Trail, as were Ang Lee's controversial *Brokeback Mountain*, *Legends of the Fall*, and *The Assassination of Jesse James*, starring Brad Pitt. What happened in Mayerthorpe on March 3, 2005, continues to haunt the RCMP and the country.

The official story began the day before on March 2 at around 3 p.m., after two bailiffs approached the padlocked gate to the rural property of James Roszko. The men were there to execute a civil court order to seize his white Ford pickup truck. Roszko was the town bully, a man with a long record of criminal behaviour, sexual deviance, and violence. He had been imprisoned for two and a half years earlier for sexually assaulting his underage stepbrother. When he saw the bailiffs, Roszko got into his truck and confronted them at the gate. He then released two of his guard dogs before driving away across a field to the other side of his property.

The bailiffs knew how dangerous the situation might be. In an affidavit sworn days later, one of them wrote that he feared Roszko would shoot anyone on his property, adding: "The debtor is quite dangerous, has a long history of assaults, is in possession of a number of firearms . . . and is known to have booby-trapped land. We just never went out there alone . . . because of his reputation."

Before going onto the property, the bailiffs called the RCMP for help.

At 3:25 p.m., Corporal James Martin, along with Constable Peter Schiemann, arrived at the Roszko farm to assist the bailiffs. By then, Roszko had left the area in his white truck. Schiemann was a budding drug investigator. The Mounties had long suspected that Roszko was growing marijuana in his metal Quonset hut. This suspicion was bolstered by the fact that power company officials had noted spikes in his electrical usage which they'd reported to police. The Mounties, eager to see what was inside the Quonset hut, accompanied the bailiffs over the fence and into the building. There they found stolen vehicles, "chopped" truck parts, a stolen generator, and a modest marijuana-growing operation.

The bailiffs left and the RCMP took control of the property. Spokesmen for the force said the Mounties tried to find Roszko that afternoon and evening, but could not. However, Diane Romeo, a local resident, told police she had seen Roszko at around 4 p.m. driving on a road near his farm. Although an alert was put out for Roszko and his vehicle, it's not clear how much effort was put into a further search.

Shortly after 4 p.m., Martin and Schiemann left two other RCMP constables, Julie Letal from Mayerthorpe and Trevor Josok from nearby Whitecourt, to guard the property. Martin and Schiemann returned to their detachment to draw up Criminal Code and narcotics search warrants and have them approved. Letal was nervous about being there, not knowing where Roszko was at the time. It was known in the community and by the RCMP that Roszko had vowed to kill a Mountie rather than be arrested and sent back to jail.

There was a further complication that the Mounties seemed willing to ignore. Canadian law dictates that the police cannot use a civil warrant to conduct a criminal investigation and search. The bailiffs had an order to seize only the white truck, which they knew was no longer there. Whatever the Mounties found in the Quonset hut would likely be deemed tainted, something the wily Roszko likely knew as well.

Corporal Martin returned at 8:40 p.m. with a search warrant that was valid until 8 p.m. the next evening. During a related search of Roszko's residence, the police found handwritten lists itemizing the names of RCMP members from Mayerthorpe, Whitecourt, and Evansburg detachments. Beside each name was the call sign of the police car normally used by each RCMP member and the cellular telephone numbers assigned to each car. The police also found ammunition, but no weapons, which should have been an ominous sign that Roszko was armed.

The Edmonton RCMP Auto Theft Section was called to attend and complete a detailed examination to identify which vehicle parts had been stolen. Constables Garrett Hoogestraat and Stephen Vigor said they would be at Roszko's property the following morning to conduct their investigation. Vigor was the part-time ERT member who had been at the shooting of RCMP dog handler James Galloway, eight months earlier in Sherwood Park, Alberta.

Before Constable Letal left the scene, she warned her colleagues to be careful. "I told the boys to make sure everything's clear, because he's watching us," Letal said. Her concerns and warnings were ignored. The big boys were going to take care of it.

During that evening, various police units arrived to search, collect evidence, and plan strategy for the next day. Mayerthorpe detachment commander Sergeant Brian Pinder, the so-called "police chief" of the town, mapped out a plan for the next day with one of his corporals. The last investigators left at 3:30 a.m. They took with them 280 marijuana plants. Left behind on the scene were two junior members, Constables Anthony Gordon, 28, who had joined the force two and a half years earlier, and Leo Johnston, 33, who had been a Mountie for four years. Their job was to sit out on the cold, dark night and protect the scene until investigators returned in the morning. No one knew where Roszko was. RCMP procedures dictated that since Gordon and Johnston were not under immediate threat they could not carry long arms. Stashed in the trunks of their patrol cars were a .308 calibre rifle and a .12 gauge shotgun.

The plan devised by Sergeant Pinder was that two other junior officers would relieve the Mounties in the morning after the auto-theft team was scheduled to arrive from Edmonton. Shortly before 9:00 a.m., Corporal Martin checked with Constables Gordon and Johnston. The constables told Martin they had not seen Roszko during their watch. No one knew where he was. But still no one heeded Constable Letal's intuition that Roszko was watching them.

Constable Schiemann, who had instigated the investigation the previous day, had planned to travel to Edmonton, one and a half hours away, to buy some work-related equipment and supplies. The 25-year-old Schiemann had been a Mountie for a little more than four years. He was primarily a highway patrolman. In plain clothes and unarmed, he drove 29-year-old Constable Brock Myrol, who had only been a Mountie for three weeks, to the Roszko property.

A few minutes later, Constables Hoogestraat and Vigor, the Edmonton based auto-theft investigators, showed up. They stopped near the road waiting for another team to arrive. They saw that two of the young Mounties were on top of a shed, a short distance from the Quonset hut. The two other men were administering a mild sedative to Roszko's dogs. The four Mounties then walked to the Quonset hut and entered it through a door.

Sometime during the evening Roszko had slipped back into the building. The police suspect that he had covered himself with a white blanket as he crawled across the snow-covered field. As the four Mounties entered the hut, Roszko cut down all of them—Gordon, Johnston, Myrol, and Schiemann—in a blaze of gunfire. He was armed with a Heckler & Koch model 91 semiautomatic rifle. He was also carrying a .308 rifle with a 20-round detachable clip. The Mounties didn't stand a chance. Only Johnston managed to get off a shot, but he hit nothing.

Hoogestraat and Vigor heard the shots and then saw Roszko emerge from the building carrying his weapons. He began to fire at the Mounties, just missing them. Vigor fired back with his handgun, wounding Roszko. The gunman fled back into the Quonset hut, and shortly afterward a single shot was heard. Roszko had committed suicide.

Hoogestraat and Vigor called for assistance. They tried to raise the four Mounties inside on their radios. There was no response; just dead silence. Vigor decided to exercise caution and not charge into the Quonset hut. It had only been eight months since the last time he had been in a similar situation. At that time the decision had been made to attack the suspect, which ended up in the death of Constable James Galloway. It was now just after 9 a.m.

Calls for assistance were made and the RCMP leapt into action, such as it was. The first official RCMP description of what had taken place read:

> Cst. Vigor and the second Auto Theft member took cover and called for assistance. Due to lighting and positioning the Auto Theft members were not able to see into the Quonset and efforts to communicate with anyone inside was met with negative results. The RCMP Edmonton Emergency Response Team was immediately deployed

with the Red Deer Team called to provide additional support and back-up. The RCMP Police Service Dog and handler, RCMP Explosive Disposal Unit, Edmonton Police Service's Air One and Stars Air Ambulance were all immediately dispatched.

At 2:00 p.m. on March 3, 2005, members from the RCMP Explosive Disposal Unit deployed their Remote Mechanical Investigator, a robot, to enter and assess the inside of the Quonset. At 2:15 p.m. the command was given for the Emergency Response Team to enter and secure the Quonset. This process involved removal of the bodies of our fallen members to positions outside the structure for further medical assessment and to address officer safety inside the Quonset. Despite previous efforts to describe this process images captured of the bodies outside the Quonset have left some believing that some or all of the officers were shot while outside. This is not the case.

The entire property was ordered locked down and treated as a crime scene. RCMP "K" Divisions Major Crimes were called in to conduct the criminal investigation. Investigative resources from across the country were called in to provide assistance.

At some point in time James Roszko sustained a gunshot wound before re-entering the Quonset and taking his own life. . . .

Canada was in shock.

It was the worst slaughter of Canadian police officers in living memory. Regimental funerals were held for each of the members, with police officers from across the continent in attendance. The parents of the dead Mounties were taken under the wing of the force and consoled. As they publicly lamented the loss of their loved ones, the families rallied behind the RCMP. Any suggestion that laxity, incompetence, and indifference by the RCMP might have been a factor in the four deaths was dismissed. No criticism of the RCMP would be entertained.

The RCMP immediately flooded the area with officers from around the country trying to get answers to the looming questions about what had happened. As the funerals were being arranged, a search warrant was drafted in an attempt to find possible co-conspirators, people who might have helped and assisted Roszko while he was hiding from the police that night.

As the investigation continued, the RCMP went into its by-now-familiar requiem mode. Public testimonials were made about each of the four dead men. Constable Schiemann, who had driven Constable Myrol to the Roszko property, was described this way by the RCMP: "Schiemann was not on duty, he was not in uniform and not armed. In the true spirit of dedication and professionalism Cst. Schiemann volunteered to drive Cst. Myrol to the scene before traveling on to Edmonton." Everyone was a hero in the eyes of the RCMP, but many policing experts had come to another conclusion almost from the moment the shots had rung out. These people suspected that the four dead Mounties were needless victims of the RCMP's broken culture.

The RCMP's official story was deftly painted in shades of truth. Roszko was a madman who had sneaked back into the building and murdered the Mounties. That much was true. The RCMP blurred the truth to the point of cooperating in a made-for-television movie which the force vetted "for accuracy."

First broadcast in February 2008, *Mayerthorpe* began with a disclaimer by the filmmakers that the characters and events being depicted were fictional. Once the slow-moving story began, the audience was plied with many false impressions and distorted information. The most significant distortion was the suggestion that the RCMP's efforts to control Roszko in the past had been stymied by a liberal and ineffective justice system. The four victims were portrayed in cameo appearances as being little more than jesters providing comic relief. But the movie had its intended effect. The next day's radio talk shows across the country were filled with invective about the judicial system and how prosecutors and the courts had all but fired the fatal shots.

The true story about Mayerthorpe could not be told because the RCMP would never allow it.

Like so many RCMP tragedies and missteps, Mayerthorpe had many more layers than were first apparent. What is clear is that the debacle revealed much that was defective with the RCMP and its culture—the tyranny of business efficiency, poor training, inadequate procedures, and the ever-present cover-up mentality. It was obvious to anyone who had any police training that the RCMP had done just about everything wrong, including the following:

- In the made-for-television movie about the incident, one RCMP officer was depicted as dogging Roszko for at least 13 years. However, the character was a composite. In fact, due to chronic short-staffing and high turnover in Mayerthorpe, the RCMP had all but lost track of Roszko. There was no institutional memory of him.

- The original search conducted with the bailiff during which the Quonset hut was entered by the police was illegal and would likely not stand up in court. Roszko should have been a known threat to police, but the Mounties were surprised during their search to find the names and addresses of police officers, as well as ammunition, but no guns. Constable Julie Letal sensed the danger, but nothing was done about her concerns. None of the young officers could refuse the order to undertake the mission. To do so would risk their careers. The RCMP did not have control of either Roszko or the property. They knew he was hostile and likely armed, and had no idea where he was while two lightly-armed officers were left overnight to guard the area. The rifles and shotguns, as per RCMP policy, were in the trunks of their patrol cars.

- An unarmed police officer, Schiemann, was allowed to enter the site, a violation of even the RCMP's own rules. In spite of all this, there was no supervisor onsite. The RCMP's emergency response team should have been called in the evening before, but was not. RCMP policy is to charge a fee to a detachment for the use of such special services, a fee that would be counted as an expense on the budget of a sergeant hoping to impress his superiors and win promotion. Getting by is the RCMP way.

- The ERT teams within the RCMP were still not cohesive units, but made up of members scattered around a wide area. In spite of the death of dog handler Jim Galloway 13 months earlier, not that far away in Edmonton, and the obvious inadequacy of the ERT system, nothing had been done to rectify the problem.

- After the shootings, the RCMP took *five* hours to get a team together capable of entering the Quonset hut where the injured or dead officers were lying in their own blood. All procedures were followed. Bravery was discouraged.

As usual, the RCMP's official story about the incident seemed a little too disingenuous for even some of its own members. Several days after the shooting, one Mountie called into an Alberta-wide radio show and said that the closest ERT team was in Calgary, not Edmonton or Red Deer, as the force had claimed.

Another Mountie who was called to the scene of the shootings to help with the investigation said the physical evidence did not match the story. "Leo Johnston's vehicle was all shot up. It looked like he was hiding behind the car and that there was a gun battle, and he was killed right there," the Mountie said. "The brass says all the members were killed inside the building, and that his body was dragged out by the first ERT members who got there, five hours after he had been shot. That doesn't jive with their training. They were obviously all dead. No cop was going to disturb the crime scene."

Producer Scott Anderson of *the fifth estate* spent nine months in Mayerthorpe and environs trying to figure out what had happened. *The fifth estate* was forced to mount a six-month-long court battle to get access to the search warrants obtained by the RCMP after the murders. The RCMP had asked the courts to seal the documents.

Anderson found that the story contained in the search warrants showed that the police knew almost immediately after the murders what Roszko had been doing before and after the event. The police knew who he was seeing between the time he left his farm and when he committed suicide after killing the police officers. Anderson had seen a number of search warrants over the course of his career and he did not find these ones to be all that remarkable. He couldn't figure out why they had been sealed.

Anderson didn't yet appreciate just how wily the RCMP was. History has shown that what the RCMP always does in a controversial matter is devise ways to stall for important time: time for the heat to die down, time to move culpable officers out of the line of fire, time to massage and whitewash the official story, a process which could go on for many years. For their efforts, Anderson and *the fifth estate* were trashed in a local newspaper for trying to make the RCMP look bad, which was seen to be disrespectful to the four dead Mounties.

By 2007, the Mayerthorpe incident would still not go away. In spite of a dubious government study which found that worker safety had not been compromised, the force was being pressed for answers by some of its own members.

"Mayerthorpe is a ticking time bomb for the RCMP," Montréal lawyer James Duggan predicted in a 2007 interview. As the longtime legal representative of the 3,000 RCMP members seeking the right to form a union, Duggan had been pressing for more answers. At the time this book was being written, he said that he had been privy to some of the evidence in the case. "I can't say what it is at this point, but some time in the future, probably late 2008 or early 2009, it's all going to come out, and it's not going to look good for the RCMP."

Sealing the search warrants was only one of the RCMP's stalling tactics. The force has also had a long history of attempting to refocus the public's attention by changing the subject with a dramatic announcement. In the past when facing a swelling controversy, the RCMP has often fought back by trumpeting major initiatives like a new organized crime unit or the arrest of some high-profile criminal. To astute observers of the RCMP, such announcements have become all too predictable.

When William Elliott was named to take over as the civilian commissioner of the RCMP, on July 6, 2007, the public was torn about whether or not it was a good idea. Even the Mayerthorpe families, coddled as they were by the force, expressed their concerns in the media. Two days after Elliott's appointment, on a Sunday no less, a day in which a tornado narrowly missed the town, the RCMP called a press conference. It announced that after a long undercover operation, two more men had been arrested in the case. Deputy Commissioner Bill Sweeney, the commanding officer of "K" Division and soon to be Elliott's right-hand man in Ottawa, issued a release that addressed the difficulties of the case, the force's high motives, and its extraordinary diligence. It read, in part:

> The twenty-eight-month long criminal investigation has been conducted utilizing the principles of Major Case Management (Team Leader, Lead Investigator and File Coordinator), a proven investigational technique used to ensure that no aspect of evidence or potential witnesses is overlooked. In part, this process treats every tip, witness and piece of evidence as a separate investigation within the primary investigation. Accordingly, all aspects of the investigation are carefully monitored to ensure the highest degrees of investigational standards are maintained. "To leave no stone unturned."
>
> This investigation has been conducted in the same manner as any serious investigation especially those addressing the loss of life, any life.
>
> The RCMP is committed to providing Canadians with timely updates on matters such as the Mayerthorpe investigation. While we understand the overwhelming need to know, we must ensure that our actions do not interfere with nor are perceived to interfere with the administration of justice.

The diligence, dedication and professionalism exercised by investigators, support personnel and supervisors involved in the Mayerthorpe investigation has been exemplary. Every step of the investigation was conducted in a professional manner, subject to the same review, approval and management principles applied in any serious criminal investigation. The fact that it took twenty-eight months to reach this point speaks to the fact that every case is unique, some will be concluded in short order, some may take years to solve and some may never reach a point of successful conclusion.

After twenty-eight months of investigation including a lengthy undercover operation and continuous support and consultation with our colleagues in the Provincial Crown's Office, Dennis Keegan Rodney Cheeseman, age twenty-three, and Shawn William Hennessey, age twenty-eight, of Barrhead, Alberta, have been charged with four counts of first degree murder, one count each for the deaths of Constable Anthony Gordon, Constable Leo Johnston, Constable Brock Myrol and Constable Peter Schiemann. Cheeseman and Hennessey are charged as a party to the offences committed by James Roszko. Section 21 of the Criminal Code addresses parties to offences and states:

21. (1) Every one is a party to an offence who
(a) Actually commits it;
(b) Does or omits to do anything for the purpose of aiding any person to commit it;
(c) Abets any person in committing it.

(2) Where two or more persons form an intention in common to carry out an unlawful purpose and to assist each other therein and any one of them, in carrying out the common purpose, commits an offence, each of them who knew or ought to have known that the commission of the offence would be a probable consequence of carrying out the common purpose is a party to that offence.

Cheeseman and Hennessey are scheduled to appear in Mayerthorpe Provincial Court on July 12, 2007.

The Mayerthorpe investigation is ongoing as investigators continue with their efforts to ensure every element is thoroughly investigated, documented and processed.

Today we have been able to provide Canadians with the first

significant update on the Mayerthorpe investigation. It is truly recognized that many questions remain unanswered. As addressed earlier we have an obligation and responsibility to respect due process. While the investigation is winding down two very important processes, criminal charges before the court and a Fatality Inquiry must be respected. As each process moves into the public domain we will then have additional answers to many more outstanding questions.

Deputy Commissioner Sweeney, Commanding Officer of RCMP "K" Division would like to specifically thank the families of the fallen four for their patience throughout this most difficult time. I would also like to thank the Canadian public and the membership of the RCMP for their patience and support throughout the course of the criminal investigation, as well as those in the media that have exercised patience, discretion and professionalism.

The media that night and the next day blasted the story across the country, but Scott Anderson, obviously one of the journalists, in the RCMP's opinion, who had not exercised "patience, discretion and professionalism," was appalled by the announcement and the way that even his own organization, the CBC, had covered the story.

"The RCMP made it look like it took them 28 months to track down Cheeseman and Hennessey, but everything they had done was in the original search warrants," Anderson said. "We reported on that in 2006, but even the CBC seems to have forgotten what its own staff had done. It was all bull."

If the intent of the arrests was to make the force and its new commissioner look like they were on top of their game, it did not work. Few believed the charges would stick. Roszko had been feared in the community. No one would stand up to him. Cheeseman and Hennessey were not even at the scene. First-degree murder seemed like a stretch.

When the two men were arraigned in court, the community rallied behind them, creating a scene at the courthouse. John Cotter of the Canadian Press reported that one distraught man, "his face flushed and his body shaking with sobs, startled the courtroom when he stood up and asked for people's attention. 'I am an ambassador of Jesus Christ, we need to pray.'" Mayerthorpe resident Chris Gordon was quoted as saying: "It is just a big political thing because they have got lots of pressure to come down on somebody. It's a bunch of crap. So far, they are being portrayed as cop killers, as haters. They are respectable people in the community. They work hard every day. They've got families."

The courts seemed to agree. Before their preliminary trial began in May 2008, a judge allowed each man to post bail and get out of jail. With the snail-like pace of the Canadian justice system, the charges bought the RCMP more time before it had to reveal the true story behind Mayerthorpe, but it did not make the force any smarter about the safety of its own officers.

✝ ✝ ✝

On June 3, 2005, three months to the day after the Mayerthorpe shootings, the string of deaths of RCMP members continued. Constable Jean Minguy, 46, a 23-year RCMP veteran, fell off a Zodiac into Okanagan Lake, near Vernon, B.C. He was in full uniform and not wearing a life jacket. His body was recovered four days later.

A month later, on July 4, 2005, Constable Jose Agostinho was performing one of the most dangerous jobs for any police officer, sitting in his patrol car investigating an accident on a busy highway. A transport truck being operated by a driver who was believed to have been asleep at the wheel crashed into the RCMP vehicle south of Edmonton, crushing Agostinho.

It would take a year for the next two Mounties to die, once again in circumstances that are still under a cloud. The murders of Constables Marc Bourdages, 26, and Robin Cameron, 29, near Spiritwood, Sask., echoed the Mayerthorpe murders. Each officer had about five years' experience. They had been called to investigate a domestic dispute that turned into a prolonged chase across the grid roads of Saskatchewan. Curtis Dagenais, the man they were chasing, was a loner with a long history with the police. In many ways, he was the Jim Roszko of his community.

The police chase of Dagenais was eventually joined by a lone female RCMP officer in her patrol car. She was behind the car containing Bourdages and Cameron, which collided with the vehicle driven by Dagenais. The two Mounties were shot in the head while still in their vehicle. The third officer fired at Dagenais but missed. He ran across the fields and escaped. Bourdages and Cameron died within hours of each other nine days later, on July 15 and 16, 2006. Dagenais eventually turned himself in and was charged with the murders.

Prime Minister Harper issued the typical statement Canadians have come to expect from its leaders in such a situation. "Today, on behalf of all

Canadians, I wish to pay tribute to both Marc Bourdages and Robin Cameron. They have made the ultimate sacrifice in the service of their fellow Canadians.... Throughout their careers, both officers brought a level of professionalism, commitment and courage that was admired and respected by their colleagues, friends and the lives of other Canadians they touched.... I express my sincere condolences to the families, friends and fellow colleagues of these brave officers who have been touched by this terrible tragedy. This is truly a sad day for all Canadians. This tragic event is a sad reminder of the sacrifice and bravery of the men and women who serve in our national police force and all those who dedicate their lives to protecting our country and our communities, often working under extreme circumstances, and in conditions of great danger. Our thoughts and prayers are with their families and loved ones in this, their time of need."

Cameron, the mother of an 11-year-old daughter, was lauded for the contributions she had made to her community, the Beardy's Okemis First Nations near Duck Lake in northern Saskatchewan. She became a particularly notable saint in the RCMP pantheon, but how she got there was never made clear.

Once again, the RCMP put a lid on any discussion about what had really happened at Spiritwood. Inside the force, the issue of training and resources came up again and again. Some believed that Bourdages and Cameron might have rammed the vehicle Dagenais was driving. If so, it was a tactic that most police services prohibit, unless the police vehicle is properly equipped with heavy ramming bars, like those some police forces use on highway patrol vehicles. The bars are designed to prevent air bags from engaging after a frontal impact. However, the Mounties' vehicle did not have ramming bars. As a result, the air bags were released, stunning and temporarily incapacitating the two constables, making them sitting ducks for Dagenais. The RCMP hid behind the criminal investigation and trial, which would take years, and would not comment about what had actually happened. That did not go unnoticed.

"For the RCMP, it seems there's no statute of limitations for answers," *Globe and Mail* reporters Katherine Harding and Dawn Walton wrote in a story at the time.

They went on to quote Bill Pitt, a former Mountie, who was now a criminology professor at the University of Alberta. Pitt told the *Globe* that the RCMP's "culture of secrecy," is deeply ingrained. "On occasion, he said, the force's contempt for public disclosure about its actions is 'taken almost to the point of absurd.'"

By this point one might have expected that governments would be conducting reviews of RCMP procedures and that there would be public pressure to improve the situation, but nothing like that happened. Public opinion was still behind the force. Giuliano Zaccardelli was gone. The death of Robert Dziekanski at Vancouver airport was still a year away. Bill Sweeney had escaped the Mayerthorpe mess and had risen to number two in the force, charged with overseeing its future. As long as it kept saying that it would improve, as long as it kept saying that it would allow itself to be held accountable, as long as it kept saying it was the best in the world, the RCMP did not have to do much.

The RCMP just kept burying its dead, holding elaborate funerals, sticking to the status quo as if nothing much had happened and there was nothing more it needed to do.

Six days before Dziekanski succumbed at the hands of the RCMP, the 19th Mountie since September 2000 died in the line of duty. On October 6, 2007, 30-year-old Christopher Worden was on call in Hay River, a community of almost 4,000 residents near Great Slave Lake in the Northwest Territories. Like the typical Mountie, Worden—originally from Ottawa— was a stranger in a strange land. He had joined the RCMP five years earlier. Hay River, to which he had recently moved, was already his third posting in the North. An isolated community, 1,067 kilometres north of Edmonton and 494 kilometres south of Yellowknife, Hay River was far from tranquil. A rowdy place bolstered by the oil and diamond boom in the region, it was infected with criminal elements from Edmonton.

Worden was the officer on call at 4:58 a.m. that morning when a woman called police for help. The call went to the RCMP's operational communications centre in Yellowknife. The woman told the operator that someone was threatening to commit suicide in an apartment complex. The police knew the complex to be a centre of criminal activity, particularly drug trafficking. At 5:03 a.m., Worden responded alone to the call.

RCMP Chief Superintendent Tom Middleton, the commanding officer of "G" Division (NWT), held a press conference the next day to describe what happened. He was accompanied by RCMP media relations Officer Sgt. Larry O'Brien.

"Words can never convey the sorrow that is felt when a member of the Royal Canadian Mounted Police pays the ultimate sacrifice," Middleton said. "Chris Worden was a valued member of this community—a husband, a father, a son, and a fine young peace officer. . . . On behalf of the RCMP family, of the law enforcement community and of our country, I extend my deepest sympathies to Chris' wife Jodie and her relatives, Chris and Jodie's young daughter, as well as to Chris' parents and siblings. Our hearts hurt as well for the community and for the many employees here, in 'G' Division and elsewhere who knew Chris. In the north, the word family takes in a lot of people. Our thoughts and prayers are with everyone that has been touched by this tragedy."

Middleton then moved on to describe what had happened to Worden. "What we can tell you so far is this," Middleton said, describing the call at 4:58 a.m., the dispatching of Worden, and the ongoing communication up to the point that he entered the apartment complex. Then Middleton said: "Contact was lost and shortly thereafter additional Hay River Detachment members were dispatched to the scene. Constable Worden was located in a wooded area outside the home and transported immediately to Hay River Hospital, where he was pronounced dead. The Division's Emergency Operations Centre was immediately activated and the location secured. Specialized RCMP teams from 'G' Division and 'K' Division [Alberta] were deployed to Hay River and remain in the area in an integrated response. I can also tell you that our investigation is active and very much ongoing."

The RCMP had a suspect, Edmonton drug dealer, Emrah Bulatci, who was on the loose.

Witnesses said that Worden had resolved the suicide threat and was heading out of the apartment when he was shot three times by the 23-year-old Bulatci. Middleton had said in his press conference that the Mounties had sent out someone to find Worden immediately after he could not be raised on his radio. The RCMP story soon began to unravel.

Three days after the shooting, Sgt. O'Brien, the media relations officer, pressed by reporters, conceded that the force's response might not have been as timely as first had been suggested: "I can say that it did take time for the members to locate him when they arrived at the scene," O'Brien told CBC News.

Getting the RCMP to admit what had happened in Hay River was like pulling teeth. The force wanted the media to concentrate on the RCMP's efforts to find Bulatci, but reporters wanted to know more about what had really happened to Worden. The questions kept coming and the Mounties refused to tell the truth. Bulatci was captured after six days and charged with the murder. The real story finally came out and it was more horrifying than anyone could have suspected.

As it turned out, after Worden failed to respond to his radio, two RCMP members set out to find him. They arrived on the scene two hours after a witness had first heard the shots. TWO HOURS! Middleton had deliberately left the impression that the RCMP had responded quickly and that every effort had been made to save the life of the mortally wounded Worden. None of it was true. The poor Mountie was found curled up in a ball and covered in his own blood.

The RCMP, sadly, had become almost maudlin in its public grief. Once again, the brass dusted off their red serge, pinned on their latest medals, and filled the airwaves with platitudes. They didn't have the honesty, integrity, courage, respect, accountability, or professionalism to admit that what they had done was to help make Worden just another saint. When confronted about its actions and inaction, the entire force curled up into a defensive ball. It had nothing to say because of the "ongoing criminal investigation," its favourite cover-up mechanism. It would not comment on what had happened. Although sending officers out alone without backup has long been abandoned by other police forces, the Mounties have long refused to adopt such practices because they're "too expensive." The lone, brave Mountie was a symbol of the force—and cheaper, too.

If there is one attribute more than any other that the RCMP had developed over the decades, it was imperviousness to public opinion, and reality. Steeped in its traditions and myths, there exists an institutional arrogance of astounding proportions. The RCMP continued, against all odds, to be confident about what it was doing. No matter how much flak it might take, it stubbornly refused to become distracted from what it perceived as its mission, that is, providing "efficient" policing to all of Canada, no matter the human cost to victims and its own members. That it was anything but efficient in every way was a great verity to be ignored. The RCMP way, like the cult of Scientology, was to weather the flap of the day and after it had died down, change the subject and press on. And, yet another young saint would be created.

A month after Worden was murdered, another Mountie was gunned down in eerily similar circumstances. This time it was another Ontario stranger patrolling the far North—20-year-old Douglas Scott. Born in Lyn, near Brockville, in eastern Ontario, Scott had graduated from Depot less than six months earlier. He had been immediately posted to a two-man detachment in the Baffin Island hamlet of Kimmirut, in Nunavut Territory. That fact alone raised eyebrows in the police community—a raw cadet thrown into a pressure cooker as if he were an experienced adult. There was no better recipe for disaster, but the RCMP was desperate for warm bodies to fill all those empty slots across the country.

On November 5, 2007, Scott was responding to a report of an impaired driver and a possible car crash. Kimmirut was officially a dry town—the sale of alcohol was prohibited. It was 11 p.m. After his partner could not raise him on the radio, he went out to search for Scott. He found him at 11:45 p.m. He had been gunned down near the community arena. A local man was arrested five hours later after a standoff, and charged with Scott's murder.

The usual shock and grief ensued. "The death of any of our members is deeply felt," Chief Supt. Martin Cheliak, the RCMP's commanding officer in Nunavut, told a news conference. "But when, once again, it occurs in one of our close-knit communities in the North, the pain of that loss seems even greater."

After the Mayerthorpe slaughter, the RCMP had been able to manage the families of the dead, but Christopher Worden's wife would have none of that. Still grieving for her own husband, Scott's compelled Jodie Worden to break the silence. She went on national television and radio and spoke with newspaper reporters about how her husband and Scott would be alive if it were not for the RCMP's antiquated policies. "The RCMP as an organization is not doing enough to keep the members safe," Worden told CBC News. "They have no idea of the demands and the expectations that are put on regular members up in the North. They need to send two members to every call. That's just an officer safety issue. What they're doing needs to be changed and it needs to happen now."

Under fire, the RCMP promised to review its policy and implement new procedures for its officers in such situations. But what could it really do? The force did not have enough manpower to cover all its responsibilities, was losing staff at a precipitous rate, and could not possibly train enough new members to fill all those gaps in the near to mid-future.

Being a Mountie from September 2000 to the present has proven to so many that it was, indeed, "a career nowhere near ordinary."

PART 3

THE CONTINUING CRISIS IN CANADA

"If they can get you asking the wrong questions,
they don't have to worry about the answers."
—Thomas Pynchon

[20]

FEDERAL POLICING
—THE BIGGEST SCANDAL?

O n a late summer's day in Ottawa, RCMP patrol car 222 is parked
near the West Block of the Parliament Buildings. A Mountie's Stet-
son is resting on the dashboard. Its owner is nowhere in sight.
Around Parliament Hill six other RCMP patrol cars are parked here and
there. Near the East Block two Mounties have parked their cars side by side
and are carrying on a conversation. On the streets around Parliament, there
are more marked RCMP vehicles. An unmarked car whizzes past carrying
another Mountie. Around Ottawa there are more Mounties parked at the
prime minister's residence, at Rideau Hall, the Governor General's residence,
and near various embassies. During the day, some of these Mounties in full-
dress uniform will take up their station near the Parliament Buildings and
pose for tourists eager to capture the moment. It looks like Canada, its sovereignty, and leaders are so well protected.

All these RCMP members are part of the Protective Branch, delegated to
provide security for the Parliament Buildings, dignitaries, and other very
important people. For decades, the 500 members who sit in those cars and
pose for photographs have done no real policing. Nevertheless, while they
pose for photos, each one is gaining seniority which allows them to rise
through the ranks of the RCMP. Some stay in protective services but most
cross over and become members, even supervisors, of elite specialized units
or criminal investigation detachments in some backwater locale.

One might think that these fully-paid members of the RCMP would be
the first to be called upon to beef up short-staffed federal police, but in the
twisted world of the RCMP, that is precisely how things do not work. If contract policing is the RCMP's first priority, protective policing has been its

second. Whenever dignitaries come to town for something like the G8 summit or a visit by the U.S. president, federal police are routinely pulled off their assignments, no matter how important or how delicate, ordered to don the red serge, and become security guards too. But what kind of security do they really provide?

Everyone knows by now how the RCMP let a burglar get over a fence and through a window into 24 Sussex and make his way to the prime minister's bedroom door before being caught. But when push comes to shove, even our own leaders don't trust the Mounties to do the job.

In November 2004, U.S. president George W. Bush took up an invitation from then-Prime Minister Paul Martin to visit Ottawa and address a joint session of the House of Commons and the Senate. Martin was determined to repair the perceived damaged relationship between the two countries, which had recently been aggravated by some critical statements about George Bush by Liberal MP Carolyn Parrish. Parrish had made a number of critical statements about Bush, calling him "war-like." She had even appeared on the comedy show, *This Hour Has 22 Minutes*, and stomped on a Bush doll. She renounced her loyalty to the Liberal Party and was booted out of caucus.

Even though Parrish had promised not to heckle Bush during his address, the American president declined to speak to Parliament, worried about an incident. "We didn't see the need and, frankly, we didn't want to be booed. There are other, better venues," said one U.S. official.

The U.S. authorities were so fearful of the mood on Parliament Hill that U.S. Ambassador Paul Cellucci impressed upon the Canadian government that Bush would come to Parliament Hill under only one condition—if the U.S. Secret Service could be armed inside the Parliament Building. The Canadian government held its collective nose and acceded to the demand. It did not have much choice, having set a precedent in the Arar case by allowing the FBI and CIA to wander freely in the country. The RCMP stowed its bullets and patrolled the grounds outside while the U.S. agents took control of Parliament for a day.

"So, who was really in charge within our Parliament buildings?" asked Edgar MacLeod, Cape Breton Regional Police Chief.

"It was outrageous to have done that," said one high-ranking Mountie familiar with the situation. "This is our country and our police force. If the Americans can't trust us in our own seat of government, what kind of trust is there between us? The members were really upset about it, but the clamp came down. No one was allowed to say a word about what had taken place.

It was just another example of how the politicians use the RCMP for their own political purposes and how the RCMP brass won't stand up to them."

The relationship between the government and the police is all about politics. Federal policing is about sovereignty, the security and integrity of the nation, the protection of its treasury and financial markets, the suppression of organized crime, and the defence of the rule of law. The RCMP is a showcase police force, but once you get past the dancing horses and fancy uniforms, there is a resounding hollowness.

✛ ✛ ✛

"The biggest scandal in Canada today is the state of federal policing," said Halifax Police Chief Frank Beazley during an interview in August 2007. "The entire country has been left exposed to incredible dangers because the RCMP has proven itself unwilling and unable to do the one job it is supposed to be doing, federal policing."

In the clubby atmosphere of Canadian policing, Beazley is a rarity, one of only a handful of police leaders in Canada who have had the courage in recent years to speak openly about the RCMP. Others might think like Beazley, but never go public with their views, largely out of fear of having the RCMP come down on them bent upon enforcing their "partnerships" and "mutual cooperation." Even Beazley eventually bent to that pressure. During another interview in December 2007, he said he had much to say about the RCMP, but asked if he could go off the record. "I don't want Commissioner Elliott breathing down my neck over something I said."

As the chief constable of one of Canada's most important port cities, Beazley and his police force are regularly exposed to the full pantheon of domestic, interprovincial, and international crime. The Halifax Regional Police must work closely with the RCMP, which is the contract provincial police force in Nova Scotia. Over the years, Beazley has seen the RCMP's ability to perform at the level required in this day and age seriously decline.

"They are just not there," Beazley said in the earlier interview. "Our municipal force and our municipal taxpayers have been asked to shoulder the burden of federal policing in our community. We are stretched to the bone trying to meet our everyday responsibilities, but we are continually being asked to do more of the RCMP's work, without extra manpower or compensation. We need the RCMP to be a strong federal police force, but it has shown that it isn't interested in federal policing."

The federal policing the RCMP is interested in performing comes with its contract positions, and therein lies an absurdity in Canadian public policy. Ottawa pays a subsidy to most communities that hire the RCMP on contract. That money is intended to offset time spent by officers on federal work like drug enforcement and border patrol. But most municipal police forces in Canada have the same responsibilities. Why does Ottawa not provide subsidies for them, as well? It is an argument which has been seized upon by municipal police chiefs and local politicians across the country, but to date one which Ottawa has ignored.

Instead of bolstering the dedicated federal force as it has promised to do for more than three decades, the RCMP has been in retreat. In 2007, for example, the RCMP shut down nine federal detachments in Québec, including productive units in outlaw motorcycle gang territories such as Rivière du Loup. Québec nationalists were not about to complain about a federal entity shrinking in their province, and neither would the criminals. "They were productive units where a lot of illegal drugs are produced," said Staff Sgt. Gaétan Delisle. "I don't know what they are thinking."

In Halifax, one of the foremost concerns for Police Chief Beazley is the city's port. In 1997, at the same time the Chrétien government was getting ready to turn the port of Vancouver over to one of Li Ka-Shing's companies, it disbanded the Ports Canada Police, at the time the oldest police service in Canada, in the name of efficiency. Jurisdiction for the ports was handed over to municipal police and the RCMP in its federal capacity, but the RCMP rarely showed up for work. The Canada Border Services Agency drops in and out of shipping container facilities, but its mandate is primarily to evaluate the contents of shipments and collect duty. Occasionally, it stumbles onto drugs in the course of its travels.

"The ports of Canada are one of the biggest security threats for this country, but the RCMP has just picked up and left," Beazley said. "We have to police it because nobody else is, even though we don't have the proper tools for the job. To police the ports, you need an overseas intelligence capability. You need manpower to conduct searches of ships and containers. You need things that we just don't have. The ports are wide open. National security is a joke." Beazley's strong words are nothing new.

"The Mounties are absolutely useless," says Ron Parks, a Vancouver forensic accountant who has seen the RCMP's work close up for decades. In 2003, after it became abundantly clear that the RCMP had no idea how to investigate and prosecute commercial crime, the Liberal government promoted the establishment of Integrated Market Enforcement Teams (IMET) in Toronto, Montréal, Calgary, and Vancouver. The teams comprised RCMP investigators, federal lawyers, provincial securities regulators, local police, and forensic accountants in what is intended to be a nimble and coordinated attack on market wrongdoing.

Fourteen months after the IMET teams were formed, the RCMP announced its presence by conducting a highly publicized daylight raid on the Bank of Nova Scotia in the heart of Toronto's business district. It was seeking documents related to Royal Group Technologies Ltd., linked to the politically connected Sorbara family. At the time, Greg Sorbara was Ontario's finance minister and was forced to resign his cabinet post after being linked to the investigation. It was IMET's first performance designed to make headlines.

"They're sending a message to investors ... 'We're going to clean up the markets and you can depend on us,'" Richard Powers, professor at the University of Toronto's Rotman School of Management, said at the time.

Four years later, the IMET teams had managed to get just one conviction in Vancouver and were considering four others in Toronto. Vancouver stockbroker Kevin Steele was jailed for six years for defrauding investors out of $10.3 million. The Royal Group investigation was still continuing although Greg Sorbara had successfully fought the RCMP in court. Ontario Superior Court judge Ian Nordheimer found the naming of Sorbara in the warrant "premature." In a blistering condemnation, he accused the RCMP of not doing enough investigative work before seeking the search warrants and of tainting certain transactions to bolster their case before the judge who signed the warrants. He said that the RCMP provided no evidence to back up two property deals it had construed to be unusual. "It raises the concern that the characterization of the transactions as unusual was made in order to taint the transactions ... and thus bolster the ultimate argument that the transactions were fundamentally suspicious," the judge wrote in his decision.

The high-profile IMET units had quickly proven themselves to be a waste of time for both victims and taxpayers, mainly because they embodied all that was wrong with the RCMP. There was no expertise and no continuity in investigations. Supervisors were rotated through the units, as were investigators, and many were not replaced. Fully 21 percent of the IMET positions were vacant in 2007. The entire reporting structure was poorly designed and obstructive. Finally, the force came to the job with an attitude that had infected it years earlier: that commercial crime and fraud were victimless crimes.

"They have no capability to investigate complex financial crimes," Parks said. "Their entire approach is wrong. Sophisticated criminals mask what they are doing in subtlety and apparent truths, but the Mounties only think in black and white. They don't understand subtlety. It's beyond them. They tend to build massive files and take an enormous amount of time doing it, overlooking the key elements in a fraud. It's as if they are constantly in search of reasonable doubt, looking for ways not to prosecute offenders."

Vancouver lawyer Robert Gardner, who does not know Parks, holds similar views. Gardner and his partners lost millions of dollars after investing in a dubious company, Getty Copper Corp., in Coquitlam, B.C. The RCMP spent three years investigating the case before suddenly dropping it in early 2007, after the Justice Department expressed its reluctance to prosecute.

"This case involved the Hell's Angels," Gardner said. "The evidence was right there, but the RCMP couldn't figure it out. I've been to the IMET offices. I've seen them work. All they do is sit around all day behind a desk. They haven't got a clue."

Where the RCMP excelled, as it were, in its incompetence has been in the investigation and prosecution of socially and politically connected miscreants. Strange things aplenty have happened. Investigations have never been started when one might think the police would be all over an irregularity like the sponsorship scandal. It has not been unusual for cases to dissolve mysteriously into the ether, like that of Conrad Black, the overly erudite former Canadian international press baron and author who forsook his citizenship in favour of a seat in the British House of Lords.

In August 2005, after two full years of controversy in Canada and the United States over the alleged milking of $500 million in shareholders' money from Black's business dealings at Hollinger Inc. and related companies, the RCMP made its report. "After conducting a thorough review, it was determined that no Canadian investigation was required," RCMP Cpl. Michele Paradis told the *Toronto Star*. The Mounties said they could find no evidence of a crime and planned to do nothing more. Shareholders had seen their investment shrink by $1.85 billion under Black's direction. Black's army of supporters in the Canadian establishment supported that position, all too quickly.

A week later, Black's right-hand man, David Radler, appeared in a Chicago court and pleaded guilty to the precise charges that would have and should have been laid in Canada. In return for a 29-month sentence, Radler agreed to testify against Black, which more than indicated that Radler believed a crime or two had been committed.

The Americans quickly rounded up the snarly, surly Lord Black of Crossharbour, and tried and convicted him of three charges of fraud and one of obstructing justice in December 2007. Black received a "light sentence" by recent American standards—just six and a half years in a Florida federal prison. He had to return $6.1 million and pay a $125,000 fine, but was allowed to keep his $38 million mansion in Palm Beach.

"What were you thinking?" Judge Amy St. Eve asked Black rhetorically while passing sentence. "I frankly cannot understand how somebody of your stature could engage in the conduct you engaged in and put everything at risk, including your reputation.... No one is above the law." She obviously did not know much about how the wealthy are treated in Canada.

Two of Black's co-accused, accountant Jack Boultbee and Hollinger executive Peter Atkinson, received lesser terms, while lawyer Mark Kipnis was given two years probation. Black protested his innocence to the end and said he planned to appeal. No matter how down he seemed to be, Black continued to enjoy support from those at the top of the food chain, even from his priest, Father Raymond J. De Souza. The priest wrote how he admired Black's defiance to the very end, pointing out to Judge St. Eve that his great newspaper had been destroyed by those who had replaced him, certainly not him.

"To the end, he was telling the truth," Father De Souza wrote. "Even Lord Black's most vociferous critics, those who will drink a toast to his imprisonment, should see a measure of nobility in that. He did not play games with the justice system, seeking refuge from extradition. He faced the charges against himself. He defended himself. And he did not change his story to seek advantage during the whole sorry saga. He was convicted of fraud, but he faced his trial as an honest man.... He is a man of words. And he would not say he was guilty simply to make life easier, because he respects the words too much. Is that not what a man of his word should do?"

One might have thought the priest was talking about Mother Teresa.

Meanwhile, during the previous decade, in France, Spain, Australia, and especially in the United States, many decorated kings of capitalism ended up being brought down and jailed for long periods. One minute Dennis Kozlowski, chairman of Tyco Industries, was on the cover of *Business Week* as the leading U.S. entrepreneur. The next, he was doing 25 years in a federal prison near Utica, NY. President George Bush's close friends and supporters at Enron got similar treatment after that company's $25 billion meltdown. Canadian-born Bernard Ebbers received a 25-year sentence in a steamy

Louisiana cell for his part in the $11 billion Worldcom fraud. The most famous businesswoman in the United States, Martha Stewart, spent several months in jail and six more under house arrest after being convicted of covering up an illegal series of transactions by which she had profited.

Prosecutions and sentences of prestigious, politically influential people like that do not happen in Canada, at least not on Canadian soil. While Canadian citizens naturally believe that they should be investigated, charged, and tried under Canadian laws in Canadian courts, the government doesn't always operate at that idyllic level. Throughout the early 1990s, Canada refused to pursue powerful lawyer and hockey agent Alan Eagleson despite numerous complaints and detailed stories by Russ Conway, a sports journalist in Lawrence, Mass., and Bill Houston in *The Globe and Mail*. Finally, U.S. authorities charged Eagleson in 1994 with several crimes of which he was later convicted. The Canadians only charged Eagleson after the Americans were done with him.

Did Black and Eagleson, among others, get help from an invisible hand? While there have been some close calls in history, no politician has ever been caught directly telling a Mountie what to do, or not do as the case might be. Since there has been no hard evidence, the Canadian political establishment and the RCMP have embraced plausible deniability in stating that the police have acted at all times without fear, favour, or affection toward politicians and their friends. In politics, however, no rational person would expect to find a smoking gun, because politics is the very definition of murkiness. Everything a successful politician and government says and does is carefully couched in terms and actions that afford it such protection. The only thing certain in Canada is that nothing is for sure.

The weakness and incompetence of the RCMP as a federal police service had not gone unnoticed. In recent years, leading U.S. financial authorities in both the private and public sector warned Americans about the increased risks of investing in Canada because of the high degree of fraud, weak law enforcement, and the virtual indifference of the judicial system. Some experts believe that the rest of the world actually discounts the value of stock in Canadian-owned companies by ten percent or more because of the "fraud factor." Others have called Canada "an enforcement-free zone."

Public Safety Minister Stockwell Day tried to address the problem in March 2007 with one of his first one-man fixes, à la William Elliott and David Brown. Nicholas Le Pan was named as an expert adviser to the RCMP on its IMET units. Le Pan was not a fraud investigator or a prosecutor, but rather a career bureaucrat in Ottawa. He had spent the previous five years as Superintendent of Financial Institutions, more an actuarial position than an investigative one. Le Pan was commissioned to conduct a study of the IMET units and to report back in the fall. In announcing Le Pan's appointment, Day said that the RCMP would now be "better equipped to investigate and prosecute serious commercial crimes."

Finance Minister Jim Flaherty added: "Strong enforcement is critical to protect investors and promote healthy capital markets in Canada. Mr. Le Pan brings a unique skill set to this task, and has the knowledge and experience to carry it out."

Whatever value Le Pan brought to the RCMP's reputation in the short term did not staunch the criticism. In the fall of 2007, *Canadian Business* magazine published a damning cover story, slamming the force for its shoddy federal police work, "A Good Country for Crooks: Canada's Losing War against White-collar Crime." The story focused on the views of two former RCMP officers who ran the Integrated Market Enforcement Team, Bill Majcher, "West Coast Billy," whom we've already met, from Vancouver and Craig Hannaford from Toronto.

Senior writer John Gray wrote: "Canada isn't having much luck cleaning up its image as a country that is soft on white-collar crime.... Canadian authorities are still licking their wounds after the recent acquittal of former Bre-X chief geologist John Felderhof on civil charges of insider trading. It wasn't supposed to be this way. Four years ago, the RCMP launched its Integrated Market Enforcement Teams, or IMETs, elite squads of investigators who were supposed to work together to crack down on white-collar crime. The results have been disappointing, to say the least. While the U.S. Justice Department has racked up more than 1,200 convictions against high-level executives and scammers in the past five years, the IMETs have managed just two—against the same person."

Majcher described Canada's justice system this way: "The system is pretty much non-existent. You can fix something that is hemorrhaging, but if the body is already lifeless, you have to start fresh. We need politicians to admit that the system is broken from the top to the bottom. Canadians have to understand that we have a two-tiered justice system, where people with money can play the system. Show me a person who has gotten any sort of satisfaction from going to the authorities after being victimized by a white-collar fraud ... who got their money back in a timely fashion and didn't go through a lot of grief. I can't think of a single person like that.

"Canada is seen as a haven for criminals," Majcher said. "We have strong trust laws, a strong and stable banking system, strong privacy legislation and weak enforcement.... Canada is seen as a soft touch. In a global criminal or terrorist organization, it's very useful to have a Canadian nexus. Then the whole network has the protection of the Canadian charter. If you can show that the Canadian police are involved in an international investigation, you can serve a disclosure application and the Canadian police can be compelled to disclose all the information captured in an investigation—information—even the information provided by other law enforcement or intelligence agencies. Canada is absolutely an Achilles heel for international criminal and terrorist investigations. That's making it harder for Canadian police to work with investigators from other jurisdictions because they view us as a big sieve of information.

"I'm in the investment industry now, and I see how this hurts Canada," Majcher continued. "I have talked with money managers and investors who have told me they will not invest in Canada. One multibillionaire I met recently, who has extensive private holdings in Canada, says he won't invest in Canadian public companies because there is no recourse if anything goes wrong. Canadians believe this Pablum we are fed that we have a trade surplus and our economy is doing great, but it's doing well because the world wants our raw materials. Where is the investment in research and development, biotech, manufacturing and other things that make a diversified economy? What happens when the commodity boom starts to bust?"

Hannaford added: "This is not a quick fix. The delays in these cases are just terrible. There is no reason why it should take 10 years to get a resolution in the Bre-X case. Can someone please tell me why Livent has dragged on for so long? Charges in that case were laid in 2002. Here we are, five years later, and there is still no resolution."

There is no national securities regulator in Canada, but there's plenty of political resistance to creating one. Enforcement is carried out by as many as 30 mostly self-regulating bodies. The largest is the Ontario Securities Commission in which the RCMP exerts its negative influence in a more vicarious way.

"Almost all the OSC investigators are ex-RCMP," said Avi Shachar, a former lieutenant colonel who spent 16 years in senior roles with the Israeli military intelligence service. Shachar, who operates his own company, Sprylogics International Inc., is recognized as an expert on intelligence, early warning, terrorism, and securities fraud. Shachar spent many years at the OSC.

"There are some great people in the RCMP, amazing people who are incredibly dedicated, but they come with a mindset that no one can change," Shachar says. "They don't know how to get to the bottom of a case quickly. They are timid and fearful of making mistakes, so they are always looking for that one more thing, the reasonable doubt, even when there is no reasonable doubt to avoid a criminal prosecution. They are absolutely intransigent about change. As a group they have been the largest drag on reform of the OSC to make it more effective."

In the first week of December 2007, the *Toronto Star* picked up the issue with a four-part series in which, once again, the opinions of former Mounties Majcher and Hannaford were prominently featured. One OSC case cited involving Mascan Corp., a defunct property developer, had been going on for 23 years and was still an active file. "The RCMP wanted no part of it," lawyer Edward Waitzer told the *Star*.

Another case was the infamous YBM Magnex stock fraud which the FBI had found involved the Russian mafia. In 2003, OSC investigators ruled that the case wasn't about organized crime and only involved regulatory infractions, a favourite out for those afflicted with RCMP investigative vision.

Star reporter Tyler Hamilton quoted a variety of reputable sources in his front-page story. Here is a sample of what he wrote:

> The OSC is Ontario's investment watchdog. It has ultimate authority over the Toronto Stock Exchange, pension funds, mutual funds and investment dealers. Across Canada, everyone from the tiniest investor to online day traders and retirees on a company pension is affected by transactions—right or wrong—under its jurisdiction.
>
> It's accountable by definition. But academics, lawyers and forensic accountants interviewed for this story say accountability is sorely lacking when it comes to securities enforcement, whether it's regulatory matters overseen by the OSC or violations of criminal law overseen by police.
>
> They also cite a lack of focus, and the sense of urgency that makes enforcement an effective deterrent to breaking the rules. The decades-old Mascan case, they say, illustrates much of what's wrong with the system.
>
> More recently, many believe the OSC and Canadian authorities dropped the ball on their investigation of Conrad Black, who will be sentenced later this month in Chicago after a speedy U.S. trial.

"For me, the hardest part about the Conrad Black trial has been explaining why it happened in Chicago and not in Toronto," former Ontario premier Bob Rae wrote recently in his blog.

All this is no surprise to Utpal Bhattacharya, a finance professor at the Indiana University's Kelley School of Business and author of a report comparing the enforcement records of the OSC and the U.S. Securities and Exchange Commission (SEC). "We found the enforcement in Ontario was pathetic," said Bhattacharya. "Canada is a first-world country with second-world capital markets and third-world enforcement."

Many high-profile cases of stock-market meltdown or corporate fraud in recent years have left investors fuming that authorities have either failed to hold people accountable or taken way too long to apply justice.

"I think delay is a big source of frustration for investors," said Poonam Puri, a law professor who teaches about white-collar crime at Osgoode Hall Law School.

Although the RCMP has paid lip service over the years to its commitment to commercial crime investigation, it has really been doing everything it could do to get out of that business, such as it was. For the past 15 years, the truth about serious fraud in Canada is that victims are in large measure made to pay for the investigations. It began as part of the RCMP's outsourcing of criminal investigations in the nineties under then-Commissioner Norman Inkster. Since the RCMP could not do the job, forensic accountants and private investigators were handed the work. The leading private investigators chasing this new pot of gold were almost always ex-RCMP officers— with their full pensions stashed safely in their mattresses.

In the outside world, these ex-RCMP officers went to work inside government, banks, and private investigation services. One of the country's leading private investigators, who became wealthy working for victims over the past 15 years, was the same man who created the concept: Norman Inkster, who retired at the end of 2007.

In the private-investigation world, these ex-RCMP members tended to use the same approaches they had employed when they were police officers— build huge files at an enormous costs without a conclusion. "Too many of them can't see the trees for the forest," said Vancouver forensic accountant

Ron Parks. "They think they have to know everything, when in many cases all that is required is one or two things. They drive up the costs and make it impossible for anyone to get true justice."

When it comes to the investigation of organized crime, RCMP Staff Sgt. Gaétan Delisle says the force is equally at sea. The RCMP's own statistics estimated that there were 750 organized crime gangs actively operating in Canada, but it only had the resources to deal with a handful of them in any given year. To cover up its shortcomings, the force has tended to mount massive, high-profile cases involving dramatic busts of leading organized crime figures. But the investigations are usually not as smooth or as well-conceived as the RCMP would lead the public to believe. Two big cases involved the Rizzuto crime family in Montréal and members of the Cuntrera-Caruana Sicilian Mafia, who were considered by Italian authorities to be "The Rothschilds of the Mafia." While the RCMP led Canadians to believe that the investigations were homegrown, in fact the impetus for each of them came from Italian and U.S. authorities who were much farther down the field in their cases and demanding action in Canada.

"We tied up 300 officers for more than three years in one investigation," Delisle says. "We were running around everywhere, but the entire investigative plan was wrong. Criminals know how we operate and they have adapted over the years. No longer is there a central command. Everything is done in silos. One group steals a truck and leaves it for the next group which uses it to pick up the drugs. The payment is made by a third group. The drugs are deposited somewhere and another group distributes it. There are no obvious connections linking anyone. In the case we did, we spent three years wasting a lot of time, and when the case was broken, the key evidence actually came from a much smaller, unrelated investigation, but the RCMP didn't say a word about that. No, they went out and got the big headlines for their grand accomplishment and then went back to sleep. We have no idea how to deal with organized crime. It's everywhere."

During the fall of 2007, with all that was going on in the daily press regarding the Robert Dziekanski incident and the other RCMP debacles, *Maclean's* magazine hit the streets with another RCMP exposé: "What's Really Killing the Mounties—Dangerous Work. No Backup. Nasty Bosses. Vicious Infighting. The RCMP is in Ruins." The reporters were Jonathon Gatehouse and Charlie Gillis, who was still on the RCMP file despite the public slagging over a previous story he had written a year earlier. They opened their story with a tale about an important drug bust in southern Ontario that wasn't prosecuted because the RCMP federal officers, based in Hamilton, were all off the job due to stress.

"It was billed as a major drug bust, significant enough to put a crimp into southern Ontario's cocaine trade. A seven-month undercover sting that culminated in the July 2005 seizure of two kilos of coke, $144,000 in cash, a silencer-equipped .22-calibre pistol, and the arrest of four men alleged to have ties to the Hells Angels, Persian mob, and, as the press release put it, 'traditional' organized crime.

"But this past Sept. 27, the accused—Trifu Margan, David Lawrence, Randy Singh, and supposed kingpin Sharame (Sean) Sherzady—walked out of a Burlington courthouse scot-free, without ever having to answer the charges. After months of delays, the Crown withdrew the case on the day their preliminary hearings were scheduled to begin because the chief witnesses—five RCMP officers who were at the centre of the investigation—were unavailable to testify.

"Officers Claim Illness, Drug Charges Dropped," said the headline in a local paper.

"The prosecutor and various police agencies—the bust was the work of the elite Golden Horseshoe Combined Special Forces Enforcement Unit (CSFEU)—expressed disappointment. But no one seemed willing to address the reasons a bunch of battle-tested cops have been off the job on stress leave for close to 20 months, or ask why the Mounties appeared willing to let four accused mobsters walk rather than fix the problem."

Gatehouse and Gillis went on to describe in withering detail the internal problems within the force, especially how the five RCMP officers at the 11-member Stoney Creek federal detachment had been driven out of their jobs by an abusive supervisor. Instead of dealing with that superior, the RCMP tried to operate the detachment with its remaining staff, and he was eventually promoted.

One of the most important components of federal policing is national security. The RCMP and CSIS are supposedly working together to protect the country. In recent years, Canada has become a haven for at least 60 jihadist organizations believed to be raising money for Islamic terrorist operations around the world. In November 2007, Lord Peter Levene, chairman of the worldwide insurance syndicate Lloyds, told the Empire Club in Toronto that Canadian businesses and installations such as hydro, nuclear, pipeline, oil, forestry, and mining might soon be targeted by Islamic terrorists. "Canada's risk profile has changed and its role is shifting from a hub for fundraising and planning attacks outside the nation to a credible target in its own right," Lord Levene said.

Canada says it is prepared, but is it?

A few weeks after September 11, 2001, the government moved quickly to fight the terrorist threat. One of the new measures introduced was Fintrac—the Financial Transactions and Reports Analysis Centre of Canada. Over the intervening years, the government regularly touted the effectiveness of Fintrac in tracing illicit cash transfers. In February 2008, however, the Canadian Press news agency obtained a year-old internal CSIS study which showed that CSIS and the RCMP were operating largely in the dark when it came to tracking funds earmarked for terrorism. "A generally accepted model for terrorist financing would provide a clear and common strategic understanding of how terrorist financing operates and a sound basis for deciding how to respond to it," read the 2007 study from CSIS's Integrated Threat Assessment Centre. "Currently, no such model exists."

As immigrants swarm to Canadian cities from around the world, among them are members of dangerous international criminal organizations such as the El Salvador-based Mara Salvatrucha or MS-13 gang. Police sources say that MS-13 and other gangs like it are building bases in Canada but are not even on the radar of the RCMP. "In 2007, I asked the RCMP about the MS-13 presence in Toronto," said one police officer who asked for anonymity, "and they replied back—'Who?' Anyone who has watched any U.S. news show over the past decade can't help but know about MS-13. There are signs of them being in Toronto, which should be of grave concern to anyone."

There are alarming indications that Canada's own institutions are being subjected to intimidation by brazen criminals. In June 2007, retired federal tax court judge Alban Garon, his wife, and a neighbour were brutally murdered in the Garons' apartment. Prior to the murders, which remain unsolved, judges across the country were complaining about threatening behaviour toward them by criminals. Judges have found themselves being openly followed or surveilled in clear attempts of intimidation by organized crime figures—particularly members of outlaw motorcycle gangs.

That same kind of intimidation is going on in Canada's penal system where correction officers are regularly threatened or find themselves boldly hounded by criminals openly lurking near their homes.

Calls for help to the RCMP by both groups have all but been ignored.

Effective federal policing depends upon gathering and analyzing criminal intelligence, and then acting on the information, a long-lost talent in the

RCMP. When Guiliano Zaccardelli took over as commissioner in September 2000, he recognized that the RCMP's federal operations had been allowed to wither on the vine. It was a purely reactive force which had all but abandoned gathering criminal intelligence. One of the first things Zaccardelli tried to do was to repair the intelligence-gathering section, but his efforts were largely in vain because he had to work within the promotion rules of the RCMP—call it the Car 222 syndrome.

In the RCMP, promotion is all about seniority and the ability to pass examinations, not about unique abilities, interests, or specialization. The very good RCMP officers—of whom there are many—too often find themselves trapped in units where their colleagues or superiors are virtually incompetent, merely passing through on the promotion carousel.

The second problem in gathering intelligence, one which afflicts most police departments, is the ingrained belief that good investigators make good intelligence officers, which is not true. Investigating is more of a science, whereas intelligence gathering is more of an art.

"One of the weakest areas in Canadian law enforcement is that there are no properly trained criminal intelligence people," said Avi Shachar, the former senior Israeli intelligence officer, who used to run operations in northern Israel and in Lebanon. "You can't just take an investigator and tell him that he is now in the intelligence business. That doesn't work in Israel and it doesn't work here. The best investigator in the world can be a lousy intelligence officer. Investigators are used to gathering facts, building cases, and going to court. In intelligence, there are no facts, no black and white; everything is grey. You must have a feel for the information and an ability to read between the lines and extrapolate. I believe the best intelligence officers are journalists. They have the proper mindset. That's who police forces should be recruiting for intelligence."

The lameness of the RCMP at the federal level is a glaring reflection of all the issues that bedevil the RCMP and Canadian governments. In the past, the force has rationalized that its structure is the perfect blend of tiered policing—federal, provincial, and municipal—all under one roof.

Never shy about patting its own back, the RCMP continued to tout its wonderful reputation, as it did in this 2007 statement: "The RCMP is recognized internationally as an example of the efficient deployment of police services, far surpassing the patchwork model employed in many other countries, because of its structure and service-delivery model. The RCMP has also pioneered a number of innovations in integrated policing, major case management, forensic sciences and behavioural sciences, all of which are recognized world-wide for being on the leading edge of police work. . . ."

The 10,000 RCMP contract police officers are "the eyes and ears" of the force, passing information up the ladder with no inter-agency overlaps getting in the way. It might sound great in theory but in practice the claim is little more than a scam perpetrated on the public. The RCMP does not police any of Canada's major urban areas—with the exception of parts of the B.C. Lower Mainland and relatively small Moncton, N.B. Canada's serious criminal and national security threats can be found in its big cities. Criminals and terrorists are urban animals. The RCMP is, for the most part, a police service composed of small-town men and women policing small-town men and women—hicks policing hicks. What useful federal criminal intelligence could the contract cops be collecting in the boonies? What national security threats are being hatched in New Ross, Fort Smith, or 100 Mile House? The eyes and ears are gathering information for a force that has proven itself to be as blind and deaf as its political masters.

The problems within the RCMP are so evident and so enormous as to be considered catastrophic. There has been an abject refusal by governments to recognize that contract policing has been allowed to become the RCMP dog, and federal policing its tail, when it should be the other way around, with a docked tail at that. This dearth of concern and insight by politicians and the public about dealing with the structure and performance of the force seems inexplicable. One reason for that may well be the inordinate influence of small-town, rural politicians on the political process. They represent fewer people than urban members, but they have an equal voice. They are the champions, for the most part, of maintaining the status quo at any cost, with their "Don't fix it if it ain't broke" mentality and "We love our Mounties" blind allegiance.

Or is it all something more sinister? The RCMP has survived in its present form because it has managed to create a brand name for itself—an untouchable symbol of Canada, virtually infallible. But has the modern RCMP been designed to be precisely what it is—incompetent and ineffective? In spite of all the evidence to the contrary, the RCMP and its defenders have continued to stand behind the monolithic force and to promote its model of policing as one of the best in the world, both efficient and effective.

The RCMP has argued that the lack of a clear distinction between its various roles is a bonus for Canadian taxpayers. But the blurring of its various roles has helped to create a murkiness that has prevented governments and the public from seeing the real picture. The current debate over the poor quality of RCMP federal policing is not a new one. For almost three decades, others have had criticisms similar to those raised in this book, but there has been no sense of urgency among the vast majority of Canadians, politicians, the public, and the media. One reason for this is that most Canadians don't appear to understand the difference between the terms "federal" and "national."

As you have just read in the RCMP press release above, the two words are used interchangeably by the RCMP and in public discussions about the RCMP, a confusion the RCMP has promoted to its own benefit to ensure its survival. When it uses the word national, the RCMP wraps itself in the flag, reminding Canadians of its mythical roots and supposedly iconic stature. By most definitions, however, the RCMP is still aspiring to be a national police force, because until now it has been one in name only.

✠ ✠ ✠

The best example of a truly national police force in a democratic county is the French Police Nationale. France has 61 million people, twice the population of Canada, in a country whose land mass is equal to Manitoba's. With 126,000 employees, the Police Nationale is five times larger than the RCMP. It provides uniformed officers and investigators in every city and large town in France. This ubiquitous force is divided into 11 directorates and central departments. Tiers of officers and agents have different duties and powers. Under the Napoleonic Code of law, the state is responsible for protecting persons and property, maintaining public order, and enforcing the law. The Police Nationale and the Gendarmerie Nationale, a 90,000 member agency which is an integral part of the country's armed forces, are used to conduct investigations under the direction of a magistrate.

They are not the only police services in France operating at the national level. Two other important forces are Customs and Excise and the Competition, Consumption, and Fraud Office, both of which are departments of the Ministry of Finance.

Among other democratic countries, Sweden has a national police force but it also has a separate federal force for investigating fraud and financial crime. In many countries, the concept of "national police" is seen to be anti-democratic and is often associated with dictatorships and second- and third-world countries.

The United Kingdom does not have a national police force, but is divided into 53 large regional or "territorial" forces. The largest territorial force is the Metropolitan London Police—Scotland Yard, as it is popularly known—which employs 13,500 uniformed officers. Within its jurisdiction is the smallest territorial service, the City of London Police, whose jurisdiction is the square mile at the heart of the city. These forces are supplemented by what are effectively federal forces whose jurisdiction is the entire realm. These include the Serious Fraud Office, the Serious Organized Crime Agency, British Transport Police, and the Ministry of Defence Police. There are also separate local forces for police ports and parks.

Australia is divided into federal and state jurisdictions. The Australian federal police are supplemented by five other effectively national law enforcement agencies: the Competition and Consumer Commission, the Australian Crime Commission, Customs Service, Quarantine and Inspection Service, and Securities and Investment Commission.

The concept of a national police force is anathema in the United States, where vigilance about excessive government power is almost paranoid. In the United States more than 16,000 police agencies operate at federal, state, and local levels. There are 60 different federal police services, as well as 13 intelligence agencies, which are considered law enforcement agencies, as well as military police in each of the armed services. If there was a national police force in the United States, it would be the Justice Department, which houses four of the big eight federal agencies. Within the Justice Department, there is the Federal Bureau of Investigation, the Drug Enforcement Agency, United States Citizenship and Immigration Service, and the U.S. Marshals. In the Treasury Department, there is Alcohol, Tobacco and Firearms, Customs, the Internal Revenue Service, and the Secret Service. One of the most effective federal police forces is the U.S. Postal Inspection Service, which investigates and prosecutes approximately 90 percent of all fraud cases in that country. The U.S. Securities and Exchange Commission also has investigative and enforcement powers.

The claim by the RCMP that it is more efficient than police forces in other countries is one of its favourite defence mechanisms. RCMP spokespeople regularly tout the U.S. model as being a cumbersome mishmash of overlapping agencies, each with its own agenda and priorities. There is some truth in that view. The FBI is not all it is cracked up to be—Friendly But Incompetent as RCMP members sarcastically refer to it. For example, the

ATF created the Waco disaster, and the DEA is seen by many to be somewhat ineffective.

The bottom line, however, is that in the United States cases usually get investigated quickly and prosecuted successfully by the federal police, in spite of all their jurisdictional belly-bumping. Every other civilized country in the world has more than one federal police service, except for Canada and New Zealand. What the RCMP really means when it claims to be the most efficient is that, from its perspective, even two federal police forces in Canada would be one too many.

In Canada, the RCMP is usually the point of contact with police from other countries, but not always. International police forces deal regularly with other Canadian police services, bypassing the RCMP. The RCMP calls itself a national police force because it is stretched across the country in its contract capacity and because it operates crime labs and other technical support services for all Canadian police services. But as a contract force, it does not police large urban centres and is virtually invisible in central Canada, where two-thirds of Canadians live, not including the National Capital Region.

As a contract police service, like a national police force, its 10,000 officers in the boonies take their ultimate direction from and report to a central command in Ottawa. But in the confusing Canadian political equation, the RCMP central command is not seen to be functioning as a national police service, but rather as a federal one with responsibility for administering the contracts. Therefore, the RCMP is just as much a pretend national police service as it has been a pretend federal service, like its practice of labelling the seizure of small amounts of drugs during a traffic stop in one of the provinces a federal offence.

As a federal police force, the RCMP has more jurisdictions than any single police force could hope to serve. Under the RCMP Act, the Mounties have been empowered to detect, investigate, and, if an offence occurs, to provide evidence for either administrative sanction or a criminal prosecution for the federal government. By September 2007, the Canadian government had 656 statutes on its books that required enforcement and 3,358 regulations. Each year it adds another 30 or so new laws and even more regulations. The RCMP has jurisdiction not only to enforce the Criminal Code of Canada, but also 118 federal statutes. It had 18 Memoranda of Understanding with various government departments to provide enforcement for those laws and other regulations. Smaller, limited-purpose entities such as the Canada Border Services Agency, Fisheries and Oceans, the Department of Transport, and others have enforcement functions, but each must call upon the RCMP for criminal investigations and prosecutions. Here is how the RCMP described its federal mandate on its own website in November 2007.

Federal Enforcement Program

The Federal Enforcement Program is a component of RCMP Border Integrity and encompasses three distinct federal mandates: the Federal Enforcement mandate, the War Crimes mandate, and the Airport Federal Enforcement Program mandate.

Federal Enforcement Mandate:

The Federal Enforcement mandate encompasses numerous federal statutes and regulations. It is enforced through a combination of proactive and reactive strategies implemented within community-based policing principles. The proactive program is a well-balanced approach of prevention, education and enforcement measures partnered with affected client communities. Reactive investigations are initiated in response to requests for RCMP assistance received from other federal departments. These requests could be in relation to any one of 118 federal statutes and are contingent on the provisions of approximately 18 Memoranda of Understanding with other government departments. This mandate is enforced through four sub-programs: Public Safety; Environmental Crime and Wildlife; Financial Loss to the Federal Government; Consumer Protection.

The public safety sub-program is responsible for operational policy pertaining to safe boating on Canadian waters, safe transportation of dangerous goods, safe transportation in air, rail, water and by pipeline and the safe storage and handling of explosives in magazines. The main statutes under this sub-program include the Canada Shipping Act, Migratory Birds Convention Act and the National Capital Act.

The Environmental Crime and Wildlife sub-program is responsible for operational policy pertaining to environmental protection including coastal fisheries, waste disposal and the dumping of pollutants into the ecosystem. The RCMP works with Environment Canada, for example, to enforce legislation relating to wildlife/endangered species. Another example under this sub-program is the

MOU with Parks Canada that defines the roles of the RCMP and Park Wardens regarding the enforcement of laws in Canada's national parks. Primary statutes under this sub-program include the Canadian Environmental Protection Act, the Quarantine Act, the Canada National Parks Act and the Wild Animal and Plant Protection and Regulations of International and Interprovincial Trade Act.

The Financial Loss to the Federal Government sub-program aims at combating the financial loss to federal government revenues and funds through criminal conspiracies, frauds, forgeries and/or misappropriation of funds. The main statutes that fall under this mandate are: Canada Pension Plan Act, Canada Student Loans Act, Family Orders and Agreements Enforcement Assistance Act and the Old Age Security Act.

The Consumer Protection sub-program is focused on criminal infringement of copyright and trademarks, criminal frauds pertaining to motor vehicle odometer tampering, illegal decoding or theft of television signals by commercial enterprises, retaliatory actions by employers where the employee is the victim (relative to Canadian human rights violations) as well as criminal frauds, forgeries, and conspiracies pertaining to animal pedigrees. The main statutes under this sub-program are the Copyright Act, the Trade-marks Act, the Animal Pedigree Act, the Weights and Measures Act and the Radio-communication Act.

War Crimes Mandate:

The RCMP works with partners such as Department of Justice (DOJ) and Canada Border Services Agency (CBSA) to ensure that Canada does not become a safe haven for those involved in crimes against humanity or war crimes. The War Crimes Program includes initiatives aimed at: preventing war criminals from entering Canada, deportation and revocation of citizenship of war criminals in Canada involved in such acts, and criminal prosecution when appropriate.

The main statute under this mandate is the Crimes Against Humanity and War Crimes Act (CAHWCAct).

Airport Federal Enforcement Mandate:

RCMP investigators work with their partners and other existing federal authorities at Vancouver, Toronto and Montréal international airports to investigate federal statutes to combat organized criminal groups. Since its inception in 1999, the Airport Federal Enforcement Program has been very successful and, in conjunction with its partners such as the Canada Border Services Agency, has seized over $500 million in contraband at these three airports.

In its own words, the RCMP is the agency with an irrepressible "can do it all" attitude. By 2005, while the country was in the throes of the post-September 11 national security threats, financial crime was out of control and the force admitted that it did not have the resources to tackle the vast majority of organized crime groups. Yet during that same period, the RCMP deliberately starved its federal operations of manpower and money. The auditor general reported that year that fully one-quarter of positions in federal policing had gone unfilled. Many believe the actual number was higher than that, perhaps closer to one-third of positions left vacant. The manpower it did have was being used to provide traffic cops in the Lower Mainland of British Columbia and elsewhere where it had contracts.

As one might expect, it is all but impossible to determine how many Mounties are actually dedicated to federal policing. Its own numbers seem deliberately confusing. When I wrote *The Last Guardians* in 1998, I used the RCMP's own estimates of spending as a guide, a copy of which was given to me by then-Commissioner Philip Murray. In those estimates, the numbers seemed clear and definitive. RCMP planned spending on federal policing from 1996 to 1999 declined from $526.6 million to $393.4 million. Actual spending on federal services for the 1997–98 fiscal year was $312.7 million or a little more than $10 per Canadian per year.

In 1998–99 the total RCMP budget was $1,767,400, down almost $70 million from the previous year and almost $160 million less than in 1996–97. Even those numbers are misleading because the RCMP generated almost half as much in income from contract policing, monies that flowed back into government treasuries.

Nine years later, the numbers are not so clear. By the 2006–2007 fiscal year, the RCMP global budget had ballooned to $3.3 billion and the force expected to spend $3.8 billion in 2007–2008. Once again, these numbers were offset by revenues from contract policing and other income streams, which generated $1.2 billion in 2006–2007 and an expected $1.4 billion in 2007–2008. The true total federal government investment in the RCMP, therefore, was $2 billion in 2006–2007 and an expected $2.3 billion in 2007–2008.

In its own estimates, the RCMP now lumps together federal and international policing, and does not break down the numbers, further blurring the data. The RCMP gross budget in 2007–2008 for "Quality Federal Policing" was $796.4 million, almost double what it was in 1997–98, but the numbers lie because it is all but impossible to determine if that money is being directly spent on federal policing or if the monies are being used to further subsidize the provinces and municipalities who buy RCMP contract services. What is clear is that the quality of federal policing in Canada is at its lowest point ever, no matter what the budgets might suggest.

The true test is the number of the RCMP's 16,000 sworn members who are dedicated only to federal policing assignments. Statistics Canada reported in 2006 that the RCMP had approximately 26,000 employees, 16,000 of whom were sworn police officers. Of those, 4,063 were dedicated federal police officers on the job across the country, although, to reiterate, one-quarter of those jobs were vacant. Another 10,000 or so members are working in contract policing.

A useful comparison between today's RCMP and the RCMP of the past can be found in the 1990 report by Auditor General Kenneth Dye. He reported that the RCMP had 20,000 employees, approximately 13,000 of whom were sworn officers. In 1990, when the RCMP budget was $1.5 billion, the auditor general found that the RCMP employed 3,887 members in federal policing. Over the next 16 years, with all that has happened in the world, with all the national and international pressures on Canada to improve its federal policing, the RCMP has done nothing to improve federal policing. Staffing levels are about the same and there seems to be less focus than ever on what it should be doing. Most of the 6,000 additional employees hired since 1990 were directed to either contract policing or to the burgeoning RCMP bureaucracy.

The observations of Halifax Police Chief Frank Beazley and like-minded observers, that the state of federal policing in Canada is a scandal, are not new. Since the McDonald Commission in 1981, there have been repeated calls for the RCMP to either beef up federal policing or for the policing structure in Canada to be reformed, but nothing has been done.

After the McDonald Commission recommended that a separate civilian counter-intelligence agency be created outside the walls of the RCMP, attention became focused on federal policing. Government studies in 1975 and

1978 had detected serious problems within federal law enforcement, which impaired both efficiency and effectiveness. The most significant problem was that the compulsively secretive RCMP had created many conflicts with other agencies, which led to a general lack of communication and cooperation. An internal RCMP study in 1978 confirmed these findings.

As early as 1981, the auditor general's report stated: "A major influence on the RCMP's federal law enforcement responsibilities is a somewhat ambiguous mandate in relation to many of the federal statutes." The report also said that, "In the past two decades, many federal departments and agencies have assumed more active enforcement roles with objectives differing from those of the RCMP."

In 1984, the government directed the solicitor general to undertake a study entitled Federal Law Enforcement Under Review (FLEUR). Then-RCMP Commissioner Robert Simmonds drafted an extensive but controversial plan for the RCMP, one that would put him at odds with the entrenched members of his own force. Simmonds had a vision of an RCMP that was solely a federal police service, operating with an agent-like structure similar to the FBI. Simmonds had seen that the hybridized RCMP could no longer continue to serve the public interest with the structure that had evolved. At the very least, Simmonds believed, the RCMP should get out of protective policing. Guarding buildings and politicians was not police work. That should be left to a separate agency. The government was not interested in what he had to say.

Auditor General Kenneth Dye reported in 1990: "The FLEUR report was completed in 1986, and again it revealed the same problems raised by the three previous studies. However, the government did not accept FLEUR's main proposal which was to establish a federal law enforcement commission to co-ordinate and standardize the federal law enforcement system. Instead, in 1987 the government established an Interdepartmental Committee of Deputy Ministers to oversee the development and implementation of solutions to the problems that FLEUR had identified. Unfortunately, the major weakness that FLEUR and earlier studies have pointed out, namely, the role and responsibilities of the RCMP for enforcing federal laws, remains unresolved."

In that 1990 report, Dye focused on the RCMP's crazy promotional structure in which experience in a certain area had nothing to do with promotion. "RCMP management has recognized that in many areas of federal enforcement its members lack the experience and expertise needed to carry out complicated investigations," Dye wrote. "This problem has resulted from a high turnover of personnel caused by the Force's 'generalist' approach to human resource development, and the related promotion, rotation and staffing policies. The delivery and management of the Economic Crime and Customs and Excise (C&E) Programs have been particularly affected by the high rate of turnover."

Dye added: "The RCMP determined that an 'unreasonably high' turnover of its C&E Program personnel had caused the value of seizures to decrease from $15.7 million in 1980 to $6.1 million in 1986. One study showed that staff in the C&E unit of the Québec City Detachment had, on average, nine months experience."

The turnover rates in Toronto in 1988 and 1989 were 87 percent and 65 percent. In Montréal, it was 50 percent and 64 percent. During those years, fewer than 40 percent of the members of the Toronto Commercial Crime Section had the two years of experience considered by the RCMP as the minimum required for officers to be effective. In 1989, a divisional audit of the Commercial Crime Branch in Toronto found that the lack of management continuity had also affected the program adversely to a significant extent.

The auditor general found that "the high turnover has also frustrated training efforts. In the past five years, although 522 members have gone through the basic C&E training (that is, an effort equivalent to training the entire C&E staff of 180 almost three times over), 61 percent of the C&E personnel in 1989 had not had any basic C&E training. Many officers had been transferred out of C&E units soon after they had received their training."

The RCMP moved its members around so much that in 1988, the C&E section of the Trois-Rivières detachment spent 70 percent of its resources on drug enforcement and other secondment work.

The auditor general said that "RCMP management is aware of these basic problems and has been contemplating the possibility of 'specialization' of its federal law enforcement personnel. Both the Economic Crime and Enforcement Services Programs have upgraded the standards for selecting their staff. However, they have encountered difficulties in implementing these new standards. The RCMP should examine the turnover rate in federal law enforcement. If it is adversely affecting performance, the Force should take steps to reduce or minimize it."

One of the protocols of an auditor general's report is that the agency being targeted be given an opportunity to reply. The RCMP response to all the above was: "Agree. This will be examined as part of the RCMP strategic action plan for enhancing human resource management."

In every report made by the auditor general in the years between 1990 and 2008, the RCMP has responded with the word "Agree," with few minor exceptions, to every critical finding. It has agreed and promised action over and over again. Agree. Agree. Agree. That is what has passed for accountability. The RCMP reads, agrees, and then does virtually nothing. Time after time after time, the federal government has allowed the RCMP to resolve its own problems. Some accountability.

On October 25, 2007, Nicholas Le Pan, the expert adviser to the RCMP's Integrated Market Enforcement Teams, submitted his 77-page report to Commissioner Elliott. The RCMP sat on it for six weeks before releasing it on December 3, where it was all but lost in the midst of the latest revelations about the payoffs by Karlheinz Schreiber to Brian Mulroney in the Airbus scandal. In his report, Le Pan had dissected the IMET unit and what he found was more of the same. The picture he painted was a scaled-down masterpiece of all that ailed the entire force. In his executive summary, Le Pan wrote:

Many people take for granted the integrity of the financial system. Sometimes I was told that capital markets fraud is not the same as other crimes. This is wrong. Fraud is not a victimless crime. Confidence in the integrity of capital markets translates into real benefits for our economy and for individual Canadians.

The IMET program is operating in a very challenging environment that it needs to be better equipped to succeed in. Public and policy maker expectations are extremely high and Canadian credibility on enforcement issues is low to start out with. Start-up knowledge was far from ideal about the challenges and risks the program faced in dealing with major complex capital markets cases. Even reasonable glitches or errors were magnified. Those being investigated or charged will understandably bring substantial high-quality resources to bear to defend themselves. The Program is "playing in the big leagues" and needs to act that way.

Legitimate criticisms center on the lack of results and questioning whether the Program and its partners have the sense of urgency needed to succeed. Nor has IMET demonstrated the leadership, tone from the top, results focus, nimbleness or consistent cohesion of action or communication among the players (including within the

RCMP and PPSC and among the federal players) that is necessary to succeed. The Director did not have clear authority to oversee. There are also frustrations building internally. There is too high a vacancy rate and turnover, and significant key-person risk.

Expectations for IMET sometimes confuse regulatory enforcement with criminal enforcement, without realizing that the latter has a much higher bar for laying charges or for conviction. Expectations of U.S.-style results are unrealistic, given Canada's different legal environment. For example, our lack of ability to compel those not being investigated to provide information, documents and data pre-trial, hampers investigations compared to the U.S. or U.K. Also, as an example, charging people in stages in a major investigation, as is done in the U.S., is not feasible in Canada due to rules on full disclosure of the Crown's case to accused.

Under-promising and over-achieving should become the watchwords for IMET, not the other way round.

Le Pan didn't use David Brown's phrase "horribly broken culture," but he could have if he wished. Le Pan had found that in spite of all the hype from the RCMP, fighting capital market fraud was not a priority of the force, as it is with dedicated financial crime agencies in the United States and Great Britain. "Indications suggest that there is reason for the critics' concern, particularly if IMET and its partners cannot achieve more results soon," Le Pan wrote.

"In the U.S., for example, the President's Corporate Fraud Task Force that was created in mid-2002 (following the Enron collapse) reported over 250 criminal convictions or guilty pleas in its first year, rising to some 500 by the end of its second year. This was greatly increased from the year before. Of course, those agencies were investigating many smaller cases as well as the more limited number of complex cases that is IMET's mandate. However, even a complex case like Enron took 4.5 years from start of investigation to trial conclusion. The first charges were six months after the investigation started. Nineteen people had been charged, including some senior officers, within 18 months. All charges were laid within 2.5 years," Le Pan found.

"The Serious Fraud Office (SFO) in the U.K. regularly reports results. For example, in its most recent annual report (2006–07) it had just over 60 cases under investigation or where proceedings commenced. Eleven cases were completed, involving trials with 21 defendants, of whom 15 were convicted. Several of these they classify as major cases. The SFO publishes its targets for a long-run average investigation-stage length of 16.5 months and a long-run average prosecution-stage length of 14.5 months."

The average IMET investigation was 2.8 years and climbing, without a resolution in sight, Le Pan said. Within the RCMP, he found there was no leadership on the issue, little cooperation with others, and infighting among divisions. There were no clear lines of accountability. No oversight. No results-based system to monitor efficiency and effectiveness. Le Pan was particularly harsh about RCMP Human Resources. He found that there was no commitment to specialization, no career development plan, and no succession planning within the IMET unit. Mounties who were promoted to the squad often arrived with no experience, interest, or talent for the work. Many of them soon transferred out and were not replaced. Twenty-one percent of the positions were vacant. In just four years, all the supervisors had left and been replaced and some of them replaced again.

The RCMP response to this was little different from the ones it had been giving for decades to critical reports about its operations and performance— agree, agree, agree. In finally releasing the report to the public, Commissioner Elliott stated: "The RCMP welcomes the recommendations contained in the report and is committed to enhancing our effectiveness in combating capital markets crime. We have already begun to implement the recommendations and I welcome the ongoing involvement of Mr. Le Pan in our implementation efforts. . . . I believe that this report reflects a number of challenges the RCMP and other Canadian law enforcement agencies face in investigating complex capital markets crime and makes realistic recommendations for improvements. Although I do not expect immediate dramatic results, clearly we can and must do better. The report notes that the IMET Program continues to make progress in investigations and the RCMP is committed to moving ahead quickly with enhancements to the IMET initiative. Fighting capital markets crime more effectively is one of the RCMP's key priorities. I believe that we must achieve enhanced results for Canadians and I will be actively monitoring our progress."

At the insistence of the RCMP, the Le Pan report eschewed neat headline-making catchphrases. With the resulting lack of prominence in the news, combined with the timing of the release in the midst of the renewed Airbus controversy, the RCMP received a bit of a reprieve. The report was buried in most newspapers, and appeared to be just another rap on the RCMP's knuckles, when it actually said so much more.

[21]

AIRBUS I—LE CERCLE OF DISTURBING BENEFACTORS

Karlheinz Schreiber was a German émigré who lived and excelled on the dark side of the ethical spectrum. His story in Canada would play out over three decades, and Schreiber would forever be linked to Brian Mulroney and the Airbus scandal. For a man whose life plan had been to stay in the shadows and keep a low profile, Schreiber became famous for his misdeeds, exposed in three Canadian books: *Presumed Guilty: Brian Mulroney, the Airbus Affair, and the Government of Canada* by William Kaplan in 1998; *The Last Amigo: Karlheinz Schreiber and the Anatomy of a Scandal*, co-authored by Stevie Cameron and Harvey Cashore in 2001; and *A Secret Trial: Brian Mulroney, Stevie Cameron, and the Public Trust*, also by William Kaplan, in 2004. In those books, and in countless newspaper stories, and groundbreaking television pieces by Cashore and host Lynden MacIntyre for *the fifth estate* since 1995, Schreiber's life became an unlikely addition to Canadian political folklore.

Schreiber's cover story was that he was a "money-greaser" for German businesses. There was even an official name, *schmiergelder*, a person designated under a German tax law that permitted middlemen to deduct from their incomes bribes or any other payments to foreigners to secure the sale of German products. One of his major clients was Thyssen AG, Germany's largest mining and steel conglomerate. In the seventies, Thyssen began to branch out into other industries around the world, including building and construction materials, elevators, and light tanks. The controlling Thyssen family, known as the Rockefellers of the Ruhr, had been the original financiers of Adolph Hitler's Nazis at a time when other German industrialists were leery of the political movement. In the thirties, the Thyssens had purged their company of Jews, although some members of the family eventually broke with the Nazis during the Second World War over the extermination camps. Thyssen AG, only one of Schreiber's stable of clients, paid him $35 million over a 15-year period, ostensibly to purchase political influence around the world in favour of its products.

In 1978, Schreiber moved from Germany and settled in Calgary, where he opened a real estate business and set out to make powerful, political friends in his adopted country. In his covert capacity as a representative for a number of German corporations, he had an instinct for identifying not only the powerful but also those who might rise to power. Schreiber immediately began to get cozy with the local politicians through a friend, cabinet minister Horst Schmid. He set up a company, A.B.S. Investments Ltd., and named former provincial cabinet ministers Hugh Horner and Bill Dickie, and former Conservative MP Bill Skoreyko, to its board. A former executive assistant to Schmid was hired by Schreiber in 1980. The group's secret plan was to buy up large tracts of land in the undeveloped areas around a booming Edmonton, which was about to expand its municipal boundaries.

One person Schreiber could not get close to was Alberta Premier Peter Lougheed, the most recognized right-wing conservative in Canada. Many believed Lougheed would someday seek to become prime minister, but he eschewed that opportunity despite the encouragement and support of Canadian business leaders. In 1979, Schreiber even stalked Lougheed to Switzerland, where he "accidentally" had a chance run-in with the Alberta premier on a ski hill. After dining with Schreiber that day, Lougheed became wary of him and later described him as "poisonous." Lougheed never revealed what Schreiber had told him, but later events suggest that it might well have been something entirely nefarious. Lougheed ordered his colleagues to stay away from Schreiber, but some did not.

Eventually Schreiber's secret land grab—fuelled with insider knowledge—led to a public and political furor and the calling of a nationally publicized inquiry by Justice William Brennan in 1981. In his 60-page report in the spring of 1982, Brennan found no fault with Schreiber's land speculation but, as Susan Ruttan later described in the *Edmonton Journal*, "the judge issued a stern warning to those who speculate financially on decisions to be made by government, and any former politicians they hire as lobbyists." A number of Schreiber's investors also lost their shirts in the gambit, lawsuits were launched, and Schreiber was all but *persona non grata* in Alberta. He shifted his attention east.

In Germany, Schreiber was a confidant and partner of Bavarian Premier Franz Josef Strauss, who was also the chairman of the newly-formed European airplane manufacturing consortium, Airbus Industrie. Strauss wanted Airbus to break into the North American market dominated by Boeing, the giant U.S. aircraft manufacturer. Canada would be, as Strauss himself put it, his "Trojan horse." He paid his friend Schreiber to come to Canada in the hope that he could convince the Canadian government to buy the European airplanes.

Almost as an afterthought, Schreiber would later say, Strauss put money into a campaign to engineer the downfall of Progressive Conservative leader and former prime minister Joe Clark. The plan was to help install Brian Mulroney as the party leader, a necessary step to making him prime minister. On the surface it seemed like an audacious and ambitious sales strategy for the chairman of an aircraft manufacturing company. Getting overtly involved in the political process was not something business people normally do. The treachery and double dealing required made such a proposition extremely dangerous. So why did Franz Josef Strauss do this? Was there more to the story than merely selling aircraft?

Since it was first revealed that something sinister had taken place in the overthrow of Joe Clark and the subsequent rise of Brian Mulroney, successive Canadian governments have been adamant about not pursuing the issue. The attitude could be summed up with the maxim "let's not dwell on the past." As it turned out, there were other reasons why the federal government has not wanted to dig into what had happened.

Any investigation that led back to Franz Josef Strauss could get messy. Strauss was a complex individual. After serving in the German army in the Second World War, he was appointed county president of Schongau by the American occupiers. Strauss won a seat in the first German parliament in 1949 and quickly rose to high levels under the tutelage of then-Chancellor Konrad Adenauer. In 1962, Strauss was forced to resign from cabinet after he admitted he had lied to parliament about the reasons for the arrest and 103-day incarceration of Rudolf Augstein, the owner and editor-in-chief of *Der Spiegel* magazine. The outraged Strauss compared his own treatment to that of "a Jew who had dared appear at a NSDAP [Nazi] party convention."

In 1965, Strauss cemented his right-wing credentials with the publication of a slender but influential book, *The Grand Design: A European Solution to German Reunification*. In it, Strauss articulated the need for "a massive drive to achieve, step by step, a European political federation," a United States of Europe, as it were.

This leads us into the tricky area of what has commonly been derided as "conspiracy theory."

✜ ✜ ✜

There are those who believe that everything important that happens in the world is controlled by one or another group of powerful individuals and secret organizations. Some think these people are capable of pulling the strings of politicians to implement policies favourable to some master plan. For example, was John F. Kennedy just killed by Lee Harvey Oswald, and Oswald only by Jack Ruby two days later? Or was it all a massive conspiracy?

The popular media rarely delve into the realm of conspiracy theory, no matter how persuasive the evidence might be in some instances. But not all conspiracy theories are theories; some are fact.

George Orwell's dystopian classic *1984*, published in 1949, satirized the notion of perpetual war—"War is peace." When he left office in 1961, U.S. president Dwight D. Eisenhower did not hide behind fiction. He warned in his farewell speech of the growing power and incipient danger of what he dubbed "the military–industrial complex." Eisenhower, a great general in the Second World War, had come to believe that the growing link between U.S. business and its armed forces meant that the United States would inevitably be dragged into a series of wars as a means of propelling its economy forward. Without war, the massive U.S. arms industry would be rendered redundant. Millions of workers would lose their jobs. Eisenhower believed wars were only meant to be conducted when needed, not for profit. Similar warnings were sounded later by, among others, industrial sociologist Seymour Melman in his 1983 book *Profits Without Production*. Melman argued that by abandoning the intrinsic, wealth-creating power of manufacturing for a perpetual war economy, the United States was creating an illusory economy doomed to fail. Every U.S. president since Eisenhower has found his way into a war or two.

In Italy in the 1960s and 1970s, many Italians were perplexed by the seemingly incongruous behaviour of their government, justice system, and police. There was a perception that the country's institutions were corrupt, but no one could find the key. The country's leaders dismissed any suggestion that there was a conspiracy that had its grip on the country. Then the worst fears of the Italian people were found to be anything but imaginary.

In the same early eighties time frame during which Schreiber was skulking around Canada, the Banco Ambrosiano collapsed in Italy. The banking arm of the Vatican, it was found to have been controlled by a Masonic lodge, Propaganda Due (P2). An investigation by Italian authorities determined that the lodge's members included aristocrats, high-ranking politicians, current and former military, intelligence, and police officers, businessmen, journalists, and members of the Italian Mafia—a government within a government. The bank was being used to finance secret activities in Italy and around the world. Among the documents found in a police raid on the villa of P2 "Worshipful Master" Licio Gelli was a "Plan for Democratic Rebirth," which called for a consolidation of the media, the suppression of trade unions, and the rewriting of the Italian constitution.

The P2 Lodge was eventually implicated in the murder of Italian journalist Mino Pecorelli and banker Robert Calvi. It was also suspected of killing Albino Luciani, Pope John Paul I, who was aware of what was going on inside the Vatican bank and had planned reforms. Luciani, who was in good health, died mysteriously on September 28, 1978, just 33 days after being elected Pope. The P2 investigation resulted in prosecutions against dozens of high-ranking business executives and politicians, including former Prime Minister Bettino Craxi, former Justice Minister Claudio Martelli, and former Olivetti Chairman Carlo di Benedetti.

Closely linked to the Vatican scandal was another mysterious organization, Opus Dei, the extreme right wing of the Catholic Church, made famous in Dan Brown's extraordinarily popular novel, *The Da Vinci Code*. Opus Dei was seen to be the modern reincarnation of the Knights Templar, which was disbanded in 1312 by Pope Clement.

In modern times, the goals and activities of secret societies like the Bavarian Illuminati, founded in the eighteenth century, have been the subject of much speculation. But no groups have been more reviled and feared by conspiracy theorists from across the political spectrum than the Bilderberg Group and the Trilateral Commission—and their overlapping offshoots like the Pilgrims, the 1001 Club, and the Bohemian Grove. The Bilderberg Group was started in 1954, when leading government, business leaders, and intellectuals from Europe and North America met at the Bilderberg Hotel in Amsterdam. They envisioned their conference as a think tank to thrash out the issues of the day and to plot a course of action that might prove mutually beneficial. The Trilateral Commission, set up in 1973 by David Rockefeller, was an overlapping group heavily weighted by private banking interests that included Japan. Each group has been described as part of a shadow world government and, like P2, a government within governments.

These various entities have one thing in common—to keep alive and vibrant such old-world concepts as the British and Holy Roman Empires, powerful political-economic-military alliances. The driving force behind these groups is leading industrialists, the descendants of European and British royal families, and New World tycoons like Canada's Paul Desmarais.

No one knows where Bilderberg's meetings are held or what is said. Minutes are kept of meetings but names are not recorded, although lists can be found on the Internet. In 1976, Bilderberg almost collapsed after, in an indicative revelation, it was publicly disclosed that Prince Bernhard had approached the Lockheed Corporation with an offer to use his official position to influence Dutch defense procurement policies in return for a financial consideration.

One of the frequent and important attendees at Bilderberg was David Rockefeller, the U.S. billionaire and former chairman and chief executive officer of Chase Manhattan Bank, one of the supporters of the World Bank. Now in his nineties, Rockefeller is still considered by many to be the most powerful man in the United States—the "kingmaker."

A lifelong globalist who preached sustainable growth, Rockefeller became frustrated by the refusal of the Bilderberg Group to include Japan in its meetings. After reading Zbigniew Brzezinski's 1970 book *Between Two Ages: America's Role in the Technetronic Era*, Rockefeller opted for a new direction. It was then he created the Trilateral Commission. At the time Rockefeller was chairman of the U.S. Council on Foreign Relations, an independent, non-partisan organization which, nevertheless, is still considered to be the most powerful arm of U.S. foreign policy after the State Department. In 1973, Rockefeller set up the Trilateral Commission and invited Japan to the conference table. The Trilateral Commission membership overlapped the Bilderberg Group, but included journalists and publishers, as well. It was heavily weighted by private banking interests.

In subsequent years, Bilderbergers and Trilateralists have risen to power in western governments and bureaucracies and have been relied upon heavily for advice and to help implement policies. Some critics assert that the overriding interest of the Trilateralists is the protection of the private banking system, particularly during national and international debt crises. Extreme right-wingers like U.S. commentator Pat Robertson have labelled both Bilderberg and the Trilateral Commission as vehicles for one-world-government that have sprung "from the depth of something evil." The far left is afraid that the Trilateral Commission is promoting corporatization over democracy.

The commission even became a fixture of Gary Trudeau's popular comic strip *Doonesbury*. In one classic example, a slightly paunchy businessman announces to a bartender that he is in the mood to celebrate because he has just been accepted as a member of the Trilateral Commission—"It is a powerful coterie of statesmen and international financiers which periodically meets in secret to shape the destiny of the western world. My job is to set zinc prices."

In a 1998 tribute to Rockefeller, longtime Trilateral Commission member Henry Kissinger said: "David's function in our society is to recognize great tasks, to overcome the obstacles, to help find and inspire the people to carry them out, and to do it with remarkable delicacy. . . ." In other words, Rockefeller was the invisible hand of all invisible hands, looking out not so much for the greater good as for the good of all those who perceived themselves to be greater.

David Rockefeller, therefore, had all the requisite credentials—power, influence, and friends everywhere—to get what he wanted done behind the scenes, without leaving his fingerprints. He was the kind of person who had the motive, the means, and the opportunity to overthrow governments, if he so desired, and to install as leaders people who shared his vision.

In 2002, he published *Memoirs*. In that book Rockefeller made light of the Trilateral Commission's reputation. He related how his own son Richard had told him that his Harvard friends thought it was "a nefarious conspiracy." *Memoirs* was criticized because Rockefeller raised a number of issues but then left so many loose ends. One of those was a vignette found on pages 412 and 413:

"Consorting with Reactionaries"

Bilderberg overlapped for a time with my membership in a relatively obscure but potentially even more controversial body known as the Pesenti Group. I had first learned about it in October 1967 when Carlo Pesenti (Banco Ambrosiano shareholder), the owner of a number of important Italian corporations, took me aside at a Chase investment forum in Paris and invited me to join his group, which discussed contemporary trends in European and world politics. It was a select group, he told me, mostly Europeans. Since Pesenti was an important Chase customer and he assured me the other members interesting and congenial, I accepted the invitation.

Jean Monnet, Robert Schuman, and Konrad Adenauer were founding members of the group, but by the time I joined, they had been replaced by an equally prominent roster that included Antoine Pinay, a former French president, Giulio Andreotti, several times Prime Minister of Italy, and Franz-Josef Strauss, the head of the Christian Social Union in Bavaria and a perennial contender for the chancellorship of the Federal Republic of Germany.

The discussions were conducted in French, and usually I was the sole American present, although on a few occasions when the group assembled in Washington, Henry Kissinger, at the time President Nixon's national security advisor, joined us for dinner. Members of the Pesenti Group were all committed to European political and economic integration, but a few—Archduke Otto of Austria, the head of the House of Hapsburg, Monsignor Alberto Giovanetti of the Vatican and a prominent member of Opus Dei, the Conservative Catholic organization, and Jean-Paul León Violet, a conservative French intellectual—were preoccupied by the Soviet threat and the inexorable rise to power of the Communist parties of France and Italy.

Pesenti set the agenda for our thrice-yearly meetings, and Maître Violet, who had close connections with the Deuxième Bureau of the Services des Renseignements (the French CIA), provided lengthy background briefings. Using an overhead projector, Violet displayed transparency after transparency filled with data documenting Soviet infiltration of governments around the world and supporting his belief that the threat of global Communist victory was quite real. While all of us knew the Soviets were behind the "wars of national liberation" in Asia, Africa, and Latin America, I was not personally convinced the Red Menace was quite as menacing as Maître Violet portrayed it to be, but my view was a minority one in that group.

Even though I found some of the discussions fascinating, the ultraconservative politics of some participants were more than a bit unnerving. My Chase associates, who feared my membership could be construed as "consorting with reactionaries," eventually prevailed upon me to withdraw.

David Rockefeller had stumbled into a snake pit of an organization that seemed to have been ripped from the pages of Frederick Forsyth's chilling 1972 novel *The Odessa File*. The group was dominated by Old World aristocrats and "stay-behind" fascists, so-called because they were still scheming to achieve their failed Second World War objectives. Fascism may have been defeated in Europe, but it was not dead. Supporters of the movement had faded into the tapestry of society, but had not lost sight of their vision for Europe and their hatred of socialism. The secret organization was so scary that it appeared to have turned Rockefeller into a conspiracy theorist.

Although Rockefeller called it the Pesenti Group, the group was actually called Le Cercle Pinay or the Pinay Circle, named after Pinay, a French statesman who briefly had served in 1952 as Prime Minister of France. The key players were Antoine Pinay, Jean-Paul Leon Violet, and Franz Josef Strauss. Its driving force was French lawyer Violet. Before the Second World War, Violet had been a member of the Comité Secret pour l'Action Revolutionnaire, a secretive fascist group. That group was also known as the Cagoule, "the hooded ones," and was considered to be an important branch of the legendary Synarchist Movement of Empire which had worked to undermine the French Republic for the Nazi invasion during the Second World War. Both Pinay and Violet were also members of Opus Dei. In recent years, Le Cercle Pinay has come to be known simply as Le Cercle.

The religious tie is an interesting one. Le Cercle has much the same lofty ambition as present-day fundamentalist Muslims who dream of building a world caliphate to restore the boundaries of their one-time empire. One of Le Cercle's founding members was Austrian aristocrat Otto von Habsburg, head of the Paneuropa Union. Von Habsburg was also a central player in underground Vatican movements. These movements are linked by a common dream—the reunification of Europe and the re-establishment of a modern Holy Roman Empire, which would include all western democratic countries.

Not much has been written about Le Cercle in the popular media for reasons which should become obvious. In 2004, an interest group in the Netherlands began to collect information for a project called the Project for the Exposure of Hidden Institutions (PEHI). Its work is published on the Internet. Conceived by Joël van der Reijden, PEHI gathered the known and convincing public evidence of Le Cercle's existence, members, and activities.

Among van der Reijden's findings was a story published in 1975 in a London magazine *Time Out*, which had been leaked 1,500 documents from the British Institute for the Study of Conflict. Soon after the story appeared, the leaked documents mysteriously disappeared from the *Time Out* office. The story, however, was picked up by the German magazine *Kronket*, and later by the popular newsmagazine *Der Spiegel*.

The *Time Out* documents revealed much about how Le Cercle worked. At that time, The Institute for the Study of Conflict was being headed by ex-CIA agent Brian Crozier, who was also the current Le Cercle chairman. Le Cercle had also provided funding for the Institute. Crozier was also revealed to be a member of an even more clandestine group, simply called "The 61."

The *Time Out* documents showed that the original goal of Le Cercle was to fight off the Soviet Union and to unify Europe, but by the seventies it had become dedicated to installing right-wing governments in power not only in Europe, but throughout the western world. Its membership was described as being "a secretive, privately-funded and transnational discussion group which regularly meets in different parts of the world. It is attended by a mixture of politicians, ambassadors, bankers, shady businessmen, oil experts, editors, publishers, military officers and intelligence agents, which may or may not have retired from their official functions. The participants come from western or western-oriented countries. Many important members tend to be affiliated with the aristocratic circles in London or obscure elements within the Vatican, and accusations of links to fascism and Synarchism are anything but uncommon in this milieu." Although lesser known, its membership, with people like former U.S. Secretary of State Henry Kissinger, overlapped with that of groups such as the Trilateral Commission and the Bilderberg Group, among others.

The *Time Out* documents contained correspondence between a senior German intelligence officer and Hans Langemann, head of Bavarian state security. Langemann, alarmed by what he was hearing, went public. He related tales of old-world alliances, ex-Nazis and other fascists, the CIA, and plans for manipulating democratic processes and having their chosen people elected to power. In those documents, Le Cercle came to the realization that the easiest and most effective way to implement its ideas and plans was to identify a like-minded leader in a country and then to throw all its efforts into getting him or her elected. It took credit for engineering the election of Strauss as Bavarian premier, the first step in an unsuccessful plan to have him elected chancellor.

Le Cercle also claimed to have orchestrated the election of Margaret Thatcher in 1979, through a covert advisory committee called Crozier's Shield. The *Time Out* documents revealed that "Crozier put together Thatcher's election campaign by adopting Jean Violet's Psychological Action program, a technique to find quick, short answers to three basic questions: What do people want? What do they fear? And what do they feel strongly about? Shield also completely convinced Thatcher about the severe threat of domestic communist subversion [in] their paper 'The diabolical nature of the Communist conspiracy.' Thatcher's reaction was, 'I've read every word and I'm shattered. What should we do?'"

Think about the simplistic campaigns of conservative governments over the past 20 years around the world: What do they want? Lower taxes. What do they fear? Threats to their security. And what do they feel strongly about? Pick your country, choose your answer. Universal health care. Right to bear arms. Campaigns are focused around those three little questions with no discussion about the real issues or policies.

In its campaign to implement its all-but-fascist vision, Le Cercle and its hidden members were implicated in the smearing, undermining, and defeat or attempted defeat of politicians such as Harold Wilson in Great Britain, Jimmy Carter in the United States, François Mitterrand in France, Olaf Palme in Sweden, and Gough Whitlam in Australia, among others. They considered Canadian Prime Minister Pierre Trudeau to be a Communist and targeted him as well.

Van der Reijden further reported: "Additional subjects covered in the Langemann papers include the "involvement of the main intelligence and security agencies both as information sources and as recipients for information in these institutions" as well as "undercover financial transactions for political aims" that would be utilized by conducting "international campaigns aiming to discredit hostile personalities or events," the "creation of a (private) intelligence service specialising according to a selective point of view" and the "establishment of offices under suitable cover each run by a coordinator from the central office. Current plans cover London, Washington, Paris, Munich and Madrid." The plans also called for "provision of contributions by certain well-known journalists in Britain, the U.S. and other countries" and the "organisation" of "public demonstrations in particular areas on themes to be decided and selected." Le Cercle and their chairman, Crozier, clearly had lined up a whole strategy of political "actions" that were not only known about, but approved by the western intelligence community, in addition to leading political figures, including Prime Minister Thatcher and presidential candidate Reagan.

In the mid-seventies, according to Van der Reijden, Le Cercle extended its reach to North America with the opening of the Washington Institute for the Study of Conflict, headed by George Ball, former Undersecretary of State (1961–66), a member of the Trilateral Commission and the Council for

Foreign Relations, and on the steering committee of the Bilderberg Group.

In 1979, Maurice Tugwell formed the Canadian Centre for Conflict Studies. Brigadier Tugwell, a former British army intelligence officer, arrived in Canada on the heels of a controversy in Great Britain in the aftermath of the "Bloody Sunday" massacre in Derry, North Ireland. On January 30, 1972, members of the Derry Housing Action Committee, supported by the Northern Ireland Civil Rights Association, were conducting a protest march when they were confronted by members of the 1st Battalion of the British Parachute Regiment. Twenty-six people were shot. Fourteen of them died. Five had been shot in the back. Tugwell was the chief communications officer for the British Army and went on television after the shootings saying that eight of those shot were wanted by British authorities.

He was soon linked to a black propaganda unit which operated out of Lisburn, Northern Ireland, which came to be known as the Lisburn Lie Factory. Tugwell's unit was an army propaganda unit that specialized in psy-ops (psychological operations), conducting disinformation under the guise of press information. At the subsequent Widgery Tribunal which investigated the matter, Tugwell was questioned extensively about the propaganda unit, but denied that he was involved in any such work. It was not until a second inquiry was called in 1998, chaired by Lord Saville of Newdigate, that Tugwell withdrew his assertion about the eight so-called suspects.

Meanwhile, back in Canada in 1979, Tugwell's Centre for Conflict Studies quickly earned contracts working for both the RCMP and the Department of Defence. In 1986, Tugwell formed the privately funded, non-profit Mackenzie Institute for the Study of Terrorism, Revolution and Propaganda, a right-wing think tank in Toronto. The institute's stated mission was: "to provide research and commentary on a subject matter, to promote informed public debate, and to hold to the proposition that our liberal democratic tradition must be safeguarded and fostered." In published materials the institute has also stated that it intended "to provide Canadians with a source of information on psychological warfare" and was also "concerned with the social and political stability of Canada, and works to enhance it when it can." Over the past decade, the MacKenzie Institute, now under the direction of John Thompson, has become a high-profile, influential fixture in Canadian public discourse.

In recent years there has been little mention of Le Cercle in the popular press. In 1997, the following headline, "Aitken dropped by the Right's secret club," was published in the respected British newspaper *The Independent*.

The story was about British Privy Councillor Jonathan Aitken, a former Minister of State for Defence, who had been reportedly kicked out of Le Cercle. *The Independent* wrote: "Formed in the Fifties . . . One of the most influential, secretive, and it goes without saying, exclusive political clubs in the West . . . One member contacted by this newspaper said he could not talk about it 'even off the record.' Another simply put the phone down. . . . The source of its funding is a mystery."

It should not have been a mystery. In 1994, in the second of his three-volume *Diaries*, former British Defence Minister Alan Clarke, another former member of Le Cercle, said unequivocally that the organization was financed by the CIA. Clarke died in 1999.

With this background, let us continue with the story of Karlheinz Schreiber.

✝ ✝ ✝

When Karlheinz Schreiber first came to Canada, the obvious place to look for a right-wing politician was Alberta, but he found that he could not seduce Peter Lougheed.

After spending enough time in Canada, he realized there was one tried and tested route for taking effective control of the federal government—through Québec. As we have already seen, Québeckers had become extremely adept at insinuating themselves at the intersections of power in Ottawa.

In his search for a candidate, Schreiber found former Newfoundland Premier Frank Moores. Moores led Schreiber to Brian Mulroney, a well-known Québec labour lawyer at the upscale firm Ogilvy Renault. Through his legal work, Mulroney had become close to then-Québec Premier Robert Bourassa. As John Sawatsky revealed in his 1991 book *Mulroney: The Politics of Ambition*, Mulroney protected Bourassa from testifying before the Cliche Commission, a 1974 public inquiry into organized crime influence and labour violence at the province's James Bay hydroelectric project. One thread of the commission's investigation led to the premier's office, but Mulroney, a counsel to the commission, argued that Bourassa did not have to testify, citing "executive privilege."

It was a revealing gambit for a future prime minister to take. Most Canadians consider themselves to be part of a country of equals governed by the rule of law. However, Canadian elected leaders and their legal counsels have proven they are not bound by that proposition.

During the seventies, the RCMP found themselves in one confrontation after another with leading politicians. A distinct pattern of misconduct, recognizable to this day, emerged during that period.

For example, in 1974 the RCMP found that federal contracts were being rigged for the dredging of the St. Lawrence River, among other projects. One of the leads led directly to Bourassa. Other associated cases led to members of Bourassa's extended family and political allies. Bourassa used all the powers of the provincial government and justice system to thwart the RCMP investigators, to the point of threatening to arrest and charge Rod Stamler, the lead RCMP investigator. It was clear that there was no love lost between the Québec establishment and the federal police.

Former Newfoundland Premier Joey Smallwood had come under scrutiny after the RCMP raided a Montréal hotel room and found evidence that Smallwood had been paid at least $375,000 by fraud artist John C. Doyle to hand over valuable mining concessions in the province in the 1960s. "I would make a deal with the devil himself, if it were for the good of Newfoundland," Smallwood had said at the time, and he did. Later, among other dealings with Doyle, Smallwood was named as an accomplice in a massive Doyle-inspired swindle known as Canadian Javelin, which bilked investors out of $10 million. The case was dismissed on a legal technicality.

Former New Brunswick Premier Richard Hatfield became so incensed at an RCMP investigation into a kickback and toll-gating system by his government that a few years later, in 1976, he set up his own short-lived New Brunswick Highway Patrol to deny the Mounties the contract work. His government also enacted an unprecedented regulation that no RCMP investigation could proceed until it was vetted by a provincial prosecutor, which allowed the politicians to see what the police were planning to do. As reported in *Above The Law*, Hatfield even went so far as to rig a public inquiry conducted by Chief Justice C.J.A. Hughes to exonerate himself and his government of all the "insinuation, implication and innuendos."

In 1976, Mulroney came out of the blue and took a wild run at the leadership of the Progressive Conservative Party, pouring an unprecedented $500,000 into his campaign. Québec had long been a stumbling block for the Tories, who were seen to be the party of English-Canadian business interests. Mulroney championed himself as a non-French Québecker who could win over the skeptical *"pur laine"* traditionalists in the province. His slick Cadillac campaign was too much for English-Canadian Conservatives and he finished out of the running. He was defeated by the little-known

Joe Clark, so obscure a choice that a newspaper headline the next day read: "Joe Who?"

Mulroney returned to his job as a lawyer at Ogilvy Renault but soon took on new duties as president of the Iron Ore Company of Canada. After battling alcoholism and depression, he reorganized the company and then, as would be his wont, sold it off to foreign interests. He also went back to work for his self-described mentor in business, Paul Desmarais.

In March 1978, Mulroney emerged from the shadows of business and attended a fundraising dinner in Toronto for Sam Wakim, a Progressive Conservative candidate who had been his roommate in university. In his 1991 book about Mulroney, Sawatsky quoted an unnamed *Globe and Mail* reporter's story about what had taken place. "Brian Mulroney re-emerged as a politician last night for the first time since that Sunday afternoon in February 1976, when he lost in his bid for the leadership of the federal Progressive Conservative Party. What he said was that Joe Clark was the best man to lead the Tories to victory in the next election. It was an admission that was a long time in coming. Yet, there still is an inclination not to take Mr. Mulroney at his word."

I was that *Globe and Mail* reporter, the only reporter there that night. It was the first time I had seen Mulroney live in action and I can remember the event it as if it were yesterday. As charming as he seemed to be, there was something disingenuous about Mulroney that bothered me, and I said so. Perhaps it was the devious twinkle in his eyes, the furrowed brow, the curl at the corner of his mouth as he spoke, all but laughing at his own fiction as he spoke.

Becoming prime minister, however, would prove to be difficult, especially after Clark won a surprise victory in 1979 over Pierre Trudeau and became prime minister. But Clark soon stumbled into a Liberal parliamentary trap, lost the confidence of the House, and was brought down several months later. He was voted out of power in 1980, but was still the leader of the Opposition. The scene was set for the elect-Mulroney plot to shift into the next gear.

By 1981, Karlheinz Schreiber had settled in Canada and had been granted citizenship. Schreiber was used to working in the grey areas between the laws of a country and the powers of a country's leaders. There was no greyer time in Canada.

The RCMP Security Service, its counter-intelligence wing charged with detecting spies and other threats to Canada, was under the very public scrutiny of the McDonald Commission. The Service was rendered all but useless.

Schreiber gathered around him a circle of friends—Moores, Austrian Walter Wolf, Montréal lawyer Michel Cogger, and New Brunswick politico Fred Doucet, among others. Franz Josef Strauss, the Bavarian premier, and his family interests, began to funnel money to them. The stated plan was to set up potentially lucrative businesses which could manufacture expensive military and aviation products for the government. The real reason was to rearrange the government of Canada, a by-product of which would be to facilitate those sales.

Cogger set up a company in Montréal in 1981, the majority of which was owned by Schreiber and Strauss. In 1982, Moores sold some land in Newfoundland to the company run by Schreiber and Strauss. The $370,000 in foreign money was then used to finance Mulroney's bid for the leadership of the Conservative Party by first undercutting Clark. In January 1983, the Conservatives called for a leadership review to be held at a convention in Winnipeg. Clark, for some inexplicable reason, declared that he would need 70 percent of the vote or he would step aside. He received 67 percent, more than enough in any democracy, but kept his word and resigned—an old-fashioned honourable man.

At that convention, Richard Cléroux of *The Globe and Mail* learned that many of the delegates from Québec had had their entire airfare, hotel accommodations, and shopping expenses paid for by Walter Wolf, the Austrian, if they promised to vote against Clark. Their contribution was seen to have tipped the balance and changed the course of Canadian history.

This should have been the first clue to the nefariousness of Mulroney and his backers. In the supposedly gentlemanly world of Canadian politics, Mulroney was the equivalent of baseball's underhanded home-run king, Barry Bonds, his political muscle artificially enhanced by the steroid of ill-gotten money. Mulroney also had an old boys' network raising funds for him in the United States that was run by Boston insurance executive Robert Shea. He was allowed to get away with that, too.

The next year John Turner won the Liberal party leadership to replace Pierre Trudeau and became prime minister. Before leaving his job, however, Trudeau saddled Turner with more than 200 patronage appointments which, despite a public outcry, Turner approved. Four days after getting the job he called an election he believed the party was sure to win. Turner then appointed longtime Liberal cabinet minister Bryce Mackasey, another Québecker with a colourful history, to the post of Ambassador to Portugal.

Mackasey was a rascal in his own right and had his own place in the political mafia. He had served in Ottawa as a cabinet minister under Trudeau and had resigned twice. Once out of office, he had returned to Québec where he won a seat in the provincial assembly. He resigned that job and went back to Ottawa in 1976 and tried again to get back into federal politics. When he failed to win in that election, the government appointed him chairman of Air Canada, a Crown corporation. In 1983, Mackasey had been caught in a scandal of his own. *Montréal Gazette* reporter William Marsden revealed that Mackasey, hiding behind a numbered company, had been acting as a lobbyist for other businesses seeking work from the federal government and taking kickbacks.

The Honourable Mr. Mackasey tried to assert his parliamentary privilege to protect himself. When that did not work he resorted to enormous libel suits, seeking tens of millions of dollars. Nevertheless, he was charged with fraud and influence peddling by the RCMP. The charges were soon thrown out by a Québec judge in a convoluted and controversial judgment. Marsden subsequently wrote that the RCMP was not all that interested in the Mackasey investigation because they sensed it would be a waste of their time. "They are all a bunch of whores," a Mountie said. It would be a portentous comment.

During the election campaign, months later, Mulroney stuck to Jean Violet's psychological action program. What do they want? Lower taxes. What do they fear? Free trade with the United States—"It would be like a mouse getting in bed with an elephant." What do they feel strongly about? National unity. Mulroney won a majority government that September, surprising even himself.

A slip of the tongue along the way by Mulroney, however, revealed a little more about his nature than he might have wanted the public to see. In commenting on Mackasey's ambassadorial appointment, Mulroney said: "There's no whore like an old whore. If I'd been in Bryce's position, I'd have been right there with my nose in the public trough like the rest of them."

Mulroney knew of what he spoke. Schreiber, Moores, Cogger, and others were creating corporate entities and lobbying companies to win government business for high-ticket items like helicopters, tanks, and airplanes. Lobbying had been a small business in Ottawa until Mulroney arrived, fewer than ten companies. In a few short years, there were almost one hundred companies, the most important of them being Government Consultants International (GCI) operated by Moores. GCI was unlike any other lobbying firm. It openly promised its clients that it could influence government decisions and it quickly built a track record to prove it. The transformation of Canadian institutions was well underway.

On March 7, 1985, one of the Schreiber group of companies, International Aircraft Leasing (IAL) of Liechtenstein, signed a secret contract with German aircraft manufacturer Messerschmitt-Bölkow Blohm (MBB) to sell helicopters to the Canadian Coast Guard. The contract stated that IAL would get eight percent on every helicopter sold in Canada. A year later, Canada purchased 12 helicopters for $27 million and the commission was paid to IAL.

Five days later, on March 12, Mulroney fired the board of directors of Air Canada, and appointed a new board which included Frank Moores. Moores would be forced off the board five months later after a political controversy over his continuing lobbying efforts through GCI.

Another critical deal for the group involved Thyssen AG and its plans to build light armoured vehicles near Bear Head Island in impoverished Cape Breton, Nova Scotia. The project promised 500 needed jobs and was backed by one of Nova Scotia's own, Mulroney cabinet minister Elmer MacKay. His son Peter, who would later go on to be a federal cabinet minister, went to work for Thyssen. Canadian Jewish groups, among others, had complained the tanks were being made for the enemies of Israel and protested. Although the Bear Head project never went ahead, for reasons which have never been revealed, the negotiations had gone far enough down the track to trigger a $3.9 million secret commission for Mulroney's friends.

It wasn't until 1988 that the group finally struck real gold. In March 1988, rumours were swirling that Air Canada was about to order a bevy of new commercial airliners from Airbus Industrie. At the same time, there were other rumours and questions in the House of Commons about hidden Tory government connections to the deal. The *Toronto Star* published this headline on March 15, 1988: "MP questions Tory links to big jet deal." Fifteen days later, on March 30, the Air Canada board of directors agreed to pay $1.8 billion to buy 34 Airbus A320 planes. Franz Josef Strauss was a happy man and so were his Canadian secret agents. Airbus handed Schreiber $20 million for his work on the sale, to be distributed to all those who had worked in the background to make the deal happen. Back in Canada, as reported in *The Last Guardians*, Mulroney even put pressure on Air Canada to pay Frank Moores's company, GCI, an additional $5 million commission, although GCI had done nothing. The money was not paid out.

On April 12, 1988, Transport Minister Don Mazankowski announced that the government intended to privatize Air Canada, another potentially lucrative deal for the insiders who would then not have to deal in the future with government oversight.

Throughout all this, scandal after scandal rocked the Mulroney government. Mulroney had campaigned against free trade with the United States, but once in power moved quickly, manipulating the negotiation process with U.S. President Ronald Reagan to make free trade law in 1988.

One of the long-forgotten stumbling blocks to the ratification of the free trade deal had been a complaint filed by Boeing, the giant U.S. aircraft maker, to the FBI. Boeing, which had its own well-placed security and intelligence infrastructure, said it had evidence of influence peddling by Canadian politicians and kickbacks in the Airbus deal. Boeing alleged that as much as $12 million had been paid out in secret commissions to unknown Canadians by Airbus and its intermediaries. Everyone in the world seemed to know about the grease money floating around—everyone but the Canadian government and the RCMP.

The RCMP launched an investigation into the Boeing complaint, but just as it was getting underway the Mulroney government announced that it had weakened the powers of the Foreign Investment Review Board. One of the first deals approved under the new regime was Boeing's purchase of the assets of de Havilland of Canada, the country's venerable airplane manufacturer. Boeing then dropped its complaint about the Airbus payoffs and stopped talking to the police. The FBI also lost interest in the matter.

By now, even some of Mulroney's own caucus members were calling him Lyin' Brian. Mulroney deftly shifted attention away from all the corruption by focusing on national unity. He portrayed himself as the saviour of Canada, the one man who could appease Québec. In the fall of 1988, many Canadian voters were swayed by Mulroney's promises. Led by Québec and Alberta, Mulroney won a second majority government, albeit with a reduced majority. The very next day, October 3, 1988, the man who helped engineer his rise to power, Airbus chairman and Bavarian premier Franz Josef Strauss, died.

Although the electorate had given him a second chance, Mulroney did nothing to alleviate the stench in his government or cement a reputation for being an honourable man. A few days after winning his second term, Mulroney unilaterally approved a Canadian banking license for American

Express—without debate. It was an unprecedented act under suspicious circumstances. The RCMP wanted to investigate but no one filed a complaint with the force.

The RCMP and a handful of news reporters were investigating case after case of slippery dealings involving Tory backbenchers, party hangers-on, and businessmen and women, mostly with ties to Québec. Mulroney's longtime university friends and social circle, people like Lucien Bouchard, Bernard Roy, Michael Meighen, Gary Whelan, Gary Ouellet, Jean Bazin, and Peter White, began to be scrutinized. But no matter what happened through the years, the focus always returned to one case—Airbus.

By the early 1990s, the Mulroney shine had worn off on the Canadian public. His popularity plummeted to 17 percent in opinion polls. His party was all but destroyed. Whispers about big payoffs in the 1988 Airbus deal continued to circulate, but no one could find the evidence. Mulroney left office in 1993, and returned to practising law at Ogilvy Renault. He said his decade in politics had drained his savings, and that he was broke, desperate for money. He began to call on friends for help, but he didn't look as down and out as he claimed to be or as unpopular as the polls might have suggested.

He must have done something right for someone. Back in Montréal, a group of anonymous businessmen, not the least being the Desmaraises, collected $4 million, which they gave to the distressed Mulroney. He used $1.6 million to purchase a mansion in Mount Royal in Westmount, the bastion of the English establishment in the city. Along the way, the Mulroneys spent another $600,000 or so in renovations on their mansion. As Stevie Cameron reported in *On The Take,* most of it was paid in cash, as the couple went on a mad spending spree. They were also looking at buying a condo in Florida with the magic money they said they didn't have. It looked like Mulroney had gotten away with it all—with a little help from his friends.

In every democratic country around the world during this period, there were numerous cases of corrupted, powerful politicians being investigated, prosecuted, and jailed for taking bribes from corporations, but only a small fish or two in Canada. Were Canadian politicians more honest and ethical than the politicians of other countries? Why were police forces in other countries so successful at similar investigations in their respective countries, but not the RCMP in Canada? Was the justice system corrupted too? What had gone wrong with the RCMP? The problems began at the top of the force.

✛   ✛   ✛

Brian Mulroney was the first Canadian prime minister to have effective political control over the RCMP.

Commissioner Robert Simmonds was an old-school cop, who many believe was over his head as commissioner. Simmonds was the first RCMP commissioner to serve as a deputy solicitor general in the regime created after the McDonald Commission. He was quickly seduced by the trappings. "I'm a deputy minister," he said, reminding his underlings, "We are public servants and we have to accept the decisions of our political masters." After the turmoil and disruption of the McDonald Commission inquiry, Simmonds lost sight of the fact that in a democracy the master of the police was supposed to be the law and the courts, not politicians. Government was responsible for the administration of the police force, not law enforcement. This point was well enunciated in *Above the Law* by former RCMP Deputy Commissioner Henry Jensen who worked under Simmonds at the time. Jensen was still active in policing in 2007, as chairman of the Ottawa Police Services Board. He says his view today has not changed. Here is what he had to say in 1994:

> After the McDonald Commission there was far more top-down vigilance, control if you would, of the force. There was detectable nervousness in the Commissioner's Office. I guess the politicians made almost compelling reasons for information to be drawn to the top. I think it led to information improperly being disclosed to political officials or to officials of the minister. To me, that's wrong. No one should know outside of the police who is under investigation.

The "detectable nervousness" of the commissioner had much to do with the fear of controversy. By its very nature, police work sparks controversy—people do not like to be investigated, especially people with something to hide. "The police go out on a limb from time to time, but they do it because they believe they have to do it. They have to do it to live up to their oath of office," says Jensen. "The role of the police is not to please any government. The role of the police is to live up to their obligations to society, to enforce the law."

Under Simmonds, the practice of providing the solicitor general with information about investigations became formalized. There were two sets of briefing books, one for the commissioner and the other for the minister. When a Mountie program director saw a headline in a newspaper related to his area of responsibility, he had to write up a report on the matter, including possible questions that might be asked of the appropriate minister and suggested responses. There was even a liaison officer between government and RCMP headquarters who handled the paperwork. The Mounties at headquarters thought that the liaison officer, although a Mountie, was acting like a ferret for the government as he often came back with further questions about a case. There was a constant flow of information up to the minister and his political staff.

Rank-and-file Mounties had been co-opted into acting as political advisers to politicians, but the police had no avenue of protest. Simmonds believed there was nothing wrong with the practice. "You know, being a deputy minister is a powerful position, without question," says Jensen. "And once you see in your mind that you're a deputy minister, it affects your role as a policeman. You cross the line." It was an intolerable situation for the police and it continues to exist.

The relationship between the RCMP and government during the first three years of the Mulroney reign was a contentious one. By 1987—a year before the Airbus purchase—the RCMP was already investigating multiple cases of political corruption involving members of Mulroney's government and his own associates. As the investigations mounted, the government was getting uncomfortable. Conservative MP Michel Gravel was convicted of accepting bribes and influence peddling, the first sitting member of Parliament to have been jailed in 25 years. Another Conservative member from Québec, Richard Grisé, was headed for the same fate. All the bad publicity was forcing the hand of the government. Something had to be done. One might think that an ethical leader would root out the political kleptocrats and support the efforts of the police. Instead, Mulroney sought to get more control over the federal police.

At a routine meeting of the solicitor general's committee in 1987, Simmonds found himself sandbagged by Québec members who demanded that he speak French, which he couldn't. Mulroney's Solicitor General James Kelleher then used the incident as a catalyst to search for a new commissioner. A committee empowered to find candidates ended up choosing one of its own, Norman Inkster, the force's director of human resources. Kelleher moved Inkster into an office next to his in the solicitor general's department.

As we have already seen, the RCMP was a police force in distress in the late 1980s and 1990s. To choose as the new commissioner the force's human resources officer, the man who oversaw hiring, promotion, and discipline, sent a message to some that the government wanted to improve the RCMP by raising its standards. That was precisely what did not happen.

Inkster brought two qualities to the job which made him the perfect choice for Mulroney. First, Inkster was keenly political in everything he did. Fellow Mounties used to marvel at his smoothness and image control, right down to attending public functions with his adopted Jamaican daughter at his side. The other thing that attracted Mulroney was purely Machiavellian. The RCMP had been in distress for years, spinning its wheels in the mud. What better way to perpetuate that failed model than to appoint to the highest position in the force the very person who had helped construct it—the negative application of political control, as it were.

From the RCMP's perspective, Inkster was a disaster from the moment he took over. After 1987, RCMP federal investigators were run off their feet chasing down a virtual feeding frenzy of unethical behaviour and suspected malfeasance by those close to Mulroney. The public treasury was being milked in a variety of ways. Mulroney was selling off Crown corporations, government assets, and buildings at a furious pace, while equally eager to purchase expensive goods and services for the government, often at hugely inflated prices.

For his part, Inkster set up a special federal enforcement investigations unit in Ottawa to look into all the corruption, but made sure that the operation was situated, not in "A" Division where it should have been, but at headquarters, where he could keep a close eye on its work. The individual Mounties in the special investigations unit first thought they were part of an elite squad, but soon found themselves being moved around, promoted, or ordered to do VIP protection at a moment's notice. It was all but impossible for them to bring continuity to any investigation.

As the RCMP struggled to do its job, investigators found strange things were happening. In one investigation in the late 1980s, investigators left a document they had found in a federal department. When they returned the next day with a search warrant, it was gone. On another occasion, they were issued a search warrant in Ottawa for the office of a Québec Conservative MP only to find a copy of the warrant in her office desk in Montréal the next day. The police were justified in their actions but the politicians continued to cry foul. The eager-to-please Inkster was all too willing to hear them out.

In June 1989, the Standing Committee on Justice and the solicitor general wanted to question Inkster about political interference in the force. The committee members wanted to know why charges against Conservative MP Grisé were not laid before the November 1988 general election. It looked like an apparent favour to the Mulroney government.

Inkster first denied the force had done anything wrong. However, the next time he appeared before the same committee, he elaborated on what had happened, but then went on to reveal something he should not have talked about. He told the committee that since 1985, the RCMP had investigated 30 people appointed or elected to Parliament. He said there were 15 active investigations. "Most of these investigations have been carried out amidst great public debate," Inkster said. "Yet in each case I can find no evidence that members of the force did other than their duty without fear, favour or affection of or towards any person. The RCMP enforces the law and should not be subject to criticism from those who wish to deflect their embarrassment or use the force in an attempt to further embarrass a political opponent. Political partisanship may be an essential feature of representative government, but it is not essential to discredit the RCMP to serve political purposes."

It all sounded high and mighty, but Inkster had done the unthinkable. He had revealed to the government and the public what RCMP investigators were doing. The suspects in the 15 cases knew who they were. Inkster had given them ample warning to get rid of any damaging evidence the police might be able to find and use against them.

One of those being investigated was Michel Cogger, who had been Mulroney's best man at his wedding. Despite all the controversies surrounding Cogger, Mulroney appointed him a senator. The RCMP had known about Cogger's activities since at least 1984, when he did something decidedly unwise. As reported in *Above The Law*, Cogger had randomly been assigned a seat next to RCMP Assistant Commissioner Rod Stamler on a transatlantic flight from England. At the time, Stamler was head of the force's drug enforcement section. Stamler never revealed his identity to Cogger, other than to say he worked for the government. Cogger opened up to the Mountie and told him about what he had been doing in the Channel Islands and Bermuda. He talked about how he and Walter Wolf had opened a bank account with an opening deposit of $50,000 to secretly finance Mulroney's election campaign. He bragged that he was the person who had knocked off Joe Clark as the Tory leader. Stamler reported the conversation to the force after arriving home.

By the late eighties, there were so many indications of corruption in the Mulroney government that it was all but impossible to keep track. Two mysterious break-ins in Montréal were being investigated. Mulroney's personal papers from the 1976 leadership bid were stolen from the office of Mulroney adviser Roger Nantel. The party headquarters in Montréal had also been broken into by unknown thieves. That investigation led to the discovery of a third, otherwise unreported, break-in at Voyageur Marine Construction in the Montréal suburb of Pointe Claire. Cogger was a director of the company and Wolf was one-third owner. The unknown thieves had stolen a photocopy of a cheque for US$80,231. To the police it looked as if someone was out to try to prove Mulroney's illegal offshore funding, something he had always denied.

In October 1988, Takayuki Tsuru, a Japanese businessman, filed a sworn affidavit, complaining he had been duped out of $39 million by a Montréal-area businessman named Guy Montpetit. Tsuru said Cogger had been paid $114,000 to lobby the federal government for a $45 million contract, which never materialized.

The RCMP investigation was suddenly cancelled after a mysterious telex—ostensibly signed by Deputy Commissioner Jensen—ordered the Mounties in Montréal to end the probe. Jensen said he never sent the telex and to this day does not know who did. But the decision to end the Cogger investigation was left to stand.

But Cogger soon came under RCMP scrutiny in another case. This time he was a suspect in the possible bid-rigging of a $160 million communications system for the department of External Affairs. The RCMP was also suspicious that Cogger was involved in offshore money laundering. As the Mounties closed in on him in January 1990, a headline in the *Ottawa Citizen* caught Mulroney's eye: "Cogger 'Sting' Target: Agent." That morning, Mulroney could not contain his contempt for the force any longer, and lashed out at his RCMP escorts: "You dizzy, stupid bastards."

A few weeks later, the diminutive Cogger got up in the Senate, tears flowing, and portrayed the Mounties as being biased, prejudiced, part of a criminal plot against him, out of control, undisciplined, unprofessional, and prone to leaking information to the media.

Inkster reacted to Cogger's unsupported allegations—which Cogger never repeated outside the safe and legally protected confines of the Senate—and stopped the investigation. Among other things, Inkster took the unprecedented step of asking a judge, René Marin, to hold an inquiry into the RCMP investigation—effectively ending police efforts. A year later, in 1991, Marin reported that the Mounties had done nothing wrong, but had been "manipulated" by an undercover operator.

By the mid-1990s, the RCMP Airbus investigation had long gone dormant. As was typical within the RCMP, the Airbus investigation was like a story begun by one writer, picked up by another, and then a third, and so on. There had been so many changes in personnel that it was all but impossible for any one officer to pick up the thread.

Mulroney's successor, Jean Chrétien, had no interest in having the police pursue the matter. The government did not care that Canada had paid $20 million more than necessary for the Airbus planes or that at least $10 million of that money had landed in the hands of unknown Canadians—courtesy of Karlheinz Schreiber. Such an investigation would certainly lead the police to the depths of institutionalized, third-world style corruption in the country.

When I interviewed Inkster during this period he said that there was no Airbus investigation because "No one has filed a complaint." Inkster was subsequently replaced by Philip Murray, another RCMP human resources officer, who continued running the force in much the same way as his predecessor but, arguably, even worse.

With the police largely neutralized and government uninterested in getting to the bottom of the Mulroney miasma, it was left to the media to track down the story and keep the issue alive.

[22]

AIRBUS II—LYIN' BRIAN
AND HIS MEDIA "ENEMIES"

From the very first moments he began to stumble in 1984 to his political demise, Brian Mulroney tried to create the impression that a cadre of renegade journalists was out to get him. He even labelled the work of some journalists as personal attacks motivated by hate. He complained that these people did not understand either him or his policies and suggested some were agents with a secret agenda and political motives. By the spring of 2008, one of his spokespersons went as far as to call on Canadian journalists to stop their "jihad" against Mulroney.

But to fully understand how difficult it was for Canadians to learn the truth about the Airbus case, one must first appreciate that not only the RCMP, but also important voices in the media, had been brought under effective political control.

By the mid-nineties, the Canadian media had fallen under the same neo-conservative spell and had come to suffer from the same malaise—an all-encompassing focus on the bottom line, at least on the surface. Inside newsrooms something more nefarious was going on. There was all but universal support for right-wing politics and politicians.

When Mulroney became prime minister in 1984, the leading newspaper in Canada was *The Globe and Mail*, Canada's self-described national newspaper, based in Toronto. Its guiding principle was expressed daily at the top of its editorial page, a quotation from the obscure English writer known as Junius: "The subject who is truly loyal to the Chief Magistrate will neither advise nor submit to arbitrary measures." It suggested that *Globe* journalists brought a sense of independence to their work and that their ultimate focus was the defence of the public interest. It was not a pretty newspaper, but it was powerful, a must-read for the social, business, and political elite as well as those who cared about the important issues of the day. The *Globe* saw itself as a newspaper of record and to that end covered the institutions of power in depth. It constantly tried to probe beneath the superficiality of everyday politics and business in search of important stories. The paper strived to be a vehicle for informed and thoughtful commentary. To that end, it was the engine that set the agenda for news coverage across Canada.

Many thought that the paper was conservative because of its readership base, while those in power thought it too liberal. When homosexuality became an issue in the 1970s, for example, a *Globe* editorialist wrote: "The state has no place in the bedrooms of the nation." Prime Minister Pierre Trudeau picked up the line and used it to ban the prosecution of homosexuality.

In 1978, *Globe and Mail* owner Kenneth Thomson signalled the pending transformation of newspapers in the country when he hired A. Roy Megarry as publisher. A registered industrial accountant, the Irish-born Megarry had come from the canned-soup business and had no previous experience in journalism. He entered journalism as an agent of change in the early days of the computer revolution, determined to modernize newspaper processes. It was a calling he did not really seem to understand. For example, one day he wandered into the newsroom and mused out loud: "Why do we have all these copy editors here? We pay reporters a lot of money and we expect them to get the stories right when they write them. Why don't we just use spell-checker programs?" He did not appreciate the need for the layers of brain power required to achieve excellence.

Megarry was so unfamiliar with normal Canadian pastimes that when he attended his first Toronto Blue Jays game in 1984, he was surprised by the number of people who paid to go to baseball games. When a batter struck out in mid-game, he asked: "Where is he going?"

Megarry was a leader in the Club of Rome and an acquaintance of the Aga Khan and was influenced by the writing of right-wing thinkers such as Herman Kahn and his 1976 book *Reshaping the International Order*. He believed that business coverage—not news—was the *Globe*'s primary mandate. The reason for this, he said at the time, was because advertising in the paper's *Report on Business* brought in a disproportionate amount of revenue. It was his view that the news department was a cost centre to be tolerated, not encouraged.

Throughout the eighties, Megarry forced the *Globe* to embrace technology and expanded the reach of the paper across Canada with satellite publishing centres. At the same time, he squeezed the budget for news gathering in favour of business coverage and fluffy, glossy magazines.

The newspaper's editor-in-chief was Norman Webster and its managing editor, Geoffrey Stevens. Together they mounted a subtle, guerrilla warfare campaign against the publisher and his wishes. During their tenure, from late 1982 to 1989, the *Globe* continued to excel at and even expand its capacity to uncover hidden stories which inevitably blossomed into major controversies. Toronto-based reporters like Peter Moon, Victor Malarek, Jock Ferguson, Stevie Cameron, Linda McQuaig, and Andrew McIntosh, to name some, had done groundbreaking work in a variety of important areas across the country. Cameron and McIntosh had exposed many of the Mulroney government scandals. Malarek had uncovered how the prestigious Toronto law firm, Lang Michener, had become involved in a sordid series of deals with Hong Kong businessmen eager to gain Canadian citizenship. Ferguson showed the close hidden links between land developers and politicians in the Toronto area. Ferguson's work led to McQuaig and columnist Michael Valpy uncovering a system of illegal political financing in which money was funnelled through a Jewish charity to the governing Liberal party in Ontario led by Premier David Peterson. The resulting Patti Starr Affair, named after the head of the charity, led to nine cabinet ministers losing their jobs on one day—unprecedented in Canadian history.

The *Globe* was good at making waves and getting to the real stories about how Canada really worked. For years the *Globe* had captured just about every possible award for its work, including the prestigious Michener Award for disinterested public service journalism three of the previous four years.

The journalistic successes did not count for much with Megarry. *Globe* reporters and editors were regularly smeared by right-wing commentators and members of the Canadian establishment for being "too left-wing." The allegations were both unfair and untrue.

In late 1988 and early 1989, Megarry ruthlessly got rid of Webster, then Stevens. He chose ultra-right-wing intellectual William Thorsell to become the paper's editor-in-chief. The Alberta-born Thorsell had once worked as an assistant to a dean at Princeton University. In 1975, at the age of 30, he made the leap into the newspaper business, becoming an editorial writer for the *Edmonton Journal*. In the intervening years, he had gone back and forth between the *Globe* and the *Journal*, always as an opinion writer, before landing the *Globe* editor's job. He had never worked as a reporter.

In his maiden speech in the *Globe* newsroom, Thorsell took issue with the previously cited Junius quotation. "What does that mean?" he asked rhetorically. He also challenged one of the traditional tenets of an independent newspaper: "Comfort the afflicted and afflict the comfortable."

"Why would we want to afflict anyone?" Thorsell asked, answering his own question. "Many of my best friends are comfortable."

It was the advent of the "good-news story," as reporters were told to find happy stories that would help offset "all the negativism" in the newspapers. By its very nature, news is about change and change usually involves conflict. Good-news stories are more often than not the antithesis of news, manufactured to take up space that might be better used for stories in the public interest. As longtime *Globe* reporter, editor, and columnist Murray Campbell once put it, ever so dryly, the news was about to become "less facts intensive."

Thorsell revealed himself to be such a right-wing polemicist that another *Globe* columnist, Trent Frayne, said "he dragged sand." Thorsell would become one of only a handful of Canadian journalists invited to attend the Bilderberg Conference. He proudly admitted to being a confidant of Prime Minister Mulroney—"I talk to him just about every day."

One of Thorsell's "innovations" was to have senior news editors sit in on off-the-record meetings with the editorial board, which is the convention in some newspapers. At the *Globe*, news reporters and editors did not attend such meetings because they want everything said to be on the record. Out of curiosity, however, in my capacity as national editor, I attended two such meetings in 1989, one with David Peterson and the other with Mulroney.

We all sat in a circle that day. Mulroney was directly across from me. For an hour Mulroney charmed everyone with his gravelly voice and humorous anecdotes as he defended his decision to implement freer trade with the United States. Near the end of the session, Thorsell noticed that I had—uncharacteristically—not said anything. He asked me if I had any thoughts. I did.

"I have studied your government and the statements by you and your colleagues, and I only have one question: Who in your government speaks for Canada?" I asked.

Mulroney glowered at me and then broke into a smile, as if to say, "Who is this guy?" By his facial expressions, I sensed he was making a mental note about me. He laughed and joked but never answered the question.

The next day, his friend and confidant Sam Wakim called me out of the blue. "So I see you met Brian yesterday. . . ." It was clear by the brief conversation with Wakim that I had entered dangerous territory—once again.

Thorsell had come to power at the *Globe* just as the Patti Starr imbroglio was dying down. One day he paid me a not-unexpected visit in my office and closed the door behind him. He began to upbraid me for the Starr coverage, which I had supervised. It had run daily for almost a month.

"You took twenty-two straight days to do that story, when it could have taken three," Thorsell said. "You deliberately tortured the government."

The "torture" phrase was an interesting one because it had come from one of our inside sources to Premier Peterson during a conversation in the midst of the series. I could only imagine where Thorsell had gotten it.

"We just followed the story where it took us. I'm sorry it was so effective," was all I had to say.

My career at *The Globe and Mail* was soon over, as were the careers of many others. As was the case in most industries of the day, an entire cohort of wise, knowledgeable, and experienced reporters and editors were soon shown the door through buyouts and not-so-subtle coercion.

In the context of this story, the circumstances surrounding the final days at the *Globe* of two reporters is worth noting.

With her Nancy Drew-like enthusiasm and circle of socialite friends, Stevie Cameron seemed like an unlikely investigative reporter. In 1989, she had published a Canadian bestseller, *Ottawa Inside Out: Prestige and Scandal in the Nation's Capital*. The gossipy book showed Canadians the minutiae of the Mulroneys' high living, right down to the number of designer shoes in Mila Mulroney's closet. Shortly after the book was published, Cameron became involved in an investigation about a young man who said he had been sexually abused at a private boy's school. Although Cameron was blessed with intuition and energy, one of her weaknesses was a penchant for getting too close to her sources. In this instance, she believed too much, and her editors, eager to prove themselves, did not push her for more evidence. The story ran as Cameron had written it and the boy's school was destroyed. A libel suit was launched and it was later revealed that the boy was actually working as a secret agent for the owner of a rival private school that wanted the business. Cameron's days at the *Globe* were done. Her editor was promoted.

Jock Ferguson, who would play a key role in the Airbus story, met his *Globe* demise in a similar fashion. He and the paper were sued over errors in a story that should have been caught by his editors. The resulting court case cost *The Globe and Mail* more than $1 million in damages and costs—and sapped much of its courage in the years to come. Ferguson was expendable. His editor was promoted.

By the nineties, fear of litigation trumped investigative journalism in the new world of corporate journalism. The media became averse to ground-breaking, sometimes controversial, storytelling, even though there was much to report.

One reason for this was that despite decades of protests, and the findings and recommendations of public inquiries, both the Mulroney and Chrétien governments refused to intervene as media concentration in the country became more intense. The neo-conservative agenda was that the stock market should decide which enterprises live and die. Advocates of the primacy of the stock market like to argue that the system puts control in the hands of the many rather than the few, but the opposite is true. With interlinked boards of directors, a very few can effectively control just about everything in an economy, most important the supposedly free media. Before long, every major enterprise in the country, with the exception of the publicly-owned CBC, had become part of a publicly-traded conglomerate.

Who was being allowed to buy up the media and control it? It was the very same individuals whom Mulroney had appointed in 1992 as privy councillors to honour Canada's 125th year: Paul Desmarais, who controlled *La Presse*, the largest French-language daily in Québec and the second largest in the world. He also had large stakes in many other major newspapers and media outlets across the country. The French-language media he did not own was controlled by Pierre Peladeau and his family, who worked closely with Power Corp.

In 1993, through Hollinger Inc., Conrad Black began to take control of the Southam newspaper group and its virtual monopoly of large- and small-city newspapers in English Canada. The Southam papers accounted for more than half of Canada's newspaper circulation.

Another privy councillor who got his hands on the media was former bureaucrat Robert Rabinovitch. He became chief executive officer of the Canadian Broadcasting Corp. Michael Sabia had worked inside the Privy Council before becoming the chief executive officer of Bell Canada. His company subsequently bought both CTV News and a majority share of *The Globe and Mail* and created CTVglobemedia.

All these business tycoons running the Canadian news business were part of a cozy, powerful club, privy to official secrets and sworn to keep them.

In 1998, Mulroney ally Black eventually bought out the entire Southam chain and, in some respects, improved them. But he put a right-wing stamp on it all, dramatically changing the atmosphere for reporters who worked in those newspapers. Black's accountant, Jack Boultbee, reminded his editorial staff one day: "You think your business is selling news. Your business is selling ads." As we know now, Boultbee, along with Black and three of their colleagues, would be convicted of fraud in 2007, and jailed in the United States.

The Toronto Star, the country's largest newspaper and also publicly traded, was not all that interested in political muckraking, especially with its chosen party under Chrétien in power. The rest of Canadian papers were largely concerned with the parochial matters of their provincial towns, with the exception of the business-friendly *Financial Post*. At that paper, reporter Philip Mathias continued to pursue stories in decidedly hostile surroundings.

When it came to political coverage, the private television and radio stations showed little initiative in generating new stories, but depended upon veteran Ottawa insiders like Mike Duffy to comment on events. Political coverage, such as it was, was relegated to phone-in show hosts. The CBC had its own struggles as it defended itself against constant attacks from free enterprisers both inside and outside government for being too left-wing and inefficient. Successive governments had reduced the CBC's budgets, making it more and more difficult for the Corp, as it is widely known, to undertake the kind of in-depth work for which it had become renowned.

There was even an attempt to shut down *the fifth estate* and create a show that was flashier and more upbeat, but that show failed. Like everything else being privatized during the time, the ultra-conservatives were advocating that the CBC be sold off to "level the playing field" for the massive commercial stations, who had shown little interest or proclivity for disinterested public interest journalism.

A final step in the devolution of quality disinterested journalism was the tight controls placed on newsrooms, not only in their budgets, but also in the pursuit, organization, and presentation of the news. The stated intention of redesigning newspapers was to attract a new generation of readers and more women. The net effect was smaller newspapers with less news content in rigid formats. There was a place for everything and everything in its place, if approved.

There were two particularly insidious developments during this period. The first was the overt management of news by corporations and government: controlling the message. By its very definition, controlling the message is about limiting debate or criticism by bypassing the filter of quality journalism. Reporters were expected to be stenographers—which many of them became—particularly in the cloistered confines of parliamentary news bureaus. It became routine for those who dared breach the protocol to be cut off from information or even ostracized.

The second development was the way columnists began to be treated. For example, in the past, in newspapers, a columnist could drive an issue for days on end to the point where the public would have time to consider and reflect upon what was being said. Under the above-described Thorsell rule, three days was more than enough for any story, no matter how large, and even that was rarely done. Newspapers were more than eager to change the subject for government to the point where the cynical political manipulators could expect that no story would be more than a predictable flap that soon would be overtaken by other news—sometimes manufactured—and then all but forgotten.

In its place a system developed in which the media became filled with the opinions of commentators in the artificial pursuit of balance. Whereas a columnist like Michael Valpy all but brought down the David Peterson government with a stinging series, by the mid-nineties few columnists in the country were allowed to write on consecutive days or about the same subject for any period of time. Enforced variety and the appearance of balance blunted the reach and effect of public interest journalists. It became all but impossible to hear what the few dedicated, disinterested writers had to say, lost in the cacophony of shouting voices—some of them propagandists with hidden political agendas—from all sides of the political spectrum.

The media, therefore, had become organized in an entirely ironic fashion. The publicly financed Canadian Broadcasting Corporation was often attacked for being in the pocket of government when it had a proven track record of non-partisanship. Meanwhile, the significantly larger private media—supposedly free of government influence—was, with a few exceptions, transformed into a stenographers' pool for the use of government and politicians. The coverage of Airbus proves this point.

In the private media, investigative reporting had become a dying art. Stories were done here and there about Airbus, but there was little, if any, commitment by the news industry in Canada to pursue in any meaningful way deep-seated corruption in business and government. Because of that, it looked as if Brian Mulroney and his light-fingered acquaintances were off the hook. The RCMP had been placed in a box under lock and key. The Canadian media had all but been neutralized, and time was on Mulroney's side. It had been seven years since the Airbus deal in 1988. It looked as if it was smooth sailing ahead for Mulroney, but new life was breathed into the story after a most unusual set of events.

✠ ✠ ✠

Almost from the moment the $20 million in secret Airbus commissions had been paid out to Schreiber, there had been a falling out among the thieves. In Canada, some of Frank Moores's accomplices had begun to complain as early as 1988 that he had received more than his fair share of the money. All the players were known to the media and public suspicion was high about what had happened, but everyone involved denied any hint of wrongdoing or involvement. The dissension in the ranks was kept largely under control because there was always more business to do.

In Europe, meanwhile, Karlheinz Schreiber had come down hard on his Swiss accountant, Giorgio Pelossi, claiming that he also had taken too much of the Airbus commissions for himself. Schreiber put pressure on Pelossi to pay back the money. The accountant was miffed. He stewed about the matter for a while and when Schreiber would not relent, Pelossi decided to exact his revenge by going to the media. In 1995, he contacted Mathias Muller von Blumencron, a senior editor at *Der Spiegel*, the German newsmagazine, and laid out the story for him.

Pelossi told von Blumencron about how Schreiber had been the conduit for millions of dollars of grease money which was being directed to politicians in Germany and Canada. He even provided evidence of a meeting in August 26, 1991, when Schreiber met two men in a pizzeria parking lot in St. Margrethen, Switzerland. The two were Walther Leisler Kiep, the long-time treasurer of Chancellor Helmut Kohl's Democratic Union party, and Horst Weyrauch, Kohl's trusted party accountant. Schreiber had handed them a briefcase containing US$500,000 in German banknotes. The money had come from Thyssen AG to enlist political support for the sale of 36 tanks to Saudi Arabia.

In Canada, Pelossi said, Schreiber had set up a network which had set up shell companies in Liechtenstein and elsewhere. They would be used to conceal the secret commissions from German companies that were funnelled to Canadian politicians and their acquaintances. Pelossi provided documents to prove Airbus had paid millions of dollars in secret commissions to Canadians to secure the sale of its aircraft to Air Canada. He could also show that Thyssen paid money to International Aircraft Leasing for the Bear

Head project and that Messerschmitt-Bölkow Blohm had paid commissions in the helicopter sale to the Canadian Coast Guard.

Von Blumencron recognized that Pelossi had opened a door to the biggest political scandal in post-Second World War German history. He also wanted to pursue the Canadian angle, but needed help. He had recently attended the Investigative Reporters and Editors Annual Conference, a gathering of investigative journalists from around the world. He contacted its organizers looking for the name of a reporter in Canada who could do some legwork for him. He was given the name of Jock Ferguson, who by now was almost out of the journalism business, unable to find similar work in Canada. Ferguson was employed as an investigator for a forensic accounting firm in Toronto.

After conferring with von Blumencron, Ferguson was in a quandary about who to bring the story to in Canada. His old paper, still under the grip of Mulroney confidant Thorsell, was out of the picture, as were all the other Canadian papers. Ferguson's only real choice was the Canadian Broadcasting Corp. He contacted Susan Teskey, senior producer at *the fifth estate*, with the story idea.

As it turned out, *the fifth estate* producer Harvey Cashore was working on a similar story. Television documentaries like those undertaken by *the fifth estate* are both time- and labour-intensive. In a good year, Cashore might get two or three stories to air. The story he was chasing came from a tip by an airline industry executive about shenanigans involving Boeing-owned de Havilland aircraft. The allegation was that de Havilland was paying secret commissions to land a contract with Bahamas Air. Cashore and his researchers, Howard Goldenthal and Morris Carp, thought it was an interesting story. When they set out to pursue it, the aircraft executive told him about another one, even more scandalous. "The big one was Airbus," the man said. "It was the mother of all bribe deals. It was so secret, nobody knew about it."

Cashore went to Teskey's office to tell her what he had been told just as she had finished her briefing by Ferguson about the *Der Spiegel* investigation. Ferguson and Cashore were assigned to work with von Blumencron. "It was really that simple," Cashore said in an interview. "People seem to think we had done a lot more, but it just landed in our lap." Cashore did not realize it at the time but the story would occupy him on and off for the next 13 years.

Cashore came to the story with a unique advantage. He had been John Sawatsky's research associate for his 1991 book on Mulroney. For that comprehensive book, Sawatsky had used journalism students at Carleton

University to gather information about Mulroney. More than 600 interviews were conducted, overseen by Cashore. He therefore knew a lot more about Mulroney than most reporters starting out on a story.

Like any television producer, Cashore set out to find archival footage where the co-conspirators might have been captured on videotape. While perusing an old German magazine, he found a photo of Brian Mulroney at a luncheon in Germany with Chancellor Helmut Kohl. He called the CBC archive department which combed through its files. The CBC did have footage shot at the luncheon—which was scheduled to be erased a week later as part of a routine purging. As Cashore viewed the film, someone on the soundtrack is heard to shout in the background, "Herr Schreiber, Herr Schreiber," followed by a dream shot—Mulroney, Schreiber, and Kohl laughing it up like old buddies.

In March 1995, *Der Spiegel* published "The Tycoon from Alberta" detailing Schreiber's activities in Canada and Germany, including his unseemly relationships with Kohl, Kiep, and Weyrauch.

A few weeks later, *the fifth estate* followed up with its version of the story, "Sealed in Silence," the first Canadian revelations about the Airbus payoffs to Schreiber and Frank Moores. Questions were raised about a mysterious bank account, code-named Devon, which had been set up by Schreiber. Who was Devon? One of the limitations of a television broadcast is how little can really be said in a one-hour format. With commercials, intros, and extros, there are really only 40 minutes of storytelling time. It is an all but impossible medium in which to explain complex stories with multiple threads. There is no flexibility. One show a year on any one topic, with an update or two, was considered to be fair and balanced—anything more, no matter how warranted, might be construed as a bias or campaign. Mulroney, Moores, and company pooh-poohed the CBC and *Der Spiegel* stories, saying there was nothing to them.

After the *Der Spiegel* article was published, German police swung into action. They soon tracked down Pelossi, who was ready to sing to the police about everything that had gone on. What emerged from this point on might well be called a tale of two countries.

The German authorities followed the money trail and were soon onto the scope of political corruption in Germany, including secret bank accounts run by Kohl, which showed that at least $16 million had been deposited over time. Kohl would never admit the sources of the money. At one point he described it as coming from secret benefactors, while another time he said the money came as donations from Holocaust survivors. Some of the money was clearly used to finance right-wing governments and parties around the world.

Kohl, his successor Wolfgang Schauble, Kiep, Weyrauch, and others were eventually charged and convicted in Germany. In 1999, four years after the *Der Spiegel* revelations, the Germans issued a warrant for the arrest of Karlheinz Schreiber and sought his deportation back to his native country. If the Germans thought the Canadians were going to be helpful, they had been sadly mistaken.

Business Week magazine reported in February 2000 that Germans saw the ongoing scandals, trials, and convictions in a relatively positive light: "Many see the Kohl scandal as part of a broader transformation in German society. Germans have made it clear that they no longer believe in the paternalistic political machines that made the country an island of stability during the cold war. The era of consensual politics, where the border between government and business was often blurred, is over. Says a top German fund manager: 'The country really needed shaking up, and this could be the catalyst.'"

Until Pelossi's revelations, the official position in Canada was that no crimes had been committed in the Airbus deal and that it was all just a matter of questionable business ethics. But Pelossi could not be ignored. Soon after the story broke in 1995, the RCMP dusted off its old Airbus file. A team of investigators began to fly all over the place tracking down leads, especially Pelossi. The singing accountant was opening doors for the German police and was more than willing to help the Canadians too. One might presume that the investigation would go smoothly, as it did in Germany, but Canada is not Germany. In Canada, when it comes to the investigation of the members of the country's establishment, there are no sure things no matter how strong Pelossi's evidence was.

On September 29, 1995, Department of Justice lawyer Kimberly Prost sent a confidential letter to Swiss authorities requesting their assistance in investigating alleged corrupt activities by Karlheinz Schreiber, Frank Moores, and Brian Mulroney while he was prime minister. In that letter she referred to "an ongoing scheme by Mr. Mulroney (and others) to defraud the Canadian Government of millions of dollars." In another part of the letter, she wrote: "This investigation is of a serious concern to the Government of Canada as it involves criminal activity on the part of a former Prime Minister."

On October, 26, 1995, Swiss officials seized the bank accounts and safety deposit boxes of Karlheinz Schreiber and Frank Moores. Schreiber and

Moores received copies of the Canadian Letter of Request. Schreiber's copy of the letter was written in German, which is important to note.

According to a timeline constructed by *the fifth estate* (from which I will borrow liberally in the next few pages), the next week Schreiber was joined in Switzerland by his Alberta lawyer Robert Hladun, upon whom Mulroney had bestowed the honour Queen's Counsel. Schreiber called Fred Doucet and asked him to tell Brian Mulroney about the Canadian government investigation. Doucet contacted Mulroney at the Royal York Hotel and told him that Schreiber said Mulroney was at the centre of an RCMP probe. Mulroney contacted Schreiber later that night in Montréal where he was told about the letter and that "there are things in here that involve you." Mulroney and Schreiber later spoke on the phone a number of times after the initial conversation about the Letter of Request.

Schreiber's lawyer, Hladun, also spoke with Mulroney by phone. Hladun told Mulroney that he had reviewed Schreiber's Swiss banking records and told Mulroney there was nothing in the records that mentioned him. "Nothing at all."

The next day, November 3, 1995, Mulroney received a translation of the Canadian Department of Justice letter which had been prepared by Schreiber's Swiss lawyers. One of his lawyers now was Roger Tassé, who over the years had been involved in a number of controversies in which the RCMP had become involved. As a former federal deputy solicitor general in 1976, he was the point man in government when Québec Premier Robert Bourassa was trying to block RCMP investigations in that province that might well have led to him. The next year, as deputy attorney general, Tassé was the first person in government to meet with Soviet spy Gilles Brunet and listen to his stories about the wrongdoings of the Security Service. He was also one of the people who recommended calling the McDonald Commission to investigate the RCMP back in 1977.

Now acting as Mulroney's lawyer, on November 5 Tassé sent a letter to Justice Minister Allan Rock and the RCMP commissioner, objecting to the wording of the Letter of Request. He reminded the minister that Mulroney had offered to cooperate with the RCMP and said Mulroney was "astonished that the RCMP has not even chosen to meet with him before making such grave accusations."

On November 10, Swiss television news program *Zen Von Zen* aired an item about the secret commissions paid to Karlheinz Schreiber's International Aircraft Leasing by Airbus for helping sell 34 of its planes to Air

Canada. Pelossi was interviewed in shadow about Schreiber's control of IAL and the $20 million it received in secret commissions. The report also revealed that Frank Moores and Schreiber opened Swiss bank accounts and that it was suspected that the money deposited in them was used for Canadian politicians.

The heat was building and the media were beginning to focus on the obvious—the Brian Mulroney connection. On November 13, CBC's *The National* aired a story on speculation the RCMP might ask the Swiss government to freeze the bank accounts of individuals involved in the sale of Airbus airplanes to Air Canada. The news report mentioned the earlier *the fifth estate* program about IAL, Schreiber, and the secret Airbus commissions. The item also references the *Zen Von Zen* report. The CBC also informed Mulroney's longtime spokesman, Luc Lavoie, that Mulroney was the Canadian politician being investigated by Swiss authorities.

Inside the government, the Mulroney counter-attack had already had its effect. The day after the CBC call to Lavoie, the Department of Justice sent a second letter to Swiss authorities saying the original Letter of Request contained only allegations against Mulroney and that they should treat the matter confidentially citing the "considerable media interest regarding this investigation."

The pressure mounted on Mulroney and there was not much he could do but deny everything, which he did at every turn. Mulroney set up a command centre at Montréal's Queen Elizabeth Hotel to manage the crisis. Meanwhile, behind the scenes and out of public view, lawyers for Frank Moores confirmed to Revenue Canada that they had filed a voluntary disclosure on money held by Moores in a foreign bank. The income Moores disclosed had come from Schreiber. As part of his public relations campaign, Mulroney disclosed to the media that his lawyer, Harvey Yarosky, had written a letter to Swiss authorities promising his complete cooperation.

On November 20 came a most Machiavellian twist. A copy of the translated, original, confidential Letter of Request to Swiss authorities had been leaked to both Philip Mathias at the *Financial Post* and William Thorsell at *The Globe and Mail*. It was an interesting choice. One can readily infer that if the letter had only been sent to Thorsell, Mulroney's confidant, suspicions would be raised. Sending it to his competitor, Mathias, blurred the matter, although Mathias had become all but a shill for the Mulroney camp. The other effect was that *The Globe and Mail* and the *Financial Post* were the bibles of the business world and the establishment elite. This would come in handy for what was to follow hours later.

Both papers ran the story about Mulroney being named, which the all-too-devious Mulroney team immediately used to their advantage. Mulroney could not sue the government over the confidential letter to the Swiss, because he could not be libelled by words not made public, but he could now that it had been aired in the newspapers. By the time the two stories hit the street, the lawsuit had been drawn up.

That very same day, Lavoie arranged a press conference for Mulroney's lawyers to announce they were filing a suit in the friendly confines of the Québec justice system against the federal government. Mulroney was claiming $50 million in damages. The Mulroney team had clearly manipulated events in such a way as to argue that the former prime minister's name had been smeared where it counted most—among the country's elite.

Mulroney lawyer Harvey Yarosky said: "Mr. Mulroney categorically and unequivocally states he had nothing to do with Air Canada's decision to buy Airbus. Nor did he receive a cent from anyone. He was simply not part of any conspiracy whatsoever."

In the statement of claim, Mulroney stated: "[The] plaintiff has never received any of the alleged payments, in any form, from any person, whether named or not in the Request for Assistance, for any consideration whatsoever."

The fifth estate fired back with an updated story. In it, Pelossi provided additional information about the Devon account. He said he was told by Schreiber that the account had been set up for Mulroney, but he also said he did not know if Mulroney was aware that the account had been set up for him. Lavoie went on the fifth estate and categorically denied that Mulroney had received money from the Devon account or Moores's other Swiss bank account, code-named Frankfurt.

Meanwhile, Frank Moores told the Toronto Star that he would be vindicated and called the journalists who were pursuing the story "scumbags." The suggestion in the smear was that authors and journalists Stevie Cameron, Harvey Cashore, and Jock Ferguson were biased and promoting a vendetta against Mulroney and his friends. The journalists all laughed it off, but the attack had only just begun.

An objective observer might have thought that a democratic government operating as a guardian would have recognized the ruse—but not the Canadian government. Prime Minister Chrétien would later say that he was "sick" about what had happened to Mulroney—a former prime minister.

"The minister of justice called me and he said that in the trial [lawsuit] here in Montréal the former prime minister swore that he never had any business with Mr. Schreiber and we could not prove the contrary. So the RCMP looked like it made a mistake and we settled out of court," Chrétien said. On another occasion, he said: "I had to accept his word because he had been a prime minister of Canada."

The fact was that the RCMP had not yet interviewed Schreiber, so the government had acted without any evidence from the police.

Chrétien and his justice minister, Allen Rock, quickly cut a deal with Mulroney and paid him $2.1 million for his legal fees, along with abject apologies from both the government and the RCMP.

"I was so relieved," Chrétien said afterward, implying that Canada was lucky to have a man as honourable, munificent, and understanding as Mulroney as one of its elder statesmen.

The RCMP continued with its investigation, such as it was, and kept building files. Pelossi met with the investigators and told them everything he knew, including when and where bank accounts had been set up, but that was not enough for the gun-shy Mounties. No matter how much information the police gathered, it was never enough to file charges. The Mulroney file just kept growing.

Meanwhile, Schreiber was eagerly awaiting a visit from the investigators—but they would never come.

Throughout this period, Mulroney and his corporate and political friends devoted themselves to restoring his good name, propelling him back into proper social and political circles as if nothing had taken place.

In 1998, lawyer William Kaplan convinced McClelland & Stewart, one of Canada's most reputable publishing firms, to publish his sensational book *Presumed Guilty: Brian Mulroney, the Airbus Affair and the Government of Canada*. Kaplan promised to show how Mulroney had been framed by his political opponents and had become a victim of a vendetta by overzealous, somewhat unscrupulous and under-supervised reporters. There was only one problem with the story. Kaplan brought all the talents of a defence lawyer to the project and none of a journalist. The naïve quasi-journalism was seen by many for what it was—hagiography. Nevertheless, Kaplan's conclusions were trumpeted by Mulroney and his supporters as vindication, but not for long. Most of the Canadian media might have been tranquillized by the settlement and Kaplan's book, but not Harvey Cashore.

On January 28, 1999, Switzerland released the contents of Schreiber's bank accounts to German authorities. These were the same accounts Pelossi had told the RCMP about three years earlier. In the documents, the German police found a series of coded sub-accounts for various Canadian and German politicians and businessmen. Sensing the danger, Mulroney's friends began to throw up more smoke.

By now, the *National Post* was entirely owned and controlled by Conrad Black. It had absorbed the *Financial Post* and was the flagship of the former stable of Southam dailies and other newspapers across the country. In Canada's biggest cities, the only other independent non-right-wing papers were in Toronto, Winnipeg, and Halifax.

The editor-in-chief of the *National Post* was Kenneth Whyte, who had many of the attributes of his counterpart William Thorsell at *The Globe and Mail*. Each was an Alberta neo-conservative who had attended the Bilderberg Conference, among other right-wing international forums.

Under Whyte's direction, the *National Post* became anything but an unbiased, disinterested newspaper. It had an agenda and was not afraid to say that it was the conservative house organ, the facts be damned if required, as you shall learn.

To fight off the latest allegations against Mulroney, former Transport Minister John Crosbie attacked the RCMP in the *National Post*, stating: "They'll be giving the final proof of the incompetence, and the errors, and mistakes they've made in their handling of the investigation, and even of starting it in the first place."

In the House of Commons a few days later, former Thyssen employee Peter MacKay stood up for his former leader and said: "Brian Mulroney is innocent of all wrongdoings and yet the Liberal government will not cease and desist the RCMP investigation. The Liberal government has a vendetta against the former prime minister which stems from the Liberals' days in opposition. There are growing concerns that the current prime minister's legacy might pale by comparison. The Liberals' plot for revenge is continuing to cost the taxpayers significant dollars—$4 million and counting."

Like an arm of the Mulroney propaganda machine, the *National Post* continued its attacks. It complained that Ottawa had not withdrawn the Letter of Request sent to the Swiss. Justice Department spokesperson Pierre Gratton said: "We have informed the Swiss on three occasions that [the letter contained] allegations only and we have apologized for the language used in the letter . . . If the RCMP were to request that the letter be withdrawn we would comply."

On April 2,1999, a *National Post* editorial attacked the RCMP investigation again: "Mr. Mulroney was not the only victim of the Canadian government's slander. Karlheinz Schreiber, the financier, was also tarred as a crook in the infamous letter."

The next day the *National Post* published an interview with Frank Moores who alleged the RCMP was dragging out the Airbus investigation as revenge for having to apologize to Brian Mulroney in its settlement with him. Moores said: "I just can't understand it. But if you ask them, they say there is still an ongoing investigation . . . It is total madness as far as I am concerned. It is unbelievable." Two days later, the *Post* contended in an editorial that relations between Canada and Switzerland could be harmed because Ottawa was withholding information.

In Germany, on May 3, 1999, Thyssen managers Jurgen Massmann and Winfried Haastert were arrested for tax evasion on money given to them by Karlheinz Schreiber. Four days later, the German newspaper *Süddeutsche Zeitung* expanded on that story by reporting how Schreiber had paid millions of German marks to high-ranking members of the Christian Democratic Union.

Former Mulroney cabinet minister Elmer MacKay immediately flew to Switzerland and provided an airline ticket for Schreiber to return to Canada to MacKay's home in Nova Scotia. MacKay later told reporters at Schreiber's first bail hearing that Schreiber's flight and the arrests of the Thyssen executives were coincidental.

Six days later, on May 14, Elmer's son Peter raised the Airbus issue in Question Period: "Mr. Speaker, the last time I checked the RCMP was under the ministry of the solicitor general. Canadians are tired of excuses and want action. It is a fact that the RCMP is suffering from a severe lack of funding due to Liberal budget cuts, yet as Bre-X gets swept under the rug the partisan obsession against Brian Mulroney continues to cost millions. The *National Post* described it perfectly. It said that the government was intent on finding something to do with someone about a crime yet to be established in order to prove that it was not entirely wrong headed in its pursuit of Airbus rumours in the first place. Letting this case fester and bumble on is not an option. The solicitor general should tell Canadians when he will put an end to this futile investigation."

A few weeks later, Peter MacKay got into a heated debate with Jacques Saada, the parliamentary secretary to the solicitor general and deputy prime minister, Herb Gray.

MacKay said: "The atrocious Airbus investigation makes the Canadian justice system the laughing stock of the international community. The government continues to waste millions of taxpayers' dollars on an investigation where the supposed prime suspect has not even been interviewed. The Liberals continue to find money for this investigation by cutting the RCMP, limiting the fight against organized crime and importation of drugs. How can the Liberal government call itself accountable as it sits back and allows a foreign country to embark on an unlawful exercise of search and seizure when it knows full well that the exercise is not permitted under Canadian law?"

Saada replied, "Mr. Speaker, the only cases that I am aware of where the legislative branch tells the judicial branch what to do are in banana republics. I do not think Canada qualifies as a banana republic."

MacKay kept pushing: "Mr. Speaker, this debacle continues and the Department of Justice continues its attempts to cover its tracks in what could go down in history as the biggest political witch hunt of all time. It is an international embarrassment. While the astronomical costs of this ridiculous, ill-founded investigation and litigation continue to mount, the Minister of Justice sits idly by, as did her predecessor. When will the government cease and desist in its malicious and vindictive obsession to besmirch a former prime minister, from whom it plagiarized most of his policy initiatives?"

Then Herb Gray weighed in: "Mr. Speaker, the Conservative Party may have interfered with police investigations. That may have been its approach. I do not know if it was, but in any event it is not our approach. We do not intend to have political interference with arm's length police investigations."

The police activity in Germany was clearly making everyone in Canada nervous. Mulroney gave an interview to the CBC's Brian Stewart, a respected journalist in his own right, but suspect to some because he was an old school friend of Conrad Black and continued to be his friend. Mulroney told Stewart that "the RCMP can investigate until the cows come home, they won't find a single, solitary thing because nothing, as far as I'm concerned, was ever done wrong."

The ever-loyal Peter MacKay followed up in the House of Commons in a reprise of his earlier battle with Saada and Gray. MacKay said: "Mr. Speaker, serious allegations of wrongdoing involving private holdings, campaign donations and questionable use of taxpayer money continues to plague the Prime Minister. As evidence mounts and the plot thickens, the grey fog rolls in to present the Liberal spin to cloak the facts and cover the tracks. Now that the shoe is on the other foot, when will the government withdraw this spurious letter of baseless allegations against Mr. Mulroney sent to Swiss authorities and call an end to the ill-founded Airbus investigation?"

Saada would not bend: "Mr. Speaker, my colleague opposite has a hard time understanding the answers we give day after day to his questions, which are always the same. I will repeat for the 51st or 52nd time the same answer: the federal government has no intention of meddling in the decisions of the RCMP, of conducting an inquiry or of stopping an inquiry. It is not our role. Ours is a legislative role. The RCMP's is an investigative role. We have no business meddling, especially since this investigation was recognized in the agreement reached with Mr. Mulroney at the time. I really do not understand why my colleague opposite cannot comprehend that."

MacKay continued: "Mr. Speaker, Canadians have come to expect stonewalling and delay every time they come in conflict with the Liberal government. When issues arise citizens face a barrage of government lawyers intent on foot dragging and legal manoeuvring. A second named party in the Airbus debacle now has a $50 million lawsuit pending against the Canadian government. My question is for the architect of Airbus, the deputy prime minister. Does the Liberal government intend to settle this matter the way it did with Mr. Mulroney, or does it intend to be dragged kicking and screaming through the courts before facing a final costly, humiliating verdict?"

Herb Gray responded: "Mr. Speaker, the lawsuit to which the Honourable member referred that was settled involved Mr. Mulroney absolutely dropping his claim for damages. Second, what was paid was simply the legal costs. In the written minutes of settlement signed on behalf of Mr. Mulroney, he recognized that the RCMP had a perfect right to begin the investigation and to carry it out. The hon. member ought to read the minutes of settlement and pass on to some other matters of real concern to Canadians."

MacKay was all but desperate in his attack. He told the *Toronto Star* that the investigation of Mulroney was politically motivated: "I think the Prime Minister is battling shadows and it is a narcissist chasing his nemesis. He is very, very concerned that Mr. Mulroney has rehabilitated his reputation almost entirely and is going to continue to do so."

Mulroney continued with his public attempts to show that he had nothing to hide. His aide, Fred Doucet, told the ever-compliant *National Post* reporter Mathias that Mulroney had called him from South Africa and asked him to arrange a conversation with Schreiber through an intermediary. Mulroney wanted Schreiber to release any confidential banking records he had because he had nothing to hide. He just wanted to clear the air.

On August 30, 1999, Schreiber was taking a stroll with Mathias in Toronto's fashionable Yorkville district, near Schreiber's condominium. He was confronted by Mounties and arrested, at the request of German authorities. Schreiber was held for extradition to face numerous series of charges in Germany over his activities there.

A week later Schreiber was released on bond. Elmer MacKay and Schreiber's lawyer, former Liberal Finance Minister Marc Lalonde, each put up $100,000. MacKay testified that he helped Schreiber return to Canada and that he had done nothing to conceal that fact. MacKay further said that Schreiber came to Canada at his request.

It still looked like Mulroney was going to escape, but then Harvey Cashore got his hands on Schreiber's bank documents. The paperwork revealed the existence of numerous coded bank accounts, which German authorities deciphered as the names of politicians and businessmen associated with Karlheinz Schreiber. One of the accounts was code-named BRITAN. The immediate suspicion was that Britan referred to Brian, just as the previously discovered Frankfurter account referred to Frank Moores. The RCMP knew this in 1996.

Mulroney, nevertheless, continued to hide behind the sometimes nasty and combative Luc Lavoie. After Cashore informed Lavoie about the Swiss documents, Lavoie said he wanted more information before making a comment. He promised Cashore that he would not reveal what he learned from him to any other reporter in the world. In another conversation with Cashore, Lavoie said Schreiber must have been using Mulroney's name in bank records for his own purposes.

Lavoie then said—off the record—to Cashore: "Karlheinz Schreiber is the biggest fucking liar the world has ever seen. That is what we believe. . . . There never was any money. And to think otherwise is really to not know Mulroney. He is too smart to do something like that. It is just too dummy. It is too damn stupid. He wouldn't do that."

Lavoie further asked Cashore for some consideration for Mulroney: "If only for human reasons, try and see if we can deal with it this weekend . . . Nothing is going to happen beyond you and I and he. But I am trying to help his life a little bit here. He is going nuts."

Cashore and Lavoie also discuss what happened to the money that was paid in secret commissions to Schreiber's International Aircraft Leasing (IAL). Lavoie said: "It didn't go to Mulroney."

Cashore: "I want to find out where the money went, wherever it went."

Lavoie: "Yeah, well."

Cashore: "Wherever it went. Wherever it went."

Lavoie: "Yeah, okay, it didn't go to Mulroney."

Cashore: "I want to find out where the money went, wherever it went."

Lavoie: "Yeah, but it didn't go to him."

Cashore: "You say that, and I've heard you say it."

Lavoie: "He said it himself, under oath."

Cashore: "Right."

Lavoie: "So it would be major perjury right?"

Cashore: "But why does that mean that I can't ask a question about where the money went. Why can't I ask that question?"

Lavoie: "Sure, you did, and I told you, I don't know where it went. It didn't go to him."

A few days later, Lavoie said he had spoken to Mulroney: "His perspective is pretty fucking clear. He never received a p—He never received a penny connected with any of this stuff."

On October 17, 1999, Mulroney contacted Schreiber's lawyer Robert Hladun and asked him to ask Schreiber for a written statement indicating that at no time did Mulroney solicit or receive compensation from Karlheinz Schreiber. Lawyer Gerard Tremblay phoned Hladun and asked for a letter to keep on file from Schreiber, which was not to be disseminated. Tremblay wanted comfort from Schreiber so that he could fire off a letter on behalf of Mulroney to the CBC which "would in his opinion shut down the airing of the next *the fifth estate* story on Airbus."

Mulroney then personally contacted Hladun and told him he had instructed Tremblay to send a letter to *the fifth estate* "indicating that if there was the slightest implication that Mr. Schreiber, Mr. Moores and Brian Mulroney were involved in any way then there would be terrible consequences." Mulroney said that he would issue the letter but first wanted an assurance in writing from Mr. Schreiber that Mulroney had not solicited or received money from Schreiber. Mulroney called Hladun again that same day, at which time Mulroney was told that Schreiber was hesitant about drafting such a letter.

On October 18, 1999, Tremblay sent a letter to the chair of the CBC board of directors threatening to sue every board member if the upcoming *the fifth estate* program was defamatory.

Somehow, two days later, the *National Post* was made aware of what was transpiring. The uninquisitive Mathias wrote another friendly story in which both Schreiber and Mulroney each denied that any money had passed between them. An accompanying editorial, headlined "Gone fishing," complained that *the fifth estate* would be broadcasting a story that night, which the *National Post* had not yet viewed. Nevertheless, the editorial concluded, the show contained allegations about Mulroney that were "false" and "preposterous."

The leak to the *National Post* proved, however, to be a poor strategy for the Mulroney team.

Lavoie had spoken off the record with Cashore and had promised not to tell anyone else what was going on. The CBC decided that he had breached that agreement and decided to use Lavoie's comments, particularly the one about Schreiber being "the biggest fucking liar in the world."

Schreiber watched "The Mysterious Dealmaker" that night as Linden MacIntyre described the trail to the "Britan" account. He and his family heard Lavoie's attack on him. Schreiber was embarrassed and furious. He had mistakenly assumed that they were all partners in the cover-up, but now he was being hung out to dry. He threatened to sue Lavoie.

In Germany the criminal cases were moving forward with the arrest of former CDU treasurer Walther Leisler Kiep. He admitted to having accepted one million German marks from Karlheinz Schreiber, touching off the biggest postwar scandal in German history. Chancellor Helmut Kohl would be the next to come under scrutiny.

A month later it appeared that the RCMP was making headway in Canada. Investigators finally obtained a search warrant to raid the headquarters of Eurocopter in Fort Erie, Ontario. The police were looking for information about secret commissions paid on the purchase of MBB helicopters for the Canadian Coast Guard.

On Boxing Day 1999, Schreiber visited the home of Fred Doucet, having receiving an unexpected invitation. There, he told Doucet to relay a message to Mulroney: "You tell your friend if under what circumstances ever I have to testify, I am not going to commit perjury for him. Make this very clear to him."

The next day Doucet and Schreiber met again. Doucet gave Schreiber a paper and asked him to sign it. It was an agreement between Schreiber and Mulroney which belatedly set out the former prime minister's relationship with Schreiber. It read:

> to provide a watching brief to develop economic opportunities for our companies, including traveling abroad to meet with government and private sector leaders to assist in opening new markets for our products and to report regularly to us in this regard. In this context,

priority should be given to opportunities relating to Canadian based manufacturing of peace keeping and/or peace making military equipment in view of Canada's prominence in this area. The mandate will be for a period of three years. The fee to cover services and expenses is set at _____ for the period.

The RCMP had been chasing Mulroney and Schreiber in slow motion for four years—which had not proved to be much of a problem for them. The CBC, however, was giving them fits. Schreiber filed a $2 million lawsuit against *the fifth estate* over "The Mysterious Dealmaker" episode. One of the things Schreiber said contributed to the libel was that *the fifth estate* "connected the name BRITAN with Brian and in particular, Brian Mulroney." Schreiber later dropped the suit. The CBC won $55,361.61 from him in legal costs.

The legal machinations to protect Schreiber, Moores, and others continued. In 2000, Cashore discovered a secret court hearing in Toronto involving a case dealing with the hidden commissions paid by MBB Helicopters/Eurocopter in obtaining contracts to sell helicopters to the Canadian Coast Guard in the mid-eighties, which would lead to another broadcast.

In public, Mulroney continued on the offensive, pun intended, to rebuild his reputation and deal with the constant flow of rumours. In September 2000, he once again sat down with the CBC's Brian Stewart, who played the willing role of a stooge, never once expressing an ounce of the skepticism felt by so many Canadians about Mulroney.

"Mr. Schreiber was never a good friend of mine," Mulroney told Stewart. "He's a man I knew. . . . He was introduced to me and he had a reputation of accomplishment. And things have to be placed in perspective. You have to look at this now seven years earlier, and his reputation was unflawed, he had achieved a great deal in the business community. And what is sad about this, is the assumption people presume guilt on his part and on the part of others. Mr. Schreiber should be presumed to be innocent. And moreover, he has a wife and a family. And the personal dimension of this should not be lost on people. He is a Canadian citizen who has the right to be presumed to be innocent. And yet because of all of the rumours and gossip and innuendo there is a tendency to presume that people have done something untoward. And so, look, life takes its toll on all of us. And this has not been a pleasant experience for anybody, and I'm sure not for Mr. Schreiber and his family, and I believe that they, too, are entitled to the presumption of innocence as I was and as other people are."

While the judicial process in Germany was in high gear, in Canada the RCMP was now trying to do a sting on Schreiber—which he recognized from the outset.

In 2001, however, *National Post* reporter Mathias, who had been the primary conduit for the well-spun Mulroney cover-up story, was suddenly confronted with real news. Schreiber told him that he had given Mulroney $300,000 in cash, the first payment coming two days before Mulroney was about to give up his seat in Parliament. Mathias was in a quandary. It looked like the confirmation of the story everyone had been pursuing for years, but his own editor, Ken Whyte, was not interested in publishing it.

Mathias went to see lawyer-author William Kaplan, whose 1999 book had "exonerated" Mulroney. Seeing Mathias's evidence, Kaplan was furious that everyone had lied to him about what had happened.

In March 2001, *the fifth estate* returned to the air with a story about the MBB helicopter deal. In that broadcast—18 years after the fact—it became the first media outlet to report how money from Germany had been used to undermine and defeat former Progressive Conservative Party leader Joe Clark in 1983. The story focused on Franz Josef Strauss, Schreiber, and others, and made it appear that the entire thing was part of the Airbus sales strategy and not something more sinister like the Le Cercle plot, previously described.

The fifth estate story, however, landed with a thud—as did the subsequent book *The Last Amigos*, written by Cashore with Stevie Cameron, and published later that year. Nobody in Canada, it seemed, cared anymore about the ever-aging story.

Two years later, on April 22, 2003, the RCMP announced it had ended its eight-year investigation.

"After an exhaustive investigation in Canada and abroad, the RCMP has concluded its investigation into allegations of wrongdoing involving MBB Helicopters, Thyssen and Airbus. The RCMP has now concluded that the remaining allegations cannot be substantiated and that no charges will be laid, beyond the charge of fraud already before the Courts. Today's announcement fulfills a commitment made by former Commissioner Phil Murray to announce the results of the Airbus investigation once the RCMP concluded its investigation."

Many of those RCMP officers involved in the second failed Airbus investigation received the same treatment as those from the first one—they were promoted.

The story seemed effectively dead. Meanwhile, the *National Post* had been hemorrhaging money. The entire chain was sold off to CanWest Global Communications, controlled by the Winnipeg family of Israel (Izzy) Asper, which had corporate director links with the Desmarais family and Power Corp.

Ken Whyte and many of his underlings were shown the door by the Aspers but he did not go long without work. Whyte's upper-crust-society and corporate friends took care of him, and he managed to live for another day, eventually returning as editor of *Maclean's* magazine. But the next leg of the story, which had begun in Whyte's own newsroom with reporter Mathias, was soon going to become public after another odd twist.

Lawyer-author William Kaplan tracked down Mathias's lead about the $300,000 payoff and wrote a second book: *Brian Mulroney, Stevie Cameron and the Public Trust*, published by the University of Toronto Press. After being embarrassed by his first book, McClelland & Stewart was not interested in publishing the second. Kaplan performed an amazing turnabout—he went from being an advocate for Mulroney to building the case against him in true lawyerly fashion.

Before it was published, however, Kaplan took the Mathias story to the *National Post*'s archrival, *The Globe and Mail*. Its own in-house Mulroney guardian angel, William Thorsell, had left in 2000, on to a greater reward, running the Royal Ontario Museum. *The Globe and Mail* ran four massive excerpts from the Kaplan book on its pages, hoping, some suspected, to make up for all those lost years of missed opportunity. The story came and went. *The National Post* and its sister papers in almost every big city across the country and most small ones too, ignored the story. Kaplan's book was equally dismissed. His borrowed news from Philip Mathias about the $300,000 in payoffs was offset by his scurrilous, not entirely undeserved, shoot-the-messenger attack on Cameron.

The assaults on Cameron continued after documents uncovered through access to information indicated that RCMP Superintendent Al Matthews had listed her as being a confidential police agent in the investigations against Mulroney. Cameron, who, as noted earlier, had a tendency to get too close to her sources, had done the unthinkable for a journalist. She had taken information from Georgio Pelossi, copies of which she had received from Jock Ferguson, and given them to the RCMP. "If anyone finds out about this, I'm dead," she told the Mountie, according to a source.

Although she denied the allegations and later said that she had only given Matthews already-published materials, little worse could be said about a reporter. Her former employers, *The Globe and Mail*, seemed to take particular delight in attacking her. Cameron's fight to clear her name took her out of the Airbus story, blurring the larger, real issue. The story was about who got the money from Schreiber, not what Stevie Cameron did or did not do. She did not take cash from Schreiber, Mulroney did.

By 2005, Schreiber was still in Canada fighting extradition to Germany. In that country, heads continued to roll. Former German Deputy Defence Minister Holger Pfhals admitted in court to taking $2.4 million in bribes from Schreiber. The Germans badly wanted Schreiber. In Canada, there was abundant evidence that Schreiber alone had distributed $25 million, but the entire focus was on the $300,000 that Mulroney had denied getting.

Finally, in late 2005, Schreiber decided to sit down with Cashore and tell him his story on camera, which was broadcast in February 2006. In the segment, "Money, Truth and Spin," Schreiber detailed how he had made three cash payments to Mulroney, each containing envelopes of $100,000 in $1,000 bills. The money had come from the Britan account at a Swiss bank. The payments had been made in 1993 and 1994.

The new revelations meant that Mulroney had lied about not knowing Schreiber well or having taken any money from him, the basis for the government's $2.1 million settlement with him as well as the subsequent apology from the government and the RCMP. But government officials decided that there was not enough evidence to overturn the settlement and claw back the money.

It seemed that nothing Cashore, Mathias, or Kaplan could uncover would ever be enough to force the government to take action. It would take almost another two years before a climax, of sorts, would be reached. During this period, Mulroney had inexplicably become one of Prime Minister Stephen Harper's most trusted advisers and confidants.

Schreiber, meanwhile, continued to fend off extradition orders, which he had been doing successfully for almost eight years. Mulroney was about to publish the first volume of his life story, *Brian Mulroney: Memoirs: 1939–1993*.

One of his chief propagandists in the media was there to lend a hand, as usual. In March 2007, William Thorsell poured on the perfume in his description of Mulroney and his soon-to-be-published memoirs in a *Globe and Mail* column: "Brian Mulroney is much too vigorous to haunt us—too present in the news, too active in public life, too insistent on participation in the debates about his legacy and the course on which Canada is headed now. Brian Mulroney lives, whether some people like it or not. It is we who haunt Brian

Mulroney. It is we who, he asserts, miscomprehend his nature and his record and who, he fears, may confine him unjustly to a purgatory of history, a victim of superficial and paranoiac vendettas. He will have none of this. He will not be haunted forever, as the writing of his *Memoirs*, to be published next week, asserts. He will pester us, he will court us, he will guide us on a certain trip through time with a narrative ripe in flavour and detail meant to exorcise the demons, correct the records, instruct the scribes and settle the accounts. No leading Canadian politician has worked so assiduously to write his story from the inside, with his own pen, a fact for which alone we should thank him."

All Thorsell's efforts, however, could not hide the odour of the swine. Schreiber went to civil court in March 2007, and filed a $300,000 lawsuit against Mulroney, claiming that he had not fulfilled his obligations under their contract. Mulroney ignored the suit. Schreiber quickly moved to gain a $740,000 default judgment against the former prime minister. That decision was quickly quashed, but then *the fifth estate* waded in with one more devastating blow against Mulroney's credibility.

In "The Unauthorized Chapter," a cheeky reference to Mulroney's new book—in which he had failed to mention Airbus or Schreiber—*the fifth estate* nailed down once and for all the $300,000 in payments to Mulroney. The show proved that Mulroney had taken steps to cover up the transaction. One of those was his voluntary tax remittance to the Canada Revenue Agency for the money, although he could not explain clearly how he had earned the money. Over the years, Mulroney's various explanations have included an investment in a pasta operation, consulting, and general advice. He provided no documents and claimed no expenses for the work he had supposedly done. *The Globe and Mail* published the story in tandem with the CBC.

Harper had ignored the implications of the Schreiber lawsuit filed six months earlier, and continued with his blind loyalty to the treacherous Mulroney, but that relationship was now threatening to bring down the prime minister himself. The public confirmation of the tax payment showed that Mulroney had taken the money while he was still a member of Parliament and that he had lied in 1995 about his relationship to Schreiber. Those lies had been the foundation of the $2.1 million settlement to him and the public humiliation of the RCMP.

Finally, Prime Minister Harper had to be seen to be doing something. He banned members of his party from having any contact with Mulroney, and called for another one-man, third-party "independent" investigation of the matter. Harper said he would be calling a full public inquiry, but as soon as he had done so, he began to climb down the other side of that high hill. He later clarified his position, stating that whatever the chosen investigator found would define the proposed inquiry, *should one be necessary.*

Harper's choice this time was David Lloyd Johnston, the president of the University of Waterloo. Independent? Johnston had once been appointed by Mulroney as the founding chair in 1988 of the National Round Table on the Environment and the Economy. In that capacity, he reported directly to Mulroney. In 1984, Johnston had been the moderator of a televised debate in which Mulroney hammered then-Prime Minister John Turner over his acceptance of the patronage appointments foisted on him by Pierre Trudeau. "You had a choice, sir," Mulroney had bellowed, waggling his finger at Turner.

While Harper was trying to make it look as if he was determined to get to the bottom of the Mulroney-Schreiber controversy, it was evident that his heart was not in it. He promised an inquiry, but his every statement and action was couched in phrases that suggested that if he could find an easy way out for himself and Mulroney, he would leap at the chance.

While Johnston began to ponder the need for and scope of a public inquiry, Schreiber continued his fight against extradition to Germany. Housed in a Toronto jail, he was on the verge of being sent to his native country, where he faced a life sentence for his crimes. The Harper government took the position that there was nothing it could do to keep Schreiber in the country, which was not true.

The Senate Committee on Ethics immediately called Schreiber to attend as a witness. There was only one way to keep him in the country, the use of a rarely invoked Speaker's Warrant, which was now employed to have him transported to Ottawa in December 2007.

Mulroney, meanwhile, told people he could not wait to clear his name. On November 13, 2007, he spoke at a fundraiser in Toronto for one of his alma maters, St. Francis Xavier University in Antigonish, Nova Scotia. He said:

> The half-truth, innuendo and smear are the insidious weapons of the political stalker or defamer. No clear accusations are ever made, just a series of sly suggestions. Hint, hint, nod nod. If only I could tell you the whole story. All from anonymous, dubious sources. And a vendetta surreptitiously works its way up to the next plateau. The difficulty with such people in the process, it's like punching jello in a pool. The only

way to confront them, the only way is to confront them. Directly, put them under the spotlight and force them to testify under oath so that their conduct and their motives can be fully analyzed.

It is for this reason that last night I called for a full-fledged Royal Commission of Inquiry into the so-called Airbus affair. This inquiry, its terms of reference, must begin from the beginning in 1988. The conduct of all high elected officials, advisors, lobbyists, public servants, police officials and those few members of the media who played a role in this matter. There can be no exceptions, and there can be no exclusions. I'm very pleased to find that Mr. Harper today agreed to appoint such a commission.... So I'm grateful to the Prime Minister for announcing his intention to appoint this royal commission of inquiry and when that commissioner is appointed and these sessions begin, I want to tell you tonight that I, Martin Brian Mulroney, the 18th Prime Minister of Canada, will be there before the Royal Commission with bells on because I've done nothing wrong and I have absolutely nothing to hide.

It was Lyin' Brian at his best and most manipulative. That Brian Mulroney was calling for an inquiry into his own activities suggested he had nothing to hide. It was all too evident, however, that he and his lawyers had already worked out the terms of any inquiry—with the agreement of the prime minister. As the O'Connor Commission proved, narrowing the scope of an inquiry can be exceedingly useful in limiting damage and controlling an intended message. It is the Canadian way.

The Airbus story told us so much about Canada and its leaders. For two decades, Brian Mulroney and his supporters—particularly those highly placed, shameless ones in the media—had insisted that nothing untoward had happened during his time in office. Together, they mercilessly attacked and smeared anyone who dared challenge the official story—Opposition members, the police, and the few reporters and editors who had the courage and tenacity to fight through the fog.

Right to the end—even after some of the truth trickled out—many continued to stay the course. Mulroney was summarily declared innocent by them and Schreiber, desperate to save his own skin, labelled a contemptuous liar.

Mulroney's defenders conveniently overlooked the fact that at the heart of every fraud is a lie and that every participant in that fraud is a liar. Mulroney's depiction of Schreiber echoed Conrad Black's of turncoat David

Radler—who had pleaded guilty to fraud before Black and his co-accused were brought to trial. Radler admitted committing criminal acts but that did not mean he was not telling the truth about how the schemes had worked—and the court agreed.

In the four days he testified before the House of Commons Ethics Committee in December 2007, Karlheinz Schreiber proved to be entertaining and a little enlightening. He told the public that he had originally set aside $500,000 for Mulroney but had decided not to pay him the money because Mulroney would not do anything to earn it. He said that the money had not come from the $20 million in Airbus commissions he had been paid. He said he did not pay money to anyone else in Canada. He talked about the campaign to overthrow Joe Clark—which changed the course of politics in Canada—but none of the politicians were too eager to follow up on that one. Canadians, unlike Germans, did not seem eager to know what was going on in their own country.

Schreiber harboured nothing but ill will for his one-time buddy, Mulroney. He expressed his sense of betrayal by reading to the committee a letter he had once written to Mulroney: "I was deeply embarrassed when people called you Lyin' Brian." He put down the letter and said: "Today Mr. Mulroney, I have to tell you Brian, if a lie itself looks for a proper label it would choose your face and your name."

As for Mulroney—grey, weary and haggard—he showed up at the committee with his family in tow, looking much the worse for wear. For four hours he tried to clear his name and set the facts straight. He said he wished he had never met Karlheinz Schreiber, whom he had spent years denying that he knew. He reiterated that Schreiber was a liar. He said he was sorry. He said he had made mistakes and he took responsibility for that. He said that he had not taken $300,000 from Schreiber, but *only* $225,000. He tried to explain why he had put the money in a family safe. No longer was the money for a pasta business, as he had once described it—now it was for his lobbying of international leaders to buy the products Schreiber was selling. He could not explain why he had not reported the income for six years, not until the truth was about to be told. He said he had long ago destroyed any documentation of receipts he might have had for expenses, so he had paid the taxes on that money as well—some businessman.

When Mulroney was finished testifying, he said he felt confident that he had refuted all Schreiber's allegations. He said there was no need for a public inquiry because he had told the truth.

The Canadian public, however, told pollsters that they believed Schreiber more than Mulroney. And that was how it ended after two decades. It didn't. The Airbus case promised to continue well beyond the publication date of this book. *Toronto Star* columnist James Travers skeptically described the process thus: "As is its habit, official Ottawa will nosily chase the truth without ever quite running it to ground."

True to the expectations of the skeptical, on January 11, 2008, independent investigator Johnston submitted to Harper his report and recommendations. Johnston concluded that any public inquiry should be limited to the nature of the relationship between Mulroney and Schreiber, beginning with Mulroney's acceptance of cash from Schreiber just two days before Mulroney resigned his seat in Parliament. Johnston suggested 17 questions that might be asked. "In determining the scope of any public inquiry, the government must make a 'cost benefit analysis' to determine how wide-ranging the public inquiry should be," Johnston wrote. "In this case, I conclude that the integrity concerns described above do not warrant a lengthy inquiry into matters that have been investigated by the RCMP since 1995. Nor should there be an inquiry with respect to facts already known."

Johnston rejected a full-scale inquiry into the allegations of $10 million in kickbacks being paid by Schreiber to unknown Canadians in the 1988 sale of Airbus jets to Air Canada, as well as the more recent allegations that Harper had ignored information provided by Schreiber.

Johnston went on to say that any public inquiry should not go over the "well-tilled ground.... The public inquiry should not be used to repeat what already had been done in the extensive RCMP investigation and other litigation and investigations that have been pursued for many years without leading to any charges."

It was as if Johnston had magically answered the prayers of both Harper and Mulroney, who had each called for a tailored public inquiry like the O'Connor Commission—so limited in its scope that the truth could be hidden.

A public opinion poll had also found that a majority of Canadians did not favour another inquiry which should have come as no surprise. Canadians did not really know or appreciate the underlying issues. After being bombarded with so many interminable and inconclusive inquiries in the past, inquiry fatigue had likely set in.

Harper immediately stated that he would not set up the inquiry until after the House of Commons ethics committee had completed its hearings into the matter, which happened in mid-February 2008. Nothing much of substance was learned then, since there were few members of the ethics committee who had either the legal skill or political will to ask probing questions and force revealing answers. Frustrated in its attempts to wade through faulty memories, conflicting stories, and apparent lies, the committee asked Harper to call his inquiry. But he indicated that he was not eager to do so and continued to stall.

Perhaps the most outlandish conclusion by Johnston was that no further investigation was needed of the Airbus Affair because the RCMP had already done it and found nothing—"the well-tilled ground." As Canadian history has repeatedly shown, just because the RCMP conducted investigations does not mean there had been a conclusive probe. The Mounties were past masters at finding nothing in politically sensitive cases.

"To say the ground had been well-tilled was outrageous," said Harvey Cashore, *the fifth estate* producer whose persistence and professionalism had exposed the many lies of Mulroney. "The RCMP had not even scratched the surface. It might have looked like an investigation, but it wasn't. The RCMP had not even interviewed Schreiber before the government settled with Mulroney."

By trying to avoid a full-scale inquiry into the Airbus Affair, the Harper government seemed to be showing that it had no interest in finally getting to the real issue—the offshore financing of Joe Clark's demise and Brian Mulroney's ascendancy. Harper wasn't curious about the bribes Schreiber had paid to unknown Canadians, presumably politicians and other influential people. One could not help but conclude that an invisible hand or two had touched Harper on the shoulder and reminded him of the ugly consequences of turning over these rocks—the entire system of government might require an examination or, perhaps, an exorcism.

Finally, on June 13, 2008, as Parliament was about to rise for the summer break, Harper announced the appointment of Jeffrey Oliphant, the associate chief justice of Manitoba's Court of Queen's Bench, to head the inquiry he had promised. Oliphant would be given a year to hold hearings and make his report.

The Airbus-Schreiber-Mulroney scandal suggested that something was seriously wrong in Canada, but it was not the only example. It is now time to return to Project Sidewinder.

[23]

PROJECT SIDEWINDER:
THE "POWER" BEHIND THE THRONE

When Stephen Harper was elected prime minister in February 2006, like his immediate predecessor Paul Martin he inherited a satchel of poisonous snakes from Jean Chrétien and Brian Mulroney. Chrétien had shown no interest in dealing with Mulroney's seedy legacy, in particular the overt corruption and the nefarious manner in which Mulroney had won power.

Recall that on his watch Chrétien racked up his own dubious collection of misdeeds: the so-called Shawinigate Scandal, where he had become personally involved in getting loans for his friends, and the phony federal sponsorship program or Adscam as it was known, which benefited more of his political friends, and is still before the courts. One scandal shared by Mulroney and Chrétien overlapped with Airbus, but did not receive as much publicity. It was a case that brought together a volatile combination—the RCMP and CSIS—Canada's only federal police force and its sole counterintelligence agency. As the world has learned since the Air India mass murder in 1985 and the recent Arar case, when CSIS and the RCMP worked together the RCMP often came out bruised and battered.

The investigation would come to be known as Project Sidewinder. Like Airbus, it involved offshore money and political influence, but in many ways Project Sidewinder revealed something even more sinister than Franz Josef Strauss and his ruthless European ultra-conservatives installing their own chosen leader in Canada. Project Sidewinder threatened to expose the deadly cancer at the centre of the Canadian political system as well as the fundamental and disturbing differences between Canada and most other democratic countries.

As you will recall from Chapter 2, in September 2000, five days into his new job as commissioner of the Royal Canadian Mounted Police, Giuliano Zaccardelli had given an extraordinary press conference in which he stated, without getting into specifics: "For the first time in this country, we are seeing signs of criminal organizations that are so sophisticated that they are focusing on destabilizing certain aspects of our society. There are criminal organizations that target the destabilization of our parliamentary system...."

The next day, the *National Post*, controlled by the uncurious, strident privy councillor Conrad Black, whacked Zaccardelli up the side of his head. It dismissed his views as being "alarmist" and suggested that the commissioner was trying to be political. He was, but not in the way the *National Post* editorialists had suspected. Zaccardelli had used the threat of a renewed Sidewinder investigation to extract from the prime minister a commitment to let him run the RCMP as he saw fit. For his part, Chrétien was more than happy to do that, and protect his own reputation, as well as his personal and business interests in China.

To understand the significance of Project Sidewinder, one must first appreciate the milieu in which it took place. After the death in 1976 of Chinese Communist Party Chairman Mao Tse-Tung, an unlikely new leader, Deng Xiaoping, emerged in 1978. Deng immediately began to change the way the Chinese thought about themselves and the rest of the world. "To get rich is glorious," he told his people, as he introduced economic reform and concepts such as "Socialism with Chinese characteristics" and "socialist market economy." In his Wikipedia entry, Deng is quoted as saying: "We mustn't fear to adopt the advanced management methods applied in capitalist countries.... The very essence of socialism is the liberation and development of the productive systems.... Socialism and market economy are not incompatible.... We should be concerned about right-wing deviations, but most of all, we must be concerned about left-wing deviations."

One of Deng's first initiatives was to invite Paul Desmarais to lead a high-powered corporate delegation to China. Desmarais took up the offer later in 1978. The opening up of China's massive, untapped economy dovetailed with thinking in the West, where the market seemed exhausted. The West was in a massive recession. Interest rates were approaching 20 percent and more. To get economies moving again, new markets were needed. China was the biggest one in the world, a perfect partner to help develop supply-side economics from a mere conservative idea to economic reality.

World economic leaders, like those who attended the Trilateral Commission and the Bilderberg Group, were promoting the importance and value of international trade. Tycoons everywhere were salivating at the prospect of opening up the enormous Chinese market and profiting from it. At the same time, the Chinese were eager to invest in western economies.

To facilitate trade with the West, the Chinese set up the China International Trust and Investment Corporation (CITIC) in 1979. It was based in Hong Kong. Original funding for the company came from a number of sources. These included the Chinese government and the bank of the People's Revolutionary Army. CITIC's initial aim was to "attract and utilize foreign capital, introduce advanced technologies, and adopt advanced and scientific international practice in operation and management." By 1984, a number of others joined CITIC, the most significant being Hong Kong billionaire Li Ka-Shing.

Although seen to be a paragon of capitalism, since 1979 Li had enjoyed a working relationship with the government of Communist China. He was considered to be a business mentor for the communists. Over the years, a number of Li's associates have been linked by police organizations around the world as being members of one of the 500 or so criminal Triads.

U.S. Congressman Dana Rohrabacher is an outspoken critic of Li. Rohrabacher, a Republican from California, told Congress in 1999 that there was evidence to support the allegation that Li is not a Hong Kong businessman, but a Communist Chinese businessman based in Hong Kong. Rohrabacher testified that: "The U.S. Bureau of Export Affairs, the U.S. Embassy in Beijing and the Rand Corporation . . . have identified Li Ka-Shing and [his company] Hutchison Whampoa as financing or serving as a conduit for Communist China's military for them to acquire sensitive technologies and other equipment."

In Canada, there were never any political concerns about dealing with Li and the Chinese. With Desmarais as the front man, diplomatic and trade relations between Canada and China blossomed, beginning in the early eighties.

In January 1984, Zhao Zhiyang, premier of the State Council of China, paid an official visit to Canada. Later that year, a Canadian parliamentary delegation visited China.

In July 1985, Li Xiannian became the first president of China to pay a state visit to Canada. He met with Governor General Jeanne Sauvé and Prime Minister Brian Mulroney. Twenty months later in March 1987, Sauvé travelled to China. The next month, a Canadian parliamentary delegation also visited China to meet with its leaders. A month after that, in May 1987, Yang Shangkun, vice-chairman of the Central Military Commission of China, came to Canada to meet with Mulroney and Foreign Affairs Minister Joe Clark. And so it would go. There were high-level visits between the two countries in 1988, 1989, 1993, 1994, and 1995. In 1996, Chrétien led his first "Team Canada" trade mission to China.

By the mid-nineties, there was a new businessman promoting the mutual interests of Canada and China. He was Chrétien's son-in-law, André Desmarais. In 1996, André had taken over the reins of Power Corporation from his father, Paul. Power Corp. had extensive business interests in China, going well beyond its involvement in the monumental Three Gorges Dam project. The younger Desmarais soon became a highly-placed adviser to the Chinese government, among his many important Chinese connections.

In 1997, ownership of the British colony of Hong Kong, the economic engine of the region, reverted back to China. Hong Kong had also served as the base for criminal Triads, many of which had conclusive links to Chinese intelligence and military agencies—as well as the government. The Triads were essentially secret societies with branches in business and government and were considered "patriots" by the Chinese and their leaders.

André Desmarais was appointed in 1997 as a director of CITIC, and through him Power Corp. was allowed to buy four percent of the Chinese company's stock which would prove to be an enormous windfall. CITIC Pacific, as it came to be called, was on its way to becoming an international conglomerate. Over the next few years, it bought up international banks and high-technology and resource companies in a number of countries. Desmarais was also appointed by the Chinese to be a member of the Hong Kong Chief Executive's Council of International Advisers in the years 1998–2005. During this period, he also became a director of The International Council of the JP Morgan Chase Bank, David Rockefeller's old bank. Like his father Paul, André was now a powerful man in his own right.

During this same time frame, democratic countries around the world were expressing their concerns about violations of human rights by the Chinese government, but not Canada. Chrétien took the position that even though it was China's third largest trading partner, Canada was too small a country to influence China. Chrétien argued that "quiet diplomacy" was the best way to deal with the situation. To that end, Canada became a supporter of China as it tried to gain entry into the World Trade Organization. On

May 11, 1995, Foreign Affairs Minister André Ouellet announced a significant change in Canadian diplomacy, stating that the country would no longer judge a trading partner by its human rights record. Ouellet said "sanctions were counter-productive." Two years later, in 1997, International Trade Minister Art Eggleton argued that the WTO should not consider issues such as human rights when evaluating China's commercial interests. The Canadian position was that ending China's isolationism would eventually have a "value-added" effect—the Chinese would eventually have to become more lenient toward their own people.

It was Chrétien's view that increased trade with China was the only important priority. What this came to mean, however, was that for the sake of business relationships Canada would never allow itself to be seen to be critical of the Chinese government. Furthermore, Canada went as far as turning a deaf ear to the many critics of the Chinese government. In the following astute analysis—written when she was a law student at Pace University in 1999—U.S. lawyer Ellen Javor summed up the Canadian position, its implications, and how others viewed the country's policy:

> To date, many have considered "value-added diplomacy" a failure. For many critics, especially in the human rights community, the dual track approach has, in effect, constituted the abandonment of Canada's traditional emphasis on human rights....
>
> In response to this kind of criticism, the Chrétien Government has stressed that "quiet diplomacy" in matters of trade in the end will be the best way of improving human rights conditions. Chrétien has long acknowledged that Canada does not always agree with China on policy matters, but is reluctant to impose its values on that nation. Critics have cited the Government's fear that criticizing China's poor human rights record could negatively impact upon Canadian trade and influence....
>
> One of the Government's severest critics has been the well-known Chinese dissident, Wei Jingshen, who has commented that the Canadian policy of engaging China through closer trade has been ineffective, and that Chrétien's view that Canada lacks leverage is "foolish." Advocating strong public diplomacy, he has commented that China will never bow to logic, only pressure.
>
> Critics of the Government's "value-added" diplomacy have, moreover, pointed out that Canada's abandonment of its human

rights agenda can also be perceived in its policy towards Indonesia. It has been noted, for example, that the Chrétien Government failed to raise human rights concerns to Indonesian officials during high-level foreign trade missions, prior to the fall of the Suharto regime in 1998.

Significantly, however, because of China's growing dependence on international trade it is entirely unclear whether it would react negatively to criticism in such a way as to actually rupture trade relations. In 1997, for example, Denmark sponsored a resolution in the United Nations Commission on Human Rights specifically criticizing China's human rights record. In reaction to Denmark's activism, China is said to have threatened to repudiate Danish contracts with Chinese state companies, but never, in fact, carried out the threat. Indeed, during the following year, Denmark's trade with China actually increased. Criticizing China on human rights abuses, therefore, does not necessarily translate into that nation's restricting bilateral trade.

Observers have commented that not only has Canada abandoned a human rights agenda as part of its bilateral relations, but appears to have abandoned public diplomacy through international organizations where Canada has had influence. In 1997, Canada broke ranks with the U.S., Britain, Denmark and several other nations, by failing to endorse their resolution submitted to the UN Commission on Human Rights, condemning China's human rights practices. Critics have also observed the Canadian Government's reluctance to meet with Wei Jingshen to discuss the plight of other Chinese dissidents. Canadian trade missions, likewise, have been criticized for failing to raise China's human rights record to Chinese officials. Missions aimed at improving trade and investment relationships in recent years have not been used as vehicles to press Canada's human rights concerns.

The pandering by the Canadian government made for smooth relations with the Chinese. At various times, President Jiang Zemin described Chrétien as being "an old friend" and "a personal friend." Jiang travelled to Canada for five days in 1997, ostensibly as part of his ongoing effort to promote international trade and economic integration. The most telling thing about his visit, however, was that Jiang spent just one and a half days in meetings with politicians and government officials. For the next three and a half days he camped out at Paul Desmarais's retreat in the Laurentians. There, his RCMP security detail saw just how close Desmarais and the Chinese had become. Of all the art in the magnificent house, the most impressive were two life-sized terra cotta Chinese soldiers, part of the most significant collection of artifacts ever found in China. The sculptures were discovered near Xi'an in 1974 and dated from the 3rd century B.C., the reign of Qin Shi Huang, the first emperor of all China. The entire collection comprised 7,000 soldiers, horses, and equipment, each piece remarkably different. Since a museum was opened on the site in 1979, the collection has become one of the leading tourist attractions in China.

In a later press release, the Ministry of Foreign Affairs of the People's Republic of China made no mention of the sojourn with Desmarais. Instead, the Chinese focused on how Jiang's close relationship with Chrétien "strengthened China's economic stature abroad, attempting to establish cordial relations with countries whose trade is largely confined to the American economic sphere." In a separate release, the Chinese government stated: "The visit further promoted the bilateral economic and trade cooperation. The two sides also signed many agreements during the visit: the Consular Agreement between the two governments, the MOU of Cooperation in Tourism between the National Bureau of Tourism of China and the Tourism Committee of Canada, and three MOUs on development aid and the exchange of notes on increasing the number of consulates-general. The visit achieved the purpose of deepening understanding, enhancing friendship, facing future challenges together and expanding cooperation and laid a firm foundation for the stable, friendly and cooperative bilateral relations in the 21st century." The Chinese said they were our friends, but they had a strange way of showing it.

There had been abundant warnings from knowledgeable observers around the world that any country dealing with the Chinese had to be wary about their methods and true intent. The Chinese were past masters at deception, subterfuge, and infiltration—skilled in the art of corruption. If it served their interests, they were prepared to bend and even break the rules.

While the Canadian and Chinese diplomats dined on canapés in the mid-eighties, the Chinese began to make themselves at home in Canada. Government, businesses, and "patriotic" organized crime factions—which often operated in unison—had long been targeting Canada by taking advantage of the country's porous immigration policy, poor security, and lax law enforcement.

Their approach could be summed up by this instruction from Chinese general and military strategist Sun Tzu, who wrote *The Art of War* some time between 300 and 600 B.C. "Be so subtle that you are invisible. Be so mysterious that you are intangible. Then you will control your rival's fate."

What the Chinese were doing, however, was not entirely invisible. In 1977, a CBC documentary *The Quiet Dragons* revealed that 40 corrupt Hong Kong police officers were living in Canada, many of them illegally. The Canadian government had turned a blind eye to their presence.

In 1986, while experts were writing that Canada was rapidly becoming one of the world centres for Chinese organized crime and espionage, RCMP Commissioner Robert Simmonds declared that there were no Triads operating in Canada.

As part of the opening of relations between Canada and China, Li Ka-Shing began to buy up huge tracts of property in the Lower Mainland of British Columbia in the mid-to-late eighties. An original prime target was the B.C. Expo Lands in the heart of Vancouver. The 80 hectares of prime real estate had been partially developed for the 1986 World Exposition on Transportation and Communication.

In 1988, *Globe and Mail* reporter Robert Matas found that B.C. Premier William Vander Zalm and one of his cabinet ministers, Peter Togo, had been openly cavorting with Li and his associates. When Matas was ready to publish his story, Li threatened the *Globe* with a pre-publication lawsuit seeking $225 million in damages. The *Globe* ran the story and the lawsuit never materialized. The story had no effect on what was to take place. Despite a local controversy, the B.C. government charged ahead and sold the property that year to a Li-controlled company, Concord Pacific Development Corporation, for a fraction of its original cost. Vander Zalm argued at the time that there were no other buyers for the Expo lands.

That same year, *Globe and Mail* reporter Victor Malarek uncovered a scheme by Hong Kong business people to bypass Canadian immigration and gain landed immigrant status by pretending to be living in properties they had purchased in Canada. The illegal venture had been orchestrated by Martin Pilzmaker, a lawyer at the prestigious Lang, Michener law firm in Toronto, along with other members of the firm. Pilzmaker was eventually charged, but committed suicide in a Florida hotel room before facing trial.

None of these threads made a cohesive story until Brian McAdam stumbled onto something unusual in the Canadian consulate in Hong Kong. A foreign services officer in the Canadian diplomatic corps since 1965,

McAdam arrived in 1989 for his third stint there. He had spent 25 years overseas working for the Canadian government with three separate postings to London and two each to Barbados and Copenhagen. In between, he had been given temporary six to eight-week duty assignments in Glasgow, Helsinki, Dublin, Bogota, Bangkok, and Amman. McAdam had received a string of superior and outstanding appraisal reports over the course of his career and was considered by law enforcement agencies around the world to be an expert on Asian organized crime. His reports were widely read and distributed and he was called on as a speaker and adviser by a number of western countries.

In 1991, McAdam began a two-year stint as an immigration and control officer in Hong Kong. One day he logged onto his embassy terminal and tried to bring up the file of an Asian gangster trying to get into Canada. He said in an interview that as he scanned the file it slowly evaporated and disappeared. When he tried to run another suspected gangster's name, the same thing happened. To McAdam it appeared that the embassy's proprietary Computer-Assisted Immigration Processing System, or CAIPS, had been breached.

McAdam called in then-Staff Sgt. Garry Clement, who was the RCMP liaison officer in Hong Kong. Clement—who would run the Almalki–Arar investigation in Ottawa nine years later—confirmed what McAdam had found—at least 788 files of suspected Chinese gangsters had been penetrated and corrupted. The system had been compromised, apparently by Hong Kong-based organized crime elements with links to the People's Republic of China.

"I would not go as far as to say that they evaporated on the screen," Clement said in an interview, "but they were definitely erased. There was no question that there was a serious problem. It had all the hallmarks of organized crime and possible money laundering activity. It was evident that the immigration system had been corrupted and that Chinese criminals were flooding into Canada. This required an immediate and full investigation."

In most other democratic countries, immigration authorities are peace officers with the power to investigate and make arrests, but not in Canada. All federal policing power is vested in the RCMP which, as we have already seen, makes it that much easier for investigations to be politically controlled and manipulated. In 1992, based on Clement's recommendation, the RCMP began an investigation. It sent Sergeant John Conohan and David Balser, a data processing expert, to check out the situation. Balser confirmed

McAdam's conclusions that the CAIP system in Hong Kong had been penetrated—at least six years earlier, in 1986, just as Sino–Canadian relationships were warming up. Balser discovered that Hong Kong nationals employed by the consulate gained illegal and unauthorized access to CAIPS and had erased at least 2,000 names from the database. He recommended changes to the system to ensure this did not happen again, but there was more going on than the computer breach.

In all, McAdam had found 70 different threads of suspected or actual criminal behaviour in the Hong Kong Consulate. One of them led back to the Consulate of Lesotho, a small African nation. This consulate was cooperating with Chinese criminals by issuing fake visas which helped the criminals to get into Canada. McAdam's work led to the Lesotho Consulate being closed in 1992.

In the Canadian offices, the Mounties found fake visa authentication stamps for countries like Panama in the desk of a female employee who was a Chinese national. Before the RCMP could talk to her she fled to Taiwan. Conohan found that the woman's brother was heavily involved in gambling and indebted to a powerful organized crime faction in Hong Kong. Eventually, the woman moved to Canada as a landed immigrant and opened up an immigration consulting business in North Vancouver.

As Malaysian-born Fabian Dawson of the *Vancouver Province* would later report, corruption seemed to be rampant at the Canadian embassy. One officer there received a Rolex watch as a going-away gift from a local millionaire. Another Canadian immigration officer got $300,000, while yet another was given expensive coins to be used as a gift for his family whom he was going to visit. Canadian immigration officials were regularly invited to the horse races, where they were each handed "a little red packet" containing money.

"I expressed trepidation—about the invitation to the races—to my immediate boss, but was told the people inviting us were not asking for visas to go to Canada," McAdam told the *Province*. "When my wife and I arrived at the VIP room at the race track, Granny Pong, the matriarch of this family, thrust little red envelopes into our hands, as she did for every other couple. This greatly disturbed me because I knew this was an old technique to bribe people," said McAdam. "Why would multimillionaires constantly invite all newcomers from the Canadian mission's immigration section, as well as locally engaged staff, to the horse races and give them thousands of dollars?"

In each of his two little red packets, McAdam said he found HK$1,000. McAdam said he took the issue up with his superiors the next day and was assured that such a thing would not happen again. "But I was told I could not return the money because it would be taken as a great offence," he said. McAdam said he sent the cash to the Save the Children Fund, saying it was courtesy of Granny Pong, and gave his boss a copy of the letter.

McAdam's reports, lobbying, and recommendations to the government led to the first organized crime legislation being promulgated in 1993— subsection 19 (1) (c.2) of the Immigration Act, which has since prevented at least 2,000 criminals from entering Canada.

It was a small victory for McAdam because the original Hong Kong investigation was shut down shortly after it had begun in 1992, by an order believed to have been issued by then-Commissioner Norman Inkster. Sergeant Conohan was transferred to other duties. As we have already seen, during Inkster's tenure as commissioner from 1987 to 1995, many politically sensitive cases were made to disappear.

McAdam said that after the RCMP investigator left he found it all but impossible to keep known Chinese criminals from immigrating to Canada. "I would reject them three, four and even five times, but my recommendations kept being overturned until it was clear that there was no use continuing the fight."

Nevertheless, McAdam continued to investigate and the more he did the more he uncovered.

McAdam found that the Canadian diplomats in Hong Kong were on a feeding frenzy and willfully blind to the company they kept. He found that wealthy Chinese families were showering 30 Canadian diplomats with gifts and cash.

"I reported that some of the Canadian diplomats were also associating with persons who were Triad leaders and who had direct linkages with China's intelligence services, some of whom owned gambling-casinos and brothels," McAdam said. "I even discovered that the tailor making suits and measuring the diplomats in their offices was a senior office bearer in the Sun Yee On Triad. I reported that some locally-engaged staff was involved in scams. The security screening abroad of the Chinese migrants is usually carried out by locally-engaged staff, whose loyalties and trustworthiness are always suspect. It has always been common practice for Communist countries to implant locally-engaged staff in embassies for espionage activities. Foreign Affairs learned there were 197 cases of corruption by locally-engaged staff from 1996–1999 at its missions abroad, and many more were discovered later."

When he reported all this to his superiors, the Canadian government hired a consultant to investigate. As it turned out, the consultant had his own conflict: he had received a "Friendship" award from Communist China.

The consultant concluded in his report that the Canadian diplomats were justified in accepting the Chinese largesse. "He said," McAdam recalled, "it was natural for Chinese who viewed Canada as an escape route prior to Beijing's takeover of Hong Kong to cultivate friendships with Canadian immigration officers. None of the diplomats were ever prosecuted. Many of them were promoted and a few are now ambassadors."

It became obvious to McAdam that while he was trying to uphold his oath to serve his country, his superiors were not as fanatical about the concept. "I reported that senior diplomats, including the head of post, set the tone at the consulate by regularly associating with Triad leaders, despite being warned who they were. They were introducing these people without comment to Canada's members of parliament and business leaders who visited Hong Kong. I became a major irritant to many who were making millions of dollars from the immigration investor schemes because I was exposing their scams."

McAdam continued to file reports. He tried to warn the government that some of the world's largest drug traffickers were entering Canada and laundering billions of dollars in the country, but he said the government did not want to hear what he had to say. It flew in the face of the official government line that Canada faced no threat from increased ties with China.

"My work caused many bureaucrats and some politicians great distress," McAdam said. "Some of my reports were hidden and destroyed."

Perplexed by the government inaction and apparent intransigence, McAdam had failed to appreciate how quickly pro-Beijing Chinese tycoons and criminal Triads had forged deep ties with both the Canadian government and key businesses. "Through my investigation I learned that these very same people were linked to Communist China's espionage goals and acting as agents of influence and surrogates of the Communist Chinese government. They had successfully infiltrated Canada."

Despite the first setback, McAdam pressed on. "After the career crisis I experienced after my return, I went to incredible lengths to launch an investigation into the destruction and suppression of my work and the corruption I had witnessed," he said.

McAdam went directly to the associate deputy minister of Immigration who assigned the task to Assistant Deputy Minister George Tsai "who dithered and delayed," according to McAdam. After Conservative MP David Kilgour wrote a letter to Prime Minister Chrétien an RCMP investigator was sent to meet with McAdam.

It looked as if the RCMP was now serious about the matter, but not for long. The RCMP would not give the Mountie or another investigator permission to travel to Hong Kong. Almost as soon as that "investigation" had begun, the RCMP used one of its favourite derailing devices—the lead investigator was reassigned to other duties. "I was duped into believing something was being done, but in reality nothing was ever investigated," McAdam said.

The Canadian government forced McAdam out of the foreign service in 1993, telling him that he "had embarrassed senior management." A smear campaign was begun against him by Foreign Affairs, Immigration, CSIS, and the RCMP. It was suggested, among other things, that he had carried out illegal acts.

Now on the outside looking in, McAdam would not give up. With Chrétien now in power, he caused two more RCMP investigations in 1994 and 1995, but those too went nowhere. Once again, the RCMP brass sabotaged efforts from the beginning by rotating a dozen officers through the investigations. No Mountie was given the time or resources to corroborate any of McAdam's complaints. Finally, McAdam, fed up with the RCMP, went directly to CSIS.

Michel Juneau-Katsuya was the chief of the Asia–Pacific desk at CSIS. His own research had shown that the Chinese were mounting an assault on the Canadian economy and its political institutions. What started out as a small investigation for him and another CSIS agent, Peter Lung, blossomed into something more wide-ranging and disturbing.

"In 1987–88, Brian Mulroney created a new class of entrepreneur category by which Chinese tycoons could buy Canadian citizenship for an investment of $250,000, which they can still do today," said Juneau-Katsuya. "We could see that several of the people taking advantage of the entrepreneur program were in fact criminals. The more we looked at the situation the bigger it got. We began to see known criminals and Chinese intelligence agents meeting with each other in Canada. Before long, we learned that the criminals, tycoons and the Chinese government, including its intelligence agencies, were working together. It was a multi-faceted problem and raised issues of criminal activity, economic security and corruption. We quickly identified hundreds of Chinese front companies which were being used to acquire Canadian companies, which gave them ownership over their technologies and patents. The Chinese were sucking profits out of the companies and leaving them dry. For example, in 1995 CITIC reported doing $95 million in business in Vancouver and expected to do $150 million the next year. It only employed 13 people in Canada. The Chinese government is sucking the money out of the country. A national tragedy was happening before our very eyes, but the Canadian government took the position that in the name of capitalism, nothing can be done to interfere with capitalism."

After having met with McAdam, Juneau-Katsuya found the immigration investigator had independently confirmed the same findings coming from another direction. Juneau-Katsuya and Lung checked with intelligence agencies in other English-speaking countries and in Europe in an attempt to verify their suspicions. They learned that the Chinese were attempting to do the same things in those countries.

Juneau-Katsuya and Lung found that the Chinese government was flooding western countries with spies, usually through what is known as the United Front Work Department. Juneau-Katsuya said:

"The problem for western intelligence agencies was that they had grown up during the Cold War with Russian spy techniques and were trying to apply those to the Chinese, which didn't work. The Chinese take a much different approach. Their approach to spying is much more sophisticated. Everyone in China has been brought up with the theories of Sun Tzu. *The Art of War* is a slim book with only 13 chapters, but the last chapter is about the value of spies in ultimately winning a war."

He said westerners have failed to recognize and to appreciate how good the Chinese are at exploiting targets, how many resources they will dedicate to an attack, and how well they can execute their plans. "The Chinese believe in the concept of *guanxi*, which describes the relationship that exists between people. These are often hidden, trusted relationships based on the notion of honourable debt. The Chinese might ask for a favour or grant a favour to someone who they do not know, but who has been vouched for by a third party each person knows. They might give you money and not request repayment immediately. That debt might be passed down from generation to generation but eventually they will try to collect on it in one way or another. Li Ka-Shing owns more than six percent of Vancouver and is not a Canadian citizen, but he can call up the mayor of Vancouver or the premier of the province and those men will immediately come to the phone. Meanwhile, ordinary Canadians could never get that service or respect. They'd be left holding their breath forever."

When it comes to the Chinese collecting information, Juneau-Katsuya used the following analogy: "If you tell a Russian that there is a grain of salt on a beach, an agent will come in at night with a shovel and pail and try to scoop up as much sand as he can before the sun comes up. The Chinese, on the other hand, would send a thousand people to the beach during the day where they would lay in the sun and act normally. At night, they will all return to the same room and shake out their towels."

As Juneau-Katsuya tried to explain this to his own superiors, he met with the same level of resistance McAdam faced in foreign affairs. "Many of them took the position that I was criticizing them for being inept, but I wasn't. I was merely trying to show them how the situation had evolved and how we needed to adapt."

As all this was going on inside the walls of CSIS, public controversy about the problems in Hong Kong caused yet another investigation to be mounted. In late 1995, a fifth RCMP investigation was begun—Project Sidewinder. This time it was a joint venture between the Mounties and CSIS. The CSIS agents were Juneau-Katsuya and Peter Lung. For CSIS it was a golden opportunity because it gave the agency access to the treasure trove of data stored away in RCMP files—the kind of information it rarely gets its hands on.

Project Sidewinder was a most peculiar effort. In what appeared to be a massive assault on Canada by a coordinated offensive by the Chinese government, businesses, and criminals, the RCMP did not assign a team of high-level investigators. Instead, the lead investigator was Corporal Brian Read, from the force's immigration and passport section.

"They thought Read would not do a good job, but I think he surprised everyone with the excellence of his investigation," Juneau-Katsuya said.

With the help of McAdam, Read pieced together what had happened. Data processing specialist Balser told Read that he had been ordered by the government to "obfuscate" his original report from 1992.

The investigators soon found they were being pressured by their superiors to file a report. Although they asked for time to perfect their information, their superiors said they could not wait.

On June 24, 1997, Read and Juneau-Katsuya submitted an unedited 30-page draft—*Sidewinder: Chinese Intelligence Services and Triad Financial Links in Canada*—to the RCMP–CSIS Joint Review Committee The original draft report which can be viewed online at www.primetimecrime.com was designed, not as an indictment, but as an overview based on available criminal intelligence and experienced analysis.

The Sidewinder report detailed what they had found and suspected. It also recommended a course of action they believed should be taken. "This is what happened," Read told his RCMP superior. "The original case was covered up."

Other Mounties familiar with the case knew that Read had merely uncovered the tip of an iceberg. Read had focused on two incredibly explosive scenarios. The first involved possible payoffs to Brian Mulroney and those around him by the Chinese. The second cited the Power Corporation–Chrétien–China triangle. One of the associated subtexts alleged Chrétien's direct involvement in certain immigration files and possible payoffs being made through an intermediary.

Read described how Chinese immigrants had insinuated themselves into other countries, such as Thailand and Malaysia, and, beyond their apparent economic means, had taken control of those respective economies. He said their seemingly successful "entrepreneurship" had less to do with hard work and much to do with the flow of illegally gained monies being laundered by the Chinese government and criminal organizations. Hong Kong tycoons, Triads, and the Chinese intelligence service "have been working for 15 years in concert with the Chinese government, and some of their 'financial ventures' in Canada serve to conceal criminal or intelligence activities." The activities described included money laundering, heroin trafficking, and the transfer of economic, high technology, and intelligence data to Beijing under the guise of legitimate business activities.

"Because of its strategic alliance with some important and influential Hong Kong business people, and with organized crime syndicates, the Chinese leadership appears to be today in a position to develop a potential of influence over the international market and particularly on the Canadian economy and political life of the country," the Sidewinder report stated.

"Why Canada?" McAdam asked. "Because Canada has always been somehow favourable in China. It has also an important Chinese community and very important economic ties with Hong Kong. Having bought significant real-estate holdings and established companies in Canada [and] gaining some access to political leaders and business people, it is now in a position to seek power by influence. What makes it difficult to argue against is the fact that most of it has been done legally. Even more, the threat is manifold and elaborated in a complicated web of businesses. It diffuses itself through a not so tangible network. If you look at a single individual, the threat does not seem to be there. But because of their associations and their alliances with China, one cannot look at individuals in isolation. The facts analyzed lead us to believe that a gain of influence has been the object of a concerted plan and that could constitute a threat to Canada."

The Sidewinder report made it clear that the Triads, tycoons, and Chinese intelligence agencies had learned that the quick way to gain influence in Canada was to provide financing to the main political parties. "China has obtained access to influential figures who are now or once were active at various levels of Canadian society."

The Sidewinder report made reasonable recommendations under the circumstances:

1. An expanded task force including analysts from at least the RCMP, CSIS, the Department of Foreign Affairs and International Trade, Immigration Canada, and Revenue Canada should be formed to pursue the research begun in this document.

    To assess the actual control of Chinese companies over the Canadian economy;

    To review who the influential Canadian figures are on boards of the Canadian companies;

    To consult with the FBI, which has recently undertaken a similar study, such consultation could prove mutually beneficial.

2. Support a series of presentations to CSIS regional directorates and RCMP divisions to alert operational managers to the need to investigate Chinese activities the better to grasp the links among the Chinese Intelligence Service, the triads, and enterprises in the service of Chinese companies.

3. Organize a series of presentations for senior members of the Canadian security and intelligence community.

4. Organize presentations for specific government departments affected by the problem other than those in the intelligence community, such as Justice and Industry.

5. Undertake review of security companies which have installed security systems for federal government departments and Crown corporations to determine the real control and ownership of the companies and the potential risk to the integrity of the systems.

6. Carry out thorough research to determine the extent of contributions

to Canadian political parties by Chinese companies established in Canada.

7. Produce a strategic analysis of the activities and involvement of the Government of China and the triads in Chinese entertainment and media in Canada.

If Read and Juneau-Katsuya thought their agencies would be excited by their good work they were absolutely mistaken. Civilian analyst Robert Fahlman and Corporal Norm Rioux, two relatively low-level members in the intelligence directorate, tried to push the case forward but without success. The upper echelons of the force were not all that excited by the prospect of taking on the prime minister and the powers that be. It soon became clear to Read that neither his immediate superior nor the rest of the force was interested in what he had found. "As the months went on it occurred to me that the RCMP were going to continue this cover-up which, I believed at that time, was perpetrated by Immigration and Foreign Affairs."

Later in 1997, Read filed an obstruction complaint against his superior which only served to isolate him further within the force. While he was in the trenches fighting for Canada, he was accused of breaching the Mountie Code of Conduct by not being loyal to and protecting the image of the force. He went on sick leave for six months. When he returned, he found that his duties had been reduced to those of a filing clerk.

The Sidewinder report meanwhile had been handed over to the Security Intelligence Review Board, the governing body of CSIS, where it was to be evaluated. It should have been a criminal investigation but now it was transformed into an issue of national security. Pushing the Sidewinder Report to SIRC placed it in the hands of the Privy Council—where Paul Desmarais and other Power Corp. associates were members.

One of the CSIS evaluators was former Ontario New Democratic Party leader Robert Rae, who might have looked like a socialist, but had proven himself in power to be anything but. John Rae, his brother, was a longtime executive of Power Corp. Rae himself would later seek the leadership of the federal Liberal Party, but fail. (In a by-election held March 17, 2008, Rae, running as a Liberal in the riding of Toronto Centre, won a seat in Parliament.)

One of the other supposedly "independent" members of the SIRC board was James Andrews Grant. He was a director of the Canadian Imperial Bank of Commerce and chairman of the executive committee of the Toronto law firm Stikeman, Elliott. Li Ka-Shing was the largest single shareholder of CIBC stock and the law firm acted for him in Canada. Neither man bothered to recuse himself.

While some RCMP members were still eager to pursue Project Sidewinder, as Zaccardelli had indicated in his maiden press conference in September 2000, CSIS had no appetite for such a venture. As a compromise to stop all the warring CSIS commissioned a junior officer to create another, slimmed down version of the Sidewinder report. It was called Project Echo.

Meanwhile, Juneau-Katsuya went through the Sidewinder report line by line, providing sourcing and substantiation for every word in the report. He created three binders, one for the RCMP, another for Barry Denofsky, his boss at CSIS, and one for himself.

In 1999, the Security Intelligence Review Committee interviewed everyone involved in the file. When Juneau-Katsuya's turn came he went into the meeting with a CSIS "babysitter—for my own protection," he said. Under questioning, he referred to the binder he had given to CSIS and the RCMP. The SIRC members said their copy had apparently been misfiled and lost.

"If I had been faster on my feet I would have realized that intelligence agencies do not lose files, but I answered too quickly," Juneau-Katsuya said. "As I began to tell them that I had another copy, my babysitter began to kick me under the table, warning me to shut up, but it was too late. At the lunch hour my superior, Dale Neufeld, berated me for what I had done and ordered me to give him the binder. It somehow got misfiled, too, and was never seen again, although I believe the RCMP still has a copy of it."

SIRC eventually suppressed the Sidewinder report as well as the Project Echo report, clearly part of the grand plan. SIRC ordered all copies and background materials destroyed. SIRC argued that the allegations were "deeply flawed . . . a loose, disordered compendium of 'facts' connected by insinuations and unfounded assertions. Overall, the document is rich with the language of scare-mongering and conspiracy theory."

The SIRC's slander of Read, McAdam, Juneau-Katsuya, and Lung was undoubtedly calculated. "We were forced to provide a draft to them and not given the time to perfect it, and then we were criticized for not being perfect," Juneau-Katsuya said. "It was quite clear that this was the plan all along."

Two days before the general election of June 2, 1997, the SIRC report denouncing Projects Sidewinder and Echo was suspiciously leaked to the *National Post*, a clear benefit to Chrétien, whose Liberals won a slim majority.

"Canadians were relieved to get rid of Mulroney and embrace Chrétien as the better man, but from what my colleagues and I could see all we did was go from crooked to crooked . . . er," says Juneau-Katsuya. "As for Neufeld, he went on to become director of CSIS, after Ward Elcock left."

⊹ ⊹ ⊹

Meanwhile, on the surface at least, Canada mounted a public relations effort to offset the Sidewinder controversy, making it appear that Canada was intent on dealing with Chinese crime. In 1999, the Canadian government was embroiled in a dispute with the Chinese government over Lai Changxing, whom we met in a previous chapter. As you may recall, China's most-wanted man had fled to Canada after operating a multi-billion-dollar smuggling racket, which involved military and government officials. Many people were convicted and some sentenced to death, but Lai and his wife, travelling on Hong Kong passports, were allowed to enter Canada.

In April 1999, Canada entered into a Memorandum of Understanding in which it expressed its intent to work with China for five years in combating a list of international crimes including money laundering, forgery, smuggling, terrorism, illegal immigration, trafficking in weapons, drugs, art treasures, or human beings and "any other area of mutual interest." Under the memorandum, the two countries pledged to help each other locate criminals, suspects, witnesses, and missing persons, and to exchange information about crimes, whether planned or in progress. The memorandum expired in 2004, and was not renewed, likely because Canada would not turn over the one man China wanted—Lai Changxing, who is still in Canada.

Corporal Read could no longer hold back and decided to go public with what he knew, releasing to the media a copy of his Sidewinder report which he had not destroyed as ordered. He complained about the cover-up, which prompted yet another RCMP investigation. This time the police found that while there were documents missing from the file and there had been curious behaviour by a number of people in Hong Kong, there was no evidence of a crime or a threat to national security. The number two diplomat in Hong Kong, for example, suddenly and without warning left his post that year. Afterward, it was learned that he had received at least $1 million from an unknown source.

As it turned out, the only person who ended up being targeted by the RCMP was whistle-blower Read, who was alleged to have violated the cultish Mountie Code of Conduct. He was accused of embarrassing the force and being disloyal to the RCMP. He was suspended with pay and charged with divulging confidential information. He was convicted in 2002 and dismissed from the force. "I had suspected the original investigator from the RCMP was in fact on the take or corrupt or something else," Read said afterward. "From my trial, however, I can see that he was following orders when he covered up the whole affair in his files."

The RCMP External Review Committee later exonerated Read and ordered that he be reinstated to the force, but Commissioner Zaccardelli refused to do that. Read was gone and Zaccardelli made sure he stayed gone, which left a bad taste in the mouths of many Mounties, but clearly made Chrétien happy. To some it looked as if a fifth column was working inside the force, protecting the political interests of the government, but the media, with its hummingbird attention span and predetermined heroes and villains, had moved on, ignoring the issue. Read's final appeals were rejected by the Federal Court of Appeal and, finally, the Office of the Commissioner for Federal Judicial Affairs in May 2006.

[24]

CANADA'S UNDERMINED NATIONAL SECURITY

The Canadian government had always denied there were any problems with Chinese espionage or organized crime in the country. In recent years the Foreign Investment Review Agency had been reduced to little more than a paper tiger. Chinese businesses and government entities have continued to gobble up Canadian property and corporate interests. The Chinese were focused on the financial sector, utilities, and natural resources such as potash and the Alberta oil patch.

The government allowed Li Ka-Shing, through his company Hutchison Whampoa, to buy a controlling stake of Husky Energy Inc., an oil producer and refiner. In 2007, through Cheung Kong Infrastructure Holdings Ltd., his road building and energy company, Li was allowed to buy TransAlta Power LP for $629 million, gaining a foothold in North America.

Successive Canadian governments continue to assert that there is nothing to worry about—insisting that the RCMP and CSIS are on top of their games. The message is that we are safe.

Throughout the rest of the western world, however, police and counter-intelligence agencies have not only been warning about Chinese-based espionage and criminal enterprises, they have actually been doing something about it. Much of the information the United States has used to arm itself came from a Canadian, Brian McAdam, who caused Project Sidewinder to happen.

In 1996, the *Washington Post* and the *Los Angeles Times* each raised questions about an effort by the People's Republic of China to influence the outcome of the presidential and congressional elections. That year the Chinese directed massive illegal contributions to Democratic party incumbents Bill Clinton and Al Gore. *Washington Post* reporters Bob Woodward and

Brian Duffy showed that the Chinese embassy in the U.S. capital was coordinating the contributions.

The Chinese denied all the allegations, however 22 people were eventually convicted for fraud or for funnelling Asian funds into the United States elections. A number of the convictions came against longtime Clinton–Gore friends and political appointees.

Among those implicated in the illegal financing scheme in the United States was Wang Jun, the chairman of CITIC. Norinco and Poly Technologies, CITIC's armaments subsidiaries, had recently been caught attempting to smuggle 2,000 AK-47 assault rifles into California. Police said the weapons were destined for street criminals and Native groups in Canada.

In recent years, Wang, the son of Wang Zheng, had been a leader of the hard-line government faction that ordered the Tiananmen Square massacre in 1989. In recent years he has been associated with the smuggling of guns and missiles to Pakistan, Sudan, Iraq, and Iran.

In 1997, a report by the Rand Corporation noted that CITIC acts as a front for the People's Liberation Army. "CITIC does enter into business partnerships with and provides logistical assistance to PLA and defense-industrial companies," the report stated. In addition, Rand Corporation said, CITIC is the umbrella for Poly Technologies, Ltd., founded in 1984, ostensibly as a subsidiary of CITIC. Poly Technologies was later exposed by U.S. intelligence to be the primary commercial arm of the PLA General Staff Department's Equipment Sub-Department, according to the *China Reform Monitor*.

In March 2000, the CIA and FBI issued a joint report which stated: "China's spy services are stepping up military spying against the United States while using Chinese students as intelligence agents and 'political influence' programs to manipulate U.S. policy." U.S. officials also said that China had 3,000 front companies in that country whose purpose was to gain technological and commercial secrets. Much of the U.S. knowledge was based on McAdam's work which the Americans realized was at least a decade ahead of their own. A number of other Chinese spies were arrested in the intervening years.

In July 2005, the British newspaper the *Telegraph* reported: "A network of Chinese industrial spies has been established across Europe as the Communist government's intelligence agencies shift their resources and attention" toward espionage "aimed at achieving global commercial dominance. The extent of the spying was laid bare after a leading Chinese agent defected in Belgium. The agent, who has worked in European universities and companies for more than 10 years, has given the Sûreté de l'Etat detailed information on hundreds of Chinese spies working at various levels of European industry."

In June 2005, Chen Yonglin, former first secretary at the Chinese consulate in Sydney, Australia, defected, claiming that China had 1,000 spies in Australia and another 1,000 in Canada. A week later, Chinese security agent Hao Fengjun also defected in Australia and backed up Chen's claims. Hao also had information about what was going on in New Zealand.

In August 2005, former CSIS agent Michel Juneau-Katsuya spoke to CBC Radio about the Canadian situation. He said, "[If] Canadian intelligence agencies weren't preoccupied with Islamist terrorists these days they would realize the greatest threat to Canadian security comes from China.... We estimated at CSIS that we were losing $1 billion a month, $12 billion a year, due to industrial espionage." Nothing was done.

The Chinese have done little to hide their activities.

In 2007, the United Front Work Department which oversees the secret agent workforce saw its budget increased by $3 billion. Over the past seven years, every western democratic country, in particular the United States, Great Britain, France, Germany, Sweden, Belgium, Australia, and New Zealand, has tackled the Chinese espionage issue as a serious threat to national security. Every country but Canada, that is. In Canada, it appeared that the government knew what has been going on, but was reluctant to do anything about it for diplomatic, commercial, and the careerist reasons of the country's bureaucrats. If the Canadian government had hoped that the subject would be forgotten, it was disappointed.

In the United States, on July 31, 2005, Chen Yonglin testified before a joint hearing of Senate and Congressional members. They were investigating China's war on the Falun Gong movement, and human rights in general, in that country. In the context of what would happen later in Canada, it is important to note that the Americans took Chen seriously. The joint hearing included the Subcommittee on Africa, Global Human Rights, and International Operation, the Subcommittee on Oversight and Investigations, and the House of Representatives Committee on International Relations.

The Falun Gong is a Buddhist-like, meditative religion whose practices are similar to Qigong. The movement has a relatively small following in China and an unknown number of members around the world, most of them in the United States, Australia, and Canada. The Chinese government has declared that Falun Gong is its greatest internal security threat.

Before Chen spoke that day in Washington, U.S. State Department official

Gretchen Birkle testified that the evidence of brutal behaviour by the Chinese government was indisputable. Birkle cited a 2004 State Department report, released in February, 2005, that concluded the Chinese government continued to commit numerous human rights abuses, including torture, mistreatment of prisoners, and denial of due process. She said Chinese authorities were quick to suppress religious, political, and social groups perceived to be threatening to government authority or national stability. The entire system, Birkle said, was designed to "perpetuate the rule of the Chinese Communist Party."

Laws and regulations were broad and arbitrarily enforced, Birkle said. In fact, China was using the global war on terror as an excuse for cracking down on its own citizens—particularly Uighur Muslims—charging them with "subversion, loosely defined state secret crimes and other crimes" for peacefully expressing their dissent. In Tibet, the Chinese had been particularly intolerant and repressive but, Birkle said, it was the Falun Gong who were the targets of the greatest wrath. The Chinese had declared Falun Gong a cult, a term used indiscriminately for any religion that was not officially approved. Birkle provided an insight into how the Chinese government and bureaucracy work:

> Some of the harshest treatment meted out by China's criminal and administrative justice system has been directed against practitioners of the Falun Gong, who have been the target of a harsh government-wide crackdown since the spiritual movement was banned in China in July 1999 as an "evil cult." Under article 300 of the criminal law, cult members who disrupt public order or distribute publications may be sentenced to three to seven years in prison, while cult leaders and recruiters may be sentenced to seven or more years in prison. What is and is not a cult is determined by government authorities, based on no discernible criteria other than the government's desire to maintain control.
>
> At the National People's Congress session in March 2004, Premier Wen Jiabao's Government Work Report emphasized that the government would expand and deepen its battle against cults, including the Falun Gong. During the past year, thousands of individuals continued to be subjected to arrest or detention, and some were incarcerated in psychiatric facilities.
>
> Over all, more than 100,000 practitioners have been detained since 1999, not only for engaging in Falun Gong practices, but also

for merely admitting that they adhere to the teaching of Falun Gong or refusing to criticize the organizer and founder, Li Hongzhi. Mere belief in the practices of Falun Gong, even without public expression of its tenets, is sufficient grounds for practitioners to receive punishments, ranging from loss of employment, mandatory anti-Falun Gong study sessions designed to force practitioners to renounce the Falun Gong, to imprisonment. The reeducation-through-labor system is regularly used to incarcerate Falun Gong practitioners. Some national observers believe that at least half of the 250,000 officially recorded inmates administratively sentenced to the country's reeducation-through-labor camps are Falun Gong adherents.

After the release from these camps, hundreds of Falun Gong adherents who have refused to recant their beliefs continue to be held in legal education centers, another form of administrative detention. Falun Gong cases are often handled outside of normal legal procedures by a special ministry of justice office, known as the 610 Office.

During the past year, the 610 Office was implicated in many allegations of abuse. As a result of the government's campaign against the group during the past year, very few Falun Gong activities were conducted publicly within the country. But Falun Gong practitioners outside of China continue their efforts to focus international attention on the plight of fellow practitioners in China.

When he testified, Chen used documents to illustrate how China has used its burgeoning economic power in an attempt to manipulate and persuade foreign governments like Australia's to say and do as it wishes. He described it as the "Grand Border Concept—a strategy for obtaining Australia's natural resources and its political compromise." Chen went on to say: "The Consulate in Sydney has cultivated intimate relations with a lot of federal and state officials by inviting them to visit China, promoting their individual business ties with China and hosting dinners for them."

Chen said that there is a coordinated Chinese government strategy to smear the Falun Gong as an evil or dangerous cult and that he provided documents that described the "eyeball to eyeball" fight that was part of the plan. He said that Chinese intelligence agents are actively monitoring Falun Gong communities and its members, many of them citizens of their respective countries. He also said the Chinese are actively gathering information about the

Falun Gong, subverting their efforts, and lobbying federal and local governments to suppress their influence and activities.

"Each year, there are numerous Chinese officials visiting Australia," Chen stated. "They have the task to use all the official occasions to denounce the Falun Gong. Mr. Wu Bangguo, chairman of the National People's Congress of the Chinese Communist Party regime visited Sydney in May 2005, and did not forget to denounce the Falun Gong as an 'evil cult' in his speech to some pro-CCP people of the Chinese community, though there is no Falun Gong demonstration during his visit."

Chen continued: "Carrying out the policy to fight eyeball to eyeball with the Falun Gong, the consulate successfully defeated the attempt of the Falun Gong to participate in the Chinese Spring Festival parade. The consulate has consecutively forced the NSW Railway Authority and Sydney International Airport Company to take down the large lamp billboard with the Falun Gong slogan "Truth, Forbearance and Tolerance." In order to prevent Sydney Minhui School (whose principal is a Falun Gong practitioner) from being sponsored by the NSW Department of Education and Training, the Chinese Consulate put enormous pressure on the Department of Education and Training. That debate continues. After talking with the Fairfield City Council, the Chinese Consulate forced the cancellation of a "Truth, Forbearance and Tolerance" festival. Chen said the lobbying and coercion has been so effective that even in Australia—which is officially concerned about Chinese spying—there exists a "black list" of Falun Gong practitioners used for border checking and surveillance in the country.

After Chen had finished his presentation, Chairman Christopher Smith said: "Your testimony is absolutely explosive. For a man who worked for the Government of the People's Republic of China to come before House Committees that deal with human rights and oversight, and to tell us in such clear and unambiguous words that there is a war on the Falun Gong going on in China that is not just within the confines of the People's Republic of China and is worldwide, and to give us the insights that you have given us, I hope that every member of the press, whether it be AP, AFP, Reuters, or all of the Chinese language press that are here, will take full note of your testimony." Others on the committee called Chen a man of courage and honour.

When Chen came to Canada in June 2007, however, he received quite a different welcome than those he had enjoyed in Australia and the United States. The Canadian government did not invite Chen—he had received a private invitation and stayed with Brian McAdam at his Ottawa home. If

Chen had hoped that Canadians were willing to hear what he had to say, he was in for a big surprise.

"Chen told me that the Sidewinder Report was one hundred percent correct," McAdam said. "We tried to arrange a meeting with CSIS. They sent over an agent who spent five minutes with him and then left. The RCMP refused to see him. Foreign Affairs refused to see him. The Senate Committee on National Security was considering hearing from him but at the last minute decided against it. I then learned that the Committee's security advisor who apparently was consulted and advised against it was Barry Denofsky. When Denofsky was at CSIS he was the person who killed the Sidewinder report in the first place. We sent out a release announcing a press conference on Parliament Hill but only one current and one former member of Parliament showed up. We lined up interviews for him with various media, but few seemed interested."

"*The Globe and Mail* wrote a story about him, but he was otherwise roundly ignored," McAdam said.

Project Sidewinder, however, continued to make news. Andrew Mitrovica was one of the few reporters in Canada who knew much about the case. Now a freelancer and journalism instructor at a Toronto area community college, Mitrovica had in the past written extensively about Sidewinder and other security issues related to CSIS. In December 2007, he published a story in the *Toronto Star* about how the British government had recently issued an extraordinary alert to 300 top executives and security chiefs at banks, accounting, and law firms warning of an "electronic espionage attack" from "Chinese state organizations." Mitrovica revisited some of Chen's allegations and then went on to write:

> None other than Jim Judd, the head of Canada's spy service, CSIS, appeared to confirm Chen's portrait of the scope and character of Chinese spying in Canada during testimony before the Senate Committee on National Security and Defence this past April. Judd told the panel that China is the agency's most formidable adversary, preoccupying almost half of CSIS's counter-intelligence apparatus.
>
> Judd's testimony was surprising for a number of instructive reasons. It represented a striking about-face by CSIS mandarins concerning the threat posed by Chinese espionage to Canada's national security.
>
> A few years earlier, Judd's predecessor, Ward Elcock, had publicly

dismissed the findings of a joint RCMP–CSIS probe into China's espionage in Canada, dubbed Project Sidewinder, as an "interesting theory" that couldn't withstand scrutiny.

In the late 1990s, the Sidewinder analysts produced a report that mirrored the central thrust of recent "revelations" by Chen and Judd. Rather than being feted as prescient, the team was disbanded at the behest of CSIS over the objections of RCMP brass who insisted that the civilian spy service had effectively torpedoed the hush-hush probe.

In internal correspondence, the Mounties accused senior CSIS officers of having "compromised the integrity" of intelligence reports to Ottawa about existing and emerging security threats and charged that CSIS analysts had been forced to bury their findings.

In fact, CSIS officials had ordered the initial Sidewinder report to be softened and documents related to the study destroyed.

The question remained, therefore, were the allegations of Read and McAdam in the Project Sidewinder report valid or just a product of their overactive imaginations? Ongoing events elsewhere supported the Sidewinder theory.

In February 2008, U.S. authorities announced four more arrests involving Chinese espionage. One case involved Gregg W. Bergersen, 51, a weapons systems analyst at the Defense Security Cooperation Agency, which is part of the U.S. Defense Department and coordinates weapons sales abroad. Bergersen was alleged to have been befriended by Tai Shen Kuo of New Orleans, a naturalized U.S. citizen who was working for the People's Republic of China. Bergersen purportedly received payments for providing information about the projected sales of weapons and military equipment to Taiwan. Tai used a female intermediary, Yu Xin Kang, to communicate with the Chinese government.

A second case involved U.S. citizen Dongfan (Greg) Chung, a weapons analyst at Boeing Corp. in Seattle, who was also sending secret information to the Chinese.

Kenneth L. Wainstein, assistant attorney general for national security, told a news conference in Washington on February 11, 2008, the following: "While there are entities from over a hundred different countries trying to get access to our secrets or our controlled technology, there are a number of countries that have proven themselves particularly determined and methodical in their espionage efforts. The People's Republic of China is one of those countries. . . . In the last six months, we have filed charges in a half-dozen cases involving [Chinese] efforts to acquire different types of technology, ranging from battlefield night-vision equipment to accelerometers used in the development of smart bombs and missiles."

One of those was Chi Mak, a Chinese-trained engineer and spy, who spent more than two decades as a "the perfect sleeper agent," infiltrating a U.S. defence contractor's operations. Chi, a married, hard-working American citizen living in Los Angeles, told authorities he began his mission in the seventies. He gradually gained top security clearances which he used to gain access to sensitive plans for navy ships, submarines, and weapons. He sent the information to China via courier before being caught. In April 2008, Mak was convicted and sentenced to 24 1/2 years in federal prison.

"Chi Mak acknowledged that he had been placed in the United States more than 20 years earlier, in order to burrow into the defense-industrial establishment to steal secrets," Joel Brenner, the head of counter-intelligence for the Office of the Director of National Intelligence, said in an interview with the *Washington Post*. "It speaks of deep patience," he said, and is part of a pattern.

The Canadian government, meanwhile, has attempted to convince the country that complex matters of espionage and subversion are delicate and must always be dealt with in the shadows—"quiet diplomacy."

Concerned Canadians such as Read, McAdam, and Juneau-Katsuya— who had bravely and unselfishly put their careers and health on the line in the defence of their country—were seen to be fair game, and were marginalized and smeared. Read, still subject to surveillance and dirty tricks long after he had left the force, was left all but a broken man. His friends say he finds it difficult to believe that the RCMP, to which he had sworn an oath of loyalty, had been entirely disloyal to him.

"Now they've managed to have me and the others written off as conspiracy theorists, so that nobody will listen to us," McAdam said in an interview. "The Sidewinder report was dead-on and subsequent events have proven me to be right, but Ottawa is controlled by a small group of people who do not want this story told."

Canadian leaders would like the world to believe that Chinese government, business, and criminal elements have not been working in concert to subvert the Canadian parliamentary system and the country's economy as Commissioner Zaccardelli had alleged in his September 2000 press conference.

Maybe that is so. Maybe selling off key parts of our economy to foreign interests is worth the return in more Wal-Marts, flimsy toasters, and cheap pens that don't work. Or maybe Canada is just Potterville writ large, governed by the greed and the self-interest of the few.

"We are selling our country out from under ourselves in the name of open markets to a country that does not play by the rules," says former CSIS agent Juneau-Katsuya. "They are buying our companies and taking the blueprints, patents, and profits home. We are losing our competitiveness, our share of the world market, and the rights to our own land. At the end of the day we will be reduced to renting our own country, unless something is done."

The country's leaders have proven themselves disinclined to hear such arguments. Canada seems prepared to do whatever pleases China.

For example, on March, 12, 2008, Foreign Affairs Minister Maxime Bernier delivered a speech in which he said Canada believed in the "one-China" policy, which meant that it would not support Taiwan's proposed referendum on membership in the United Nations. Stephen Harper's longtime support of Taiwan had inexplicably been reversed.

China has long claimed that Taiwan is part of mainland China. Lost in the mists of time is evidence to the contrary. Taiwan was originally settled by Malays and Polynesians. China conquered the island, then known as Formosa, in the seventeenth century, but after losing the first Sino–Japanese War, from 1894 to 1895, ceded its rights in perpetuity in the Treaty of Shimonoseki. The Taiwanese eventually shook off the Japanese and became rulers of their own land.

The Canadian announcement of its one-China policy was greeted with enthusiasm in Beijing. *Xinhua*, the official government news agency, reported that Chinese Foreign Ministry spokesman Qin Gang applauded Bernier's speech. Qin was quoted as saying that China values its relations with Canada, and always maintains that the growth of China–Canada relations accords with the fundamental interests of both nations and their peoples. Qin hoped that the two nations, based on the principles of mutual respect, equality, mutual benefits, and non-interference in each other's internal affairs, would make concerted efforts to promote the healthy and stable development of China–Canada relations. A few days later, the Chinese launched their controversial crackdown on dissidents in Tibet.

The larger, more disturbing issues have remained unaddressed, left festering in Canadians' consciousness. We know by his own words and records that Karlheinz Schreiber had distributed at least $10 million in secret commissions to unknown Canadians, including $300,000 to Mulroney (or $225,000, if one chooses to believe Mulroney). All that was chicken feed compared to what the Chinese have shown they are willing to pay for what they want. Have the Chinese bought off Canadian politicians, bureaucrats, police, and others to look the other way or exert needed influence to assist them as they gobble up this country's resources and technology like starving piranhas? Mulroney might have received $300,000 from Strauss and company, but in the circumstances a legitimate question is, did he receive even more from the Chinese? Who else might have benefited from such underhanded behaviour? These are reasonable questions to ask.

Opening this door, however, leads to other, even more delicate, questions. If Franz Josef Strauss thought the government of Canada was for sale, who else in the world thinks that way?

This line of questioning goes beyond matters of mere corruption and strikes at the heart of a fundamental issue—what is national security? It is evident from the track record that, unlike democratic governments elsewhere, Canadian governments have taken the position that international trade and anything associated with it—including kickbacks or bribes—are not criminal matters but rather legitimate national security issues.

Who is defending Canada?

✝ ✝ ✝

There is only one guardian institution in Canada empowered to protect Canadians from such criminal behaviour: the RCMP. CSIS and the CSE (Communication Security Establishment), as arms of the government, do not investigate crime and operate entirely under a blanket of secrecy. Yet the flow of information and the levels of accountability, such as they are, require the RCMP to deal with CSIS on virtually every matter related to international affairs, be they criminal, economic, or political.

These guardian institutions have been organized in such a way as to allow political influence over their activities under the guise of national security. As you have already seen in this book, when any controversy involving even a hint of so-called national security has erupted in Canada, a detectable pattern of misconduct has emerged. The rule of politics has always trumped the rule of law.

In cases such as those of Maher Arar, Airbus, and Project Sidewinder, the RCMP investigators set out to do the right thing and conduct an impartial investigation, only to have it derailed internally by some invisible hand like the Security Intelligence Review Board. Since their inception in 1984, CSIS and SIRC have proven to be the most vigilant and politicized protectors of the government and its principals. They have not acted as guardian institutions empowered to defend the public interest.

From the Air India case onward, CSIS has shown that it has been all too willing to destroy evidence of criminal behaviour. CSIS destroyed or withheld vital documents from the RCMP in the Air India investigation, Project Sidewinder, and the Arar debacle, among others.

CSIS directors and agents have not been held accountable for incredible lapses. A female CSIS agent who left a computer disc containing the names of informants in a telephone booth in 1999 was never reprimanded. Another who had his briefcase containing sensitive documents stolen from his car was fired, but informed sources say the theft was a sting by CSIS agents who were out to get one of their own. There are no checks and balances. The entire system is designed for "regime protection"—the concealment of individual wrongdoing by powerbrokers—not defence of the state.

When Australia undertook a series of reviews of its intelligence agencies in recent decades, the issue of "regime protection" was seen to be "a sign of decay in an intelligence system." Before we examine the Australian experience in the next chapter, it seems abundantly evident that the Canadian system is not functioning as intended. Successive governments have done nothing constructive to fix the situation because to do so would not be in their self-interest.

It has been left to the RCMP and CSIS to work out their problems themselves, as if it were all some kind of game. But it is an uneven battle. The RCMP does not stand a chance of getting its way, the defence of the rule of law, because CSIS controls all the high cards in its defence of the rule of politics.

Internal documents from CSIS and the RCMP obtained by Ottawa researcher Ken Rubin show that historically the two forces have been at odds over what their respective mandates should be. The two institutions do not trust each other but have always lied about it to the public, asserting that their working relationship is sound.

For example, a 2005 briefing note for Public Safety Minister Anne McLellan about the RCMP–CSIS relationship after September 11, 2001, acknowledged considerable media reporting about perceived difficulties between the RCMP and CSIS. McLellan went on to say: "Over the years, however, the relationship has significantly improved and many of the issues that had previously caused difficulties have been addressed. The media periodically reports that there are continued problems between CSIS and the RCMP, however, the former CSIS director and the commissioner of the RCMP have repeatedly testified in front of parliamentary committees that the two agencies have complementary—though distinct—mandates and that they work well together in achieving their respective objectives."

Contrast that with a briefing note a year later, in February 2006, just after Stephen Harper had been elected prime minister. The subject of that document was a revised memorandum of understanding between the RCMP and CSIS. The two forces were operating under an outdated 1990 agreement. Attempts to update the agreement in 1998, 2002, 2003, and 2005 had been unsuccessful.

"Both CSIS and the RCMP agree in principle with revising the MOU, however, the issue of how information is shared between organizations remained a stumbling point," the briefing note read.

Two decades after CSIS had been created, the two forces were still waiting for the government to devise a policy framework for them. The mandate of CSIS was to defend national security. It had no mandate to conduct criminal investigations. Every piece of information it gathered was deemed to be intelligence. CSIS presumed that everything the RCMP gathered was evidence, but might be intelligence. CSIS, therefore, consistently took the position that it could not reveal anything to the RCMP because the RCMP might be compelled under Canadian law to reveal everything in court. The flow of information is expected to be one-way—from the RCMP to CSIS and on to the government—which the RCMP has tried to resist.

"For these reasons we are not proceeding with the MOU until our relationship is defined," the RCMP stated in the briefing note.

The two forces even tried an exchange of employees in an attempt to indoctrinate them in each others' culture. The CSIS agents seconded to the RCMP complained afterward that they were treated badly, but in many ways they were treated no differently than the RCMP treated its own members. The report read: "Secondees frequently report the RCMP does not make good use of CSIS secondees and their treatment could be significantly improved (e.g., inconsistencies in agreements, lack of clear roles and responsibilities, mismatching of skills and job requirements, disrespectful remarks, etc.)."

In the end, the evidence versus intelligence conundrum was never resolved.

The two forces even sought help from FBI Director Robert S. Mueller III about how to improve the situation, but the problem proved intractable. In public, their own leaders and their political masters would continue to attest to their mutually beneficial relationship and the good job they were each doing, but everyone inside knew the truth. Some of the truth finally came out at the Air India inquiry in 2007.

Former Deputy Commissioner Henry Jensen blamed politicians for not having the foresight to recognize that by gutting the RCMP of its counter-intelligence responsibilities in 1984, it had left Canada virtually defenceless. Jensen blamed CSIS for the bungled Air India investigation. "I've always carried the view that this is the biggest and most disastrous civil intelligence failure that Canada has faced," Jensen told former Supreme Court justice John Major. "I firmly believe that. I, for one, feel that somehow, somewhere, there were some dots that could have been linked and should have been linked. And had that been done, then who knows, it might have been prevented."

Former commissioner Robert Simmonds, who retired in 1987, later testified that he had been in favour of the creation of CSIS, but did not believe the RCMP should have been gutted of its power to investigate national security matters. "I think it was quite essential that in our Criminal Intelligence Branch, which was old and established in terms of organized crime and so on, we needed to create an organization that was dedicated to looking at these issues connected to terrorism," Simmonds said. "The only real difference is motive between organized gangs of criminals and terrorists. Murder is murder whether it is done in the name of a political cause or whether it is done in the name of a criminal cause and the police . . . almost fail in duty if they are not looking hard into those operations."

The inquiry was able to show the controlling mentality, power, and influence of the Security Intelligence Review Committee which issued a report in 1986 that said the RCMP was deemed to be not capable of investigating sensitive security issues. "We also have questions about the security intelligence capability of the RCMP, which might operate in parallel with CSIS duplicating or even conflicting with the service's primary role mandated by Parliament," the report stated. "As a committee we have no oversight powers respecting the RCMP directly . . . indeed there is comparatively little independent oversight of the RCMP."

At that time, in 1986, Simmonds had tried to fight back by sending a strongly worded 13-page letter to Solicitor General James Kelleher, objecting to SIRC's comments. He argued that SIRC had ignored the fact that all police investigations are overseen by prosecutors and judges when they go to court.

"It is absolutely essential that we have the information that we need in an effort to prevent serious crime and to investigate serious crime. The suggestion that there is not sufficient supervision over the RCMP I find somewhat difficult because it totally dismisses the court and the judges," Simmonds said. "If it leads to a trial—there is nothing you can hide—you have to justify all that you have done and to a very large extent how you did it."

In spite of all that has transpired between 1986 and today, SIRC's position that the RCMP cannot be trusted to do national security investigations continues to be advanced, with the implicit support of government.

One of the disturbing facts about all this is that since it was created in 1984, CSIS has bungled one thing after another. Yet it has been the RCMP that has absorbed the brunt of criticism and political attack.

Former commissioner Norman Inkster was the next to testify before the Air India inquiry. Recall that Inkster had been made deputy commissioner of RCMP operations soon after the bombing. In that role for two years and as commissioner until 1995, Inkster directly oversaw the Air India investigation. Inkster talked about the frustrations of dealing with CSIS, about how important documents had been "lost in the mail." Most important, the ever-political Inkster blithely described the culture, which has prevented Canadians from getting a true picture about how their guardian institutions operate.

Inkster told the inquiry that the RCMP was "gun-shy" about asking for information from CSIS on the Air India bombing and had difficulty in getting CSIS to cooperate. But that was not how the government portrayed the relationship to the public and government.

Inkster testified that during a review by the Security Intelligence Review Committee in 1992, he played down the problems because he and Reid Morden, the new director of CSIS at the time, were trying to repair the strained relationship between the two forces. It was Inkster's view that the Canadian public need not hear the RCMP and CSIS publicly criticizing each other. It was the same attitude adopted by the RCMP in its relationships with other Canadian police services.

"We undertook to do everything we possibly could to cooperate as fully as we could," Inkster testified. "No one wanted to say anything to upset that relationship . . . So we wanted to put a positive front on it as best we could, while recognizing we had very different mandates."

Former RCMP Commissioner Giuliano Zaccardelli then told the inquiry that the entire relationship with CSIS was fatally flawed from the start in 1984, a problem, he said, which continued to the present day. Zaccardelli said government expectations that both institutions would freely share information never materialized. He testified that the country's entire approach to national security should be revamped because it was all but impossible for the country to defend its national security with the present set-up.

"Unless you fundamentally change how they operate, or the structure under which they operate, the tendency is to continue to behave in the same way," Zaccardelli testified. "There is exchange of information, and good cooperation takes place, but the legislation and the policies around the legislation and the creation of CSIS actually forced the men and women of CSIS and the RCMP to work under a very difficult and almost unworkable regime. That's the essence of the problem here. So the exchange takes place. But every time it was a laborious process. It was a very difficult and frustrating process for both organizations."

Zaccardelli's solution to the problem—that the federal national security response be fused under a single governing body—was a predictable one. "If you're on the same team, you tend to share and collaborate," Zaccardelli said. "If you see each other as competitors for those scarce resource dollars . . . then to enhance yourself, you've got to put somebody down. . . . I know you may have to use a bit of an autocratic style to make this happen, but sometimes to get things done, you do have to be a bit autocratic and force the issues and force the change of culture."

Zaccardelli's vision for a single entity guarding Canada's national security interests was merely an extension of the traditional view of how the country should be policed. Canada has always leaned toward minimalization in policing and security. Once there was only the RCMP. After 1984, there was just the RCMP and CSIS. This view of the policing and security of the country has dominated the political agenda throughout Canada's history. It put the entire scope of the policing and security establishment into the hands of an extraordinarily few people—the public safety minister, the prime minister, chosen bureaucrats, and hand-picked oversight committees. Everything is wrapped in layers and layers of secrecy.

By every measure, the structure has been a failure—organized criminals operate with impunity, financial crime is rampant, and national security is a joke. In spite of the considerable evidence to the contrary successive governments have argued that the Canadian system is efficient and effective, the best model for a huge, thinly populated country like ours.

But is it?

[25]

THE AUSTRALIAN MODEL: CONSTANT EVOLUTION

The hubris of the RCMP is that it is the best police force in the world, and many Canadians believe that. When that view has been challenged, the RCMP points to all the people it regularly puts in jail, as if that alone were an indicator of competence. That's what all police forces do. Some just do it better and more equitably than others.

The RCMP, in spite of the abundant evidence to the contrary, has consistently denied that the problem is its very structure. When critics have argued that it's stretched too thinly across the country and was failing in its federal responsibilities, the RCMP has repeatedly refused to admit there is a problem.

The confusion about the force and its mandate in Canada is exemplified by its own insignia—Maintiens le Droit: Maintain the Right, or uphold the law. The vagueness in wording, however, makes it sound like a driving instruction or political mantra. Does it mean that the goal of the force is to protect big-business interests and prop up conservative-minded political parties?

Whenever it is confronted about its many ambiguities, the RCMP usually wraps itself in the flag, plays on its so-called iconic status, and charges ahead. The force and its political supporters imply that changing the RCMP is tantamount to changing the country and its traditions, as if Canada would no longer be the same.

Canada is not an over-policed country. From 1984 to the late 1990s, the Mulroney and Chrétien governments reduced the number of police and security personnel in Canada to a point where the United Nations noted in a 2004 report that Canada ranked 25th among 29 nations surveyed for the number of police officers per capita. Statistics Canada found in its 2006 and 2007 reports on police resources that while the raw numbers in this country have increased, the per capita percentage remains unchanged.

For example, until the mid-eighties, Canada and the United States used to employ approximately the same ratio of police officers per capita. By 2007, however, Canada had 19 percent fewer police officers per capita than the United States. Canada was 12 percent lower than Australia and 28 percent lower than England and Wales.

Federal policing in Canada has been the most visible weakness of the force. Successive auditors general from the early eighties to today have pointed out that the force has serious shortcomings in virtually every area of its federal operations. One can only conclude that federal policing has been very much a planned disaster.

The RCMP's national laboratories and identification services cannot keep up with the work. The RCMP has proven it cannot fully meet its contract requirements in the provinces and territories. Its very structure has corrupted its promotion system—too many people have woven their way through the massive structure to the top without any deep policing experience.

When confronted with changing its monolithic structure, the RCMP uses the same straw man to make its point—the U.S. system. In the United States there are more than 100 federal police services and more than 15,000 separate police services, 800 of which are one-person operations. In the RCMP view, the U.S. system is fragmented, inefficient, and not all it's cracked up to be, which in many ways is true.

That storyline has been successfully used to gain continuing political support and to reinforce and perpetrate its role as the "Everypolice." In the context of Canadian needs, however, the U.S. comparison is a fraudulent one. Some have said that Canada should adopt the British system, described in Chapter 15. But the more analogous comparison is to Australia.

Like Canada, Australia, with nearly 21 million residents, has a relatively small population spread out over a huge and often inhospitable area. In total land mass, Australia is the sixth largest country in the world, almost as large as the continental United States. In Canadian terms, the east-to-west distance from Brisbane to Perth is about the same as the distance from Halifax to the Alberta border. In terms of north to south, from Darwin to Adelaide, the distance is comparable to that from Moosonee, 1,000 kilometres north of Toronto, near James Bay, to Disney World in Orlando, Florida.

Although similar to Canada in some ways, Australians do not think like

Canadians. Australians have shown themselves to be determined not to be overrun by the rest of the world and have been unafraid to adopt measures to protect their sovereignty, security, and strategic interests.

For example, while Investment Canada, the foreign investment review agency, has rubber-stamped every major corporate takeover by a foreign company in recent years, the Australian Foreign Investment Review Board decides whether a deal "is contrary to the national interest."

In recent decades, Canada has shown little interest in protecting home-grown industries. A notable exception occurred in March 2008. After a public outcry and talk of a revolt in Parliament, the Harper government belatedly moved to block the $1.325 billion sale of the space division of MacDonald, Dettwiler and Associates to Alliant Techsystems of Minneapolis. The Canadian company had long taken advantage of Canadian tax credits and subsidies to develop technologies such as the Canadarm robot used on U.S. space ships and Radarsat-2, a spy in the sky satellite system. Canadian taxpayers invested more than $430 million in the development of Radarsat-2. The possible sale of McDonald, Dettwiler was likened to the abandonment of the Avro Aero jet project by the Diefenbaker government on February 20, 1959, so-called Black Friday in Canada.

In Australia, meanwhile, such decisions are not made in such an ad hoc fashion. Australia vetoed two takeovers in 2007 and set serious conditions on others. When Australia's BHP merged with British-owned Billiton, creating the world's biggest mining company, the Australians made a definitive ruling. The new company—BHP Billiton—had to continue to be an Australian entity managed in Australia and listed on the Australian Stock Exchange. Australia even demanded that the global headquarters of the company not only had to be in Australia but also that BHP Billiton had to publicly acknowledge that fact in all its significant public announcements and public documents. Furthermore, the merged company's chief executive officer and chief financial officer had to have their principal residences, offices, and key supporting functions in Australia. The majority of all regularly scheduled board meetings and executive committee meetings each year were also to be held in Australia. "These requirements are specific enough to ensure that the Australian office will be a true executive office, keeping executive jobs, industry expertise, and supporting professional services and capital markets that might have been lost should the global headquarters have moved from the country," wrote the *Toronto Star*'s David Crane, quoting from a consultant's report.

When it comes to politics and policing, Australia—like Canada—has been heavily influenced by both the United States and Great Britain. Australia has faced many of the same political, criminal, and security problems and threats as Canada, if not more.

Australia's military support of the United States in Afghanistan and Iraq has made it a target of Islamic fundamentalist terrorists. On October 12, 2002, the Al-Qaeda-linked Jemaah Islamiyah extremist group bombed Paddy's Pub in Bali, Indonesia. Eighty-eight of the 202 people killed were Australian.

Being so similar to Canada, one might expect Australia would have a similar system of policing and security but it does not.

In Canada, power has been centralized in the hands of a few—one federal police service, one counter-intelligence agency, and one unified military. Successive Australian governments have striven for quite the opposite over the past three decades. In Australia, there has been a constant evolution, with an expanding number of players participating in a system of overlapping responsibilities, oversight commissions, and codified checks and balances.

In the mid-seventies and throughout the eighties, Australia held a number of public inquiries to review its security apparatus. During the same period in Canada, a similar task was handed to the McDonald Commission. Canada made the decision to split the RCMP Security Service from the police force, creating CSIS. Both institutions were placed under strict political control. The third major player is the Communications Security Establishment (CSE) which monitors the airwaves.

Canada has seen no need to have its own foreign intelligence-gathering service, as if we, alone in the world, are too embarrassed to spy on others to protect our national interests. The government instead shares information with a group of English-speaking democratic countries, the United States, the United Kingdom, Australia, and New Zealand. They call themselves the Five Eyes. In the context of the Five Eyes, Canada is a net exporter of intelligence information and relies entirely on its allies to tell it what is going on in the rest of the world. It depends on the U.S. CIA, the British Secret Intelligence Service, or MI-6, and the Australian Secret Intelligence Service, among others. The Australians rejected that approach for themselves.

In Australia, the most prominent and important of the public inquiries were two Royal Commissions in the seventies and eighties, each headed by Justice Robert Hope. Until it was exposed by the British press in 1972, the Australian Secret Intelligence Service (ASIS) had been operating for more than two decades entirely in secret. Hope recognized that one of the most critical priorities for Australia was the open support of a strong foreign intelligence gathering service. "It would be naïve to imagine that overseas governments will always tell us everything they know about a particular matter," Hope wrote. "The position they take is quite neutral and we should face up to it realistically."

In his reports, Justice Hope set out the essential philosophy underlying Australian agencies engaged in international intelligence, a philosophy that was accepted by subsequent inquiries and successive governments. Here is a summary of Hope's recommendations:

> Australia needs its own independent and robust intelligence assessment and collection capability; Intelligence assessment should be separate from policy formulation; Intelligence collection functions should be separate from intelligence assessment and the collection of human and signals intelligence should be undertaken by different agencies; The Office of National Assessments, as the principal assessment agency for foreign intelligence, should enjoy statutory independence; In addition to assessing, on a continuing basis, international developments of major importance to Australia, ONA should keep under review the activities connected with international intelligence that are engaged in by Australia; In respect of security intelligence, the responsibility of ASIO, collection and assessment should be separate from law enforcement. ASIO also needs access to intelligence available in and from other parts of the world; Ministers, and subject to them the Secretaries of Departments, should be actively involved in providing guidance to and monitoring the intelligence community; All intelligence activities should be conducted in accordance with the laws of Australia.

ASIS operates under strict guidelines and reporting structures. Its domestic counterpart is the Australian Security Intelligence Organization (ASIO) which, like CSIS or Great Britain's MI-6, conducts internal counter-intelligence investigations. Unlike the relationship between CSIS and the government of Canada, ASIO is not a policy arm of the government. It has a clearly proscribed mandate and is subject to a regime-defined series of checks and balances.

In his 1984 report, Hope recommended there be some overlap between ASIO and ASIS, so that the internal agency could also gather foreign and domestic intelligence as well as provide protective security advice to government.

Hope also recommended that the security-related activities that ASIO should investigate be redefined; references to subversion and terrorism be removed and replaced with the term "politically motivated violence"—involving attacks on Australia's defence system and the promotion of communal violence. Hope recommended that a separate office, Inspector-General of Intelligence and Security, be established to provide a layer of oversight. At the same time, he believed amendments to the ASIO Act were needed to provide safeguards against unlawful surveillance. "It is not the purpose of the Act that the right of lawful advocacy, protest or dissent should be affected or that exercising those rights should, by themselves, constitute activity," Hope wrote.

In addition to the ASIS and ASIO, Australia also employs a Defence Intelligence Organization and a Defence Security Branch. Each wing of the military also has its own intelligence and security units. All these entities report to different masters, including Parliament, the prime minister, the Department of Foreign Affairs and Trade, the Defence Department, the Attorney, as well as oversight boards.

The Australian government describes the Inspector General of Intelligence and Security, a position created in 1986, as "a key element of the accountability regime for Australia's intelligence and security agencies." That office oversees the activities of the Australian Secret Intelligence Service, the Australian Security Intelligence Organisation, Defence Imagery & Geospatial Organisation, Defence Intelligence Organisation, Defence Signals Directorate, and the Office of National Assessments.

The mandate of the Inspector General of Intelligence and Security is "to provide independent assurance to the Australian government, the Parliament and the people that the agencies conduct their activities within the law, behave with propriety, comply with ministerial guidelines and directives [and] have regard to human rights."

When it comes to the development of intelligence gathering over the past three decades Australia has clearly taken a thoughtful and proactive approach to protecting its national interests. As Justice Hope put it, to do otherwise would be "unrealistic."

Why has Canada allowed the spies of other countries to tell us what dangers exist in the world? Are we naïve? Or is that part of some unknown, unfathomable, grander plan?

CSIS has admitted that since 2001 it had covertly sent as many as 50 agents out of the country, mostly to the war theatre in Afghanistan, technically a violation of its mandate. The extent of the restrictions on its international mandate became evident in 2007. CSIS was planning an overseas investigation involving communications intercepts of ten suspects, nine of whom are Canadians or immigrants to Canada. CSIS had previously investigated the suspects in Canada, but they had all since left the country. CSIS was so fearful of its agents being prosecuted that it took the bizarre step of applying in advance to the courts for permission to conduct an investigation outside the country. *The Globe and Mail* revealed that CSIS's attempt to extend its operations to the surveillance of the ten unnamed suspects was rejected by the Federal Court of Canada. In his decision, Justice Edmond Blanchard wrote: "I find that this court is without the jurisdiction to issue the warrant sought. Accordingly, the request is denied." The judge ruled that such an investigation might violate the rights of the suspects under the Charter of Rights and Freedoms or the Criminal Code.

Reporter Colin Freeze wrote that "compounding the problem is the fact that Canada's wiretap agency, the Communications Security Establishment, was created to eavesdrop outside of Canada, but cannot listen in on citizens of Canada inside or outside of the country." CSIS spokeswoman Manon Bérubé told Freeze that though Blanchard had raised questions about whether CSIS has the mandate to operate outside Canada, his decision was not binding. Other federal agencies, she said, have recognized the need for CSIS to work abroad. She said today's "threat environment" has caused CSIS to re-examine its methods. "Those wishing to cause harm to Canada do not restrict their movements to Canada's borders," she said.

The craziness in thinking extends to policing. In Canada, as we know, the RCMP has clung to its mandate as the Everypolice, its tentacles reaching into every aspect of policing function.

The major police force in Australia is the Australian Federal Police, formed October 19, 1979. The AFP was created in response to an emergency, the bombing the year before of a hotel in Sydney. Australia recognized that its system of policing had become antiquated and ineffective, so it amalgamated the Commonwealth Police, the Australian Capital Territory Police, and the Federal Bureau of Narcotics of the Australian Custom Service into the Australian Federal Police. The AFP employs about 4,500 dedicated federal officers, at least 500 more than the RCMP, in a country that has less than two-thirds the population of Canada.

The federal police are responsible for patrolling the streets of the capital, Canberra, under a separate but included entity, the Australian Capital Territory Police. ACT employs about 600 sworn officers.

A further restructuring of the Australian Federal Police occurred in 1984, when the government decided that the force should no longer be responsible for protective services; that is, providing security at government installations and for dignitaries. Unlike Canadians, the Australians recognized that protective service work was antithetical to the concept of federal policing and created problems within the internal promotions system. A separate entity, the Australian Protective Service, was created to carry out those duties.

Later, Australia decided to hive off other police-associated responsibilities which, in Canada, the RCMP desperately tries to manage. In 2000, the government created CrimTrac, a separate national agency, whose mission was to enhance community safety by delivering and maintaining high-quality, timely, and cost-effective national policing information services, advanced national police investigation tools, and national criminal history record checks for accredited agencies.

In Canada it is impossible to call a central agency for the criminal history of an individual, even though it is the precise reason criminal records were created in the first place. In Canada, such information is protected by privacy legislation.

Another mandate of CrimTrac was for it to keep abreast of the latest developments in forensic science, information technology, and communications advances. The agency also supports policing by providing information and investigative tools for faster suspect identification, clearing the innocent, and shortening investigation times. The common goal is to free police to investigate and solve more crimes.

CrimTrac was further charged with delivering four new systems to improve information sharing for police, including an improved National Automated Fingerprint Identification System, a National Criminal Investigation DNA Database, a National Child Sex Offender System, and the provision of rapid access to national operational policing data. All this is in addition to the National Institute of Forensic Science, located in Melbourne.

The AFP is not the only enforcement agency in Australia at the federal level. Its work is supplemented by five other badge-carrying law enforcement agencies: the Competition and Consumer Commission, the Australian Crime Commission, Customs Service, Quarantine and Inspection Service, and Securities and Investment Commission.

Created in January 2003, the Australian Crime Commission has a mandate to work with both police agencies and the private sector. It describes itself this way in its own literature: "Using intelligence and investigative strategies, the ACC endeavours to better position Australia to meet and respond to threats posed by serious and organised crime groups. The ACC is seeking to work collaboratively with the Australian community and private security sector to make security services more hostile to criminal penetration and to develop strategies to reduce the impact of organised crime groups within the private security industry."

In its first four years of operation, the ACC has been responsible for numerous successful prosecutions involving organized crime, drug trafficking, money laundering, and stock-market fraud.

Ironically, one of the major contributors to the development of Australian organized crime legislation was Brian McAdam, the Canadian foreign affairs officer who sparked the Project Sidewinder investigations.

At the local level, the Australian policing system developed around its states and territories. The oldest and largest police service in Australia is the New South Wales Police Force, formed in 1788. Its name changes over the years reflect the continuing evolution in thinking about policing in Australia. With the passing of the Police Service Act in 1990, the New South Wales Police Force changed its name to the New South Wales Police Service to reflect the emerging concept of community policing, involving the community in crime control. It was the policing fad of the day in democratic countries around the world.

During that same time frame in Canada, police forces became police services. The philosophy was that the police should not be seen as a paramilitary organization, but more like gentle and friendly civil servants with guns or, as Giuliano Zaccardelli sarcastically referred to it, "Boy scouts marching hand in hand across the country."

The comic image of the community policing model adopted by most communities around the world beginning in the late eighties and nineties confused both residents and the police. For example, Community Watch programs became the rage as the police cut back on patrols in an attempt to deal with more serious issues. Among its many faults, the concept overlooked the reality that in the vast majority of families, both adults must work. Entire neighbourhoods were left defenceless during the daylight hours and thieves knew it. Property crime rates exploded in community policing jurisdictions.

For the police, the other message embodied in so-called community policing was a softer, gentler approach. The police were commanded to enforce the laws "politely" in a world where most criminals don't mind their manners. In many respects, community policing caused the police to lose focus and purity of purpose. Police department slogans like "Protecting with Pride" and "Community Commitment" were attempts to portray the police as something they are not and never should be. The police are enforcers of the law; Enforcers! Not social workers. Society pays them to do a dirty, difficult, and often soul-destroying job. Those who do it know that, but that is what they choose to do. The very definition of their job is public service. They didn't have to be reminded by silly, contrived, consumer-friendly names like the Oxford Community Police Service, as one Ontario force calls itself.

In Australia, the loss of this sense of purity of purpose was addressed in 2002 by Michael Costa, the minister for police. He introduced an amendment to the Police Service Act: "I do not believe we need the word 'service' in the name of the police force. I do not accept the argument that we need the word 'service' in a community-based policing approach," Costa told Parliament.

From then on, the word service was dropped and the police department became known as the New South Wales Police, but not for long. In 2006, a further amendment was introduced to change the name back to the original New South Wales Police Force to better reflect both the intention and the attitude of the police in that state. The new–old name better reflected the Latin insignia of the New South Wales Police: "Culpam poena premit comes" which translates as "Punishment follows close on guilt." In New South Wales, the message is clear—the police are not afraid to advertise exactly what their job is and the criminals know what they are up against.

The New South Wales Police Force currently employs about 13,500 sworn officers, almost the size of the RCMP. It has more than 500 offices and detachments in New South Wales and employs its own security and counter-intelligence units. There are six other large police forces in the country, effectively national police forces patrolling the cities and towns of each state. There are also a number of smaller territorial and Aboriginal police services. Each of these police services has layers of oversight and clear lines of accountability.

Corruption in both the public and private sectors has long been of concern to Australian governments. They have tried to meet this challenge with strong laws. In 1988, the Australian government passed the Independent Commission Against Corruption Act (ICAC) to "protect the public interest, prevent breaches of public trust and guide the conduct of public officials" in New South Wales. The ICAC Act defines corrupt conduct as:

> a: any conduct of any person (whether or not a public official) that adversely affects, or that could adversely affect, either directly or indirectly, the honest or impartial exercise of official functions by any public official, any group or body of public officials or any public authority, or, b: any conduct of a public official that constitutes or involves the dishonest or partial exercise of any of his or her official functions, or c: any conduct of a public official or former public official that constitutes or involves a breach of public trust, or, d:. any conduct of a public official or former public official that involves the misuse of information or material that he or she has acquired in the course of his or her official functions, whether or not for his or her benefit or for the benefit of any other person.
>
> (2) Corrupt conduct is also any conduct of any person (whether or not a public official) that adversely affects, or that could adversely affect, either directly or indirectly, the exercise of official functions by any public official, any group or body of public officials or any public authority and which could involve any of the following matters: official misconduct (including breach of trust, office fraud, nonfeasance, misfeasance, malfeasance, oppression, extortion or imposition), bribery, blackmail, obtaining or offering secret commissions, fraud, theft, perverting the course of justice, embezzlement, election bribery, election funding offences, election fraud, tax evasion, revenue evasion, currency violations, illegal drug dealings, illegal gambling, obtaining financial benefit by vice engaged in by others, bankruptcy and company violations, harbouring criminals, forgery, treason or other offences against the Sovereign and homicide or violence.

In the nineties and afterward, the ICAC investigated and prosecuted many high-profile cases of corruption. It also promoted prevention through education programs. Yet governments found that all this was not enough to deal with the secretive world of the police in New South Wales.

After a huge police corruption scandal in New South Wales was uncovered, the Australian government did not try to explain away the problem. Instead, in December 2006, the federal government created another powerful, independent oversight agency to deal with the police—The Australian

Commission for Law Enforcement Integrity. Its mandate was to detect, investigate, and prevent corruption in the federal police and the National Crime Commission, as well as to oversee state and other police.

In the Law Enforcement Integrity Commissioner Act, corruption was defined as "applying to three categories of activity by a law enforcement officer: an abuse of office; conduct that perverts the course of justice; or corruption of any other kind. The integrity commissioner is to give priority to dealing with serious corruption and systemic corruption."

The integrity commissioner can launch a corruption investigation in the following ways: The head of a law enforcement agency within ACLEI's jurisdiction must notify the Integrity Commissioner of any corruption issue that relates to the agency, and provide all relevant information and documents if it is a significant corruption issue.

The Minister for Justice can refer a corruption issue to the integrity commissioner or request the commissioner to conduct a public inquiry into corruption or integrity in law enforcement agencies.

Any person or government agency (e.g., the Commonwealth Ombudsman) can refer to ACLEI an allegation or information raising a corruption issue. A referral can be anonymous, or on behalf of another person. A person in custody can make a referral by a secure communication channel.

The integrity commissioner can commence an investigation on his or her initiative.

What is clear about the Australian approach to policing is that when it comes to policing and security, the country believes in purity of purpose. Everyone has a specific job to do and is expected to do it well, all in the public interest. There have been problems and scandals but the general attitude of governments has been to improve, invent, and strengthen the country's institutions.

The Australians have recognized the need and value for specialization and have taken steps to ensure that the integrity of the country's institutions is protected so that the rule of law governs the country, not the rule of politics. Given that the Australian population is less than two-thirds that of Canada in a country almost the size of the United States, how could it afford such seeming luxuries?

Part of the answer to that question is that Canada's so-called efficient system is anything but. While Australia has striven to create layers of policing and accountability in recent years, Canada has been headed in the diametrically opposite direction, as if the entire democratic world but it is out of step.

[26]

THE LURKING DANGERS
OF "INTEGRATED POLICING"

If one were to accept the proposition that the RCMP has failed in its mandate; that it has become a largely unaccountable police force susceptible to political influence and control; that the laws of the country are being enforced *with* fear, favour, and affection; that the safety and security of the country and its democratic principles are at risk; and that the public interest of Canadians is not being served as well as it should, then Canadians should be deeply concerned about the direction the form and function of our guardian institutions are headed in Canada.

It has been more than four decades since Canadian governments put their minds together and dealt with the issue of the organization of police in the country. The Québec-centric federal government and its provincial partners have shown no leadership when it comes to policing. Governments have failed to keep up with the times to implement policies and initiatives that are desperately needed.

In her 2000 report on the RCMP, Auditor General Sheila Fraser observed: "The arrangement between the federal government and the provinces set in 1966 for these services needs to be rethought. It is time for a clear agreement among all the players in the law enforcement community—in the federal, provincial and municipal governments—on level of service, funding arrangements, user input, management and accountability. A new agreement will require the collaboration of all parties."

The last time the federal government bothered to deal with the RCMP, or any substantive police policy issue, had been in 1981, with the release of the tainted McDonald Commission report. Since then, the police have been left on their own, making it up as they go.

Québec, which once had the most dysfunctional and corrupt system of policing in Canada, has used this period to transform the administration and operation of its police forces into what many believe is the single best system in the country. As part of an ongoing program to amalgamate and consolidate municipalities, Québec has created a tiered policing system with the Sûreté du Québec, the provincial police, at the top. The Sûreté is followed by agglomerations of large municipal and regional forces down to policing in the smallest communities and villages. The division of police organization and practices in the public safety ministry oversees the implementation of laws that relate to policing and promotes and coordinates police activities. The police in Québec have a plan and protocols for every conceivable situation so that no community is left without effective security. The underlying problem, however, is that no matter how good the police are in the province, the Québec justice system is still designed to be political. Those at the highest ranks of society can still count on "executive privilege" to get them off the hook, should the police come knocking at their door.

After the murders of four Mounties at Mayerthorpe in 2005, Alberta Solicitor General Harvey Cenaiko moved immediately to promote change in the province, where the RCMP was chronically short-staffed. Cenaiko, a former Calgary police officer, turned his attention to the ex-Mounties who ran the police services branch within the public safety ministry, as is the case in every other RCMP contract jurisdiction. Cenaiko hired his one-time Calgary police partner, Brian Skeet, to be the assistant deputy minister in charge of police services. Skeet soon brought in others like him from the Calgary and Edmonton police forces. Their first initiative was to transform the 400-member provincial sheriff's department from one that merely guarded and transported prisoners to and from court into a secondary police service that would do many of the jobs the RCMP was failing to do. It cost less than $100,000 per officer to put a sheriff on the road, compared to the almost $160,000 it cost Alberta for each Mountie.

The sheriffs began to patrol secondary highways and do traffic enforcement. By 2007, the program had already expanded to include traffic enforcement on major highways, four surveillance teams, and protective services. Many have seen the expansion of the sheriff's program as a stalking horse for a provincial police force in Alberta, which Skeet has repeatedly denied. The downside is that the sheriffs are being asked to do police work without police training, which many police experts believe is a recipe for disaster. Manitoba is currently considering a similar program.

As provinces and communities struggle to find a cost-effective policing model that works for them, it has become all but impossible for anyone to figure out how many police are needed, and where. Politicians, bureaucrats, and police leaders alike have shown a propensity for interpreting statistics in whatever way might best support the case at hand.

One of the most abused statistics is crime rates. Even the police admit, confidentially, that when they need more police officers, crime rates tend to go up. When they want to cut costs, crime rates mysteriously shrink. The problem with using crime rates and clearance rates of cases by police as an absolute is that there is no absolute measure. The RCMP and other forces interpret crime rates and clearance rates differently.

For example, prior to the 911 emergency system, the crime-rate concept was an abstract one because many crimes were not being reported. After 911, the vast majority of crimes were called in to police, providing a truer measure of criminal activity. The police, however, soon found themselves overwhelmed by the volume.

To address this problem, the RCMP in B.C.'s Lower Mainland began a program in late 2006 in which all calls for help are subjected to a "harm assessment." As Deputy Commissioner Gary Bass described it in an interview, a senior officer would determine how and when to respond to a call for help. The downside was that the police would no longer respond to some situations.

"If a person reports a car stolen, there's no value to us sending a patrol car to look at the empty parking spot," said Assistant Commissioner Alistair Macintyre in the same interview. "Instead we will be concentrating on the likely suspects."

Because of such police initiatives, some police experts believe that victims are no longer fully reporting property crimes, especially those that might affect their insurance rates. The police talk about crime deterrence but are incapable of or unwilling to back it up with a consistent and visible presence.

Finally, police leaders often rail against the problems with the justice system. In large measure, however, the most egregious laws have been created by the judicial response to the inappropriate actions of the police. A solid police investigation never resulted in bad law.

Against this confusing backdrop, the RCMP has been left to drive Canada's national policing agenda with the support of often ill-informed and often short-sighted bureaucrats and politicians. Over the past several years, police and governments at every level have adopted one word to describe their planned approach to policing and the justice system. That word is "integrated." It has become part of the ongoing dialogue about policing and justice in Canada. Almost every day we read or hear about integrated homicide units, integrated fraud squads, integrated intelligence units, or an integrated justice or social services system. To the unwashed, it might sound as if our political leaders have conducted studies on the issue, reflected on all the possible consequences of integration, and are doing the right thing to be more efficient and economical.

In fact, the opposite is true. In the past, police departments have always worked together at some level. For major projects and investigations, joint forces operations were and continue to be common. In a joint forces operation, police from a variety of police agencies work together, usually from a common site, for a period of time to undertake a complex investigation or solve a crime. When the investigation is over, the individual officers return to their respective departments.

The modern concept of integrated policing takes the joint-forces approach and attempts to make such relationships permanent. Memoranda of agreement are drawn up in legal language and are designed to be enforced to keep all participants in line. There is no room for criticism or complaint—any integrated unit is compelled to speak "with one voice."

The rationale for integration is that we live in an age where crime crosses jurisdictions, not only in a physical sense but also in an ethereal one, via the Internet. That being the case, the argument goes, any police force will find itself dealing with suspects and issues that are trans-provincial, transnational, or international. The premise is that by having all levels of policing working together it will cost less, which strikes a chord with the taxpaying public. But all is not as it seems.

Criminals have always operated across jurisdictions. Al Capone was not just a Chicago mobster and bootlegger; his empire was international in scope. He virtually owned the French islands of St. Pierre and Miquelon. He had safe houses in Canadian cities like Guelph, Ontario. Bank robbers, murderers, and every other brand of criminal usually like to spread out. They go where the money is and stay where they hope they can't be found. Historically, the police in Canada have always chased criminals as far as they had to go to catch them, often with the help of other agencies. They all worked together with a common interest—law enforcement.

In other nations, the police are organized in tiers to deal with every sort of situation, and when something not foreseen arises, a new agency might be created, such as the National Crime Commission in Australia.

In Canada, integrated policing has been promoted by the RCMP for two purposes: to hide the reality that the RCMP has abrogated its federal policing responsibilities and to extend the reach, power, and influence of the RCMP and the federal government into provincial and municipal police forces across the country. The implications are potentially horrendous, yet there has been no public debate about it, although a handful of police leaders have tried to raise the alarm.

✜ ✜ ✜

Meet Edgar MacLeod. A police officer for more than three decades, MacLeod began his policing career in 1973, after graduating from the Atlantic Police College in Prince Edward Island. All MacLeod's police service was undertaken in some of Canada's smallest communities—historic Shelburne on the south shore of Nova Scotia, Charlottetown, PEI, and New Waterford on Cape Breton Island, where he served as police chief. In 1993, he was appointed the police chief of Sydney. A small-town guy, perhaps, but MacLeod has been a big-time thinker when it comes to policing in Canada.

"People talk about federal this and provincial that, but it all comes out of one municipal taxpayer's dollar," MacLeod said. "The municipal taxpayer through their individual property taxes pays for the majority of government expenditures but municipal governments have little or no say on how that money is spent. People have reached the point of tax fatigue. We can't keep going on the way we have. We have to be smarter."

When Nova Scotia mandated the amalgamation of the greater Sydney area in 1995, the RCMP placed a bid on the contract to police the region. The RCMP lobbied hard to take over all the policing duties in the community, arguing that it could do the job better and more efficiently, partly because it wasn't unionized.

MacLeod met that challenge head-on, sitting down with the police union and hammering out a consensus.

"Police associations, like any union, are out to get the most for their members, but we all knew the economic realities of Cape Breton," MacLeod said in an interview. "There is a dwindling tax base and the community cannot afford to pay big city salaries. I told them, 'You could have beer flowing from the fountain at city hall and live it up if you want, but you are going to put yourself out of work.' We worked out an agreement. They had to trust me and I had to trust them. We knew we had to work together."

MacLeod's side won the support of the local council and the Cape Breton Regional Police was formed in 1995. MacLeod was named its first chief of police.

The RCMP predicted doom and gloom but MacLeod and his team built the Cape Breton Regional Police into a high-tech, modern, and efficient police service with a stellar reputation in its community. The Cape Breton force became so successful and respected by its citizens that the tables were turned. When the RCMP contract to police Membertou, a First Nations territory near Sydney, came up for renewal in 2007, the community's leaders asked the Cape Breton Regional Police to submit a bid, which it won. It was the first time the RCMP had lost a contract to a municipal force for such work. The key to MacLeod's success was that he is a straight shooter who has been unafraid to break with his police counterparts when it comes to serving the public interest. And he was all too familiar with the shades of truth in which the RCMP usually spoke.

"The Membertou nation had seen enough of the Mounties, or not enough, as it were," MacLeod said. "They knew that we would be a full service, a fully accountable police service, and that's why they chose us."

MacLeod has long been a thorn in the side of the RCMP. In his capacity as a vice-president of the Canadian Association of Police Chiefs (CACP), the lobby group of the chief constables in the country, he took the job seriously. Instead of treating each annual CACP convention as an opportunity to reconnect with old buddies and play a lot of golf, MacLeod pounded away with regularity at the underlying problems facing policing in Canada. It was not a universally popular subject. The police chiefs liked to take positions on criminal justice and law reform, but when it came to lobbying the government to be more conscientious about its own role in policing, MacLeod sometimes ran into a brick wall.

"Many of these people run large police forces. They see themselves as the policy makers, and they absolutely do not want government dictating to them what they should do and how they should do it," MacLeod said.

Nevertheless, in 2003, he had been instrumental in having the CACP commission the consulting firm of McInnes and Associates to conduct a study of the factors influencing police resources and to examine any resulting governance issues that may emerge.

It had become evident to Canadian police chiefs that the cost of policing had hit a ceiling in Canada but that the public's expectations for expanded and high-quality police services continued unabated. At the time, municipal police budgets across Canada accounted for 56.2 percent of the total monies spent on policing. Provincial and federal policing were 22.5 and 21.3 percent respectively.

The McInnes report, completed in June 2003, identified that one of the main drags on the delivery of police services in the country was government policy decisions. Since the seventies, governments at all levels have regularly demanded that police take on new undertakings and programs, to move beyond their traditional law enforcement role into areas of social policy. Rather than just chasing and catching criminals, the police were being asked to participate in government initiatives such as youth justice, domestic violence, and restorative justice, to name a few.

As governments piled on the work for the police, budgets were not increased to reflect the added burden. This was exacerbated by court decisions, usually based on the Charter of Rights, that required the police to devote significantly more time and paperwork to a variety of issues, from the content of search warrants to the procedure for dealing with domestic violence issues.

The McInnes report stated that police managers were often forced to reallocate existing resources to meet the new priorities. Governments had not taken into consideration the changing demographics of the country and the pressures being placed on core services such as investigation and enforcement. The police found themselves between a rock and a hard place, unable to fight crime or meet governments' social policy agenda by maintaining and forging new community relationships.

The McInnes report pointed to the problems with the country's National Crime Prevention Strategy "which aims to 'reduce crime and victimization by tackling crime before it happens. The National Strategy is based upon the principle that the surest way to reduce crime is to focus on the factors that put individuals at risk: factors like family violence, school problems, and drug abuse.' Resource constraints reported by policing leaders are impacting the police community's ability to fully engage in such important policy initiatives."

At the heart of the McInnes report was the assertion that governments had no plans and little interest in improving the situation. Everyone knew the issues. Meetings were regularly held and there was lots of talk—but nothing was being done to address the underlying problems. Solutions, such as they were, were being devised on an ad hoc basis. The police were left to work out the problems for themselves with no overriding sense of direction from above.

In their conclusions, the consultants quoted "the renowned philosopher Yogi Berra [who] once said, 'If you don't know where you're going, you'll wind up somewhere else.'" They went on to say:

It is clearly a time for Canada to create a policing public policy framework to address the goal of inter-agency cooperation and juris-dictional challenges that have been identified as major challenges by policing leaders. The framework should be endorsed by all levels of government and developed around the concept of collaboration and systemic accountability. It should seek to:

- Delineate roles and responsibilities
- Establish an appropriate management structure
- Establish authority and control equal to responsibility
- Establish a dispute resolution feature
- Establish a funding formula aligning with established roles & responsibilities
- Embrace innovation and efficiency recognizing that there is but one taxpayer

The McInnes report landed on deaf ears in government and the RCMP. "Delineating responsibilities" was the kind of phrase that struck at the core of all that was wrong with the RCMP. With its obvious and myriad prob-lems, the force could not withstand an objective examination of the country's policing structure. The logical conclusion of any such effort would be the deconstruction and reconfiguration of the force, something that would change not only the RCMP, but Canada as well.

In August 2004, at a most critical time, MacLeod was elected president of the Canadian Association of Chiefs of Police. The RCMP was entering the latest phase of its inexorable struggle to meet its commitments to the Canadian public. As the self-appointed national policing leader, the force charged into the policy gap identified by the McInnes report. It devised and began to implement its own solution to the problem, one that would not only guarantee the survival of the force in its current structure but even expand its reach.

In his 2003–04 directional statement, Commissioner Giuliano Zac-cardelli embraced "Integrated Policing" as one of the RCMP's key strategic priorities. Zaccardelli described it as a concept that "defines how we must work day-to-day and how we must respond to our changing and dynamic environment." He said the strategy was grounded in the need for collaboration by all levels of police and law enforcement to address matters of community, municipal, provincial, federal, and international importance.

While the RCMP and, by extension, the federal government were pushing integrated policing, Canadian mayors and police chiefs, in large measure, were alarmed by what was happening. Many paid lip service to the concept, but no one, not even the RCMP, could explain precisely what it meant by integrated policing. In one of its own descriptions of the term, the RCMP said it was "somewhat vaguely defined." The RCMP added that the term integrated policing was intended to describe "police agencies working together at the ascending tactical, operational and strategic levels."

In 2004, the Federation of Canadian Municipalities (FCM) passed a resolution, "A New Deal for Canadian Cities and Communities." In that document, municipal leaders demanded a seat at the table with the federal and provincial governments when it came to the issue of finances. Tired of having the senior levels of government telling them what they could or could not do, the local politicians wanted to be consulted before decisions were made on issues affecting them. They sought "improved coordination of policies and programs related to such issues."

Although the resolution did not speak directly about policing, Edgar MacLeod made sure that municipal politicians were brought up to speed about what was going on in his world.

MacLeod made sure that the Canadian Association of Chiefs of Police rallied behind the mayors. The CACP did so by passing a resolution calling upon "all levels of government in Canada to join together with police and governance associations in a public policy discussion on policing in the 21st century, with the intention of defining the roles and responsibilities of each order of government and establishing a governance structure to support police agencies and their bodies operating within Canada's multi-level policing environment."

In effect, the police chiefs were calling on the federal and provincial governments to wake up and recognize that there was a serious problem with the administration and operations of police in Canada. They were also not-so-subtly warning governments that the RCMP-driven grand plan for integrated policing was not a solution, but an aggravation of the existing situation.

Ottawa City Councillor Herb Kreling was chairman of the Ottawa Police Services Board in November 2004 when U.S. President George Bush visited Parliament Hill. The RCMP later congratulated itself on how well everything had gone, how all six police forces had worked in such an "integrated fash-ion." (The Mounties never mentioned that the only ones allowed to have guns on Parliament Hill were the Americans.)

Kreling recognized that while nothing had gone drastically wrong dur-ing the visit, there had, nevertheless, been serious problems which went to the heart of the integrated policing concept. The six police services in Ottawa that day had applied security measures in different ways. Both politicians and the public had complaints about how they had been treated. Kreling rec-ognized that the root of the problem was that no government policy frame-work existed to clarify the various roles and mandates of the police agencies involved. There was also no mechanism for accountability.

Now aware of that problem, in 2005 the Federation of Canadian Munic-ipalities called on the federal government to establish "a task force (with mu-nicipal input) to develop a model for national unified police governance that will clearly identify the roles and funding responsibilities of each level of gov-ernment and ensure a process that will work effectively and efficiently across the three levels of government."

Inside the tight fraternity of Canadian police, however, the most power-ful police chiefs would never speak out publicly about the RCMP. They were masters of their own fiefdoms and were part of a collegial, mutual back-slapping network that in many ways has been more interested in its own survival than the greater good of the country.

For example, when I tried to approach Ontario Provincial Police Com-missioner Julian Fantino in the summer of 2007 about a national framework for policing and about the perceived problems and dangers of integrated policing, his eyes narrowed and he looked out the side of his face at me, as if I had asked him if he had killed his wife. "Talk to Edgar MacLeod about that," was all he had to say.

Any discussion about the contentious issue was left mostly to the little guys, like MacLeod, Frank Beazley of Halifax, Paul Shrive of Port Moody, B.C., and Jack Beaton of Calgary. They had all been trying to get answers from government to several simple, but fundamentally important, questions: What is integrated policing? What does it mean for law enforcement? How should it work? Who is going to pay for it? How are the police going to be held accountable? Is it really such a good thing? What are the short-, medium-, and long-term implications?

Richard Bruce, the police chief in Brandon, Manitoba, succinctly summed up his misgivings about integrated policing in seven words: "We are *Corner Gas*, not *CSI Miami*."

In other words, what the municipal police want the RCMP to do is what it should be doing—taking the big view by providing dedicated, quality federal policing across Canada in support of local police departments.

"Right across the country efforts are being made to integrate policing, but no one really knows what it means," MacLeod said. "At a practical level—while the RCMP talks about and promotes integrated policing—there has been no definition of what that is, no model that brings the abstract concept into reality and no policy framework from government that sets out the roles, responsibilities and accountabilities.

"Governments are encouraging the idea of integrated policing because to the public it sounds as if it speaks to professionalism, excellence, a forward-looking approach, efficiencies and economies," MacLeod said. "The public expects the police to work together, across agencies and jurisdictional boundaries. Citizens see police, as they see other services, through one taxpayer's eyes. But governments, at all levels, do not see policing in the same way. They see policing as having distinct levels. At the same time as they expect police to integrate efforts and systems, they have failed to provide leadership in terms of integrated policing policy. In fact, there is a risk that the public may over-estimate the extent to which police are collaborating and integrating their efforts in the fight against organized crime and terrorism. The police chiefs of Canada are very concerned about this risk."

The RCMP culture is substantially different than that in other police forces. RCMP members are trained differently than most other police officers. The RCMP conducts investigations differently than most other police officers. The RCMP does not willingly share information with other police forces, and is forbidden to do so in national security investigations. Most important, in every case where RCMP and other police forces work together, the RCMP presumes that it will be in charge, no matter how small its involvement in a project or investigation.

In these start-up years of integration, police forces around the country have found that working with the RCMP has been no different than in the past—that is, all but impossible. "When you look at any integrated unit across the country, it would be fair to say that the one force not holding up its end of the bargain in every situation is the RCMP," said one police chief, who asked for anonymity.

The history of integrated police operations in the lower mainland of British Columbia illustrates well the problems with the concept.

In 1974 the RCMP investigated the creation of the Coordinated Law Enforcement Unit (CLEU). Its mandate was to work with the police forces, gathering intelligence on organized crime groups and initiating operations against them. It had a staff of about 150 officers. Over the next two decades the RCMP regularly trumpeted the supposed successes of CLEU, in spite of obvious shortcomings. Internal bickering and myriad failures, however, led to the creation of a three-man committee headed by former attorney general Stephen Owen to review the CLEU concept. In 1998, the Owen Committee reported back that CLEU was all but clueless in fighting organized crime.

In 1999 a new entity was created: the Organized Crime Agency of British Columbia. The agency was set up with a command structure that largely took control out of the hands of the RCMP. What did the Mounties do?

Over the next five years the RCMP undercut the operations of the crime agency, actions which caused it to become largely ineffective. On April 1, 2004, the agency was integrated with the RCMP as a "federal-led" Combined Forces Special Enforcement Unit, along with an Integrated Gang Task Force. Since then the new structure seems to have done little to abate either rampant organized crime in the Lower Mainland or gang activity.

In 2005, the Canadian Association of Chiefs of Police passed a resolution aimed specifically at the question of integrated policing. It called upon the federal and provincial governments to:

1. Pursue studies and analyses on the costs, and operational and strategic implications, of current policing arrangements;
2. Confirm roles and responsibilities of each order of government consistent with Canada's constitution and governments' stated commitment to municipal engagement on public safety issues;
3. Jointly, with representatives of the municipal order of government, establish a policy framework to support police agencies in operating within Canada's multi-jurisdictional policing environment; and
4. Define integrated policing as a concept and analyze the implications of this concept applied respectively at the tactical, operational, and strategic levels.

Over the next three years, there would be a series of meetings held to discuss need for a policy framework for policing in Canada. In February 2005, the so-called Sussex Circle met in Ottawa bringing police and bureaucratic leaders together. In June 2005, federal and provincial deputy ministers met to pore over the issue. They called for "an integrated policing policy framework" to be developed by all orders of government. The Chrétien government was not interested in the subject. In May 2006, the Sussex Circle met again and recommended government leadership, but with Harper now in power, the stall took on a new dimension. The focus of all levels of government was now on the renewal of RCMP contracts, which were set to expire in 2012. And so it went. The RCMP continued to forge ahead trying to make agreements with various police forces and thereby to present governments with a *fait accompli*. As one might expect, what happened in the interim was that the RCMP has used its muscle to control and mute the very important debate.

In 2006, MacLeod began to promote the idea of a "New Deal for Police" in his public presentations, speeches, and written articles. To both the RCMP and its masters, the federal government, it was a dangerous concept, even if it made some sense. Like the FCM's new deal for municipalities, any discussion about creating a new regime for policing in Canada carried with it an important subtext—an implicit review of the structure and mandate of the RCMP.

The RCMP began to fight back. Until then, the annual conference of the CACP had been largely ignored by the Mounties, who looked down their collective noses at the city cops. The commissioner and some of his deputies and a regional commander or two might show up at a CACP meeting, give a speech, and amuse themselves. But at the meeting in St. John's, Newfoundland in 2006, the Mounties showed up in large numbers. Their reason for being there was to attack the "dangerous" ideas coming out of the CACP about integrated policing and the new deal for police. In St. John's, the RCMP began to argue that the police must speak with "one voice." It began to lobby for changes to the wording of documents, toning things down, and putting heat on MacLeod, Beazley, Shrive, and Beaton.

At the CACP convention in Calgary in August 2007, the chiefs of police were astonished to see a flood of RCMP members arrive that Sunday night for the meet-and-greet at the Hyatt Convention Centre. New Commissioner William Elliott, on the job just a few weeks, was surrounded by putative RCMP police chiefs from the rank of superintendent and up. Most were part of the force's contract regime. Each had purchased memberships and, therefore, was allowed to participate in discussions and voting. MacLeod's plan to deliver an updated paper on the issues at hand was vetoed by a committee after strong arguments were made by RCMP attendees.

The lid was back on the debate. Afterward, the RCMP continued with its bullying efforts, coercing the CACP to remove from its website papers by MacLeod and others that addressed the integrated policing issue and the new deal. Nevertheless, the CACP's new president, Winnipeg Police Chief Jack Ewatski, continues to call upon government to implement a national framework for policing.

Like so many RCMP-driven initiatives, the one about integrated policing is long on promise, promotion, and marketing and short on effectiveness, true efficiencies, and the chance of success in the real world.

Like so many RCMP-driven initiatives, the presumption is that the RCMP knows best how to operate a police force, solve crimes, and defend the rule of law, when the reality is that the Mounties have proven their lack of professionalism, incompetence, and duplicity over and over again.

Like so many RCMP-driven initiatives, there are also the seeds of suspicion, the real possibility of a dark and sinister maneuver, hidden in plain sight, as it were, being constructed before our very eyes.

When one analyzes the so-called integration of police services, it all comes down to one cold, hard, indisputable scenario. The RCMP has shown that it has had no will or intention to maintain a strong, properly functioning, and effective federal police service. Its priority has been contract policing, but contract policing, as we have seen, has left the majority of the force out in the wilderness, the gendarmerie of the boonies. Integration, on the other hand, is the introduction of federal police in a coordinated way into municipal police forces in the large urban areas, where most people and criminals live.

If one accepts that all this is a good thing, there is yet another set of problems.

Like many other police chiefs in Canada, MacLeod saw the so-called integration movement as an attempt by the federal government and the RCMP to download in a sly fashion the cost and responsibility for federal policing and other services onto the backs of municipal taxpayers. For example, the federal government has declared that it is responsible for policing Canada's borders, but who is going to do that work?

In 2006, in one of his first initiatives as prime minister, Stephen Harper ordered that Canadian Border Agency members be trained to carry guns, which they began to do in 2007. The RCMP had tried to argue that borders were its jurisdiction, even though successive reports over the previous decades showed that the RCMP was incapable of providing policing at border crossings. Everything was being left up to the unarmed border guards who had to call for help, if they needed it, a call that was often not treated as a priority and even went unanswered on occasion.

In Surrey, B.C., the jurisdiction of the RCMP municipal detachment runs to the Washington State border. Many other Canadian cities and towns are on or near the border, but there are no Mounties there. Airports are borders. In Ontario and Québec, the Mounties no longer do that job. Ports are borders, but no Mounties again. To a large extent, all those "federal" responsibilities are being left to local police or the RCMP in its local contract role.

"What they are really doing is transferring the cost of federal policing to the municipal taxpayer, without any accountability or policy framework," said MacLeod. "We have no idea how any of this should work, who should be in charge, who should pay for what and who gets held accountable when things go wrong, which is bound to happen. They use the word integration, but some of us wonder if the real intention is amalgamation."

Now that is an interesting notion—the Everypolice everywhere. In the Soviet Union they called that force the KGB.

The RCMP has long had a penchant for sucking up information and building files, not cases. It has always promised to serve the public interest while at the same time carrying out other, sometimes nefarious, agendas. Because of the lack of accountability built into the system it has always been able to escape scrutiny for its actions.

In February 2008, federal Privacy Commissioner Jennifer Stoddart issued her first report to Parliament. She found that the RCMP had for decades defied government and civilian overseers by illegally collecting and storing tens of thousands of files in two "exempt" data banks—the Criminal Operational Intelligence Records and National Security Investigation Records. These record caches were designed to hold the most sensitive national security and criminal intelligence information, but Stoddart uncovered information on ordinary Canadians which she deemed should not be secret, and should have been destroyed years earlier.

The files contained unsubstantiated allegations against individuals and were hidden so deeply inside the force that, if asked about any of them, it would neither confirm nor deny that any existed. In fact, a similar audit two decades earlier had discovered the same problems with the data banks. At that time, the RCMP promised to fix the problem and even went as far as adopting a form to describe and account for information, but the force, with a few exceptions, continued to skirt privacy legislation.

"These finds are particularly concerning given that, with few exceptions, the audit was conducted on randomly selected files already examined by the RCMP as part of an internal review," Stoddart said in a news release accompanying the report. Stoddart said the large number of files being kept secret was not only unjustifiable but also illegal. The files should have been captured and evaluated as part of the RCMP's internal review regime, but were not. "Compliance with the policy was largely ignored prior to 2006. Of the exempt bank files opened prior to 2004, approximately 70 percent of the national security files and 90 percent of the criminal operational files that we examined had not been subject to ongoing review. . . . Of the 116 files that we examined, approximately 50 percent of the national security files and 60 percent of the criminal operational intelligence files did not, in our view, meet the established threshold for continued exempt bank status under RCMP policy. . . . We also observed files the inclusion of which in an exempt bank was assessed as questionable."

After Stoddart released her report, the RCMP, once again, pledged that it would do the right thing. "We will be implementing every one of this report's recommendations," Chief Superintendent Dan Killam said in a news release. He said that the force would re-examine the files retained in the two data banks.

The RCMP's pack-rat mentality should be of grave concern to everyone, given its past, poor performance, its documented susceptibility to political control and pressure, and its deceptive practices. The threat of the RCMP covertly insinuating itself into municipal policing and expanding its dominion into all sectors of policing, therefore, is no small issue. But governments, particularly the federal government, seem uninterested in the topic.

The inherent danger to the rule of law in Canada posed by a systemized regime of integrated policing should be all too evident. It cannot be seen only in its positive sense—integrated groups of police officers working together to do something good for the country. Canadian police leaders have shown they are absolutely reluctant to rock the boat and are determined to speak "as one voice." Because of that penchant for uniformity, their agreements with the RCMP binding them together must be seen as contrary to the rule of law. If all the police are playing on the same team, there exists a very real threat of negatively applying the concept of integrated policing, and that is the potential for selective investigation or non-investigation of important matters. In Canada, no agency is empowered to oversee other police in a disinterested, objective role. Everyone is working together. With only one group, opinion about what is a crime, who is a criminal, and who should be pursued or not, the danger to any democratic society should be obvious.

To further argue, as the police themselves have, that all that would be needed to make such a system work are policies, rules and, perhaps, civilian oversight, is to be so disingenuous as to be ridiculous. No paperwork system or group of political appointees could possibly overcome the power of those memoranda of understanding between cooperating police forces. No paperwork system or group of political appointees could defeat the righteousness, bunker mentality, and shared spirit of brotherhood that would conspire to have all police involved in controversy to bind together—united against the world. Simply put, integrated policing places too much power where it should not be, without viable checks and balances. This should be cause for grave and immediate concern.

The organization of Canadian police, therefore, should not only be viewed in terms of service models, cost, and perceived efficiency, but also in terms of freedom, equality under the law, and public safety and security. Without overlapping, tiered, and clearly accountable police jurisdictions with multiple federal police forces—each imbued with a purity of purpose, as is the case in Australia and elsewhere—Canada will be opening its doors wide to the risk of tyranny. It might not happen right away and it might not be in an historically recognizable form—but the groundwork is being laid. No matter how well-intentioned the promoters of the concept of integrated policing might be, a federal police force which has the means, motive, and opportunity to direct, manipulate, and control all other police forces is the very definition of tyranny: antithetical to the rule of law.

[27]

A NOT-SO-INVISIBLE HAND, AFTER ALL

Into this cauldron of duplicity, Stephen Harper was deposited. When he participated in writing the Alberta Firewall Letter in 2001, Harper had a vision for what he believed Canada should be. He thought that there should be clear lines of authority and accountability between the federal and provincial governments.

Once in office, however, he found himself pummelled from all sides by the dirty fallout from the Chrétien and Mulroney governments. He was saddled with the Arar affair and its explosive secrets, the RCMP pension scandal, and the multitude of failures by the RCMP. All this was further aggravated by the resurfacing of the Airbus payoffs to Harper's good friend Brian Mulroney, Harper's own dithering over that, and, of course, the lingering, hidden power of the Desmarais family. Whether one agrees with Harper's policies or not, it cannot be denied that so many traps had been set for Harper that it would be all but impossible for any single leader to escape unblemished.

Harper's own actions seemed to hurt him as well. He appeared insular, mean, controlling, and petty to the point of being a stooge for Mulroney, particularly when it came to the subject of the CBC. The public broadcasting company had been the only media outlet that didn't give up on the Schreiber story.

The Harper government's paranoia about the CBC reached apoplexy in mid-December 2007, when Bloc Québecois founder and former Liberal cabinet minister Jean Lapierre revealed that a question by Québec Liberal Pablo Rodriquez to Mulroney during the ethics committee hearings had actually been crafted by CBC reporter Julie Van Dusen. It was not uncommon on

Parliament Hill for that to happen because the reality of the situation is that when it comes to certain subjects, reporters often know more than the politicians. The Conservatives tried to use the revelation as an example of the CBC's ongoing campaign against Mulroney, as if Van Dusen had taken the money from Karlheinz Schreiber.

Harper then showed how unmagnanimous he could be. When it came to doling out his year-end interview time, he treated the vast operations of the CBC as if it were a local radio station. He went as far as refusing to be interviewed by Kathleen Petty, the host of the CBC national radio show, *The House*. He was piqued over criticisms about him and his government on the show.

The disinformation campaign continued with the Conservative Party's year-end fundraising efforts. The party tried to make a big issue about the Van Dusen question in its literature. The message to party loyalists had some effect.

"Look at this," a Nova Scotia Conservative organizer said as she handed me the fundraising paperwork during a holiday season visit to her home. "Something has got to be done about the CBC to bring it under control."

Harper borrowed a page from U.S. Republicans, twice rolling back the GST—lopping off two percent—thereby starving the federal treasury of tens of billions of dollars in revenue. Only time will tell if he did this as a short-term measure to pander to voters or as part of a larger scheme to justify arguments to be made later that the federal government could no longer afford to subsidize the provincial and municipal governments for services such as RCMP contract policing outside Ontario and Québec.

Harper's popularity in national opinion polls was stagnant. Hiding behind cabinet ministers had not served him well. No matter what he did, the majority of the electorate remained cool about him. Only a little more than a third of voters expressed support for him. Every other week, Harper threatened to force an election.

The ongoing crisis in the RCMP, which Harper had promised to address quickly, had quietly been shoved to the back burner.

Recall that in July 2007, Public Safety Minister Stockwell Day had empowered a five-person panel, headed by David Brown, to recommend changes to the RCMP. It remained to be seen how far the prime minister was prepared to go to deal with the crisis inside the walls of the RCMP. Would he do as others had done—pretend to implement change while maintaining the status quo? Or would he deal with the important issues at hand and begin the much needed process to restructure and transform the RCMP and policing in Canada? The opportunity had come for Harper to stand up for what he believed.

✠ ✠ ✠

With Giuliano Zaccardelli forced out of the commissioner's office in December 2006, the Harper government tried to make it look like it would be the first one in Canadian history to tackle the issue of the RCMP head-on. The scope of the problems inside the force was delineated in June 2007, when special investigator David Brown issued his headline-catching "horribly broken culture" report. To reiterate, that conclusion had been based upon two studies by professors Linda Duxbury and Chris Higgins, conducted in 2001 and 2004. The Brown report had led to the appointment of William Elliott as the first civilian commissioner of the force.

Elliott immediately hired Professor Duxbury to conduct another quick-and-dirty study of the RCMP, a follow-up to her two earlier reports. If Elliott and the government had expected that Duxbury would conclude the RCMP ship had miraculously righted itself after Zaccardelli had been shoved out the door, they would be severely disappointed.

On November 2, 2007, Duxbury delivered to Elliott her new 158-page report: "The RCMP Yesterday, Today and Tomorrow: An Independent Report Concerning Workplace Issues at the Royal Canadian Mounted Police." The report was never made public. Duxbury's key conclusions described how damaged the RCMP culture continued to be:

> The RCMP is not, by any accepted measure, a change-ready organization; the RCMP will have tremendous difficulty recruiting and retaining "the best" in a tight labour market, as the organization cannot be considered best practice with respect to [accepted] human resources practices (training, learning, career development and performance management); RCMP culture is not one that supports change. Nor is it one that promotes workplace health or provide competitive advantage. The RCMP may be victim of the "success spiral," which occurs when an organization holds on too long to a culture in the belief that what has worked in the past will continue to confer a competitive advantage in the future. This report indicates that the RCMP has failed to realign its organizational culture to take into account new environmental realities. This has resulted in key elements of RCMP culture being liabilities as the organization moves forward with reforms; changes undertaken in the last couple

of decades have resulted in an organization: which is more vulnerable and under intense public scrutiny; that lacks expertise, depth, corporate knowledge in key areas; that is stretched with respect to certain key competencies; in which employees are change weary, skeptical and cynical about the motivations behind change; in which employees wonder who is in charge and who to trust . . .

Finally, I can only conclude that the RCMP must undergo fundamental transformational change in order to re-engage its workforce, improve its state of change readiness and re-establish itself in order to attract the talent it will require in an increasingly complex environment. Changing structures and systems will not suffice however—the changes required go much deeper and will require fundamental shifts to organizational culture.

Duxbury said that most of the now-28,200 RCMP sworn members, civilians, and government workers found their work personally fulfilling, but she saw trouble ahead. She disparaged the force's human resources system for being inconsistent, inequitable, underfinanced, and burdened with too many priorities. "There is only one high importance HR area where the RCMP is currently meeting expectations: the area of pay and benefits."

She was also critical of the training process in the force: "Regions and divisions dedicate different levels of resources to training. This means that training . . . depends on where you are and who your senior manager is. There is no equity. There is no linkage between training, development and strategic planning . . . nor are there any links between the strategic priorities and the funding of training."

Duxbury said the RCMP should be concerned about the high number of employees who plan on retiring before reaching full pension. "These people can be considered fleeing the RCMP." She added: "A disturbingly high number do not feel respected or trusted by their employer and, in turn, do not trust the organization."

"The RCMP is in a very low state of change readiness," Duxbury wrote. "The organization has undertaken a number of changes in the past several decades and the way that these changes have been managed and led have resulted in a culture that is change adverse [sic] and a workforce who is change fatigued and cynical."

Duxbury went on to provide the following advice to Elliott: "The Commissioner can expect a great deal of resistance, largely from employees at all levels who have learned that in most cases they can 'out wait' the change. Additionally, the added complexity that public scrutiny will bring further complicates the change. As such, I offer the following specific advice to the Commissioner: Proceed with Caution . . . you never get a second chance to make a first impression; Ensure that the Government of Canada will make sure that the critical success factors for change of this nature are provided. . . ."

As damning as all the above might seem, Duxbury's caveats to her findings were perhaps the most revealing comments of all: "In the time allowed I could not look at everything. I cannot say that I have not missed key documents. Nor can I say that I completely understand how the RCMP works. As an outsider I had no way of knowing the validity and veracity of much of the information provided me by the RCMP."

After conducting three studies over a six-year period on the RCMP, Duxbury had come to appreciate the extent of the institution's dysfunction, all the awards for its great management aside.

Duxbury's comments that she neither fully understood the inner workings of the RCMP nor trusted the information she received from it should have raised alarm bells everywhere. Her findings were a complete rebuke of the legacies of both Norman Inkster and Philip Murray, the two former human resources chiefs who became commissioners and made the force what it is today.

In the days and weeks leading up to his first report in June 2007, Brown had consistently downplayed what he was going to say. He left Canadians and the RCMP with the entirely wrong impression, that all he would do would be to suggest a few minor changes—and then he dropped his bombshells.

Prior to "Rebuilding the Trust," his second report released December 14, 2007, Brown indicated that he and his four colleagues on the task force, including Inkster, would be recommending "drastic changes" to the RCMP. He said the group had spent five months travelling around the country, where they had met with more than 2,000 RCMP members and many other people before arriving at their conclusions and writing their report. Hard workers!

"In releasing my previous report this past June, I said the Force has a culture, management structure and corporate governance that isn't working," Brown said. "Five months later and with the benefit of my colleagues on this Task Force—I can confirm that the problems facing the RCMP today are deep and fundamental. . . . Fundamental change is required to create a modern, accountable and healthy national police force that is the pride of members and Canadians alike."

Brown's latest report was all but dripping in emotion as he described the pathetic situation that existed within the RCMP.

> We ... witnessed despair, disillusionment and anger with an organ-
> ization that is failing them. With remarkable, but disturbing consis-
> tency, we heard of chronic shortages of people and equipment, of
> overwork and fatigue, of issues of wellness, health and even safety.
>
> We learned about basic human management systems that
> haven't worked for years: mandatory unpaid overtime; discipline
> and grievance systems that don't work; a promotion system with
> little or no credibility; a sometimes embarrassing record of account-
> ing to the people they serve.
>
> These and many other issues came tumbling out through
> poignant stories of personal experiences related to us personally and
> in over the 500 confidential emails we received.
>
> What emerged was a picture of an honourable and revered
> Canadian institution with rank and file members and employees
> struggling to do their best under the tremendous burden of an inef-
> ficient and inappropriately structured organization.
>
> Our first reaction was to craft solutions to each of these prob-
> lems—some of which were blindingly obvious. But as the issues piled
> up, we realized that these were merely symptoms of a much larger
> issue encompassing the organization, governance and culture of the
> institution; that treating the symptoms alone would not provide a
> lasting cure.

Brown made three major recommendations: establishing the RCMP as a separate entity and separate employer from government; creating a new board of management to oversee all organization and administration of the RCMP; and creating a new independent complaints and oversight commis-sion with extended power and authority. His report also recommended the creation of an implementation council to ensure that the recommendations of the task force were implemented as intended—within a defined time frame.

The task force indicated that without addressing the three core recom-mendations, implementing the additional 45 detailed recommendations included in its report would be very difficult. Those included issues such as: human resources, funding, culture, governance, ethics, capacity, admin-istration, bureaucracy, compensation, safety, health, wellness, disclosure, discipline, recruitment, training, education, promotion, transparency, and communication.

"Through our consultation and research, we clearly realized that continuing to simply treat the symptoms ailing the RCMP was not going to fix anything and would only serve to compound the issues for future generations," Brown said. "But I am heartened—and I am confident that the recommendations we have made today will rebuild this national icon into a modern-day police force. I believe that lost trust among rank and file members will be restored. I believe that shaken trust among Canadians will be regained."

Brown and his colleagues—Inkster, Richard Drouin, Linda Black, and Larry Murray—waxed eloquently about how the new and improved RCMP would better serve Canadians. It was refreshing to hear them say that the RCMP should not be "mired in endless bureaucracy and administration with the federal government. The RCMP is not just another federal department— nor should it be."

They hoped that the new civilian management board and an oversight board would make the RCMP more efficient and effective, as well as more transparent and accountable.

It was envisioned that the proposed Independent Commission for Complaints and Oversight of the RCMP (ICCOR) would be established by legislation, would be truly independent of government, would report publicly on recommendations and findings, and would have the capacity in appropriate circumstances to consider complaints and initiate and conduct investigations with the power to summon witnesses and compel testimony.

"In many ways," Brown said, "the RCMP's approach to governance has been based on a model and style of policing developed from—and for—another era. We believe that our reforms will produce a modern RCMP, well equipped to meet today's—as well as future—challenges. A modern-day RCMP will have the tools to do their job properly, free from unnecessary government constraints—while being driven by a professional management team and maintaining accountability to Canadians through independent civilian oversight. . . . A modern-day RCMP will shed its cloak of secrecy while protecting the fundamental rights of Canadian citizens. It will build on its world-class expertise fighting organized crime and terrorism. It will better inform Canadians about its activities and in turn, rebuild trust through greater transparency. A modern-day RCMP will attract new, young Canadians who want to serve their community and country. It will be an institution steeped in education and training for the entire duration of their careers. It will focus on the safety and professional growth of its members. It will promote leaders who have been trained in strong management and ethics. Existing and new leaders will run the RCMP as an organization that combines good policing, good governance and good business."

Brown concluded: "[A] modern-day RCMP is not simply an aspiration—an ideal. It is the only acceptable destination from where we are. We now have a plan to fundamentally fix the RCMP and restore trust in this institution—but the path we have laid out is not for the faint of heart. Our years of collective experience have taught us that the best plans—without a detailed implementation plan—can often get shelved or go awry. In this case, the Task Force believes that a rapid but orderly implementation of our recommendations is essential to enable the RCMP to provide the effective policing services expected of it. The scope of the changes we have recommended is substantial. New entities must be created and new capacities must be built within the RCMP to manage its human resources and financial affairs. New authorities must be delegated from existing governmental entities to the RCMP. 'Rebuilding the Trust'—identifies the core and fundamental issues facing the RCMP today and recommends clear, decisive—and definitively tough—solutions to fix these problems—once and for all. Failure is not an option."

Brown had promoted his report by using the words "drastic changes." He made it appear as if the government was finally going to be doing something constructive with the RCMP—but was it? There was little "drastic" about the report. The fine hand of Inkster could be seen protecting the image of the force.

A drastic action would have been restructuring and refocusing the RCMP—getting it out of contract policing and protective services. Another drastic action would have been to amend the RCMP oath so that officers swore their allegiance to the country—not the police force.

The entire exercise, however, was superficial. It was grounded in the dual premises that the structure of the monolith that is the modern-day RCMP is sound and that it was only the force's employees who were messed up and confused, in spite of what Professor Duxbury found. The task force concluded, in spite of abundant evidence to the contrary, that all that was needed to fix the force was a few good managers, a little hard work, and time.

The proposed civilian oversight board would be the sole controlling entity to monitor the force. Meanwhile, Canadian history and the experiences of other countries have shown that police forces and intelligence agencies are extremely adept at avoiding scrutiny, if it serves their interests.

In the weeks and months that followed the release of the Brown report in December 2007, media interest in the RCMP waned, to be replaced by, among other things, the war in Afghanistan, the ongoing Airbus revelations in the House of Commons ethics committee, and suggestions of impropriety by one of the prime minister's aides.

The RCMP had become old news, so much so that the restoration of Giuliano Zaccardelli's reputation and the resumption of his policing career went unnoticed. It had begun quietly with his retirement ceremony on February 21, 2007. While everyone there thought Zaccardelli was headed out to pasture with a bell around his neck, he was already plotting his return. One of the speakers that night was Ronald K. Noble, an American who was the secretary general of Interpol, the international policing organization. Noble lauded Zaccardelli for his great career and contributions to policing, as if nothing untoward had ever happened. In April 2008, Noble announced in a another speech in Ottawa that: "I am thrilled to announce that the distinguished former commissioner has agreed to be the director of Oasis Africa." It was a plum four-year appointment for Zaccardelli based in Lyon, France. His mission is to organize and coordinate African police forces to fight crime.

As James Travers reported in the *Toronto Star*, "Thrilled and distinguished are not words often associated with Zaccardelli.... Bad experience and lingering suspicion ensure a sigh of relief will follow Zaccardelli out of town. But neither explains his safe landing."

"How can we trumpet in Africa the arrival of someone who left here with our police service in disarray?" asked David Christopherson, the NDP member of the justice committee who witnessed Zaccardelli's implosion.

Zaccardelli sold his Ottawa-area house four hours after the real estate listing was posted. He told friends that he hoped the new job would be a springboard to him becoming the Interpol secretary general after Noble's term expired in 2010.

A few weeks later, Deputy Commissioner J.G. Harper Boucher, one of Zaccardelli's New Brunswick underlings who had been running the force in Eastern Canada, left the RCMP. He had ridden to the top of the RCMP on Zaccardelli's coattails and the ride wasn't over. Boucher landed a job at Interpol in New York to work as a liaison with the United Nations.

Harper's popularity, meanwhile, continued to slip in the polls. At one point, he was even lagging behind the uninspiring Liberal leader Stéphane

Dion, each man being favoured by fewer than a third of the electorate. Nevertheless, Harper continued to posture, challenging the other parties to defeat his government and force an election over proposed anti-crime legislation, the future of the war in Afghanistan, or minor tax policy issues, "cheap politics" as *The Globe and Mail*'s Lawrence Martin described it.

Across the country, the RCMP focus was clearly set on 2012, when its 20-year provincial and municipal contracts were set to expire. In light of Harper's previous positions about federal and provincial jurisdictions, he, inexplicably, gave no indication that the federal government was planning to cut federal subsidies for RCMP contract policing.

The RCMP, in fact, was continuing to pursue contracts in all its jurisdictions and protect its business lines. No consideration was given inside the force to moving it out of contract policing, protective policing, or some of the other functions it has proven itself to be incapable of running competently. The RCMP boasts that it operates like a business but in the real world, any business would divest itself of non-performing or counterproductive divisions—not the RCMP.

As the Harper government fiddled with the RCMP, the larger policing and security issues were not being addressed. There was not even a hint that the government was prepared to consider a policy framework for policing in Canada or the long-term implications of an RCMP-driven integrated policing protocol.

In February 2008, an RCMP-orchestrated forum of government, civic, and police leaders was held in Vancouver to discuss the possible implementation of a regional policing system in the metropolitan area. Some, like Vancouver Police Chief Jim Chu and West Vancouver Police Chief Kash Heed, argued for a regionalized service at the expense of their own high-paying jobs. Others were happy with the RCMP: "We love our Mounties."

To reiterate, what was there to love? As a contract force, the RCMP is accountable to Ottawa, not local or provincial law. Local municipalities have no say over who their police officers will be. The RCMP is a more expensive police force than any other in Canada. There were well-publicized reports about future recruiting problems for the RCMP which meant that chronic short staffing of RCMP detachments would not only continue but might get worse. The ramifications of Duxbury's finding that it might take ten years or more—if ever—to repair what ailed the RCMP was not even publicly discussed.

All the available evidence indicates that the Mounties are not capable of doing all the jobs the force is trying to do. Who in their right mind would want to hire them for another 20 years?

Public Safety Minister Stockwell Day had argued in December 2006 that the situation within the RCMP was so urgent that matters had to be expedited. He said there was no time for public inquiries or Parliamentary deliberation. Although Day had promised to move forward on the Brown report and implement changes immediately, it took another three months to announce anything.

By April 2008, 16 months after Zaccardelli's departure, not much substantial progress had been achieved inside the force. There had been no massive overhaul, as promised. William Elliott proved to be an all-but-invisible head of the force. Like Prime Minister Harper, he delegated controversy to his subordinates.

Behind the scenes, Elliott had begun instituting Brown's recommendations, such as they were. Elliott was moving to undo some of the errors of the Norman Inkster and Philip Murray years and to re-centralize the command structure—by putting more power back in Ottawa. However, the very same people Zaccardelli had groomed and promoted for the top jobs were still running the RCMP. In fact those same people, such as Deputy Commissioner Pierre-Yves Bourduas, were in charge of implementing the new grand plan. The government's stated desire to implement change immediately had been transformed into "change through attrition." The new approach served only to freeze in place even those who intended to leave the force.

"No one wants to retire right now because the timing is bad," said one high-level source. "Everyone is afraid of being seen as part of the house cleaning."

One unpublicized initiative Elliott began to implement involved a way to improve the RCMP's promotion system. The changes were designed to ensure that future promotions would be based more on merit than esoteric qualities such as length of service, social skills, and bilingualism. The French-language factor had long been a sore point inside the force. Just being able to muddle along in another language was not going to be good enough anymore for someone to rise to the top in the RCMP.

On March 20, 2008, the Thursday before the Easter long weekend, Day announced the appointment of a five-person RCMP Reform Implementation Council to supervise the "overhaul" of the force as set out by the previous Brown committee. To call the council a curious collection of individuals would be to seriously understate the choices made.

Heading the council was David McAusland, a prominent Québec lawyer and businessman who was a former president of the Montréal Chamber of

Commerce. Since the late nineties, he had been the mergers and acquisitions specialist at Alcan Inc., the giant Québec-based multinational aluminum and mining concern.

Alcan had been the pride of Québec. It employed more than 60,000 people in the province and around the world. A number of the top executives of Alcan and some of its board members were longtime members of the Trilateral Commission, movers and shakers at the global level, almost on a par with the Desmarais family. McAusland became available to oversee the Mounties after he engineered the $38.1 billion cash sale of Alcan in 2007 to British-controlled Rio Tinto, creating the world's largest aluminum company.

For his efforts, McAusland was named by one magazine as Canadian Corporate Counsel Newsmaker of the Year. He said at the time that he was cleaning up the loose ends in that deal and he was eager to move on. "I'm trying to get out of Dodge as they say, and it's like one of those horror movies where the hand keeps coming up from the grave and pulling me back," he joked.

What the gunslinger McAusland knew about policing in Canada was anyone's guess. He certainly did not look like the kind of guy who was going to shake things up and change the status quo.

Another appointee was Jean-Claude Bouchard, a career public servant, who had recently headed the Canadian Environmental Assessment Agency. Since 1971, Bouchard had worked for the government with a brief stint in the private sector. He had returned to government in 2000 and was appointed assistant deputy minister of Industry Canada in charge of the operations sector. According to his official biography, "In that capacity, he led efforts to stimulate a competitive and innovative private sector in Canada and to promote confidence in a fair and efficient Canadian marketplace."

Bouchard later became associate deputy minister of Fisheries and Oceans Canada, where he was responsible "for managing all aspects of the department in cooperation with the Deputy Minister in addition to providing leadership on the international fisheries governance file. He also had direct responsibility for the Audit and Evaluation Directorate and the Centre for Values, Integrity and Conflict Resolution." What did Bouchard know about the big picture?

A third person with Québec business ties was Jocelyn Côté-O'Hara, president of a Toronto-based consulting firm that specialized in corporate strategy and communications. Just what the RCMP needed—someone to help them spin their mythical story even better.

Next came Kevin McAlpine, one of the more obscure members of the Canadian policing community. McAlpine had served as the police chief of two Ontario communities, Peterborough and Durham Region, the urban–rural sprawl east of Toronto, whose largest communities are Oshawa, Whitby, Pickering, and Ajax. Described as a hard-nosed, difficult-to-get-to-know kind of police leader, sources say he was not well-liked in Durham. "He never opened up on anything," said one of his colleagues. He left that job to become a professor in the school of justice at tiny Durham College, but had strong links to the Conservative party.

Finally, there was former RCMP Interim Commissioner Beverley Busson. Though well-respected within the ranks of the RCMP, Busson came with her own baggage. Under her command in British Columbia, the RCMP was all but a disaster. She seemed like an unlikely candidate to implement reform.

In her brief seven-month stint as commissioner in 2007, Busson had been cited by Paul Kennedy, chairman of the RCMP Commission for Public Complaints, for interfering with the process. Kennedy stated in a report to Parliament that Busson, like her predecessor Zaccardelli, had intervened to change a number of adverse reports against RCMP officers by challenging findings, questioning witness credibility, reweighing evidence, introducing new evidence, and substituting her own findings of fact in the cases.

Kennedy said at the time that the refusal of the RCMP commissioners to accept the findings of commission reviews over Mountie actions "strikes at the core of civilian accountability of the RCMP. More than half of the commission's adverse findings have been overruled by the RCMP commissioner, enabling the RCMP, in effect, to ignore the merits of the commission's recommendations." The Kennedy report added that the resistance "significantly undermines" civilian review of the RCMP and is "inherently biased" against the person who has lodged the complaint.

The Canadian media dutifully reported the news without comment—and collectively headed off for the Easter weekend. The public was left with the impression that the government was working diligently behind closed doors to fix the RCMP.

"The whole list seems to be a little funny," said former RCMP Superintendent Garry Clement. "My sense is that if the government were truly intent upon reorganizing and realigning law enforcement in Canada, there would be people there with a strong background in the prosecutorial and judiciary worlds. I don't see how these individuals bring a value-added component to the mix. I don't know what the government is thinking, but to me it looks like a cover-up."

A few weeks later, on the afternoon of Friday, April 25, 2008, the RCMP finally announced its long-awaited personnel moves in an internal broadcast to the force by Commissioner Elliott. By then, Zaccardelli's number-one acolyte, Deputy Commissioner P.Y. Bourduas, had quietly left the force after 33 years of service, his lifelong aspiration of becoming commissioner dashed. He got to keep all his medals and honours, including being a Member of the Order of Merit of the Police Forces, a decoration conferred on him by the Governor General in 2006.

Elliott said Deputy Commissioner William Sweeney, who was only going to be on the job for eight months when he was appointed the previous summer, had been named senior deputy commissioner. Sweeney decided to stay in Ottawa as Elliott's right-hand man. His greatest debacle, the Mayerthorpe massacre in 2005, had yet to be explained.

Three new deputy commissioner positions were created, for federal policing, contract policing, and support services for other police forces. Those posts were filled by others who had risen to the top under Zaccardelli—Raf Souccar, Darrell Madill, who had been the commanding officer in Manitoba, and Tim Killam. Assistant Commissioner Bernie Corrigan was appointed commanding officer of national headquarters where he would also oversee the Musical Ride. Two other Zaccardelli students from New Brunswick, twin assistant commissioners Mike and Pat McDonell, were put in charge of "O" Division (Ontario) and Protective Policing, respectively. It was as if nothing had changed.

Not only was there a dearth of new blood at the top, there was also something more ominous afoot.

In his recommendations, David Brown had urged that the RCMP operate as a separate entity from government. Recall his recommendation that the RCMP should not be "mired in endless bureaucracy and administration with the federal government. The RCMP is not just another federal department— nor should it be." He also said: "A modern-day RCMP will shed its cloak of secrecy while protecting the fundamental rights of Canadian citizens."

In his announcement, Elliott said he would be creating another new position—assistant deputy minister in charge of public affairs. By definition, an assistant deputy minister works for the government, not the police. The Harper government had claimed the power to vet everything the RCMP could and could not tell the public, gaining even more control over the police.

There had long been concerns within the RCMP about the commissioner being a deputy minister and the unseemly proximity to government. With two key people positioned at the top of the RCMP beholden to the prime minister, Harper had cemented the seal on the force while slipping another potential controversy past the somnambulant media.

"That's Margaret Bloodworth's work," said one Ottawa observer familiar with what was going on. "Bloodworth is the problem. She is the national security advisor. She's in the Privy Council Office. She is determined to control everything."

As we already know, there was much information to control.

Elliott's announcement was sent to RCMP offices in Canada and around the world, but a press release was never issued. I took it upon myself to do something about the assistant deputy minister position by contacting *Globe and Mail* columnist Lawrence Martin. It took a week for the RCMP to answer Martin's questions about the new position. Here is what Martin wrote on May 15, 2008 under the headline: "A plan to muzzle the RCMP? This demands an explanation."

The Commissioner's announcement stood for almost three weeks. Then, when it appeared that news of it would get out—I had begun making inquiries—there came a sudden change of mind. The Commissioner made another internal announcement to the force Tuesday and forwarded the text to me.

"As announced we intend to move forward to create a new senior position," he said. "However the position will not be an Assistant Deputy Minister's position as had been indicated. The title Assistant Deputy Minister is not an appropriate one for a position within the RCMP and the misuse of this title in my broadcast has raised questions about the role and reporting relationship of the position."

He termed his April 25 statement a "miscommunication," adding that "there is no intention for the position to be under the authority or direction of anyone other than the RCMP."

It was a remarkable about-face. It's possible there was a crossing of signals and an honest mistake was made in the initial broadcast. But before we decide to accept this version of events, more facts should be considered.

In the first place, a move to assert control over Mountie communications would be hardly out of character for this government.

Second, if the position was not to be that of an ADM, how did Mr. Elliott miss this mistake? A former ADM himself (for Transport Canada), he is well aware of the position's significance. In the RCMP context, he would have known it should signal outside monitoring.

Third, if it was indeed a simple matter of erroneous use of language in his April 25 statement, wouldn't the government have cleared it up in a matter of days—not almost three weeks later, after prying by the media had begun?

A more likely explanation is that the plan for the information czar had been put in place by Public Safety Minister Stockwell Day and the Prime Minister's Office. When fears arose that it would touch off a firestorm of protest, the new statement was issued.

The "reforms" the government said it was making to the RCMP were anything but.

Sources say the person Harper wanted to insert into the RCMP hierarchy was Keith Beardsley, one of his key advisors who had set up and operated a political war room for the Prime Minister. In an underhanded fashion, Harper was clearly seeking absolute control over the police.

It did not take long for William Elliott to create enemies in the force. After less than a year on the job, many senior RCMP officers were longing for "the good old days of Zac," as one put it. "Zac was an authoritarian, but he was also a gentleman. He treated you with respect. Elliott is a screamer. He reams senior officers out in public and belittles them. Some of us are ready to pack it in all because of him."

No matter what Elliott did, Harper would be deaf to the criticisms. Elliott was his man. Harper clearly had lost his appetite to address the form and function of the RCMP, to restructure and demythologize the force. There was no recognition by him, his government or, to be fair, the opposition parties of the fact that the RCMP is a national disaster. It neither serves its members nor the public interest all that well. Instead of depoliticizing the force, Harper's instinct was to increase political control and the opposition cheered him on.

That Canada's political leaders continue to ignore the obvious can only suggest one thing—our leaders don't want real change no matter how desperate the need. Having the RCMP as a captive police force *is* the grand plan.

As Jeffrey Simpson ably pointed out in his 2001 book *The Friendly Dictatorship*, Canada is a country where there is no system of checks and balances. Simpson wrote:

Prime Ministerial power is now more centralized than ever, and the centralization is increasingly out-of-step with the operating practices of other major institutions, the needs of modern government and the expectations of citizens. . . . The only checks that do exist are more nebulous ones: the shifting sands of political opinion, the possibility of adverse media coverage and potential conflict with provincial premiers, although a clever Prime Minister can turn those conflicts to his advantage. The Prime Minister has it both ways. He is not only primus within the governing party, where he exercises dominant power, but the Canadian political system provides no effective check or balance to the exercise of that power.

Nothing has changed since Simpson wrote that book seven years ago. There are those who believe the situation is even worse today.

✛   ✛   ✛

In March 2008, retired judge John Gomery had stepped into the fray. Gomery had overseen the public inquiry three years earlier into the sponsorship scandal. He was subsequently attacked by Chrétien for his comments and findings. Speaking to the government operations committee on March 11, 2008, Gomery warned about the growing concentration of power in the Prime Minister's Office and the incipient danger to Canadian democracy. "It should be remembered that the political staff in the Prime Minister's Office are not elected," Gomery said. "They are not subject to any rules or laws of which I am aware, and they have the ear of the most important and powerful person in Canadian government. . . . I suggest that this trend is a danger to Canadian democracy and leaves the door wide open to the kind of political interference in the day-to-day administration of government programs that led to what is commonly called the sponsorship scandal."

Gomery went on to criticize Harper for ignoring the 19 recommendations he had made in his report on the Liberal government scandal. "I expected that in due course the recommendations contained in our report would at some future time be studied and, at least to some degree, acted upon," Gomery said. "Unfortunately, that was not the case."

One of his other observations was that the Harper government had not even waited for his report before drafting and deciding upon its proposed

Accountability Act. But, as we have seen so many times in this book, public commissions, judicial inquiries, and special investigators have become mere decoys in Canadian politics, designed to distract the attention of the public while the government, unilaterally, does what it wants to do.

By March 2008, the slimy underbelly of Canadian politics was further revealed in a new book *Like a Rock: The Chuck Cadman Story* by Tom Zytaruk. Zytaruk asserted that the Conservatives had tried to bribe the independent Cadman in May 2005. They hoped Cadman would side with them in a crucial Parliamentary showdown two days hence. Cadman was dying of skin cancer at the time and eschewed the offer to help topple Paul Martin's Liberal government. He died two months later.

It was not the first time Harper's government had been caught trying to improve its fortunes without going to the voters. In 2006, Ottawa mayoral candidate Larry O'Brien met with his opponent, Terry Kilrea, and promised him a federal appointment if he would step out of the race. Kilrea went as far as meeting with Conservative MP John Reynolds, Harper's fixer, before declining and going to the police. O'Brien has been charged with bribery.

Reynolds was also the bagman in a $50,000 alleged payoff to Conservative candidate Alan Riddell, who withdrew from the 2006 election in favour of Alan Cutler. Reynolds also admitted that he may have met with Cadman. Two other top Conservatives who said they met with Cadman in the May 2005 time frame were two of Harper's top advisers, Tom Flanagan and Doug Finley.

Zytaruk described the form of the attempted bribe as a $1 million insurance policy, which Cadman and his wife seriously considered accepting, but soon rejected. Why insurance on a man soon to be dead? If Cadman did not run, his wife's benefits would be cut in half. But Cadman was an honourable man and declined the offer.

More important, Zytaruk interviewed Harper about the matter, and he seemed to know what had been going on.

"I don't know the details," Zytaruk quoted Harper as saying. "I know that there were discussions, uh, this is not for publication?"

Zytaruk assured Harper that it was for a book, not a newspaper story. He said Harper went on to say: "I can tell you that I had told the individuals—I mean, they wanted to do it—but I told them they were wasting their time. I said Chuck has made up his mind he was going to vote with the Liberals. I know why, and I respected that decision, but they were convinced there was [sic] financial issues . . . but I said that's not going to change the decision. I said: 'Don't press him, I mean, you have this theory that it's, you know, financial insecurity, and . . . if that's what you say, make the case, but I said, don't press it.'"

The Opposition tore into Harper and many accusations were made both inside and outside the House of Commons, including a Liberal Party website. The Cadman affair was clearly a political issue, but Harper began to fully reveal himself as the next logical successor to Brian Mulroney and Jean Chrétien. When cornered, forget politics and kick up the dust by invoking the courts to advance your case.

On March 13, 2008, Harper filed a libel suit seeking more than $2.5 million in damages and legal costs against the Liberal Party of Canada, the Federal Liberal Agency of Canada and "the unnamed author or authors of the statements published on the party's website two weeks ago." It was the first time a sitting prime minister had sued the Opposition for libel.

"I have every right, as does my family, to defend our reputation, and the Liberal party will, as I said, come to regret engaging in this illegal and untruthful behaviour," Harper later told the House of Commons.

Two months later, on cue, the RCMP announced it could find no evidence of criminal wrongdoing in the Cadman affair.

In April 2008, acting for Elections Canada, the RCMP raided the offices of the Conservative Party in Ottawa over more allegations that the party had used illegal transfers between candidates and the party to skirt the law during the 2006 election campaign. The Conservatives denied any wrongdoing and suggested, once again, that the action by the watchdogs at Elections Canada was motivated by politics.

Like clockwork the scandals continued to roll in. Foreign Affairs Minister Maxime Bernier became the focus of attention after it was learned his well-endowed girlfriend Julie Couillard had previously been connected to outlaw bikers in Québec. The woman he ordained his "love of my life" was linked to a biker who had been murdered. Harper defended Bernier's choice of companions until it was revealed in late May 2008 that Bernier had left sensitive NATO briefing notes in Couillard's apartment and forgotten about them. Only after his breakup with Couillard did she reveal the existence of the documents, which forced Harper to finally fire Bernier. It seemed that Harper was so willfully blind and naïve that he did not consider the possibility that Couillard might have been a secret agent—the Mata Hari of the 450 as she came to be called. It was a reference to the telephone area code in which she lived. A few weeks later, it was revealed that Couillard had cozy relationships with others close to the government and may have been acting literally as an undercover lobbyist for a Quebec land developer who was interested in winning federal government approval for a controversial project.

Harper had come to office with a pledge of making government more transparent. Instead he seemed determine to block the public from knowing anything about the operations of government—like his move in May 2008 to quietly shut down a database called the Co-ordination of Access to Information Requests System. Created in 1989 and revamped in 2001, the CAIRS database is a monthly compilation of all access requests received by federal agencies. Canadians could use it to see the information that had already been made public or was in the process of being released, and could then make a request to see the documents themselves. Harper told the House of Commons that the database was "deemed expensive, it was deemed to slow down the access to information, and that's why this government got rid of it. This is a government that has actually widened access to information," he said straightfaced to a chorus of jeers by the Opposition.

Harper portrayed himself as being an independent, courageous, ethical, and modern man in touch with his country, the kind of guy who listened to Blue Rodeo and the Tragically Hip on his iPod. He had promised to make things better. Instead, he either underwent a conversion on the road to Ottawa or merely revealed himself to be, not so much a fan of Blue Rodeo but, tragically, more likely Richard Wagner.

Once in office, Harper looked no different than his predecessors Chrétien and Mulroney—desperate to hold on to power and defend the status quo. Like them, he showed he was willing to hide behind dubious legal actions rather than confront issues head on. Like them, he adopted a bunker mentality and ignored the need to repair and strengthen institutions like the RCMP—when the need for action was obvious. Like them, he pandered to Québec and big business interests at the expense of other Canadians.

The intention of this book has been to illustrate how profound Canada's problems are. I believe I have made a sound case that our public institutions—the guardians of our freedoms and way of life—have become worrisomely compromised by anti-democratic forces.

That being so, why have Canada's political leaders been so reluctant to fix what is clearly broken?

You might try asking Power Corporation that question.

[afterword]

ON HONOURABLE PERSONS
AND HONOUR

My fellow Canadians, I am not an honourable person. In Canada, parliamentarians can refer to each other as honourable members, but the actual title comes with the better jobs—prime minister, cabinet minister, and judge, among others. Members of the Privy Council are also called honourable. Based on the history and performance of our parliamentarians I would never last long as an honourable man because I could not accept being party to so much that has been so dishonourable.

Each honourable person is vested with extraordinary powers in a democratic society and his or her place in Parliament is a matter of public trust. The code for Members of Parliament expects that they will, among other things: "fulfill their public duties with honesty and uphold the highest standards so as to avoid real or apparent conflicts of interests, and maintain and enhance public confidence and trust in the integrity of each Member and in the House of Commons." Another expectation is that they will "perform their official duties and functions and arrange their private affairs in a manner that bears the closest public scrutiny, an obligation that may not be fully discharged by simply acting within the law."

At the very heart of the definition of the term is the notion that all honourable men and women must act at all times in the service of their country and within its laws—even in the face of what might be daunting political imperatives and self-survival. There is no room for self-interest in being honourable, only disinterest. The Public Office Holders' Code dictates that each such person "shall act with honesty and uphold the highest ethical standards so that public confidence and trust in the integrity, objectivity and impartiality of government are conserved and enhanced." Furthermore, "Public office holders have an obligation to perform their official duties and arrange their private affairs in a manner that will bear the closest public scrutiny, an obligation that is not fully discharged by simply acting within the law."

In other words, doing what might be technically legal but morally unethical does not get a parliamentarian off the hook. Therefore, if an honourable person finds himself in an untenable political position or conflict of interest, the tradition has been that he or she must recuse themselves from a situation or resign, either as a point of principle or to protect the good name or reputation of the institution of government.

In 1959, RCMP Commissioner Leonard Nicholson resigned to protest political interference by Prime Minister John Diefenbaker in the operations of the police. Since then, with the evolving corporatization of government and the police, and all the incumbent thought processes, the concept of honour has been allowed to deteriorate and wither away. Think about how Jean Chrétien and Brian Mulroney—each caught in murky personal dealings—loudly proclaimed their innocence and vindication after being cleared of wrongdoing by legal technicalities or, as in Mulroney's case, through outright lies and obvious collusion. Each of these men should have recognized the moral imperative, to resign with honour. But for them and for so many of our guardians, the acquisition, maintenance, and entrenchment of power and individual wealth and comfort have become the sole measures of honour. An obvious exception is the much maligned Joe Clark—at least he did the honourable thing when he stood by his word and stepped down as leader of his party when he did not get the level of support he deemed to be a mandate.

Taking a stand on a point of principle has, in large measure, become a negotiating tool by which to extract mutually beneficial terms for both the perceived aggrieved and aggrievor. So much of what we see and hear, therefore, is all role-playing filled with deception, distortion, and manipulation—the tactics of modern political discourse. Is it any wonder that ordinary people have become cynical and feel so helpless?

Canada has long been seen as a paragon of good will and a land of untold wealth. During the Second World War at the massive Auschwitz-Birkenau concentration and extermination camp in Poland, there was one area known as Canada. It was called Canada because the inmates saw it as heaven. It was the place in Auschwitz where all the wealth and material goods from the soon-to-be murdered victims were separated and catalogued.

But as we have come to know, Canada has been less than heaven for so many of its residents. Our governments and politicians preach about transparency, but among democratic governments, Canada's is one of the most secretive in the world. In every election campaign, our prospective leaders promise greater openness and accountability, but once in office find it all too easy to slip into the shadows. No matter the political stripe, everyone in Ottawa is seen to be working to protect each other—the Opposition acts in name only.

How has this come to be?

In my first book, *Above the Law*, I focused on a relatively subtle change introduced by the Mulroney government in the way Parliament functions. Since Confederation the Board of Internal Economy had overseen the expenditures of Parliament, including salaries and other contingent expenses. Traditionally, the board had been chaired by the Speaker and consisted of four ministers. In 1985, under Mulroney the governing Act was amended to enlarge the board's membership to nine. The number of cabinet ministers was reduced to two, and the other seven members were backbenchers and representatives from each of the opposition parties. The board continued to meet in secret. Its records were not published.

At the time I interviewed him in 1993, Marcel Pelletier, who had served as law clerk and legal counsel to Parliament during the Mulroney years, predicted the change to the Board of Internal Economy would have a muzzling effect on the Opposition. He predicted that in matters of great dispute, all the parties could end up on the same side of an issue, and not necessarily on the side of the public interest.

Isn't that what has happened?

In so many obvious ways, Canada has become brutal and corrupted, its economy dominated by large, enormously wealthy individuals and corporations, working together to stifle innovation and diversity. Its vast resources should be enough to create a vibrant, self-sustaining, and multi-faceted economy, but those resources are being mined for the benefit of others, without long-term benefits for the people of Canada.

Our most important guardian institutions have become corrupted and we as a nation have been all but oblivious to that fact. Some even seem to believe that corruption is not an important social, economic, or political issue, but merely a by-product of success—to the winners go the spoils. Yet history has shown conclusively that corruption and the complacency that allows it to breed are the enemies of democracy. Plato wrote more than 2,400 years ago that in the Ideal State, "Justice rules, the people are content and well cared for, corruption is unthinkable, and the government acts with the willing consent of the governed." When the Ideal State fails, it "gradually becomes corrupted, passing through many stages until it finally evolves into anarchic tyranny." As we should know by now from events in other countries, Plato's words hold true today.

Our public and important private institutions are our watchdogs. Each has a role in protecting our democracy, but each has lost its purity of purpose.

Of particular concern should be the state of the media in Canada. Back in 1989, when I was national editor of *The Globe and Mail*, I wished I had had the power to change the way politics and government was being covered in Canada. One particularly dark fantasy was to drop a neutron bomb on Ottawa, thereby eliminating the people but leaving the buildings intact— perfect for starting over. The moment passed but my concerns did not. To me back then, the Parliamentary Press Gallery was a virtually useless exercise filled with too many reporters and commentators who seemed to judge their individual success by the lack of distance between themselves and the people they were meant to cover. Real stories were not getting done because the reporters falsely assumed they had a higher understanding of any situation due to their proximity to the politicians and other power brokers. Journalist and author Andrew Coyne has deftly described their attitude as being "like bored socialites at a tennis match."

Those who get too close tend to merely repeat the words and positions of those in power—without ever daring to doubt anyone's veracity. It is a problem not unique to Canada. Frank Rich of the *New York Times* has called it "the cloistered echo chamber of our political journalism's status quo."

As bad as things seemed to be back in 1989, I believe the situation in Canada is much worse today. You may recall from Chapter 20 how both the P2 movement in Italy and Le Cercle each believed that consolidation of the media was a necessary goal to achieve their stated globalist political and economic ends. In Canada, that has come to pass. Ownership of the private media has been allowed to become so concentrated in right-wing hands that newspapers, radio, and television stations have all but become arms of government and industry—sycophantically doing their bidding at almost every turn. There are good reporters and editors everywhere but their efforts are all too often stymied in either subtle or overt ways. So many of them tell me about their frustrations and the road blocks they face in trying to serve the public interest with their work.

Meanwhile, the Canadian Broadcasting Corporation, though not perfect by any means, has emerged as one of the few pure defenders of the public interest. Yet it is the CBC that has been singled out as a partisan, politicized entity, particularly by the right wing with their dubious, not-so-hidden agenda of untrammeled capitalism. The dumbing down of the media and the incessant barrage of corporate and political propaganda, combined with the muffling and muzzling of clear voices and criticism, only serves the interests of those who do not believe in democracy.

Disinformation, scurrilous attacks, and outright lies cause us to live our lives in fear of challenging authority when we should. Without the proper functioning of our institutions—guided solely by their duty to serve the public interest—Canada's democracy is at risk and its wealth left exposed to plunderers and modern-day carpetbaggers.

It is no accident that most of the serious problems within Canada detailed in this book, almost without exception, can be traced back to one common root—Québec. The status of the province of Québec and the persistent demands of its mythically oppressed original francophones have dominated Canadian federal politics for four decades—to the detriment of the entire country. Canadians must come to terms with the fact that the people of Québec have a distinctly different view of how society and the economy should be run. Québec thinks about Québec first and that is contrary to how the rest of Canada thinks. Through accommodation, appeasement, and complacency, Canada has allowed its institutions to be manipulated and controlled by this Québec-first attitude. For them, Canada is an afterthought—if a thought at all.

We have chosen leaders from Québec to lead Canada largely because we have been given no other real choice. Our political system has been cleverly leveraged to guarantee that the interests of Québec and its elite are of primary concern to the entire nation, even if it comes to the defiance of the rule of law.

With their thuggish behaviour and rule by fear, Brian Mulroney and Jean Chrétien consolidated this power. They used it to shield their own activities and promote the interests of their wealthy benefactors, not the least being the Desmarais family and Power Corporation. Despite his promises of "reform," Stephen Harper, by his own actions, has allowed himself to fall into the same camp as his two notorious predecessors.

The Canadian political structure, therefore, has become an oligarchy in all but name. Canada is being ruled by a fantastically small group of people and their agents who exercise influence over, or actually have the power to direct, important guardian institutions like the Privy Council and the Security Intelligence Review Committee. This group has shown conclusively that it has the motive, the means, and the opportunity to control the government, the Royal Canadian Mounted Police, and the Canadian Security Intelligence Service. Far too many strange things have happened in Canada these past few decades to argue otherwise.

In his oft-quoted 1887 letter to Bishop Mandell Creighton, Lord Acton wrote: "Power tends to corrupt and absolute power corrupts absolutely." What exists in Canada today is the very definition of absolute power. It rests within the narrow confines of the Prime Minister's Office, the Privy Council Office, and the elite of the bureaucracy, where the intertwining of corporate and political interests is largely hidden from view by a thick fog of secrecy.

This ruling junta has done little, if anything, to defend our sovereignty. Our institutions have been organized in such a way as to not defend the country, its people, and their assets, yet our politicians and governments seem stunningly oblivious to that fact. That we have been and continue to be manipulated by outside forces goes unquestioned. Spies and subversive elements have been allowed—hidden as they are—to become all but part of the Canadian democratic process. One cannot help but surmise who they all might be and where they might be placed in government, the public and, most importantly, the media. This is not paranoia speaking. It is grounded in fact. Spies have been found to exist in those areas in every other country in the world and in many cases their presence has been uncovered—but not in Canada.

The current-day RCMP has been victimized by multiple foreign espionage manipulations and shaped by it. That has never been publicly debated and remains hidden behind the all-but-impervious wall of national security.

Our politicians have let us down badly. Too many have shown themselves all too willing to compromise in an effort to protect their status, pensions, and creature comforts—at the expense of the rest of the country.

In these trying and dangerous times, who is there to stand up for Canada? Who speaks for Canada? If there is no one to speak up for us, we may well cease to be us.

Who among us has the courage to defy the powers that have gained such a stranglehold? Who is prepared to ask the right questions, not just the ones government invites us to ask?

We need intelligent politicians with fire in their bellies and honesty in their hearts. We need bureaucrats with steely integrity who can resist the temptation of politics. We need a truly independent justice system that cannot be manipulated. We need police leaders who are independent-minded enough to see the big picture and who are unafraid to enforce the law for everyone—including self-aggrandizing business leaders, politicians, and other police.

Print journalism is under siege by television and the Internet, yet print journalism in any form is the engine of information in a democratic society. Without it, the other media would be left with little important to say.

We need publishers, editors, and journalists who are cognizant of the important public trust bestowed upon them. We need publishers, editors, and journalists who come to their work with a sense of duty—entirely disinterested people who can rise above the stenography of modern journalism. We need publishers, editors, and journalists who are truly competitive and fiercely so in pursuing not only profits but also the real news—not just stories that bleed. In other words, we need more facts-intensive journalism.

It used to be that newspapers competed to tell a story better than their rivals. Today, important stories in the public interest are often ignored simply because a rival has generated them—the negative application of competition. This attitude only serves to protect vested powers, not the public interest.

Every second of every day we are being bombarded with information from every direction but much of that information is useless, even in the traditional media. There is only the appearance of plenty. Thousands of new books are published every year. Fat newspapers and glossy magazines abound. But so much of what passes for news is fed to us without context, leaving people starved for knowledge.

That there is valuable information to be found through the Internet is indisputable, but the quality of so much of that information cannot be relied upon because it is unedited, out-of-context, and subjective, therefore largely unreliable.

I—and many like me—do not want to read another self-help book. Canadians, use your brains. Think and help yourselves.

I do not want to read another self-serving autobiography like so many of those by our leading and former politicians. All too often, they have only skimmed over the surface, inevitably portraying themselves as selfless heroes. Meanwhile, they conveniently ignore the Airbus debacle and Karlheinz Schreiber (Mulroney) or the sponsorship scandal (Chrétien).

I do not want to read another piece of hagiography by some captive author or journalist out to make a quick buck. I am tired of all the spin, marketing, and toying with the public's emotions. All I want to know is the truth, as best as it can be discerned at a particular moment in history because, as has been said many times before, only the truth will set us free.

Only by establishing a framework and set of rules that everyone can understand can we defeat apathy, fake competition, and contrived partisanship, and restore the concept of honour in our leaders and ourselves. The only way our leaders in government and business will be held wholly accountable for their actions is if the public and its media are informed, objective, and vigilant—and the police truly independent of the political process. Only then can we rise above the superficial sniping of modern fear-mongering disingenuous politics.

At the time of writing, it appeared that a federal election would be forced in 2008, even though public opinion polls had given no leader enough support for a majority. The problem for the relatively unpopular Stephen Harper, mired in minority government, is that he cannot govern unilaterally as his predecessors Mulroney and Chrétien did with their strong Québec political and business ties. The obstacle confronting the Liberals is that their leader, the erudite Stéphane Dion, is seen to be the Joe Clark of his party, someone who had won the leadership in December 2006 by coming up the middle and defeating the establishment favourite, the even more erudite Michael Ignatieff.

In late 2007 and early 2008, Dion's advisers seemed to be pushing him to force an election he could not win. Why? This would set the stage for a leadership review and the likely candidacy of Ignatieff and the newly-elected Bob Rae.

In some ways, Ignatieff, an accomplished writer and thinker in his own right, has looked like a saviour of the country. He even has a pedigree. His mother is the sister of philosopher and historian George Grant whose 1965 essay *Lament for a Nation* first addressed the diminishment of Canada in the face of the power of its neighbour, the United States of America.

But in other ways, Ignatieff looked like more of the same, the natural extension of the Desmarais extended family. Ignatieff had all the appropriate globalist qualifications, both in his work with the United Nations and as a longtime member of the Trilateral Commission and the Bilderberg Conference, among other globalist ties.

Where are our Barack Obamas, our inspirational leaders who can get everyone involved in politics and government? Where are our leaders who are not slaves to the Trilateral Commission and Bilderberg Conference or their secret society offshoots, replete with their hooded robes and hoary rituals? Which party is prepared to build an election campaign around what really matters—the integrity of our public institutions—and carry out its promises once in power?

Once again, who will speak for Canada?

No matter who that person might be, he or she faces a great challenge. If Canada is to be all that it can possibly be, a vibrant and safe home for our children and their children, a welcoming land for immigrants to join us and build their lives with us, and for all of us, then Canada's institutions must be reformed and strengthened to reflect our mutual desires and to protect us all under the rule of law.

To realign our country and put it back on course we must set aside our petty regional grievances and jealousies and see the big picture for what it is. Each of us must look into our own souls and ask the tough questions most of us avoid. As John F. Kennedy put it: "Ask not what your country can do for you, ask what you can do for your country." In this way we might be able to confront and defeat the narcissism and apathy that bedevil us.

Making Canada confident and strong might well invite controversy, discomfort, and hardship. However, if we do not collectively have the will and courage to do something to take back Canada, we will be forever reduced to a country of mere waiters, salespeople, and advisers—hookers on the stroll of the global economy.

We have the means and power to become what we once were—a nation of courageous thinkers, hard workers, and builders who united a continent. A good start might be starving all those big-box stores to death, along with the sinister things sometimes hidden inside their packaging. Otherwise, there is a real danger that our country and its way of life will be destined to fade into history.

We must tap into and encourage the strength, common sense, and ingenuity of Canadian people and give them, their families, and their communities a fighting chance in the future.

Our public institutions have been under attack for more than three decades by outside forces determined to eviscerate our laws and regulations. Our institutions need to be strengthened, not weakened. Our laws and the application of those laws need to be reconsidered so that the playing field in Canada is levelled for all.

Control of our media must be broken up and freed from the oligarchs, otherwise we are doomed to a future of biased, useless news designed to entertain, but not inform, us. We must become eager to challenge those who ply us with pseudo-information that is suspect—intended to serve someone's agenda or the hidden interests of others. We must demand pertinent information—in context, with perspective—that can serve our best interests.

We desperately need our society to be educated about the crucially important but different roles played by commerce and guardians in society. History has shown us conclusively that in a fair, vibrant, and successful society, each has its place, but there must be balance. Neither is evil when in balance, but when the balance is lost, a society will find itself under the thumb of tyrants, be they protective totalitarians or enterprising fascists.

We desperately need to understand the meaning of the word "disinterested" and learn to encourage and value those people who are disinterested, that is, unbiased by personal interest or advantage. Truly disinterested citizens have no hidden agendas. They operate on observation, insight, and action and are dangerous, but in a good way.

All this could well be the subject of another book or two. In the threads of the stories contained in this book, I can envisage several others. I invite others to pursue those stories with objectivity, intelligence, and vigour.

The very fact that this book has been published shows that our great country still has a chance, but its future depends on all of us. We must not only make ourselves more aware of what our honourable men and women are doing in government but we must also hold them to a higher standard of performance. Unless we all are prepared to do more for our country, it is all but guaranteed that our governments will continue to do less for us. By their words, deeds, and actions over these past three decades, far too many of our honourable men and women have shown the world that they are not there for us, my fellow Canadians, most assuredly, not for us.

ACKNOWLEDGEMENTS

The idea for this book came from Robert Lecker, a Montréal literary agent. Amid all the scandal in which the RCMP had become involved in late 2006 and early 2007, Lecker believed someone should write a book about it. He approached Lee Lamothe, one of his clients, who had written a number of books about organized crime. He was then working on a novel.

Lamothe suggested my name to Lecker, who did not know about my previous and continuing work on the RCMP. Thank you, Lee.

Lecker worked with me on my original proposal which was admittedly not strong. In the preamble to that proposal, I stated that the story was continuing to unfold and that writing about it would be like trying to hit a moving target.

Janie Yoon at Key Porter Books recognized the potential of the story. She was lured away by another publisher, but in her new role she continued to provide me with valuable advice.

Managing editor Jonathan Schmidt took over the project while it was still in its infancy. Jonathan provided tremendous encouragement and support through the many challenges and somewhat difficult times we both experienced in completing the project. Thank you to Jordan, Jonathan, copy editor Gillian Scobie, and the rest of the Key Porter team.

I could not have undertaken such an intensive project without the absolute support of my wife and business partner, Sharon McNamara. Our businesses—Kiln Art, Chez Glass Lass, and Sharon McNamara *et al.*—were entering the busiest period of the year. But Sharon believed in me and the story. "For as long as it takes, I don't want to see you at the shop, unless there is a special request for the things you make," she told me. "I will run every-thing." And she did. We both ended up working seven days a week, including Christmas Eve, Christmas Day, Boxing Day, New Year's Eve, and New Year's Day. This book could not have happened without her unconditional support, cogent advice, and love, although there were trying moments. "Are we in danger?" she asked me a couple of times. I thank Sharon and our wonderful employees for picking up the slack—Jan Melvin, Karen Lowe, Susan Robar, Melissa Bond, Jackie Langille, Bev Nauss, and Kate Melvin. Last—but certainly not least—was our special weapon, the irrepressible and talented Katie Gorman.

Over the years I have been fortunate to meet and befriend police officers capable of taking the big view. They have helped me immensely. Foremost among them was former RCMP Deputy Commissioner Henry Jensen, currently the chairman of the Ottawa Police Services Board. I cannot thank him or his wife Lois enough for their insights and for their hospitality.

Others who were helpful and generous with their time were former Toronto Police Chief William McCormack, then-Cape Breton Regional Police Chief Edgar MacLeod, former Vancouver Police Chief Bob Stewart, Halifax Police Chief Frank Beazley, Alberta Assistant Deputy Minister Brian Skeet, and Geoff Gruson of the Police Sector Council.

Many other current and former police officers and intelligence agents helped shape this story. Those who can be named are: Gary Bass, Alistair Macintyre, Dr. Allen Castle, Brian McAdam, Michel Juneau-Katsuya, Julian Fantino, Garry Clement, Graham Muir, Bill Majcher, Al Sauve, Kim Armstrong, Mark Lalonde, Gaétan Delisle, Pete Merrifield, Natalie Deschenes, Rob Creasser, Patrick Douek, Michel Funnicello, Ross Woronka, and Dave Moore.

Tony Cannavino and Dale Kinnear from the Canadian Police Professional Association and Dean Secord and Mike Donovan from the New Brunswick Police Association provided me with many useful insights. Ottawa researcher Ken Rubin and private investigator Kevin Bousquet of the Corpa Group, Burlington, Ontario, provided invaluable information. LeJune Pier of Clarity Intelligence Services, London, Ontario and Ron Thibault of Mo-Ro Inc., Montréal also made significant contributions.

Then there were those with other police or legal expertise and experience which included: Scott Newark, Dorothy Ahlgren Franklin, James Duggan, Laura Young, Wally Craig, Heather Robertson, Allen Stern, John Olah, Ron Parks, Robert Gardner, Dr. Steven Kent, Horst Baender, John and Peggy Findlay, my brother, Dave Palango, my daughter, Lindsay Palango, and Keith Perrault.

Along the way I met Brent Beleskey who proved to be a tireless (and unpaid) researcher. Brent seemed determined to provide me with as many points of view and more reading material than I thought possible to absorb. A special thank you, Brent.

The international scope of the story took me into uncharted territory, where I was helped by many others, including: Avi Shachar, Jonathan Halevi, "George Samuel," Dr. Rachel Ehrenfeld, John Loftus, Clare Lopez, Leo Knight, Paul Williams, Brent MacLean, Robbie Cressman, and Wayne Roques.

In the course of gathering material I talked to many ordinary citizens who ended up contributing much to my greater understanding of the story. They included Marco D'Onofrio, Pierre Rigolli, and Ray Berkovits in Montréal as well as Sandy MacDonald, Blanch McCleave, and Wendy Barry.

Information from a number of journalists was also helpful. Among them were: Leslie McKinnon, Charlie Gillis, Susan Delacourt, Harvey Cashore, Scott Anderson, Colin Freeze, James Travers, and Naheed Mustafa. I would also thank those in the media who gave me visibility during this process, which often led to new sources and leads. Those people include the CBC radio syndication service and its hosts, such as Margaux Watt, Peter Brown, and Russ Knutsen. In the private sector were, most notably, Rob Breckenridge, Bill Good, Christy Clark, Arlene Bynon, Paula Todd, and Mike Duffy.

Working with computers always presents difficulties—more than I could ever have dreamed in this case. Thank you to the technical staff at Eastlink Internet Services for their time, patience, and professionalism—and to my personal technician, Michael Harnish.

Having sat in the same spot for more than eight months I could not have done this without Dr. William Smith, the official chiropractor of this book.

I would also like to thank Connal McNamara and Steve Jarrett, who took the time to read my first draft and who each offered valuable suggestions.

Finally, I would like to thank those closest to Sharon and me for their love and support: our parents, Arnold and Lea Palango and John and Bonnie Ensing, my sister, Carol-Anne Hoard, and my nephew, K.C. Hoard, for their hospitality, and, of course, our children, from oldest to youngest: Hilary Gorman, Lindsay Palango, Ryan Gorman, Virginia Palango, and Katie Gorman.

INDEX